A History of Literacy Education

A History of
Literacy Education

Waves of Research and Practice

Robert J. Tierney
P. David Pearson

TEACHERS COLLEGE PRESS

TEACHERS COLLEGE | COLUMBIA UNIVERSITY
NEW YORK AND LONDON

Published by Teachers College Press,® 1234 Amsterdam Avenue, New York, NY 10027

Front cover illustration: Curling pages by ZimaNady_klgd, newspaper background by Olga_Z, both via iStock by Getty Images.

Library of Congress Cataloging-in-Publication Data

Names: Tierney, Robert J., author. | Pearson, P. David, author.
Title: A history of literacy education : waves of research and practice / Robert J. Tierney, P. David Pearson.
Description: New York, NY : Teachers College Press, [2021] | Includes bibliographical references and index.
Identifiers: LCCN 2021007237 (print) | LCCN 2021007238 (ebook) | ISBN 9780807764633 (paperback) | ISBN 9780807765760 (hardcover) | ISBN 9780807779682 (ebook)
Subjects: LCSH: Literacy—History. | Reading—Research. | Educational change.
Classification: LCC LC149 .T54 2021 (print) | LCC LC149 (ebook) | DDC 372.6—dc23
LC record available at https://lccn.loc.gov/2021007237
LC ebook record available at https://lccn.loc.gov/2021007238

ISBN 978-0-8077-6463-3 (paper)
ISBN 978-0-8077-6576-0 (hardcover)
ISBN 978-0-8077-7968-2 (ebook)

Printed on acid-free paper
Manufactured in the United States of America

Contents

Introduction
An Overview

Over the past 50 years, we have been part of the global reading and literacy education research community as it has experienced some monumental shifts. These shifts have occurred as new insights have been acquired into the nature of reading/literacy and its development. Our list includes:

- the shift from behaviorism to cognitive and psycholinguistic perspectives;
- the advent of research on reading comprehension and especially learning to learn and metacognition;
- the connecting of reading with writing and the unfolding of literacy;
- increased attention and growing awareness of the social and cultural processes involved in literacy;
- the rise of critical traditions especially tied to post-structuralism, feminism, racism, etc.;
- shifts in assessment paradigms;
- reading reforms;
- digital developments; and
- global shifts, especially related to epistemologies, decolonization, and indigeneity.

These shifts might be conceived as *turns, zeitgeists,* or *revolutions.* Our preference is to coin them as *waves* because like ocean waves, they are stirred by different and often opposing forces. They have different shapes or contours, assume different proportions and trajectories, vary in their crest, surge, and impact. They have variable durations, merge with one another, stir undercurrents, and break in different ways. Finally, and very much like waves they are difficult to separate or pin down within fixed time frames or shapes.

These waves of development have been quite consequential. They have prompted significant changes in our thinking, orientations, and perspectives. The ripple effects of these changes extend to human affairs and societal matters—consistent with literacy's role in the broader contexts of developments in culture and communications, societal participation, legal affairs and governmental matters, our ways of knowing, and the nature of protocols and memorials. In terms of intellectual thought, they represent developments in behaviorism, cognition, sociocultural thought, sociology, linguistics, psycholinguistics, artificial intelligence, literary theory, and critical thought. Their synergies with our human affairs befit literacy's role in defining learnedness and authorization—that is, as a license to participate in community rituals and governance. These developments even reveal roots in periods in our histories of epoch proportion, such as the Reformation, the Enlightenment, nation building, colonization, and liberation movements.

This book traces these developments, especially in modern times, in ways that attempt to animate reading across the ages through discussions of integral research, theories, practices, and other developments. Foregrounding each discussion is the notion of an imagined reader that is emblematic of the changing times. Our umbrella-like characterizations of readers over time are intended to set a theme rather than to define or restrict; they fit with the emphases and conditions for reading that occur at the hand of different wave-like developments. They are shaped in part by the politics of the time, sometimes by educational design concepts or changing concepts of meaning making and expectations for readers—or by all these threads. You may see yourself in the characterizations in ways that might be enlightening but also provocative and educative.

The history of reading is intertwined with the broader history of learning—and, perhaps even more so, the history of meaning making so central to our participation in the world. Reading occurs at the nexus of language, thought, and praxis as learners navigate their pursuits in the world. We know of no other field of study so absorbing as the study of readers and reading, especially during the last hundred years, when the nature of reading has moved from the printed page to a home in multimedia digital networks. This history has drawn a range of scholars (psychologists, linguists, educators, anthropologists, philosophers, and sociologists) to explore how readers make meaning with texts, how they develop, and in turn, how they are, or should be, taught (all of which has changed significantly during these times). Indeed, the study of readers has been preoccupied the sciences over the last century. It has been the site for scholars to delve into the complex nature of meaning making and language development—especially in how readers enlist reading in their everyday lives.

LOOKING BACK

This book begins with what might be considered precursors, dating back across the millennium to literacy's role in religion, legal systems, statehood and the age of empires, colonization, and nation building. In this regard, the notion of the *enculturated reader* is discussed as reading served as a way to ensure that members of communities or nations or congregations share unified views, values, and understandings. Literacy has been the means and object of philosophical discussions dating back thousands of years across the globe. It served as a vehicle to advance religious and moral thought, a means of enshrining protocols and rituals for societies, and a means of social and political control. It was central to the Reformation, the scientific revolution, systems of colonization, and shifts in social thought, including revolutions.

From the late 19th, through the 20th, and into the 21st century, psychology, first as a budding and eventually as a mature science, has shaped literacy substantively. Psychology studied literacy as a site of laboratory-based research focused on the role of the mind and the eye (e.g., eye movement tracking studies, response times, etc.). Psychology spurred an emphasis on observable measurable behavior that pervaded reading theories and pedagogy for most of the 20th century. In turn, reading tests emerged and coupled with a reductionistic detailing of the component and related subskills of reading, along with a developmental orientation tied to stages of reading and skills-based reading curricula. As developments involving system analyses and mass production became foundational in industry, mastery models of reading emerged. It was as if reading development became tied to a carefully controlled and measured diet of graded reading material accompanied with a scope and sequence of skills that were taught, practiced, and tested in a fashion not unlike a *manufactured/assembled reader.*

WAVES OF DEVELOPMENT

The influence of these aforementioned waves persisted and had residual influences through the 1960s and arguably beyond. At the same time, if you were an educator in the late 1960s and early 1970s, you were living in a time where the great society was touted, the space race had fueled competition among nations, and you were seeing a rise in civil rights movements and criticisms about Western involvement in Asia—especially Vietnam. Indeed, societal concerns were at a boiling point. If you were a reading educator, you were not a bystander, but engaged in exploring these social matters in your classrooms and in seeking various initiatives for better ways to meet your students' needs and compete on the global stage (e.g., through educational advances measured by achievement tests). Indeed, research on teaching reading was the major focus of educational research at this time. Reading programs were seen as the front line for addressing the gaps in achievement or opportunities that varied across communities in the United States and other countries.

Essentially, the search for the best method of teaching reading became education's equivalent of the space race. The 1960s were preoccupied with the search for a silver bullet or the best approach to teaching reading. Hence, there was a proliferation of different methods of teaching reading; horse race studies were conducted to find the champion approach. Key contenders were approaches that advocated phonics taught synthetically (versus phonics taught analytically), as well as more meaning-centered and eclectic approaches such as basal reading series (with carefully leveled or graded stories) and the Language Experience Approach, which put a premium on using children's oral language to leverage a transition to mastering the print code. In an effort to respond to this cry for answers, there were massive investments in research that compared approaches. Partially spurring these developments were popular books decrying the failure of reading programs, with Rudolph Flesch's 1955 popular press version, *Why Johnny Can't Read*.

The search for a panacea somewhat abated with the first major study of beginning reading approaches, the *Cooperative First Grade Studies*. The findings of the study confirmed the views from a popular book, *Learning to Read: The Great Debate* by Jean Chall. With Chall's work came the realization that there was no silver bullet or panacea—indeed, no single approach was better than any other. Instead, what seemed key were teachers' abilities to meet the needs of their students with a solid understanding of reading. Nevertheless, despite these developments, the teacher was still often positioned as a mechanic manufacturing readers along an assembly line. Integral to the "production" of readers were the component skills and regimen of reading program—the scope and sequence of skills and a diet of reading material of ever-increasing difficulty.

In the 1970s, debates and "wars" over the best approach to teaching reading were calmed and replaced by a focus on studies of language acquisition and early reading and writing development. Indeed, interest in understanding language development and reading drew the attention of scholars from a range of disciplines (cognitive psychology, linguistics, sociolinguistics) resulting in stunning insights—including the growing interest in how children, especially early readers, learn language. Major breakthroughs began occurring in understandings and appreciation of how students acquire language, including how they learn to read and write. Emerging scholars of reading were introduced to studies of early reading and writing by scholars such as Carol Chomsky, Charles Read, Emilia Ferreira, and Dolores Durkin—studies that illuminated the linguistic awareness and prowess of young children as they learned to speak, listen, read, and write. Views of reading also shifted to accommodate psycholinguistics with the release of Frank Smith's book *Understanding Reading* and Kenneth Goodman's breakthrough notion of *Reading as a Psycholinguistic Guessing Game*.

At the same time, interest in reading development turned to reading comprehension. Historically, the ability to learn from text was viewed as a by-product of maturation aligned with the nature of the reading experiences and challenges afforded to readers. The 1970s witnessed a shift in foundational thinking about reading comprehension processes, especially a move to thinking about reading comprehension strategies as teachable. Foreshadowing these developments was increased interest in learning from text and content reading, as seen in the work on comprehension by Harold Herber, Russell Stauffer, and others in the learning sciences, such as Ernest Rothkopf and David Ausubel.

These developments and others formed a confluence and what many consider a zeitgeist. Indeed, cognition replaced the hundred-year-plus stranglehold on reading by behaviorism. It changed the goals and practices in literacy classrooms and was foundational to the subsequent digital revolution. By the late 1970s, views of meaning making were aligned with schema-theoretic notions of the reader and aspirations for *constructivist readers*. The revolutionary nature of this wave paralleled other revolutions of the times—the civil rights movements throughout the world, the end of the Vietnam War, landmark developments brought by digital technologies, and developments in the arts and sports.

Not surprisingly, these cognitive-based notions of reading merged with other waves of development that seemed equally as revolutionary. In the 1980s, a focus on improving reading comprehension became coupled with the notion of learning to learn, metacognition, and the aspirational goal of a *strategic reader*. Whereas our past aspirations for reading comprehension development were tied to views that were maturational—as if reading comprehension abilities were pre-set (i.e., comprehension could be unfolded or enhanced)—thinking shifted to a view of reading comprehension abilities as less fixed. Reading comprehension (reader-based and text-based strategies) became viewed as teachable and focused on developing independent, sustainable, flexible, transferable, and (above all) nimble learning strategies that enhanced a reader's comprehension.

Furthermore, concurrent with the cognitive wave in reading, writing research and practices were moving along at a similarly rapid pace. A number of reading educators—ourselves included—were enthralled with how these developments could complement and illuminate reading. That is, we looked at how reading might piggyback on the developments in research on the writing process and studies of authorship and writing pedagogy. In turn, the *writerly reader* emerged as an aspiration, in concert with a weaving together of reading–writing in classrooms beginning in the early grades through college. These developments spurred a shift in thinking of reading more as production than reception and corresponded with the shift from reading being treated in isolation to reading and writing and other forms of representation, communication, and exploration being considered under the umbrella of literacy.

Other major waves of development followed as interests shifted to the dynamics of meaning making as a social process. In the 1980s, social views of literacy assumed an increasingly important role, no longer being viewed as a variable influencing literacy development but as integral to reading and writing processes. Our models of literacy moved to views that encompassed elements and processes that were outside the head, including interactions with others, collaborations, cooperative meaning making, and other participatory forms of learning. The aspirations for reading embraced the notion of *social readers*.

In turn, growth in interest in sociology led to literacy becoming scrutinized more closely and diversely in the late 1980s through to today. Sociopolitical considerations, especially critical theoretic frames tied to race, gender, ethnicity, and sexuality, became increasingly salient. These waves of interest created frames or aspirations for readers informed by different movements in critical race and feminist theories. These frames inspired critical readings, unmasking and interrogating prevailing systemic forces in play in our texts, our reading, and our writing. This wave advanced the notion of what might be labeled broadly as *critical advocates* or, more specifically, readers who enlist critical frames such as critical race theories and feminist theories.

Simultaneously, other waves of development ebbed and flowed and merged with these developments. A range of new forms of assessments, grounded in a classroom and learner-centered orientation, emerged. There was a growing interest in *self-assessing readers* who reflected on their own development and processes (corresponding with some of the concepts undergirding strategic readers and writerly readers, with their shift away from positivist emphases on behavior and measurement). Unfortunately, some of these developments were overridden by others, including growing government interest in accountability as a means of managing and overseeing educational progress. In many countries, periodical testing on a large scale replaced more organic forms of assessment. Coupled with curriculum mandates and standards, reading instruction became increasingly aligned with top-down controls and reforms related to what was taught and tested, and when. Readers became what seem best labeled as *regulated readers*.

With the new millennium, we have experienced or are witnessing other waves tied to major shifts in our text worlds and our engagements, especially across digital, online, and social media spaces, and across borders. The final waves represent two currently emerging areas for teachers and students to grasp—the *digital readers/meaning makers* and the *global reader/meaning makers*. Included in the digital discussions are historical developments, including online reading and learning, gaming, social media, and embodiment. The discussion of the global wave extends to transliteracies, cosmopolitanism, global citizenship, language revitalization, indigeneity, epistemologies, and open access publishing.

As a quick preview of what the book holds in store, here is a chapter-by-chapter account of the major threads you will encounter as a reader.

Part I: Looking Back

Chapter 1. Beginning Traces: Early Science and Cultural Concerns

The first section begins with a look back over the last 150 years to some of key antecedents, especially the influence of psychological studies of reading and the connections to German psychologist Wilhelm Wundt and William James in the United States, who mentored some of the world's leading reading scholars. It looks at Edmund Huey, who wrote the first textbook focused on reading research, along with the authors of the first reading tests, and examines the dominant influence of behaviorism and measurement that persists somewhat today. The depiction of the *encultured reader* attempts to capture an imagined reader reflecting the emphases during this period.

Chapter 2. The Persistence of Pedagogy

The second section on the *assembled reader* and the "Search for Best Method" followed a period of intensity spurred by concern that reading failures were on the rise and a belief that researchers should identify the best method for teaching beginning reading. It was as if there was a race between approaches in search of a "silver bullet." The race was fraught with difficulties and problems that provided more questions than answers. In terms of readers, it was a period when reading development involved a scope and sequence of skills as if readers could be assembled.

Part II: Waves of Development

Chapter 3. The Cognitive Wave

The first major wave discussed is related to the *constructivist reader* and the *cognitive turn*. The shift to cognition over behaviorism is viewed by many as the major zeitgeist of the last hundred years and led to major shifts in our views of the mind and learning as well as reading. Spurred by studies of language development, the advent of psycholinguistics, research on text comprehension and artificial intelligence, major shifts in our theories of reading occurred together with our practices. These were exciting times wherein fervent developments in reading occurred and major changes in our theories of how readers *construct* meaning proactively rather than just receptively.

Chapter 4. The Learning to Learn Wave

Learning to learn and metacognition address a major vexing matter—the issue of whether or not comprehension and reading development can be enhanced and accelerated by teaching focused on strategic learning and reader awareness. This wave explores what we learned from research on developing independent and *strategic readers*—especially comprehenders.

Chapter 5. The Reading–Writing Wave

Reading and writing development explores major changes in our thinking and practices as writing researchers and educators reconceptualized reading and writing as composing processes that worked together. These developments marked major changes in our thinking on the nature of reading development and its separation from writing and the beginnings of reading and writing intertwined as literacy. These signaled a shift from reading to literacy and introduced the notion of the *reader as composer* and *writerly reader*.

Chapter 6. The Social Wave

The social turn shifts our views of reading and writing from "inside the head" to social processes involving acts, practices, people, and events as integral to the meaning making that occurs and goals that are pursued. The reader was viewed as involved in a range of social negotiations with social systems, peers, and authors.

Chapter 7. The Critical Wave

Critical literacies bring to the study of literacy work in sociology, especially by Marxist scholars and French sociologists who examined how position and power are intertwined with our engagements with texts. The critical wave brought to literacy a recognition of the pervasive traces of power and privilege inscribed in texts used to teach literacy and methods. It also brought to the fore *critical advocates* who enlisted feminist perspectives, critical race theories, and other ways of unearthing as well as challenging the privilege and bias in our materials and practices.

Chapter 8. The Assessment Wave

Beginning in the 1970s, coinciding with the birth of the National Assessment of Educational Progress in the United States, the role of testing received intense scrutiny as its impacts on teaching and learning were questioned. The interrogation of testing practices led to major shifts in what was assessed, why, how, and by whom. It led to developments around authentic assessment, portfolios and student-led assessment and *readers involved in self-assessment* at the same time as high-stakes assessment achieved more traction.

Chapter 9. The Reform Wave

In the last 25 years, in various countries, we have seen a rising wave in government reform of education where governments have exerted controls over what is taught and how under the banner of accountability. To ensure compliance, schools have been audited and students tested in terms of their mastery of the pre-set standards of skills. These reform efforts tied to testing and standards evoked traces of the form of criterion-based teaching and testing indicative of the assembled reader of an earlier era where outcomes and accountability dominated. And, in turn, teaching practices were realigned with testing and student learning became increasingly *regulated*.

Chapter 10. The Digital Wave

The nature of literacy has changed seismically in recent years as the digital wave has moved us toward new forms of literacies, new practices for sense-making, a range of mediums for social exchanges, and new lenses for critiquing texts and understandings. Print on paper, once the singular medium of representation, has had to make room for multiple forms of representation and a decidedly *digital reader.*

Chapter 11. The Global Wave

Amid the global flow of people and goods and an increased appreciation of the importance of our diversity both ecologically and epistemologically, *global meaning making* involves exploring our reading of the world and in the world, including our reading of the systems that operate and provide affordances that shape our multiple identities as we traverse cultures and languages across spaces and time.

Part III: Ebb and Flow

Chapter 12. Research Currents

As the research lenses enlisted by researchers and theorists have shifted, so our understandings of literacy have changed. The waves of development in literacy education research represent shifts in the frames of reference that govern inquiry. These different frames of reference befit what some might consider theoretical constructs, paradigms, or shared orientations, acting like crosscurrents with the various waves. In this crucible of debate over epistemology and method, certain methodologies have dominated for short periods, only to be forced into sharing the spotlight with complementary or sometimes opposing perspectives. Just after WWII, the emphasis on correlational studies dominated, but later merged with quasi-experimental investigations and multiple correlational approaches. While these persist even today, beginning in the 1970s, they have had to share the spotlight with an ever-shifting stream of epistemologies and methods spurred by an increased acceptance of tools from the learning sciences as well as sociocultural and critical perspectives on what counts as scholarship. New complementary traditions have included advances in qualitative, formative, and design-based research as well as studies seeking transformative change.

Chapter 13. History Unaccounted: A Personal Retrospective on Waves of Development

Rob's and David's collective and independent journeys took place across many years and in many spaces around the globe, affording them the opportunity to partake of and witness amazing changes that they have characterized as waves. They are keen to acknowledge the book as an account and to apologize and acknowledge the idiosyncrasies of their experiences for the personal and restricted perspectives in which they have indulged.

Please access the related website (literacyresearchcommons.org: username *TCPWavesofLiteracy*, password *Tierney&Pearson*), which includes video lectures, taped conversations between the coauthors, and an invitation to extend our literacy research commons.

One cautionary note to all readers: As carefully as we have tried to marshal evidence to warrant the claims we make about these waves, as conscientiously as we have tried to explain both the consistent patterns and the dramatic shifts, we realize all too well the possibility that not all literacy scholars, even those who came onto the scene with us as peers in the late 1960s and early 1970s, would tell the same story as the one we have crafted for you as readers. While we believe our history to be trustworthy and valid, we make no claims about truth, only meaning. We hope you find our story useful and meaningful in explaining where as a field, we are, have been, and maybe will be in the future. In the final analysis, it is our story, our history. Enjoy!

References

Bond, G. L., & Dykstra, R. (1967). The cooperative research program in first-grade reading instruction. *Reading Research Quarterly, 2*(4), 5–142. doi: 10.2307/746948

Chall, J. (1967). *Learning to read: The great debate* (1st ed.). McGraw-Hill.

Goodman, K. S. (1967). Reading: A psycholinguistic guessing game. *Journal of the Reading Specialist, 6*(4), 126–135. doi: 10.1080/19388076709556976

Smith, F. (2012). *Understanding reading: A psycholinguistic analysis of reading and learning to read* (6th ed). Routledge. Original work published 1971.

Part I

LOOKING BACK

1 Beginning Traces—Early Science and Cultural Concerns

1.1 THE ENCULTURATED READER

How we engage with text and how we are taught to respond to text is not insignificant. Historically, our engagement with reading and writing has been embedded in social systems, with affordances that represent forms of enculturation. Enculturation may be self-determined or, alternatively, imposed or mandated by the institutions that guide and govern us. In today's societies, our engagements with text involve a constant barrage of material. While some of this material is self-initiated or explored, the rest is directed at us via the platforms of the institutions within which we allow ourselves to be embedded as we increasingly tether ourselves to the media. As shown in the recent elections in various countries, inadvertent or planned forms of enculturation may occur via web-based and social media platforms. The forms may range from marketing to attempts to frame, construe (or misconstrue), or somehow influence the cultural beliefs and behavior of users, readers, and viewers operating within these digital realms.

Reading as a form of enculturation (bringing members of the collective in line with cultural norms) has occurred across societies for thousands of years. In Australian Aboriginal communities, the world's oldest continuous society, learning to read one's world has historically involved learning about place and one's place in one's community and world through art. Integral to these readings is a mode of learning in the company of elders, who guide one's understanding of symbols as well as one's license and responsibility as a meaning maker alongside members (present and deceased) of communities and place.

In many of the world's faith communities, participation often involves reading or listening to scriptures as guides to moral decisionmaking and the learning of values—with or without license for interpretation. For Christians and Muslims, key texts are the Bible, the Quran, or other ordained guides. As Martin Luther (1986) stated:

> Above all things, let the scriptures be the chief and most frequently used reading group in both primary and high schools and the very young children should be kept in the

3

gospels. Is it not proper and right that every human being, by the time he has reached his tenth year, should be familiar with the holy gospels, in which the very core and marrow of his life is bound? (pp. 15–17, S. 321)

Likewise, in the interest of shaping communities or a national identity, schools have prioritized some texts and forms of responding to text over others. In her landmark history of American reading, Nila Banton Smith (1934) commented on the important role of reading in nation formation beginning after 1776:

> While the greatest concern of the church had been saving souls and making good communicants, the foremost goal of the state was the building of national strength and making good citizens. . . . To develop loyalty to the new nation, its traditions and institutions, its occupations and resources; and to indicate the high ideals of virtue and moral behaviour which were considered so necessary a part of the general program of building good citizenship. (p. 37)

Looking Back at the Study of Reading by Examining the History of Writing Systems

The history of the study of reading as a vehicle for enculturation can be traced to the advent of writing systems that goes back perhaps over 150,000 years. Reading became integrated into our exchange of goods and ideas. Markings on seashells and the use of tokens were among the earliest forms, as people enlisted systems for trade and ceremony. Print systems followed and became integrated with cultural, economic, educational, social, and political interchanges. The significance of these systems (as records of negotiations, artistic expressions, everyday practices, historical events, and spiritual guidance) is apparent in the rise of repositories for such records—as evidenced by documentation of the philosophic debates and literary works of antiquity, the creation of the first libraries (e.g., Alexandria, 200 BCE), and eventually the first universities (e.g., University of Bologna, 1088 CE, and the University of Timbuktu, circa 1100 CE). It was further propelled by various religious developments—especially the rise in Christianity, Buddhism, Islam, and Protestant Christianity—as well as the expansion of empires in the 1600s and the growth of a science of ideas during the Enlightenment. Throughout this development, the role of text as a tool of subjugation or liberation was not without debate, as evidenced in the portrayal by the Greek philosopher Plato of Socrates's concern for the displacement of a dialectic (by the shift to written texts as advocated by the Sophists; see box). Also attesting to the growing recognition of the power of text as an agent in the enculturation in society was the dismissal, destruction, and appropriation of what was read and written, and how expectations for engagement have evolved from ancient times through to present day.

Breakthroughs that occurred in printing, including wood-block printing in China (circa 200 CE) and later, the Gutenberg printing press in Europe (circa 1450 CE), fueled a rapid rise in the distribution of texts throughout the public sphere but also signaled increased uniformity in thought and ideology, as many religious orders and schools demonstrated an interest in constraining what was read (as well as why, where, and how). Perhaps one of the ironies of the explosion of writing on the planet was the use of print by institutions (e.g., governments, churches, and schools) to impose their values, histories, and practices on individuals and societies by inscribing them in print. Studied examinations of reading and writing were used as the basis for planned approaches to enculturation, colonization, and control by institutions. In many societies, texts were assigned an elevated role, often serving as a binding record of transactions, in keeping with the notion that "the pen is mightier than the sword."

The advent of the printing press thus corresponded with increased access to print—especially in schools—but also with prescriptive forms of meaning making. The mode of text, as well as its position in relation to authorship and representation, carries consequences. As Socrates suggested, written text may imply more authority than oral text, potentially blunting readers' disposition for dialectical and critical engagement. Similarly, as research has shown, the persona of a text may prompt a certain ethos or truthfulness. In schools especially, texts have not been prepared for multiple interpretations but instead to provide a citizenry with shared experiences, understandings, and values, thus serving as a potential tool for leaders aspiring to promote imperialistic, national, or spiritual aims.

Socrates's (469-399 BCE) views arose at the intersection of a network of earlier Greek philosophers who were considered to be the first Western philosophers. He was quite adamantly opposed to philosophers labeled Sophists, who had positioned themselves as teachers of argumentation without regard for truth and were tied to modes of persuasion devoid of the debate or dialectic that Socrates deemed so crucial. It was in this vein that Socrates discussed concern over the displacement of an oral tradition with a written tradition—specifically, the loss of engagement of speakers with their audience (through which arguments could be debated and discussed in a fashion consistent with a search for truth) to a Sophist persuasion supported by writing. Socrates did not write down his views, but they were discussed or represented by later Greek philosophers who were his followers and students—as seen in work by Plato, especially in his dialogues that he ascribes to Socrates.

Schools as Sites of Enculturation

In schools, reading and writing are aligned with aspirational goals for individuals to advance and become moral citizens. Indeed, for high schoolers, reading and

writing are aligned with cultural canons that are in turn tied to admissions requirements of key universities, curricula set by government authorities, or both.
Reading in this model has emerged as a cultural gauntlet, in which selected texts
are assigned to be read in a fashion that elevates the status of both the texts themselves and the ideologies they represent. In China, for example, the advent of the
national examination system hundreds of years ago focused on memory of the
writings of Confucius, thereby elevating the *Analects*. Similarly, throughout the
English-speaking world, texts by Shakespeare and other British authors are required reading. Indeed, in the British Empire during the early 1900s, it was estimated that 70% of high schoolers would have read Shakespeare's *Julius Caesar*.
Even with the introduction of multiculture standards for text selection, secondary English curricula in America tend to reflect an informal canon across states
and schools that is heavily focused on European authors (Applebee, 1993). Due to
this tendency, world history curricula in English-speaking countries have focused
largely on Europe, limiting treatment of Eastern and Southern countries primarily
to their involvement in the European empires of the last 500 years.

The canonization of selected texts in different cultures has also extended to
family and community life. In the Islamic world, the Quran dominated, read either
silently or aloud. In the Christian world, the Bible along with a few other books
were initially the most common reading materials in homes. For example, when
Alexis de Tocqueville traveled the United States in the 1830s, he found that the
typical reading fare in frontier homes included the Bible, the works of Milton, and
Shakespeare's plays. A thirst for books, even in many small settlements aspiring to
libraries, eventually led to individual collections of reading repertoires.

Reading and Empire

Clearly, in general there is a reverence for the written word. In education, books
have been seen both as a source of information and as a means of enculturation
as a result of a shared cultural experience and immersion. In school, students'
reading experiences were standardized in terms of what was read and how readers
were expected to respond. Reading became institutionalized, and readers became
stamped by the books that they were expected to read and the manner in which
they were expected to read them. Books and oral reading comprised an individual's passport to education and constituted a test for citizenship.

As John Willinsky (1998) notes in *Learning to Divide the World: Education
at Empire's End*, reading and writing have served as tools for empires to assimilate or displace cultures and individuals in the interests of the metropole. Empires
routinely destroyed or removed cultural artifacts and practices, replacing them
with their own. If you were living in the British Empire or Commonwealth, you
would be taught British history and read the poems, novels, and plays written
by canonical British authors. For students enrolled in colonial schools, the texts
and related curricula were anchored in the empire, highlighting how the world
was divided. In his book *Learning to Divide the World: Education at Empire's End*,

John Willinsky (1998) ended his unmasking of the imperialistic underpinnings of educational developments worldwide by examining our identity in the context of this legacy with a view to ourselves as foreigners. At the same time, he warned us not to become cathartic about identity and not to shy away from operating across cultures or globally.

Pedagogy of Reading

For centuries, teachers and clergy defined what, why, and how we read—in ways that resembled indoctrination and enculturation. In Christian settings, what people read was pre-set or standardized in the interest of devout allegiance, patriotism, or the development of moral character. The approach to reading in this context—in which oral reading was the predominant mode—also appeared to engender a reverence for the text itself rather than the reader's own meaning making. Before the advent of the printing press, a lack of access to texts was a factor in this approach. Yet even well after the invention of the printing press, the advent of psychological considerations of reading tended to position reading as behavioral and mechanical, as if readers were expected to do close and overt reading of the text itself rather than engage in their own thought processes. While the pedagogy of reading has been the subject of much debate since the 1900s, especially with contested approaches in the early grades, reading overall has been aligned with psychological studies that tout oral reading as a way of observing, measuring, and advancing targeted learning skills (Pearson & Goodin, 2010).[1] Consequently, despite the virtues of being able to revisit and reread written texts, there has been a tendency to align print with pre-set forms of meaning making and uniformity.

Indeed, considered historical, print text has been linked to the imposition of institutional norms on texts. Despite the rise of constitutional monarchies, the independence of the United States, the advent of liberalism, and the growth of pamphlets, newspapers, and sites to the free engagement and debate with ideas, school-based texts have frequently been mandated—perpetuating a fixed representation of ideas rather than a model of free-flowing discussion. Norms and expectations for reading those texts varied by context (e.g., religious and/or schooling); depending on the text and reading circumstances, there are likely to be different views on the authority of the writer (including the writer's scribe, publisher, etc.) and the responsibility or expectation of the reader. Adding to these dimensions are different agencies (e.g., governmental or educational) advocating different standards for reading texts. Politicians, curriculum developers, and scholars are implicated in this positioning as tools that continue to shape cultural norms, values, and allegiances.

In Closing

Oscar Wilde is reputed to have coined the phrase, "We are what we read." We would suggest that we are *embedded* in what we read. That is, we are constantly

SOME OF THE KEY DEVELOPMENTS OF
READING AND WRITING IN SOCIETY

Here are some of the key developments pertaining to reading and writing in societies:

- The use of tokens as a means of representing exchange of goods including the use of clay holders for storing (e.g., 9th to 2nd millennium)
- The creation of images to communicate, to record observations, and to transact and engage with one's environment and community (e.g., cave paintings in France, circa 30,000 BCE)
- The advent of texts as advancing rituals sometimes deemed as sacred
- The development of writing systems (e.g., America, 300 BCE; China, 1200 BCE, Northern Africa, 3100 BCE)
- The growth of universities (e.g., University of Timbuktu, 1200; University of Bologna, 1088) and libraries (e.g., Alexandria, 300 BCE)
- The introduction of the printing press and the expanded access to text (e.g., China, Tang Dynasty woodblocks, 200 CE; Europe, Gutenberg press, 1440 CE)
- The role of religious developments and texts (e.g., Islam/Muhammad, the Quran, 500 CE; Christianity, the Catholic Church, and the Protestant Reformation, 16th century)
- The Enlightenment (1650) and the circulation of texts in the public sphere (e.g., newspapers and pamphlets) as well as sites where ideas might be shared and debated (e.g., parlors and clubs)
- Global imperialism and empires as related to the spread and control of information and culture
- The growth of an educational textbook industry, especially the advent of readers (e.g., hornbook primers, etc.)
- The advent of oral reading of texts as a means of sharing and placing constraints on variation
- The pursuit of reading repertoires in communities with libraries and in homes through individual collections
- The institutional uses of text to enculturate (e.g., via nomination of certain texts and prescribed ways of engaging with texts as tools of cultural learning and moral development, economic self-sufficiency, and participatory decisionmaking)
- The advent of web-based resources, digital media, and social media platforms with architecture that heightens participation with others in, with, and around our worlds via intelligent engineering for designed purposes

engaged with reading our worlds as we pursue our everyday activities and interact with a range of media sites and other reading and writing materials. The texts that we read or write embody a range of goals and interests, from personal sustenance to economic, social, and political concerns. Hence, to study reading is to study ideas, representations, reflections, negotiations, and communication, and the ways in which individuals and groups contemplate, seek expression, or negotiate through art, text, or tokens. Reading occurs at the confluence of culture, language, and thought, amidst individuals and people, functioning economically, physically, socially, spiritually, and politically. The history of reading is the history of ideas and records—including debates over reading itself—as well as the use of text to support developments on a number of fronts (see box). It is through reading that ideas are expressed and debated but also given permanency and legality. It is through reading that cultures are given expression and people become enculturated. It is through reading that people become participants in, rather than observers of, their futures.

The last 75 years have brought a period of rapid change with respect to text, especially with telegraphed technologies, the integration of print and image, and the networking of ideas and people. These changes include letters and notes replaced by email and text messages of various forms; the worldwide expansion of wirelessness; memory storage and processing capabilities increasingly miniaturized; the growth of global video conferencing; an increasing immediacy and virtuality to our communications; changes to public and social spheres; and an increased use of robotics, avatars, simulations, and artificial intelligence to create new social relations. As we engage with or in these worlds—shaping ourselves and these networks in the process—we may also be engineered to the enculturation goals of others. Indeed, reading and writing can fuel our advancement or our subjugation.

References

Applebee, A. (1993) *Literature in the secondary school: Studies of curriculum and instruction in the United States.* National Council of Teachers of English.

Beach, R., & Tierney, R. J. (2017). Toward a theory of literacy meaning making within virtual worlds. In S. E. Israel (Ed.), *Handbook of research on reading comprehension* (2nd ed., Vol. 2, pp. 135–165). Guilford. doi: 10.1177/1086296X18803134

Dale E., & Chall J. (1948). A formula for predicting readability. *Educational Research Bulletin, 27,* 11–20 + 28.

Gray, W. S., & Leary, B. W. (1935). *What makes a book readable.* University of Chicago Press.

Lively, B., & Pressey, S. (1923). A method for measuring the "vocabulary burden" of textbooks. *Educational Administration and Supervision, 99,* 389–398.

Luther, M. (1986). *Luther's small catechism with explanation.* Concordia Publishing House.

Pearson, P. D., & Goodin, S. (2010). Silent reading pedagogy: A historical perspective. In E. H. Hiebert & D. R. Reutzel (Eds.), *Revisiting silent reading: New directions for teachers and researchers* (pp. 3–23). International Reading Association.

Schmandt-Besserat, D. (1978). The earliest precursor of writing. *Scientific American, 238*(6), 50–59. doi: 10.1038/scientificamerican0678-50

Schmandt-Besserat, D. (1986). The origins of writing: An archaeologist's perspective. *Written Communication, 3*(1), 31–45. doi:10.1177/0741088386003001003

Scribner, S. (1984). Literacy in three metaphors. *American Journal of Education, 93*(1), 6–21. doi: 10.1086/443783

Scribner, S., & Cole, M. (1978). Literacy without schooling: Testing for intellectual effects. *Harvard Educational Review, 48*(4), 448–461. doi:10.17763/haer.48.4.f44403u05l72x375

Smith, N. B. (1934). *American reading instruction: Its development and its significance in gaining a perspective on current practices in reading.* International Reading Association. Silver Burdett and Ginn.

Street, B. (1999). The meanings of literacy. In D. A. Wagner, R. L. Venezky, & B. V. Street, (Eds.), *Literacy: An international handbook.* Westview Press.

Taylor, D. (1997). *Many families, many literacies: An international declaration of principles.* Heinemann.

Thorndike, E. L. (1917a). Reading as reasoning: A study of mistakes in paragraph reading. *Journal of Educational Psychology, 8*(6), 323–332. doi: 10.1002/rrq.87

Thorndike, E. L. (1917b). The understanding of sentences. *Elementary School Journal,* 1917, 18, 98–114.

Tierney, R. J. (2017). Populism and literacy consciousness in uncertain global times. *Journal of Literacy Research, 49*(3), 4–7. www.academia.edu/32174097/Populism_and_Literacy_Consciousness_in_Uncertain_Global_Times

Willinsky, J. (1998). *Learning to divide the world: Education at empire's end.* University of Minnesota Press.

Willinsky, J. (2006). Access to power: Research in international policymaking. *Harvard International Review, 28*(2), 54–57. www.jstor.org/stable/42763114

1.2 THE FOUNDATIONAL YEARS OF READING

Reading is anchored in a formative history that dates back to the advent of symbolic representation over 4,000 years ago—during which time it was used as a vehicle for records and the pursuit of negotiations, through print and its antecedents such as tokens used for trade and ceremony (a practice that goes back perhaps over 150,000 years). The significance of these systems (as records of commercial transactions, legal negotiating, artistic expressions, everyday communications [letters, notes, lists], historical events, and spiritual guidance) is evidenced by documentation of the philosophic debates and literary works of antiquity, the creation of the first libraries (e.g., in Alexandria, 300 BCE), and eventually of the first universities (e.g., University of Bologna, 1088 CE, and the University of Timbuktu, circa 1100 CE). Print itself became the vehicle for inscribing rituals and laws, designating rights of ownership, liberties, and citizenship. At the same time, the notion of reading texts became an object of study among prominent philosophers, who debated whether texts were tools of subjugation or liberation. For instance, as captured in Plato's *Meno*, Socrates related his concern over the displacement of a dialectic with written text. Philosophers thus debated the merits of oral and written renditions and intended meanings among scholars, priests, and their disciples.

Literacy was further propelled by technologies, most notably various systems of representation, tools such as various scribing tools, and—of course—the invention of the printing press. Additionally, the spread of religions (Christianity, Buddhism, Islam) and the expansion of empires beginning in the 1600s propelled the range of potential literacy participants. In terms of literacy's intellectual "DNA," one of the strongest influences on literacy research was the advent of the field of psychology in Germany in the 1800s; perhaps most influential for reading was the laboratory of Wilhelm Wundt, whose work was aligned with positivism, behaviorism, and observational studies tied to measurement of a plethora of human attributes and performances. Consistent with the metaphor of a wave, the influence of psychological studies on views of reading has been and remains substantial. Indeed, despite the growth of sociocultural considerations, psychology has remained a mainstay in terms of our theoretical conceptualizations of reading and their applications to pedagogy, largely because many American scholars traveled to Germany to be apprenticed in this new "science" and brought its theories and methods back to the United States. Specifically, our theories, research, and practices in literacy and literacy education were (and in some cases, still are) heavily influenced by *behaviorism*, a restricted research regimen tied to largely *correlational studies* of variables. Such studies emanated in particular from the advancement of *testing* technologies and new measures of reading, intelligence, and various other variables. In turn, literacy was separated into reading, writing, speaking, and listening, and was further broken down into subskills within those categories. Rooted in behavioristic views, it was focused on rote learning of skills isolated from, rather than integrated with, one another. Essentially, reading was

THE 1800S: THE ORIGINS OF PSYCHOLOGY AND READING RESEARCH

Studies of reading in the early 1900s to some extent reflected an aspirational researcher trend to be scientific and was rooted in a psychological experimental tradition dating back to the global fathers of psychology: namely, Wilhelm Wundt (1832–1920), who founded the first formal laboratory for psychological research at the University of Leipzig in 1879; and William James (1842–1910), who trained as a physician but has been deemed America's foremost philosopher and the founder of psychology. James is also purported to have written the first book on psychology and taught the first course on the subject offered at a university. Over time, these leaders and their students shaped the new field of psychology and, in turn, the study of reading.

Wilhelm Wundt's students included:

- James McKeen Catell (1860–1944), who had tenure at Columbia and the University of Pennsylvania. Catell's students included Edward Thorndike and Arthur Gates, both of whom interacted with and mentored notable reading researchers such as Guy Bond, Ruth Strang, Ernest Horn, and David Russell. Gates's work also extended beyond his focus on testing to a wide range of interests reflected by others with whom he worked, such as David Russell (who worked in the areas of reading and thinking).
- Charles H. Judd (1873–1946), who taught at the University of Chicago and guided William S. Gray (1885–1960) in his studies and pursuits, leading to Gray's PhD in 1916. Gray, who also received a master's at Columbia with Thorndike, was the author of the first diagnostic test in reading and the Scott Foresman Curriculum Foundation Series that dominated American reading instruction with Dick, Jane, and their nuclear family. He was the first president of the International Reading Association and author of several books on teaching reading.

William James's students included:

- Edward L. Thorndike (1874–1949), the leading U.S. experimental psychologist of the early part of the 1900s, who earned a master's degree with James before earning a PhD at Columbia with Cattell.
- Granville Stanley Hall (1844–1924), with whom John Dewey also studied when Hall was a professor at Johns Hopkins University); Dewey did not study in residence with James, but was heavily influenced by both James's pragmatic philosophy and his new perspectives on psychology. Besides Dewey, Hall, after he moved to Clark College in Worcester, Massachusetts, mentored Lewis Terman

(of IQ fame), Arnold Gesell (America's leading developmental psychologist), and Edmund Burke Huey, who went on to write *The Psychology and Pedagogy of Reading* in 1908, which was deemed the first book focused on reading research and in which he reviewed various experimental studies, including his own work examining eye movements.

viewed mostly as reception rather than as a form of meaning making or production. It was as if readers were expected to glean the meaning of the explicit text by operating within the four corners of the text, without any integration with the background knowledge that readers brought to the text. These views changed dramatically with the cognitive turns and other shifts in the 1970s.

The influence of the fledging field of psychology aligned with its bias toward measurement, behaviorism, and positivism was foundational from the mid-1800s on (see box). Reading researchers from 1850 until the 1960s (and many still today) have been primarily psychologists, seeking recognition of their field as a "true" measurable science. Thus, in terms of reading, eye movement research and ways to test reading flourished. As early as the 1880s, eye movement research has flourished at several sites in Europe: with Louis Émile Javal at the University of Paris, B. Erdmann and R. Dodge at the University of Halle, and J. M. Cattell at Leipzig. Beginning in the 1900s (Pearson, 2000; Venezky, 1984), it became popular in the United States: with C. H. Judd at Yale, J. M. Cattell at Columbia, and W. F. Dearborn and J. O. Quantz at Wisconsin) (see Venezky, 1984).[2]

There were several foundational developments in the early 1900s. First, we saw the advent of the first tests in reading and other areas. William S. Gray developed the Gray Oral Reading Test, widely recognized as the first diagnostic reading test and which, in turn, became the model for a number of diagnostic instruments designed by others (see box). E. L. Thorndike was involved in developing entrance examinations for universities (which some have suggested included a pre-set bias to exclude certain ethnicities). Alfred Binet was involved in developing the first intelligence test. All of these tests exist in some form today and gave rise to a proliferation of testing and research tied to these tests, including a surge in correlation studies as a basis for predicting reading success.

Second, from some of the correlational studies emerged the notion of reading readiness, which included notions of a prerequisite mental age and the necessity of select pre-reading skills such as letter name or alphabet knowledge (i.e., skills that had been shown to be highly correlated to reading ability). This work coupled with other work by developmental psychologists appearing in the 1920s (e.g., Gesell, Halverson, Thompson, Castner, Ilg, Ames, and Amatruda, 1940), who undertook extensive observational studies of reading development and argued for a view of reading as unfolding over time in accordance with a gradient that they proposed. Informing this work were Jean Piaget's interview and observational studies of

> The first edition of the Gray Oral Reading Tests (GORT) involves a test wherein the reader answers questions based on passages that are read aloud by the test administrator. The reading of these passages continues until a ceiling is reached in terms of accuracy. The GORT was designed to measure oral reading abilities (i.e., Rate, Accuracy, Fluency, and Comprehension) of students in grades 2 through 12. The test was originally published in 1923 and again in 1967, with revisions in 1986 (GORT-R), 1992 (GORT-3), and 2001 (GORT-4). The later published edition (e.g., GORT-5) included updated developmental norms extending from 6 years 0 months to 23 years 11 months; more streamlined basal and ceiling rules; revised items that were passage dependent; and additional studies showing evidence of psychometric properties. However, shortcomings remain. It could be argued that the method of measuring oral reading performance had not been informed by miscue research, the passages to assess comprehension were quite short, the ceiling was likely to cut off students prematurely, and the reliabilities befitted group comparisons but not those of individuals (Tierney, 1990).

how children assimilate and accommodate ideas or knowledge, based on their existing schema and across stages from egocentrism to socio-centrism, reflection, abstraction, and complex reasoning.[3]

Third, simultaneously, notions of readability emerged as a corollary to using scores to compare students and match them with books that fit their reading ability. Beginning in the 1920s, a number of scholars published word lists and various formulae in an attempt to assess the difficulty level of material or design material for students at different levels (e.g., Lively & Pressey, 1923). This involved well-known researchers such as E. L. Thorndike, Edgar Dale (Dale & Chall, 1948), and William S. Gray (Gray & Leary, 1935).

Fourth, studies correlating various variables with reading comprehension indicated that vocabulary was one of the best predictors of reading comprehension, leading to the assumption of the importance of teaching vocabulary as a precursor to the development of reading comprehension. As we stated above, methodologically, correlational studies tended to dominate, while their findings—highlighting key relationships—in turn influenced practice. These led to such emphases as the teaching of vocabulary, reading rate, and such select pre-reading skills as alphabetic knowledge. Their influence remained in place despite subsequent studies suggesting that such findings were more indicators of reading ability than essentials for learning to read or improving comprehension.

At the same time, developments that were sidelined but later became foundational included a shift from behaviorism to cognition. For example, studies of reading comprehension seemed somewhat overlooked despite the challenge they presented for the emphasis on oral reading and widely held views of reading comprehension. Specifically, in 1917, Thorndike conducted a highly heralded study of the "errors" in the meaning making of a paragraph, highlighting that reading involved reasoning tied to a careful balancing and weighing of ideas. He argued that teaching practices should place more emphasis on oral reproduction of the text and on reasoning via opportunities to read silently for understanding. As he stated: "Understanding a paragraph is like solving a problem in mathematics. It consists in selecting the right elements in the situation and putting them together in the right relations, and also with the right amount of weight or influence or force for each" (Thorndike, 1917, p. 329).

The prediliction to behaviorism precluded other views. For example, most scholars, some from ignorance and others from rejection, did not take up the work of social psychologist Frederic Bartlett at the University of Cambridge (especially his landmark 1932 book *Remembering*) on the nature of remembering. Bartlett delved into the nature of shifts in schema (abstract representations of knowledge in memory), the nature and role of imaging, and the ongoing reconstructive nature of remembering to highlight the influence of past and ongoing experiences on meaning making. Indeed, his work indicated a major break from the notion that meaning is something one derives from the text; rather, he posited, it is what one brings to the text. It would take a 1970s revolution in psychologists' theories and methods for studying the very nature of cognition for Bartlett's work to become foundational to the cognitive turn and perhaps among the most cited studies. In a complementary initiative, this period saw the beginning of efforts to teach machines to think and the growth of informational sciences tied to a major shift to understanding meaning making. This development was somewhat popularized by the 1990s film *Breaking the Code* (and again later with the 2011 TV movie *Codebreaker* and the 2014 film *Imitation Game*), which introduced film audiences to Alan Turing's efforts at utilizing binaries to program machines to think during the 1940s.

Behaviorism and 20th-Century Models of Reading Instruction

In the 1950s, under the influence of William S. Gray (the most influential reading scholar of the day), a diet of reading selections with teacher guidance and supplemental activities became the mainstay of reading in the United States and elsewhere. While Gray's views on reading across cultures touted notions of meeting local needs, his studies and overall approach reflected more of a skill-based than experientially based orientation to reading curricula. The curricular models of reading instruction focused on a scope and sequence of reading skills that were taught in concert with a diet of reading material leveled in accordance with readability measures. Teachers were expected to deliver a pre-set reading curriculum specified by educational governing bodies using published materials such as basal readers. Accordingly, this standard curricular model deemed a basal reader approach for teaching reading skills focused on a diet of reading material befitting a canon of approved selections, a regimen of skill and drill activities, along with an emphasis on reading aloud, some silent reading, and teacher questioning as a check on accuracy of understanding.[4]

Undergirding curricula (as is still evident in many curricular models today) was the notion that "learning to read" preceded "reading to learn" [see box], and J. Chall's 1983 *Stages of Reading Development*), with the switch occurring at about the transition from grade 3 to grade 4. Further, as is still touted today, reading was viewed by some as a form of meaning making closer to translation than to reader-based understanding.

A Typical List of Skills in a Basal Reader

Readiness skills	Primary reading skills	Comprehension (literal, inferential, interpretative, and critical)	Study skills
Letter names and sounds	Word recognition skills	Details	Making notes
Alphabet	Phonics	Main ideas	Varying reading speed
Visual discrimination	Sight words	Causal and temporal relationships	
Auditory discrimination	Context clues	Making inferences	
Left-to-right sequence	Syllabification	Drawing conclusions	
		Identifying themes	

The widespread alignment with this model of curriculum resulted in the separation of reading from writing, the notion of reading as reception, and an emphasis on learning to read prior to reading to learn. In general, the approach to reading development was based on a canon of reading material representing selected values (middle-class White Anglo-Saxons). The core of the reading lesson was a guided reading of selections, which included some pre-teaching of vocabulary, creating interest, and setting purposes for reading, followed by the reading of the selection with a teacher questioning to assess comprehension. Follow-up activities focused on teaching skills related to the reading selection and occasionally involved additional skill instruction (if needed), independent work, or suggestions for independent reading by the students. To meet the needs of different students, especially students of diverse abilities and with different needs, classes would be broken down into three to five reading groups of differing overall abilities (with selected individuals sometimes receiving small group or individual attention). Informal and standardized tests were often enlisted to suggest these classroom groupings and identify students with specific needs. Estimates suggested that the majority of classrooms utilized this type of program—that is, a reading curriculum built on a model of learning to read *before* reading to learn (a model that, by the end of the 1950s, was about to be challenged). This curriculum engendered forms of teaching reading that concentrated on skill and drill to mastery and, more and more, relied on what was tested.

In terms of teaching reading, these developments suited the creation of methods informed by a mix of aspirations tied to enculturation and teaching

JEANNE CHALL'S STAGES OF READING DEVELOPMENT

Jeanne Chall's (1983) stages of reading have had a strong influence on views of the progression of reading, especially from "learning to read" to "reading to learn." Building on a Piagetian approach to development and a potpourri of research support (but not a longitudinal study), Chall postulated that reading development followed a certain progression. Though she did claim that the stages aligned with chronological age, suggesting that they occurred in a defined order, she also suggested that students might shuttle back and forth between stages. The stages:

- Stage 0. *Prereading*: The learner gains familiarity with the language and its sounds—that is, recognizes sound similarities between words, learns to predict the next part in a familiar story, and may start to recognize a few familiar written words.
- Stage 1. *Initial Reading* or *Decoding Stage*: The learner becomes aware of the relationship between sounds and letters, and begins applying this knowledge to texts.
- Stage 2. *Confirmation, Fluency*: The learner, now familiar with basic sound–symbol relationships and a greater number of words, improves decoding skills, expands the number of words recognized by sight, and builds fluency.
- Stage 3. *Reading for Learning*: The reader has enough reading skill to focus on content and learn new information and facts from reading.
- Stage 4. *Multiple Viewpoints*: The reader at this stage begins to be able to analyze what they read, understand different points of view, and react critically.
- Stage 5. *Construction and Reconstruction—A World View*: The reader has the ability to select reading material and is building a personal view or model of the world and truth.

Longitudinal studies have since raised concerns about the rigid sequence Chall outlined, arguing that readers often are engaged in stages 4, 5, and 6 from the outset of their reading and that it is beneficial instead to approach reading in a meaning-centered fashion (Tierney, 1992).

and learning undergirded by largely behavioristic science—largely, in ways that were perhaps piecemeal and assembled toward curricular that were akin to elaborate systems intended to enculturate learners with a shared heritage. In most countries, the teaching of reading was aligned with (1) canons of selected works intended to advance patriotism, religions, or the values of the motherland; and (2) earning a scope and sequence of prescribed skills deemed essential for reading.

References

Chall, J. (1983). *Stages of reading development*. McGraw Hill.

Dale E., & Chall J. (1948). A formula for predicting readability. *Educational Research Bulletin, 27*, 11–20 + 28.

Gesell, A., Halverson, H. M., Thompson, H., Castner, B. M., Ilg, F. L., Ames, L. B., & Amatruda, C. S. (1940). *The first five years of life: A guide to the study of the preschool child, from the Yale Clinic of Child Development*. Harper and Bros.

Gray, W. S. (1956). *The teaching of reading and writing: An international survey*. UNESCO.

Gray, W. S., & Leary, B. W. (1935). *What makes a book readable*. University of Chicago Press.

Huey, E. B. (1908*). Psychology and pedagogy of reading: With a review of the history of reading and writing and of methods, texts, and hygiene in reading*. Macmillan.

Ilg, F., Ames, L., Haines, J., & Gillespie, C. (1964, 1965, 1972, 1978). *School readiness: Behavior tests used at the Gesell Institute*. Harper and Row.

Lively, B., & Pressey, S. (1923). A method for measuring the "vocabulary burden" of textbooks. *Educational Administration and Supervision, 99*, 389–398.

Pearson, P. D. (2000). Reading in the twentieth century. In T. L. Good (Ed.), *American education: Yesterday, today, and tomorrow. Yearbook of the National Society for the Study of Education* (pp. 152–208). University of Chicago Press.

Pearson, P. D., & Goodin, S. (2010). Silent reading pedagogy: A historical perspective. In E. H. Hiebert & D. R. Reutzel (Eds.), *Revisiting silent reading: New directions for teachers and researchers* (pp. 3–23). International Reading Association.

Piaget, J., & Gabain, M. (1932). *The moral judgment of the child*. Kegan Paul, Trench, Trubner & Co.

Piaget, J., & Tomlinson, J. & A. (Trans.) (1929). *The child's conception of the world*. Routledge. Originally published as an article, 1925.

Piaget, J., & Warden, M. (Trans.) (1926). *The language and thought of the child*. Kegan Paul, Trench, Trubner & Co.

Reutzel, D. Ray, & Mohr, K. A. J. (2015). 50 years of *Reading Research Quarterly* (1965–2014): Looking back, moving forward. *Reading Research Quarterly, 50*(1), 13–35.

Thorndike, E. L. (1917). Reading as reasoning: A study of mistakes in paragraph reading. *Journal of Educational Psychology, 8*(6), 323–332. doi: 10.1002/rrq.87

Tierney, R. J. (1990). Test of reading comprehension and Gray Oral Reading Test, revised. In J. C. Conoley & J. J. Kramer (Eds.), *The tenth measurements Yearbook* (pp. 337–338). Buros Institute of Mental Measurements, University of Nebraska-Lincoln, University of Nebraska Press.

Tierney, R. J. (1992). Studies of reading and writing growth: Longitudinal research on literacy acquisition. In J. Flood, J. Jensen, D. Lapp, and J. R. Squire (Eds.), *Handbook of research on teaching the language arts* (pp. 176–194). Macmillan.

Tierney, R. J. (2015). Integrative research review: Mapping the challenges and changes to literacy research. *Annual Proceedings of the Literacy Research Association, 63*, 20–35.

Venezky, R. L. (1984). The history of reading research. In P. D. Pearson, R. Barr, M. L. Kamil, & P. Mosenthal (Eds.), *Handbook of reading research* (pp. 3–38). Longman.

NOTES

1. This view was challenged by Thorndike (1917) in his discussion of reading as reasoning—based on his examination of reading comprehension and others (see Pearson & Goodin, 2010).

2. See Venezky, R. L. (1984). The history of reading research. In P. D. Pearson, R. Barr, M. L. Kamil, & P. Mosenthal (Eds.), *Handbook of reading research* (pp. 3–38). Longman; and Pearson, P. D. (2000). Reading in the twentieth century. In T. Good (Ed.), *American education: Yesterday, today, and tomorrow. (Yearbook of the National Society for the Study of Education)* (pp. 152–208). University of Chicago Press.

3. For influential work in development psychology, see: Gesell, A., Halverson, H. M., Thompson, H., Ilg, F. L., Castner, B. M., Ames, L. B., & Amatruda, C. S. (1940). *The first five years of life: A guide to the study of the preschool child.* Harper and Row; Ilg, F., Ames, L., Haines, J., & Gillespie, C. (1964, 1965, 1972, 1978), *School readiness: Behavior tests used at the Gesell Institute.* Harper and Row; Piaget, J., & Warden, M. (Trans.) (1926). *The language and thought of the child,* Kegan Paul, Trench, Trubner & Co.; Piaget, J., & Tomlinson, J. & A. (Trans.) (1929). *The child's conception of the world,* Routledge. Originally published as an article, 1925; Piaget, J., & Gabain, M. (1932). *The moral judgment of the child.* Kegan Paul, Trench, Trubner & Co.

4. See Pearson, P. D., & Goodin, S. (2010). Silent reading pedagogy: A historical perspective. In E. H. Hiebert & D. R. Reutzel (Eds.), *Revisiting silent reading: New directions for teachers and researchers* (pp. 3–23). International Reading Association.

2 The Persistence of Pedagogy

2.1 THE MANUFACTURED/ASSEMBLED READER

In the 1960s, there was a growing interest in developing detailed systems for education. This was in part fueled by research that speculated about components that might be sequenced and mastered sequentially in order for one to learn. These systems drew their rationale from theories of learning (e.g., Gagné, 1965; Bloom, 1968) that featured optimal and/or typical sequences of skill acquisition and assessments designed to measure each step along the way. Reading was not spared this approach, as developmental approaches shifted to those that reconfigured learning as an assembly line rather than a well-directed orchestra. Instead of likening reading to an ever-maturing orchestration of skills and resources under the direction of a skillful conductor, progress in reading was modeled after systems analyses tied to mass production models or assembly lines, with the reader transported from one isolated component skill to the next until the product was fully assembled and ready to operate (Guthrie, 1973). This approach did not appear overnight; to the contrary, there was a long tradition of separate, decontextualized skill instruction dating back to at least the 1930s and perhaps to the founding era of the field of educational psychology in the very early years of the 20th century.

Skills-Based Curricula

In the early 1900s, curricula began to focus on the teaching of reading. Primarily, this shift was based on educators' efforts to dissect reading and writing development into a presumed set of subskills needed to read. These subskills or component skills were expected to be comprehensive in scope, and learning them in sequence was viewed as being both necessary and sufficient for reading development. The skills covered several areas, including reading readiness, decoding, word recognition, comprehension, critical reading; literary understandings; and study skills. In some cases, the number of skills across these areas was in the hundreds (Otto, 1977; Otto & Chester, 1976); when differentiated further—to account for subskills sequenced for mastery—they could exceed a thousand (see Johnson & Pearson, 1975).

The articulation of many of these skills emanated from studies that identified and measured subcomponents that were shown to correlate (even modestly) with reading achievement (typically measured by oral reading accuracy or reading comprehension performance). Such studies arose from the advent of psychology and its application to reading (see Hartman & Davis, 2008; Huey, 1908), together with the growth of developmental studies (e.g., Gesell & Ilg, 1949). This work placed a great deal of trust in (1) the suggestive causality of correlational relationships, (2) the viability of subjective judgments that undergirded their sequencing, and (3) the validity of measures of mastery.

Most skills were expected to be mastered in the order in which they were prescribed and applied across texts of increasing difficulty. The difficulty level of a selection was determined by vocabulary and syntactic complexities, or by readability formulae based on these or other features, to suggest an approximate grade level. The expectation was that if students engaged in mastering the component skills and applied them to what they read, they would make steady, almost inevitable, progress. Most reading lessons at the elementary consisted of two parts: skill instruction and story reading. Sometimes story reading would precede the skill lessons; at other times, the skills would precede the stories.

Again the regimentation of this standard or assembly-line approach to curriculum resembled an assembly line (Guthrie, 1973), embracing the view that the quality of reading would be assured if the sequenced skills were mastered (see box). Skills were taught separately, then integrated into a lesson plan or into a set of guided steps for reading short selections.

When David was a relatively new assistant professor at the University of Minnesota, he moved his field-based reading course to an elementary school in suburban Minneapolis. They had just adopted a popular assembly-line curriculum system dubbed Wisconsin Design for Reading Skill Development. The curriculum consisted of (a) a set of mastery tests for each of the 50 or so skills at each grade level and (b) extensive packets of worksheets geared to each skill in the testing system. Students took tests on all the skills in a unit. If they passed all the tests, they went on to the next unit to take another set of pre-tests. If they failed some tests, they received packs of worksheets to allow them to practice the skills to get ready for a retest. When they passed all the tests at a pre-set level, say 80%, they went on to the next unit to take more tests and practice more skill worksheets. This is what mastery learning looked like in the 1970s. It was done in the name of individualized instruction. The truth is that it was isolated instruction. Today's version of this sort of assembly-line learning might well be standards-based instruction.

These selections were chosen from a compilation of leveled or graded readers. To a large extent, this approach to reading development still exists today; most reading programs adopt an extended list of skills that are sequenced and tied to a set of graded readers.

Many of the elements identified in studies as being correlated to achievement were later found to contribute to improvements in reading achievement or to have a causal connection to improving reading achievement. Troubling these findings, however, were two noteworthy exceptions: letter-name knowledge and vocabulary. The former was related to initial reading achievement, but did not improve reading achievement if taught. The latter was related to reading comprehension, but not in a fashion that was causal.

Other aspects of the skills-focused approach were also questionable. Many of the skills were difficult to isolate as separate, and therefore not teachable in a piecemeal, decontextualized, or sequenced fashion. Additionally, many of the comprehension skills identified as needing to be taught were outcomes of reading comprehension rather than prerequisites to comprehension. Perhaps for that reason, they were taught in a fashion that was more definitional than explanatory.

Implications for Readers and Teachers

So, what did this mean for the reader? The reader as the "product" to be manufactured through this approach represented a sum or a set of parts—assembled, in theory, by mastering each skill separately rather than in a fashion that was more nuanced, differentiated, or concurrent. Mastering a set of separate skills was viewed as a prerequisite or equivalent to learning to read. If the measure of reading was indicated by a student's performance on tests (i.e., tests of the subskills), then the student would likely perform well on such test tasks. If the measure of reading was to use the skills together, nimbly, and in a range of passages, however, the students were not prepared—unless they learned to do so despite the classroom emphasis on decomposed and decontextualized skill mastery.

In terms of comprehension, the basis for the curriculum development was built on some overly simple notions, hierarchies that were later shown as ill-conceived. Many of the approaches to comprehension relied on set comprehension outcomes, from arbitrarily and ill-fitting sequences of literal to inferential, interpretative to critical, and questions for readers drawn from a pre-set skill sequence. For example, the concept of main idea and other comprehension outcomes might be defined and tested at the same time that a diet of sequenced questions or purposes for reading were provided. For better or worse, it was as if comprehension, literacy, understanding, and critical reading were merely being tested. It was more or less a practice makes perfect approach, rather than facilitating the intentional acquisition of a repertoire of strategies and practices for making and monitoring meaning that emerged from the later influence of constructivism on pedagogy.

In the classroom, reading instruction was largely routinized to include a mix of assigned workbook activities focused on skill development. These exercises occurred in conjunction with guided readings of selections of stories. The guided reading of selections involved a protocol of steps (i.e., preparation for reading the selection, including pre-teaching key vocabulary and setting purposes, followed by directed reading of segments of the selection, orally or silently) and concluded with a series of questions. Follow-up activities included further questions, discussions, or targeted skill development. At times, quizzes were enlisted to assist (or assess) the mastery of skills (Pearson & Goodin, 2010; Venezky, 1984).

Management of this process by the teacher also included grouping the students in accordance with informal assessments of their reading skills. An informal sampling of a student's reading of selections was enlisted to suggest the appropriate level of graded reader that the student could read and, by extension, the best group within which to place them for directed reading. Students deemed to be reading at the instructional level usually exhibited 90 to 95% oral reading accuracy and 75% comprehension accuracy. To read independently, the student needed to have near perfect oral reading accuracy and comprehension. If the student performed poorly in terms of oral reading and comprehension, the student would likely need to be given a lower-graded reader and be placed in a lower-graded reading group. The spread of reading levels across most classrooms spurred a tendency to group students within each class by ability, with three groups being commonplace.

With some exceptions (e.g., problem- or project-based approaches) the same regimen for reading development was used in most elementary schools and across all grade levels. While there were variations in the design elements and specific story selections of different reading programs, the basic protocol or framework remained the same. Variations in the design elements were largely tied to the approach to teaching initial reading skills (i.e., whether the approach involved a synthetic learning of phonemic elements or phonemic awareness was approached analytically, from words). These differences were related to much-debated issues around reading to learn—specifically, whether it occurs concurrently with or after learning to read.

The assembled reader was a reader who was moved along an assembly line and required to adapt to whatever skills the curriculum dealt him at every stage. The curriculum was never asked to adapt to the student. In her review of two longitudinal studies of early readers, Dolores Durkin (1966) highlighted how curricula had become more focused on the particular reading regimen than on actually learning to read—as if the proxy of the assembly line became not only the process but also the goal. Challenging the widely accepted yet unfounded belief that out-of-school early reading (prior to school instruction) would result in long-term problems, Durkin's review suggested that help with reading at home not only benefited early readers in the long run but also came in a range of informal styles and approaches (unlike standardized school-based materials). The notion of success in school was therefore limited, Durkin claimed, to learning how to learn to read in accordance with each school's approach.

References

Bloom, B. S. (1968). *Learning for mastery.* Evaluation Comment, 1.

Durkin, D. (1966). *Children who read early: Two longitudinal studies.* Teachers College Press.

Gagné, R. M. (1965). *The conditions of learning.* Holt, Rinehart, & Winston.

Gesell, A., & Ilg, F. L. (1949). *Child development: An introduction to the study of human growth.* Harper.

Guthrie, J. T. (1973). Models of reading and reading disability. *Journal of Educational Psychology, 65*(1), 9–18.

Hartman, D. K., & Davis, D. H. (2008). Edmund Burke Huey: The formative years of a scholar and field. In K. Youb, V. J. Risko, D. L. Compton, D. K. Dickinson, M. K. Hundley, R. T. Jiménez, K. M. Leander, & D. W. Rowe (Eds.), *57th yearbook of the National Reading Conference* (pp. 41–55). National Reading Conference.

Huey, E. B. (1908). *Psychology and pedagogy of reading: With a review of the history of reading and writing and of methods, texts, and hygiene in reading.* Macmillan.

Johnson, D. D., & Pearson, P. D. (1975). Skills management systems: A critique. *The Reading Teacher, 28,* 757–764.

Otto, W. (1977). The Wisconsin design; A reading program for individually guided elementary education. In R. A. Klausmeier, R. A. Rossmiller, & M. Saily (Eds.), *Individually guided elementary education: Concepts and practices.* Academic.

Otto, W. R., & Chester, R. D. (1976). *Objective-based reading.* Addison-Wesley.

Pearson, P. D., & Goodin, S. (2010). Silent reading pedagogy: A historical perspective. In E. H. Hiebert & D. R. Reutzel (Eds.), *Revisiting silent reading: New directions for teachers and researchers* (pp. 3–23). International Reading Association.

Venezky, R. (1984). The history of reading research. In P. D. Pearson, R. Barr, M. Kamil, & P. Mosenthal (Eds.), *Handbook of Reading Research* (pp. 3–38). Longman.

2.2   THE SEARCH FOR BEST METHOD

Shifting Political Contexts and Debates

In the 1960s, standard curriculum remained dominated by approaches to skill development that involved a diet of graded reading materials tied to a scope and sequence of skills to be mastered across the grades. The approach to reading research remained heavily influenced by psychologists who used various tests to explore the relationship between variables and overall reading achievement. Indeed, a testing regimen increasingly dominated research, resulting in correlational studies, studies exploring aspects of reading difficulties, and research on and development of curriculum (including comparisons of different approaches to beginning reading that relied on test scores or testimonies to assess respective merits).

Shifting political contexts also motivated some of the research designs. Concerns for civil rights in different countries, the emergence of the Cold War, and the beginnings of the space race influenced an increased warlike fervor among educators and the public for certain beginning reading approaches over others. Students' reading performance became the focus, with books such as Rudolf Flesch's 1955 work *Why Johnny Can't Read: And What You Can Do About It*. Flesch suggested that there was a decline in American reading scores at a time when countries around the world were touting the importance of education as fuel for economic, social, and political development. It should be noted, however, that the media and some books of the time overlooked the reality that the evidence for this decline was questionable; in fact, there were indications that students, including more students from diverse backgrounds, were doing better.

These developments coincided with the view that one of the keys to improving student achievement was preschool education and what became a widespread belief that we should begin the teaching of reading earlier. One report by Jerome Bruner (1960)—sponsored by the U.S. National Academy of Science—promoted a rethinking of teaching and development in science and more broadly. Appearing in Bruner's 1960 publication, *The Process of Education*, the report challenged Piagetian (see Piaget & Warden, 1926) maturational views and concepts of readiness and argued for a spiral curriculum, citing a very provocative hypothesis. The hypothesis was, as Bruner stated, "that any subject can be taught effectively in some intellectually honest form to any child at any stage of development" (p. 33).

In terms of reading development, given recognition of the importance of home–school connections as a key foundation to reading development, reading readiness was promoted as a way to build stronger bridges between successful reading at home and through schooling. A 1966 study by Dolores Durkin focused on children who read early received a lot of attention confirming these views and reinforced the growing interest in beginning formal schooling at an earlier age (and finding the best methods to do so). Indeed, in the United States we saw the advent of the Headstart program along with the emergence of a competition over best method of teaching reading and other subject areas; there was, for instance, concern over the neglect of science teaching in the early grades, in addition to heated debates as to the merits of different approaches for teaching both reading and mathematics.

As we have suggested, commitments to varying approaches for beginning reading involved what some have characterized as an ideological fervor that prompted the label "the reading wars." As this debate over phonics versus meaning-centered approaches heated up, mathematics experienced a similar debate over how mathematics should be taught (i.e., skill-based or meaning-centered). On the one hand, these debates were useful in terms of advancing different approaches to research and development and engaging the public in these matters. On the other, their frequent alignment with political ideologies and the fervencies of the discussions seemed to contribute to a partisan-like divide with entrenched views.

Developments in Reading Research Methods and Design

The increased interest in reading marked a period of increased activity in reading research that came to dominate educational scholarship. In 1956 The International Reading Association, headed by its first president, William S. Gray (see Gray, 1956), became the first U.S.-based professional organization focused on reading; notably, 10 years later, *Reading Research Quarterly* became the first research journal devoted solely to reading research. The journal also included an annual summary of research in reading—initially by Helen Robinson, a student and colleague of W. S. Gray. Overall, this research ranged from detailed studies of sub-skills—such as reading rate, visual and auditory discrimination, and the phonics generalizations thought to merit teaching—to readability studies of the stories enlisted to prompt teacher questioning or student grouping strategies (see box on p. 27).

During this period there was also evidence of the emergence of an interest in critical reading, with the advent of the Watson-Glazer Critical Thinking Appraisal and a major study of the components of critical reading undertaken at the Ohio State University (King et al., 1967; Wolf et al., 1967). Building on the work of Dolores Durkin, some scholars focused on early reading. Still others followed the guidance of Helen Robinson and Marion Monroe and focused on reading diagnosis and disability (e.g., the utility of different tests and the saliency of a reader's modal preferences, lateral dominance, and intelligence). With the exception of a UNESCO survey and other occasional studies of illiteracy, most of the international research was undertaken in Western nations, was tied to various analyses of the aforementioned issues, and enlisted similar methods.

Landmark Studies of Reading

Befitting the interest in best methods, beginning approaches proliferated (see Aukerman, 1971), tied to a range of rationales and claims of their benefits. Some

As Robinson and her colleagues (Robinson et al., 1965, 1967) noted, in the 1960s we experienced a significant increase in reading research across an expanding number of areas, including: (1) detailed examinations of predictors of reading achievement; (2) studies of the effectiveness of programs (especially primary programs) for students in different settings; and (3) research on study skills as well as secondary and college reading skills.

At the same time, there were significant developments expanding reading research focused on factors related to: (1) the reader (e.g., sub-abilities, interests, attitudes, personality, and behavior); (2) text characteristics (e.g., readability, legibility); (3) teachers (e.g., their pacing, questioning, and knowledge); (4) tests (e.g., informal, such as IRI [Informal Reading Inventory] or cloze procedure, and standardized tests); and (5) the role of pre-set curriculum (especially basal programs) and the effectiveness of variations of these programs (phonics or meaning-centered approaches) and their subcomponents.

Robinson et al. also noted that three areas were more researched than others. They included visual perception, reading disability, and beginning reading. As Robinson et al. (1965) stated:

> The studies are divided into six major categories. Forty-three fall within the first category of summaries of specific topics. The second major category, relating to teacher preparation, reveals a marked increase in attention. The third category, sociology of reading, continues to be short with major contributions from other fields. Increased interest was shown in three aspects of the psychology of reading: 1] intellectual abilities included four studies of creativity; 2] personality and reading; and 3] readability, with major focus on the cloze procedure. Under the fifth category, teaching of reading, a marked increase in volume of research was found at the primary-grade level.

spurred a large set of comparative studies. Unfortunately, as they represented a mixed bag of pursuits and results, they made viable comparisons and syntheses across these studies difficult, if not impossible.

Nevertheless, the concern for some kind of winner in the competition over the best method contributed to a strong interest in convergence and, in turn, led to two landmark studies intent on addressing the potpourri of research findings in search of an answer to what might work best. The first was a study by Jeanne Chall (1967), conducted with funds from the Carnegie Corporation and later reported on in her work *Learning to Read: The Great Debate*. For this study, she and her team reviewed beginning approaches to reading, detailing the histories of such approaches as well as analyzing the results of studies of these methods. Chall et al. also pursued observations in Great Britain and U.S. schools, interviewing teachers and advocates of various methods. Any acceptance of her discernments requires a leap of faith and a trust in the viability of extrapolations from an array of studies (i.e., studies that varied due to approaches, treatment conditions, and tests). While Chall acknowledged limitations (i.e., that correlational relationships were not causal; that some results were not comparable), she gave the overall nod to methods that stressed the code emphasis, although she did not privilege some code approaches (e.g., synthetic letter-by-letter decoding) over others (e.g., analytic phonics focusing on examining parts of whole words). Further, she made recommendations for curriculum developers, teacher educators, test makers, and researchers.

The second landmark study was tied to the report of the Coordinating Center of the Cooperative Research Program in First Grade Reading Instruction (i.e., the Cooperative First Grade Reading Studies; see Bond & Dykstra, 1967). The Center, housed at the University of Minnesota, attempted to coordinate 20-plus separate studies across the United States; each of the studies examined some facet of different methods for teaching 1st-grade reading. The goal was to compare their results across all of these studies using a common set of pre-test and outcome measures. The approaches under examination included Basal; Basal plus Phonics; the Initial Teaching Alphabet; Linguistic; Language Experience; and Phonic/Linguistic. While some projects administered more measures than others (e.g., in San Diego's Language Experience initiative an attitude measure was enlisted as well), they were all committed to gathering and providing identical information for each project. Information ranged from test data on selected measures to teacher, school, and community characteristics. At the same time, they were committed to common experimental guidelines across all the studies. As is always the case, perfect parallelism and treatment fidelity were not possible—either because of implementation drift or the reality that some projects were at different stages of development than others (and, in some cases, in purer forms that befit their label).

Given that this study was conducted in an age of hard copy (i.e., data cards), one can only imagine the massive coordination required to analyze data that were generated across the 27 projects on several premeasures, background variable measures, and outcome measures (administered approximately 140 days into the project).

Essentially, the cooperative study was a study of the studies of best methods. Its findings suggested that results will vary by settings, teachers, and other variables. Three questions were pursued:

1. To what extent are various pupil, teacher, class, school, and community characteristics related to pupil achievement in first grade reading and spelling?
2. Which of the many approaches to initial reading instruction produces superior reading and spelling achievement at the end of the first grade?
3. Is any program uniquely effective or ineffective for pupils with high or low readiness for reading? (Bond & Dykstra, 1967, p. 115)

Table 2.1. The Cooperative 1st-Grade Studies: Summary of Correlations Between Key Pre-Measures and the Stanford Paragraph Meaning Test for Each of the Six Treatments

Measures	Basal	Initial Teaching Alphabet	Basal + Phonics	Language Experience	Linguistic	Phonic/ Linguistic
Murphy Durrell Phonemes	.46	.53	.52	.41	.50	.57
Murphy Durrell Letters	.52	.58	.55	.51	.55	.59
Metropolitan Word Meaning	.30	.38	.44	.19	.27	.32
Metropolitan Listening	.23	.29	.38	.18	.27	.33
Pitner-Cunningham Intelligence Test	.42	.52	.56	.43	.48	.52

For each approach, correlations between the various measures were pursued. Results of the correlation analysis revealed that the ability to recognize letters of the alphabet prior to the beginning of reading instruction was the single best predictor of 1st-grade reading achievement. As shown in Table 2.1, the best predictor of reading performance was letter name knowledge, regardless of approach.

In terms of the search for the best method, the results presented a mix of findings with regard to comparisons made to the traditional basal approach and moreover a tendency across studies to generate significant within-project difficulties. The analysis of differences in beginning approaches indicated that the various non-basal instructional programs tended to be superior to basal programs when measured by the word recognition skills of pupils after one year of reading instruction. However, differences between basal and non-basal programs were less consistent when measures of comprehension, spelling, rate of accuracy of reading, and word study skills constituted the criterion of reading achievement. The findings of the variance and covariance analysis suggested that there were effects of the approach on some measures but not others—as well as some gender differences and other differences tied to the project, such as where an approach was initiated. The analysis of treatments according to level of readiness for reading revealed that no method was especially effective or ineffective for pupils of high or low readiness as measured by tests of intelligence, auditory discrimination, and letter knowledge.

The cooperative study thus highlighted situational differences, underscoring how differences within projects or treatments are as substantial as differences across treatments. In other words, the effectiveness of a method will likely vary at the hands of different teachers, in different settings, with different students, and so on. The study pointed to two major implications: (1) The failure of a clear winner in the horse race suggests a one-size-fits-all approach or the search for a best approach for all students in all setting may be misguided; and (2) "Eclecticism," or a mix of approaches, may be advisable (a suggestion that essentially displaces notions of theoretical purity).

According to some participants, the developments that occurred related to methods, especially by those engaged in the implementation of the Language Experience Approach were one benefit of the research. Interestingly, a nugget within this work was a statement about writing. As reported by Bond and Dykstra (1967) in the Cooperative First Grade Studies, writing was highlighted as one of many advisable approaches to primary reading programs:

> A writing component is likely to be an effective addition to a primary reading program. In the first place, the Language Experience approach, which involves considerable written expression, was an effective program of instruction. In addition, programs such as i.t.a. and Phonic/Linguistic, both of which were relatively effective, encourage pupils to write symbols as they learn to recognize them and to associate them with sounds. This appears helpful to the pupil in learning sound–symbol relationships. Furthermore, it is likely that writing such common, but irregular, words as "the" helps the child to commit them to his sight vocabulary. (p. 124)

In terms of an overall conclusion of the various studies, the researchers suggested a move away from a comparison of methods (akin to a horse race) and advocated a set of recommendations directed at other considerations. As they stated:

> Future research might well center on teacher and learning situation characteristics rather than method and materials. The tremendous range among classrooms within any method points out the importance of elements in the learning situation over and above the methods employed. To improve reading instruction, it is necessary to train better teachers of reading rather than to expect a panacea in the form of materials.
>
> Children learn to read by a variety of materials and methods. Pupils become successful readers in such vastly different programs as the Language Experience approach with its relative lack of structure and vocabulary control and the various Linguistic programs with their relatively high degree of structure and vocabulary control. Furthermore, pupils experienced difficulty in each of the programs utilized. No one approach is so distinctly better in all situations and respects than the others that it should be considered the one best method and the one to be used exclusively. (Bond & Dykstra, 1967, p. 123)

Subsequent Paths of Inquiry

To some extent, the search for best method in reading also spurred further work on teacher effectiveness—that is, the search for the characteristics (i.e., knowledge, behaviors, thought processes, attitudes, and preparation) of effective teachers. Numerous studies enlisted various observation procedures and other tools to delve into the behavior of teachers and the responses (e.g., cognitive, affective, and social) of students; specifically, they focused on the questioning practices of teachers in reading classrooms and the response patterns of students. In our estimation, the search for effective teaching in some ways fell into the same traps of the search for best methods. In particular, the global search for an effective teacher based on achievement scores yielded little in the way of consistent results. On the other hand, it successfully avoided those traps. For instance, the closely scrutinized relationship between teaching behavior and the types of initiatives and responses of students revealed some interesting patterns.

We would argue that the most significant shift following the search for the best method was a new emphasis on comprehension development, especially for younger students in 2nd grade and below (Pearson, 2000). Contributing to this shift were studies of reading performance over time. These demonstrated that students' early successes in reading were not often sustained when the emphasis shifted to reading to learn. In a number of longitudinal studies, those students taught using a code versus more meaning-centered approaches often floundered as more emphasis was given to reading for understanding. They might have performed well on tests that emphasized word and letter level skills but did poorly on passage level reading (see Tierney, 1992; Tierney & Sheehy, 2003, for a review).

Conclusion

Looking back and digesting the developments made during this period, we did witness some major advances as reading research received increased attention and careful study. Certainly, the number of studies focused on reading surpassed those on other skills or fields of study. But there were other significant advances as well. For example, research foci shifted away from a search for best method as attention turned to teacher research. At the same time, studies of early literacy became more developmental and open-ended as a new respect for the learners' own strategies and approaches to learning developed. Interests in comprehension also began to appear—although these were still largely undersubscribed, as there remained an emphasis on reading comprehension as an outcome rather than as a process.

Across these new paths of inquiry, the limitations of correlation findings became more apparent. As intervention studies proceeded, they raised questions about causal hypotheses for different elements (e.g., teaching the alphabet, teaching vocabulary, etc.). Reading scholars became less prone to accept correlation as causality and became more interested in looking at reading development differentially. This period contributed to many of us seeking a closer examination of the interplay of teaching with student learning across different situations. For many of us, these developments contributed to a shift toward forms of formative studies of teaching and learning, and also studies that examined less broad effects. While standardized tests continued to be used as one measure of student achievement, other measures were also employed—measures that were more focused, situated, and, in turn, more likely to show changes or effects.

One should not discount the merits of the search for the best method of teaching reading, despite its failure to identify the best method for all situations. The search yielded valuable insights about studying method, shifting researchers away from a horse race mentality and into studies that were more formative than summative. A student's performance on a standardized test was no longer viewed as the gold standard; indeed, most researchers recognized that the use of large-scale standardized testing would be unprofitable in the search for the effects of different approaches or reading experiences. Such tests appeared to be insensitive to the effects that researchers might be pursuing. Instead, researchers realized that the new gold standards were long-term effects, sustainable development, and students' ability to apply or transfer what they had learned.

Lastly, it should be noted that the search for the best method of teaching reading was not the sole preoccupation of all reading researchers during this period. Many other pursuits in different areas continued as well, leading to other shifts, including the emergence of special education and a focus on adapting teaching to the specific learning needs of students consistent with the emergence of the notion of learning disabilities (Allington, R. & McGill-Frnzen, A. (1989; 1994)); a major interest in language development and how students learn language (sophistication as a learner had been revered but not fully understood by linguists); and an interest in teaching reading in the content areas. Simultaneously with these developments, a number of scholars shifted their focus from learning to read to studies of reading and thinking as well as reading to learn—especially within the context of secondary education and content area learning. Most notably, the University of Syracuse with Harold Herber (e.g., Herber, 1970) became an epicenter for work regarding content area reading, and the University of Delaware (Stauffer, 1969) became the site that launched practices such as the Directed Reading-Thinking Activity.

References

Allington, R., & McGill-Franzen, A. (1994). Compensatory, remedial, and special programs in language and literacy. In A. Purves (Ed.), *Encyclopedia of the English studies and language arts*. Scholastic.

Allington, R., & McGill-Franzen, A. (1989) Different programs, indifferent instruction. In A. Gartner and D. Lipskey (Eds.), Beyond separate education. New York: Brookes.

Aukerman, R. C. (1971). *Approaches to beginning reading* (1st ed.). Wiley & Sons.

Bond, G. L., & Dykstra, R. (1967). The cooperative research program in first-grade reading instruction. *Reading Research Quarterly, 2*(4), 5–142. doi: 10.2307/746948

Bruner, J. S. (1960). *The process of education*. Harvard University Press.

Chall, J. (1967). *Learning to read: The great debate* (1st ed.). McGraw-Hill.

Durkin, D. (1966). *Children who read early: Two longitudinal studies*. Teachers College Press.

Flesch, R. (1955). *Why Johnny can't read: And what you can do about it* (1st ed.). Harper and Row.

Gray, W. S. (1956). *The teaching of reading and writing: An international survey*. UNESCO.

Herber, H. L. (1970). *Teaching reading in content areas*. Prentice-Hall.

King, M., Ellinger, B., & Wolf, W. (1967). *Critical reading*. Lippincott.

Pearson, P. D. (2000). Reading in the twentieth century. In T. L. Good (Ed.), *American education: Yesterday, today, and tomorrow. Yearbook of the National Society for the Study of Education* (pp. 152–208). University of Chicago Press.

Piaget, J., & Warden, M. (Trans.) (1926). *The language and thought of the child*. Kegan Paul, Trench, Trubner & Co.

Robinson, H. M., Weintraub, S., & Smith, H. K. (1965). Summary of investigations relating to reading, July 1, 1964 to June 30, 1965. *Reading Research Quarterly, 1*(2), 5–126.

Robinson, H. M., Weintraub, S., & Smith, H. K. (1968). Summary of investigations relating to reading, July 1, 1966 to June 30, 1967. *Reading Research Quarterly, 3*(2), 151–301. doi: 10.2307/747092

Stauffer, R. G. (1969). *Directing reading maturity as a cognitive process*. Harper and Row.

Thorndike, E. L. (1917). Reading as reasoning: A study of mistakes in paragraph reading. *Journal of Educational Psychology, 8*(6), 323–332. doi: 10.1037/h0075325

Tierney, R. J. (1992). Studies of reading and writing growth: Longitudinal research on literacy acquisition. In J. Flood, J. Jensen, D. Lapp, and J. R. Squire (Eds.), *Handbook of research on teaching the language arts*. Macmillan.

Tierney, R. J., & Sheehy, M. (2003). What longitudinal studies say about literacy development/what literacy development says about longitudinal studies. In J. Flood, J. Jensen, D. Lapp, & J. R. Squire (Eds.), *Handbook of research on teaching the English language arts* (2nd ed., pp. 171–191). Erlbaum. www.academia.edu/9764833/

Watson-Glazer Critical Thinking Appraisal. Pearson. www.watsonglaser.com.au/index.html

Wolf, W., Huck, C., & King, M. (1967). *Critical reading ability of elementary school children*. The Ohio State University Research Foundation.

Part II

WAVES OF DEVELOPMENT

3 The Cognitive Wave

3.1 THE CONSTRUCTIVIST READER

Constructivist notions of meaning making turned long-held views of comprehension upside down. They highlighted that the reader, not the text, is the key determinant of meaning (Anderson & Pearson, 1984). The reader does not extract meaning from the text by some form of translation; rather, constructivist readers draw on their knowledge of the world, including their existing awareness of such elements of characters (e.g., traits, motivations, and most likely actions), events (i.e., their possible antecedents and outcomes), and settings (e.g., the nature and influence thereof).

For educators and curriculum developers, constructivism brought to the fore a number of flaws in researchers' notions of comprehension, such as the tendency both to align instruction with a hierarchy (i.e., from literal to inferential to interpretative) and to assume that a reader's meanings could be fixed and deemed accurate without regard to likely variations (i.e., due to background knowledge and perspectives).

The Shift for Readers

Constructivism moved us from notions of reading as extracting meaning to reading as constructing meaning. The previous assumption was that the meaning is in the text and the job of the reader is to extract it in order to understand it. The constructivist assumption was that meaning lies in the interaction among the reader, the text, and the context in which the reading takes place; the job of readers is to construct a model of meaning by integrating text-based information with knowledge from memory while taking into account the context (e.g., studying for a text versus reading for pleasure). The interaction might be spurred by the text, but the true driver of meaning making is the reader—stemming from their background knowledge and views of the world. The reader is the meaning maker—assessing what make sense and how ideas fit together and judging what is salient to their interests, purposes, and perspectives. Informational text, expositions, or arguments are understood in terms of whether the ideas suggested by the text are viable in relationship to the reader's experience. Readers also use their knowledge to monitor their emerging models of meaning, looking for congruence between their account of text meaning with their prior knowledge.

The shift to constructivism and the constructivist reader represented a shift of the locus of control from the text or teacher to the reader. Likewise, it represented a shift of authority from a set of predetermined answers or interpretations to a respect for meaning making that evolves from the interactions between the reader and the text. Judging the understandings and interpretations of readers requires a consideration of the plausibility rather than the correctness of a reader's answers. And, to judge such plausibility requires an appreciation of readers' interactions with the text, especially in terms of their background knowledge, purposes, and sense of what the task requires.

A constructivist reader is not engaged in an effort to read by translating the words into meaning. At the outset of reading, constructivist readers are asking their own questions, making predictions, and scoping possible ideas. As they move forward, they formulate hypotheses shaped by their own experiences and the ideas presented with their reading of the text, the plot suggested, and the discoveries that they have discerned—all while enlisting and adjusting their preexisting schema or knowledge structures. They do not proceed one brick at a time, but holistically fit the pieces into what they deem to be the most reasonable whole. This process involves repeated cycles of forward inferencing and predicting, combining prior knowledge with prompts and clues suggested by the text. Meaning making thus entails shuttling back and forth between the whole and the parts as plausible and coherent understandings are sought.

In a constructivist model, a reader's agency is paramount. Accordingly, reading comprehension through this lens is concerned with how readers weigh elements suggested by the text differentially, depending on the possible meanings and their unique fit with the successively refined model of meaning they are building. In other words, according to Collins et al. (1980), reading comprehension requires a progressive refinement model. They suggest readers make meaning for a text that unfolds as follows:

> text-understanding proceeds by progressive refinement from an initial model to more and more refined models of the text.... The initial model is a partial model, constructed from schemata triggered by the beginning elements of the text. Successive models incorporate more and more elements from the text. The models are progressively refined by trying to fill the unspecified variable slots in each model as it is constructed. As the questions associated with the unfilled slots in more refined models become more and more specific, the search for relevant information is constrained more and more.... people pursue the refinement process until it converges on a solution that satisfies a number of conditions for a plausible model. (pp. 387–388)

Likewise, notions such as a reduction of uncertainty and psycholinguistic guessing games have been used by scholars in an effort to capture meaning-making processes. In accordance with such a model, constructivist readers may be

Considered in terms of processes, constructivist readers are repeatedly doing the following:

- Accessing relevant background knowledge to help them suggest possible meanings
- Asking questions as they read about what makes sense
- Making predictions
- Checking the fit of new ideas with what they know and what they have already constructed for the text they are reading
- Judging plausibility, coherence, fit, and comprehensiveness

engaged in what might be described as a form of detective work—using their understanding of the world and knowledge of events and people to discern patterns or instantiations of what took place or is occurring (see box).

In other words, constructivist reading is not passive. Constructivist readers are engaged and actively enlisting strategies to relate ideas to their world, recognizing how patterns and ideas occur differently and in various contexts. In other words, constructivist readers ask questions, relate what they read to the worlds they discern, adopt different perspectives, and perhaps visualize and make predictions. Whereas assembled and enculturated readers might be limited by a set of prior questions—assigned a text to read, sometimes quickly, either silently or aloud, and then asked questions about it—constructivist readers are initiators engaged in generating questions, moving in, out, and around the text. They contemplate the saliency of ideas as they consider meanings that they deem pertinent.

From the outset, every reader is occupied in making inferences based on their understanding of the world, their purposes and perspectives, using these inferred understandings to weigh either the poignancy or the comparative insignificance of that which others might simply take as literal. In other words, the pathway to reading for understanding is not a direct route from literal to inferential to evaluative; it can just as easily begin with the inferential and evaluative. Likewise, the reader is immediately critical, contemplating and judging the feasibility and integrity of ideas in ongoing ways. Constructivist reading—really any reading for understanding—does not proceed from the literal to the inferential to interpretive to critical; it can move and morph in a variety of directions depending on how a particular reader's model of meaning evolves.

The constructivist readers are also apt to use cues from the text that go beyond the word or the sentence. They tend to know that ideas are presented with key words within and across sentences, but also that these ideas are connected across texts structured in predictable ways. Stories follow an event structure tied to key characters. Informational texts will often enlist variations on familiar structural templates that organize information within and across paragraphs and section: problem solution, compare and contrast, conflict resolution, sequences of events, steps, or stages, and so on. Constructivist readers use their knowledge of text structures and genres as checks on ideas as they move across and between texts.

Finally, the understandings developed by constructivist readers may be difficult to judge without understanding the purposes they chose, the perspectives and background knowledge they activated, and the monitoring routines they enacted to check the fit of the new to the known, and their sense of what is appropriate and necessary in the context in which they are doing the reading. Answers will vary, befitting the range of meanings that arise from the interactions between the ideas suggested by the text and those that the reader brings to the process. If teachers are to assess constructivist reading, they need to adjust their judgments in ways that acknowledge and affirm the various meanings readers are apt to construct.

References

Anderson, R. C., & Pearson, P. D. (1984). A schema-theoretic view of basic processes in reading comprehension. In P. D. Pearson (Ed.), *Handbook of reading research* (pp. 255–291). Longman.

Bransford, J., Brown, A. L., & Cocking, R. R. (Eds.). U.S. National Research Council Committee on Developments in the Science of Learning, Division of Behavioral and Social Sciences and Education, & Board on Behavioral, Cognitive, and Sensory Sciences. (2000). *How people learn: Brain, mind, experience, and school.* National Academy Press.

Collins, A., Brown, J. S., & Larkin, K. (1980). Inference in text understanding. In R. J. Spiro, B. C. Bruce, & W. F. Brewer, (Eds.), *Theoretical issues in reading comprehension: Perspectives from cognitive psychology, linguistics, artificial intelligence, and education* (pp. 385–410). Erlbaum.

Goodman, K. S. (Ed.). (1968). *The psycholinguistic nature of the reading process.* Wayne State University Press.

Neisser, U. (1976). *Cognition and reality: Principles and implications of cognitive psychology.* W. H. Freeman.

Pearson, P. D., & Johnson, D. D. (1978). *Teaching reading comprehension.* Holt, Rinehart, & Winston.

Spiro, R. J. (1980). Constructive processes in prose comprehension and recall. In R. J. Spiro, B. C. Bruce, & W. F. Brewer (Eds.), *Theoretical issues in reading comprehension: Perspectives from cognitive psychology, linguistics, artificial intelligence, and education* (pp. 248–275). Erlbaum.

Tierney, R. J. (1990). Redefining reading comprehension. *Educational Leadership, 47*(6), 37–42.

3.2 THE COGNITIVE TURN: CONSTRUCTIVISM AND SCHEMA THEORY

Some Background on the 1970s

The political context for developments in the late 1960s and early 1970s involved major global tensions around civil rights and the war against communism, which persisted in countries like Vietnam and in political events around the world. While we saw the end of the Vietnam War and a peace accord between Egypt and Israel, various countries were still in struggle. The world seemed to be balanced on the precipice of change, yet it remained embattled within and across nations. In some countries where the political climate seemed to be in a state of flux, there also appeared to be a shift from social mindedness to individualism.

- In the United States, the civil rights movement continued forward on a path despite the assassination of Martin Luther King, Jr., in 1968 and the preponderance of white flight across communities. Civil rights movements spurred developments in women's rights (e.g., the landmark decision of *Roe v. Wade*), the change of the voting age to 18 years (via the 26th Amendment), and increased access to education for handicapped students (i.e., the Education for All Handicapped Children Act, passed in 1975). The United States also began secret talks to end the war in Vietnam in 1972, finally withdrawing in 1973. Meanwhile, impeachment proceedings against President Nixon began in 1973, which ended with his resignation in 1974.
- In Canada, Prime Minister Pierre Trudeau became involved in the establishment of a bilingual country with the 1969 Official Languages Act, established Canada's relationship with China, and pursued his vision of a "Just Society" with the charter of rights across Canada.
- Australia withdrew from the war in Vietnam in the early 1970s and voted in a socially progressive labor government under Gough Whitlam (1972 to 1974). (This was dismissed, however, in a form of parliamentary coup d'état at the hands of conservative interests and with the aid of a British-appointed governor-general). Aboriginal Australians were given right to vote in Commonwealth elections in 1962, but the struggle for rights persisted.
- In Europe we saw the gradual expansion of the European Union.
- The Middle East experienced the oil crisis and more violence involving Israel.
- In China, the period between 1966 and 1976 marked the Cultural Revolution, which caused an enormous and brutal upheaval to families and society structures in the name of reestablishing a Marxist-influenced

doctrine. (The election of Deng Xiaoping in the later 70s represented a shift away from such strong ideologically driven policies to a new openness to the West and a market economy. In 1972, Nixon visited China; by the end of the decade, relationships between China and the United States were restored.)

- In South America, the assassination of Salvador Allende and the rise of a junta under Pinochet changed the government in Chile.
- Africa continued on a path of decolonization with independence for Angola and Mozambique and the removal of Ethiopia's longtime ruler. Trade union strikes, student-led protests, and participatory socialism were emerging as challenges to South African racism and other inequities.

Universities As Sites for Social Activism and Innovation

In the Western world, especially the United States, universities were sites where an increasing proportion of the population was accessing higher education, including postgraduate education. Universities were meccas for intense debates over social issues (e.g., civil rights) and sites for opposition to the war in Vietnam. They were also places where people and ideas were less segregated, and where major developments offered a diverse set of new frameworks for the mind—including many that challenged the dominance of behaviorism in the social sciences. Ironically, some of the funding for—and productivity in enhancing—advances in the social sciences was tied to military funding and institutions interested in improving human performance, such as the U.S. Navy.

Numerous scholars using a range of lenses (e.g., psychological, linguistic, and social) were interested in the nature of learning and readily drawn to studying meaning making in complex learning environments, including reading. They moved beyond solely syntactical accounts of text to more semantic, logical, and pragmatics-focused frameworks to account for meaning making (see Austin, 1962; Fillmore, 1968; Grice, 1975; Searle, 1969). As research in cognition emerged, they formed new scholarly areas—including psycholinguistics, cognitive science, and text linguistics (see Pearson & Cervetti, 2015, 2017).

At the same time, a number of scholars became more and more interested in unraveling the mystery of meaning making. On the one hand, this was spurred by the advent of artificial intelligence and technology, which began to assume a more prominent role (e.g., Schank, 1982). During this period we saw the beginnings of modern computer systems as advances in hardware and software coupled with attempts to mimic human reasoning. These included:

- The world's first general microprocessor, Intel 4004 (1971).
- Programming language that was simple, flexible, and interfaced with other languages moving forward.
- Storage shifts to floppy disks, mouse-held devices, and optic fibers.

- Other major advances in hardware with the introduction of handheld calculators, early personal computers, VCRs, video game consoles, mobile phones, the Sony Walkman, and microwave ovens.

Increasingly, scholars were interested in natural language processing and whether they could model text comprehension. And, to this end, researchers were exchanging ideas across their institutions in ways that pulled together the thinking of different disciplines. Of relevance to reading, a range of scholars from sociologists to anthropologists to linguists and psychologists to computer scientists focused on reading and literacy development. As they did so, major shifts in our understanding and views occurred.

Early Cognitive Developments

The shift away from behaviorism became more and more discernable as the inadequacies of behaviorism to explain complex phenomena became increasingly apparent. Though the cognitive turn in education did not gain traction till the early 1970s, its antecedents can be traced back to Immanuel Kant, Jean Piaget, and Gestaltists (see box). For example, in his book *Critique of Pure Reason*, Immanuel Kant (Kant et al., 1998) discussed innate structures in the mind for perceiving the world. Piaget (1926), in his discussion of young children's thinking, coined the term "schema" and suggested that mental frameworks— constantly under construction by assimilation and accommodation—served as vehicles for perceiving and interpreting our worlds and building concepts. Gestaltists (around the turn of the 20th century), in terms befitting emerging cognitive thinking, proposed that the mind acts as a global whole with self-organizing principles.

In his 1985 readable account of these developments, *The Mind's New Science: A History of the Cognitive Revolution*, Howard Gardner cites George A. Miller in suggesting that the beginning of what he referred as a zeitgeist, or the emergence of cognitive science, began on the second day of the Massachusetts Institute of Technology's Symposium on Information Theory. As Gardner indicates, this day— September 11, 1956—may represent a key date on which the rising tide of interest in alternatives to behaviorism was foreshadowed by three key papers. Specifically, Noam Chomsky presented a landmark paper detailing the shortcomings of previous linguistic attempts and behaviorism to explain the language-learning capabilities of young children; Newell and Simon presented their efforts to simulate complex processing on a computer; and Miller presented his work on memory organization and processing, in which he postulated that memory could only cope with seven plus or minus two chunks. These papers foreshadowed the mounting multidisciplinary interests in new views of knowledge structures and processes— precursors to the burgeoning field of informational processing, which became known as cognitive science. This was a change of epic proportions, especially for theoretical notions of reading and approaches to research (i.e., what, why, and how

Here are some landmark developments in psychology leading to the cognitive revolution in reading and learning more broadly construed:

1932 Frederick Bartlett publishes a landmark book, *Remembering*, which resurfaced as foundational to the cognitive turn.

1956 George Miller publishes his paper "The Magical Number Seven, Plus or Minus Two."

1959 Noam Chomsky publishes his review of B. F. Skinner's *Verbal Behavior* critiquing behaviorism.

1959 Lawrence Kohlberg completes his study of moral development.

1962 Albert Bandura publishes *A Psychology of Being*.

1964 Jean Mandler and George Mandler publish *Thinking: From Association to Gestalt*.

1965 Herbert Simon publishes *The Shape of Automation for Men and Management*.

1967 Marvin Minsky publishes *Computation: Finite and Infinite Machines*.

1967 Ulric Neisser founded cognitive psychology.

1972 Endel Tulving distinguishes episodic and semantic memory.

1972 Vygotsky Circle's scholar Alexander Luria publishes *The Working Brain*.

1977 Albert Bandura publishes *Social Learning Theory*.

1978 The term "cognitive neuroscience" is invented.

1977 John Flavell publishes *Cognitive Development*.

1977 Richard Anderson, Rand Spiro, and William Montague publish *Schooling and the Acquisition of Knowledge*.

1979 John Bransford publishes *Human Cognition*.

1985 Howard Gardner publishes *The Mind's New Science*.

research was conducted) as well as theories and developments in reading practice (i.e., what was taught, and how).

As Gardner's description suggests, this shift gathered momentum in the 1950s and 1960s due to the confluence of work by a range of scholars (including computer scientists, linguists, communication theorists, psychologists, and psycholinguists). First separately and later together, they were motivated to go beyond behaviorism to understand the complex meaning-making processes occurring across different contexts as readers encountered paragraphs and texts. In summary:

- Computer scientists were interested in modeling meaning making for purposes of computer simulation and developing applications ranging from playing chess to summarizing news stories.
- Linguists were keen to extend their analyses of language to complex texts and extended everyday discourse by enlisting semantic and logical frameworks, such as case grammar.

range of interest in cognitive science

- Communication theorists complemented this work with pragmatic analyses, including speech act theory (e.g., Austin, 1962; Searle, 1969).
- Psychologists were so frustrated by the ineffectiveness of complex behaviorist models to explain how language works for either adults or for the language acquisition by children that they became open to new models, such as Chomsky's top-down account of language expertise and development and the notion of nativist constructs, such as a language acquisition device.
- Equally important to psychologists was the role of meaning making and nature of memory, especially in terms of schema theoretic notions. Originally spurred by Frederick Bartlett (1932/1995), this interest was also advanced by influential cognitive psychologist Ulric Neisser (1967, 1976) via his discussions of the workings of re-episodic memory in recalling events (e.g., the Challenger explosion) as well as by David Ausubel's views on and approaches to meaningful learning. Ausubel (1968) stated that "if [he] had to reduce all of educational psychology to just one principle, [he] would say this: The most important single factor influencing learning is what the learner already knows. Ascertain this and teach him accordingly" (p. vi).
- The advent of psycholinguistic perspectives (e.g., Miller, 1963, 1975) linked language and cognition, especially in terms of how language was used and understood and its indeterminant nature. Such pursuits were foundational to applications of artificial intelligence to language processing but also a shift to enlisting a linguistic lens, especially in terms of language development.
- These developments, in turn, spurred psycholinguistic models of reading and gave credence to notions of hypothesis testing, risk taking, predicting, and child-directed learning—displacing mastery and rote routines as models for learning. Kenneth Goodman's (1967) study of oral reading—using semantic and syntactic miscue analyses of oral reading to undercover meaning making—challenged notions of strict reading accuracy. Goodman's notion of reading as a psycholinguistic guessing game was complemented by the writings of Frank Smith (1973, 2012); and James Britton (1970); together, their psycholinguistic notions constituted key bridges to reader-centered views of meaning making that aligned with transactional notions of meaning making touted by Rosenblatt (1978). Indeed, their views both foreshadowed and became foundational in the shift toward a view of learners as actively engaged in figuring out their world—that is, a view of the learner as more productive than receptive, and more purposeful and self-determined than directed and rote.

Accordingly, the cognitive revolution in reading was linked to a series of developments in the field in the early 1970s—especially in those interdisciplinary gatherings of scholars on the state of the field. In part, these gatherings were sponsored by the U.S. National Institute of Education (NIE), which provided much of the leadership and funding for learning research during this period. Two such serious attempts funded by NIE led directly to the funding of the Center for the Study of Reading at the University of Illinois and the Institute for Research on Teaching at Michigan State University.

Among most reading educators, the adoption of a cognitive perspective for reading comprehension seemed to have a somewhat fitful history. Arguably, early traces of a cognitive perspective were apparent in the analyses of paragraph reading by E. L Thorndike in 1917 and in the discussion of memory for text by Edmund Burke Huey in 1908. But while Thorndike and even Huey acknowledged the nature of the reader's meaning making, they tended to extol the importance of a close authorial reading of the text. They seemed to espouse the belief that the reader needed to arrive at some kind of literal understanding of the text before beginning to infer, interpret, or evaluate. The modeling of comprehension in the first half of the 1900s also emanated from the psychometric work tied to correlational analyses and factor analyses (see Frederick Davis, 1971, 1972). The factor-analytic model building of reading comprehension and related measures, though impactful (for instance, by contributing to the teaching of vocabulary as a key factor in comprehension development), tended to be tied to models of reading that were more reductionistic than synergistic.

By the 1960s and 1970s, interest in reading comprehension among reading educators had gained momentum as a result of increased interest in teacher questioning and scaffolding of reading comprehension. This interest was evident in Frank Guszak's 1967 study of teacher questioning in reading, in Harold Herber's work in 1970 on teaching reading in the content areas, Russell Stauffer's (1969) directed reading–thinking teaching approach, and other discussions of process-oriented comprehension as problem solving that appeared in articles by Herbert Simon (1971), Jill Olshavsky (1976), and Roberta Golinkoff (1975).

Key to what became viewed as the cognitive revolution was research emerging from studies of models of meaning making challenging behaviorism and analyses of meaning rooted in the grammatical deep structure of texts. Notably, David Rumelhart proposed a shift from linear models of comprehension to an interactional model involving top-down (reader-based) and bottom-up (text-based processes) (Rumelhart, 1983). Keith Stanovich (1980; 1984) provided an interesting twist on Rumelhart's interactive model by proposing an interactive-compensatory model positing that readers who struggle often place greater emphasis on top-down than bottom-up resources to compensate for shortcomings in their foundational skills. John Bransford, a graduate student at the University of Minnesota at the time, and his colleagues (see Bransford, 1979; Bransford & Johnson, 1972) did some of the most extraordinary experiments demonstrating the power of schemata. His work highlighted that new meanings are developed as readers enlist their knowledge of the world to formulate meanings with the text—in other words, meanings do not come from the text or author, but from the progressive refinement of meanings suggested by the ideas gleaned or put forward by the reader. It is the reader's knowledge of the world and the relationships between ideas that prompt the reader to predict meanings suggested by the text; thus, schema access, activation, and instantiation by the reader are vital for meaning making.[1] Take the example offered by Bransford and Johnson (1972) in which readers were asked to make sense of the following text.

> If the balloons popped, the sound wouldn't be able to carry since everything would be too far away from the correct floor. A closed window would also prevent the sound from carrying, since most buildings tend to be well insulated. Since the whole operation depends on a steady flow of electricity, a break in the middle of the wire would also cause problems. Of course, the fellow could shout, but the human voice is not loud enough to carry that far. An additional problem is that a string could break on the instrument. Then there could be no accompaniment to the message. It is clear that the best situation would involve less distance. Then there would be fewer potential problems. With face-to-face contact, the least number of things could go wrong. (Bransford & Johnson, 1972, p. 719)

By triggering—or not triggering—a reader's schema (via pictures and topics), Bransford and Johnson were able to demonstrate the importance of a reader's schema in the process of meaning making. Without triggering, the participants (who were not given the picture ahead of reading the passage) could not make sense of the passage and did not recall it very well. However, when a schema was triggered (by providing a picture before the text), readers had no problems making sense of the text and recalled the passage well (see Figure 3.1).

In a second study reported in the same article, Bransford and Johnson (1972) similarly demonstrated the importance of schema access and activation prior to reading. Participants were presented with the following passage:

> The procedure is actually quite simple. First you arrange things into different groups. Of course, one pile may be sufficient depending on how much there is to do. If you have to go somewhere else due to lack of facilities that is the next step, otherwise you are pretty well set. It is important not to overdo things. That is, it is better to do too few things at once than too many. In the short run this may not seem important but complications can easily arise. A mistake can be expensive as well. At first the whole procedure will seem complicated. Soon, however, it will become just another facet of life. It is difficult to foresee any end to the necessity for this task in the immediate future, but then one never can tell. After the procedure is completed one arranges the materials into different groups again. Then they can be put into their appropriate places. Eventually they will be used once more and the whole cycle will then have to be repeated. However, that is part of life. (Bransford & Johnson, 1972, p. 722)

This second study again demonstrated the power of schema to facilitate meaning making. Essentially, the topic (doing laundry) served to activate the relevant schema. Students given the schema (doing laundry) had a coherent understanding, while those without the schema floundered. Similar demonstrations of the nature and role of schema emerged from other studies. For example, a study by

**Figure 3.1. Adaptation of Image Used to Trigger Schema by
Bransford & Johnson (1972)**

Source: Adapted from Bransford and Johnson, 1972.

Anderson et al. (1977) enlisted an ambiguous text (about wrestling) to illustrate the role of schema in shaping meaning.

The nature of cognitive processes during reading is vividly illustrated by this classic example from Collins et al. (1980); it demonstrates the nature of schema selection and modification.

The text begins: "He plunked down $5 at the window." As Collins et al. (1980) detailed, oftentimes readers will be prompted to infer that the text involves an exchange at a ticket office between a female ticket clerk and a purchaser. However, as the text proceeds, the reader's understanding may become confounded when it reads next: "She handed him $2.50 but he refused to take it." It is not until the reader shifts his schema, which will likely occur when he reads remainder of the text, that he settles on an understanding that is coherent and plausible: "So when they went inside she bought him a bag of popcorn."

As Collins et al. (1980) outlined:

The theory states that text-understanding proceeds by progressive refinement from an initial model to more and more refined models of the text. . . . The initial model is a partial model, constructed from schemata triggered by the beginning elements of the text. Successive models incorporate more and more elements from the text. The models are progressively refined by trying to fill the unspecified variable slots in each model as it is constructed. As the questions associated with the unfilled slots in more refined models become more and more specific, the search for relevant information is constrained more and more. . . . people pursue the refinement process until it converges on a solution that satisfies a number of conditions for a plausible model. (pp. 387–388)

Finally, a study by Reynolds et al. (1982) highlighted the same overriding impact of cross-cultural background knowledge with a comparison of different readings of the following passage by African American and Anglo-American 8th-grade students. The passage illustrates African American language play in phrases such as "sounding" and "doing the dozens" (pp. 358–359).

Dear Joe,

I bet you're surprised to be hearing from your old friend Sam. It's been a long time since you moved away so I thought I'd drop you a line to catch you up on what's going on around here. Things haven't changed much. . . . School has been going O.K. but I did get in some trouble last week.

It started out as a typical Thursday. Typical that is until lunchtime; at that point things started to get interesting. But don't let me get ahead of myself. I'll start at the beginning. Renee, my sister, and I were almost late for school. . . . We barely caught our ride and made it to school just as the tardy bell rang.

Classes went at their usual slow pace through the morning, so at noon I was really ready for lunch. I got in line behind Bubba. As usual the line was moving pretty slow and we were all getting pretty restless. For a little action Bubba turned around and said, "Hey Sam! What you doin' man? You so ugly that when the doctor delivered you he slapped your face!" Everyone laughed, but they laughed even harder when I shot back, "Oh yeah? Well, you so ugly the doctor turned around and slapped your momma!" It got even wilder when Bubba said, "Well man, at least my daddy ain't no girlscout!" . . . The next thing we knew we were all in the office. The principal made us stay after school for a week; he's so straight! On top of that, he sent word home that he wanted to talk to our folks in his office Monday afternoon. Boy! Did I get it when I got home. That's the third notice I've gotten this semester. As we were leaving the principal's office, I ran into Bubba again. We decided we'd finish where we left off, but this time we would wait until we were off the school grounds.

Well I have to run now. . . . Write soon and let me know what's going on with you.

Later,

Sam

Their study generated findings that highlight how differences in understanding are culturally anchored. In particular, Reynolds et al. examined how 8th-grade students (White and Black) treated the material and interpreted the encounter. They noted the response of one student in particular who, "on being told that white children understood the letter to be about a fight instead of sounding, . . . looked surprised and said, 'What's the matter? Can't they read?'" (p. 365).

The schema that a reader activates and accesses is tied not only to their background knowledge; there are also other dynamics at play. Some of the dynamics may be quite interpersonal, involving the relationship between the reader and the author or fellow readers, or tied to the reader's embodied relationship with what might be (for the reader) an enlivened plot or narrative elements. As researchers such as Pichert and Anderson (1977) and Jose and Brewer (1984) found, the perspective of the reader had an impact on their focus as well as on the amount and details of their recall (in one of their studies, they compared the recall of readers who were asked to read a text from one character's perspective [e.g., a burglar] with that of readers who were not assigned any particular point of view). This work underscored how perspectives not only heighten recall of the text but also trigger different views and criticisms of the ideas presented— highlighting how a reader's positionality, purposes, identity, and perspective might engineer specific forms of enhanced meaning making. With this in mind, one could create the circumstances that ensured success or failure based on the match or mismatch with the background, experience, and the perspective prompted by the text.[2]

Discussions of background knowledge extended to the propositions represented in the text and how they might be structured (i.e., in terms of genre, rhetorical conventions, and a reader's expectations for and knowledge of the semantic and logical constitutions of text structures) (see Kintsch & van Dijk, 1978; Pearson & Johnson, 1978; Tierney & Mosenthal, 1982). In conjunction with this work, a number of scholars turned to analyzing readers' schema for text by unpacking the structure of both narratives and expository text with the intent to study the influence of readers' experiences and expectations. In particular, a number of studies examined key elements of narrative structure, such as setting, plot, or event structures (see Figure 3.2; Stein & Trabasso, 1981; Trabasso et al., 1984; Whaley, 1981).

Additionally, they looked at exposition using various forms of structural analyses including hierarchies and flowcharts (see Figure 3.3; Armbruster & Anderson, 1980; Dansereau, 1979; Geva, 1983; Marshall & Glock, 1978; Meyer, 1975; Meyer et al., 1980).

So What?

Together these studies represented major shifts in our understanding of the nature of meaning making—especially with regard to the importance of access to and activation of background knowledge or pre-existing schema in encoding meaning. For reading educators, these findings challenged many of the traditional assumptions about reading comprehension, including:

Figure 3.2. Narrative Structure

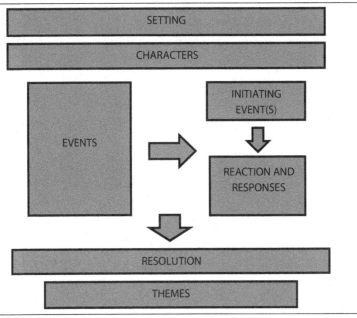

Figure 3.3. Expository Text Map Example

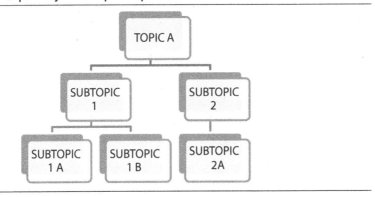

- The notion that reading is an act of reception, wherein the reader's task is to decipher the author's meaning;
- The belief that meaning involves translating words into meaning—and that there is a single meaning for (and in) the text that has to be unlocked by the reader;
- That meaning involves first the literal then the inferential processes needed to build a model of meaning.

Perhaps the most powerful revelation was the notion that readers create meaning—whether their goals are to learn from text or to engage with the images or ideas suggested by authors. In turn, we came to recognize that inferencing was the core of meaning making, not a by-product or an adjunct to what appeared to be explicit meaning presented in the text. Meaning making required activating, accessing, maintaining and refining a reader's background knowledge and schemata. This was akin to suggesting that the text is in part generated by the reader—that meanings represent a mix of explicit and inferred cues interlaced with views of what the author was intending. In other words, meanings emerged from negotiations or composites of orchestral proportions—often with elastic qualities, but difficult to separate from one another.

The ramifications for testing were also profound. Unfortunately, standardized tests and other large-scale assessments of reading comprehension often stack the deck against cultural and linguistic minorities by emphasizing a particular psychometric dimension, the discrimination index. The discrimination index is the correlation between performance on a single item (right or wrong) and the overall test score; it is used to weed out items with low correlations between an item score and the overall score. But consider the implications of that practice. Items with low discrimination indices are those that low-scoring students tend to perform better on relative to their high-performing peers. And who are the students who do better on the low-discriminating items? Those who score low on the overall test. And who scores lower on the overall test—linguistic, cultural, and economic minority students. The implication? The very use of the discrimination index is likely to be a source of bias against minorities, however we define them, in the assessments. It systematically excludes items that might benefit students who might not be performing as well. Indeed, the background knowledge effect has a broad and overriding influence, regardless of how well a reader measures on standardized tests. On culturally diverse material, for instance, otherwise well-performing cultural minority readers may not do as well, displaying characteristics of normally poor-performing readers and vice versa.

This key shift in views of meaning making in turn prompted additional pursuits. These included exploring in more depth the dynamics of how readers employ background knowledge not only to address a range of problems (especially complex knowledge domains) but also to explore the nature of complex knowledge and how it is acquired and built. These shifts in understandings also prompted an interest in cognitive engineering, learning to learn, or what developmental psychologist John Flavell (1977) termed "metacognition."

At the same time, there was increased recognition that we had neglected work on reading comprehension. We were seeing a decline in students' reading performance beyond the 3rd grade, and an orientation to teaching reading comprehension that appeared to be geared toward testing rather than understanding the nature of comprehension for extended text or its development.

In reading education, the combination of developments in psycholinguistics and cognition, along with various conscious efforts to focus on reading comprehension, began occurring in research and the literature as well as in research funding. Simultaneously, a number of new studies and books began to focus on reading comprehension, including *Schooling and the Acquisition of Knowledge* (1977), edited by Richard Anderson, Rand Spiro, and William Montague, and *Teaching Reading Comprehension* (1978), written by David and Dale Johnson.

Another key development involved the creation of a major research center, The Center for the Study of Reading at the University of Illinois. It was there that an interdisciplinary group of scientists (psychologists, linguists, psycholinguists, literacy education researchers, and artificial intelligence scholars primarily from Bolt, Beranek, and Newman) focused their research on reading comprehension examined from a cognitive perspective. These scholars—as well as others around the world—quickly energized the field and advanced our understanding of reading comprehension as seen from a cognitive and text linguistic perspective. Among the numerous notable scholars in this group were Alice Davison, Allan Collins, Andrew Ortony, Ann Brown, Bertram Bruce, Bonnie B. Armbruster, Debra Genter, Diane Schallert, Dolores Durkin, George McConkie, Georgia Green, Jerry Morgan, Joseph Campione, Richard Anderson, Stella Vosnaidou, Thomas Anderson, William Brewer, and the two of us, Rob and David.

Getting Personal

As reading researchers in this era (actually, David is just about a half-decade ahead of Rob in terms of age and entry into the field), both of us were keenly interested in probing the nature of meaning making. We became captivated by the burgeoning field of work and the promise it had for challenging our practices and understanding of reading.

Rob's story (Tierney)

Rob was an assistant professor at the University of Arizona, with colleagues such as Joseph Vaughan, Wilbur Ames, William Valmont, Patricia Anders, Diane Schallert, and Ken and Yetta Goodman.

As I began probing the nature of meaning making through a constructivist lens, I was immediately conscious of mismatches with our teaching and testing practices. Indeed, constructivist notions of reading comprehension suggest that the normalcy of unstable measures of reading comprehension for a reader or across readers depends on the relevance of the passage to the reader and the nature of the probes. The pertinence of these findings for testing were apparent in the responses of different students to the rich assortment of passages included in the U.S. National Assessment of Educational Progress in the 1970s and early 1980s. Student performances were quite varied in accordance with what appeared to be the shifting relevance of different passages for different students.[3]

The difficulty in standardizing forms of reading comprehension also emerged in a study I conducted with colleagues (Peterson et al., 1978), in which we analyzed the use of the Informal Reading Inventory (widely used by teachers to place students at a reading level for instructional purposes). The Informal Reading Inventory assumed that if a student answered a carefully developed set of questions with 75% accuracy, that student could be seen as handling those materials and could be given other material at that readability level. However, assuming the accuracy of the aforementioned cognitive studies in reading comprehension, a student's "reading level" is in reality prone to fluctuations in topics, texts, and the reader's purposes for reading—as well as the probes enlisted. Accordingly, across three parallel sets of questions to the same reading passage, we found that student performance was incredibly erratic. For one set of questions a student might attain a perfect score and be placed at a certain reading level; for a parallel set of questions on the same passage, that same student might perform quite differently and be placed at a different level. Essentially, the volatility of the assessment was predictable if you adopted a constructionist (or re-constructionist) view of meaning making.

As views of reading shifted, we realized the need for approaches that tapped into readers' constructions as they engaged with text. In an effort to discover what readers do as they engage with extended text for themselves, many of us began to use retellings, think-alouds as they read, and other means of opening windows into their process. At the same time we asked students to respond to a range of texts, we also went to great lengths to pin down what, arguably, was the author's representation of text through detailing its explicit and implicit semantic, logical, and pragmatic features. To this end, I was drawn to Carl Frederiksen's (1975) rather comprehensive system for analyzing text en route to understanding a reader's understanding.

Together with two of my colleagues (Connie Bridge and Mary Jane Cera, who were pursuing graduate studies at the University of Arizona at the time), I spent countless hours trying to apply semantic and logical analyses in pursuit of what was always somewhat elusive—namely, the author's representation of meaning, In the end, Connie, Mary Jane, and I pursued a study of the discourse processing operations of 3rd-graders, applying Frederiksen's text analyses to two texts as the bases for examining students' recalls. Laboring through this text analysis was educative, and we quickly became aware that texts are suggestive rather than definitive when it comes to delineating their meaning. We came to realize that meanings are always in the eyes of the beholders and can be quite varied. We would suggest that text analyses require inferences as to what writers are trying to do—even writers are not fully aware of that, purposely or otherwise. When you ask for and analyze a student's retelling, you have introduced yourself as an audience to the reader—you are a reader once again. Certainly, we could label text as fitting certain grammatical functions—or in terms of agents, objects, actions, modifiers, and so on—but meanings are derived only when readers apply their knowledge of the world to these elements. And, as a researcher, you realize that your studies of readers are apt to be readings of their readings.

Despite these limitations, the text analysis did provide an important basis for our study. By comparing the retellings of the 3rd-graders to our propositionally based author's representation, we were able to demonstrate that readers of varying abilities are engaged in a rich mix of inferential operations as they fill out the meanings, and that they do so regardless of ability level. Of relevance to notions of reading comprehension at the time, the findings dispelled the view that inferential comprehension followed from literal comprehension of text, that poorer readers were not ready to engage inferentially until they had addressed the literal. The findings yielded what now may seem obvious:

- All readers (good and poor) recall a mix of explicit and inferred information tied to their rendition or meaning spurred by the text;
- Various factors may contribute to the amount and nature of a reader's recall, including background knowledge and confidence.

Perhaps one of the most notable research studies with which I was involved was one that my doctoral advisee at the time, David Hayes, pursued with me. Building on discussions of the role of background knowledge as it relates to the sport of cricket, David studied the role of analogies as a means of building background knowledge for the reading of unfamiliar text (see Hayes & Tierney, 1982). The study highlighted the types of issues that grew out of schema theoretic views of reading and learning, as well as some key methodological concerns. Specifically, the study presented passages on cricket—resembling a news account that might appear in an Australian newspaper—followed by questions and predictions of what might follow. Perhaps predictably, as evidenced in the recall and other measures, the findings confirmed how knowledge of a familiar topic (e.g., baseball) afforded a schema that bridged to an understanding of an unfamiliar topic (e.g., cricket).

For example, the study was able to demonstrate the important role of background knowledge by presenting readers with passages mimicking press releases on cricket similar to the following:

Today's cricket

The bowlers placed their men in slips and covers, but to no avail. The batsmen hit one four after another as well as an occasional six. Not once did their ball hit the stumps or get caught.

The research highlighted the extent to which a student's background knowledge (activation and access) is at the center of meaning making and comprises the fuel of readers' schema for developing plausible and coherent meanings.

They also highlight the extent to which background knowledge may account for one's reading successes or shortcomings, as well as how curriculum and tests might intensify a student's existing privilege or disadvantage by accommodating only certain reader experiences. Moreover, they underscore the pragmatics of meaning making that inform readers' attempts to make sense of the ideas suggested to them by the text.

Based on these emerging insights, along with my foray into schema theory and speech act theory, my colleagues and I pursued other studies that contributed to a number of papers discussing basic postulates of reading (e.g., Tierney & Spiro, 1979). With James Mosenthal, there were studies investigating the nature and role of text especially differentiating between cohesion and coherence (e.g., Tierney & Mosenthal, 1982, 1983; Mosenthal & Tierney, 1984) and with Diane Schallert several studies exploring the nature and role of secondary text material in history and science (e.g., Schallert et al., 1984). In papers with Jill LaZansky (e.g., Tierney et al., 1987), we explored the reader–writer relationship and what might be a reasonable band of allowable interpretation emerging from a transactional view of meaning making. In a study I carried out with Taffy Raphael (Raphael & Tierney, 1981), we demonstrated how the meaning making of readers acknowledges and may compensate for inconsistencies, especially in familiar and concrete text forms. We explored the ability of 5th-grade readers to detect inconsistencies (or obvious misinformation) purposely placed in parallel texts that we constructed and deemed familiar or unfamiliar, narrative or nonnarrative. The approach involved asking readers to respond to requests for free recall and probes directed at inconsistencies to an array of parallel texts (Table 3.1).

The study highlighted the reader's own role in meaning making and how the readers were not constrained by authors—especially when the ideas were familiar or presented in the context of everyday interactions, such as written accounts of conversations. For example, the readers in the study, unless dealing with unfamiliar text, maneuvered around inconsistencies in their retellings. When interviewed about their treatment of theses, they indicated a consciousness of the contradictions, which many attributed to authorial oversight.

While these pursuits helped me rethink reading, I was aware that there were major loose ends. When I look back at these developments, I believe that cognitive views of reading should more fully explore issues of prediction or forward inferencing, persona, identity, imagery, and affect. I was increasingly interested in perspective taking (see Neisser, 1976; Pichert & Anderson, 1977; Jose & Brewer, 1993), author–reader relationships (see Bruce, 1980; Pratt, 1977), and the extent to which students were engaged in visualizing (Pressley, 1976, 1979; Sadoski & Paivio, 2001; Schallert, 1980; Tirre et al., 1979; Waltz, 1979), as well as what Michael Benton had described as a kind of secondary world experience (Benton, 1992). I would find myself intrigued by the sparkle in readers' eyes and a sense of magic when readers talked about the images they formed as they read and the vicarious nature of the journey with which they engaged as well as the tug-of-war-type relationship with the author.

Table 3.1. Passages Enlisted by Raphael & Tierney, 1981

Familiarity	
Familiar	**Less Familiar**
Mary had a problem. This is a story about how she solved it (could not solve it). There were two things that Mary had always wanted. One was a place to be alone and the other was a place that she could use for bird watching. Mary decided there was one way that she could get both of these things. Her family was renting a home in the big city and in the backyard there was a large tree. . . .	The Poly Plastic Bag Company had a problem. This is a story of how they solved it (could not solve it). There were two things that the Poly Plastic Bag Company had always wanted. One was a factory of their own and the other was offices that were out of the city. They decided that they could get both of these things. They were currently renting a factory in a big city. But near a quiet river outside the city, they owned a block of land. . . .
Discourse Style	
Non-dialogue	**Dialogue**
All over the world children like (hate) different games. In some countries, children enjoy playing a game called Fly. It gets its name because to play the game you need to be able to leap through the air. The game is easy to learn and play. The only equipment you need is six sticks that are similar in style and about as long as a person's foot and wide as a thumb. After the sticks are found, they are placed on the ground. . . .	Lisa and Mike were bored. It was Saturday and they did not know what to do, until Lisa had an idea. "I know a game we can play that they play in some countries. You know children all over the world like (hate) to play different games," Lisa said. Mike was interested and asked, "What is the game?" "It is called Fly, because to play the game you need to be able to leap through the air," Lisa said. "You only need six . . ."

My interviews of young readers and writers highlighted the primacy and saliency of these experiences. There was a kind of dreamlike, impressionistic quality to the images that readers formed as they read. Further, they often burrowed into a story or assumed a perch within the story world and usually moved around in a story as if they were able to project themselves into it—as if they were operating with a homunculus or something like an avatar of themselves. With Patricia Enciso, who had overlapping interests, a background in drama education, and a wealth of knowledge of children's literature, I pursued this sense of embodied participation with 4th-graders across a number of stories. We presented the material at the National Reading Conference, but I regret that we never published this research. Fortunately, Pat Enciso went more deeply into these pursuits with her thesis, and some of her subsequent work that included a very innovative procedure (Symbolic Representation Interview) she developed enabling students to display their participatory engagements with stories (Enciso, 1990; 1996). I remain convinced that understanding reading is a frontier not fully explored in terms of these dimensions.

David's Story *Pearson*

My (David's) story comes in four short chapters. Graduate student days at Minnesota, a post-doctoral fellowship in linguistics and psycholinguistics at the Univrseity of Texas-Austin, a study leave at Stanford in 1976, and an unplanned move from Minnesota to the Center for the Study of Reading at the University of Illinois at Urbana-Champaign in 1978. In each of these chapters, the theoretical ground on which I was standing was compromised if not destroyed.

Chapter 1. In grad school I was never too enamored of all the early reading issues that dominated the culture there (it was, after all, the home of the coordinating center for the infamous First Grade Studies of the 1960s and featured among its faculty were Guy Bond, Bob Dykstra, John Manning, Ted Clymer, and Jay Samuels—all bonded by an abiding interest in K–1 reading). Having been a 5th-grade teacher, I wanted to know more about comprehension and language. So I traveled across the quad to the Psych Department to take Jim Jenkin's year-long seminar on the newly exploding field of psycholinguistics. There I got immersed in that community and past and current research about how little (and bigger) humans learn to use their language to enter into the family of humankind. Met three post-docs (John Bransford, Jeffrey Franks, and Bill Brewer). When I read and listened to reports of their paradigm-shifting research, it changed my life. I would never again be able to look at a behaviorally grounded S-R (stimulus-response) bond with a straight face. Understanding consists of synthesis and integration, not analysis and decomposition. I never looked back.

Chapter 2. In the fall of 1969, I defended my dissertation at Minnesota, loaded up our brand-new Ford Torino (just like Clint Eastwood's!) with my wife Mary Alyce and whatever we could shove into the back seat and roomy trunk, and headed off to take a postdoc in psycholinguistics in the Psych Department at UT Austin. Met a lot of famous language researchers (Phil Gough and Donald Foss) and linguists (Emmon Bach, Robert Wall, and visitors like Noam Chomsky, George Lakoff, Charles Fillmore, and James McCawley) whose ideas and approaches to language study and analysis shook not only my behaviorist learning theories but my faith in positivistic searches for truth and unqualified causality. I also met and began a lifelong collaboration with Michael Kamil.

Chapter 3. I returned to Minnesota in 1970 to take up a professorship and started to do a number of classic psycholinguistic experiments in which we varied language features and looked at their impacts on understanding and/or word identification. By the fall of 1975, I had earned the right to a single quarter study leave, so on New Year's Day of 1976, Mary Alyce and I stuffed what we could into the back seat and less commodious trunk of our 1974 Fiat Sedan, leaving room for two interim acquisitions (4-year-old Matthew and 2-year-old Susan), and headed for Stanford for three months *not* in the Minnesota winter. Bob Calfee was the sponsor of this postdoctoral study leave. I found three seminars at once that again changed my worldview, not by upsetting it, but by deepening it and providing it with an even richer theoretical underbelly. The first was a course offered by Terry Winograd (he was at both Stanford and Xerox Research Park—the site of ground-breaking work that became the backbone of cognitive science) on the computer-ized analyses of both the semantic and syntactic foundations of text. The second was Gordon Bower's advanced studies of cognition; and the third was Robert Calfee's course on advanced statistical designs for these burgeoning approaches to the close examination of text and knowledge as the primary determinants of comprehension. I returned to Minnesota in April 1976 armed with new ideas and methods that would literally change my life and career path.

Chapter 4. In the spring of 1978, right after Dale Johnson and I published our twin books, *Teaching Reading Vocabulary* and *Teaching Reading Comprehension*, I got a call from Jean Osborn from the newly funded Center for the Study of Reading (CSR) at the University of Illinois, inviting me to come as a visiting scholar for a year to help them carve out an agenda on how to teach reading comprehension. By 1978, 2 years into their first cycle of funding, CSR had astounded the reading research community with seminal studies, some of which we have already described in the early parts of this chapter, but they had not yet done much work on the pedagogical part of their five-year work plan. I would get to help them craft that agenda. Fresh off the book, how could I turn that down? I didn't. So Mary Alyce and I packed up our two cars (the sole Fiat had been replaced by a classic 1976 Olds Cutlass hard-top convertible and Mary Alyce's "king of the road" golden VW Scirocco sporty sedan) with whatever they could carry besides 7-year-old Matthew and 5-year-old Susan. Changed my life. Changed our lives—those of Mary Alyce, Matthew, and Susan as well.

My Minnesota grad student, Taffy Raphael, came with me, and we started a line of work that 3 years later had morphed into her now famous QAR (Question-Answer-Relationship) work. I got to know *so much more* about schema theory and developed an even more knowledge-centric view of comprehension than I came with. Got hit between the eyes with the emerging work on metacognition by Ann Brown and Joe Campione, the schema work of Dick Anderson and colleagues and Alan Collins, the work on metaphor by Andrew Ortony, the work of Rand Spiro on how schema control and are controlled by the comprehension process, the work on stories by Bill Brewer and Chip Bruce—it was a never-ending list, just went on and on. And a year later Rob came as my partner in moving the peda-gogical agenda along. That was the start of another lifelong collaboration—the end result of which is the volume you are reading now.

That's my conversion story from the 1970s. Life changing. Career shaping. Never looked back.

Closing Remarks

The 1970s and the cognitive turn signaled significant shifts in the study of reading comprehension and spurred a large number of studies of reading comprehension

---

CONSTRUCTIVISM: THE CONFLUENCE OF DEVELOPMENTS

Essentially, constructivism marked a shift in the zeitgeist with a confluence of influences, including:

- a decline in behavioristic frames for thinking about and studying reading;
- building on studies of language development, an increased interest (by linguists) in nativist views of language learners (i.e., that learners are wired to make sense of their world);
- a growing interest in the pragmatics of language (i.e., how language is used, as well as semantic and logical analyses of language), along with an interest in studying the nature of extended text—especially narrative and expository forms;
- a rediscovery and reincarnation of schema theoretic notions that dated back to Kant and extended to Bartlett, 1995/1932; Piaget, 1926; and Gestaltist views (e.g., Wertheimer, 1945);
- the stimulus of discussions among selected cognitivists, including Jerome Bruner (1986), Ulric Neisser (1967), and a number of young researchers such as John Bransford (1979) and Rand Spiro (1980);
- an interest in unraveling the scripts we use to understand our worlds that might be enlisted as a means of building machines that could think (e.g., Schank, 1982);
- an interest in the nature and role of teaching and learning, following David Ausubel's work on advanced organizers (1960), Harold Herber's work on scaffolds (e.g., structured overviews) (1970), Russell Stauffer's reading-thinking approaches driven by prediction making (1969; 1970), and Anthony Manzo's work on reciprocal questioning (1973);
- key developments and reconceptions of reading in conjunction with the rise of interest in psycholinguistics in the early 1970s; and
- concerns about students' reading comprehension performance.

---

processes. Many of these studies connected to and extended previous studies, but did so in ways that challenged past views and approaches (i.e., previously used frameworks and methodology). The confluence of studies represented a shift of monumental proportions; as many concur, it represented a zeitgeist in thinking that exploded traditional models, including past notions of reading comprehension abilities as fixed acts of reception rather than productive, dynamic, and creative transactions with oneself and others (see box). The studies reflected encounters with texts from the real world by adventurous and creative researchers who were themselves changing—in their views of meaning making as well as in the range of studies they were pursuing with a new openness for explanatory frames.

Constructivism also reinforced theoretical developments emanating from psycholinguists, who argued that reading involved a transaction between reader and the text in a fashion that befitted the reader's natural language-processing abilities. At the same time, it supported a growing corpus of work that examined the role of scripts, schemas, and knowledge processes—including studies by cognitivists and artificial intelligence scholars that aligned readers' recalls and responses with various forms of text analyses. For a large number of reading researchers, constructivism shifted attention away from a code emphasis in the early grades to a meaning orientation across all of the grades.

As constructivism advanced and the cognitive turn proceeded, attention shifted to previously unheralded past research and theory developments that highlighted the natural learning prowess of readers. This was especially the case for nativist views of readers—that is, that readers are wired to make meaning—as well as developmental views of learners tied to schema theoretic notions (e.g., Immanuel Kant; Jean Piaget, 1926; and Frederick Bartlett, (1932/1995) and cognitive perspectives offered by Ulric Neisser (1967), Jerome Bruner (1986), and Gestaltists (e.g., Wertheimer, 1945). This past research substantiated learning approaches emanating from the work of pedagogical scholars such as David Ausubel (1960), Harold Herber (1970), and Russell Stauffer (1969, 1970).

The end result was that studies of reading comprehension, and especially how to teach and facilitate it through pedagogy, proliferated. A large number of studies of readers' meaning making with extended text used retellings and oral reading miscues as a basis for examining the hypotheses and inferencing made by readers as they read. Rather than employ syntactic or phonological analyses of words, researchers shifted to using semantic and pragmatic analyses of readers' transactions with texts. Rather than being overly text-driven, constructivist studies therefore highlighted the agency of the reader and the role of perspective taking.

Despite this proliferation of studies, many elements of meaning making that were mentioned nevertheless remained undeveloped or limited. The roles of visualization and schema development were only partially formulated during this period. In terms of limitations, cognition remained a model of meaning making that was individualized and contained primarily "within the head." Research therefore tended to focus on an individual's meaning making without regard to the influence of social transactions with others; further, the relationship between meaning and one's multiple selves was neglected. The models of meaning making also tended to be quite verbocentric—ignoring the kinds of engagements that are participatory and aesthetic as readers travel vicariously within the animated, "material" world of the text in the company of others (including characters, authors, or fellow readers).

References

Anderson, R. C. (1984). Role of the reader's schema in comprehension, learning and memory. In R. C. Anderson, J. Osborn, & R. J. Tierney (Eds.). (1984). *Learning to read in American schools: basal readers and content texts* (pp. 243–258). Erlbaum.

Anderson, R. C., & Pearson, P. D. (1984). A schema-theoretic view of basic processes in reading comprehension. In P. D. Pearson (Ed.), *Handbook of reading research* (pp. 255–291). Longman.

Anderson, R. C., Reynolds, R. E., Schallert, D. L., & Goetz, E. T. (1977). Frameworks for comprehending discourse. *American Educational Research Journal, 14*(4), 367–381. doi: 10.3102/00028312014004367

Anderson, R. C., Spiro, R. J., & Montague, W. E. (Eds.). (1977). *Schooling and the acquisition of knowledge.* Erlbaum.

Armbruster, B. B., & Anderson, T. H. (1980). *The effect of mapping on the free recall of expository text.* Center for the Study of Reading Technical Report No. 160. University of Illinois. hdl.handle.net/2142/17929

Austin, J. L. (1962). *How to do things with words.* Clarendon Press.

Ausubel, D. P. (1960). The use of advance organizers in the learning and retention of meaningful verbal material. *Journal of Educational Psychology, 51*(5), 267–272. doi: 10.1037/h0046669

Ausubel, D. P. (1968). *Educational psychology: A cognitive view.* Holt, Rinehart, & Winston.

Baker, L., & Brown A. L. (1984). Metacognitive skills and reading. In P. D. Pearson, R. Barr, M. L. Kamil, & P. Mosenthal (Eds.), *Handbook of reading research* (pp. 353–394). Longman.

Bartlett, F. C. (1995). *Remembering: A study in experimental and social psychology* (Reissued ed.). Cambridge University Press. First published 1932.

Bransford, J. (1979). *Human cognition: Learning, understanding, and remembering.* Wadsworth.

Bransford, J., Brown, A. L., & Cocking, R. R. (Eds.). U.S. National Research Council Committee on Developments in the Science of Learning, Division of Behavioral and Social Sciences and Education, & Board on Behavioral, Cognitive, and Sensory Sciences. (2000). *How people learn: Brain, mind, experience, and school.* National Academy Press. doi: 10.17226/6160

Bransford, J. D., & Johnson, M. K. (1972). Contextual prerequisites for understanding: Some investigations of comprehension and recall. *Journal of Verbal Learning and Verbal Behavior, 11*(6), 717–726. doi: 10.1016/S0022-5371(72)80006-9

Britton, J. (1970). *Language and learning.* Penguin Books.

Brown, A. L. (1987). Metacognition, executive control, self-regulation and other more mysterious mechanisms. In F. E. Weinert & R. H. Kluwe (Eds.), *Metacognition, motivation and understanding* (pp. 65–116). Erlbaum.

Bruce, Bertram C. (1980). Plans and social actions. In R. J. Spiro, B. C. Bruce, & W. F. Brewer (Eds.), *Theoretical issues in reading comprehension: Perspectives from cognitive psychology, linguistics, artificial intelligence, and education* (pp. 367–384). Erlbaum.

Chomsky, N. (1959). Review of *Verbal behavior* by B. F. Skinner (1957). *Language, 35*(1), 26–58. doi: 10.2307/411334

Collins, A., Brown, J. S., & Larkin, K. (1980). Inference in text understanding. In R. J. Spiro, B. C. Bruce, & W. F. Brewer (Eds.), *Theoretical issues in reading comprehension: Perspectives from cognitive psychology, linguistics, artificial intelligence, and education* (pp. 385–410). Erlbaum.

Dansereau, D. F. (1979). Development and evaluation of a learning strategy training program. *Journal of Educational Psychology, 71*(1), 64–73. doi: 10.1037/0022-0663.71.1.64

Davis, F. B. (1972). Psychometric research on comprehension in reading. *Reading Research Quarterly, 7*(4), 628–678. doi: 10.2307/747108

Davis, F. B. (Ed.). (1971). *The literature of research in reading with emphasis on models: Final report*. Graduate School of Education, Rutgers State University, and National Center for Educational Research. files.eric.ed.gov/fulltext/ED059023.pdf

Enciso [Edmiston], P. (1990). *The nature of engagement in reading: Profiles of three fifth graders' engagement strategies and stances*. (Unpublished doctoral dissertation). The Ohio State University.

Enciso, P. (1996). Why engagement in reading matters to Molly. *Reading and Writing Quarterly, 12*, 271–294.

Fillmore, C. J. (1968). The Case for Case. In E. Bach & R. T. Harms (Eds.), *Universals in linguistic theory* (pp. 1–88). Holt, Rinehart, & Winston.

Flavell, J. H. (1977). *Cognitive development*. Prentice-Hall.

Frederiksen, C. H. (1975). Representing logical and semantic structure of knowledge acquired from discourse. *Cognitive Psychology, 7*(3), 371–458. doi: 10.1016/0010-0285(75)90016-X

Gardner, H. (1985). *The mind's new science: A history of the cognitive revolution*. Basic Books.

Geva, E. (1983). Facilitating reading comprehension through flowcharting. *Reading Research Quarterly, 18*(4), 384–405. doi: 10.2307/747375

Golinkoff, R. M. (1975). A comparison of reading comprehension processes in good and poor comprehenders. *Reading Research Quarterly, 11*(4), 623–659. doi: 10.2307/747459

Goodman, K. S. (1967). Reading: A psycholinguistic guessing game. *Journal of the Reading Specialist, 6*(4), 126–135. doi: 10.1080/19388076709556976

Goodman, K. S. (2000). Ken Goodman on his life in reading. *History of Reading News, 23*(2). www.readinghalloffame.org/node/276

Goodman, K. S. (Ed.). (1968). *The psycholinguistic nature of the reading process*. Wayne State University Press.

Grice, P. (1975). Logic and conversation. In P. Cole & J. Morgan, *Syntax and semantics, vol. 3: Speech acts* (pp. 41–58). Academic Press.

Guszak, F. J. (1967). Teacher questioning and reading. *The Reading Teacher, 21*(3), 227–234.

Halliday, M. A. K. (1973). *Explorations in the functions of language*. Edward Arnold.

Halliday, M. A. K. (1975). *Learning how to mean: Explorations in the development of language*. Edward Arnold.

Halliday, M. A. K., & Hasan, R. (1976). *Cohesion in English*. Longman.

Hayes, D. A., & Tierney, R. J. (1982). Developing readers' knowledge through analogy. *Reading Research Quarterly, 17*(2), 256–280. doi: 10.2307/747486

Herber, H. L. (1970). *Teaching reading in content areas*. Prentice-Hall.

Hilgard, E. R., & Bower, G. H. (1966). *Theories of learning* (3rd ed.). Appleton-Century-Crofts.

Jose, P. E., & Brewer, W. F. (1984). Development of story liking: Character identification, suspense, and outcome resolution. *Developmental Psychology, 20*(5), 911–924. doi: 10.1037/0012-1649.20.5.911

Kant, I., Guyer, P., & Wood, A. W. (Eds.). (1998). *Critique of pure reason*. Cambridge University Press. Original work published 1781.

Kintsch, W., & Van Dijk, T. A. (1978). Toward a model of text comprehension and production. *Psychological Review, 85*(5), 363–394. doi: 10.1037/0033-295X.85.5.363

Manzo, A. V. (1969). The ReQuest procedure. *Journal of Reading, 13*(2), 123–126.

Marshall, N., & Glock, M. D. (1978). Comprehension of connected discourse: A study into the relationships between the structure of text and information recalled. *Reading Research Quarterly, 14*(1), 10–56. doi: 10.2307/747293

Meyer, B. J. F. (1975). *The organization of prose and its effects on memory*. American Elsevier Publishing Company.

Meyer, B. J. F., Brandt, D. M., & Bluth, G. J. (1980). Use of top-level structure in text: Key for reading comprehension of ninth-grade students. *Reading Research Quarterly, 16*(1), 72–103. doi: 10.2307/747349

Miller, G. (1963). *Language and communication.* McGraw Hill.

Miller, G. (1975). *The psychology of communication.* Harper and Row.

Mosenthal, J. H. (1984). *Instruction in the interpretation of a writer's argument: A training study* (Doctoral dissertation, University of Illinois at Urbana-Champaign). ProQuest (Order No. 8502253).

Mosenthal, J. & Tierney, R. J. (1984). Misnotions of text: The cohesion concept and its ramifications. *Reading Research Quarterly,* 19, 2, pp. 240–243.

Neisser, U. (1967). *Cognitive psychology.* Appleton-Century-Crofts.

Neisser, U. (1976). *Cognition and reality: Principles and implications of cognitive psychology.* W. H. Freeman.

Olshavsky, J. E. (1976). Reading as problem solving: An investigation of strategies. *Reading Research Quarterly, 12*(4), 654–674. doi: 10.2307/747446

Pearson, P. D. (2013). The effects of grammatical complexity on children's comprehension, recall, and conception of certain semantic relations (reprint). *Journal of Education, 193*(1), 1–16. doi: 10.1177/002205741319300102

Pearson, P. D., & Johnson, D. D. (1978). *Teaching reading comprehension.* Holt, Rinehart, & Winston.

Peterson, J., Greenlaw, M. J., & Tierney, R. J. (1978). Assessing instructional placement with the IRI: The effectiveness of comprehension questions. *Journal of Educational Research, 71*(5), 247–250. doi: 10.1080/00220671.1978.10885083

Piaget, J., & Warden, M. (Trans.) (1926). *The language and thought of the child.* Kegan Paul, Trench, Trubner & Co.

Pichert, J. W., & Anderson, R. C. (1977). Taking different perspectives on a story. *Journal of Educational Psychology, 69*(4), 309–315. doi: 10.1037/0022-0663.69.4.309

Pratt, M. L. (1977). *Toward a speech act theory of literary discourse.* Indiana University Press.

Pressley, G. M. (1976). Mental imagery helps eight-year-olds remember what they read. *Journal of Educational Psychology, 68,* 355–359.

Pressley, G. M. (1979). Imagery and children's learning: Putting the picture in developmental perspective. *Review of Educational Research, 47,* 585–622.

Raphael, T. E., & Tierney, R. J. (1981). The influence of topic familiarity and the author–reader relationship on detection of inconsistent information. In M. L. Kamil & M. M. Boswick (Eds.), *Directions in reading: Research and instruction, 30th yearbook of the National Reading Conference* (pp. 40–50). National Reading Conference.

Reynolds, R. E., Taylor, M. A., Steffensen, M. S., Shirey, L. L., & Anderson, R. C. (1982). Cultural schemata and reading comprehension. *Reading Research Quarterly, 17*(3), 353–366. doi: 10.2307/747524

Rosenblatt, L. (1978). *The reader, the text, the poem: The transactional theory of the literary work.* Southern Illinois University Press.

Rumelhart, D. (1983). Toward an interactive model of reading. In H. Singer & R. B. Ruddell (Eds.), *Theoretical models and processes of reading* (3rd ed., pp. 722–750). International Reading Association.

Sadoski, M., & Paivio, A. (2001) *Imagery and text: A dual coding theory of reading and writing.* Erlbaum.

Schallert, D. L. (1980). The role of illustrations in reading comprehension. In R. J. Spiro, B. C. Bruce, & W. F. Brewer (Eds.), *Theoretical issues in reading comprehension*. Erlbaum.

Schallert, D., Ulerick, S., & Tierney, R. J. (1984). Relational mapping as a discourse analysis method. In C. D. Holley & D. Dansereau (Eds.), *Spatial learning strategies: Techniques, applications and related Issues* (pp. 255–275). New York: Academic Press.

Schank, R. C. (1982). *Reading and understanding: Teaching from the perspective of artificial intelligence*. Erlbaum.

Searle, J. R. (1969). *Speech acts: An essay in the philosophy of language*. Cambridge University Press.

Simons, H. D. (1971). Reading comprehension: The need for a new perspective. *Reading Research Quarterly, 6*(3), 338–363. doi: 10.2307/747124

Smith, F. (1973). *Psycholinguistics and reading*. Holt, Rinehart, & Winston.

Smith, F. (2012). *Understanding reading: A psycholinguistic analysis of reading and learning to read* (6th ed). Routledge. Original work published 1971.

Smith, F. (2015). Twelve easy ways to making learning to read difficult, and one difficult way to make it easy. In F. Smith *Landmarks in literacy: The selected works of Frank Smith* (pp. 13–26). Routledge. doi: 10.4324/9781315744490

Smith, F., & Goodman, K. S. (2008). Profiles and perspectives: On the psycholinguistic method of teaching reading, revisited. *Language Arts, 86*(1), 61–65.

Spiro, R. J. (1980). Constructive processes in prose comprehension and recall. In R. J. Spiro, B. C. Bruce, & W. F. Brewer, (Eds.), *Theoretical issues in reading comprehension: Perspectives from cognitive psychology, linguistics, artificial intelligence, and education* (pp. 248–275). Erlbaum.

Spiro, R. J., Bruce, B. C., & Brewer, W. F. (Eds.). (1980). *Theoretical issues in reading comprehension: Perspectives from cognitive psychology, linguistics, artificial intelligence, and education*. Erlbaum.

Stanovich, K. (1980). Toward an interactive-compensatory model of individual differences in the development of reading fluency. *Reading Research Quarterly, 16*, 32–71.

Stanovich, K. (1984). The interactive-compensatory model of reading: A confluence of developmental, experimental, and educational psychology. *Remedial and Special Education, 5*(3), 11–19.

Stauffer, R. G. (1969). *Directing reading maturity as a cognitive process*. Harper and Row.

Stauffer, R. G. (1970). *The language-experience approach to the teaching of reading*. Harper and Row.

Steffensen, M. S., Joag-Dev, C., & Anderson, R. C. (1979). A cross-cultural perspective on reading comprehension. *Reading Research Quarterly, 15*(1), 10–29. doi: 10.2307/747429

Stein, N. L., & Trabasso, T. (1981). *What's in a story: An approach to comprehension and instruction*. Center for the Study of Reading Technical Report No. 200. University of Illinois. www.ideals.illinois.edu/bitstream/handle/2142/18031/ctrstreadtechrepv01981i00200_opt.pdf

Tierney, R. J. (1990). Redefining reading comprehension. *Educational Leadership, 47*(6), 37–42.

Tierney, R. J., Bridge, C., & Cera, M. J. (1978). The discourse processing operations of children. *Reading Research Quarterly, 14*(4), 539–573. doi: 10.2307/747262

Tierney, R. J., LaZansky, J., Raphael, T., & Cohen, P. (1987). Authors' intentions and readers' interpretation. In R. J. Tierney, P. L. Anders, & J. N. Mitchell (Eds.), *Understanding readers' understanding: Theory and practice* (pp. 205–226). Erlbaum.

Tierney, R. J., & Mosenthal, J. (1982). Discourse comprehension and production: Analyzing text structure and cohesion. In J. A. Langer & M. T. Smith-Burke (Eds.), *Reader meets author: A psycholinguistic and sociolinguistic perspective* (pp. 55–104). International Reading Association.

Tierney, R. J., & Mosenthal, J. (1983). The cohesion concept's relationship to coherence of text. *Research in the Teaching of English, 17*(3), 215–229.

Tierney, R. J., & Spiro, R. J. (1979). Some basic notions about reading comprehension: Implications for teachers. In J. Harste & R. Carey (Eds.), *New perspectives in comprehension*, Monographs in teaching and learning, no. 3 (pp. 132–137). School of Education, Indiana University.

Tirre, W. C., Manelis, L., & Leicht, K. L. (1979). The effects of imaginal and verbal strategies on prose comprehension by adults. *Journal of Reading Behavior, 11*, 99–106.

Trabasso, T., Secco, T., & Van Den Brock, P. (1984). Causal cohesion and story coherency. In H. Mandl, N. L. Stein, & T. Trabasso (Eds.), *Learning and comprehension of text* Erlbaum.

Waltz, D. L. (1979). On the function of mental imagery. *The Behavioral and Brain Sciences 2*, 569–570.

Whaley, J. F. (1981). Readers' expectations for story structures. *Reading Research Quarterly, 17*(1), 90–114. doi: 10.2307/747250

Winograd, T. (1972). *Understanding natural language.* Academic Press.

NOTES

1. The salience of a reader's background knowledge aligns with the correlational studies of the relationship between vocabulary knowledge and reading comprehension. Indeed, a measure of background knowledge outperforms vocabulary as a predictor of reading comprehension while correlating strongly with the vocabulary measure itself.

2. Nevertheless, several strands in measurements of reading ignore and override such findings. They tout culture-free tests when they may be excluding cultural variability. For example, the use of latent trait theory to develop tests (which assume reading performance will be one-dimensional) has and could continue to perpetuate an approach to testing that excludes items that do not operate in support of mainstream differences.

3. The shift of NAEP to a model driven by a desire to provide a single scale undermined a differential approach to reading assessment that afforded the possibility of illuminating sociocultural considerations.

4   The Learning to Learn Wave

4.1   THE STRATEGIC READER

A key tenet of being strategic stemmed from the work of developmental psychologists such as John Flavell (1977), who introduced the notion of meta-memory—a precursor to metacognition that became synonymous with the ability to read strategically across a range of situations independently. In turn, the focus shifted to a learner's self-awareness—the ability to judge and read a task or situation, to bring strategies to the task in order to address that task and its specific features, to adapt to circumstances, to monitor and adjust progress, and to consider a task's relevance to one's world. As the focus shifted to helping students learn how to learn, the goals of reading development extended to developing their metacognitive skills and strategies so they could in turn employ them independently and in different circumstances. While the notion of independence in reading was not new, its marriage to reading comprehension was (see box).

Being a strategic reader extended and complemented the notion of a constructivist reader to address learning to read to learn—in ways that were independent (they could do it on their own) and transferable (they could do it not only on the text in which you taught the strategies but also in the next text they encountered on their own) (see box). Schema theoretic notions of reading heralded the

The new standard for readers was not whether or not they could comprehend what they read, but whether or not they were strategic comprehenders—savvy enough to reason their way out of a dead end in comprehension. Were readers equipped with a repertoire of skills that enabled them to engage in a range of meaning-making processes, including assessing goals, gathering relevant resources, initiating an array of strategies to generate questions, identifying and distinguishing key ideas, making connections, judging the merit of meanings gleaned, monitoring their meaning along the way to see if it made sense, using and applying ideas, and adjusting strategies as needed (or based on assessment of the adequacy of their pursuits)?

It was generally agreed that past practices were more directed at testing students' comprehension than on ways to improve how they comprehend. Those past practices also reflected an approach tied to a mastery orientation rather than a flexibility stance. Further, the orientation to comprehension enhancement emphasized the provision of pre-set adjuncts to support learning. Observations of classroom reading and subject area practices suggested that reading comprehension instruction consisted primarily of teachers questioning students on what they read—again and again and again. The questions were purportedly based on taxonomies, such as Bloom's; however, in practice, most questions—such as recall questions to which students responded and the teacher judged their answers—focused on literal details. When targeted skill development did occur, it tended to require students to define textual elements, such as the main idea, or to draw conclusions and locate evidence in the selections they read or in their assigned paragraphs. Unfortunately, there were a number of faulty assumptions undergirding these practices, including:

- Comprehension ability (i.e., the student's potential) is predetermined and in accordance with mental ability, a proxy for which is the student's listening comprehension performance across graded selections.
- Reading comprehension is a receptive act intent on discerning the author's or the text's meaning.
- Comprehension proceeds sequentially, from the literal to inferential to interpretative and then critical.
- Acquiring the skills of comprehension involves mastering a subset of skills related to outcomes rather than developing adroit strategies of meaning making.
- Reading development can be measured and reported on a grade-level scale of the challenge readers are capable of reading successfully, as if grade-level reading or a standardized score on a test were a reasonable, credible, and generalizable appraisal of reading ability.
- Readability can be defined in accordance with the student's overall reading grade level and by what is discerned to be the difficulty level of the material (based on some index of vocabulary and syntactical complexity).

In a survey of over a thousand secondary school students that Rob conducted with Diane Schallert in the early 1980s, they uncovered the extent to which high schoolers approached reading in a fashion that was flawed and naïve. Most read their texts only once, often as quickly as possible, and as they did so they tried to remember as much as possible. Not surprisingly, these same students complained about how tedious reading was and the poverty of their recalls (Schallert & Tierney, 1982).

importance of building, activating, and enlisting background knowledge to keep the comprehension process alive. To be strategic meant knowing when to enlist certain strategies to enhance their learning in different situations with different texts or reading sources, as they pursued one text or project along the way. As is needed in different situations, strategic readers are capable of setting goals and orchestrating practices that might include gathering resources, posing their own questions, enlisting forward inferencing abilities, adjusting foci and perspectives, moving around in the text, zooming in and out, pausing, re-reading, revising, rethinking, self-correcting, and applying. They have understandings whereby they can notice features and patterns; they are engaged in knowledge building; they can chunk and situate ideas and relate these ideas to their current task. Strategic readers are also self-initiating—their approach is not lockstep but adaptive and nimble, as they flexibly seek to engage ways to make meaning. They contemplate the task, the nature of their meaning making, and their deployment of strategies as they accrue understandings and in turn judge and adjust their approaches.

Essentially, like constructivist readers, successful strategic readers are not passive but are actively engaged in a form of ongoing meaning making driven by curiosity, predictions, anticipations, self-questioning, and forward thinking. These readers engage in connecting ideas and considering patterns, themes, and the coherence and plausibility of ideas as they self-monitor, consider relevance and possibilities. Strategic readers develop "muscle memory" that they marshal for critically reflecting on their processes for making meaning, the ideas and understandings they might glean.

Again, consistent with an emphasis on learning to learn—or what was termed metacognition—self-monitoring skills became a focus. In the past, students were supported in terms of their comprehension with scaffolding by the teacher (by way of prompts, etc.) and encouraged to use adjunct aids, such as noticing headings and taking notes. With the shift to strategic reading, this support was seen as not developing in students a repertoire of strategies that they could employ independently or transfer to other circumstances (see Clay, 1998; Paris et al., 1983, 1984, 1992; Pearson & Gallagher, 1983; Tierney & Cunningham, 1984). Research and development on strategies to enhance readers' awareness of their reading tasks (i.e., strategies that they might employ flexibly and selectively) took hold. In turn, a new set of strategies and heuristics for teachers were adopted in an effort to help readers use them for themselves (see Tierney & Readence, 2005). For example, Donna Ogle (1986) developed KWL (i.e., what do you *know*, what do you *want* to learn, and what you did *learn*), and Taffy Raphael (1982) developed a task analysis procedure for readers called the Question Answer Relationship (QAR). Other researchers extended the strategy developments already in place. For example, Annmarie Palincsar (Palincsar & Brown, 1984) built on Anthony Manzo's (1969) ReQuest (for reciprocal questioning between teacher and student) procedure in which teacher and students traded turns playing the teacher role (what they termed Reciprocal Teaching).

Likewise, text-based approaches were suggested from flowcharts by Dansereau (1979), mapping (see Armbruster & Anderson, 1980; Schallert et al., 1984), explicit teaching of structures (e.g., Meyer et al., 1980; Stein & Trabasso, 1981), or more author-based analyses by James Mosenthal (1984).

The envisioned ideal was a reader who could selectively and independently enlist appropriate strategies and skills (i.e., planning, researching, inquiring, formulating, contemplating, and monitoring) that reflected their reading goals and whatever reading activities they might pursue in trying to achieve those goals. This idealized reader would be able to access strategies and skills deftly and seamlessly—just as a pull-down menu provides support for digitally based writing, video, and other projects. In essence, they would develop a tool kit, a repertoire of strategies that would support their reader-based and text-based needs with different texts and goals of reading.

References

Armbruster, B., & Anderson, T. (1980). *The effect of mapping on the free recall of expository text.* Tech. Rep. No. 160. University of Illinois, Center for the Study of Reading.

Baker, L., & Brown A. (1984). Metacognitive skills and reading. In P. D. Pearson, R. Barr, M. L. Kamil, & P. Mosenthal (Eds.), *Handbook of reading research* (pp. 353–394). Longman.

Clay, M. M. (1998). *By different paths to common outcomes.* Stenhouse.

Cunningham, P. M., Hall, D. P., & Defee, M. (1998). No ability-grouped, multileveled instruction: Eight years later. *The Reading Teacher, 51,* 652–664.

Dansereau, D. F. (1979). Development and evaluation of a learning strategy training program. *Journal of Educational Psychology, 71*(1), 64–73. doi: 10.1037/0022-0663.71.1.64

Flavell, J. (1977). *Cognitive development.* Prentice-Hall.

Fountas, I. C., & Pinnell, G. S. (1996). *Guided reading: Good first teaching for all children.* Heinemann.

Harste, J. C., Short, K. G., & Burke, C. L. (1988). *Creating classrooms for authors: The reading-writing connection.* Heinemann.

Herber, H. L. (1970). *Teaching reading in content areas.* Prentice-Hall.

Manzo, A. V. (1969). The reQuest procedure. *Journal of Reading, 13*(2), 123–126.

Meyer, B. J. F., Brandt, D. M., & Bluth, G. J. (1980). Use of top-level structure in text: Key for reading comprehension of ninth-grade students. *Reading Research Quarterly, 16*(1), 72–103. doi: 10.2307/747349

Mosenthal, J. H. (1984). *Instruction in the interpretation of a writer's argument: A training study* (Doctoral dissertation, University of Illinois at Urbana-Champaign). ProQuest (Order No. 8502253).

Ogle, D. M. (1986). K-W-L: A teaching model that develops active reading of expository text. *The Reading Teacher, 39*(6), 564–570.

Palincsar, A. S., & Brown, A. L. (1984). Reciprocal teaching of comprehension-fostering and comprehension-monitoring activities. *Cognition and Instruction, 1*(2), 117–175. doi: 10.1207/s1532690xci0102_1

Paris, S. G., Cross, D. R., & Lipson, M. Y. (1984). Informed strategies for learning: A program to improve children's reading awareness and comprehension. *Journal of Educational Psychology, 76*(6), 1239–1252. doi: 10.1037/0022-0663.76.6.1239

Paris, S. G., Lipson, M. Y., & Wixson, K. K. (1983). Becoming a strategic reader. *Contemporary Educational Psychology, 8*(3), 293–316. doi: 10.1016/0361-476X(83)90018-8

Paris, S. G., Wasik, B. A., & Turner, J. C. (1991). The development of strategic readers. In R. Barr, M. L. Kamil, P. Mosenthal, & P. D. Pearson (Eds.), *Handbook of reading research,* (Vol. 2, pp. 609–640). Longman.

Pearson, P. D., & Gallagher, M. C. (1983). The instruction of reading comprehension. *Contemporary Educational Psychology, 8*(3), 317–344. doi: 10.1016/0361-476X(83)90019-X

Raphael, T. E. (1982). Question-answering strategies for children. *The Reading Teacher, 36*(2), 186–190.

Schallert, D., & Tierney, R. J. (1982). *Learning from expository text: The interaction of text structure with reader characteristics.* Report prepared for the National Institute of Education, NIE-6-79-0167.

Schallert, D. L., Ulerick, S. L., & Tierney, R. J. (1984). Evolving a description of text through mapping. In C. D. Holley & D. F. Dansereau (Eds.), *Spatial learning strategies: Techniques, applications, and related issues.* Academic Press.

Short, K. G., Harste, J. C., & Burke, C. L. (1996). *Creating classrooms for authors and inquirers* (2nd ed.). Heinemann.

Stauffer, R. G. (1969). *Directing reading maturity as a cognitive process.* Harper and Row.

Stein, N. L., & Trabasso, T. (1981). *What's in a story: An approach to comprehension and instruction* (Center for the Study of Reading Technical Report No. 200). University of Illinois. www.ideals.illinois.edu/bitstream/handle/2142/18031/ctrstreadtechrepv01981i00200_opt.pdf

Taylor, B. M., Pressley, M. P., & Pearson, P. D. (2002). Research-supported characteristics of teachers and schools that promote reading achievement. In B. Taylor & P. D. Pearson (Eds.), *Teaching reading: Effective schools, accomplished teachers* (pp. 361–373). Routledge. doi: 10.4324/9781410612489

Tierney, R. J., & Cunningham, J. W. (1984). Teaching reading comprehension. In P. D. Pearson, R. Barr, M. L. Kamil, & P. Mosenthal (Eds.), *Handbook of reading research* (pp. 609–656). Longman.

Tierney, R. J., & Readence, J. E. (2005). *Reading strategies and practices: A compendium* (6th ed.). Pearson.

4.2   LEARNING TO LEARN WITH TEXT

The cognitive revolution of the 1970s extended beyond studies of readers making meaning for a particular text to addressing the question, Is it possible to improve a reader's comprehension for texts that they have not yet read? The significance of this question should not be underestimated. Inherent in asking it is a challenge to the notion that intelligence is fixed and possibly innate. It raises the possibility that intelligence, or at least some important self-learning processes, can be improved for transfer to future learning situations. But what would it take? Is it tied to teaching certain related elements such as vocabulary? Does it entail developing background knowledge? Should we teach students how to follow and connect ideas to infer, evaluate, synthesize, and so on? How might we do so, and how would we judge when we succeeded? It seemed the real test would be to measure readers' abilities to enlist and apply these strategies across various situations, on their own or independently. Such a standard went beyond improving test scores.

The notion of learning to learn inspired the imagination of many of us, especially those focused on teaching and learning, and extended our attention beyond studies of comprehension processes. And these questions arose at a time of significant social and technological developments throughout the world. Socially, there was significant social upheaval resulting from revolutionary developments worldwide. In China, the Cultural Revolution had ended; China opened up to the United States; African countries freed themselves from their colonial masters. In countries such as Nicaragua, there were major literacy campaigns pursued in the name of liberation. In terms of technology, we saw the development of the personal computer and the space shuttle. And in the area of health, the world was concentrating on addressing HIV/AIDS.

Certainly, in modern times, the nature and role of teaching and learning have been a major focus of several lines of scholarship, as theorists and researchers have explored and posited theories of learning and teaching, as documented in the watershed syntheses of state-of-the-art knowledge available in *How People Learn* (National Research Council, 2000) and *How People Learn II* (National Academies of Sciences, Engineering, and Medicine, 2018). As we have discussed in previous chapters, studies of reading development often involved correlational methods (referred to as process-product studies, in which frequencies of teacher behavior and student activity are related to achievement); program evaluations of schools and classrooms; and carefully controlled studies examining variations of teaching procedures (e.g., time on task) and different approaches (e.g., basal readers, language experience approaches) to student achievement and student engagement.

With the emphasis on learning to learn, the focus shifted to facilitating students' agency and their ability to deploy skills and strategies for themselves. And, while learning scientists had a history of success in improving comprehension with the aid of adjuncts and strategies, the pursuit of sustained, transferable, and independent reading strategies raised the ante significantly. Over time, it became apparent that the research approaches for doing so necessitated studies that enlisted a range of methods, which allowed for a focus on students' learning over time and across place, and enabled the implementation of various measures (i.e., online, post-measures, transfer measures) and detailed qualitative analyses of site-based learning (e.g., teacher–student and student–student interactions). They suggested a need for formative studies in collaboration with teachers and students, exploring ways to support learning to learn to read critically, creatively, strategically, and independently.

Even so, what became vexing was that attempts to help students learn to learn proved more elusive, as repeated efforts fell short of achieving these goals. Essentially, we could improve comprehension performance with guidance in place, but without scaffolding students' learning and use of strategies were not readily sustained and transferable.

Shifts

The nature, role, and advancement of learning have been major foci of several lines of literacy research. In the 1950s and 1960s, research focused on securing the best method for teaching reading (e.g., what are the attributes of an effective teacher? And how might we enlist adjuncts and use selected study skills—such as note taking and summarizing—to enhance learning from text?). By the 1970s, it was as if the cognitive turn "took pause." It was recognized that we were not teaching reading comprehension, and in terms of comprehension development there was not an easy transition from the early grades to the middle grades as the emphasis on reading to learn intensified. Dolores Durkin's 1978 observations of the teaching of reading comprehension instruction in schools (in the intermediate grades) confirmed what many of us suspected: Reading comprehension instruction was lacking in schools. Her observations of reading and social studies in classrooms in various schools across the grades revealed what other studies suggested—namely, that reading comprehension instruction was negligible, and that most teachers instead appeared more intent on assessing reading comprehension than on providing students with explanations and support (see Guszak, 1967). However, while Durkin's study made it clear that the teaching of reading comprehension was lacking if not entirely nonexistent, it did not clarify what reading comprehension teaching should be, how it should be taught, and when.

In response, there emerged a call for more classroom-based research on teaching and facilitating reading comprehension. Literacy educators responded and we witnessed a major surge in research and development on the teaching of reading comprehension beginning in the 1980s. Reviews of the teaching of reading comprehension confirmed the shortcomings of our teaching practices and offered new directions (e.g., Dole, Duffy, Roehler, & Pearson, 1991; Pearson & Fielding, 1991; Tierney & Cunningham, 1984). They spurred research on how educators might help students develop thoughtful and flexible learning strategies—that is, learning to learn, in accordance with a metacognitive framework advanced by developmental psychologists (see Baker & Brown 1984; Bransford, 1979; Bransford et al., 2000; Brown, 1987; Flavell, 1977; and Paris et al., 1991).

While the cognitive turn had a seismic impact on theories and models of reading, the research and development on learning to learn had significant influences on teaching and our goals for learning. It shifted preexisting lines of teacher research and reading to learn research, as well as classroom practices for teaching reading. These influences have also subsequently extended to and connected with cultural and critical pedagogical considerations, postcolonial theorizing, and other developments in research—especially those involved in rethinking some traditions of schooling (e.g., the ways of knowing across schools and societies).

Shifting Teacher Research

In the first three quarters of the 20th century, studies of teachers were oftentimes rather mechanistic and reductionist correlational studies. Frequencies of teacher behavior and student activity were related to achievement, to program evaluations of schools and classrooms, and to carefully controlled studies examining variations of teaching procedures. In the 1950s, process-product studies, drawing somewhat from Ned Flanders's 1970 work on classroom interactions, dominated the field. These studies tended to look at the relationship between teacher's affective or cognitive behavior (based on observational analyses) and student performance (as measured by a standardized tests). Those of us who conducted process-product research engaged in extensive observations of classrooms, noting the teachers' as well as the students' behavior every three seconds. We classified teacher behavior within categories such as giving direction, asking questions of different types, responding to students, or offering praise or criticism; at the same time, we classified student behavior as initiated or responsive, or on- or off-task. These types of studies later extended to a consideration of the correlation of different instructional models (e.g., classroom organizational patterns or instructional regimens) with proxies for effective learning (such as measures of academic engagement, on-task behaviors, content covered, student engagement and achievement) (see Rosenshine & Stevens, 1984).

On the one hand, this research suggested some consistent trends—including a treatment-by-aptitude interaction, the power of teacher-directed activities over student independent learning (with regard to academic tasks), the power of small groups over whole class-level work on student engagement, the power of a task orientation, and the positive effects of a predictable sequence of activities. These studies also suggested that successful teachers tended to be clear, flexible, and businesslike, and were inclined to offer praise, ask various questions, and afford students the opportunity to learn with structured comments (Rosenshine & Furst, 1973).

On the other hand, these studies did not closely examine teachers and students in differential and complex ways. They did, as Dunkin and Biddle (1974) suggested, shift to studying the interactions between teacher variables (teacher personality and background), context variables (class size, pupil background, community, etc.), processes (teacher and students in classrooms), and product (learning outcomes, such as test scores). But too few studies provided details of the precise nature of the task and teaching practices, and they failed to focus on different populations. From the perspective of constructivism, these early studies were predominately focused on whether or not the teacher delivered instruction and how the students responded to what they were expected to learn. They did not consider a full range of options in terms of what is taught, why, how, when, and where. Rather, they tended to focus on approaches that were more prescribed than emergent, involving a scope and sequence of skill development in conjunction with an attempt to construct a balanced diet of graded reading experiences. Project orientations were either sidelined or subordinated to such a regimen.

With the rise of constructivism in the 1970s, teacher research shifted. As Roehler and Duffy (1991) indicated, research veered away from a focus on what facts students remembered to examine instead their strategy development and how they were positioned in terms of their own learning. Studies of teaching also went beyond a model of learning tied to "the exercise model" and readers accumulating facts. Lauren Resnick (1981) described the shift as moving from a receptive model to a transformational model of learning involving conscious control by learners. Accordingly, she stated, "instruction must be designed not to put knowledge into learners' heads, but to put learners in positions that allow them to construct well-structured knowledge" (Resnick, 1981, p. 660). Lee Shulman similarly suggested that the research orientation should shift from treating students as memory machines to acknowledging their role as active meaning makers: "the consequences of teaching can only be understood as a function of what the teaching stimulates the learner to do with the material" (Shulman, 1986, p. 17). Thus, researchers who studied teaching tried to understand and uncover how teachers might achieve these new aspirations; they shifted to a more comprehensive analysis of teaching, including analyses of planning (e.g., the creation of instructional settings and attendance to material, representations, motivations, participations, direction expectations, activity structures, etc.) and actions (e.g., explanations, modeling, think-alouds, release of responsibility, participation structures, etc.).

Shifting Curriculum Frameworks

In response to these shifts, reading programs revised their approaches and began touting their alignment with constructivist thinking and classroom practices. Essentially, the core features of most reading programs involved collections of reading material—leveled books containing various stories and informational passages along with activity pages or workbooks that students were expected to read with the teacher's guidance. Teachers were provided a guide, various checklists, and packages of tests to help them do so. These leveled pupil compendiums of stories and informational text comprised the diet of daily and weekly engagements with reading. The related activities focused on skill development related to the scope and sequence of skills (e.g., word recognition, comprehension, study skills, and literary appreciation) that students were expected to master. Oftentimes students were placed in reading-level groups, established according to the level of material that their placement criteria suggested they could read comfortably (defined as approximately 90% oral reading accuracy and 75% comprehension).

Most reading programs had a similar look and feel, but some core programs were organized differently, oftentimes involving a more theme-based approach or other emphases (such as skill mastery). Such differences played out along various dimensions tied to prescribed or emergent philosophies and notions of skill development.[1] Overall, however, they followed similar routines of guided reading, teacher questioning, and related student activities. Leveled passages were introduced one at a time with a mix of teacher-led guided reading and questions (probes). Reading then involved a routine of pre-reading, guided, and post-reading, followed by related activities or those related to the students' own purposes or needs. After reading the selection, there often followed a combination of discussion, always guided by teacher questioning, and practice of selected skills (increasingly based on specific skill tests). The original and still most common lesson framework was one or another variation of the Directed Reading Lesson popularized by Betts (1946). It involved a predictable sequence as students read sections of their graded readers or assigned texts. It moved from pre-reading (with teachers setting purposes and creating student interest, along with previewing some vocabulary) to guided reading, and ended with post-reading (which consisted of discussion and skill development). Another 1970s variant of this sequence integrated writing and other follow-up engagements. Some other frameworks include the Directed Reading-Thinking Activity, developed by Russell Stauffer (1969); later variants in this same family included Guided Reading (an offshoot to Reading Recovery), developed by Irene Fountas and Gay Su Pinnell (1996); and Four Blocks, developed by Pat Cunningham and her colleagues (1998).

In the early 1980s, the realignment of reading programs led to further tinkering to acknowledge the important role played by readers' background knowledge. This acknowledgment led to a deliberate attempt to build from what students already knew, especially in pre-teaching, to enhance their understandings during guided and post-reading.

In terms of skill development, skill activities were also revamped, with more focused strategy development tied to teacher modeling. Whereas the traditional lesson frameworks required the teacher to set the stage for reading (as part of pre-reading activities), lessons began to shift toward a model of engaging students by positioning them as meaning makers. Students were asked to set their own purposes and ask their own questions. Further, while traditional guided reading asked students to read portions of the text in response to the teachers' questions (to check their comprehension), guided reading became more student-driven, intended to draw from the students' ideas and predictions in a fashion that respected their developing understandings. Lastly, post-reading activities became sites for extending students' reading strategy development, self-assessment, and application into related activities in other curricular domains, including other disciplines (science or social studies) or the arts. These shifts are portrayed in Figure 4.1.

Figure 4.1. Lesson Frameworks: Pre- and Post-Cognitive Turn and Learning to Learn

APPROACH—Pre-Cognitive
    Pre-reading activities
- Creating interest
- Introducing key concepts
- Teach Vocabulary
- Set purposes

    Guided reading
- Teacher-directed reading (with questions)

    Post-reading
- Discussion of selection
- Related skill development
- Checks

    Supplementary reading

REVISED APPROACH—Post-Cognitive
    Pre-reading
- Building bridges from what children know

    Reading
- Guided reading, including predicting and self-questioning
- Respecting students meaning, building on their responses (visualizing and connecting ideas)
- Altered approaches to questioning
- Student answers will vary

    Post-reading
- Strategy development (reader- and text-based strategies, in context)
- Cross-curricular applications

Shifting Emphases: Learning from Text to Learning to Learn

It was generally recognized that these changes in the routine and sequence of lesson frameworks were not enough, nor would a shift to study skills or adjuncts to learning suffice. Reading educators began asking what we might do beyond adjuncts, study skills, increased reading fluency, and a diet of reading selections with questions to improve reading comprehension. Though the research on reading to learn was quite impressive, it fell short in terms of addressing the shift to metacognitive abilities and learning to learn.

More specifically, most studies of reading comprehension were focused on learning from text, examining the mathemagenic or learning enhancement function of adjuncts and the use and benefits of the readers' enlistment of study-style skills. This work was often funded by the military, given their vested interests in careful responses to text. In terms of adjuncts, the nature and role of aids—such as questions, pictures, study guides, previews, and objectives before, during, and after reading—in relation to understanding were examined. In terms of studying, the roles of note taking, outlining, visualizing, and summarizing were examined.

Figure 4.2. Bransford's (1979) Tetrahedral Model of Learning

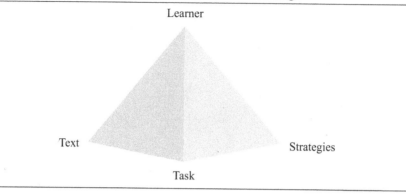

Among the most influential work during this period was that of David Ausubel (1968) on advanced organizers and Harold Herber's (1970) work on reading in the content areas (e.g., with story previews, study guides, and structural overviews).[2]

Their work provided consistent support for the power of adjuncts for enhancing memory for text. However, if the hope was to advance the reader's independent reading strategies for other texts, results were unlikely to be achieved, or even pursued. Repeatedly, efforts fell short of having readers develop flexible and deft use of strategies.

As the field focused on research intent on teaching strategies where the gold standard was independent reading (i.e., not prompted or guided), the pursuit became more demanding. Predictably, researchers scurried to find the means of supporting readers to be independent learners, equipped with a repertoire of strategies applicable across different texts and situations. Befitting the tetrahedral model formulated by Bransford (1979; see Figure 4.2), the following agenda emerged:

- Can readers formulate or assess the nature of the task and its needs or demands?
- Can they formulate, implement, and assess ways to proceed with text(s) for themselves, and do so in a fashion that is flexible and adaptable?
- What strategies do they need to do so?
- How do we develop these strategies?

Formulating the Strategies—and the Approach

These developments set many of us on a new course. Based on what we knew about meaning making and learning to learn, we asked:

- What are the strategies that readers might employ?
- When, and how?

- How might we support them in learning to employ these strategies deftly across situations and for themselves?

As researchers pursued these questions, it was apparent that the skills specified for learning to read—especially reading comprehension—were piecemeal and tied to a notion of mastery that did not match what we imagined readers needed to do. Our view was that readers needed to exercise more nimble control over their skill and strategy repertoire—to deftly select clusters of skills and strategies for meaning making. These clusters of skills would be tied to their own analyses of their meaning-making needs as they engaged in the project of reading.

In their quest to develop such clusters, some researchers provided visual metaphors or heuristics. While Scott Paris and his colleagues developed a series of extended metaphors for reading strategies (e.g., being a detective), other researchers devised heuristics (Paris et al., 1983, 1984, 1986, 1991). For example, Donna Ogle (1986) developed KWL (what do you know, what do you want to learn, and what did you learn), and Taffy Raphael (1982) developed a task analysis procedure for readers called the Question Answer Relationship (QAR). Annemarie Palincsar (Palincsar & Brown, 1983) extended the reciprocal question approach of Manzo (1969) to promote readers' control over strategies. Other researchers extended the strategy development already in place.

In accordance with a text-based approach, a number of researchers focused on helping readers enlist text structural prompts to support the reading of complex narratives and informational texts. They employed analyses of narrative and expository text features by Stein and Trabasso (see Mandler et al., 1984; Stein & Trabasso, 1981), text structure by Meyer (Meyer et al., 1980) and Bartlett (1932/1995), and the use of flowcharts by Dansereau (1979), mapping (see Armbruster & Anderson, 1980), or more author-based analyses by James Mosenthal (1984).

Undergirding these developments was a new conceptualization of reader-based and text-based strategies. Again, these compilations represented clusters of skills rather than skills isolated from one another. Over time, the list of strategy clusters also expanded to include self-assessment strategies and collaborative strategies (i.e., beyond those "inside the head" analyses). Figure 4.3 includes a partial listing.

The ideal envisioned was a reader who would selectively and independently enlist appropriate strategies and skills (i.e., planning, researching, inquiring, formulating, contemplating, and monitoring) befitting their reading goals and activities (or what might be considered their reading project). This reader would be able to access these strategies and skills deftly and seamlessly—just as a pull-down menu provides support for digitally-based writing, video, and other projects. While we drew on our studies of meaning making to identify the strategies, our understanding of how to teach them was still limited—especially if we wanted students to use strategies effectively and independently across a range of situations. Consequently, several new frameworks emerged, but their results appeared less than convincing in terms of achieving this goal.

Figure 4.3. Skill Clusters

Reader Based	Text based
Selecting/Judging sources	Flowcharting
Questioning	Story mapping
Visualizing	Outlining
Connecting ideas	Networking
Predicting	
Cross-checking	
Rethinking	
Collaborative	**Monitoring**
Seeking support	Formulating
Giving support	Assessing process, progress and outcomes
Planning together	Implementing
Networking	Reviewing
Sharing	Revising
	Considering and applying criteria
	Judging

These efforts represented a major shift in classroom-based research; nevertheless, despite carefully crafted approaches, most of the results of these efforts were somewhat modest—especially when the goals became the reader's independent use of strategies and the enhancement of learning across new situations. Researchers were often dismayed that readers did not enlist the strategies unless they were overtly prompted to do so. In other words, if the gold standard extends to independent reading of different material without prompting, then most approaches fell short. When delayed post-test and transfer tasks were used to assess whether students enlisted the strategies taught in other situations, these studies of learning to learn rarely yielded sustained or transferable influences. The studies resulted in advances of what was taught, but questions still remained in terms of the best way to scaffold and support developing independent learners—including how, when, why, and where.

Scaffolding Learning to Learn

Adopting a broad perspective, in response to the question "What are the conditions for learning that teachers should create?" educators have been intrepid in their pursuits of ways to engage students and support their learning to learn or other challenging missions (e.g., such as antiracism, bullying). Integral to their efforts they have explored various frameworks that might scaffold learning to learn, such as systematic and incidental, direct and indirect teaching, and project-based and strategy-focused approaches. The frameworks addressed different foci in terms of what is read and how it is taught. Plus, the frameworks offered different forms of scaffolds for learning that stretch along a continuum, from student-centered approaches, to teacher-centered, to a combination of the two.

Brian Cambourne (1998, 1999), and more recently Crouch and Cambourne (2020), suggested as a framework for teachers a list of tenets that are required for learning and that teachers might emulate (Cambourne, 1988, 1999; Crouch & Cambourne, 2020). Cambourne's tenets include immersion, demonstration, engagement/experimentation in risk-free environments, realistic and informed expectations of development and success, learner-based responsibility and self-direction, approximation including acceptance of mistakes and attempts, meaningful uses, and responsiveness.[3]

Other approaches advanced teacher modeling and student practice with a developmental orientation to mastery. For example, Manzo (1969) and Palincsar and Brown (1984) developed what they termed reciprocal teaching, which involves a give-and-take, or repeated rotation, between teacher modeling and student practice. David and Meg Gallagher have developed and been refining an influential model they labeled the Gradual Release of Responsibility Model (GRR) (Figure 4.4).

David and his colleagues (Pearson et al., 2019) have recently revisited the Gradual Release Model in a major "revisionist" account of its successes and shortcomings, while also accounting for its spread to other areas of pedagogy besides

Figure 4.4. Pearson and Gallagher Gradual Release of Responsibility Model

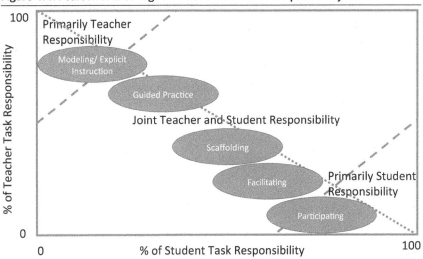

literacy pedagogy. Among other issues, they accounted for the central role of scaffolding in the model, and after reflecting on many misuses of the model, they adopted these rules of thumb for using scaffolds in instruction:

- Fade scaffolding over time.
- Vary scaffolding within a lesson.
- Vary scaffolding across lessons within a unit.
- Vary scaffolding between students.
- Scaffolding will inevitably ebb and flow over time, situations, and task demands.

Working with Dole and Duffy (Dole et al., 2019), David also accounted for some common misuses of the model, noting these in particular (from the work of Duke & Pearson, in press):

- Neglecting explicit teaching (on the assumption that students will "get it" just from experiencing it);
- Missing the middle (the collaborative stage in which students and teacher share responsibility for enacting a practice);
- The gradual rise of rigidity (insisting on a lock-step sequencing of the stages of pedagogy—and ironically cutting out the very heart of the model, its capacity for adaptability and nimbleness).

Reflecting on the future of the model, Dole et al. (2020) speculated that its future depended primarily on its adaptable character, which might allow it to morph into new forms and functions:

> As new theories of learning and instruction are developed, it is likely that the GRR model will evolve further. In the meantime, it is incumbent upon those who espouse the model to help teachers implement it in their classrooms. The dozens of professional articles, chapters in books, and indeed this book, will help teachers understand the emerging forms of the model, how to implement them, and when and where they are most useful. As long as we all regard it as a nimble and adaptable tool for guiding learning and teaching in our classrooms, the GRR model will retain its lasting legacy in our classrooms, our policy briefs, and our research journals. (p. 260)

In a similar fashion, other models have been developed. For example, drawing on Wittgenstein's notion of complex knowledge acquisition and his case study approach in medicine, Rand Spiro (Spiro et al., 2003) argued that a case study orientation was key to flexible adaptive use. Still others focused on approaches that were integrated with students' inquiry. For example, Jerome Harste, Cathy Short, and Carolyn Burke (Harste et al., 1988; Short et al., 1996) developed the author inquiry cycle, or authoring cycle, in which students are guided in their inquiries as they pursue projects with peers (Figure 4.5).

Figure 4.5. Authoring Cycle

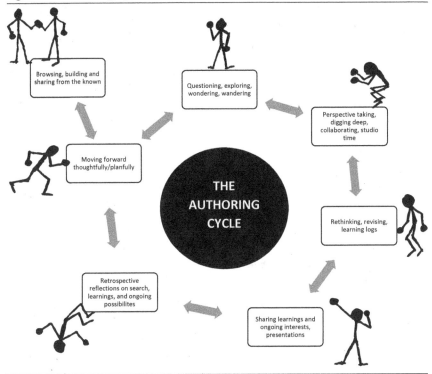

Adapted from Harste et al.'s (1988) authoring cycle.

At the core of a number of approaches has been professional development tied to an orientation toward developing readers' discernments of their meaning making in combination with forms of self-monitoring and strategy usage. For example, in the context of discussing some of the tenets undergirding Reading Recovery, Marie Clay (1998) advocated helping students develop self-improving systems that involve their enlisting strategies including a form of triangulation—that is, cross-checking their decoding and understandings as they read. Yetta Goodman (1996) similarly developed a form of critical reflection with the advance of Retrospective Miscue Analysis following oral reading.

Yet others have focused extensively on the professional development component together with enlisting an apprenticeship model for students involving a mix of project-based learning and notions of metacognition to address disciplinary learning. For example, Cindy Greenleaf and her colleagues developed the Reading Apprenticeship Framework tied to such tenets that has been used widely to enhance disciplinary reading, especially in science. As Greenleaf et al. (2011) note:

The Reading Apprenticeship framework centers on metacognitive conversation, involving explicit metacognitive routines, modeling, small-group work, and class discussions that focus, in the case of science instruction, on how to read science and why people read science materials in the ways they do as well as on the science content of what is read in science classes. These discourse routines offer students support to clarify content, discuss the processes they use in reading and problem solving, practice comprehension strategies, respond to and elaborate on content, engage in word-learning strategies, write to learn and to consolidate learning, and make connections to other related texts and topics. (p. 657)

The combination of an apprenticeship approach within a discipline foreshadowed and, in some ways, paralleled shifts to frameworks that were both situated and aligned with socio-cultural-political processes whether they were in disciplinary circumstances such as science or in efforts to import approaches to learning aligned with community or real-world practices addressed in the next section.

Lingering Questions; Ongoing Considerations; Contemplating Research on Learning to Learn for Today's World

As we strive for readers who are both connoisseurs and agents for change, our research approach might need to open itself to a fuller sense of the cognitive, social, political, and cultural elements of life and how they might factor into a reader's enlistment of insights, learnings, and strategies in ways that are critical, creative, and reflective. Our research might need to understand these worlds and support our readers and their development. To this end, perhaps we should be exploring learning to learn using research approaches that are more formative than predetermined, in the hope that we can fashion what and how we teach to students' developing needs. Perhaps we need a more recursive research cycle for doing anchored in discerning observations and well-crafted approaches. They should begin and continue with extensive observations of what students can and might do before, in conjunction with, and after reading, and work in support of initiatives directed at advancing readers' awareness and refinement of their engagements, goals and outcomes, understandings, and potential applications and extensions. Observations should keep in mind member checking or a form of debriefing readers about their changing and ongoing multifaceted developments. Perhaps as we proceed, we should examine the situatedness of such pursuits, especially the relevance to a particular group. It might be a matter of engaging with reading within fields of study—as demonstrated in the "Seeds of Science/Roots of Reading" approach, which engages students in reading as an offshoot to science projects (Cervetti et al., 2007).

Or perhaps it requires a bigger step involving a commitment to a plurality of knowledge and ways of knowing. In W. S. Gray's 1956 survey for UNESCO, *The Teaching of Reading and Writing*, he noted the failure of educational programs that did not connect what was taught to the everyday lives and work within the communities they were intended to serve. Indeed, as they stand, approaches to formal schooling may be less conducive to engaging with broader communities and traditions (i.e., those that may be less intimately embedded in local community and family spheres, depending on the powers at play). In other words, we might want to focus on building bridges between schools and communities in ways that extend local ways of knowing and are relevant. More specifically, we would hope to build on explorations of alternative models of education designed for various groups, such as Kathy Au's 1980 exploration of an educational model for Hawaiian children, Susan Philips's 1983 work on participation structures with the Warm Springs Indian Reservation community in Oregon, or the various researches conducted in Canada by First Nations educators that enlist Indigenous ways of knowing (Archibald, 2008; Hare, 2007) and some of the elements considered key in New Zealand such as Maori ways of knowing (see Bishop et al., 2014; G. H. Smith, 1997, 2002, 2015; and L. T. Smith, 1999). This may entail drawing from the work of critical theorists focused on literacy programs connected directly to community pursuits such as Freire (1995) and Boal (1979, 1995). Building reciprocal relationships between learning and communities might connect learning to learn to frameworks such as the Reggio Emilia preschool approach in Italy, which engages so intimately with communities (Edwards et al., 1993), or New Basics for Queensland (Australia) schools (Education, Queensland, 2000a, 2000b), or the Funds of Knowledge "after school" initiative proposed by González et al. (2005) from their work in Arizona.

In an age of migration and transnationality, it seems fitting to pursue educations that can move across cultures respectfully, ethically, safely, and supportively as they engage with communities and learners with a deep understanding of the local (see Ladson-Billings, 1994; Luke, 2004; Tierney, 2006). As Mike Rose (1995) discussed in his study of successful teachers in the southwest region of the United States, it was the sense of possibilities that distinguished these teachers from others: "I've come to believe that a defining characteristic of good teaching is a tendency to push on the existing order of things. This is not simply rebelliousness. . . . It's an ability to live one's working life with a consciousness of possibility, an ability to imagine a better state of things" (p. 276). And, as Rose went on to explain, this ability grew out of a cultural recognition and community development that those teachers pursued "with knowledge of individual students' lives, of local history and economy, and of sociocultural traditions and practices . . . educating themselves about the communities and cultures of the students before them, connecting with parents and involving parents in schooling, and seeing students as resources and learning from them" (p. 419).

These issues are more complex than various aforementioned pronouncements might suggest. As the Maori scholar Linda Smith (1999) noted, cultural spaces are tricky ground. Indeed, these issues are at times quite vexing, as institutional forces of schooling are more colonizing than accommodating, with assimilation as a goal. Oftentimes cultural differences are treated as an objects akin to commodities rather than as foundational to educational endeavors. For example, a bias remains in many educational institutions, despite the diversity of the student body, to engage students in a Western image or the image of the dominant society. Local or diverse knowledge is sidelined and relegated to a secondary asset or an object of study, and the knowledge that students gain in school may not bear any relationship to the developmental needs of their communities. In an age of globalization, the local can be overlooked, displaced, or subordinated rather than respected; educational relevance to people's everyday lives and cultural roots lacks systemic support. Broader considerations may need to be given to developing strategies that value and build on local interests and resources—and do so in a manner that empowers rather than manages learners consistent with the discussions of literacy learning emerging in conjunction with the social wave and global waves later in this book.

To Recapitulate

Unpacking the teaching of reading and learning to read is not just a matter of analyzing how teachers teach a set of skills and strategies that students are expected to learn. As readers face changing and heightened demands, the notion of learning to learn should not be underestimated. Given the increasingly challenging and changing sociopolitical digitally demanding worlds, readers need strategies for contributing, selecting, sorting, enlisting, interfacing, exchanging, composing, sharing, and navigating within the worlds of ideas and relevant problem solving in a manner that is flexible, critical, discerning, effective, creative, and informed by readings both from the page and beyond.

References

Armbruster, B., & Anderson, T. (1980). *The effect of mapping on the free recall of expository text.* Tech. Rep. No. 160. University of Illinois, Center for the Study of Reading.

Baker, L., & Brown A. (1984). Metacognitive skills and reading. In P. D. Pearson, R. Barr, M. L. Kamil, & P. Mosenthal (Eds.), *Handbook of reading research* (pp. 353–394). Longman.

Betts, E. (1946). *Foundations of reading instruction: With emphasis on differentiated guidance.* American Book Co.

Bishop, R., Ladwig, J., & Berryman, M. (2014). The centrality of relationships for pedagogy: The Whanaungatanga thesis. *American Educational Research Journal, 51*(1), 184–214. doi: 10.3102/0002831213510019

Boal, A. (1979). *Theater of the oppressed.* Urizen Books.

Boal, A. (1995). *The rainbow of desire: The Boal method of theater and therapy.* Routledge.

Bransford, J. (1979). *Human cognition: Learning, understanding, and remembering.* Wadsworth.

Bransford, J. D., Brown, A. L., & Cocking, R. R. (Eds.). (2000). *How people learn: Brain, mind, experience and schooling.* National Research Council and National Academy Press.

Brown, A. (1987). Metacognition, executive control, self-regulation and other more mysterious mechanisms. In F. E. Weinert & R. H. Kluwe (Eds.), *Metacognition, motivation and understanding* (pp. 65–116). Erlbaum.

Cambourne, B. (1988). *The whole story: Natural learning and the acquisition of literacy in the classroom*. Ashton Scholastic.

Cambourne, B. (1999). Conditions for literacy learning: Turning learning theory into classroom instruction. A minicase study. *The Reading Teacher, 54*(4), 414–429.

Cardenal, F., & Miller, V. (1982). Nicaragua: Literacy and revolution. *Prospects, 12*(2), 201–21.

Cervetti, G. N., Pearson, P. D., Barber, J., Hiebert, E. H., and Bravo, M. A. (2007). Integrating literacy and science: The research we have, the research we need. In M. Pressley, A. K. Billman, K. H. Perry, K. E. Reffitt, & J. M. Reynolds (Eds.), *Shaping literacy achievement: Research we have, research we need* (pp. 157–174). Guilford.

Clay, M. M. (1998). *By different paths to common outcomes*. Stenhouse.

Crouch, D., & Cambourne, B. (2020). *Made for learning; How the conditions of learning guide teaching decisions*. Richard C. Owens Publisher.

Cunningham, P. M., Hall, D. P., & Defee, M. (1998). Noability-grouped, multileveled instruction: Eight years later. *The Reading Teacher, 51*, 652–664.

Dansereau, D. F. (1979). Development and evaluation of a learning strategy training program. *Journal of Educational Psychology, 71*(1), 64–73. doi: 10.1037/0022-0663.71.1.64

Dole, J., Duffy, G., Roehler, L., & Pearson, P. D. (1991). Moving from the old to the new: Research on reading comprehension instruction. *Review of Educational Research, 61* (2), 239-264.

Dole, J. A., Duffy, G. G., & Pearson, P. D. (2019). Epilogue: Reflections on the gradual release of responsibility model: Where we've been and where we're going. In M. B. McVee, E. Ortlieb, J. Reichenberg, & P. D. Pearson (Eds.), *The gradual release of responsibility in literacy research and practice* (pp. 245–263). Emerald Group Publishing.

Duke, N. K., & Pearson, P. D. (in press). The gradual release of responsibility: Setting the record straight. *American Educator*.

Dunkin, M. J., & Biddle, B. J. (1974). *The study of teaching*. Holt, Rinehart, & Winston.

Durkin, D. (1978). What classroom observations reveal about reading comprehension instruction. *Reading Research Quarterly, 14*(4), 481–533.

Education Queensland. (2000a). *Literate futures; Report of the literacy review for Queensland state schools*. The State of Queensland, Department of Education. education.qld.gov.au

Education Queensland. (2000b). *New Basics; Curriculum organizer*. The State of Queensland, Department of Education. education.qld.gov.au

Edwards, C. P., Gandini, L., & Forman, G. E. (1993). *The hundred languages of children: The Reggio Emilia approach to early childhood education*. Ablex.

Flanders, N. A. (1970). *Analyzing teacher behavior*. Addison-Wesley.

Flavell, J. (1977). *Cognitive development*. Prentice-Hall.

Fountas, I. C., & Pinnell, G. S. (1996). *Guided reading: Good first teaching for all children*. Heinemann.

Freire, P. (1995). *Pedagogy of the oppressed* (20th anniversary ed.). Continuum.

Gardner, H. (1983). *Frames of mind: The theory of multiple intelligences*. Basic Books.

Gee, James Paul. (2003). *What video games have to teach us about learning and literacy*. Palgrave Macmillan.

González, N., Moll, L. C., & Amanti, C. (2005). *Funds of knowledge: Theorizing practice in households, communities, and classrooms*. Erlbaum. doi: 10.4324/9781410613462

Goodman, Y. M. (1996). Revaluing readers while readers revalue themselves: Retrospective miscue analysis. *The Reading Teacher, 49*(8), 600–609.

Greenleaf, C. L, Litman, C., Hanson, T. L., Rosen, R., Boscardin, C. K., Herman, J., Schneider, S. A., Madden, S., & Jones, B. (2011). Integrating literacy and science in biology: Teaching and learning impacts of reading apprenticeship professional development. *American Educational Research Journal, 48*(3), 647–717. doi: 10.3102/0002831210384839

Guszak, F. J. (1967). Teacher questioning and reading. *The Reading Teacher, 21*(3), 227–234.

Hare, J. (2007). Aboriginal education policy in Canada: Building capacity for change and control. In R. Joshee & L. Johnson (Eds.), *Multicultural education policies in Canada and the United States* (pp. 51–68). UBC Press.

Harste, J. C., Short, K. G., & Burke, C. L. (1988). *Creating classrooms for authors: The reading-writing connection.* Heinemann.

Herber, H. L. (1970). *Teaching reading in content areas.* Prentice-Hall.

Hoffman, J. V. (1991). Teacher and school effects in learning to read. In R. Barr, M. L. Kamil, P. Mosenthal, & P. D. Pearson (Eds.), *Handbook of reading research* (Vol. 2, pp. 911–950). Longman.

Johnston, P. H. (2004). *Choice words: How our language affects children's learning.* Stenhouse.

Ladson-Billings, G. (1994). *The dreamkeepers: Successful teachers of African American children.* Jossey-Bass.

Mandl, H., Stein, N. L., & Trabasso, T. (1984). *Learning and comprehension of text.* Erlbaum.

Manzo, A. V. (1969). The reQuest procedure. *Journal of Reading, 13*(2), 123–126.

Meyer, B. J. F., Brandt, D. M., & Bluth, G. J. (1980). Use of top-level structure in text: Key for reading comprehension of ninth-grade students. *Reading Research Quarterly, 16*(1), 72–103. doi: 10.2307/747349

Mosenthal, J. H. (1984). *Instruction in the interpretation of a writer's argument: A training study* (Doctoral dissertation, University of Illinois at Urbana-Champaign). ProQuest (Order No. 8502253).

National Academies of Sciences, Engineering, and Medicine. (2018). *How people learn II: Learners, contexts, and cultures.* Washington, DC: National Academies Press. doi: 10.17226/24783

National Research Council. (2000). *How people learn: Brain, mind, experience, and school: Expanded edition.* Washington, DC: National Academies Press. doi: 10.17226/9853

Ogle, D. M. (1986). K-W-L: A teaching model that develops active reading of expository text. *The Reading Teacher, 39*(6), 564–570.

Palincsar, A. S., & Brown, A. L. (1984). Reciprocal teaching of comprehension-fostering and comprehension-monitoring activities. *Cognition and Instruction, 1*(2), 117–175. doi: 10.1207/s1532690xci0102_1

Paris, S. G., Cross, D. R., & Lipson, M. Y. (1984). Informed strategies for learning: A program to improve children's reading awareness and comprehension. *Journal of Educational Psychology, 76*(6), 1239–1252. doi: 10.1037/0022-0663.76.6.1239

Paris, S. G., & Cunningham, A. (1996). Children becoming students. In D. C. Berliner & R. C. Calfee (Eds.), *Handbook of educational psychology* (pp. 117–147). Macmillan.

Paris, S. G., Lipson, M. Y., & Wixson, K. K. (1983). Becoming a strategic reader. *Contemporary Educational Psychology, 8*(3), 293–316. doi: 10.1016/0361-476X(83)90018-8

Paris, S. G., Wasik, B. A., & Turner, J. C. (1991). The development of strategic readers. In R. Barr, M. L. Kamil, P. Mosenthal, & P. D. Pearson (Eds.), *Handbook of reading research* (Vol. 2, pp. 609–640). Longman.

Pearson, P. D., & Fielding, L. (1991). Comprehension instruction. In P. D. Pearson, R. Barr, M. L. Kamil, & P. Mosenthal (Eds.), *Handbook of reading research* (Vol. 2, pp. 815–860). Longman.

Pearson, P. D., & Gallagher, M. C. (1983). The instruction of reading comprehension. *Contemporary Educational Psychology, 8*(3), 317–344. doi: 10.1016/0361-476X(83)90019-X

Pearson, P. D., McVee, M. B., Shanahan, L. E. (2019). In the beginning: The historical and conceptual genesis of the gradual release of responsibility. In M. B. McVee, E. Ortlieb, J. Reichenberg, J., & P. D. Pearson (Eds.), *The gradual release of responsibility in literacy research and practice* (pp. 1–21). Emerald Group Publishing.

Philips, S. U. (1983). *The invisible culture: Communication in classroom and community on the Warm Springs Indian Reservation.* Longman.

Raphael, T. E. (1982). Question-answering strategies for children. *The Reading Teacher, 36*(2), 186–190.

Roehler, L. R., & Duffy, G. G. (1991). Teachers' instructional action. In P. D. Pearson, R. Barr, M. L. Kamil, & P. Mosenthal (Eds.), *Handbook of reading research* (pp. 861–883). Longman.

Rose, M. (1995). *Possible lives: The promise of public education in America.* Houghton Mifflin.

Rosenshine, B., & Furst, N. (1973). The use of direct observation to study teaching. In R. M. W. Travers (Ed.), *Second handbook of research on teaching: A symposium* (pp. 122–183). Rand McNally.

Rosenshine, B., & Stephens, R. (1984). Classroom instruction in reading. In P. D. Pearson, R. Barr, M. L. Kamil, & P. Mosenthal (Eds.), *Handbook of reading research* (pp. 745–798). Longman.

Short, K. G., Harste, J. C., & Burke, C. L. (1996). *Creating classrooms for authors and inquirers* (2nd ed.). Heinemann.

Shulman, L. (1986). Paradigms and research programs on the study of teaching: A contemporary perspective. In M. C. Wittrock (Ed.), *Handbook of research on teaching* (3rd ed.). Macmillan.

Smith, G. H. (1997). *The development of Kaupapa Maori: Theory and praxis* (Doctoral dissertation, Auckland University). researchspace.auckland.ac.nz/handle/2292/623?show=full

Smith, G. H. (2002, January). Kaupapa Maori theory: Transformative praxis and new formations of colonisation. Paper presented at the Second International Conference on Cultural Policy Research, Te Papa National Museum, Wellington.

Smith, G. H. (2015, April). Transforming research: The Indigenous struggle for social, cultural, and economic justice within and through education. Presented at The American Educational Research Association Annual Meeting, Chicago, IL. www.aera.net/Events-Meetings/Annual-Meeting/Previous-Annual-Meetings/2015-Annual-Meeting/2015-Annual-Meeting-Webcasts/Transforming-Research-The-Indigenous-Struggle-for-Social-Cultural-and-Economic-Justice-Within-and-Through-Education

Smith, L. T. (1999). *Decolonizing methodologies: Research and Indigenous peoples.* Zed Books.

Spiro, R. J., Collins, B. P., Thota, J. J., & Feltovich, P. J. (2003). Cognitive flexibility theory: Hypermedia for complex learning, adaptive knowledge application, and experience acceleration. *Educational Technology, 43*(5), 5–10.

Stauffer, R. G. (1969). *Directing reading maturity as a cognitive process.* Harper and Row.

Stein, N. L., & Trabasso, T. (1981). *What's in a story: An approach to comprehension and instruction.* Center for the Study of Reading Technical Report No. 200. University of Illinois. www.ideals.illinois.edu/bitstream/handle/2142/18031/ctrstreadtechrepv01981i00200_opt.pdf

Taylor, B. M., Pressley, M. P., & Pearson, P. D. (2002). Research-supported characteristics of teachers and schools that promote reading achievement. In B. Taylor & P. D. Pearson (Eds.), *Teaching reading: Effective schools, accomplished teachers* (pp. 361–373). Routledge. doi: 10.4324/9781410612489

Tierney, R. J., Carter, M. A., & Desai, L. E. (1991). *Portfolio assessment in the reading-writing classroom*. Christopher-Gordon Publishers.

Tierney, R. J., & Cunningham, J. W. (1984). Teaching reading comprehension. In P. D. Pearson, R. Barr, M. L. Kamil, & P. Mosenthal (Eds.), *Handbook of reading research* (pp. 609–656). Longman.

Tierney, R. J., & Readence, J. E. (2005). *Reading strategies and practices: A compendium* (6th ed.). Pearson.

Wagner, D. A. (2011). What happened to literacy? Historical and conceptual perspectives on literacy in UNESCO. *International Journal of Educational Development, 31*(3), 319–323. doi: 10.1016/j.ijedudev.2010.11.015

NOTES

1. The material for reading programs was also usually influenced by government guidelines, which prescribed the curriculum in terms of its topic/issue selection, the readability of the reading materials, and the scope and sequence of the skills to be taught.

2. What became apparent from this past work was the power of design—namely, that the merits of any adjunct, from questions to illustrations, were related to its design or relation to the students, their tasks, and the material they were to learn. Carefully customized material was likely to be better than generic adjuncts. Just as correlational studies of teachers had revealed, a treatment-aptitude interaction was common, benefiting lower performing students more than higher performing students.

3. Crouch and Cambourne (2020) draw on their extensive observations of teachers pursuing a culture of learning in classrooms and capitalizing on what they deemed to be students' "natural" learning prowess. Additionally, they draw on Johnston's analyses of discerning guidance by teacher's choice words (Johnston, 2004) along with examples of complex learning offered (e.g., Howard Gardner's analysis of the Suzuki method [1983]) and James Gee's analyses of video gaming (2003).

5 The Reading-Writing Wave

5.1 THE WRITERLY READER

Amid contemplating writerly readers, we are reminded of African American scholar Cornell West's discussion of the racism, xenophobia, and bias stemming from a television comedy star's (Roseanne Barr) racist tweet.[1] He commented on one's responsibility to oneself and the need for empathy for others. Speaking on the importance of having "courage, vision," and not "conforming to the idols," he suggested we all need to "hope and to have . . . enough courage to try to change the world . . . [be] in the world but not of it; [be] nonconformist in life of love, justice, tenderness and freedom. . . . Action takes a number of different forms . . . broaden it out not just by hitting the streets. . . . Think, be a poet—[be] true to self in terms of love and integrity" (Moore, 2018).

The notion of "being in the world but not of it" and being "true to self with empathy to others" epitomizes what we think should be a key underlying tenet for the meaning maker. It highlights the view of the meaning maker as one who enlists, but is not governed by, the text or texts—as a creator of meaning, not a translator or recipient thereof.

Writerly Readers: Their Inseparability

It is difficult to separate reading from writing, for as we read, we are engaged in our own meaning making, akin to writing the text. In one of our favorite articles, "Teaching the Other Self: The Writer's First Reader," Pulitzer Prize winner and writing educator Donald Murray (1982) has suggested that when writers and readers compose a text, they negotiate its meaning with "the other self"—the inner reader who continually reacts to what the writer has written, is writing, and will write, or what the reader has read, is reading, and will read. It is this other self that acts as the reader's or writer's counsel, judge, and guide. This other self oversees what the reader or writer is trying to do, defines the nature of the collaboration or partnership between reader and author, and decides how the writer as reader and reader as writer is proceeding. It is analogous to when coauthors rework the text in accordance with their own interests. Even when one reads one's own writing, one is rewriting the text in a fashion that is akin to ongoing constructionist notions of reading. And when we write, we are reading from multiple sources as we go back and forth formulating our ideas (see McGinley & Tierney, 1989). At times, our reading and writing involves engaging in a tug-of-war with ideas and their expression. Essentially, the writerly readers are viewed as composers as they create meanings (Pearson & Tierney, 1984; Tierney & Pearson, 1983).

The notion of a writerly reader is also aligned with the proposition offered in our notions of reading as composing. Take, if you will, our discussion of revision, in which approaches to reading are pursued in ways that encourage pauses, re-thinking, consultations, and revision. As suggested,

> If readers are to develop some control over and a sense of discovery with the models of meaning they build, they must approach text with the same deliberation, time, and reflection that a writer employs as she revises a text. They must examine their developing interpretation and view the models they build as draft-like in quality—subject to revision. We would like to see students engage in behaviours such as rereading (especially with different alignments), annotating the text on the page with reactions, and questioning whether the model they have built is what they really want. (Tierney & Pearson, 1983, p. 270)

Characteristics and Responsibilities of the Writerly Reader

There seems to be a lengthy list of characteristics (and responsibilities) of writerly readers as meaning makers and co-creators of texts.

Agency and Planfulness

- Like their cousins (the constructivist and the strategic reader) in the activist family, writerly readers are agents, actively and constantly engaged in making sense of what they experience or seek to access and enlist.
- Writerly readers are contemplative and purposeful in terms of their actions and attention.

Enlarging and Integrating Understandings

- Writerly readers are involved in the use of reading and writing to progressively enlarge understandings and help with pursuits (i.e., knowledge builders and users).
- Writerly readers are constructively arrogant as they decide if a text is sufficiently newsworthy or insightful to warrant the time, attention, and energy it takes to learn from the text.
- Writerly readers will engage with the meanings suggested by (perhaps even scribed in) the text as witnesses of or participants in the events and ideas presented, as a way of appreciating the author's meaning and craft and enjoying (in the spirit of connoisseurship) engaging with the author.

- Writerly readers use their newly constructed knowledge for ongoing meaning making—predicting as they read, learning from text, harnessing new understandings to store in their knowledge warehouses.
- Writerly readers pursue integrated and coherent understandings through reading and writing—understandings that are focused yet expansive rather than scattered and piecemeal.

Reader–Author Relationships

- Writerly readers are aware of their roles in their exchanges with the world—recognizing that they serve as a catalyst for meaning making and are responsible for the support and continuation of that knowledge. Writerly readers might be thoughtful to the author and to the text, but mostly they will be thoughtful to themselves.
- Writerly readers acknowledge their authorship as they engage with the ideas and authorship of others that may spur or inform their own meaning making.
- Writerly readers will consider meanings with an eye toward their perspectives and stances as well as toward the perspective and stance of the author and those of other meaning makers and processes.
- Writerly readers seek to know the author and the author's goals, approaches, and appeals—as well as their (i.e., the writerly readers') own readership and authorship in meaning-making exchanges.
- Writerly readers can shift their focus from ideas to aesthetics to appreciate both the craft and the art of the writing (and the writer) before them.

Layered and Linked Texts

- Writerly readers are always reading between and among texts—intertextually. Writerly readers cross-cross their reading and writing, enlisting them in different ways for different purposes in a fashion that integrates ideas for layered meaning making.

Reading Oneself

- Writers are their own first readers, and readers of writers other than themselves are essentially reading their writing of the reading of another reader's writing.
- Writerly readers might pause to redevelop, rethink, revamp, or reflect on their deliberations and future pursuits.
- Writerly readers will learn to read their own writerly reading of ideas. As meaning makers engage with their own texts or the texts of others, they are engaged in a form of transaction with themselves and others. The notion of writerly readers might be viewed as equivalent to that of a readerly writer.

- Writerly readers are aware of fellow meaning makers with whom they may contend.
- Writerly readers revise—usually as they are afforded feedback or become aware of the need to do so.

Inseparability and Continuity

Reading and writing involve meaning makers' transactions across texts (i.e., those that we author as well as those authored by others). Whether we are involved in reading or writing or in a combination of the two, we are engaged in continuous meaning making as we connect and negotiate with people and events, images, and conversations. Our meaning making involves transactions with our worlds as we engage with and contemplate meanings and their relevance to what we think or might do. For both the reader and the writer, meanings are never directly given. They must be created.

References

McGinley, W., and Tierney, R. J. (1989). Traversing the topical landscape: Reading and writing as ways of knowing. *Written Communication, 6*(3), 243–269. independent .academia.edu/RobTierney/Papers

Moore, C. (Exec. Producer). (2018). Interview with Cornell West. In *Anderson Cooper 360.* CNN.

Murray, D. M. (1982). Teaching the other self: The writer's first reader. *College Composition and Communication, 33*(2), 140–147. doi: 10.2307/357621

Pearson, P. D., & Tierney, R. J. (1984). On becoming a thoughtful reader: Learning to read like a writer. In A. Purves & O. Niles (Eds.), *Reading in the secondary school* (pp. 144–193). National Society for the Study of Education. independent.academia .edu/RobTierney/Papers

Tierney, R. J., & Pearson, P. D. (1983). Toward a composing model of reading. *Language Arts, 60*(5), 568–580. independent.academia.edu/RobTierney/Papers

5.2   READING–WRITING RELATIONSHIPS

Prior to the 1980s, reading and writing were somewhat equivalent to strange bed-fellows. Reading and writing were viewed quite differently, were approached in different ways in schools and scholarly writings, and reading overshadowed writing in terms of its priority. But change was afoot, partially as a result of the growth of interdisciplinarity (see box), but also at the hands of developments in writing that represented somewhat of their own revolution. Change was looming as developments in writing processes and pedagogy began experiencing their own zeitgeist, with an array of research on writing processes and author–reader relationships. Catalyzing these developments were writing theorists and pedagogists such as James Moffatt, Donald Murray, Donald Graves, Peter Elbow, Mina Shaughnessy, and Janet Emig; cognitive scientists such as Linda Flower and John Hayes; and rhetoricians, sociolinguists, and others such as James Kinneavy.[2]

In turn, schools from kindergarten through university were increasingly invested in supporting learners' finding their "voices" through writer-centered writing practices focused on processes, audience, and so on. While developments in writing were historically separated from reading, that was about to change as reading and writing became powerful partners with enormous synergy—indeed, signaling a shift in thinking about reading, writing, speaking, listening, and media as tools for learning, exploration, expression, and discovery under the umbrella notion of literacy.

A Closer Look at These Developments

The history of reading–writing relationships can be characterized as involving three periods. The first (up until 1980) involved a separation of reading and writing in terms of research, theory, and practice. In the 1980s there was a period of crossover, when reading and writing informed one another. Then, beginning in the late 1980s, reading and writing became almost inseparable—under the inclusive field of literacy.

Pre-1980s: Reading and Writing as Separate Curricular Practices

Reading and writing education have different histories and, in turn, different views, theories, research traditions, and practices. Whereas psychologists traditionally dominated the field of reading education, a mixture of practitioners and theorists with literary backgrounds informed writing education. In schools, reading and writing were mostly taught as separate subjects, timetabled in different time slots. Mainly, teachers treated writing as a form of expression and exposition.

Reflecting this period of separation, a number of studies of reading and writing relationships focused on what reading and writing might share. Walter Loban's

(1963) study of reading and writing abilities involved detailed examinations of students' reading and writing abilities across 12 grade levels. His study suggested that reading and writing were strongly correlated, but that high-performing readers might not be high-performing writers (and vice versa) and that low performers in one area might be better in the other. Likewise, later studies of the correlations between measures of reading abilities with those of writing abilities confirmed statistically significant correlation accounts—demonstrating a shared variance between reading and writing that approached 50% (Shanahan, 1984; Shanahan & Lomax, 1986, 1988). Such findings prompted the view that reading and writing abilities interacted with one another and that advances in reading would in turn advance writing.

To a large extent, writing was not as much of a priority as reading. The focus in schools was on learning to read before learning to write, with the understanding that writing abilities would develop as reading abilities advanced. In a 1978 report for the Ford Foundation, Donald Graves described the neglect of writing in school—detailing the national obsession with reading and mathematics but not writing. Writing received less than 1 of every 100 dollars of research funding for reading and was often viewed as secondary to reading in schools. As Graves (1978) suggested, writing was viewed more as an outlet for expression than as a key vehicle for learning and thinking, as a means of preparing students to possess voices for advancing democracy, or as an important adjunct or tool for all disciplines. While his report was aligned with the notion of reading and writing as separate (including the view of reading as reception and writing as production), it might be considered a historical marker of a new emphasis on writing in research, theory, and practice—an emphasis that eventually contributed to the integration of reading and writing.

Adding to the separation of reading and writing was the relationship between writing and reading educators. Writing educators were wary of reading educators given the orientation in the reading curriculum to skill mastery and testing reading outcomes. The political benefits of testing writing were viewed as questionable when weighed against the impact such an emphasis would have on schools. In addition, traditional views of reading and writing viewed them as opposites, with writing seen as expression or production and reading as reception. Rather than a springboard for thinking, writing was positioned to follow reading in ways that afforded an outlet for thinking. Such views may have contributed to a lack of investment in research on writing (compared with reading) and a tendency to look at the two fields' influence on one another as if they were separate rather than intertwined.

Indeed, the entrance of reading researchers into the world of writing scholarship in the early 1980s was more the exception than the rule and occurred at a time when the fields were still quite separate—both conceptually and, to a large extent, in practice. Reading researchers were engaged in reading research, not writing research. Most reading researchers reflected a tradition aligned with psychology, emphasizing what was observable and measurable. In terms of practice, the teaching of reading was approached in a fashion that seemed rather mechanical. There was a scope and sequence of skills (as determined by the grade level of the material) that readers were expected to acquire as they advanced in their reading proficiency.

Writing instruction, on the other hand, was influenced by reflections by writers, practical theorists, rhetoricians, and scholars who took an interest in literary work (see box). Writing scholars seemed focused on helping writers develop their meanings with connections to studies of genre, studies of voice and persona, college writing programs, and studies of the evaluation of writing by Charles Cooper and others (e.g., Cooper, 1983; Cooper & Matsuhashi, 1983; Cooper & Odell, 1977; Odell & Cooper, 1980). At the same time, studies of the writing process were on the rise—beginning with the work of Janet Emig (1971) and spurred by Donald Murray's (1984) declaration of writing as a process. Writing scholars included practical theorists such as James Moffett (1987), Peter Elbow (1998), Ken Macrorie (1988), and Don Murray (1984); rhetoricians such as James Kinneavy (1971) and Kenneth Burke (1969) and scholars interested in writing across cultures, such as Alan Purves (1988).

A major catalyst was writing process research undertaken by a small group of cognitive psychologists at Carnegie Mellon (e.g., John Hayes and Linda Flower) and elsewhere (e.g., in Toronto, with Carl Bereiter and Marlene Scardamalia). While these researchers were not without their critics, as their approach was outside of the norm for writing scholarship, it eventually gained traction. The cognitivists used think-alouds as a basis for their proposed model of the writing process and spurred (or dovetailed with) a range of other studies examining writing and developments. To some extent, they also complemented writing practices in the elementary school that were shifting to a process orientation and a concern over voice and audience (a shift stemming from the work inspired by Donald Graves, Donald Murray, and, later, Tom Newkirk and Jane Hansen at the University of New Hampshire). Other writing studies included work by Ann Berthoff (1981) and Nancy Sommers (1980, 1982), who studied revisions. This work also connected with Mina Shaughnessy's notions of basic college writing (emanating from her work on students writing difficulties) as well as a host of contributions by writing researchers who were interested in a range of issues with regard to writing as a way of knowing and a pedagogy (e.g., David Bartholomea, Anthony Petrosky [1982], Lester Faigley [1981], Stephen Witte [1992], John Daly, Glynda Hull, Sarah Freeman, and others).

Indeed, writing research and practice flourished in ways that were distinct from reading. Within universities, academic writing received significant attention. Networks of writing programs created coalitions such as the National Writing Project (initiated by James Gray at Berkeley in 1974) for teachers to share and enhance their practice. At the same time, in conjunction with the efforts of university–school partnerships, classroom writing practice was shifting in a manner that was student-centered, process-oriented, and collaborative.

Research in writing was also quite multifaceted—bringing together communication theorists, literary theorists, and educators. The recipients of the National Council Teachers of English Promising Research Award illustrate this diverse range of perspectives. The award was tantamount to an award for the most cutting-edge dissertations during this period (Figure 5.1). The recipients present a mix of process-oriented studies along with studies enlisting rhetoric, and so on.

1980s-Reading and Writing Crossovers

Prior to the 1980s, there seemed to be only a handful of reading researchers who were interested in writing and engaging with the reading and writing-related research that was beginning to emerge. Reading educators interested in writing were certainly in the minority and were viewed skeptically both by their own reading colleagues and by writing scholars. Yet their early interest foreshadowed the crossovers from writing to reading and the subsequent significant shift as the two fields became more wedded to one another. Indeed, the 1980s might be described as a period of crossover between reading and writing, especially from writing to reading, not unlike other forms of border crossings.

Authorship and readership were areas for which there were crossovers, especially from writing to reading. Writing educators and researchers, as well as literary theorists and communication scholars, had engaged for centuries in explorations of the author's representation of meanings in written forms—delving into notions of persona, ethos, audience, and other considerations. Many of us, who were exploring the nature of reading and writing processes, were keen to understand the nature and roles (including the responsibilities) of authors and readers in relation to one another (e.g., Bertram Bruce [Bruce, 1982], James Britton [Britton, 1982] Richard Beach and his colleagues [Beach et al., 1986, 1988], and Jerome Harste, Carolyn Burke, and Virginia Woodward [Harste et al., 1981; Harste et al., 1983; Harste et al., 1984]). To this end, one of the frames used to unpack reading–writing relationships was Rosenblatt's transactional theory of meaning making as well as speech act theory—building on Paul Grice's (1975) cooperative principles, the work of John Austin (1975), and John Searle's (1969) suggestion that writers and speakers actively try to get readers or listeners to engage with what they want them to think and do.[3] There was an interest in applying these notions to extended texts (e.g., Pratt, 1977) as more and more reading scholars gravitated toward a view that readers create meaning with the support of authors, but not rigidly. The scope of meanings for a text was apt to be broadened depending on the match between the author's intents and the reader's purposes as well as other factors, including the shared knowledge or individual background experiences of reader and author and the influence of the setting within which the reading occurred (including any interactions with others). The meanings suggested by authors, texts, and readers were not fixed but rather, to some degree, elastic (see box).

Figure 5.1. Promising Research Award Winners

1985

Kathleen Ann Copeland, St. Edward's University, Austin, TX, "The Effect of Writing upon Good and Poor Writers' Learning from Prose"

Anne J. Herrington, Penn State University, "Writing in Academic Settings: A Study of the Rhetorical Contexts for Writing in Two College Chemical Engineering Courses"

Glynda A. Hull, University of Pittsburgh, "The Editing Process in Writing: A Performance Study of Experts and Novices"

1984

Deborah Brandt, University of Wisconsin-Madison, "Writer, Context, and Text"

George E. Newell, University of Kentucky, Lexington, "Learning from Writing in Two Content Areas: A Case Study/Protocol Analysis"

1983

Stephen B. Kucer, UCLA, "Text Production and Comprehension from a Transactional Perspective"

Linda Hanrahan Mauro, University of Maryland, "Personal Constructs and Response to Literature: Case Studies of Adolescent Readers"

1982

Anne Haas Dyson, University of Georgia, "The Role of Oral Language in Early Writing Programs"

Robin Bell Markels, Ohio State University, "Cohesion in Four Paragraph Types"

1981

Margaret A. Atwell, California State College, San Bernardino, "The Evolution of Text: The Interrelationship of Reading and Writing in the Composing Process"

June C. Birnbaum, Rutgers University, "The Reading and Composing Behaviors of Selected Fourth- and Seventh-Grade Students"

Lee Galda, University of Georgia, "Three Children Reading Stories: Response to Literature in Preadolescents"

Mike Rose, UCLA, "Writer's Block in University Students: A Cognitivist Analysis"

1980

Lillian S. Bridwell, University of Nebraska-Lincoln, "Revising Strategies in Twelfth-Grade Students' Transactional Writing" (*Research in the Teaching of English*, October 1980, pp. 197–222)

Colette A. Daiute, Teachers College, Columbia University, "Psycholinguistic Influences on the Writing Process" (*Research in the Teaching of English*, February 1981, pp. 5–22)

Ann Matsuhashi, University of Illinois at Chicago Circle, "Pausing and Planning: The Tempo of Written Discourse Production" (*Research in the Teaching of English*, May 1981, pp. 113–134)

1979

Sondra Perl, Herbert H. Lehman College, CUNY, "Five Writers Writing: Case Studies of the Composing Processes of Unskilled College Writers" (*Research in the Teaching of English*, December 1979, pp. 317–336)

Donald L. Rubin, University of Georgia, "Development in Syntactic and Strategic Aspects of Audience Adaptation Skills in Written Persuasive Communication"

Nancy T. Sommers, University of Oklahoma, "Revision in the Composing Process: A Case Study of Experienced Writers and Student Writers"

Renee K. Weisberg, Beaver College, PA, "Good and Poor Readers' Comprehension of Explicit and Implicit Information in Short Stories Based on Two Modes of Presentation" (*Research in the Teaching of English*, February 1979, pp. 337–352)

1978

Janet K. Black, University of Texas, Arlington, "Formal and Informal Means of Assessing the Communicative Competence of Kindergarten Children"

Marion Crowhurst, Brandon University, Manitoba, Canada, "The Effect of Audience and Mode of Discourse on the Syntactic Complexity of the Writing of Sixth and Tenth Graders"

Barry M. Kroll, Iowa State University, "Cognitive Egocentrism and the Problems of Audience Awareness in Written Discourse"

Don Nix, International Business Machines, Thomas J. Watson Research Center, Yorktown Heights, NY, "Toward a Systematic Description of Some Experiential Aspects of Children's Reading Comprehension"

Sharon Pianko, Livingston College, Rutgers University, "A Description of the Composing Process of College Freshman Writers"

As researchers attempted to advance our understanding of these dynamics and move beyond the text, they turned to alternative frames. Just as analyses of spoken conversations required intensive observations and analyses of exchanges, so analyses of reading and writing required close observation, careful analysis, and more. The dynamics of reader–writer exchanges were less visible and demanded a means of analyzing the text (i.e., what the writers provided) as well as tools to delve into the ongoing meaning making "in the heads" of readers and writers. Accordingly, many of us found ourselves enlisting a mix of approaches to make the meaning making of readers and writers visible (i.e., interview-type questions, spontaneous think-alouds, and debriefings), enabling us to align what writers and readers were thinking with the text that they read and produced (e.g., Newell, 1984).

Some of us found Walker Gibson's (1950, 1969) frame for interpreting reader, author, and subject to be quite useful in separating the dimensions of each and identifying their interactions with one another. For example, Tom Crumpler and Rob explored how researchers positioned themselves in reporting their research

by mapping how they positioned themselves relative to subjects and audiences
across their reviews of literature and their
methods, results, and conclusions. They
found researchers shifting from first person to third person—suggesting that
while they treated their research pursuits
as subjective, they presented their findings as objective. It was as if the subject,
author, and audience configuration shifted
(Figure 5.2) (see Crumpler & Tierney,
1995; Gibson, 1950, 1969).

Indeed, in a number of studies
with colleagues, Rob manipulated authors' personae—
studying the tug-of-war between authors and readers in
the context of readers responding to writers' directions
across modes of communication and text (i.e., face-to-
face, email, paper and pencil,
and telephone) (see Tierney &
LaZansky, 1980; Tierney et al.,
1987).

Process-oriented research on writing constituted a second area of major
crossover from writing to reading. In the
writing field, process-oriented approaches
emerged in practice and in research. In practice, Don Murray (1984) had im-
pressed on writing practitioners that the focus of writing should be the process,
not the product. His views and recommendations for practice impacted writing
pedagogy and, to some extent, undergirded the reinvention of the teaching of
writing at all levels. One of the most notable contributions to the process orientation to writing was the work of Don Graves (1978, 1983) and a group of teachers
in New Hampshire, which had a widespread and revolutionary impact on approaches to teaching writing in schools. Don Graves's 1983 book *Writing: Teachers
and Children at Work* described their initiative and had an impact of global proportions. Its influence should not be underestimated; as a result of Graves's work,
reading teachers made shifts to integrate writing and reading, altering their overall
approaches to reading instruction. Additionally, students who were engaged in

Figure 5.2. The Subject–Author–Reader Dynamic

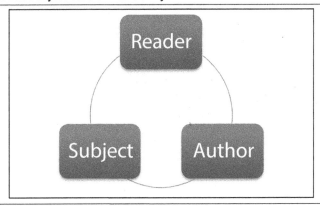

these writing experiences acquired abilities and attitudes that carried over to their engagements in reading.

Other process-oriented work in writing also had a crossover effect. In particular, the process-oriented research on writing done by Linda Flower and John Hayes (Flower & Hayes, 1981), and Bereiter and Scardamalia (see Bereiter & Scardamalia, 1984; Scardamalia, Bereiter, & Steinbach, 1984) propelled a shift in how writing was conceptualized. Flower and Hayes developed a model of the writing process based on writers' think-aloud processes (e.g., goal setting, refinement, and revision) that suggested how writing may shape thinking (see Figure 5.3).

While the Flower and Hayes model seemed to have obvious parallels to the cognitive models emerging for reading, it also suggested provocative extensions and differences—such as notions of recursiveness and revision. Unlike those process-oriented notions of meaning making by readers tied to schema access and schema selection (e.g., Collins, Brown, and Larkin's Progressive Refinement Model of Reading, in Collins et al., 1980), writing theorists delineated a composing process that more fully embraced meaning making as a process in which readers engaged, an adjustment approaching a paradigm shift. The two of us (Rob and

Figure 5.3. Flower and Hayes's (1981) Cognitive Process Model of Writing

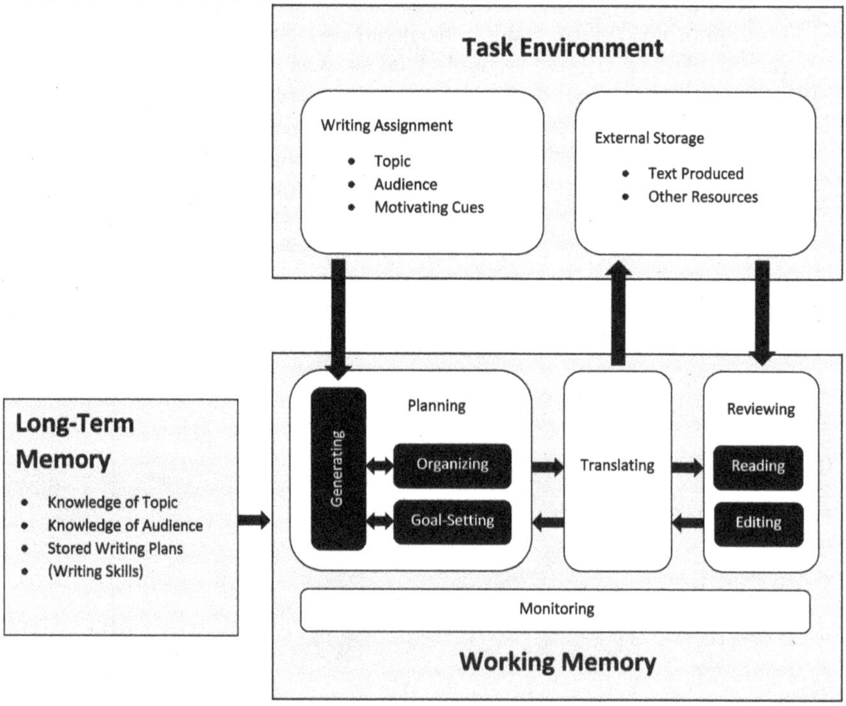

David) proposed a Composing Model of Reading (Tierney & Pearson, 1983) and also discussed the notion of learning to read like a writer (Pearson & Tierney, 1984). Both represented a key crossover from writing to reading at the time (see Figure 5.4).

Other crossovers occurred as process-oriented practices in writing and reading research advanced and as writing assumed a more prominent role (in different classrooms for different purposes) with the backing of networks of writing teachers. Writing to learn became more commonplace in science, history, and mathematics classrooms—especially as research on writing to learn made visible the positive impacts of writing on the learning and thinking in which students were engaged. For example, George Newell (1984) demonstrated that writing enhanced learning. Langer and Applebee (1987), along with a number of their colleagues (e.g., Marshall, 1987), addressed how different genres of writing shaped thinking. And, in studies of genre, a number of writing researchers (especially in Australia) such as Frances Christie and James R. Martin (see Christie & Martin, 1997) argued for the teaching of different genres as crucial to reading and writing development (as an alternative to process-based approaches).

Finally, there was a crossover in pedagogy from writing to reading in terms of interpersonal, intrapersonal, and social skills and strategies. Whereas reading

Figure 5.4. Composing Model of Reading

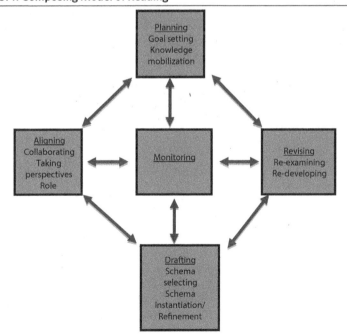

Source: Tierney and Pearson, 1983

was focused on reading skills and strategies acquired in concert with teacher modeling and guided and independent student practice, learning to write was done in concert with students engaging with their classmates as they negotiated their drafts, contemplated their next steps and strategies, and shared their emerging texts with their classmates (who were also authors and readers and learners). These conferences among students constituted sites for discussing the meaning making they were pursuing as well as for sharing the strategies they might employ in doing so. Learning to learn in writing classrooms interfaced the intrapersonal and interpersonal. It positioned writing as a social enterprise, foreshadowing or existing as a precursor to the social turn and its influence with regard to approaches to reading. Learning to learn in writing also signaled a move toward an amalgamation of reading, writing, speaking, listening, and viewing under the umbrella of literacy. Accordingly, it necessitated a shift to studying reading and writing development across individuals (i.e., not just within a single person's head), viewing meaning making as social and occurring outside the head (in a manner which not only informs an individual's meaning making but also connects those meanings with those made within and across collections of people).

Reading and Writing Working Together

As writing assumed a more prominent and dynamic role in classrooms, more teachers began integrating reading and writing. Initially this entailed employing writing activities as precursors or follow-up activities to reading; however, increasingly reading and writing began to meld as if they were crisscrossing students' explorations and projects. Lucy Calkins, who had worked with Donald Graves, detailed the critical eye that writers had for reading, arguing that writers approached published authors as authors themselves (Calkins, 1983). As she stated, young writers came to realize that books were something developed by persons, not produced by a machine. Indeed, it was apparent that reading was the potential beneficiary of writing, not only as writers read their own writing and shared it with others, but also as a result of the dialogical attitudes that it propelled.

There were other notable breakthroughs. Among the most stunning were early writing studies suggesting that young students may learn to read by writing—particularly as they transition from scribbles to invented spelling to conventional text (see Bissex, 1980; Chomsky, 1969; Ferreiro & Teberosky, 1982; King et al., 1981; Teale & Sulzby, 1986). Readers learn about written language as they experiment with writing, from labels to sentences to story to captions. Their first reading, therefore, is of the words that they write.

Also stunning to some of us was the realization of the power of the integration of texts (i.e., those read, written, viewed, spoken, etc.). As studies of the reading process moved forward to study comprehension and learning from extended text (especially in everyday settings), the mingling of reading and writing and the sharing of common sub-processes could not be avoided. Further, as studies of processes focused on meaning making across texts, the notion of reading and writing working together rather than separately was increasingly apparent. Classrooms became sites for such discoveries, and as teachers also became engaged as writers and researchers, they shared their reflections of their practices and their observations of the benefits of integrating reading and writing to enhance reading and writing abilities (as well as thinking and discovery) in ways that aligned with real-world problem solving (including the multilayered meaning making that occurs across digital environments).

The unfolding of these developments in the late 1980s seemed almost preordained as researchers explored students' reading and writing at all levels. These included studies of early readers and writers (e.g., Ann Haas Dyson, 1988; Nancy Shanklin, 1981; Deborah Rowe, 1987; Stephen Kucer, 1985); reading and writing studies at the elementary level (e.g., Jane Hansen (Graves & Hansen, 1983; Boutwell, 1983; Giaccobbe, 1982); reading and writing among high school and college students as well as among those in the workplace, with projects examining reading and writing from multiple sources (e.g., McGinley & Tierney, 1989; Spivey, 1984; Tierney et al., 1989); and studies of digital developments, which involved multilayered interfaces for meaning making. Befitting its new status, writing was highlighted as one of the cornerstones of reading development in a major U.S. national report on reading, *Becoming a Nation of Readers* (Anderson et al., 1985).

As work in this new arena advanced, it prompted (and required) the advancement of research approaches, tools, and frames to support it. Research on these matters required new norms for studies, including recognizing the importance of engagements over time and space and keeping track of the interchanges (i.e., spoken, written, and with media) across individuals. These developments required a shift to more qualitative, thick, and in-depth observations and extensive data collection and reflection. They also required lenses and frames for describing the intrapersonal and interpersonal nature of engagements among and with people who were animating ideas in multilayered and multifaceted ways. For example, Spiro (Jacobson & Spiro, 1995; Spiro & Jehng, 1990) enlisted Wittgenstein's notion of crisscrossing complex knowledge domains to examine how meaning makers engage with multilayered, multi-text environments of significant relevance in digital learning within his Cognitive Flexibility Theory. Rob together with his colleagues at Center of Reading at that time demonstrated through revisions and debriefings how reading and writing working together contributed to thinking critically (Tierney et al., 1989). Others gravitated to semiotic perspectives as well as biological metaphors to unpack these dynamics (e.g., Witte, 1992).

Overall, as reading and writing became recognizable interwoven threads in support of meaning making, "literacy" emerged as a more apt name for the resulting fabric—thus replacing the separate domains of reading and writing.

References

Anderson, R. C., Hiebert, E. H., Scott, J. A., & Wilkinson, I. A. G. (1985). *Becoming a nation of readers: The report of the commission on reading*. National Academy of Education, & Center for the Study of Reading.

Austin, J. L. (1975). *How to do things with words* (2nd ed.). Clarendon Press.

Beach, R., & Anson, C. M. (1988). The pragmatics of memo writing: Developmental differences in the use of rhetorical strategies. *Written Communication, 5*(2), 157–183.

Beach, R., & Liebman-Kleine, J. (1986). The writing/reading relationship: Becoming one's own best reader. In B. Peterson (Ed.), *Convergences: Transactions in reading and writing*. National Council of Teachers of English.

Bean, T. W., & Steenwyck, F. L. (1984). The effect of three forms of summarization instruction on sixth graders' summary writing and comprehension. *Journal of Reading Behavior, 16*, 297–306.

Bereiter, C., & Scardamalia, M. (1984). Learning about writing from reading. *Written Communication, 1*(2), 163–188. doi: 10.1177/0741088384001002001

Berthoff, A. E. (1981). *The making of meaning: Metaphors, models, and maxims for writing teachers*. Boynton/Cook Publishers.

Birnbaum, J. C. (1982). The reading and composing behavior of selected fourth- and seventh-grade students. *Research in the Teaching of English, 16*, 241–260.

Bissex, G. L. (1980). *GYNS AT WRK: A child learns to write and read*.: Harvard University Press.

Boutwell, M. (1983). Reading and writing process: A reciprocal agreement. *Language Arts, 60*, 723–730.

Britton, J. (1982). *Prospect and retrospect: Selected essays of James Britton*. G. Pradl, Ed. Boynton/Cook.

Bruce, B. C. (1980). Plans and social actions. In R. J. Spiro, B. C. Bruce, & W. F. Brewer (Eds.), *Theoretical issues in reading comprehension* (pp. 367–384). Erlbaum.

Burke, K. (1969). *A rhetoric of motives*. University of California Press.

Calkins, L. (1983). *Lessons from a child*. Heinemann.

Colvin-Murphy, C. (1986, December). Enhancing critical comprehension of literary texts through writing. Paper presented at the National Reading Conference, Austin, TX.

Chomsky, C. (1969). *The acquisition of syntax in children from 5 to 10*. MIT Press.

Christie, F., & Martin, J. R. (Eds.). (1997). *Genre and institutions: Social processes in the workplace and school*. Pinter.

Collins, A., Brown, J. S., & Larkin, K. (1980). Inference in text understanding. In R. J. Spiro, B. C. Bruce, & W. F. Brewer (Eds.), *Theoretical issues in reading comprehension: Perspectives from cognitive psychology, linguistics, artificial intelligence, and education* (pp. 385–410). Erlbaum.

Cooper, C. R. (1983). Procedures for describing written texts. In P. Mosenthal, L. Tamor, & S. A. Walmsley (Eds.), *Research on writing: Principles and methods*. Longman.

Cooper, C. R., & Matsuhashi, A. (1983). A theory of the writing process. In M. Martlew (Ed.), *The psychology of written language: Developmental and educational perspectives*. Wiley.

Cooper, C. R., & Odell, L. (1977). *Evaluating writing: Describing, measuring, judging*. National Council of Teachers of English.

Crafton, L. K., Hill, M. W., House, A. L., & Kucer, S. B. (1980). Language instruction: From theoretical abstraction to classroom implications. Occasional Papers in Language and Reading. Indiana University.

Crumpler, T., & Tierney, R. J. (1995). Literacy research and rhetorical space: Reflections and interpretive possibilities. Research monograph. www.academia.edu/9699516/Literacy_Research_and_Rhetorical_Space_Reflections_and_Interpretive_Possibilities

Dyson, A. H. (1988). Negotiating among multiple worlds: The space/time dimensions of young children's composing. *Research in the Teaching of English, 22*(4), 355–390.

Eckhoff, B. (1983). How reading affects children's writing. *Language Arts,* 60, 607–616.

Elbow, P. (1998). *Writing without teachers* (2nd ed.). Oxford University Press.

Emig, J. A. (1971). *The composing processes of twelfth graders.* National Council of Teachers of English.

Faigley, L., & Witte, S. (1981). Analyzing revision. *College Composition and Communication, 32*(4), 400–414.

Ferreiro, E., & Teberosky, A. (1982). *Literacy before schooling.* Heinemann Educational Books.

Flower, L., & Hayes, J. R. (1981). A cognitive process theory of writing. *College Composition and Communication, 32*(4), 365–387.

Fulwiler, T., & Young, A. (Eds). (1982). *Language connections: Writing and reading across the curriculum.* National Council of Teachers of English.

Galda, L. (1983). The relations between reading and writing in young children. In R. Beach & L. S. Bridwell (Eds.), *New directions in composition research* (pp. 191–204). Guilford.

Giacobbe, M. E. (1982). A writer reads, a reader writes. In T. Newkirk & N. Atwell (Eds.), *Understanding writing.* Northeast Regional Exchange.

Gibson, W. (1950). Authors, speakers, readers, and mock readers. *College English, 11*(5), 265–269. doi: 10.2307/585994

Gibson, W. (1969). *Persona: A style study for readers and writers.* Random House.

Goodman, K. & Goodman, Y. (1984). Reading and writing relationships: Pragmatic functions. In J. Jensen (Ed.), *Composing and comprehending.* National Council of Teachers of English.

Graves, D. H. (1978). *Balance the basics: Let them write.* Ford Foundation.

Graves, D. H. (1983). *Writing: Teachers and children at work.* Heinemann.

Graves, D., & Hansen, J. (1983). The author's chair. *Language Arts,* 60, 176–182.

Grice, P. (1975). Logic and conversation. In P. Cole, & J. Morgan, *Syntax and semantics, vol. 3: Speech acts* (pp. 41–58). Academic Press.

Harste, J. C., Burke, C. L., & Woodward, V. A. (1981). *Children, their language and world: Initial encounters with print* (Final report, National Institute of Education). Language Education Department, Indiana University.

Harste, J. C., Burke, C. L., Woodward, V. A., & Bouffler, C. (1983). *The young child as writer-reader, and informant* (Final report, National Institute of Education). Language Education Department, Indiana University.

Harste, J. C., Woodward, V. A., & Burke, C. L. (1984). *Language stories and literacy lessons.* Heinemann Educational Books.

Jacobson, M. J., & Spiro, R. J. (1995). Hypertext learning environments, cognitive flexibility, and the transfer of complex knowledge: An empirical investigation. *Journal of Educational Computing Research, 12*(4), 301–333. doi: 10.2190/4T1B-HBP0-3F7E-J4PN

King, M., Rentel, V., Pappas, C., Pettegrew, B., & Zutell, J. (1981). *How children learn to write: A longitudinal study.* The Ohio State University Research Foundation.

Kinneavy, J. (1971) *A theory of discourse.* Prentice-Hall.

Kroll, B. M. (1985). Rewriting a complex story for a young reader: The development of audience-adapted writing skills. *Research in the Teaching of English,* 19, (2), 120–139.

Kucer, S. L. (1985). The making of meaning: Reading and writing as parallel processes. *Written Communication*, 2(3), 317–336.

Langer, J. A. (1986a). Reading, writing and understanding: An analysis of the construction of meaning. *Written Communication*, 3(2), 219–267.

Langer, J. A., & Applebee, A. N. (1987). *How writing shapes thinking: A study of teaching and learning.* National Council of Teachers of English.

Loban, W. (1963). *The language of elementary school children: A study of the use and control of language and the relations among speaking, reading, writing, and listening.* Research Report No. 1. National Council of Teachers of English.

Marshall, J. D. (1987). The effects of writing on students' understanding of literary texts. *Research in the Teaching of English*, 21(1), 30–63.

Martin, P. (1977). A comparative analysis of reading and writing skills: Six case studies. *English in Australia*, 40, 51–53.

Macrorie, Ken. (1988). *The I-Search paper.* Heinemann.

McGinley, W., & Tierney, R. J. (1989). Traversing the topical landscape: Reading and writing as ways of knowing. *Written Communication*, 6(3), 243–269. independent.academia .edu/RobTierney/Papers

Moffett, James. (1987) *Teaching the universe of discourse.* Boynton/Cook.

Murray, D. (1984). *Write to learn.* Holt, Rinehart, & Winston.

Newell, G. E. (1984). Learning from writing in two content areas: A case study/protocol analysis. *Research in the Teaching of English*, 18(3), 265–287.

Newkirk, T. (1982). Young writers as critical readers. *Language Arts*, 59(5), 451–457.

Nystrand, M. (1986). *The structure of written communication.* Academic Press.

Odell, L., & Cooper, C. (1980). Procedures for evaluating writing: Assumptions and needed research. *College English*, 42(1), 35–43. doi: 10.2307/376031

Pearson, P. D., & Tierney, R. J. (1984). On becoming a thoughtful reader: Learning to read like a writer. In A. Purves & O. Niles (Eds.), *Reading in the secondary school* (pp. 144–193). National Society for the Study of Education. independent.academia.edu/RobTierney /Papers

Petrosky, A. R. (1982) From story to essay: Reading and writing. *College Composition and Communication*, 33(1), 19–36.

Pratt, M. L. (1977). *Toward a speech act theory of literary discourse.* Indiana University Press.

Purves, A. C. (Ed.) (1988). Writing across languages and cultures: Issues in contrastive rhetoric. Sage series on *Written Communication*. Sage.

Roen, D. H., & Willey, R. J. (1988). The effects of audience awareness on drafting and revising. *Research in the Teaching of English*, 22, 75–88.

Rosenblatt, L. (1978). *The reader, the text, the poem: The transactional theory of the literary work.* Southern Illinois University Press.

Rowe, D. W. (1987). Literacy learning as an intertextual process. In J. E. Readence & R. Scott Baldwin (Eds.), *Research in literacy: Merging perspectives.* Thirty-Sixth Yearbook of the National Reading Conference National Reading Conference.

Rubin, D. (1984). Social cognition and written communication. *Written Communication*, 1(2), 211–246.

Ryan, S. M. (1985). An examination of reading and writing strategies of selected fifth grade students. In J. Niles & R. Lalik (Eds.), *Issues in literacy: A research perspective* (pp. 386–390). *34th Yearbook of the National Reading Conference*, National Reading Conference.

Scardamalia, M., Bereiter, C., & Steinbach, R. (1984). Teachability of reflective processes in written composition. *Cognitive Science, 8*(2), 173–190. doi: 10.1016/S0364-0213(84) 80016-6

Searle, J. R. (1969). *Speech acts: An essay in the philosophy of language.* Cambridge University Press.

Shanahan, T. (1984). Nature of the reading-writing relation: An exploratory multivariate analysis. *Journal of Educational Psychology, 76*(3), 466–477. doi: 10.1037//0022-0663 .76.3.466

Shanahan, T., & Lomax, R. G. (1986). An analysis and comparison of theoretical models of the reading-writing relationship. *Journal of Educational Psychology, 78*(2), 116–123. doi: 10.1037/0022-0663.78.2.116

Shanahan, T., & Lomax, R. G. (1988). A developmental comparison of three theoretical models of the reading-writing relationship. *Research in the Teaching of English, 22*(2), 196–212.

Shanklin, N. (1981). Relating reading and writing: Developing a transactional theory of the writing process. *Monographs in teaching and learning.* Indiana University.

Smith, F. (1984). Reading like a writer. In J. M. Jensen (Ed.), *Composing and comprehending.* National Council of Teachers of English.

Smith, R., Jensen, K., & Dillingofski, M. (1971). The effects of integrating reading and writing on four variables. *Research in the Teaching of English, 5,* 179–189.

Snow, C. E. (1983). Literacy and language: Relationships during the preschool years. *Harvard Educational Review, 53,* 165–189.

Sommers, N. (1980). Revision strategies of student writers and experienced adult writers. *College Composition and Communication, 31*(4), 378–88.

Sommers, N. (1982). Responding to student writing. *College Composition and Communication, 33*(2), 148–156.

Spiro, R. J., & Jehng, J. C. (1990). Cognitive flexibility and hypertext: Theory and technology for the nonlinear and multidimensional traversal of complex subject matter. In D. Nix & R. Spiro (Eds.), *Cognition, education, and multimedia* (pp. 163–205). Erlbaum.

Spivey, N. N. (1984). *Discourse synthesis: Constructing texts in reading and writing* (Monograph). International Reading Association.

Spivey, N. N., & King, J. R. (1989). Readers as writers composing from sources. *Reading Research Quarterly, 24*(1), 7–26.

Squire, R. J. (1984). Composing and comprehending: Two sides of the same basic processes. In J. M. Jensen (Ed.), *Composing and comprehending* (pp. 23–31). National Council of Teachers of English.

Stotsky, S. (1982). The role of writing in developmental reading. *Journal of Reading, 25,* 330–340.

Sulzby, E. (1981). Kindergartners begin to read their own compositions: Beginning readers' developing knowledges about written language projects (Final Report to the Research Committee of the National Council of Teachers of English). Evanston, IL: Northwestern University.

Teale, W. H., & Sulzby, E. (1986). *Emergent literacy: Writing and reading.* Ablex.

Tierney, R. J., & LaZansky, J. (1980). The rights and responsibilities of readers and writers: A contractual agreement. *Language Arts, 57*(6), 606–613.

Tierney, R. J., LaZansky, J., Raphael, T., & Cohen, P. (1987). Authors' intentions and readers' interpretation. In R. J. Tierney, P. L. Anders, & J. N. Mitchell (Eds.), *Understanding readers' understanding: Theory and practice* (pp. 205–226). Erlbaum.

Tierney, R. J., & Pearson, P. D. (1983). Toward a composing model of reading. *Language Arts, 60*(5), 568–580. independent.academia.edu/RobTierney/Papers

Tierney, R. J., & Shanahan, T. (1991). Research on the reading-writing relationship: Interactions, transactions, and outcomes. In R. Barr, M. L. Kamil, P. Mosenthal, & P. D. Pearson (Eds.), *Handbook of reading research* (Vol. 2, pp. 246–280). Longman. independent.academia.edu/RobTierney/Papers

Tierney, R. J., Soter, A., O'Flahavan, J. F., & McGinley, W. (1989). The effects of reading and writing upon thinking critically. *Reading Research Quarterly, 24*(2), 134–173. doi: 10.2307/747862. independent.academia.edu/RobTierney/Papers

Witte, S. P. (1992). Context, text, intertext: Toward a constructivist semiotic of writing. *Written Communication, 9*(2), 237–308. doi: 10.1177/0741088392009002003

NOTES

1. See also J. Koblin (2018, May 29). "Roseanne" self-destructs with a racist tweet. *New York Times*, p. A1. nyti.ms/2GXOIFT

2. In the 1970s and 1980s, interdisciplinary teams were commonplace in efforts to address educational matters such as the priority given to advancing our understanding of reading. The creation of national centers for the study of reading—initially at the University of Illinois, later at the Universities of Maryland and Georgia and then at Michigan, Michigan State, Virginia, and the University of Southern California—involved scholars from psychology, computer science, education, linguistics, and psycholinguistics. And, as interest in writing grew, a national center for the study of writing was funded at the University of California and Carnegie Mellon University, with a similar mix of interdisciplinary scholars.

3. For a number of reading scholars, the view of the reader and writer relationship had shifted to what Louise Rosenblatt described as transactional—a better fit for studying reader–writer negotiations than the more detached interactional model of top-down, bottom-up meaning making (derived from schema theory) (Rosenblatt, 1978).

6 The Social Wave

6.1 THE SOCIAL READER

As we were revising the discussion of the social reader, we were distracted by the proceedings of the U.S. Senate Judiciary Committee regarding the contested nomination of Judge Amy Coney Barrett to assume the Supreme Court Justice appointment vacated by Justice Ruth Bader Ginsburg. We were especially struck by the position adopted by the nominee when she described her judicial role as a textualist. As reported in the *New York Times* (Fandos, 2020) on the following day:

> As questioning got underway, Judge Barrett described her judicial philosophy, calling herself a strict textualist and originalist in the tradition of her mentor, the late Justice Antonin Scalia.
>
> "In English, that means I interpret the Constitution as a law," said Judge Barrett. "The text is text, and I understand it to have the meaning that it had at the time people ratified it. It does not change over time, and it is not up to me to update it or infuse my own views into it."
>
> Asked by Senator Lindsey Graham, Republican of South Carolina and the Judiciary Committee chairman, if it would be accurate to call her a "female Scalia," Judge Barrett said that he had been a mentor. But she added: "I want to be careful to say if I am confirmed, you would not be getting Justice Scalia. You would be getting Justice Barrett, and that is because not all originalists agree." (Fandos, 2020, para. 1–3)

We may not identify with the need to approach text with the predisposition of a Supreme Court justice. Nonetheless, Judge Barrett's comments bring to the fore the social milieus surrounding any reading, not just those surrounding a reader intent on refrained interpretation. Judge Barrett's assertion that her way of reading is not a duplicate of even her mentor's acknowledges the transactional nature of reading, tacitly recognizing how readers engage in a form of interpretation that is a combination of reading cues from the author, one's own perspective, and a process of comparing and contrasting with other readers.

Indeed, her comments could be explored from a variety of viewpoints that might question her position. These views might range from formalist orientations advocating close reading and self-referent texts (e.g., I. A. Richards) to transactional views and theories (e.g., Louise Rosenblatt) and, more recently, a cadre of other theorists (e.g., David Bleich, Stanley Fish, Wolfgang Iser); educators (e.g., Richard Beach, David Bloome, Judith Green, Jerome Harste, Douglas Hartman, Theresa Rogers); feminists (e.g., Donna Alvermann, Carmen Luke); and critical race theorists (e.g., Cynthia Tyson, Violet Harris, Annette Henry, William Tate).

The study of social reading conjures up metaphors of a kaleidoscope, or an art exhibition involving various traditions. The notion of a social reader moves us beyond thinking that reading is a process that takes place only inside the head, or the notion that reading is merely an act of translation (as if meanings and language are so tightly constructed that there is no license or need to bring one's own meanings to the text). Reading, from its earliest origins, has involved transactions between people and communities, both in real time, as in a social setting, or across time and place, in a cultural setting. It is situated and entails exchanges that occur at multiple, reverberating levels as readers exchange with authors and authors exchange with readers; readers exchange with their own reading or compositions of texts and authors (as readers) exchange with their own texts; and readers and writers alike contemplate other linkages, including the systems at play. For example, behind any act of reading (e.g., reading signs, news releases, letters or emails, opinion essays, fiction), a reader considers what the authors are trying to convey, taking into consideration authorial intentions, approaches, biases, and perspectives. But readers do this as they form their own compositions and contemplate their own views in relation to the text. Meanings are not given directly (e.g., see box).

Nowadays, exchanges are situated across a range of social media and take various forms for purposes of different exchanges or engagements. And, in this digital age, we have ascribed terms such as "jazz," "bazaar-like" and more recently "mangled" to the various social dynamics at play in the myriad of ongoing exchanges between people across digital spaces (e.g., their various personae, avatars, etc.). As participants interact with one another, a form of theatrical improvisation takes place—as though there are multiple playwrights enlisting multiple characters or

---

In an illustration of how reading involves transactions between people and communities, Cynthia Tyson (1999) described her conversation with an African American 5th-grader about a fairy tale:

> During an interaction with a fifth grade male student, I asked him why he appeared not to be interested in the stories I read to the class. I will never forget his reply: "There ain't no Little Red in my hood, and I catch one of 'dem little piggies, I'm gon' have a Bar-B-Que." While his response made me chuckle, we continued to discuss why he did not like fairy tales. His comments suggested that he did not view fairy tales in the traditional ways. (p. 151)

personae in their various interactions with others. In the digital realm, our nego-tiations are mangled, collapsing and ever-changing.

In order to navigate these diverse and multifaceted processes of reading and writing, the social reader does not experience reading and writing in isolation. They are aware that as readers, they are writers; as writers they are readers; and that reading and writing are done in concert with others as one transacts meanings in pursuit of goals. The interfacing of reading and writing occurs constantly as one negotiates with oneself and with individuals or groups with whom one commu-nicates, collaborates, or engages in various ways. For readers and writers, reading and writing involves not only engaging with authors, readers, and audiences, but also navigating one's own engagement as both reader and writer. The processes of reading and writing therefore entail matters of positionality and perspective-taking, in combination. They are multilayered, intertextual, and multimodal, oc-curring across a range of spaces and time.

In other words, social readers are:

- aware of their own roles, positions, and agency;
- able to negotiate and navigate meaningful participation and communication—including being able to access resources and strategies—in ways that meet their own needs and befit the cultural norms and expectations of communities;
- conscious of and demonstrate critical reflexivity with regard to their participation with others (i.e., authors, readers, communities) in and across various communication exchanges;
- aware of their positionality in engagements;
- aware of norms and conventions—and therefore able to predict the nature, authority, and relevance of interactions;
- aware of criteria befitting the participation, and able to judge the sincerity, integrity, perspicuity, evidence, and claims appropriate to the register;
- able to discern the intentionality of authors and others;
- able to plan, organize, collaborate, and engage in collective action;
- able to engage in, navigate, and generate communications that involve transmediation across multimodal and multilayered virtual and real platforms, for a range of purposes;
- able to enlist a variety of communication tools to address personal and professional needs;
- able to develop and engage with networks—locally, regionally, and globally—for meaningful communication and support;
- able to operate across multiple planes of engagement with multiple perspectives and at different stages, simultaneously;
- able to participate morally and ethically with others, in both virtual and face-to-face communications; and
- able to enlist and enlarge their own perspectives, and willing to recognize and engage with the perspectives of others (be they similar or different).

For instance, in her introduction to *The Golden Notebook* (1973), Doris Lessing offered the following vignette.

> Ten years after I wrote (*The Golden Notebook*) I can get in one week, three letters about it.... One letter is entirely about the sex war, about man's inhumanity to woman, and woman's inhumanity to man, and the writer has produced pages and pages all about nothing else, for she—but not always she—can't see anything else in the book.
>
> The second is about politics, probably from an old Red like myself, and he or she writes many pages about politics and never mentions any other theme.
>
> ... The third letter, once rare but now catching up on the others, is written by a man or a woman who can see nothing in it but the theme of mental illness.
>
> But it is the same book.
>
> And naturally these incidents bring up again questions of what people see when they read a book, and why one person sees one pattern and nothing at all of another pattern, and how odd it is to have, as author, such a clear picture of a book, that is seen so very differently by its readers. (p. xvi)

Above all, social readers are engaged in participatory forms of communal literacy with themselves, others, groups, and their worlds. They are not reading the text just for ideas but also for how they might stage their ongoing presence, role, place, and relevance. They are not just reading what they sense an author is suggesting; they are constructing their own reading in the direct or virtual company of others, either collaboratively as sounding boards or in comparison or contrast. In some ways, reading is a form of participation in a myriad of simultaneous conversations.

References

Beach, R. (1993). *A teacher's introduction to reader response theories*. National Council for Teachers of English.

Bleich, D. (1998). *The double perspective; language, literacy and social relations*. Oxford University Press.

Enciso, P. (1997). Negotiating the meaning of difference: Talking back to multicultural literature. In T. Rogers & A. Soter (Eds.), *Reading across cultures* (pp. 13–41). Teachers College Press.

Fandos, N. (2020, October 14). Judge Barrett resists "female Scalia" label, but embraces his legal philosophy. *New York Times*. www.nytimes.com/live/2020/10/13/us/amy-coney-barrett-live/judge-barrett-resists-female-scalia-label-but-embraces-his-legal-philosophy

Fish, S. (1980). *Is there a text in this class? The authority of interpretative communities*. Cambridge University Press.

Harris, V. (Ed.). (1993). *Teaching multicultural literature in grades K-8*. Ablex.

Hartman, D. (1995). 8 readers reading: The intertextual links of proficient readers reading multiple passages. *Reading Research Quarterly, 30*, 220–261.

Iser, W. (1978). *The act of reading; A theory of aesthetic response*. Johns Hopkins University Press.

Langer, J. (1995). *Envisioning literature: Literary understanding and literature instruction.* Teachers College Press.

Lessing, D. (1973). *The Golden Notebook* (3rd ed.). Bantam Books.

Luke, C. (Ed.). (1996). *Feminisms and the pedagogies of everyday life.* State University of New York.

Petrosky, A. (1973). Response to literature. *English Journal, 66,* 86–88.

Richards, I. A. (1929). *Practical criticism.* Harcourt Brace and Jovanovich.

Rogers, T. (1991). Students as literary critics: The interpretative experiences, beliefs and processes of ninth grade students. *Journal of Reading Behavior, 23,* 391–423.

Rosenblatt, L. (1978). *The reader, the text, the poem.* Southern Illinois University Press.

Tyson, C. A. (1999). "Shut my mouth wide open": Realistic fiction and social action. *Theory into Practice, 38*(3), 155–159. doi: 10.1080/00405849909543847

6.2   THE SOCIAL WAVE

For many of us who had been immersed in cognition, the social wave was an epiphany or breakthrough that was equivalent to changing our schema for or the lens through which we examined reading, and moreover literacy. In the 1970s and 1980s, significant advances occurred in our understandings of and approaches to teaching reading and writing. At the same time, we were developing an increasing awareness of the role played by social factors in a range of psychological activities that had previously been shaped more by a consideration of individual differences than of social or cultural contexts. During this era, the social had largely been positioned by educators as a variable influencing learning to read rather than as a key facet of the nature of reading itself. The social thus tended to be studied as a separate factor (one of many) in the contextual surround and as a mediator—an explanatory means to an end, but not as an end unto itself or as integral to the nature of reading or literacy.

cognitive view

Perpetuating this orientation was a primary focus on the learning of the individual or individuals instead of the event. Our notions of learning thus tended to be tethered to an "inside the head" view of reading (i.e., related to individual skill and strategy development), a view that predominated in terms of teaching and testing. This "inside the head" perspective defined reading development as the progression of a set of skills and strategies, treating the social as fixed, separate, and external rather than integrated in the process of reading itself. The social was still seen as a relevant mediating factor; indeed, during the height of the cognitive revolution, as schema theory (Anderson & Pearson, 1983; Bartlett, 1932) became, for a brief period, the dominant paradigm, most of the key studies demonstrating the power of schemas (abstract conceptual frames hypothesized to organize knowledge in long-term memory) were based on studying the impact of social and cultural schemata, such as weddings, religious rites, or ethic discourse traditions. This was also the period in which a number of learning theorists were spurred by translations in the 1970s and 1980s of the research of Russian psychologist Lev Vygotsky and his colleagues (e.g., Wertsch, 1985), who had highlighted the nature and the significant role of the social in mediating development of the individual— the "in the head" learning. Consequently, "inside the head" views of reading largely entrenched and positioned the social as serving learning (i.e., as opposed to the integrated social model of learning), recognizing the social's mediating role in the service of reading improvement.

This emphasis on the social as a mediator to learning tended to be emphasized despite a growing interest in the connections between reading and writing. The reading and writing connection, at its very foundation, was tied to two key social dynamics: (1) the notion that meaning making involves inherently social transactions between readers, writers, readers-as-writers, writers-as-readers, and others; and (2) the recognition of the important classroom practices of dyadic conferencing and classroom communities in relation to reading and writing development. Yet despite increasing interests in and awareness of these connections—highlighting the inextricable and significant link between the social and learning to read—the orientation to an "inside the head" approach prevailed (albeit with the understanding that social elements only serve as key mediators).

Around this time there was also a heightened realization of the power of learning in the company of others (movements such as cooperative learning as promoted by David Johnson and Roger Johnson, or Robert Slavin), as well as recognition of the influence of teaching practices on students' participation (Johnson & Johnson, 1975; Slavin 1980). Accordingly, a number of researchers examining participation structures in the classroom found that classroom reading activities involved an array of structures that could be examined through a social lens. Over the decades between the unearthing of the social and cultural in schema theory to today, the situated character of learning also became a focus of study, as a new brand of cultural psychology, which eventually morphed into what is now called the learning sciences (National Academies of Sciences, Engineering, and Medicine, 2018 and Mind Brain Education science) examined whether or not approaches to teaching were aligned with how learning occurred in the real world, which is often much more social and collaborative than the highly individualized models of learning in schools. For example, based on a comparison of how learning occurs in the real world versus its occurrence in schools, Brown et al. (1989) argued for an orientation to learning that was situated and embedded in the social. Table 6.1 illustrates their comparison of learning among "just plain folks" (JPL), "students," and "practitioners."

Brown et al. argued for the importance of learning from a practitioner orientation, with forms of collective problem solving and collaboration with others. But again, the social served as a means of socially constructing skills and meaning rather than functioning as an integrated, socially based form of learning. In other words, the value of the social was in promoting better individual development.

Table 6.1. Just Plain Folk Versus Practitioner Versus Student Activity

	Just Plain Folks	Students	Practitioner
Reasoning with	Casual stories	Laws and theories	Causal models
Acting on	Situations	Symbols	Conceptual situations
Resolving	Emerging and complex problems and dilemmas	Well-defined problems	Ill-defined and complex problems
Producing	Negotiable meanings Socially constructed understandings	Fixed meanings Immutable concepts	Negotiable meanings and Socially constructed understandings

Source: Brown, Collins, & Duguid, 1989.

Making the Social Wave

Foundational to the social wave were anthropologically based perspectives applied to communication, including literacy. From the perspective of some, the advent of writing systems was deemed as a lifeline to development, advancing reasoning abilities as well as economic, social, and political advantages. Some argued that literate communities were advantaged in ways that contributed to what they deemed to be a great divide between the literate and nonliterate in terms of reasoning, apart from the social networking advantages that were afforded. (For an example, see Jack Goody's 1968 discussion of the development of writing and its social nature and consequences.) To some extent, while the social nature of literacy was highlighted, notions of a great divide were put to rest by Scribner and Cole's (1981) analyses of the unique Vai communities in Liberia (which included literate and nonliterate peoples). Their attempts to assess abstract reasoning suggested that there was little social and economic advantage or difference in reasoning abilities across literate and nonliterate populations. Countering the view that literate communities have more advanced reasoning, Scribner and Cole demonstrated how different literacies might prompt different social affordances but no distinct advantages in reasoning. In other words, there was no evidence of a literate advantage supporting the characterization of a great divide.

In a related vein, Dell Hymes and John Gumperz advanced a number of studies examining literacy in use by enlisting what they deemed an "ethnography of communication" or "interactional sociolinguistics" within selected speech communities (e.g., Cook-Gumperz & Gumperz, 1992; Gumperz, 1967, 1981; Hymes, 1964, 1976, 1994). For example, in an effort to unpack prestige language forms versus other language forms, they highlighted the prowess of speakers of less prestigious dialects, including forms of code switching that might be enlisted by speakers of less powerful dialects as they moved across codes (prestigious and less prestigious) in a form he termed "diglossic."

Discussions of differences in these codes extended to schooling. Indeed, such issues and debates were brought to the fore in discussions of language differences (as contrasted with the more common attribution of deficit) by Labov and others (1969, 1982), in conjunction with concerns around matters of dialect. One memorable example was the infamous federal court case in the United States in which African American parents sued Martin Luther King, Jr. Elementary School in Ann Arbor (Michigan) for denying their children an education as a result of interactional problems tied to their dialect (see box; Fiske, 1981). The plaintiffs in the Ann Arbor case were able to show the cumulative effects of the school personnel's ignorance of their children's backgrounds, especially with regard to language, on decisions related to opportunity and placement. They highlighted the extent to which a school or a teacher's lack of understanding and failure to apply a sociocultural lens unfairly label language differences as deficits and in turn restrict the opportunities afforded certain students. The case also highlighted how these issues manifested themselves in the views of the public. As Cook-Gumperz and Gumperz

The Ann Arbor case drew national attention. As reported in the *New York Times* (Fiske, 1981) at the time:

In his decision, Judge Joiner said that ignorance of this dialect on the part of teachers can create "a psychological barrier to learning" in students. "The child may withdraw or may act out frustrations and may not learn to read," he wrote. "A language barrier develops when teachers, in helping the child switch from the home (black English) language to standard English, refuse to admit the existence of a language that is the acceptable way of talking in his local community."

The plaintiffs hailed it as a "major victory" that could be used elsewhere to force changes in the education of poor black youngsters. The school board said it was "confused."

To implement the decision, Judge Joiner and school officials agreed to a plan under which 40 teachers at the King School, where the plaintiffs were enrolled, would undergo 40 hours of "consciousness raising" about black English. (The case did not—as many persons assumed—require teachers to use black English as the language of instruction)....

The decision aroused considerable attention in the academic community, and several national conferences have been conducted on the education of dialect speakers. By contrast, the hopes of the plaintiffs and their representatives that the Ann Arbor case would set a precedent for decisions elsewhere requiring schools to take special actions in behalf of children coming from homes where standard English is not spoken have proved vain.

One exception came in January when Federal District Judge William Wayne Justice, in ruling that bilingual programs in Texas public schools were seriously flawed, declared, "Both the language and the cultural heritage of these children were uniformly treated with intolerance and disrespect." ...

The allegation of insensitivity to the students' "home language" was based on a relatively new section of the United States Code that says students cannot be denied equal educational opportunity by the failure of a school to "take appropriate action to overcome language barriers that impede equal participation by its students in its instructional programs." (paras. 7-9, 16-17, 22)

(1992), who discussed the aforementioned Ann Arbor case and a number of other studies of learning, argued:

This work showed how these aspects of the communication system provided for or denied access to learning in situations when the actual verbalized message was only one part of the total system (Erickson, 1979; Florio, 1978; Philips, 1972). Work that continued in this vein showed that the differences in instructional practices and misunderstandings between teacher and ethnically different students were mostly the product of interactional constraints, not conscious prejudice. Misunderstanding both linguistic messages and implicit cues provided reinforcement for differential instruction and learning, unless these culturally coded messages could be understood (McDermott, 1974). These studies alerted us to the communicative character of the social system of the classroom and, most important, to the fact that access to learning opportunities is determined socio-communicatively and is not initially a matter of cognitive understanding of language differences. (p. 165)

At the same time, colleagues of Hymes and Gumperz extended their work to studies of communities and families revealing the social interaction patterns of different families as they relate to matters of schooling. Shirley Brice Heath's (1983) report of her nine-year study of two communities (which she called Trackton and Roadville) documented her explorations—through observations, conversations, and interviews—of the material differences between how parents and teachers interact and provide literacy experiences for their students. Heath highlighted how literacy is embedded in social interactions and the variety of ways in which it is constituted across communities and schools.

Relatedly, Victoria Purcell-Gates (1995) conducted an extended study of family members living in southern Ohio who were largely illiterate. Her study identified the social ramifications of illiteracy for these family members and their children, including how it influenced their interactions within the family, in the workplace, and in and with schools. These and other studies provided extended analyses of literacy embedded in and across social settings, delineating the nature of the social fabric that supports literacy. Essentially, Purcell-Gates demonstrated how literacy involves social dimensions and dynamics tied to the interrelationships of students, their families, and schools. She illuminated the possible estrangements that are likely to occur when social norms run counter to expectations and experiences not unlike the findings that emerge when readers encounter texts that are not relevant to or based on the familiar.

A number of scholars enlisted more micro-ethnographic, sociolinguistic techniques to explore classroom exchanges that delineate the social dynamics occurring between teachers and students and among students themselves. For example, in their analyses of the discourse of students in reading classrooms, David Bloome and Judith Green (2015) argued for a shift in how we conceptualize literacy to be socially constituted (in contrast to the earlier view that it was just another factor influencing individual development), as well as a change in how literacy might be studied. They argued that for a social model to be truly realized, the unit of analysis should be the event rather than the individual. Further, they contended that events should be examined across time and space, taking into account intertextualities as well as actions, reactions, and ongoing interpretations and exchanges.

An exemplar of research in this area with implications for rethinking the nature of learning has been the work of Ann Haas Dyson (1988). Her research focuses on the social construction of meaning by young children, offering an illustration of how the worlds of students are negotiated. Her work analyzed preschoolers'

As Dyson (1988) noted,

I followed Mitzi and seven of her primary-grade peers over a two-year period, observing them as they composed imaginary worlds. I focused on the inter-relationships between children's creations of written text worlds and their use of or response to forces outside those worlds but within the situational context of the classroom—particularly other symbolic media (drawing and talk) and other people (particular peers). Rather than focusing on how the children's written messages became disembedded, I examined how their use of writing was em-bedded with a network of supportive symbolic and social relationships.

Based on the project's findings, I argue here that children's major devel-opmental challenge is not simply to create a unified text but to move among multiple worlds, carrying out multiple roles and coordinating multiple space/time structures. That is, to grow as writers of imaginary worlds and, by infer-ence, other sorts of text worlds as well, children must differentiate, and work to resolve the tensions among the varied symbolic and social worlds within which they write—worlds with differing dimensions of time and space.

Surface appearances to the contrary, there is [sic] sense and order to children's apparently disorganized texts. To discover that sense, though, we must take a long view, a developmental view, considering children's past and future efforts, and a broad view considering the symbolic and social forces that surrounded and shaped those texts. (p. 356)

writings, their worlds, and the worlds of their peers—along with the various re-sources that might be merged and used to explore and construct the imaginary worlds created in their shared stories. Dyson examined how writing is embedded in networks of symbolic and social relationships. Her observations suggest that, rather than through linguistic and cognitive pursuits, children find coherence by engaging across multiple individual and collective worlds, building connections with others in a web of multiple text worlds. Her accounts underscore the extent to which social dimensions interface with and are fused with literacy, bringing the social lens to the fore of literacy research (see box).

Adding momentum to the social movement, James Gee (1990, 2000), Brian Street (1984, 1993, 1995, 2003), and others suggested the need for a new era in literacy. In particular, this perspective developed into something like a movement that even came with a name (New Literacy Studies) and a manifesto (New London Group, 1996) in which a collection of scholars from the United States, the United Kingdom, and Australia (Courtney Cazden, Bill Cope, Mary Kalantzis, Norman Fairclough, James Gee, Gunther Kress, Allan Luke, Carmen Luke, Sarah Michaels Martin Nakata) argued for a conceptual paradigm shift worthy of the New Literacy Studies (NLS) moniker, one in which literacy was redefined as encompassing social practices rather than con-stituting a set of technical skills. Growing out of their opposition to an "autonomous view of literacy," in which literacy was seen as learned outside of the social context, NLS scholars argued for an orientation to literacy practices that recognized socially constituted texts, or "discourse," thereby highlighting their social existence. Street suggested that there was need for an "ideological" reckoning with literacy's context-dependent power relationships across a system of practices. As Lankshear and Knobel (2011; see also Lankshear & Knobel, 2003, 2007) argue, "the sociocultural approach to literacy overtly rejects the idea that textual practices are even largely, let alone solely, a matter of processes that 'go on in the head,' or that essentially involve heads communicating with each other by means of graphic signs" (pp. 12–13).

Building on these notions, Barton and Hamilton (1998, 2000), who were involved in detailing literacy in everyday life, indicated that "in the simplest sense literacy practices are what people do with literacy" (Barton & Hamilton, 2000, p. 7). They suggested that "literacy practices are more usefully understood as existing in the relationships between people, within groups and communities, rather than as a set of properties residing in individuals" (Barton & Hamilton, 2000, p. 8). Accordingly, Barton and Hamilton (2000) offered six tenets of literacy:

1. Literacy involves social practices mediated by texts.
2. Different literacies are associated with different areas of life.
3. Literacy practices (their role and influence) are shaped by our social institutions and power relationships.
4. Social goals and cultural practices embed and drive literacy practices.
5. Literacy is historically situated.
6. Literacy practices are not fixed but change, and new ones form through processes of informal learning and sense making. (p. 8)

In a similar vein, Purcell-Gates—in conjunction with her Center for the Cultural Practices of Literacy Study (CPLS)—derived and analyzed data across multiple case studies in an effort to chronicle, archive, and delve into cultural practices of literacy across multiple sites. The work undertaken by Purcell-Gates and her colleagues led to the development of a model (Figure 6.1) that represents the theoretical relationship between literacy events and literacy practices (Purcell-Gates et al., 2011). As Purcell-Gates et al. describe it:

> The central, shaded layers of the model represent observable literacy events, beginning with the agent's intent for reading or writing, and then moving to the text itself. For example, a woman may read through an online employment database to identify job openings. Together, this function or communicative intent (locating job openings), along with the actual text (online employment database), mediate the agent's purpose, or social goal, for engaging in the event. In this case, the woman's purpose is to apply for (and, ideally, to obtain) a job. This immediate social goal is shaped by larger domains of social activity, which are in turn shaped by various other layers of context. Applying for and obtaining a job occur in the social domain of Working. This domain is, in turn, shaped by other contextual layers. (p. 451)

Figure 6.1. Model of a Literacy Practice

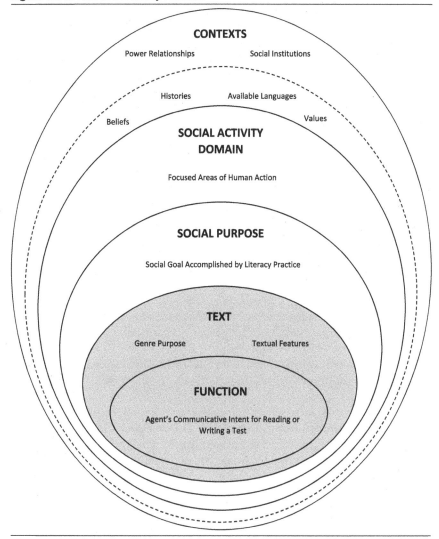

The areas shaded in gray represent an observable literacy event, while the unshaded areas represent inferred aspects of literacy practices that represent the context shaping the event.

Adapted from: Purcell-Gates et al., 2011.

Discussion

The advent of a social wave required that scholars step back and look at the nature of literacy development with the aid of sociolinguistic approaches, cultural lenses, and a variety of research tools and methodologies (i.e., ethnography, discourse analysis, historic analysis, etc.). The shift marked a new wave in literacy—from the cognitive to the socio-cognitive to the sociocultural. Indeed, psycholinguistics gravitated to a socio-psycholinguistic view of reading building on sociolinguistic and social semiotic perspectives (Harste & Burke, 1978). The end result— sociocultural perspectives had a huge impact on theories of literacy. Over time, these analyses illustrated that social dynamics and purposes themselves are integral to reading practices, not separate from them. Moreover, whereas the initial research focus on the social tended to remain primarily concerned with the role of individual cognition, the social wave shifted the focus to encompass interpersonal, intrapersonal, and collective meaning making.

These developments represented the widespread recognition that meaning making was not exclusively cognitive, nor was it just a "within the head" phenomenon or enterprise. Reading was deemed situated—in other words, inseparable from the social circumstances involved. A sociocultural perspective suggested that reading involves a network of exchanges across time and space. These exchanges extend to readers individually and collectively, as they interact with one another across and through assemblages of text, image, speech, and so on (often greatly enhanced and transformed by digital advances).

The social wave was also foundational to other developments in literacy as more and more educators applied sociological perspectives to reading and literacy (Bloome & Green, 2015). Attention began to be paid to how learners within cultures develop in their engagement in social literacy practices, the sociocultural dimensions of learning within communities. For example, a number of educators developed models for teaching and learning that attempted to bridge this divide, offering the promise of some fidelity with sociocultural ways of knowing (see Pearson & Stephens, 1993). They included the Funds of Knowledge "after school" initiative of González et al. (2006); Kathy Au's 1980 exploration of an educational model in the Hawaiian context; Susan Philips's 1983 work on participation structures in the classrooms of the Warm Springs Indian Reservation in Oregon; and work in Canada by First Nations educators enlisting Indigenous ways of knowing (Archibald, 2008; Hare, 2007). Worth noting too is the notion of productive pedagogies in Australia (see Lingard et al., 2003); Kris Gutiérrez's notion of a Third Space (2008); and the Maori education model (see Bishop et al., 2014; Smith, 1997, 2002, 2015).

In this age of globalization and increased mobility, emphasis has also been given to how one is positioned within, outside, or across worlds. Foci extend beyond local literacy to the cross-flows that occur across borders within society or with global channels, especially in the age of the Internet. Some (Brandt, 2001,

2009; Brandt & Clinton, 2002) have questioned the situation-specific notions of localized literacies proposed, arguing for a shift that also addresses how literacy practices have some transferable potential (e.g., accommodating the global flow of new literacies via online social networking and other digital engagements). These developments are discussed in later chapters focused on critical literacies, globalization, and digital literacies.

References

Archibald, J. (2008). *Indigenous storywork: Educating the heart, mind, body and spirit.* UBC Press.

Au, K. H. (1980). Participation structures in a reading lesson with Hawaiian children: Analysis of a culturally appropriate instructional event. *Anthropology and Education Quarterly, 11*(2), 91–115. doi: 10.1525/aeq.1980.11.2.05x1874b

Barton, D., & Hamilton, M. (1998). *Local literacies: Reading and writing in one community.* Routledge.

Barton, D., & Hamilton, M. (2000). Literacy practices. In D. Barton, M. Hamilton, & R. Ivanič (Eds.), *Situated literacies: Reading and writing in context* (pp. 7–15). Routledge. doi: 10.4324/9780203984963

Bishop, R., Ladwig, J., & Berryman, M. (2014). The centrality of relationships for pedagogy: The Whanaungatanga thesis. *American Educational Research Journal, 51*(1), 184–214. doi: 10.3102/0002831213510019

Bloome, D., & Green, J. (2015). The social and linguistic turns in studying language and literacy. In J. Rowsell & K. Pahl (Eds.), *The Routledge handbook of literacy studies* (pp. 19–34). Routledge.

Bourdieu, P., & Thompson, J. B. (Trans.) (1991). *Language and symbolic power.* Harvard University Press.

Brandt, D. (2001). Sponsors of literacy. In E. Cushman, E. R. Kintgen, B. M. Kroll, & M. Rose (Eds.), *Literacy: A critical sourcebook* (pp. 555–571). Bedford/St. Martins.

Brandt, D. (2009). *Literacy and learning: Reflections on writing, reading and society.* Jossey-Bass.

Brandt, D., & Clinton, K. (2002). Limits of the local: Expanding perspectives on literacy as a social practice. *Journal of Literacy Research, 34*(3), 337–356. doi: 10.1207/s15548430jlr3403_4

Bransford, J. (1979). *Human cognition: Learning, understanding, and remembering.* Wadsworth.

Brown, J. S., Collins, A., & Duguid, P. (1989). Situated cognition and the culture of learning. *Educational Researcher, 18*(1), 32–42. doi: 10.3102/0013189X018001032

Cook-Gumperz, J., & Gumperz, J. J. (1992). Changing views of language in education: The implications for literacy research. In R. Beach, J. L. Green, M. L. Kamil, & T. Shanahan (Eds.), *Multidisciplinary perspectives on literacy research* (pp 151–179). National Council of Teachers of English.

Cope, B., & Kalantzis, M. (Eds.). (2000). *Multiliteracies: Literacy learning and the design of social futures.* Routledge.

Dyson, A. H. (1988). Negotiating among multiple worlds: The space/time dimensions of young children's composing. *Research in the Teaching of English, 22*(4), 355–390.

Erickson, F. (1979). Talking down: Some cultural sources of miscommunication in inter-racial interviews. In A. Wolfgang (Ed.), *Nonverbal behavior: Applications and cultural implications* (pp. 115–129). Academic Press.

Fiske, E. B. (1981, May 5). Black English debate fades in Ann Arbor where it began. *New York Times* (National Edition), p. C00001. nyti.ms/2Ll9wdS

Gee, J. P. (1990). *Social linguistics and literacies: Ideology in discourses.* Falmer Press.

Gee, J. P. (2000). Discourse and sociocultural studies in reading. In M. L. Kamil, P. B. Mosenthal, P. D. Pearson, & R. Barr (Eds.), *Handbook of reading research,* (Vol. 3, pp. 195–208). Routledge. doi: 10.4324/9781315200613

González, N., Moll, L. C., & Amanti, C. (Eds.). (2006). *Funds of knowledge: Theorizing practice in households, communities, and classrooms.* Erlbaum. doi: 10.4324/9781410613462

Goody, J. (1968). *Literacy in traditional societies.* Cambridge University Press.

Gumperz, J. (1967). Language and communication. *The Annals. American Academy of Political and Social Science, 373,* 219–231.

Gumperz, J. (1981). Conversational inference and classroom learning. In J. L. Green & C. Wallat (Eds.), *Ethnography and language in educational settings* (pp. 3–23). Ablex.

Gutiérrez, K. D. (2008). Developing a sociocritical literacy in the third space. *Reading Research Quarterly, 43*(2), 148–164. doi: 10.1598/RRQ.43.2.3

Halliday, M. A. K. (1973). *Explorations in the functions of language.* Edward Arnold.

Hare, J. (2007). Aboriginal education policy in Canada: Building capacity for change and control. In R. Joshee & L. Johnson (Eds.), *Multicultural education policies in Canada and the United States* (pp. 51–68). UBC Press.

Harste, J. C., & Burke, C. L. (1978). Toward a socio-psycholinguistc model of reading. *Viewpoints in Teaching and Learning, 54*(3), 9–34. eric.ed.gov/?id=EJ193359

Heath, S. B. (1983). *Ways with words: Language, life, and work in communities and classrooms.* Cambridge University Press.

Hruby, G. G. (2001). Sociological, postmodern, and new realism perspectives in social constructionism: Implications for literacy research. *Reading Research Quarterly, 36*(1), 48–62. doi: 10.1598/RRQ.36.1.3

Hymes, D. (1964). Introduction: Toward ethnographies of communication. *American Anthropologist, 66*(6), 1–34.

Hymes, D. (1976). *Foundations in sociolinguistics: An ethnographic approach:* University of Pennsylvania Press.

Hymes, D. (1994). Toward ethnographies of communication. In J. Maybin (Ed.), *Language and literacy in social practice: A reader* (pp. 11–22). Multilingual Matters, Ltd.

Jacobson, E., Degener, S., & Purcell-Gates, V. (2003). *Creating authentic materials and activities for the adult literacy classroom: A handbook for practitioners.* National Center for the Study of Adult Learning and Literacy.

Johnson, D., & Johnson, R. (1975). Learning together and alone, cooperation, competition, and individualization. Prentice-Hall.

Kress, G. (2000a). Design and transformation: New theories of meaning. In B. Cope & M. Kalantzis (Eds.), *Multiliteracies: Literacy learning and the design of social futures* (pp. 153–161). Routledge.

Kress, G. (2000b). Multimodality. In B. Cope & M. Kalantzis (Eds.), *Multiliteracies: Literacy learning and the design of social futures* (pp. 182–202). Routledge.

Labov, W. (1969). *The logic of nonstandard English*. Georgetown University School of Languages and Linguistics.

Labov, W. (1982). Objectivity and commitment in linguistic science: The case of the Black English trial in Ann Arbor. *Language in Society, 11*(2), 165–201. doi: 10.1017/S0047404500009192

Lankshear, C., & Knobel, M. (2003, April). Implications of "new" literacies for writing research. Keynote lecture presented at the Annual Meeting of the American Educational Research Association, Chicago, IL. files.eric.ed.gov/fulltext/ED478121.pdf

Lankshear, C., & Knobel, M. (2007). Sampling "the new" in new literacies. In M. Knobel & C. Lankshear (Eds.), *A new literacies sampler* (pp. 1–24). Peter Lang.

Lankshear, C., & Knobel, M. (2011). *The new literacies: Everyday practices and social learning* (3rd ed.). Open University Press.

Lave, J., & Wenger, E. (1991). *Situated learning: Legitimate peripheral participation*. Cambridge University Press.

Lewis, C., Enciso, P., & Moje, E. B. (2007). Introduction: Reframing sociocultural research on literacy. In C. Lewis, P. Enciso, & E. Moje (Eds.), *Reframing sociocultural research on literacy: Identity, agency, and power* (pp. 1–11). Erlbaum.

Lingard, B., Hayes, D., & Mills, M. (2003). Teachers and productive pedagogies: Contextualising, conceptualising, utilising. *Pedagogy, Culture & Society, 11*(3), 399–424. doi: 10.1080/14681360300200181

Luke, A. (2003). Literacy and the other: A sociological approach to literacy research and policy in multilingual societies. *Reading Research Quarterly, 38*(1), 132–141.

Luke, A. (2004). On the material consequences of literacy. *Language and Education, 18*(4), 331–335. doi: 10.1080/09500780408666886

Mazak, C. M. (2006). Negotiating el difícil: English literacy practices in a rural Puerto Rican community (Unpublished doctoral dissertation). Michigan State University.

McDermott, R. P. (1974). Achieving school failure: An anthropological approach to literacy and social stratification. In G. Spindler (Ed.), *Education and cultural process: Toward an anthropology of education* (pp. 82–118). Holt, Rinehart, & Winston.

McShane, S. (2005). *Applying research in reading instruction for adults: First steps for teachers*. United States National Institute for Literacy.

Moje, E. B., Luke, A., Davies, B., & Street, B. (2009). Literacy and identity: Examining the metaphors in history and contemporary research. *Reading Research Quarterly, 44*(4), 415–437. doi: 10.1598/RRQ.44.4.7

Muth, W. R., & Perry, K. H. (2010). Adult literacy: An inclusive framework. In D. Lapp & D. Fisher (Eds.), *Handbook of research on teaching the English language arts* (3rd ed.). Routledge.

National Academies of Sciences, Engineering, and Medicine. (2018). *How people learn II: Learners, contexts, and cultures*. National Academies Press. doi: 10.17226/24783

New London Group. (1996). A pedagogy of multiliteracies: Designing social futures. *Harvard Educational Review, 66*(1), 60–92. doi: 10.17763/haer.66.1.17370n67v22j160u

Pearson, P. D., & Stephens, D. (1993). Learning about literacy: A 30-year journey. In C. J. Gordon, G. D. Labercane, & W. R. McEachern (Eds.) *Elementary reading: Process & practice* (pp. 4–18). Boston: Ginn Press.

Perry, K. (2012). What is literacy? A critical overview of sociocultural perspectives. *Journal of Language and Literacy Education, 8*(1), 50–71. jolle.coe.uga.edu/wp-content/uploads/2012/06/What-is-Literacy_KPerry.pdf

Perry, K. H. (2007). Sharing stories, linking lives: Literacy practices among Sudanese refugees. In V. Purcell-Gates (Ed.), *Cultural practices of literacy: Case studies of language, literacy, social practice, and power* (pp. 57–84). Erlbaum.

Perry, K. H. (2008). From storytelling to writing: Transforming literacy practices among Sudanese refugees. *Journal of Literacy Research, 40*(3), 317–358. doi: 10.1080/108629 60802502196

Perry, K. H. (2009). Genres, contexts, and literacy practices: Literacy brokering among Sudanese refugee families. *Reading Research Quarterly, 44*(3), 256–276. doi:10.1598/RRQ.44.3.2

Perry, K. H., & Purcell-Gates, V. (2005). Resistance and appropriation: Literacy practices as agency within hegemonic contexts. In B. Maloch, J. V. Hoffman, D. L. Schallert, C. M. Fairbanks, & J. Worthy (Eds.), *54th yearbook of the National Reading Conference* (pp. 272–285). National Reading Conference.

Philips, S. U. (1983). *The invisible culture: Communication in classroom and community on the Warm Springs Indian reservation.* Longman.

Purcell-Gates, V. (1995). *Other people's words: The cycle of low literacy.* Harvard University Press.

Purcell-Gates, V., Duke, N. K., & Martineau, J. A. (2007). Learning to read and write genre-specific text: Roles of authentic experience and explicit teaching. *Reading Research Quarterly, 42*(1), 8–45. doi: 10.1598/RRQ.42.1.1

Purcell-Gates, V., Jacobson, E., & Degener, S. (2004). *Print literacy development: Uniting cognitive and social practice theories.* Harvard University Press.

Purcell-Gates, V., Perry, K. H., & Briseño, A. (2011). Analyzing literacy practice: Grounded theory to model. *Research in the Teaching of English, 45*(4), 439–458.

Purcell-Gates, V., & Waterman, R. (2000). *Now we read, we see, we speak: Portrait of literacy development in an adult Freirean-based class.* Erlbaum. doi: 10.4324/9781410605955

Rassool, N. (1999). *Literacy for sustainable development in the age of information.* Multilingual Matters.

Rex, L. A., Bunn, M., Davila, B. A., Dickinson, H. A., Ford, A. C., Gerben, C., & Carter, S. (2010). A review of discourse analysis in literacy research: Equitable access. *Reading Research Quarterly, 45*(1), 94–115. doi: 10.1598/RRQ.45.1.5

Scribner, S., & Cole, M. (1981). *The psychology of literacy.* Harvard University Press.

Slavin, Robert E. (1980). Cooperative learning. *Review of Educational Research, 50* (2): 315–342.

Smith, G. H. (1997). *The development of Kaupapa Maori: Theory and praxis* (Doctoral dissertation, Auckland University). researchspace.auckland.ac.nz/handle/2292/623?show=full

Smith, G. H. (January 2002). Kaupapa Maori theory: Transformative praxis and new formations of colonisation. Paper presented at the Second International Conference on Cultural Policy Research, Te Papa National Museum, Wellington.

Smith, G. H. (April 2015). Transforming research: The Indigenous struggle for social, cultural, and economic justice within and through education. Presented at the American Educational Research Association Annual Meeting, Chicago, IL. www.aera.net/Events -Meetings/Annual-Meeting/Previous-Annual-Meetings/2015-Annual-Meeting/2015 -Annual-Meeting-Webcasts/Transforming-Research-The-Indigenous-Struggle-for -Social-Cultural-and-Economic-Justice-Within-and-Through-Education

Street, B. (1984). *Literacy in theory and practice.* Cambridge University Press.

Street, B. (1993). Introduction: The new literacy studies. In B. V. Street (Ed.), *Cross-cultural approaches to literacy* (pp. 1–21). Cambridge University Press.

Street, B. V. (1995). *Social literacies: Critical approaches to literacy in development, ethnography, and education.* Longman.

Street, B. V. (2003). What's new in new literacy studies: Critical approaches to literacy in theory and practice. *Current Issues in Comparative Education, 5*(2), 77–91.

Street, B. V., Pahl, K., & Rowsell, J. (2009). Multimodality and new literacy studies. In C. Jewitt (Ed.), *The Routledge handbook of multimodal analysis* (pp. 191–200). Routledge.

Wertsch, J. V. (1985). *Vygotsky and the social formation of mind.* Harvard University Press.

7 The Critical Wave

7.1 THE CRITICAL ADVOCATE

The notion of critical advocate has immediate antecedents in critical theory—especially as advanced by sociologists such as Bourdieu (1991) and Foucault (1989), philosophers such as Marx and Engels (1967), and a number of literacy scholars addressing issues of race, class, gender, and inequities using critical discourse analyses and other tools to interrogate hegemonies (e.g., Alvermann et al., 1997; Apple, 1988; Baker & Luke, 1991; Comber & Simpson, 2000; Ellsworth, 1989; Enciso, 2004; Gee, 2015; Gilbert & Taylor 991; hooks, 1994; Janks, 2010; Ladson-Billings & Tate, 1995; Luke, 1994, 2014; McLaren, 1989; Shannon, 1989; Shor, 1980; Sims, 1982; Willis, 1995). Critical advocacy is propelled by an effort to understand power and challenge hegemony. The advocacy requires one to counter discrimination, privilege, and selective/marginalizing representations of any and all groups and ideas. Accordingly, critical advocates interrogate the circumstances of our worlds through a lens that examines the politics and ideologies that govern them. The critical advocates seek to understand the political designs that undergird texts, people, and events, including how individuals and events are portrayed. Critical advocacy could be regarded as an aspect or offshoot of critical thinking (see box), but notably in a direction tied to political engagements. Arguably, elements included in discussions of critical thinking are foundational to the discernments needed for reflective considerations and well-reasoned judgments and thoughtful and deft actions and decisionmaking. Perhaps a key distinction may be differences in alignment. Whereas critical thinking often touts suspended judgment as a key disposition, critical theory is driven by ideological considerations as well as activism.[1]

Cervetti et al. (2001) differentiate critical thinking from critical literacy in terms of an approach that contrasts a liberal humanist orientation with poststructuralism and emancipatory ideology. Whereas critical reading might analyze the audience, the assumptions, arguments, warrants, and stylistic tendencies, critical literacy interrogates the positioning of ideas, especially in terms of matters of power examined in terms of sociopolitical considerations. As Cervetti et al. suggest:

> In its pedagogy, critical literacy combines poststructuralist, critical, and Freirean understandings. From poststructuralism, critical literacy understands texts as

ideological constructions embedded within discursive systems and has borrowed methods of critique. From critical social theory, critical literacy understands that texts, being products of ideological and socio-political forces, must be continually subjected to methods of social critique. Finally, from Freire, critical literacy understands that literacy practices must always have social justice, freedom, and equity as central concerns. (p. 7)

Based on tenets of liberatory pedagogy, critical advocacy is not passive critique but is aligned with transformation, social development, and protagonism (e.g., Andreotti & de Souza, 2011; Boal, 1979; Freire, 1972). This protagonism goes beyond reading and responding or reading in an evaluative fashion. Reading, analyzing, and interrogating texts might be necessary, but it is not considered enough. Critical advocates are expected to act on their readings responsibly.

These actions include pursuing transformative change in the interests of society, interrogating inequities and injustices relative to considerations of social justice and fairness. Critical readings involve seeking improvements in ways that connect with communities, inclusive of challenging the status quo—especially in terms of advocating for the rights of women, Indigenous peoples, members of LGBTQ+ communities, religious subgroups, and persons living with disabilities. Critical readings are problem-solving processes, mobilizing support, interrogating systems, disrupting hegemonies, seeding change, and pursuing advocacies, by being an ally or by protesting.

Undergirding critical advocacies are forms of critical reflexivity: reflecting on ourselves and our worlds in the company of other readers; indeed the ultimate act of critique is critique of one's own critique. Critical readers are akin to researchers, positioning themselves and grappling with their own identities as they scrutinize the world, themselves, and the cauldron of sociopolitical forces involved. Critical readers uncover what may have gone unnoticed, or that which was misunderstood or ignored (see McIntosh, 1989). They examine events, settings, characters, and issues from different perspectives as they observe and participate aesthetically, vicariously, efferently, and respectfully as advocates, allies, and activists. To these ends, critical advocates should have a sense of place with regard to different meanings that they might hold, encounter, or derive from others; they need to be aware of the gaps in their understandings and what they may need to do to take next steps. They need to be conscious of the layers of meaning through which they might travel and what these various orchestrations of meaning intend to prompt.

Ultimately, critical advocacy requires the recognition of one's own perspective and the perspectives of others, as well as an interrogation of the structures that undergird them. Hence, critical advocates need to read aggressively, not just from one source but from many, and not just with one perspective but with many and for real-world purposes. They need to examine what they know and explore alternative views prior to, concurrently with, and after any engagement, fitting or aligning their own thoughts and new information with further ideas and possibilities. They will likely have multiple readings that are collaborative, multiperspectival analyses of power and identity. Their readings should be participatory, exploring issues of positioning such as cultural affirmation, sidelining, or subjugation. And apart from being critically reflexive, they should be advocates. Their critical advocacy should extend to forms of investigative inquiry that explore the nature of specific circumstances and what might be done in support of others in need or lacking in voice or support. Critical advocates need to adopt a range of perspectives and sources as they seek understandings and pursue strategies to enhance the agency of others, doing so in ways that are self-examining and, in terms of supporting others, respectful, responsive, and not colonizing or self-serving (Smith, 2005).

The arrival of the critical wave spurred a shift in sociocultural activism: that which interrupts the systems used to perpetuate the social reproduction of privilege or advance bias and discrimination. The critical wave brought to the fore sociopolitical-cultural readings of ourselves and our worlds that challenged complacency as they exposed racism, sexism, and other inequities across systems. Moreover, critical advocacy moved beyond reflection toward action, pursuing activism and advocacy or allying with others. In concert with the civil rights movements of the 1970s—including the rise of feminism together with frameworks from sociology that examined power dynamics—the critical wave challenged our consciousness (what Freire 1972 termed our *conscientização*), especially in terms of the operating systems that perpetuate discrimination and bias. As Paulo Freire (1972) argued, critical consciousness takes action against the oppressive elements in our world illuminated by those understandings.

References

Alvermann, D., Commeyras, M., Young, J., Randall, S., & Hinson, D. (1997). Interrupting gendered discursive practices in classroom talk about texts: Easy to think about, difficult to do. *Journal of Literacy Research, 29*(1), 73–104.

Andreotti, V., & de Souza, L. M. T. M. (2011). *Postcolonial perspectives on global citizenship education.* Routledge.

Apple, M. W. (1988). *Teachers and texts: A political economy of class and gender relations in education.* Routledge and Kegan Paul.

Baker, C. D., & Luke, A. (Eds.). (1991). *Toward a critical sociology of reading pedagogy.* Benjamins.

Bernstein, B. (1977). *Class, codes, and control.* Routledge.

Bloom, B. S., Engelhart, M. D., Furst, E. J., Hill, W. H., & Krathwohl, D. R. (1956). *Taxonomy of educational objectives. Handbook I: Cognitive domain.* David McKay.

Boal, A. (1979). *Theater of the oppressed.* Urizen Books.

Bourdieu, P. (1991). *Language and symbolic power.* Harvard University Press.

Cervetti, G., Pardales, M. J., & Damico, J. S. (2001, April 2001). A tale of differences: Comparing the traditions, perspectives, and educational goals of critical reading and critical literacy. *Reading Online, 4*(9). www.readingonline.org/articles/art_index.asp?HREF=/articles/cervetti/index.html

Comber, B., & Simpson, A. (Eds.). (2001). *Negotiating critical literacies in classrooms*. Erlbaum. doi: 10.4324/9781410600288

Dewey, J. (1910). *How we think*. D. C. Heath.

Freire, P. (1972). *Pedagogy of the oppressed*. Herder and Herder.

Kohlberg, L. (1981). *Essays on moral development, Vol. 1: Philosophy of moral development*.
   Harper & Row.

Luke, C. (1994). Feminist pedagogy and critical media literacy. *Journal of Communication
   Inquiry, 18*(2), 30–47. doi: 10.1177/019685999401800200

Marx, K., and Engels, F. (1967). *The Communist manifesto*. Penguin Books.

McIntosh, P. (1989, July/August). White privilege: Unpacking the invisible backpack. *Peace
   and Freedom Magazine*, pp. 10–12. www.nationalseedproject.org/Key-SEED-Texts
   /white-privilege-unpacking-the-invisible-knapsack

McLaren, P. (1989). *Life in schools: An introduction to critical pedagogy in the foundations of
   education*. Longman.

McPeck, J. E. (1981). *Critical thinking and education*. Martin Robinson.

Rawls, J. (1971). *A theory of justice*. Harvard University Press.

Rousseau, J.—J. (1762). *Émile*. Jean Néaulme.

Shannon, P. (1989). *Broken promises: Reading instruction in twentieth-century America*. Bergin and Garvey.

Shor, I. (1980). *Critical teaching and everyday life*. South End Press.

Sims, R. S. (1982). *Shadow and substance: Afro-American experience in contemporary
   children's fiction*. National Council of Teachers of English.

Smith, L. T. (2005). On tricky ground: Researching the Native in the age of uncertainty.
   In N. K. Denzin & Y. S. Lincoln (Eds.), *The SAGE handbook of qualitative research*
   (3rd ed., pp. 85–108). SAGE.

Toulmin, S. (1958). *The uses of argument*. Cambridge University Press.

Willis, A. I. (1995). Reading the world of school literacy: Contextualizing the experience
   of a young African American male. *Harvard Educational Review, 65*(1), 30–50. doi:
   10.17763/haer.65.1.22226055362w11p5

Wolf, W., King, M. L., & Huck, C. S. (1968). Teaching critical reading to elementary school
   children. *Reading Research Quarterly, 3*(4), 435–498.

7.2   CRITICAL LITERACIES

The 1970s and 1980s saw major changes and epoch shifts, not just in terms of our understandings of and practices in literacy, but also in terms of the opening up of society as traditional power structures were being interrogated and challenged. As Marxist views, feminism, and liberatory pedagogy (especially as envisioned by Brazilian Paulo Freire) gained traction and gathered momentum, the literacy field turned the lens on itself. In so doing, it exposed its own gender bias that favored the perspectives of White males, its racial and ethnic biases against minorities (especially non-English speakers), its epistemological preference for positivism, and its lack of support for teacher professionalism, to name a few.

Some Background on the Roots and Development of Critical Theory

In many ways, the history of critical theory may be traced to a long history of progressive educators identifying the social transformative values of education for society or to that of advocates for historically disenfranchised persons. In the modern period, critical theory mostly corresponds with the advent of sociology as a field of study and the developments/shifts that occurred as a result, especially in the postcolonial period.

Critical Theory and Subsequent Developments

Essentially, critical theory and sociology draw from various fields such as history, political science, cultural studies, sociolinguistics, and philology, and includes a range of theoretical lenses, including postcolonial critiques, poststructuralism, feminism, and others. Though critical theory might have antecedents throughout history, the most recent incarnations can be traced to scholars connected with the Institute of Social Sciences at the University of Frankfurt (henceforth referred to as the Frankfurt School). The Frankfurt School, which had its beginnings in the 1920s, went into exile to the United States in World War II, affiliating itself with Columbia University. The school, rooted in Marxism (see Engels, 1969; Marx, 2000; Marx & Engels, 1975–1976) and Hegel's work (see Hegel, 2015), focused on a dialectal orientation and built on Habermas's 1987 work on communicative reason and critiques of positivism, materialism, and determinism. Initially, the Frankfurt School strove to unmask the connections between power and knowledge—specifically, by challenging the power of positivist research in its instrumentality and reasoning (i.e., the separation of facts from values and avoidance of human consciousness) and questioning the failure of science to connect theory and policy to everyday life or to concern itself with society's betterment.

Developments in other countries have also been quite influential; for example:

- In France, a number of scholars who were focusing on the subjugation by social institutions enlisted a mix of methods and frames from linguistics, philosophy, and history. Among the most influential was Pierre Bourdieu (1991), whose theories addressed issues of power and subjugation—that is, how symbolic dimensions of domination engage in ways that mask their cultural, social, and economic realities. Michel Foucault's (1989, 1995) closer examinations of power deemed these dimensions more fragmented, localized, and nuanced across institutions. These and other French critical theorists, philosophers, and sociologists (e.g., Deleuze, 1994) inspired further developments by social theorists throughout the world.
- In the UK, the work on language and social class by Basil Bernstein (1977) at the University of London and the creation of the Centre for Contemporary Culture Studies in 1964 at the University of Birmingham contributed to a range of studies examining social issues and race (e.g., Stuart Hall, 2017), including complex issues of reproduction, resistance, positioning, and agency with regard to social class (e.g., Paul Willis, 1977).
- Critical theory, especially when applied to schooling and literacy, had powerful South American antecedents with the literacy campaigns in Cuba and Nicaragua and the influence of Paulo Freire's liberation pedagogy. Appearing in the 1970s, the pedagogy of Freire (1995/1970) and his colleagues (e.g., Boal, 1979) was a major catalyst for both critiques of and challenges to oppression in schooling contexts, pointing to illiteracy used as a means of subordination and maintaining inequities. He recognized that literacy involves a combination of *reading the word* and *reading the world*. His view of literacy was tied to notions of liberation and participation as opposed to oppression and marginalization. Accordingly, Freire (1995/1970) defined literacy as a process of *conscientização*, or consciousness, connecting reading to the world for purposes of empowerment. As he stated, "Literacy makes sense only in these terms, as the consequence of men beginning to reflect about their capacity for reflection, about the world, about their position in the world, about the encounter of consciousness" (p. 106).
- In North America, several American sociologists, philosophers, cultural studies scholars, and educators enlisted the theoretical underpinnings of Marxist theorists, French sociologists, and South American scholars together with American philosopher John Dewey in their critical social critiques and arguments for egalitarian approaches to educational developments. These critical analyses began to gather a great deal of

synergy beginning in the 1980s with Michael Apple (1979, 1988, 2012); Thomas Popkewitz (1984); Henry Giroux & Peter McLaren (1989, 2000); Lankshear & McLaren (1993); Ira Shor (1980, 1987); Henry Macedo (Freire & Macedo, 1987); Elizabeth Ellsworth (1989); bell hooks (1994), and numerous other scholars who drew on a combination of French, German (especially Marxist), and American philosophers, British sociologists, and Freirean concepts in their analyses of educational matters (and, in Canada and the United States, in some of their proposals for educational change). Their analyses reflected the aim to understand power and challenge hegemony.

- In Africa, a number of scholars focused on the Western impact (through colonization) on African epistemologies, languages, and education. Building on the work of Thiong'o (1986), there has been an interest in rekindling African ways of knowing (e.g., Ubuntu), as well as applying cultural and sociological analyses to African suppression and development (e.g., Assié-Lumumba, 2016; Wright & Abdi, 2012; Rabaka, 2009).

- In Australia, critical theory gained a fertile foothold stemming from its history of racism, sexism, and classism and aligning with a rise in consciousness about prejudice, inequities experienced by and activism from Australian Aboriginal and Torres Strait Islanders. Specifically, it was propelled by the growth of socialism in the 1970s, by some of the social movements arising in the same period (i.e., anti–Vietnam War protests, feminism, and campaigns for Aboriginal rights), and by the scholarly initiatives of clusters of critical sociologists (e.g., Raewyn Connell, Allan Luke) and feminist scholars (e.g., Bronwyn Davies, Pamela Gilbert, Carol Baker, Carmen Luke) across Australia, but most notably at Deakin University and James Cook University. A number of critical theorists in Australia were particularly engaged in exploring issues of gender representation and protocols to advance critical analyses that students at all levels might do.[2] In addition, under the guidance of Michael Halliday, who moved from the United Kingdom to Australia as chair of linguistics at the University of Sydney, functional systemic linguistics rooted in sociopolitical considerations contributed to sociopolitical analyses of text, including a movement that was labeled genres of power (Halliday, 1985; Hasan, 1978). A genre approach was advocated as addressing the needs of students in terms of essential genres that were deemed likely to be neglected in approaches to text that emphasized narrative forms, especially in concert with a process writing emphasis (Christie, 1985; Martin, 1985).

- In other parts of the world, critical movements took root in conjunction with civil rights movements in the United States, South Africa, New Zealand, and Australia, and with decolonialization efforts, especially in

India and Indonesia. On a larger scale, these movements took the form of national revolutions such as the growth of socialist movements in China.[3]

The Development of Critical Literacy

Literacy has often been at the nexus of issues revolving around power and privilege, dating back to the advent of the power of the pen over the sword, its ritualistic use in society and revered status in most religions, and its gatekeeping function in the right to vote. Despite these developments and the historic noteworthiness of literacy's role, critical theory did not emerge as a substantial field of study until the 1980s. As Siegel and Fernandez (2000) noted in their contribution to the third volume of the *Handbook of Reading Research*, critical theory had been overlooked as a possible entry in prior volumes. In part, critical theory emerged as a natural extension of social and cultural developments; however, it also arose as critical theoretical tenets were applied to literacy by a number of Western scholars, including Michael Apple (1979, 1988, 2012), Carol Edelsky (1999, 2006), and Pat Shannon (1989, 1998, 2001, 2007, 2010, 2011, 2014; Shannon & Edmondson, 2005).

The focus on literacy by critical theorists became most apparent with the collection of papers in the volume *Critical Literacy: Politics, Praxis, and the Postmodern*, edited by Colin Lankshear and Peter McLaren in 1993. In their introduction to the volume, they emphasize how their use of the term "literacy" was intended to denote a shift from what they considered to be a mechanistic rendering of reading and writing (i.e., as it has appeared in schools) to practices as they are constituted in the real world. The term "critical" was meant to evoke Freirean notions of consciousness. They make clear their alignment with Street (1984, 1993, 1995, 2003; Street, Pahl, & Rowsell, 2009) in saying that they endorse the notion of "specific social practices of reading and writing . . . rather than some abstracted technology or other essence" (Lankshear & McLaren, 1993, p. xvii). Furthermore, they state:

> in addressing critical literacy we are concerned with the extent to which, and the ways in which, actual and possible social practices and conceptualizations of reading and writing enable human subjects to understand and engage the politics of daily life in the quest for a more truly democratic social order . . . make possible a more adequate "reading" of the world, on the basis of which, as Freire and others put it, people can enter into "rewriting" the world into a formation in which their own interests, identities, and legitimate aspirations are more fully present and are present more equally. (p. xviii)

Issues of identity and social structure were spurred by poststructuralism, which focused on analyzing and deconstructing texts in terms of their construction of social categories and identities.[4] As Hagood (2002) contends:

What is central to critical literacy that focuses on identity is the influence of the text and specifically of identities in texts on the reader. The text, imbued with societal and cultural structures of race, class, and gender, marks the site of the struggle for power, knowledge, and representation. (pp. 250–251)

For the critical theorist, literacy research and practice—especially with regard to the classroom and the text—became sites for analyses of books and instructional regimes relating to issues of identity, representation, and power. Notable among American scholars has been the emergence of critical race theory (e.g., Ladson-Billings, 1999, 2003; Ladson-Billings & Tate, 1995); race critiques of literacy research (Willis, 1995; Willis & Harris, 1997); feminist critiques, including Ellsworth (1989) and Alvermann et al. (1997); and discussions of gender (e.g., Blackburn, 2002). In addition, literacy practices have been interrogated in terms of their cultural representations and authenticity (e.g., in the work of Sims, 1982, 1983; Bishop, 2007, on African American children's literature) and cultural responsiveness (e.g., Philips's 1983 work with Indigenous populations). Among U.S. literacy scholars, Patrick Shannon and Carol Edelsky assumed key leadership roles with their advocacy for progressive democratic education, historical analyses of resistance and progressive education, and as their work challenging some political and corporate emphases. They made a case for reading educators being political, highlighting the challenges to teacher empowerment and analyzing the rhetoric, power dynamics, and negative influences of the dominant forces in reading instruction in U.S. schools (especially in textbooks, testing, and standards).

The role of literacy in shaping who we are and might become has been pervasive in discussions of digital literacies (e.g., New London Group, 1996; Willinsky, 1990), work on embodiment and identity drawing in part on the work of Deleuze (1994), and in recent discussions of the integration of virtual reality into conceptualizations of literacy. As Brandt (2001, 2009; Brandt & Clinton, 2002) and Moje et al. (2009) have contended—in many ways reminiscent of Dyson's (1988) discussion of how students seek coherence across multiple worlds—texts engage us in different ways, influencing who we are and imagine we might be. These scholars question the control that texts have—especially through identities perpetuated through texts, the discourses of schooling, and digital affordances. As Moje et al. suggest, readers' engagements with texts contribute to the identities and voices afforded to them (Moje, 2009). For Indigenous educators, matters of voice and identity and lack thereof are tied to their cultural alienation and subjugation at the hands of colonization, forced assimilation, and forms of epistemicide prevalent in their schooling (e.g., Battiste, 1998; Morgan, 2018; Rigney & Hattam, 2018; Smith, 2011).

Multifaceted Work by Selected Critical Literacy Theorists

The efforts of some critical literacy theorists over the last 25 years is illustrative of its scope and significance. Among modern-day pioneers, Michael Apple (2012) is one of America's most notable and widely translated critical theorists. He prefaced a collection of his selected works with the following explication of his goals: "to understand the currents in that river of democracy, the attempts by dominant groups to channel it in dangerous directions and to block its flow, and the various ways in which counter-hegemonic movements can and do offer serious challenges to dominance" (p. 16).

The scope of work, by Apple and others, has been extensive, reaching around the world. As Apple's preface in his selected works illustrates, the aims of this work—apart from a broad range of concerns analyzing issues of power and oppression as well as forms of critical reflexology of his own frames and roles—are particularly relevant to literacy, including issues pertaining to literacy textbooks and practices. For example, Apple's (2012) list of critical engagements included:

- the development of critical theories of knowledge and power;
- the necessity to move beyond reductive and essentializing approaches and to include a wider set of dynamics in order to better understand the intersections of the contradictions among class, gender, and race;
- the politics of language and the process of labeling;
- the content and form of the curriculum;
- the processes of deskilling and intensification in teachers' work;
- the power and contradiction within agency;
- the struggles over text and official knowledge;
- the importance of the state and of politics in general;
- how rightist movements get formed and how they work conflicts over issues of "common culture" and a common curriculum;
- the power of conservative religious movements in education and the larger society;
- new forms of schooling, such as home schooling and their ideological and social bases;
- the effects of globalization and diasporic populations on our understanding of the politics of culture and the education of teachers;
- and finally, the responsibilities of being a critical scholar and activist educator. (p. 16)

Similarly, the work of Allan Luke has been seminal. Luke is a critical literacy scholar with roots in the United States, Canada, and Australia. As he suggested in his entry for the *Encyclopedia on Language and Education*, critical literacy has an ongoing commitment to critique: to make change with the possible risk of becoming subject to one's own critique. As Luke (1997) stated:

Shared across contemporary approaches to critical literacy is an emphasis on the need for literates to take an interventionist approach to texts and discourses of all media, and a commitment to the capacity to critique, transform and reconstruct dominant modes of information. In their present form, they converge on the key question of representation and are increasingly being used to re-examine questions of identity and power in the textual cultures of new media and institutions. The focus of Freire's initial project remains central to the teaching of critical literacy in new social conditions: an emphasis on the capacity of literates and literacies to transform the construction and distribution of material and symbolic resources by communities and social institutions. What remains ever problematic is which directions those transformations might take, and how any new literacy can figure in relation to the emergent institutional cultures and identities, texts and technologies of postmodern economies and societies. (p. 150)

Influences of Critical Theory and Critical Literacy

Critical theory had a major impact on educational thinking, providing researchers with the tools and frameworks for delineating the political forces that were at play. It clearly established that everything can and should be looked at through a political lens that examines vested interests and power. In this regard, perhaps one of the more influential discussions was James Gee's 2015 exploration of ideologies in his book *Social Linguistics and Literacies: Ideology in Discourses*. Gee's work discusses how the notion of an ideologue emerged (and was used as a foil by Napoleon initially to suggest a form of demagogy).

Unfortunately, in the 1990s, positivism and government agencies had largely marginalized critical and more interpretive epistemologies and research paradigms by excluding them from funding because of their alleged lack of rigor and robust research designs, even accusing them of lacking objectivity. They positioned critical theoretical developments as ideologies and thus lacking the legitimacy to be used as the basis for educational policy and practices. Likewise, they took issue with the rise in teacher-based inquiry as they argued for a change to teacher accountability. The broad-based goal of engaging teachers in communities of reflective practice was replaced by a mandated list of best practices (see Callahan et al., 2008; Gore & Zeichner, 1991; Tierney, 2000–2001). This reimposed forms of top-down, totalitarian control of education, renewing advocacy for traditional empiricism as well as traditional prescriptions of government policy and practices (including standards and accountability).

Critical Cultural Analyses

While broad support for critical theoretical challenges to education were limited in the early 1990s, analyses of issues of cultural representation, educational access and graduation received some attention. Critical theorists turned the lens on themselves, employing various forms of analyses (e.g., discourse, bibliometric, and historical) of gender, race, and class, which they also applied to textbooks, reading research, issues of inequity, and policy and practice. And, increasingly, publications and various institutions scrutinized matters of access and representation in ways that began to hold theorists and educational institutions accountable. The impact has been notable in terms of bringing to light historic shortcomings, prompting shifts in schooling practice, and altering research pursuits and reports. As a result, in terms of schooling, it was as if desegregation and changes in representation extended to curricula and tests. In research studies, scholars were expected (at a minimum) to represent the diversity of the populations they studied and unpack their results to illuminate differences.

Inclusive Education

The tangible effects of critical theoretic views were apparent in the area of special education. Stemming from calls for egalitarianism, critical theoretic considerations mobilized a shift from models of special education tied to exclusion to those of inclusion, with the goal of meeting the needs of all students in regular classrooms (Boyle & Anderson, 2020). As Knight (1999) noted:

> A classroom is democratic and socially inclusive to the extent to which it welcomes all students as equally valued members of the school community. Separation and exclusion in its many forms need to be addressed by democratic education. Exclusiveness is found in the hierarchical education that has been powerfully reinforced over the past century. This hierarchy is manifest formally by tracking and ability grouping . . . and informally by differential encouragement given students by classroom teachers. (p. 7)

In the 1990s, the foundation of this momentous change was anchored in the Salamanca statement, written under the auspices of UNESCO and others, which generated support from a number of countries (UNESCO & World Conference, 1994; UNICEF, 2013). However, the replacement of exclusionary forms of special education by inclusion remains under development. Given what some consider to be a neoliberal agenda tied to school choice, alongside arguments that it is more utopian than practical, inclusion is not universally embraced. Nonetheless, even detractors or advocates of separate services admit to aspiring to such social justice tenets—despite their concerns that teachers, schools, and parents may not have the resources and expertise to fully realize them (e.g., Norwich, 2013; Kauffman et al., 2016).

Multiliteracies and Critical Theory

The advent of multiliteracies proposed a significant shift in pedagogy that aligned with tenets of critical theory, including situated, participatory literacy teaching and learning. With an interest in building on sociocultural concepts (including

NLS; see Street, 1993) and the changing digital affordances, a mix of literacy scholars with sociocultural and critical orientations came together to formulate a theory in the hope of shaping literacy practices.[5] In particular, they proposed a model that they termed "multiliteracies," which included two components: (1) the notion that global communication requires multiple channels and media; and (2) the idea that multiple literacies are constituted by, and constitutive of, the multiplicity of cultures and linguistic contexts in which literacy practices occur (New London Group, 2000).

Multiliteracies represented a way to conceptualize how literacies are situated within a changing social world—one that involves a growing diversity of literacy practices, an increasingly diverse population, and an expanding variety of exchanges that require different registers, semiotic understandings, and social engagements. The proponents of multiliteracies argued for an approach to learning that was social, situated within the embodied participation of individuals and groups, and therefore embedded "in social, cultural and material" contexts (New London Group, 1996, p. 82). In so doing, they added momentum to the social turn at the same time as they brought to it an engagement with multimodal digital developments and a design orientation, combining literacy(ies) practices with transformative, critical, and relevant engagements and overt teaching and understandings of design features. They argued for a shift from verbocentric notions of literacy to a more semiotic framing of multiple modes wherein students are engaged as the "remakers, the transformers, and the re-shapers of the representational resources available to them" (Kress, 2000a, p. 155).

Multiliteracies as a pedagogy was not without its critics. Some questioned whether it was a more prescriptive than illustrative pedagogy. As Leander and Bolt contend in their critique of multiliteracies (2013), multiliteracies have the potential of becoming more fixed than generative, more imposed than organic. Their critique raises questions about an empirical orientation, which uses examples from selected cases as de facto empirical evidence. And, as Leander and Bolt transition to a discussion of nonrepresentation, assemblages, and animation of text—in accordance with Deleuzian theory—they tout exemplars of multiliteracies that may in fact not be linked to them. Indeed, they present cases the authors of which did not tie to multiple literacy formulations—using these repositioned cases as criticism, as warrants, or as evidence of Deleuze's views in ways that may not be justified.

Ethical Considerations and Critical Research

Critical theory often faces a dilemma when some of the ascribed goals of empowerment conflict with the nature of the pursuit (e.g., if they are examined in terms of ethics with a consideration for cultures). At times, researchers act without regard to the fact that they are cultural outsiders. They seek to serve the interests of others, but with approaches that are more presumptuous than respectful. Indeed, critical theory appears to assume a form that can become somewhat narcissistic and self-promoting if and when it comes untethered from cultural understanding and practices. Arguably, in some ways critical theory and critical literacy have at times become less connected with their roots (i.e., less engaged in the work of social change) and more invested in theoretical discussions, pontification of actions that should occur, or commodified forms of critical theoretical thoughts and instantiations.

Such shifts are often riddled with ethical problems, as initiatives become detached from the communities they are intended to serve. Further, initiatives become the property of the theorists and researchers, without regard to the community being discussed (including community interests, ongoing needs, and rights such as appropriated or colonized property). Sometimes the commodification of knowledge by researchers assumes a priority or takes a precedence that displaces the everyday needs and rights of the community they mean to serve. An obvious tension, if not dilemma, arises when individual empowerment and community considerations or consultations are not aligned—especially if extending the consultation to the community might conflict with or undermine the "critical" project. Issues of ethics and critical reflexology provide important lenses for understanding and pursuing research, particularly in an age of global commodification often disguised or positioned as a form of liberatory practice.

This tricky space is apparent if one examines some of the approaches American and Oceania scholars have taken in feminist and gender studies. Australia has been a site for the advancement of critical literacy on a number of fronts, including the analyses of textbooks from a variety of perspectives, for instance, feminism, the interrogation of educational research methodologies, and concerns over systemic discrimination in conjunction with testing and teaching tied to government mandates. Yet while critical analyses have directed the attention of educators to the inequities and biases of educational policy and delivery, they seem to have fallen short in terms of advancing alternatives other than textbook material that may itself reflect a generic form of criticism or genre of teaching. In a number of cases, critical theorists have been enlisted to shape and develop curriculum and teaching procedures, only later to have those procedures prescribed or positioned as best practice without regard for their organic fit or method of engaging with communities.

Literacy education scholars such as Victoria Purcell-Gates, learning theorists such as Deborah Butler (2006; Butler & Schnellert, 2008; Butler et al., 2008), and Indigenous educators such as Graham Smith (2011), Linda Smith (1999, 2005), and Joann Archibald (2008) argue for research partnerships with communities tied to community goals that occur in consultation and collaboration with, and develop in the interest of supporting the needs and activities of, learners and communities. Oftentimes such an approach involves an emphasis on building relationships as well as participation of community members in school initiatives. (Indeed, in the international arena, William Gray's 1956 book for the UN discussed the importance of projects directed at addressing community needs, an issue more recently explored in Daniel Wagner's 2018 discussion of core literacy initiatives.) And, as one might expect, there is a history of such initiatives worldwide. bell hooks (1994) as well as others (Brown & Strega, 2005; Tuck & Yang, 2014) have called for forms of teacher empowerment and approaches to educational practice that are transgressive and, if necessary, aligned with resistance as well as teacher and student activism.

Moving Forward

Critical theory foregrounded the political nature of literacy at the same time as it advanced formative participatory research and development (what some might describe as activism) in the interest of social improvements on behalf of communities. Nowadays, critical theorists do so through a postcolonial frame, turning the lens on themselves and others with an eye to matters of identity and cultural practices. They unpack and interrogate themselves along with others as they seek forms of activism and participatory research conforming to critical theoretical tenets and critical reflexiveness, attempting to avoid self-interest as they seek to navigate the suppression or derailment of initiatives by opposing forces. Essentially, critical theorists must be attuned to and more carefully consider the means and the ends. The means might entail exposing hierarchies and changing the power dynamics so that they are more egalitarian and open. In order to establish systems that support an ecology of egalitarianism and openness and allow for ongoing organic change, the ends need to allow for diversity rather than uniformity and be aligned with considerations for the local and for community engagement.

At times, the field of literacy has realized these ends, means, and more, but efforts have been derailed or sabotaged by commercial interests or government overrides. Key to their success would be ensuring there are safeguards in place that prevent collusion and subversion. As Pat Shannon (2010) suggested, organic egalitarian educational enterprises need to recognize that changes in literacy are not psychological and linguistic but political. Addressing those political matters are integral to moving forward.

It is not surprising that a number of critical theorists have been major proponents of empowering teachers and students, arguing for a democratization of teaching and learning consistent with John Dewey's argument for egalitarian educational pursuits. When teachers are encouraged to explore improvements in their students' learning in a fashion akin to a formative research study or design experiment, they are obliged to ask critical questions about themselves, about their students' learning, and about what they may do—together with students and community members—to enhance learning experiences. They engage with their students in formative practices. Advocacy for such approaches is apparent in the work of a number of critical theorists. For example, Joe Kincheloe (1991), Ira Shor (1980, 1987), and others have argued for the importance of empowering teachers via their involvement in knowledge production and decisionmaking (i.e., as a means of challenging the top-down dictums of educational practice that relegate teachers to rather mechanistic implementations of educational practices arising from research by others). In other words, they argue for teacher research that challenges the power dynamics in play (or any other educational practices that are not inclusive) and seeks answers for new directions (Hoffman, 2020). They recognize the importance of participatory decisionmaking.

On the negative side, however, despite the ways in which critical theories and analyses have advanced multiple frames by which educators have interrogated the world, such readings have often paled in terms of their influence. Some have conjectured that many have focused more on the critique than on reform, stopping short of the ultimate goal of becoming agents of change, or sponsors or allies for others. Critical analyses thus sometimes appear to advance theories detached from communities, as theorists and researchers engage in forms of academic commodification of theories—what some have referred to as the "privatized academic" (Smith, 2011). Accordingly, the community or persons remain "guests" rather than "hosts" of such efforts (Morgan, 2018). They remain the subject of initiatives rather than overseers or participants in the decisionmaking. Critical analyses thus sometimes appear to engage in forms of exclusion of the participants and communities that the research might be intended to serve. Perhaps the positive outcome of some of this critique of critical perspectives is to establish an ethic of self-criticism among those who are engaged in critiquing other efforts.

Indeed, an ethical approach to critical literacy research therefore involves going beyond member checking to a democratization of research that is participatory, organic, and accommodating of community and individuals. It is not inconsistent with the notion of catalytic validity advocated by Patti Lather (1986, 1992) and Maxime Green (1995), or the guidelines for research suggested by Indigenous groups (see Smith, 1998, 2005) or those that befit participatory tenets (Goodwin, 2012) fostering, at a minimum, respect, reciprocity, consultation, and local decisionmaking (i.e., especially those that do not colonize the local or commodify their practices). It is consistent with the participatory design research and social justice efforts that have attended to cross-border circumstances of nonmainstream communities in refuge (e.g., Bang & Vossoughi, 2016; de los Ríos & Molina, 2020; Gutiérrez & Jurow, 2016; Patel, 2018).

In other words, while a critical literacy lens has added immeasurably to our appreciation and understanding of power dynamics—especially the systems at play—it has not always done so in ways that are participatory and respectful of local situations. Indeed, theoretically, empirically, and practically, engagement in critical theory or pedagogy or literacy involves a number of perils. For example, it should be recognized that Western versions of Marxist critique and Freirean notions of oppression and empowerment have also been criticized as having the

INDIGENOUS TRANSFORMATIVE CHANGE

Transformative change is political at various levels—within and across communities and various subgroups and individuals with the communities, various agencies that serve the communities as well as the institutions that govern the agencies.

Take, if you will, efforts at transformative change for indigenous communities. In various communities there have been countless efforts to remove the yolk of colonialization and instead breathe life into schools by moving away from standardized and culturally estranged education to culturally responsive and sustainable education. In some Indigenous communities, we have seen the development of Indigenous ways of knowing as core educational developments (e.g., New Zealand Kaupapa Māori theory; see Smith, 1990; www.rangahau.co.nz/research-idea/27/). In Australia, however, it remains a struggle as efforts for Aboriginal sovereignty are thwarted by the government and the interests of the dominant communities.

Recently, Aborigine and Torres Strait Islander advocacy has manifested itself in various forms of activism to recent efforts around the "Uluru Declaration of the Heart" that seeks formal recognition of the Aboriginal and Torres Strait Islanders and their ways of knowing (see: http://nationalunitygovernment.org/content/uluru-statement-heart). At the same time, it is apparent in communities striving for a political foothold as they represent the community interest. For example, Daryle Rigney and his Aboriginal community (Ngarrindjeri), in hopes of attaining a degree of sovereignty and self-governance, have engaged in forms of contractual relationships with the federal and state governments around their water problems. Despite being historic custodian of their land for over 50,000 years, Daryle Rigney on behalf of his community has had to plead to be involved in addressing the water issues not just for his community but for the southeast region of Australia (Rigney, Bignall, & Hemming, 2015). For Daryle Rigney, this is a tricky place to navigate at all levels of governance—federal government representing colonizing forces and even as a member of the Ngarrindjeri community. But for outsiders, this is space that would be even more tricky to negotiate and indeed, an outsider's knowledge, commitment, and vested interests might be considered suspect. Outsiders may view themselves as emancipists but be seen as having the vestiges of colonization, imperialism, racism, objectification, commodification, universalism, individualism, and simplification, which fail to address the complexities and differences in the realities, interests, histories, and epistemologies of diverse cultures. . . . activists may need to search for an ethical compass to address what seems paradoxical and a form of activism that befits the circumstances and communities being supported or partnered. . . . researchers can find themselves slipping from advocate and ally to cultural interloper engaged in a form of colonization and appropriation. Respectful critical research . . . requires practices that avoid outside imposition, the appropriation of others in the outsider's image, and the displacement of the societies, communities, and individuals the researchers might be seeking to read, study, or support.

From the perspective of Indigenous scholars, such transformative change could entail what Māori scholar Linda Smith (2005) suggested in the context of discussing ethics for Indigenous research:

> For Indigenous and other marginalized communities, research ethics is at a very basic level about establishing, maintaining, and nurturing reciprocal and respectful relations, not just among people as individuals but also with people, as collectives and as members of communities, and with humans who live in and with other entities in the environment. The abilities to enter pre-existing relationships; to build, maintain, and nurture relationships; and to strengthen connectivity. (p. 97)

Additionally, as Ali Abdi (2015) has warned, activism should advance cautiously, lest it unwittingly advance an agenda that is assimilationist. For example, in his discussion of Bolivia, Aman (2017) illustrated how Westerners not only control the words to describe but also to appropriate and control even the manner of change. In the Bolivian context, the language of the Indigenous—including words such as *interculteridad*—was enlisted in ways that detracted from its use by the Indigenous groups.

Respectful critical research and meaning making require practices that avoid outside imposition, the appropriation of others in the outsider's image, and the displacement of the societies, communities, and individuals the researchers might be seeking to read, study, or support. Accordingly, critical meaning making may need to thwart what have been the dominant research norms that have deferred to forms of standardizing rather than differentiating others, objectivity, and detachment over participation, co-operation, and consultation.

potential of being too broad when local characteristics and cultural considerations should be heeded. Concern over a one-size-fits-all approach to analyzing and proposing power has been critiqued by various groups concerned with places of intersection—especially those of race, gender, and class. It also has been criticized in terms of its reach across borders to other cultures, with the understanding that this needs to be tempered and complicated (e.g., Takayama, 2009). Indeed, critics aptly point out that many of the tenets undergirding some critical approaches fall short in terms of attributions (e.g., multiple literacies can be found in the writings of Freire and others that seem to be neglected in terms of attribution and their discussions; see Rogers, 2018).

Concurrent with these criticisms has been the emergence of various critiques representing efforts to adopt a wider variety of perspectives befitting these different strands as well as reflecting or accommodating the debates and divisions that have occurred or may be ongoing. For example, critical race theory (Tate, 1997) and feminist theory have a number of sub-strands which are themselves sites of debate over emerging theoretical postulates or appropriate methodologies. Within postmodern feminism, Judith Butler's position (2011) has been simultaneously embraced, questioned, and shifted. Not surprisingly, then, the uniform application of critical theory as a lens for use in different settings has been problematized.

With some exceptions, critical theory has manifested itself as a critique of hegemonies within academic circles with only some connections to learners in classrooms or the real world. However, as literacy connections to civic and community matters have emerged, so critical theory has become more connected to societal matters—whether through a new lens such as posthumanist or transliteracy or through the portal of schools or community centers (e.g., Lenters & McDermott, 2019; Sheehy, 2009; Stornaiuolo et al., 2017). In recent years, a number of literacy educators have involved their students in raising their critical voices

---

THE USE OF DRAMA IN TRANSFORMATIVE CHANGE

As Rob has noted in reflecting on Drama as a Transformative Tool,

> Our colleagues in fields such as drama education have much to teach us about framing and building on critical readers' engagements. Dramatists and directors from Bertolt Brecht, Konstantin Stanislavsky, David Williamson, Andrew Upton, Harold Pinter, and Quentin Tarantino to educators such as Dorothy Heathcote, Gavin Bolton, Cecily O'Neill, Brian Edmiston, and Tara Goldstein have offered forms of practical theory that have the potential to transcend our cognitive and socio-cognitive and critical theoretically based understandings of literacy. I recall on separate occasions watching Cecily O'Neill and Dorothy Heathcote move learners in a participatory fashion into scenarios or drama frames and shift the participants' positions in and out of the frame as they engaged them in experiencing worldly matters and also critically reflecting on them. Their practices transcended theorizing as they manipulated a combination of strategies and understandings with their deft skills to punctuate imagined circumstances with calls to critique, improvise, and critically reflect as preambles to pondering and pursuing transformative changes.

in conjunction with media pursuits, interrogating their worlds and the existing hegemonies. These include a number of digital video projects as well as initiatives involving theater and forms of drama education.

For example, a number of educators and community activists have adopted various forms of drama to simulate these political systems at play in peoples' lives to expose, examine, and explore ways in which they might be countered. Most notable are the interactive drama pursuits stemming from the drama frames of Augusto Boal and those emanating from the process drama work advanced by Dorothy Heathcote, Gavin Bolton, Cecily O'Neill, Michael Anderson, Brian Edmiston, Robin Ewing, John O'Toole, Tara Goldstein, and others (e.g., Boal, 1979, 1996; Bolton, 1984; Bolton & Heathcote, 1995; Edmiston, 2014; Edmiston & Enciso, 2002; Freebody et al., 2018; Goldstein, 2013; O'Neill, 1995; O'Toole, 1992; Rozansky & Aageson, 2010).

Another heartening development are studies that pursue activism and agency and how they might be achieved. Unquestionably, these pursuits of change may sometimes falter or involve a struggle. As Roger Slee (2018) lamented in his efforts to advance an inclusive education model: "the structures and cultures of schooling reinforce privilege and exacerbate disadvantage according to the taut, and taught, boundaries of the neo-liberal imagination. Accordingly, there is no shortage of data demonstrating academic underachievement and diminished educational experiences according to students' class, gender, race, ethnicity, or perceived ability or disability" (p. 31).

Certainly, critical theorists may need a long-term view. As Bregman (2017) stated: "If we want to change the world we need to be unrealistic, unreasonable, and impossible. Remember: those who called for the abolition of slavery, for suffrage for women, and for same-sex marriage were also once branded as lunatics. Until history proved them right" (p. 264).

Despite these challenges, a number of studies have been or are being pursued in an effort to understand hegemonies, resistance, and change related to matters of difference among cultures, ethnicities, genders, and sexualities (e.g., Beck, 2019; Curnow et al., 2019; McCarty & Lee, 2014; San Pedro, 2018). A growing number of research activists are exploring agency in an effort to mobilize change within their institutions and classrooms, and finding leverage to do so (see box The Use of Drama in Transformative Change; Garrett, 2018; Rigney et al., 2015; Smith, 2011).

References

Alvermann, D., Commeyras, M., Young, J., Randall, S., & Hinson, D. (1997). Interrupting gendered discursive practices in classroom talk about texts: Easy to think about, difficult to do. *Journal of Literacy Research, 29*(1), 73–104.

Andreotti, V., & de Souza, L. M. T. M. (2011). *Postcolonial perspectives on global citizenship education*. Routledge.

Apple, M. W. (1979). *Ideology and curriculum*. Routledge and Kegan Paul.

Apple, M. W. (1988). *Teachers and texts: A political economy of class and gender relations in education*. Routledge and Kegan Paul.

Apple, M. W. (2012). *Knowledge, power, and education: The selected works of Michael W. Apple*. Routledge. doi: 10.4324/9780203118115

Archibald, J. (2008). *Indigenous storywork: Educating the heart, mind, body and spirit*. UBC Press.

Assié-Lumumba, N. T. (2016). The Ubuntu paradigm and comparative and international education: Epistemological challenges and opportunities in our field. *Comparative Educational Review, 61*(1). doi: 10.1086/689922

Baker, C. D., & Luke, A. (Eds.). (1991). *Toward a critical sociology of reading pedagogy*. Benjamins.

Bang, M., & Vossoughi, S. (2016). Participatory design research and educational justice: Studying learning and relations within social change making, cognition and instruction. *Cognition and Instruction, 34*(3), 173–193.

Battiste, M. (1998). Enabling the autumn seed: Toward a decolonized approach to Aboriginal knowledge, language and education. *Canadian Journal of Native Education, 22*, 16–27.

Beck, B. L. (2019). "A different kind of activism": The University of Florida Committee on Sexism and Homophobia, 1981–1992. *American Educational Research Journal, 56*(4), 1353–1379.

Bernstein, B. (1977). *Class, codes, and control*. Routledge.

Bishop, R. S. (2007). *Free within ourselves: The development of African American children's literature*. Greenwood Press.

Blackburn, M. V. (2002). Disrupting the (hetero)normative: Exploring literacy performances and identity work with queer youth. *Journal of Adolescent & Adult Literacy, 46*(4), 312–324.

Boal, A. (1979). *Theater of the oppressed*. Urizen Books.

Boal, A. (1996). *The rainbow of desire: The Boal method of theatre and therapy*. Routledge.

Bolton, G. M. (1984). *Drama as education*. Longman.

Bolton, G. M., & Heathcote, D. (1995). *Drama for learning: Dorothy Heathcote's mantle of the expert approach to education (Dimensions of Drama Series)*. Heinemann Drama.

Booth, David. (1994). *Story drama: Reading, writing and role playing across the curriculum*. Pembroke.

Bourdieu, P. (1991). *Language and symbolic power* (G. Raymond & M. Adamson, Trans.). Harvard University Press.

Boyle, C., & Anderson, J. (2020). Inclusive education and the progressive inclusionists. In U. Sharma & S. Salend (Eds.), *The Oxford research encyclopedia of education*. Oxford University Press. doi: 10.1093/acrefore/9780190264093.013.151

Brandt, D. (2001). Sponsors of literacy. In E. Cushman, E. R. Kintgen, B. M. Kroll, & M. Rose (Eds.), *Literacy: A critical sourcebook* (pp. 555–571). Bedford/St. Martins.

Brandt, D. (2009). *Literacy and learning: Reflections on writing, reading and society*. Jossey-Bass.

Brandt, D., & Clinton, K. (2002). Limits of the local: Expanding perspectives on literacy as a social practice. *Journal of Literacy Research, 34*(3), 337–356. doi: 10.1207/s1554843 0jlr3403_4

Bregman, R. (2017). *Utopia for realists and how we get there*. Bloomsbury.

Brown, L. A., Strega, S. (Eds.). (2005). *Research as resistance: Revisiting critical, indigenous, and anti-oppressive approaches.* Canadian Scholars' Press.

Butler, D. L. (2006). Frames of inquiry in educational psychology: Beyond the quantitative-qualitative divide. In P. A. Alexander & P. H. Winne (Eds.), *Handbook of educational psychology* (2nd ed., pp. 903–929). Erlbaum. doi: 10.4324/9780203874790

Butler, D. L., & Schnellert, L. (2008). Bridging the research-to-practice divide: Improving outcomes for students. *Education Canada, 48*(5), 36–40.

Butler, D. L., Schnellert, L., & Higginson, S. (2008, April). Fostering agency and co-regulation: Teachers using formative assessment to calibrate practice in an age of accountability. Paper presented at the annual meeting of the American Educational Research Association, New York, NY. ecps.educ.ubc.ca/files/2013/11/Butler_Schnellert__Higginson_2007.pdf

Butler, J. (2011, May 27). Precarious life and the obligations of cohabitation. Presented at the Nobel Museum, Stockholm, Sweden.

Campano, G., Ghiso, M. P., & Sánchez, L. (2013). "Nobody one knows the . . . amount of a person": Elementary students critiquing dehumanization through organic critical literacies. *Research in the Teaching of English, 48*(1), 97–124.

Christie, F. (1985). Curriculum genre and schematic structure of classroom discourse. In R. Hasan (Ed.), *Discourse on discourse: Workshop report from the Macquarie Workshop on Discourse Analysis.* Applied Linguistics Association of Australia (Occasional Papers, 7), 38–42.

Cochran-Smith, M. (2000). Blind vision: Unlearning racism in teacher education. *Harvard Educational Review, 70*(2), 157–190. doi: 10.17763/haer.70.2.e77x215054558564

Coleman, J. S., Campbell, E. Q., Hobson, C. J., McPartland, J., Mood, A. M., Weinfeld, F. D., & York, R. L. (1966). Equality of educational opportunity. Report for Department of Health, Education and Welfare, National Center for Educational Statistics, Washington, DC.

Comber, B. (1993). Classroom explorations in critical literacy. *Australian Journal of Language and Literacy, 16*(1), 73–83.

Comber, B. (2006). Pedagogy as work: Educating the next generation of literacy teachers. *Pedagogies: An International Journal, 1*(1), 59–67. doi: 10.1207/s15544818ped0101_9

Comber, B. (2013). Critical literacy in the early years: Emergence and sustenance in an age of accountability. In J. Larson & J. Marsh (Eds.), *The SAGE handbook of early childhood literacy* (pp. 587–601). SAGE. doi: 10.4135/9781446247518.n33

Comber, B. (2015). *Literacy, place, and pedagogies of possibility.* Routledge. doi: 10.4324/9781315735658

Comber, B., & Nixon, H. (2014). Critical literacy across the curriculum: Learning to read, question, and rewrite designs. In J. Pandya, & J. Ávila (Eds.), *Moving critical literacies forward: A new look at praxis across contexts* (pp. 83–97). Routledge.

Comber, B., & Simpson, A. (Eds.). (2001). *Negotiating critical literacies in classrooms.* Erlbaum. doi: 10.4324/9781410600288

Connell, R. W. (2002). Making the difference, then and now. *Discourse: Studies in the cultural politics of education, 23,* 319–327.

Connell, R. W., Ashenden, D. J., Kessler, S., & Dowsett, G. W. (1982). *Making the difference: Schools, families and social division,* George Allen & Unwin.

Cope, B., & Kalantzis, M. (1993). *The powers of literacy: A genre approach to teaching writing.* University of Pittsburgh Press.

Cope, B., & Kalantzis, M. (Eds.). (2000). *Multiliteracies: Literacy learning and the design of social futures*. Routledge.

Curnow, J., Davis, A., & Asher, L. (2019). Politicization in process: Developing political concepts, practices, epistemologies, and identities through activist engagement. *American Educational Research Journal, 56*(3), 716–752.

Davies, B. (1982). *Life in the classroom and playground: The accounts of primary school children*. Routledge and Kegan Paul.

Davies, B. (1989). *Frogs and snails and feminist tales: Preschool children and gender*. Allen & Unwin.

Davies, B. (1993). *Shards of glass: Children reading and writing beyond gendered identity*. Allen & Unwin.

de los Ríos, C. V., & Molina, A. (2020). Literacies of refuge: "Pidiendo Posada" as ritual of justice. *Journal of Literacy Research, 52*(1), 32–54. journals.sagepub.com/doi/pdf/10.1177/1086296X19897840

Deleuze, G. (1994). *Difference and repetition*. Athlone Press.

Dewey, J. (1899). *Democracy and education*. Macmillan.

Dixon, K. (2010). *Literacy, power, and the schooled body: Learning in time and space*. Routledge. doi: 10.4324/9780203851487

Dyson, A. H. (1988). Negotiating among multiple worlds: The space/time dimensions of young children's composing. *Research in the Teaching of English, 22*(4), 355–390.

Edelsky, C. (2006). *With literacy and justice for all: Rethinking the social in language and education* (3rd ed.). Routledge.

Edelsky, C. (Ed.). (1999). *Making justice our project: Teachers working toward critical whole language practice*. National Council for Teachers of English.

Edmiston, B., & Enciso, P. (2002). Reflections and refractions of meaning: Dialogic approaches to classroom drama and reading. In J. Flood, D. Lapp, J. Squire, & J. Jensen (Eds.), *The handbook of research on teaching the English language arts* (pp. 868–880). Simon & Schuster/Macmillan.

Ellsworth, E. (1989). Why doesn't this feel empowering? Working through the repressive myths of critical pedagogy. *Harvard Educational Review, 59*(3), 297–324. doi: 10.17763/haer.59.3.058342114k266250

Enciso, P. (2004). Reading discrimination. In S. Greene & D. Abt-Perkins (Eds.), *Making race visible: Literacy research for cultural understanding* (pp. 149–177). Teachers College Press.

Enciso, P. (2007). Reframing history in sociocultural theory: Toward an expansive vision. In C. Lewis, P. Enciso, & E. Moje (Eds.), *Reframing sociocultural research on literacy: Identity, agency, and power* (pp. 49–74). Erlbaum.

Engels, F. (1969). Ludwig Feuerbach and the end of classical German philosophy. In K. Marx & F. Engels, *Karl Marx and Frederick Engels: Selected works* (pp. 594–632). Progress Publishers.

Ewing, R. (2019). *Drama-rich pedagogy and becoming deeply literate (Drama Australia Monograph No. Twelve)*. Drama Australia.

Fairclough, N. (1992). *Critical language awareness*. Longman.

Fairclough, N. (1995). *Critical discourse analysis: The critical study of language*. Longman.

Foucault, M. (1989). *Archaeology of knowledge*. Routledge. doi: 10.4324/9780203604168

Foucault, M. (1995). *Discipline and punish: The birth of the prison*. Vintage.

Fraser, N. (1989). *Unruly practices: Power, discourse, and gender in contemporary social theory*. University of Minnesota Press.

Fraser, N. (2009). *Scales of justice: Reimagining political space in a globalizing world*. Columbia University Press.

Freebody, K., Balfour, M., Finneran, M., & Anderson, M. (2018). *Applied theatre: Understanding change*. Springer.

Freire, P. (1972). *Pedagogy of the oppressed*. Herder and Herder.

Freire, P. (1995). *Pedagogy of the oppressed* (20th anniversary ed.). Continuum. Original work published 1970.

Freire, P., & Macedo, D. P. (1987). *Literacy: Reading the word and the world*. Bergin & Garvey Publishers.

Garrett, K. C. (2018). Lacking resilience or mounting resistance? Interpreting the actions of Indigenous and immigrant youth within TeachFirst New Zealand. *American Educational Research Journal, 55*(5), 1051–1075. doi: 10.3102/0002831218769563

Gee, J. P. (2015). *Social linguistics and literacies: Ideology in discourses* (5th ed.). Routledge.

Gee, J. P., Hull, G. A., & Lankshear, C. (1996). *The new work order: Behind the language of the new capitalism*. Westview Press.

Gilbert, P. (1992). *Gender and literacy: Key issues for the nineties*. Paper prepared for the Victorian Ministry of Education.

Gilbert, P., & Taylor, S. (1991). *Fashioning the feminine: Girls, popular culture, and schooling*. Allen & Unwin.

Giroux, H. & McLaren, P. (1989). *Critical pedagogy, the state, and the struggle for culture*. State University of New York Press.

Goldstein, T. (2008). Multiple commitments and ethical dilemmas of performed ethnography. *Educational Insights, 12*(2), 1–19.

Goldstein, T. (2013). *Zero Tolerance and other plays: Disrupting racism, xenophobia and homophobia in school*. Sense.

González, N., Moll, L. C., & Amanti, C. (Eds.). (2006). *Funds of knowledge: Theorizing practice in households, communities, and classrooms*. Erlbaum. doi: 10.4324/9781410613462

Goodwin, S. (2012, August 23–25). *Conducting action research in an "evidence-based" policy environment*. Australian qualitative research conference "Embodying Good Research: What Counts and Who Decides?" at Charles Darwin University, Australia.

Gore J. M. (1995). On the continuity of power relations in pedagogy. *International Studies in Sociology of Education, 5*, 165–188.

Gore J. M., & Zeichner K. M. (1991). Action research and reflective teaching in preservice teacher education: A case study from the United States. *Teaching and Teacher Education, 7*, 119–136.

Gray, W. S. (1956). *The teaching of reading and writing: An international survey*. UNESCO.

Greene, M. (1995). *Releasing the imagination: Essays on education, the arts, and social change*. Jossey-Bass.

Gutiérrez, K. D., & Jurow, S. (2016). Social design experiments: Towards equity by design. *Journal of Learning Sciences, 25*(4), 565–598.

Habermas, J. (1987). *The theory of communicative action (Vol. 2), Lifeworld and system: A critique of functionalist reason*. Polity Press.

Hagood, M. C. (2002). Critical literacy for whom? *Reading Research and Instruction, 41*(3), 247–266.

Hall, B. (1978). Continuity in adult education and political struggle. *Convergence: An International Journal of Adult Education, 11*(1), 8–15.

Hall, S., Davison, S., Featherstone, D., Rustin, M., & Schwarz, B. (Eds.). (2017). *Selected political writings: The great moving right show and other essays.* Duke University Press. doi: 10.1215/9780822372943-001

Halliday, M. A. K. (1985). *An introduction to functional grammar.* Edward Arnold.

Hasan, R. (1978). Text in the systemic functional model. In W. Dressier (Ed.), *Current trends in textlinguistics,* Helmut Buske.

Heath, S. B. (1983). *Ways with words: Language, life, and work in communities and classrooms.* Cambridge University Press.

Heathcote, D. (1984). *Dorothy Heathcote: Collected writings on education and drama.* Eds. L. Johnson and C. O'Neill. Media Limited.

Heathcote, D., & Bolton, G. (1995). *Drama for learning: Dorothy Heathcote's "mantle of the expert" approach to education.* Heinemann.

Hegel, G. (2015). *Encyclopedia of the philosophical sciences in basic outline.* Cambridge University Press.

Hoffman J. V. (2020). Practicing imagination and activism in literacy research, teaching, and teacher education: I still don't know how to change the world with rocks. *Literacy Research: Theory, Method, and Practice, 69*(1), 79–98. doi: 10.1177/2381336920938670

hooks, b. (1994). *Teaching to transgress: Education as the practice of freedom.* Routledge.

Janks, H. (2010). *Literacy and power.* Routledge. doi: 10.4324/9780203869956

Janks, H. (2014). Critical literacy's ongoing importance for education. *Journal of Adolescent & Adult Literacy, 57*(5), 349–356. doi: 10.1002/jaal.260

Janks, H., Dixon, K., Ferreira, A., Granville, S., & Newfield, D. (2014). *Doing critical literacy: Texts and activities for students and teachers.* Routledge.

Janks, H., & Vasquez, V. (2011). Critical literacy revisited: Writing as critique (Editorial). *English Teaching, 10*(1), 1–6.

Jiménez, R. T. (2000). Literacy and the identity development of Latina/o students. *American Educational Research Journal, 37*(4), 971–1000. doi: 10.2307/1163499

Kamil, M. L., & Taylor & Francis eBooks A–Z. (2000). *Handbook of reading research* (Vol. 3). Routledge.

Kamler, B. (1994). Lessons about language and gender. *Australian Journal of Language and Literacy, 17*(2), 129–138.

Kamler, B. (2001). *Relocating the personal: A critical writing pedagogy.* State University of New York Press.

Kauffman, J. M., Ward, D. M., & Badar, J. (2016). The delusion of full inclusion. In R. M. Foxx & J. A. Mulick (Eds.), *Controversial therapies for autism and intellectual disabilities* (2nd ed., pp. 71–86). Taylor & Francis.

Kincheloe, J. L. (1991). *Teachers as researchers: Qualitative inquiry as a path to empowerment.* Routledge. doi: 10.4324/9780203801550

Knight, T. (1999). Inclusive education and educational theory: Inclusive for what? Paper presented at the British Educational Research Association Conference, University of Sussex at Brighton, September 2–5. www.leeds.ac.uk/educol/documents/000001106.htm

Knobel, M., & Lankshear, C. (2004). Planning pedagogy for i-mode: From flogging to blogging via wi-fi. *English in Australia, 139,* 78–102.

Kress, G. (1989). *Linguistic processes in sociocultural practice.* Oxford University Press.

Kress, G. (2000a). Design and transformation: New theories of meaning. In B. Cope & M. Kalantzis (Eds.), *Multiliteracies: Literacy learning and the design of social futures* (pp. 153–161). Routledge. doi: 10.4324/9780203979402

Kress, G. (2000b). Multimodality. In B. Cope, & M. Kalantzis (Eds.), *Multiliteracies: Literacy learning and the design of social futures* (pp. 182–202). Routledge. doi: 10.4324/9780203979402

Kress, G., & Van Leeuwen, T. (2006). *Reading images: The grammar of visual design* (2nd ed.). Routledge.

Ladson-Billings, G. (1999). Just what is critical race theory and what's it doing in a "nice" field like education? In L. Parker, D. Deyhle, & S. Villenas (Eds.), *Race is . . . race isn't: Critical race theory and qualitative studies in education* (pp. 7–30). Westview Press.

Ladson-Billings, G. (2003). Foreword. In S. Greene & D. Abt-Perkins (Eds.), *Making race visible: Literacy research for cultural understanding* (pp. vii–xi). Teachers College Press.

Ladson-Billings, G., & Tate, W. F. IV. (1995). Toward a critical race theory of education. *Teachers College Record, 97*(1), 47–68.

Lankshear, C., & McLaren, P. (1993). *Critical literacy: Politics, praxis, and the postmodern.* State University of New York Press.

Lather, P. (1986). Issues of validity in openly ideological research: Between a rock and a soft place. *Interchange, 17*(4), 63–84. doi: 10.1007/BF01807017

Lather, P. (1992). Critical frames in educational research: Feminist and post-structural perspectives. *Theory into Practice, 31*(2), 87–99. doi: 10.1080/00405849209543529

Lau, S. M. C. (2016). Language, identity, and emotionality: Exploring the potential of language portraits in preparing teachers for diverse learners. *The New Educator, 12*(2), 147–170. doi: 10.1080/1547688X.2015.1062583

Lave, J., & Wenger, E. (1991). *Situated learning: Legitimate peripheral participation.* Cambridge University Press.

Leander, K., & Boldt, G. (2013). Rereading "A pedagogy of multiliteracies": Bodies, texts, and emergence. *Journal of Literacy Research, 45*(1), 22–46. doi: 10.1177/1086296X12468587

Lemke, J. (1993). Intertextuality and educational research. *Linguistics and Education 4*(3/4), 257–268.

Lenters, K., & McDermott, M. (2018). *Affect, embodiment, and place in critical literacy: Assembling theory and practice.* Routledge.

Lewison, M., Leland, C., & Harste, J. C. (2014). *Creating critical classrooms: Reading and writing with an edge* (2nd ed.). Routledge. doi: 10.4324/9781315817842

Luke, A. (1988). *Literacy, textbooks, and ideology: Postwar literacy instruction and the mythology of Dick and Jane.* Falmer Press.

Luke, A. (1997). Critical approaches to literacy. In V. Edwards & D. Corson (Eds.), *Encyclopedia of language and education* (Vol. 2, pp. 144–151). Springer Netherlands. doi: 10.1007/978-94-011-4540-4

Luke, A. (2000). Critical literacy in Australia: A matter of context and standpoint. *Journal of Adolescent & Adult Literacy, 43*(5), 448–461.

Luke, A. (2003). Literacy and the other: A sociological approach to literacy research and policy in multilingual societies. *Reading Research Quarterly, 38*(1), 132–141.

Luke, A. (2004). On the material consequences of literacy. *Language and Education, 18*(4), 331–335. doi: 10.1080/09500780408666886

Luke, A. (2009). Race and language as capital in school: A sociological template for language education reform. In R. Kubota & A. Lin (Eds.), *Race, culture, and identities in second language education: Exploring critically engaged practice* (pp. 286–308). Routledge. doi: 10.4324/9780203876657

Luke, A. (2013). Regrounding critical literacy: Representation, facts and reality. In M. R. Hawkins (Ed.), *Framing languages and literacies: Socially situated views and perspectives* (pp. 136–148). Routledge.

Luke, A. (2014). Defining critical literacy. In J. Pandya, & J. Ávila (Eds.), *Moving critical literacies forward: A new look at praxis across contexts* (pp. 19–31). Routledge.

Luke, C. (1994). Feminist pedagogy and critical media literacy. *Journal of Communication Inquiry, 18*(2), 30–47. doi: 10.1177/019685999401800200

Martin, J. R. (1985). Process and text: Two aspects of semiosis. In J. Benson & W. Greaves (Eds.), *Systemic perspectives on discourse: Selected theoretical papers from the 9th International Systemic Workshop,* 248–274. Ablex (Advances in Discourse Process, 15).

Martino, W. (2009). Literacy issues and GLBTQ youth: Queer interventions in English education. In L. Christenbury, R. Bomer, & R Smagorinsky (Eds.), *Handbook of adolescent literacy research* (pp. 386–399). Guilford.

Marx, K. (2000). *Karl Marx: Selected Writings* (2nd ed.). Ed. David McLellan. Oxford University Press.

Marx, K., & Engels, F. (1967). *The Communist manifesto.* Penguin Books.

Marx, K., & Engels, F. (1975–1976). *Collected Works.* International Publishers.

Mavers, D. (2009). Image in the multimodal ensemble: Children's drawing. In C. Jewitt (Ed.), *The Routledge handbook of multimodal analysis* (pp. 263–271). Routledge.

McCarty, T., & Lee, T. (2014). Critical culturally sustaining/revitalizing pedagogy and Indigenous education sovereignty. *Harvard Educational Review, 84*(1), 101–124. doi: 10.17763/haer.84.1.q83746nl5pj34216

McDermott, R. P. (1974). Achieving school failure: An anthropological approach to literacy and social stratification. In G. Spindler (Ed.), *Education and cultural process: Toward an anthropology of education* (pp. 82–118). Holt, Rinehart, & Winston.

McKinney, C. (2016). *Language and power in post-colonial schooling: Ideologies in practice.* Routledge. doi: 10.4324/9781315730646

McLaren, P. (1989). *Life in schools: An introduction to critical pedagogy in the foundations of education.* Longman.

McLaren, P. (2000). Paulo Freire's pedagogy of possibility. In S. F. Steiner, H. M. Krank, P. McLaren, & R. E. Bahruth (Eds.), *Freireian pedagogy, praxis, and possibilities: Projects for the new millennium* (pp. 1–22). Falmer Press.

Meacham, S. J. (2003). *Literacy and street credibility: Plantations, prisons, and African American literacy from Frederick Douglass to Fifty Cent.* Presentation at the Economic and Social Research Council Seminar Series Conference, Sheffield, UK.

Mellor, B., Patterson, A., & O'Neill, M. (1987). *Reading stories.* Chalkface Press.

Mellor, B., Patterson, A., & O'Neill, M. (1991). *Reading fictions.* Chalkface Press.

Moje, E. B., Luke, A., Davies, B., & Street, B. (2009). Literacy and identity: Examining the metaphors in history and contemporary research. *Reading Research Quarterly, 44*(4), 415–437. doi: 10.1598/RRQ.44.4.7

Morgan, B. (2018). Beyond the guest paradigm: Eurocentric education and Aboriginal peoples in NSW. In E. A. McKinley & L. T. Smith (Eds.), *Handbook of Indigenous education.* Springer. doi: 10.1007/978-981-10-1839-8

Morgan, W. (1992). *A post-structuralist English classroom: The example of Ned Kelly.* The Victorian Association for the Teaching of English.

Morgan, W. (1997). *Critical literacy in the classroom: The art of the possible.* Routledge. doi: 10.4324/9780203034323

Morrell, E. (2008). *Critical literacy and urban youth: Pedagogies of access, dissent, and liberation*. Routledge.

New London Group. (1996). A pedagogy of multiliteracies: Designing social futures. *Harvard Educational Review, 66*(1), 60–92. doi: 10.17763/haer.66.1.17370n67v22j160u

Nixon, H. (2003). New research literacies for contemporary research into literacy and new media? *Reading Research Quarterly, 38*(4), 407–413.

Nixon, H., & Comber, B. (2005). Behind the scenes: Making movies in early years classrooms. In J. Marsh (Ed.), *Popular culture, new media and digital literacy in early childhood* (pp. 219–236). Routledge.

Norwich, B. (2013). *Addressing tensions and dilemmas in inclusive education*. Routledge.

O'Brien, J. (2001). Children reading critically: A local history. In B. Comber & A. Simpson (Eds.), *Negotiating critical literacies in classrooms* (pp. 41–60). Erlbaum.

Ogbu, J. (1982). Cultural discontinuities and schooling. *Anthropology & Education Quarterly, 13*(4), 290–307.

Ogbu, J. (1994). Introduction: Understanding cultural diversity and learning. *Educational Researcher, 17*(4), 354–383.

O'Neill, C. (1995). *Drama worlds: A framework for process drama (The dimensions of drama)*. Heinemann Drama.

O'Neill, C., & Lambert, A. (1984). *Drama structures: A practical handbook for teachers*. Hutchinson.

O'Toole, John. (1992). *The process of drama: negotiating art and meaning*. Routledge.

Pandya, J., & Ávila, J. (Eds.). (2014). *Moving critical literacies forward: A new look at praxis across contexts*. Routledge.

Patel, L. (2018). Immigrant populations and sanctuary schools. *Journal of Literacy Research, 50*(4), 524–529. doi: 10.1177/1086296x18802417

Perry, K. (2012). What is literacy? A critical overview of sociocultural perspectives. *Journal of Language and Literacy Education, 8*(1), 50–71. jolle.coe.uga.edu/wp-content/uploads/2012/06/What-is-Literacy_KPerry.pdf

Perry, K. H., & Purcell-Gates, V. (2005). Resistance and appropriation: Literacy practices as agency within hegemonic contexts. In B. Maloch, J. V. Hoffman, D. L. Schallert, C. M. Fairbanks, & J. Worthy (Eds.), *54th yearbook of the National Reading Conference* (pp. 272–285). National Reading Conference.

Philips, S. U. (1983). *The invisible culture: Communication in classroom and community on the Warm Springs Indian reservation*. Longman.

Popkewitz, T. S. (1984). *Paradigm and ideology in educational research: The social functions of the intellectual*. Falmer Press.

Purcell-Gates, V. (1995). *Other people's words: The cycle of low literacy*. Harvard University Press.

Rabaka, R. (2009). *Africana critical theory: Reconstructing the Black radical tradition, from W. E. B. Du Bois and C. L. R. James to Frantz Fanon and Amilcar Cabral*. Lexington Books.

Rigney, D., Bignall, S., & Hemming, S. (2015). Negotiating Indigenous modernity: Kungun Ngarrindjeri Yunnan—Listen to Ngarrindjeri speak. *AlterNative: An International Journal of Indigenous Peoples, 11*(4), 334–349. doi: 10.1177/117718011501100402

Rigney, L., & Hattam, R. J. (2018, April). *Toward a decolonizing culturally responsive pedagogy?* Paper presented at the American Educational Research Association annual meeting, New York, NY.

Rogers, R. (2018). Literacy research, racial consciousness, and equitable flows of knowl-edge. *Literacy research: Theory, method and practice, 67*, 24–43.

Rozansky, C., & Aagesen, C. (2010). Low-achieving readers, high expectations: Image the-atre encourages critical literacy. *Journal of Adolescent & Adult Literacy, 53*(6), 458–466. December 11, 2020, from www.jstor.org/stable/25614590

Sánchez, L. (2011). Building on young children's cultural histories through placemaking in the classroom. *Contemporary Issues in Early Childhood, 12*(4), 332–342. doi: 10.2304 /ciec.2011.12.4.332

San Pedro, T. (2018). Abby as ally: An argument for culturally disruptive pedagogy. *American Educational Research Journal, 55*(6), 1193–1232. doi: 10.3102/0002831218 773488

Schnellert, L. M., Butler, D. L., & Higginson, S. K. (2008). Co-constructors of data, co-constructors of meaning: Teacher professional development in an age of account-ability. *Teaching and Teacher Education, 24*(3), 725–750. doi: 10.1016/j.tate.2007 .04.001

Shannon, P. (1989/1998). *Broken promises: Reading instruction in twentieth-century Amer-ica*. Bergin and Garvey.

Shannon, P. (1998). *Reading poverty*. Heinemann.

Shannon, P. (2001). *Ishop you shop: Raising questions about reading commodities*. Heinemann.

Shannon, P. (2007). *Reading against democracy: The broken promises of reading instruction*. Heinemann.

Shannon, P. (2010). We've always considered our work political. In P. Anders (Ed.), *Defying convention, inventing the future in literary research and practice* (pp. 214–227). Rout-ledge. doi: 10.4324/9780203844717

Shannon, P. (2011). *Reading wide awake: Politics, pedagogies, & possibilities*. Teachers Col-lege Press.

Shannon, P. (2014). *Reading poverty in America*. Routledge. doi: 10.4324/9781315858128

Shannon, P. (Ed.). (2001). *Becoming political too*. Heinemann.

Shannon, P., & Edmondson, J. (Eds.). (2005). *Reading education policy: A reader*. Interna-tional Reading Association.

Share, J. (2009). Young children and critical media literacy. In R. Hammer & D. Kellner (Eds.), *Media/cultural studies: Critical approaches* (pp. 126–151). Peter Lang.

Share, J. (2010). Voices from the trenches: Elementary school teachers speak about imple-menting media literacy. In K. Tyner (Ed.), *Media literacy: New agendas in communica-tion* (pp. 53–75). Routledge.

Sheehy, M. (2009). *Place stories: Time, space and literacy in two classrooms*. Hampton Press.

Shor, I. (1980). *Critical teaching and everyday life*. South End Press.

Shor, I. (1987). *Freire for the classroom: A sourcebook for liberatory teaching*. Boynton/Cook.

Siegel, M. (1995). More than words: The generative power of transmediation for learning. *Canadian Journal of Education, 20*(4), 4.

Siegel, M., & S. L. Fernandez. (2000). Critical approaches. In M. L. Kamil, P. B. Mosenthal, P. D. Pearson, & R. Barr (Eds.), *Handbook of reading research* (Vol. 3, pp. 141–152). Routledge.

Sims, R. S. (1982). *Shadow and substance: Afro-American experience in contemporary children's fiction*. National Council of Teachers of English.

Sims, R. S. (1983). Strong Black girls: A ten year old responds to fiction about Afro-Americans. *Journal of Research and Development in Education, 16*(3), 21–28.

Slee, R. (2018). *Inclusive education isn't dead, it just smells funny* (1st ed.). Routledge. doi: 10.4324/9780429486869

Smith, G. H. (April 2011). Transforming education: Māori struggle for higher education. Manu Oa presentation. www.manu-ao.ac.nz/massey/fms/manu-ao/documents /Graham%20Smith%20Powerpoint.pdf

Smith, L. T. (1999). *Decolonising methodologies: Research and indigenous peoples.* University of Otago Press.

Smith, L. T. (2005). On tricky ground: Researching the Native in the age of uncertainty. In N. K. Denzin & Y. S. Lincoln (Eds.), *The SAGE Handbook of Qualitative Research* (3rd ed., pp. 85–108). SAGE.

Stornaiuolo, A., Smith, A., & Phillips, N. C. (2017). Developing a transliteracies framework for a connected world. *Journal of Literacy Research, 49*(10), 68–91.

Street, B. (1984). *Literacy in theory and practice.* Cambridge University Press.

Street, B. (1993). Introduction: The new literacy studies. In B. V. Street (Ed.), *Cross-cultural approaches to literacy* (pp. 1–21). Cambridge University Press.

Street, B. V. (1995). *Social literacies: Critical approaches to literacy in development, ethnography, and education.* Longman.

Street, B. V. (2003). What's new in new literacy studies: Critical approaches to literacy in theory and practice. *Current Issues in Comparative Education, 5*(2), 77–91.

Street, B. V., Pahl, K., & Rowsell, J. (2009). Multimodality and new literacy studies. In C. Jewitt (Ed.), *The Routledge handbook of multimodal analysis* (pp. 191–200). Routledge.

Takayama, K. (2009). Progressive education and critical education scholarship in Japan: Toward the democratization of critical educational studies. In M. Apple, W. Au, & L. Gandin (Eds.), *The Routledge international handbook of critical education* (pp. 354–367). Routledge. doi: 10.4324/9780203882993

Tate, W. F. (1997). Critical race theory and education: History, theory, and implications. *Review of Research in Education, 22*(1), 195–247. doi: 10.2307/1167376

Taylor, P. (2000). *The drama classroom: Action, reflection, transformation.* Routledge/Falmer.

Thiong'o, N. W. (1986). *Decolonising the mind: The politics of language in African literature.* J. Currey.

Tierney, R. J. (2001–2002). An ethical chasm: Jurisprudence, jurisdiction and the literacy profession. *Journal of Adolescent Literacy, 46*(4), 260–277.

Tierney, R. J. (2020). Notes on global reading: Critical cultural traversals, transactions and transformations. In L. I. Misiaszek (Ed.), *Exploring the complexities in global citizenship education: Hard spaces, methodologies, and ethics* (pp. 36–68). Routledge.

Tuck, E., & Yang, K. W. (2014). *Youth resistance research and theories of change.* Routledge. doi: 10.4324/9780203585078

UNESCO & World Conference on Special Needs Education: Access and Quality. (1994). *The Salamanca statement and framework for action on special needs education (adopted by the World Conference on Special Needs Education: Access and Quality. Salamanca, Spain, 7–10 June.* UNESCO.

UNICEF. (2013). *The state of the world's children 2013: Children with disabilities.* UNICEF. data.unicef.org/resources/the-state-of-the-worlds-children-2013-children-with -disabilities/

Vander Zanden, S., & Wohlwend, K. E. (2011). Paying attention to procedural text: Critically reading school routines as embodied achievement. *Language Arts, 88*(5), 337–345.

Vasquez, V. (2001). Constructing a critical curriculum with young children. In B. Comber & A. Simpson (Eds.), *Negotiating critical literacies in classrooms* (pp. 61–72). Erlbaum.

Vasquez, V. M. (2014a). *Negotiating critical literacies with young children* (2nd ed.). Routledge.

Vasquez, V. M. (2014b). Inquiry into the incidental unfolding of social justice issues: 20 years of seeking out possibilities for critical literacies. In J. Z. Pandya & J. Ávila (Eds.), *Moving critical literacies forward: A new look at praxis across contexts* (pp. 174–186). Routledge.

Vasquez, V. M., Tate, S. L., & Harste, J. C. (2013). *Negotiating critical literacies with teachers: Theoretical foundations and pedagogical resources for pre-service and in-service contexts.* Routledge. doi: 10.4324/9780203081778

Vicars, M. (2013). Queerer than queer! In R. Gabriel & J. N. Lester (Eds.), *Performances of research: Critical issues in K-12 education* (pp. 245–272). Peter Lang.

Wagner, B. J. (Ed.). (1998). *Educational drama and language arts: What research shows.* Heinemann.

Wagner, D. A. (2018). *Learning as development: Rethinking international education in a changing world.* Routledge.

Whipple, G. M. (1934). *The activity movement. 33rd yearbook of the National Society for the Study of Education.* Public School Publishing Company.

Willinsky, J. (1990). *The new literacy: Redefining reading and writing in the schools.* Routledge. doi: 10.4324/9781351235945

Willis, A. I. (1995). Reading the world of school literacy: Contextualizing the experience of a young African American male. *Harvard Educational Review, 65*(1), 30–50.

Willis, A. I., & Harris, V. J. (1997). Expanding the boundaries: A reaction to the First-Grade Studies. *Reading Research Quarterly, 32*(4), 439–445. doi: 10.1598/RRQ.32.4.7

Willis, P. (1977). *Learning to labour: How working class kids get working class jobs.* Columbia University Press.

Wright, H. K., & Abdi, A. A. (Eds.). (2012). *The dialectics of African education and western discourses: Counter-hegemonic perspectives.* Peter Lang.

NOTES

1. Discussions of critical thinking have a history that extends back centuries, including deliberations by John Dewey (1910) and John Rawls (1971) as well as an unpacking by Robert Ennis (1996), John McPeck (1981), and numerous others (see Hitchcock, 2010). Discussions of thinking critically or critical thinking or critically framed reading involve behaviors, dispositions, perspectives, and abilities (both general and specific) tied to what Rousseau (1762) and Dewey (1910) considered to be reflective thinking befitting a form of inquiry that extends to consideration of matters of justice. In education, critical thinking or critically framed reading intersects with the taxonomic approaches undergirding curriculum developments such as the taxonomy proposed by Bloom et al. (1956) in the cognitive domain; in the affective domain proposed by Krathwohl et al. (1964); and approaches to reading literature (e.g., Wolf et al., 1968), including response to literature. Some have also

examined these matters by enlisting frameworks from the study of arguments by Stephen Toulmin (1958) and Deana Kuhn (1991), or moral stages, such as those documented by Lawrence Kohlberg (1976).

2. See work by Bronwyn Davies (1982, 1989, 1993); Pam Gilbert (1992); Gilbert & Taylor (1991); Connell et al. (1982); Connell (2002); Barbara Comber (1993, 2006, 2013a, 2013b, 2015); Comber & Nixon (2014); Comber & Simpson (2001); Barbara Kamler (1994, 2001); Allan Luke (1988, 1997, 2000, 2003, 2004, 2009, 2013, 2014). See also Baker & Luke (1991), Carmen Luke (1994), and Jenny Gore (1995).

3. In China, Marxism's modern-day roots are evident in the Three Principles advocated by Sun Yat-sen—those of nationalism (minzu, 民族), of democracy (minquan, 民權), and of welfare (minsheng, 民生)—and later in the Chinese revolution efforts to strive for a socialist state where the proletariat was eminent, aligned with efforts to emulate Marxist-Leninist and Mao Zedong thought.

4. A number of critical theorists (e.g., Foucault, Derrida, Barthes, and Judith Butler) identified themselves as poststructuralists and pursued the deconstruction of text for purposes of judging the forces at work.

5. Multiliteracies scholars bringing sociocultural and critical orientations to the field included Courtney Cazden, William Cope, Norman Fairclough, James Gee, Mary Kalantzis, Gunther Kress, Allan Luke, Carmen Luke, Sarah Michaels, and Martin Nakata. For specific publications, see: Cope & Kalantzis, 2000; Norman Fairclough, 1992, 1995; James Gee, 2015; Allan Luke, 1988, 1997, 2000, 2003, 2004, 2009, 2013, 2014. See also Baker & Luke, 1991; Moje et al., 2009; Carmen Luke, 1994; Gunther Kress, 1989, 2000a, 2000b; and Kress & Van Leeuwen, 2006.

8 The Assessment Wave

8.1 THE SELF-ASSESSING READER

Given the significant role that tests play, the term "self-assessing reader" might conjure up notions of readers as test takers, perhaps employing some of the strategies used to excel at selecting an answer from multiple choices or generating a favorably scored response. Indeed, test-taking ability befits the notion of a self-assessing reader but in a fashion that is limited. We prefer to view the self-assessing reader as a person who employs a range of strategies and practices as they engage in various literate activities in ways that are purposeful and strategic. This includes drawing on multiple forms of awareness, judgmental abilities, and attitudes while formulating and initiating appropriate engagements and applying criteria selectively as they continue to examine and judge plans, efforts, and progress.

The development of a self-assessing reader has precursors on a number of fronts that occurred simultaneously or operated somewhat in the shadows. They included some of the major waves of the development in the field, including:

- learning to learn and metacognition, with its focus on the student-strategic development (e.g., Bransford et al., 2000; Brown, 1987; Flavell, 1977);
- reading, writing, and media working together via projects, etc. (e.g., Edwards et al., 1998; González et al., 2006; Harste et al., 1988);
- the opportunities for students to examine their reading, writing, and other developments across time, such as through portfolios (e.g., Tierney et al., 1991; Tierney & Clark, 1998);
- constructivist and qualitative research and the notion of responsive evaluation—involving a commitment to participatory and reciprocal learning (e.g., Guba & Lincoln, 1989; Lather, 1986; Tierney, 1998; 2009);
- critical theoretical developments, especially those tied to reading oneself and critical reflexivity (e.g., Freire, 1970/1995); and
- the emergence of a developmental orientation that emphasized students' development of sustainable, independent, and transferable strategies, or a self-improving system (e.g., Clay, 1998; Fountas & Pinnell, 1996; Goodman, 1996; Goodman et al., 2005).

At the same time, self-assessment is not a new concept. It has roots in our everyday lives (spiritual, physical, professional) in conjunction with undertaking periodical review, setting performance goals and targets, and representing the self in these endeavors or in the search for new pursuits. On a regular basis, many of us reflect on our lives—our health needs, spirituality, exercise regimens, economic circumstances, or daily accounting for our schedules and commitments.

For those of us who are educators, forms of self-assessment may pervade our lives as we contemplate our professional plans, including our teaching activities and learning goals for our students. If one of our goals is to improve students' own decisionmaking, we are likely to focus on helping our students assess themselves. On one level, we operate with our classes in a way that somewhat resembles how a conductor oversees an orchestra, ensemble, or free-flowing jazz group. On another level, we try to advance the discerning decisionmaking of each student—perhaps leading from behind or on the sidelines with probes of learners' interests and purposes as we seek to encourage the proprietorship of the self-assessor. Explicitly or implicitly, we are involved in conversations about the criteria students might use to examine their efforts, consider their accomplishments, and discuss directions their pursuits might take. If our goal is student-led decisionmaking, we may operate with the view that the self-assessment is more important than the products or outcomes, and that the person involved in the self-assessment should take ownership of his efforts, including exploring the criteria and lens to support the self-reflective enterprise.

Our approach is not different from developing forms of meta-awarenesses and heuristics. Indeed, the context of reading is not unlike the formulation of a learning contracts approach or an approach to strategy enlistment—akin to what Marie Clay (1978) referred to a self-improving system. Our approach is more akin to the kinds of discussions that Peter Johnston has so powerfully depicted in his book *Choice Words* (2004), or what Debra Crouch and Brian Cambourne detail in their discussions of learning conditions (2020), or those discussions of project-based learning advocates in the Reggio Emilia context (Edwards et al., 1998).

The espoused notion of the self-assessing reader is tied to a view of reading that is reader-centered and diverse versus one driven by a standardized curriculum and teaching/learning for the test (see box). The notion of self-assessing readers goes beyond reading and writing themselves, affording forms of self-teaching devices. Readers should be involved in becoming discerning decisionmakers as they enlist a range of developing criteria to review both what they have already done and what they should further pursue. They are involved in judging their own efforts rather than comparing or competing with others. Self-assessing reading places assessment as a key element in learning itself. It shifts from an assessment "of" readers to an assessment "by," "with," and "for" readers. At a minimum, it entails reading oneself and being continuously engaged in a kind of formative research of reading's meaning-making strategies that one might employ, checking on and comparing understandings. As self-assessing readers engage with text, they do so planfully—considering the questions and purposes they might

Despite developments across various nations that have heightened the use of tests for accountability and high-stakes decisionmaking, challenges to the domination of traditional testing have occurred under the banners of authentic assessment and approaches to testing focused on student self-assessment. Indeed, in conjunction with the shift to constructivist notions of reading and research, a key feature of assessment shifted to recognizing that the learner is a key stakeholder, and that her own assessments of her goals, achievement, needs, processes, and so on, are of value. And in terms of pedagogy, a fundamental principle is that as a teacher, mentor, or guide, the only reason I have a right to assess you today is so that you can do it for yourself tomorrow.

pursue as they actively contemplate what they are gleaning. This involves pausing to reflect on their progress, ongoing questions, approaches, understandings, and uses of the text. It might also go further, exploring their worlds through a combination of reading and observation and project pursuits. It might involve exploring one's likes and dislikes as a reader, differences in interpretation and themes, or the nature of arguments—the evidence, claims, warrants (e.g., Murphy et al., 2018; Reznitskaya & Wilkinson, 2018: Sheehy, 2002; Wilkinson et al., 2010).

For many students, self-assessment begins with being encouraged to develop and apply a repertoire of reading and research strategies to the texts they choose. This includes strategies related to book selection (e.g., locating sources for research, inspiration, or the joy of reading, etc.), pre-reading (e.g., thinking about what they know, making predictions, and self-questioning), reading (e.g., connecting ideas, visualizing, further cross-checking ideas, questioning, and predicting), and post-reading (e.g., making intertextual links and contemplating relevance). In the context of projects, these strategies might extend to engaging in a needs assessment and the research of circumstances, as well as project planning, gathering resources, collaborations and consultations with others, implementation, and follow-up (e.g., Edwards et al., 1998; González et al., 2006; Harste et al., 1988). Portfolios, knowledge maps, peer-to-peer conferencing, rubric discussions, and other activities support the self-assessing reader. Such approaches engage learners in planning ahead what they may do and looking back at what they have done en route to contemplating their progress and being thoughtful about the next steps.

Self-assessment is consultative and collaborative amid supporters and stakeholders who are more constructive than judgmental. To some extent, self-assessments offer a time for engaging in building relationships and forging partnerships. Self-assessing readers are never alone; they have the authors and peers with whom they may share their pursuits. Plus, they might be in parallel play with classmates who are also engaged in the same critical reflexivity with themselves.

They are engaged in an enterprise done with others—sometimes as a team involved in a collaborative project, or perhaps even as they are pursuing something by themselves. Regardless, they are involved in various collaborations, both incidental and ongoing, for problem solving or for feedback. As a group member they might be involved in team planning and occasional troubleshooting with their peers. As an individual they might be using others as sounding boards or for advice. Others can provide advice as a reader wrestles with reading, or seeks input of one form or another, or as a means to compare and contrast efforts, understandings, and approach. Others can provide an alternative lens for thinking about matters or confirming or complementing a reader's conclusions. Regardless, others are integral to one's self-assessments of pursuits, as readers' input for each other may be influential even as they are engaged in their own. A self-assessing reader is learning to learn in the company of others—both seeking and offering input.

It is important to offer students opportunities to be engaged in conversations with themselves and others about their reading, with the goal of their becoming decisionmakers and self-directed learners (based on their enlistment of a repertoire of criteria for doing so). Fellow learners should be considered as consultants rather than as competitors. The approach is ongoing and formative as readers look backward and forward at what they have done or will do next. Self-assessing readers will take ownership of their development and are apt to be able to relish their progress themselves and with their peers and families. They are conscious of developing criteria that they might employ to judge and adjust their pursuits and the quality of their engagements. Readers are not just the subjects of the assessment; they are the assessors and partners in the educational enterprise for formative purposes. And above all, readers are the first and most important clients of any assessment system.

References

Bransford, J. D., Brown, A. L., & Cocking, R. R. (Eds.). (2000). *How people learn: Brain, mind, experience and schooling.* National Research Council and National Academy Press.

Brown. A. (1987). Metacognition, executive control, self-regulation and other more mysterious mechanisms. In F. E. Weinert & R. H. Kluwe (Eds.), *Metacognition, motivation and understanding* (pp. 65–116). Erlbaum.

Carter, M. (1992). *Self-assessment using writing portfolios* (Unpublished doctoral dissertation). The Ohio State University.

Clay, M. (1978). *Reading: The patterning of complex behavior.* Heinemann.

Clay, M. (1998). *By different paths to common outcomes.* Stenhouse.

Crouch, D., & Cambourne, B. (2020). *Made for learning; How the conditions of learning guide teaching decisions.* Richard C. Owens Publisher.

Crumpler, T. (1996). *Exploring a culture of assessment with ninth grade students: Convergences of meaning within dramas of assessment.* (Unpublished doctoral dissertation). The Ohio State University.

Education Queensland. (2000a). *Literate futures; Report of the literacy review for Queensland state schools*. The State of Queensland, Department of Education. education.qld.gov.au

Education Queensland. (2000b). *New basics; Curriculum organizer*. The State of Queensland, Department of Education. education.qld.gov.au

Edwards, C. P., Gandini, L., & Forman, G. E. (1993). *The hundred languages of children: The Reggio Emilia approach to early childhood education*. Ablex.

Fenner, L. (1995). *Student portfolios: A view from inside the classroom* (Unpublished doctoral dissertation). The Ohio State University.

Flavell, J. (1977). *Cognitive development*. Prentice-Hall.

Fountas, I. C., & Pinnell, G. S. (1996). *Guided reading: Good first teaching for all children*. Heinemann.

Freire, P. (1995). *Pedagogy of the oppressed* (20th anniversary ed.). Continuum.

González, N., Moll, L. C., & Amanti, C. (2005). *Funds of knowledge: Theorizing practice in households, communities, and classrooms*. Erlbaum. doi: 10.4324/9781410613462

Goodman, Y. M. (1996). Revaluing readers while readers revalue themselves: Retrospective miscue analysis. *The Reading Teacher, 49*(8), 600–609.

Guba, E. G., & Lincoln, Y. S. (1989). *Fourth generation evaluation*. SAGE.

Harste, J. C., Short, K. G., & Burke, C. L. (1988). *Creating classrooms for authors: The reading-writing connection*. Heinemann.

Johnston, P. H. (2004). *Choice words: How our language affects children's learning*. Stenhouse.

Lather, P. (1986). Research as praxis. *Harvard Educational Review, 56*(3), 257–277.

Murphy, K. P., Greene, J. A., Firetto, C. M., Hendrick, B. D., Mengyi, L., & Montalbano, C. (2018). Quality talk: Developing students' discourse to promote high-level comprehension. *American Educational Research Journal, 55*(5), 1113–1160. doi: 10.3102/0002831218771303

Reznitskaya, A., & Wilkinson, I. A. G. (2018). Truth matters: Teaching young students to search for the most reasonable answer. *Phi Delta Kappan, 99*(4), 33–38.

Sheehy, M. (2002). Illuminating constructivism: Structure, discourse, and subjectivity in a middle school classroom. *Reading Research Quarterly, 37*(3), 278–308. onlinelibrary .wiley.com/doi/10.1002/rrq.131/epdf

Short, K. G., Harste, J. C., & Burke, C. L. (1996). *Creating classrooms for authors and inquirers* (2nd ed.). Heinemann.

Tierney, R. J., Carter, M. A., & Desai, L. E. (1991). *Portfolio assessment in the reading-writing classroom*. Christopher-Gordon Publishers.

Tierney, R. J., & Clark, C. (with L. Fenner, R. J. Herter, C. Staunton Simpson, & B. Wiser). (1998). Portfolios: Assumptions, tensions, and possibilities. *Reading Research Quarterly, 33*(4), 474–486.

Tierney, R. J., & Readence, J. E. (2005). *Reading strategies and practices: A compendium* (6th ed.). Pearson.

Wilkinson, I. A. G., Soter, A. O., & Murphy, P. K. (2010). Developing a model of quality talk about literary text. In M. G. McKeown & L. Kucan (Eds.), *Bringing reading research to life* (pp. 142–169). Guilford.

8.2   THE WAVE OF NEW ASSESSMENT PARADIGMS

In characterizing the self-assessing reader, we have painted an idealistic portrait of the relationship between students and the assessments to which they hold themselves to account. Alas, the reality of the relationship between the assessments we have and the "assessed" paints a more dismal portrait, one in which students' lives and well-being are often held hostage by the assessments we use to gauge the progress of individuals and groups.

The assessment of reading and literacy performance has been regarded as a key proxy for judging advances and improvements in education. Those who have aspired to make education a science have viewed reading achievement as a highly valued and readily measurable outcome that can be indexed by simple observable behaviors such as oral reading accuracy and fluency or scores on a multiple-choice test of passage comprehension (Pearson & Hamm, 2005; Resnick & Resnick, 1988, 1992). These yielded scores by which readers and schooling could be compared for purposes of policy considerations, research, or educational planning.

Over time, since their appearance around the time of World War I, tests have assumed more and more prominence. Testing became integral to making educational policy decisions as well as being used as an aid to instructional decisionmaking by teachers, administrators, and the public at large. Tests were used by universities for admissions screenings—at some times in an effort to limit and discriminate against certain students, and at others prompted by ideals associated with meritocracy (Lemann, 1999; Willis, 2008). By World War II, tests were being used extensively to assess the preparedness of recruits for various posts. And after World War II, in the era of the space race, the media often looked to test results to assay the success or failure of schooling in terms of alleged shifts in performance. In a number of ways, tests became the gatekeepers for societies and in turn had a major impact on schooling. For many students and societies, tests served as paths to opportunities; for others, as screening filters to track, label, or prescribe. Tests do provide for the assessment of groups and the differential assessment of individuals, but the results of tests can also be used as gatekeepers. As the stakes, both for schools and for individuals, became higher and higher, tests became a determinants of what was taught and emphasized—a kind of default curriculum.

Standards for validity, reliability, fairness, and utility are intended to guide test construction and use. Notions of validity (content, construct, concurrence, predictability, and consequence) are tied to concerns about (1) whether an assessment represents the *content* (topics, processes, skills, strategies, and outcomes) of what should be measured; (2) whether the test correlates well with other assessments of the construct (that is *concurrent*) or is a good *predictor* of performance on some future criterion (e.g., alphabet knowledge at kindergarten level predicting reading achievement at the end of grade 2); and (3) whether the tests themselves and the results have *consequences* that are beneficial or problematic to those who are being assessed. Checks on the reliability of assessment instruments (test-retest, intra-test reliability) are enlisted to check on issues of consistency and the power of the tests to offer stable measures of differences among groups or individuals. In particular, test-retest reliability addresses whether performance on a test would be relatively consistent if the test were readministered; internal consistency reliability assesses whether items measure a given construct consistently. Depending on the test's degree of reliability, it might be reasonable for group use or have sufficient precision to offer safe judgments about or between individuals.

In terms of matters of interpretation, assessments are often calibrated against normative data for students from appropriate comparison groups, such as similar ages, and the skills and abilities represented by their performance on the test (e.g., the strengths, weaknesses, mastery, or other measures of performance). And, as test use has increased and tests themselves have been streamlined, responses digitized, and scoring increasingly automated, the results are available expeditiously— sometimes almost immediately.

Reading tests have almost become a genre unto themselves with features similar to one another. Reading comprehension measures are based predominantly on a reader's responses to questions after reading a paragraph or extended text; oral reading accuracy is still based on a form of read-aloud of selected passages of increasing difficulty. Changes occurred with the addition of a few dimensions informed by research and some shifts in the reading curriculum implemented in schools. For example, with vocabulary emerging as a key predictor of reading comprehension (and appearing seemingly easy to assess), vocabulary subtests became an addition to most reading assessments. In the 1930s, with the advent of the notion of reading readiness coupled with observational studies of reading development, assessments of young students expanded to include measures deemed to be predictors of early reading, such as visual and auditory discrimination and letter name knowledge.

Also commonplace were forms of testing that dovetailed with developments in readability, as well as views of reading progression aligned with a linear demarcation of the difficulty level assigned to reading material. The introduction of readability formulae fueled the view that the difficulty level of reading material could be reduced to a formula, based on assessment of the vocabulary that was used and the complexity of sentences (usually measured by length). Once reading material was assessed as corresponding to certain grade levels, educators developed procedures to place and track the development of readers. Among the most common was a subjective evaluation of reading comprehension and oral reading labeled as the Informal Reading Inventory. The key criteria for placement dated back to what was referred to as a five-finger rule, where placement in reading material was deemed to correspond to 95% oral reading accuracy (i.e., only five errors in a 100-word selection) and 75% comprehension accuracy. Nowadays the practice continues in variations of this same form of leveling and assessment. For example, in programs such as Reading Recovery, running records are used repeatedly to assess the progress and decide on the advancement of the students to more difficult reading material.

Consistent with the interest in readability, the cloze technique (with ties to journalism) became widely enlisted as a way to judge comprehension (Taylor, 1953). As the name implies, the cloze procedure required the reader to complete passages—usually a few hundred words in length—where words were deleted systematically throughout the passage (typically, every fifth word was deleted, with the first and last sentence left intact). On the assumption that the reader's accuracy to complete the passage corresponded with the reader's comfort in reading the material, it was then discerned whether or not the material was within the comfort zone or beyond the reach of the student. While systematic studies of cloze suggested that it was not without flaws, it became widely used as a quick guide for checking on whether a passage was at a suitable level for a reader (e.g., Shanahan et al., 1982).

The massive growth of various forms of tests of reading or reading-related skills, as well as protocols for testing, contributed to extensive reviews of the available tests and their properties. Indeed, ongoing testing became integral to the curriculum developments of the 1960s and early 1970s, in part as a systems approach was increasingly enlisted to monitor students' mastery of what were deemed the skills of reading. This included what is regarded as a criterion-based approach, in line with systems analyses.

Nowadays, various forms of tests are available in most curricula or as distinct tests for particular needs. The quantity and variety of tests are overwhelming; reviews of thousands of published educational tests are compiled in various volumes of the Buros Yearbook (published by The Buros Center for Testing, a nonprofit located at the University of Nebraska–Lincoln). Tests to measure reading performance still proliferate, especially because of ongoing government mandates tied to accountability. There remain periodically reviews of tests conducted by literacy educators (e.g., such as that advanced by Roger Farr), and testing has been the subject of critical reviews in most major reference works in literacy. This is especially evident in selected books or articles focused on different forms of evaluation, including comprehension assessment (Johnston, 1983), portfolio assessment (e.g., Tierney et al., 1998), or major syntheses critiquing and tracing the history of reading assessments and their relationships to learning and policy (Johnston, 1984; Calfee & Hiebert, 1991; Valencia & Wixson, 2000).

A map of the terrain of testing is now therefore quite multifaceted and somewhat multidirectional as a number of different assessment pathways are pursued. These include forms of (1) external testing for the following goals:

- Large-scale standardized or comparative assessments to monitor educational progress on the international, national, state, and regional level over time and across jurisdictions and populations, for example, countries, states, cities, rural areas, ethnicities, language groups, gender, and backgrounds (e.g., Global, PISA; United States, The National Assessment of Educational Progress-NAEP);

- Admissions testing and minimal standards testing for purposes of judging qualifications tied to tracking, acceptance, promotion, and graduations (e.g., Graduate Records Examination; TESOL, SAT);
- Screening devices for special services, such as special needs (e.g., Woodcock, ITPA);
- Periodic assessments of schools, teachers, classrooms, and students to meet the demand for local accountability tied to expectations for progress;

and (2) internal (to the classroom and school) testing for purposes of:

- Teacher assessments of students to guide instruction, including:
  - » Criterion-based measures tied to a prescribed set of skills aligned with what has become labeled RTI (Response to Instruction)
  - » Periodic informal assessments of the student's overall reading ability, including the level of reading and a profile of developments derived from a mix of ongoing teacher observations, checks, rubrics, and so on that might be related to school work and assessments emanating from running records (tied to occasional checks on reading accuracy, understandings, and strategies)
- Student-based assessments, directed at helping students deliberate on their own efforts, processes, pursuits, and achievements tied to projects, portfolios, and rubric discussions.

Some Critical Perspectives on Reading Assessments

Testing became a dimension of society that in many countries, such as China, overshadowed what was being emphasized in schools. It has been a major part of the landscape of education and has remained so despite some efforts to shift the forms and uses of tests as well as the epistemologies that undergird them. The use of testing should not be considered uncritically. Historically, assessments claim to advance meritocracy; in reality they may have served nefarious purposes. Indeed, reading assignments were used as a means of screening persons for positions and their eligibility to vote, or to define their eligibility to access opportunities both economic and social. Indeed, the entrance examinations for universities were initially intended to serve as a means of excluding certain groups or exerting social privilege and class control of education. In the interest of uniformity, tests have served as ways to impose cultural norms on others in ways that have displaced cultural ways of knowing.

While tests were claimed to be fair, they were not constructed to measure the diverse literacies of test takers, treating the need to represent the diversity within a population as secondary to the uniformity of standardization of tasks, scoring

It is troubling that many large-scale tests seem to be developed with assumptions that are not in line with the complex nature of reading or the diversity of our school populations. Particularly troubling is that they can use test discrimination coefficients to weed out items without regard for relevance or diversity.

Of course, one can ignore these complexities and be content that the tests used are an acceptable proxy for real reading, or present a reasonable approximation of real reading. Yet if the goal is to achieve a more valid measure of the construct in question, then we must decide whether the superior criterion is a correlation with another standardized measure of reading or a more direct measure of reading in the real world. In short, do we want criterion related validity or ecological validity to govern our evaluation of a test?

procedures, and interpretation. Most standardized tests had an inherent bias as a result of their efforts to ensure uniformity—a bias to mainstream communities. In particular, those involved in major test development have tended to exclude passages or items where student responses vary. Unfortunately, in the interest of aggregating scores and pursing matrix sampling, a passage may be excluded if students' performances seem erratic (despite being perhaps consistent with their background knowledge). In reality, readers will perform quite differently from one text to another, depending on the relevance to them of what they are reading. Depending on the topics chosen, any one person or group may be advantaged over another. Yet often test makers proceed almost with sleight of hand as they fit tests into their psychometric models—with pre-set biases to the view that reading ability should be homogenous rather than varied (see box).

Looked at historically, tests quickly became entrenched in what was measured, how, when, and why. It is as if they became "the tail that wagged the dog," as curricula became tied to the test and not the reverse. Despite calls to update curricula, the test dictated the path forward. Indeed, calls for revolutionary changes in curriculum were usually nullified as a result of the testing traditions that had taken hold—especially if the tests were high-stakes (e.g., tied to graduation or access to educational opportunities such as university entrance). Teachers and students, in turn, would invest time in learning for the test. What was taught was aligned with what and how reading was tested—typically in the format of multiple-choice responses to short passages.

For example, take the forms of reading that constitute many national and international tests and most standardized tests. Tests are mostly built on a sampling of texts that may or may not match the test takers' experiences or pursuits. Multiple-choice items measure a person's response to having to make a choice in accordance with the setup of the questions and the presented options from which they must choose. If tests employ questions with open-ended responses, how the questions are asked and support a response will have an influence on what a test taker provides. In tests with retellings or recall, there are differences in how comfortable readers feel when asked to freely retell the text and different degrees of responsiveness to further probes. A test's measure of reading is more a measure of what and how the test is measuring.

Indeed, if you compare reading and writing in the real world with reading and writing in the test world, there are many differences:

- Whereas in the real world, individuals encounter a wide range of materials enlisted for a range of purposes that have variable relevance, most tests are limited to a small subset of passages.
- Whereas in the real world, individuals live in the media as they engage in array of connected digital texts and environments (e.g., emails, text messages, the Internet, social networks, etc.), tests tend to use print forms or represent online copies in print forms.
- Whereas in their real worlds, individuals are engaged in texts connected to their worlds—that is, those that are culturally rich and apt to vary by gender, age, and culture—traditional testing vies to be culturally free (that is, homogenized and standardized).
- Whereas in the real world, reading is often pursued with others—in a fashion that is collaborative—tests involve reading by oneself.
- Whereas in the real world there is more acceptance and recognition of different interpretations and views of texts, in tested reading there is an assumption of correct responses only.
- Whereas in the real world reading may involve various forms of extended, incidental, and impromptu reading events integrated into ongoing literacy engagements, tests involve a limited form of reading—one that is scheduled and often laden with time constraints. Similarly, whereas real reading involves a range of purposes, from incidental to emerging to relevant, tests prescribe reading purposes.
- Whereas in the real world, we approach texts with different intentions, intensities, and approaches (tied to access and uses, including ongoing inquiry, keeping us up-to-date, or satisfying our own indulgences), tests involve responding to selected, pre-set test formats to be responded to under formalized test conditions and durations, and with the most common purpose being to answer the questions on the test.
- Whereas in the real world, our engagement with texts is more likely to represent a mixture of communications with others (i.e., ongoing projects, articles of interest, memos, emails, text messages, and web searches—akin to a messy desktop with numerous files, images, tags, and invitations for comments or feedback), our test engagements represent a restricted array of material and probes with limited connections to our lives.

- Whereas our reading in the real world is tied to our actual pursuits, tests are tied to attempts to yield scores that might predict real world reading.

The nature of reading development adds to these complexities. Test makers and curriculum developers perpetuate a false illusion that there is a set sequence to reading development, that a single score can be ascribed to the stage of a reader's development. But learning does not progress in a way that is unidimensional or linear. Development profiles of readers may be "shoe-horned" to fit a pre-set, simplified scoring system, but a truer representation would be multifaceted, multidimensional, and varied in accordance with differences among readers. If you consider your own reading development, you would probably describe your reading performance as varied—for instance as dependent on whether your reading was in areas in which you have expertise or experience or in areas in which you are less informed. Your literacy is somewhat unique, not as uniform as what and how it is apt to be measured. You may read a lot of political discussions, especially those pertaining to foreign relations or to certain politicians who intrigue you. Your reading may be tied to certain authors or to topics from sports to human interest to self-help matters. If you were to be profiled, your profile would be somewhat unique and likely to change over time. It would look different when compared with the profiles and developments of others and would not follow a prescribed sequence (see box).

> We should therefore be careful not to overgeneralize the merits of using piecemeal, step-by-step learning progressions, which might better fit the learning of a narrow set of skills and understandings (e.g., learning how to construct a PowerPoint or do certain mathematical processes). Some of our colleagues would suggest that over time we may have the research that would enable us to generate a development trajectory for which we could confidently predict individual reading outcomes and development (e.g., Shepard et al., 2009). But too often educators turn tests into instructional regimens, wherein test specifications (especially those descriptions of the characteristics or signs of reading development that undergird test designs) become blueprints for the curriculum that might well be designed to prepare students to succeed on that test.

Stepping Back

So, what are the ramifications of measuring reading?

- The reality of reading is that if your goal is to attain a true measure, your approach needs to be robust and diverse in order to match the diverse nature of meaning making across readers and circumstances for reading.

- Your measures should allow for variability across readers and acknowledge the fallibilities of tests.
- If you wish to examine growth in reading development over time, you need to capture rather than distort the complexity of construct.

Why might you choose to accept the current testing regimen?

- Tests in their present form are accepted, respected, and expected in society.
- Test developers are seeking more straightforward forms of comparison and means of aggregating individual and group performances.
- Tests are viewed as adequate proxies for more complex profiles.
- Test scores can be easily normalized and are useful for educational decisionmaking and, over time, for student learning (e.g., as checks on responses to teaching).
- You can use broad enough developmental categories and adopt statistical procedures (e.g., Item Response Theory, IRT, tied to unidimensional modeling assumptions) to force-fit or selectively pull together a set of items to conform to such a model.
- Summative test results provide help to policymakers as they make decisions.

Why might you contest the dominant regimen of most tests?

- Tests may sample texts, but their sampling represents a limited array of the types of texts encountered in the real world.
- Tests represent an interrogation of readers that is a step removed from reading in the real world.
- Tests may stagnate and narrow the curriculum, both for individuals and groups.
- Test scores are not a proxy, nor are the scores useful for educational decisionmaking or student learning, as they do not adequately represent reading in the real world.
- Summative test results may not help teachers teach and students learn.
- Test scores are tied to notions of reading development and ability as unidimensional when reading ability is decidedly multidimensional.
- Tests often marginalize minorities in what and how they test, sometimes even keeping individuals and groups invisible as tests are developed and results are reported.

Most tests may give the illusion that they are measuring reading, but they may just be measuring what is tested. Unfortunately, the illusion may be supported when we teach to the test, a practice that can sometimes drive pedagogy and curriculum to its lowest common denominator. Tests seen as representative of a form of aberrant reading, when elevated in status, do lead to a coercive and potentially erosive influence on reading development. Indeed, a test should be viewed systematically; it should measure up to ethical standards tied to judicial decisionmaking and responsive evaluation (Guba & Lincoln, 1989; Lather, 1986; Moss, 1996) in terms of its design but also in terms of how it is used. Developers and consumers of tests should view as integral to their use a consideration of the consequential validity of their measures—including the impact of tests on students, teachers, parents, communities, and society *Stephens, 1995). As Kris Gutiérrez (2004) has argued, incidences of teaching to the test involve

> a set of complex issues that defines schooling for so many students today. . . . It is an account of the consequences of narrow views of literacy and how a teacher's understanding of literacy is complicated and constrained by a mandated school curriculum that was conceptualized and implemented independently of the knowledge and practices of its students. It is an account of the ways we understand competence across racial, ethnic and class lines. It is an account of the consequences of the ways we measure what counts as literacy, especially if we only see it in snapshots in discrete moments in time disconnected from the laminated, multimodal reality of literacy activity. (p. 102)

Making Progress by Changing the Underlying Tenets of Assessment

As constructivist and sociocultural models of literacy grew in prominence and critical perspectives achieved traction, a number of educators in the 1980s and 1990s turned their attention to the nature and role of assessment. Examined from the perspectives of policy personnel, teachers, and learners, questions were asked about how well assessments served the needs of teachers and learners in all their diversity at the classroom level (see box). Likewise, literacy educators recognized that literacy assessments were dated and did not match how literacy was currently viewed in terms of the tenets of constructivist research or the growing emphasis of teachers as professionals and students as strategic learners (e.g., Valencia & Pearson, 1987). These criticisms included (1) concern that multiple-choice tests or other forms of "closed" assessments did not align with constructivist tenets; (2) the emphasis on tests was detracting from efforts to

As the U.S. Congressional Office of Technology Assessment (1992) stated in the summary of a report, "Testing in American Schools: Asking the Right Questions," "The move toward new methods of testing has been motivated by new understandings of how students learn as well as changing views of curriculum" (p. 16). They argued for forms of performance-based assessment that better fit with learning that was relevant and meaningful, intending for tests themselves to serve educative as well as evaluative functions.

advance classroom practices; and (3) if classroom practices advanced, they would not match with testing practices.

In response, education witnessed a surge in what was termed "authentic assessment" practices, including a range of tools to support their use. Project-based learning assignments with assessment components proliferated. These were accompanied by a range of teacher adjuncts, such as the use of dynamic forms of record keeping including anecdotal records (Barr et al., 1988), running records (Clay, 1993), and retellings (Irwin & Mitchell, 1983; Morrow, 1988). Also notable was the rise in the use of portfolios among educators.

These new approaches represented a form of engagement with students that dovetailed with classroom pursuits, especially forms of project-based learning. They correlated with the increased emphasis on reading–writing connections and student-based conferencing with student self-assessment. A number of educators saw the advantages of such measures over other modes of assessment, especially in terms of better representing student literacy development and processes in more complex ways than scoring systems did. Studies suggested that parents were also more apt to prefer these approaches as better representing a student's learning (e.g., Shepherd & Bleim, 1995). Studies comparing forms of performance assessment with traditional measures suggest that changes in learning are more apt to be captured by such assessments (see Shavelson et al., 1992; Tierney et al., 1998).

The Reform Movement Agenda and Setback

Despite the momentum of these developments in the 1990s, traditional approaches to assessment regained their prominence with the rise in accountability tied to school reform efforts. These were anchored in large-scale assessments within and across countries for students, schools, and populations. Indeed, policymakers seemed intent on using reports from traditional assessments to judge and plan educational progress, providing report cards of progress based on measurable outputs rather than on more diverse qualitative considerations, including inputs. Sociocultural considerations have had a tendency to be sidelined or displaced by reports of the performances of different groups by race, gender, and location. In reality, these reports, which herald, applaud, or deplore the performance of different groups, seem to ignore some of the history of testing—especially its use to exclude as well as its inherent bias tied to the erroneous notion that such tests are and should be culture-free (see box).

Tests have a history that seems almost chameleon in nature—claiming to be something other than what they are but constrained by the framework from which they are derived. Certainly, the history of reading suggests that the testing of reading has been limited to the tenets of what was observable and score-able; hence, simple additive dimensions—such as the accuracy of responses to questions or vocabulary assessment—were adopted to measure ability rather than more complex and idiosyncratic engagement. Reading tests have a history of using summative scores of ability or target scores for mastery that are quite contrived. Unfortunately, they often dictate decision-making, as if they were more trustworthy and less limited or restricted than they are. And, unfortunately, this seems to have been advanced with the marriage of test scores to standards and curriculum, as endeavors such as Response to Intervention (RTI) (Fuchs & Fuchs, 2006) and the widespread use of tests such as DIBELS (Good et al., 2001; Riedel & Samuels, 2007) have been viewed as positive, without being questioned (Goodman, 2006).

In Closing

As a number of scholars of assessment[1] and others have suggested, test developers and users should be held to standards related to a test's validity and reliability, but also to ethics—considering a test's consequences, including the social and educational ramifications (e.g., Calfee & Hiebert, 1991; Johnston, 1984). As Bruner (1990) argued, we should be "conscious of how we come to our knowledge and as conscious as we can be about the values that lead us to our perspectives. It asks us to be accountable for how and what we know" (p. 30). Examined historically, testing has had a questionable history. Literacy assessments especially have a history of playing a role in society that may be considered nefarious (Ellwein et al., 1988; Haney, 1993; Nichols & Berliner, 2007; Willis, 2008). Quite deliberately, literacy tests have excluded individuals and groups (i.e., in terms of access to voting, education, or other rights). Indeed, under the guise of being reliable and fair tests for all, tests often reflect a questionable alignment that advantages some over others. If they assume or are given a high-stakes status, there is a danger of their being extremely harmful. As Campbell (1979) stated, "The more any quantitative social indicator is used for social decision-making, the more subject it will be to corruption pressures and the more apt it will be to distort and corrupt the social processes it is intended to monitor" (p. 85).

Yet many have argued that the solution lies with improved forms of testing, and in recent years we have seen some inroads again. In an effort to pursue major improvements in the assessment of reading comprehension, the National Academy of Education released an expanded discussion of *Reading for Understanding* (*RfU*) that included a lengthy critique of reading comprehension assessment and the pursuit of what they suggested were "forward-thinking assessments that not

For example, some of the current U.S. national assessments provide pull-down, digitally based menus, the results of which can be examined according to the ethnic makeup and location of test takers. However, these sites have failed to include items that are responsive to the literacies of different groups as well as those that are up to date with the media world we inhabit. Test developers seem to have had an appetite to apply advances in technology to test reporting but have not as yet embraced these technologies as a means of supporting different, more representative sampling across various groups.

only meet the standards of educational and psychological testing, but also promise to advance both research and practice in reading comprehension for years to come (Pearson et al., 2020, p. 255). Among those assessments touted in the RfU report was what has been identified as *scenario-based assessment*, incorporating a project-based frame suited to a more realistic form of reading comprehension assessment. In concert with a shift to what is learned rather than comprehended, this enlists project-based stimuli and forms of outcomes befitting the learning goals (O'Reilly et al., 2018; O'Reilly et al., 2014; Sabatini et al., 2014a, 2014b; Sabatini et al., 2016; Sabatini et al., 2019).

Consistent with the sentiment for a new framework to guide literacy assessments, the U.S. design team for the 2025 National Assessment of Educational Progress in Reading (NAEP) has also shifted to a form of testing that is more governed by sociocultural tenets. As the design team suggests, the key components of the (ref.: sociocultural) "model—reader, text, and activity—are situated in both highly specific contexts, such as classrooms, homes, or digital spaces, and more general contexts, like communities, social networks, and nations" (NAEP, 2020, p. 19). They do so by investing in an approach to passage and task selection that is more representative of the diversity of texts and situations experienced in the real world. Enlisting a form of scenario-based testing, assessments are scaffolded (including with avatars) in an effort to mimic "real world reading." As they state:

> The most fundamental principle of the sociocultural model of reading is that, as a human meaning-making activity, reading is always situated in social and cultural contexts that shape every aspect of readers' engagement with text and influence how readers respond to and learn from the experience of reading. (p. 28)

To this end, the NAEP team is pursuing an emphasis focused on simulating situated or contextualized literacy tasks. As the team states:

> This emphasis on contextualization is present from the moment readers begin the NAEP 2025 assessment. For example, at the outset of an assessment activity, readers will be introduced to what will be called an activity structure. That introduction will specify a simulated context for traversing an entire 30 minute block, including:
> - A simulated social setting (a community setting or a classroom and perhaps some avatar classmates and even a teacher) and an explicit role for the reader
> - A purpose for engaging in the entire activity (an activity-specific instantiation of one of the two overarching Purposes (Reading to Develop Understanding or Reading to Solve Problems)
> - The disciplinary Context in which the activity is situated (Literary Context, Science Context, or Social Studies Context) (p. 29)

The pursuit of such a shift represents a major development consistent with the advances in literacy. The effort to simulate is admirable but immensely challenging, especially if outcomes are to be reported in a fashion befitting the tenets of the effort. However, the question left unanswered is whether these new assessments approach what might be considered a truer form of reading and whether their measures of different readers' performances offer representations of performance reflecting the diversity and the situatedness of literacy that they tout. In other words, replacing old tests with new tests may give the impression that change is afoot but may simply be putting old wine into new bottles.

Some would argue that to address the problems with testing, a different epistemological approach may be needed (e.g., Moss, 1996). For example, in concert with constructivist and critical research tenets, assessment would be done in a fashion that is participatory, collaborative, formative, and learner-driven. To these ends, the 1990s witnessed the rise of an orientation to assessment that involved engaging students and teachers in forms of authentic assessment, including the use of portfolios. This orientation had certain key tenets:

- Assessment should support innovative teaching and the engagement of students in strategic learning, using a range of texts for different purposes.
- Assessments should be made from the inside out, following from what students and teachers do rather than what the test imposes (i.e., from the outside in). In other words, assessments should keep up with teaching and learning, not derail it.
- Integral to any assessment should be learning to assess oneself.

Essentially, collaborative and participatory forms of assessment such as portfolios are premised on assessment practices being intertwined with teacher and student learning and decisionmaking in the classrooms or across classrooms.

In terms of benefits, these learner-based forms of assessment assumed that educators and learners would be better informed when assessments considered multiple sources of data and were done so in a collaborative, judicial, responsive, and reflexive fashion. They assumed that teachers and students have a collective understanding of achievements and progress, without the need for rigid forms of scoring and aggregation (i.e., measures derived from periodical assessments removed from the everyday). They assumed that notions of reliability can be strengthened by the verifiable nature of the evidence and grounded assumptions that could be used to generate claims. They assumed that classroom and learner-based assessments such as portfolios fit within a cultural ecological orientation that builds on, recognizes, and values local and diverse resources and knowledges. Accordingly, they also assumed that they might bridge with, respect, and credit the diverse cultural capital of communities.

Perhaps we will see a reckoning if the current resurgent interest in shifting to a sociocultural frame prevails. We might even see the emergence of assessments that traffic less in efficiencies and more in the diversity of our literacies and our students. But we must also consider the possibility that this new wave of reform, like its predecessors, will be rebuffed by the stubborn durability of the narrowly defined and deployed standardized test (see box).

Our engagements in assessment have been threefold. First, as literacy educators with an interest in how we comprehend or make meanings, we have been engaged in attempts to enlist state-of-the-art assessment techniques to study literacy, hoping to unlock the nature of meaning making and its development. Our goal has been to enlist a range of assessment tools to study reading and writing precisely, reliably, and ethically. Second, we have been keen to examine the role of testing in schools and society— especially with regard to how testing practices might be enlisted by various stakeholders to make decisions. We have examined the influences and rhetoric surrounding the growth of test-driven curricula, and we have been involved in studies of popular tests (e.g., intelligence tests; screening tests for learning disabilities; various placement tests of reading levels; and testing procedures enlisted in judicial systems, including the interrogation of language minorities) as well as in studies of tools for reading comprehension assessment and the characteristics of large-scale assessments. Third, we have been involved in helping design national and international assessments of literacy such as PISA and NAEP. Most recently, David has chaired NAEP-Reading Development Panel to guide the plans for NAEP beginning in 2026.

As such, we have been keen to study assessment's role in terms of spurring positive, generative, organic, and culturally responsive changes, via forms of evaluation, that empower teachers, students, and caregivers—perhaps even interrupt and challenge testing's historical roots. Moving forward, we would like to pursue a course that is more culturally oriented and hence more truly individually oriented. Perhaps we can step outside of the box, advance alternatives, and engage in building more credible forms of assessment for all.

References

Afflerbach, P. (2005). High stakes testing and reading assessment. *Journal of Literacy Research, 37*(2), 151–162.

Barr, M., Ellis, H., Hester, H., & Thomas, A. (1988). *The primary language record.* Heinemann.

Bruner, J. S. (1990). *Acts of meaning.* Harvard University Press.

Calfee, R., & Hiebert, E. (1991). Classroom assessment in reading. In R. Barr, M. L. Kamil, P. Mosenthal, & P. D. Pearson (Eds.), *Handbook of reading research* (Vol. 2, pp. 280–309). Longman.

Campbell, D. T. (1979). Assessing the impact of planned social change. *Evaluation and Program Planning, 2*(1), 67–90. doi: 10.1016/0149-7189(79)90048-X

Clay, M. (1993). *An observation survey of early literacy achievement.* Heinemann.

Cunningham, J., & Tierney, R. J. (1979). Evaluating cloze as a measure of cognitive change due to reading. *Journal of Reading Behavior, 11*, 287–292.

Ellwein, M. C., Glass, G. V., & Smith, M. L. (1988). Standards of competence: Propositions on the nature of testing reforms. *Educational Researcher, 17*(8), 4–9.

Farr, R., & Carey, R. (1986). *Reading: What can be measured* (2nd ed.). International Reading Association.

Fuchs, D., & Fuchs, L. S. (2006). Introduction to response to intervention: What, why, and how valid is it? *Reading Research Quarterly, 41*(1), 93–99. doi: 10.1598/RRQ.41.1.4

Good, R. H. III, Kaminski, R. A., Simmons, D., & Kame'enui, E. J. (2001). Using dynamic indicators of basic early literacy skills (DIBELS) in an outcomes-driven model: Steps to reading outcomes. *Oregon School Study Council (OSSC) Bulletin, 44*(1), 1–24. files .eric.ed.gov/fulltext/ED453526.pdf

Goodman, K. S. (Ed.). (2006). *The truth about DIBELS: What it is, what it does*. Heinemann.

Gould, S. J. (1981). *The mismeasure of man*. W. W. Norton.

Guba, E. G., & Lincoln, Y. S. (1989). *Fourth generation evaluation*. SAGE.

Gutiérrez, K. (2004). Literacy as laminated activity: Rethinking literacy for English learners. In J. Worthy, B. Maloch, J. V. Hoffman, D. L. Schallert, & C. M. Fairbanks (Eds.), *53rd yearbook of the National Reading Conference* (pp. 101–114). National Reading Conference.

Haney, W. (1993). Testing and minorities. In L. Weis and M. Fine (Eds.), *Beyond silenced voices* (pp. 45–74). SUNY.

Irwin, P. A., & Mitchell, J. N. (1983). A procedure for assessing the richness of retellings. *Journal of Reading, 26*, 391–396.

Johnston, P. (1984). Assessment in reading. In P. D. Pearson, R. Barr, M. Kamil, & P. Mosenthal (Eds.), *Handbook of research in reading* (pp. 147–182). Longman.

Johnston, P. (1997). *Knowing literacy: Constructive literacy assessment*. Stenhouse.

Lather, P. (1986). Research as praxis. *Harvard Educational Review, 56*(3), 257–278. doi: 10.17763/haer.56.3.bj2h231877069482

Lemann, N. (1999). *The big test: The secret history of American meritocracy*. Farrar, Straus & Giroux.

Morrow, L. M. (1988). Retelling stories as a diagnostic tool. In S. M. Glazwer, J. W. Searfoss, & L. M. Gentile (Eds.), *Reexamining reading diagnosis: New trends and practices* (pp. 128–149). International Reading Association.

Moss, P. (1996). Enlarging the dialogue in educational measurement: Voices from interpretive research traditions. *Educational Researcher, 25*(1), 20–28.

National Assessment Governing Board. (2020). Reading Framework for the 2025 National Assessment of Educational Progress. U.S. Department of Education. Accessed July 20, 2020, www.naepframeworkupdate.org

Nichols, S. N., & Berliner, D. C. (2007). *Collateral damage: The effects of high-stakes testing on America's schools*. Harvard Education Press.

O'Reilly, T., Sabatini, J., & Wang, Z. (2018). Using scenario-based assessments to measure deep learning. In K. Millis, D. Long, J. Magliano, & K. Weimer (Eds.), *Deep comprehension: Multi-disciplinary approaches to understanding, enhancing, and measuring comprehension* (pp. 197–208). Routledge.

O'Reilly, T., Weeks, J., Sabatini, J., Halderman, L., & Steinberg, J. (2014). Designing reading comprehension assessments for reading interventions: How a theoretically motivated assessment can serve as an outcome measure. *Educational Psychology Review, 26*, 403–424. doi: 10.1007/s10648-014-9269-z

Pearson, P. D., Palincsar, A. S., Biancarosa, G., & Berman, A. (Eds). (2020). *Reaping the rewards of the Reading for Understanding Initiative*. Washington, DC: National Academy of Education. naeducation.org/wp-content/uploads/2020/07/NAEd-Reaping-the-Rewards-of-the-Reading-for-Understanding-Initiative.pdf

Peterson, J., Greenlaw, J. J., & Tierney, R. J. (1978). Assessing instructional placement with the I.R.I.: The effectiveness of comprehension questions. *Journal of Educational Research, 5*, 244–250.

Resnick, D. P., & Resnick, L. P. (1988, April). Understanding achievement and acting to produce it: Some recommendations for the NAEP. *Phi Delta Kappan, 69*(8), 576–579.

Resnick, L. B., & Resnick, D. P. (1992). Assessing the thinking curriculum: New tools for educational reform in changing assessments. In B. K. Gifford & M. C. O'Connor (Eds.), *Changing assessments: Alternative views of aptitude, achievement and instruction* (pp. 37–75). National Commission on Testing and Public Policy.

Riedel, B. W., & Samuels, S. J. (2007). The relation between DIBELS, reading comprehension, and vocabulary in urban first-grade students (with commentary). *Reading Research Quarterly, 42*(4), 546–567. doi: 10.1598/RRQ.42.4.5

Sabatini, J., O'Reilly, T., Weeks, J., & Steinberg, J. (2016, April). *The validity of scenario-based assessment: Empirical results.* Paper presented at the annual meeting of the National Council on Measurement in Education, Washington, D.C.

Sabatini, J., O'Reilly, T., Weeks, J., & Wang, Z. (2019). Engineering a 21st century reading comprehension assessment system utilizing scenario-based assessment techniques. *International Journal of Testing, 20*(4), 1–23. doi: 10.1080/15305058.2018.1551224

Sabatini, J. P., O'Reilly, T., Halderman, L. K., & Bruce, K. (2014a). Integrating scenario-based and component reading skill measures to understand the reading behavior of struggling readers. *Learning Disability Research & Practice, 29*(1), 36–43. doi: 10.1111/ldrp.12028

Sabatini, J. P., O'Reilly, T., Halderman, L., & Bruce, K. (2014b). Broadening the scope of reading comprehension using scenario-based assessments: Preliminary findings and challenges. *L'Année psychologique, 114*, 693–723.

Shanahan, T., Kamil, M., Tobin, A. (1982). Cloze as a measure of intersentential comprehension. *Reading Research Quarterly, 17*, 229–255.

Shavelson, R., Baxter, G. P., & Pine, J. (1992). Performance assessment: Political rhetoric and measurement reality. *Educational Researcher, 21*(4), 22–27.

Shepard, L., & Bliem, C. L. (1995). Parents' thinking about standardized tests and performance assessment. *Educational Researcher, 24*(8), 25–32.

Shepard, L., Hannaway, J., & Baker, E. (Eds.). (2009). *Standards, assessments, and accountability* (Education Policy White Paper). National Academy of Education, Working Group on Standards, Assessments, and Accountability. files.eric.ed.gov/fulltext/ED531138.pdf

Stephens, D., Pearson, P. D., Gilrane, C., Roe, M., Stallman, A. C., Shelton, J., Weinzierl, J., Rodriguez, A., & Commeyras, M. (1995). Assessment and decision-making in schools: A cross-site analysis. *Reading Research Quarterly,* 30 (3), 478–499.

Stowell, L. P., & Tierney, R. J. (1994). Portfolios in the classroom: What happens when teachers and students negotiate assessment? In R. Allington & S. Walmsley (Eds.), *No quick fix: Rethinking literacy lessons in America's elementary schools* (pp. 78–94). Teachers College Press.

Taylor, W. L. (1953). Cloze procedure: A new tool for measuring readability. *Journalism Quarterly, 30*, 415–453.

Teasdale, R., Tierney, R. J., Ames, W., & Wray, R. (1978). A cross-cultural comparison of item analysis data on the Revised ITPA. *Australian Psychologist, 3*, 391–399. www.tandfonline.com/doi/abs/10.1080/00050067808254328?journalCode= taps20

Tierney, R. J. (1998). Literacy assessment reform: Shifting beliefs, principled possibilities, and emerging practices. *The Reading Teacher, 51*(5), 374–390.

Tierney, R. J. (2009). Literacy education 2.0: Looking through the rear view mirror as we move ahead. In J. Hoffman & Y. Goodman (Eds.), *Changing literacies for changing times: An historical perspective on the future of reading research, public policy, and classroom practices* (pp. 282–300). Routledge.

Tierney, R. J., Carter, M., Desai, L. (1991). *Portfolio assessment in the reading writing classroom.* Norwood, MA: Christopher Gordon Publishers. independent.academia.edu/RobTierney/Books

Tierney, R. J., Clark, C., Fenner, L., Herter, R. J., Simpson, C. S., & Wiser, B. (1998). Portfolios: Assumptions, tensions, and possibilities. *Reading Research Quarterly, 33*(4), 474–486. doi: 10.1598/RRQ.33.4.6

Tierney, R. J., Crumpler, T., Bond, E., & Bertelsen, C. (2003). *Interactive assessment: Teachers, students and parents as partners.* Christopher Gordon Publishers. independent.academia.edu/RobTierney/Books

Tierney, R. J., & Thome, C. (2006). Is DIBELS leading us down the wrong path? In K. S. Goodman (Ed.), *The truth about DIBELS: What it is, what it does* (pp. 50–59). Heinemann.

Tierney, R. J., Wile, J. M., Moss, A. G., Reed, E. W., Ribar, J. P., & Zilversmit, A. (1993). *Portfolio evaluation as history: A report on the evaluation of the history academy for Ohio teachers* (Occasional Paper). National Council for History Education. files.eric.ed.gov/fulltext/ED371978.pdf

U.S. Congress Office of Technology Assessment. (1992). *Testing in American schools: Asking the right questions.* Congress of the United States, Office of Technology Assessment.

Valencia S. W., & Pearson, P. D. (1987). Reading assessment: A time for change. *The Reading Teacher, 40*, 726–732.

Valencia, S. W., & Wixson, K. (2000). Policy-oriented research on literacy standards and assessment. In M. L. Kamil, P. Mosenthal, R. Barr, & P. D. Pearson (Eds.), *Handbook of reading research* (Vol. 3, pp. 909–935). Longman.

Willis, A. (2008). *Reading comprehension research and testing in the U.S.: Undercurrents of race, class, and power in the struggle for meaning.* Erlbaum.

NOTE

1. Including Gordon Stanley, Lee Cronbach, Gene Glass, and more recently, David Berliner, Robert Linn, Lorrie Shepard, Ernest House, Pamela Moss, and Sean Reardon.

9   The Reform Wave

9.1   THE REGULATED READER

Over the last 25 years, readers have become increasingly regulated in terms of what they experience in their literacy learning. In various countries, we have seen a rise in government-inserted controls on what is taught and how. Further, to ensure compliance with mandates, schools are audited and students are tested on their mastery of pre-set, skill-based standards. The end result is that school efforts to build on and bridge from the diversity of students' lived experiences are displaced by those in favor of uniformity.

Reform efforts tied to testing and standards suggest a return to a form of criterion- and referenced-based teaching and testing, where literacy learning is more akin to coaching students to march in unison. Such orientations to education displace goals of innovation and adaptation and access and opportunity with set outcomes and accountability. They impose prescribed sets of skills and standards on learning and involve an ongoing monitoring of teachers and their students. Figure 9.1 outlines the stated purposes and key elements for standards-driven assessment advocated by the U.S. National Association of School Boards of Education (NASBE). The goals of literacy in such a framework become aligned with a predetermined set of skills and tests, displacing arrays of meaningful literacy engagements such as project-based learning and the integration of reading with writing.

The consequences of aligning literacy education with regulatory approaches can be grave. Indeed, our colleague Kris Gutiérrez (2004), in writing about her experiences with her own son after moving to Los Angeles, offers a cautionary tale.

> When my son, Scott, entered the second grade, he was a confident and fluent reader and writer. Several months after his entry to the school, I received an urgent call from his teacher requesting an immediate meeting with me. I sat nervously in his classroom trying to imagine what had prompted this urgency. I was concerned, as the school and its participants had had some difficulty adjusting to its first Latino (he is Chicano/African-American) to ever enroll in the school.
>
> Our meeting began. Leaning forward, her voice in a whisper as if not embarrass me, the teacher shared her concern that Scott might not make it through the second

Figure 9.1. Standards-Driven Assessment Principles, National Association of School Boards of Education (NASBE) Study Group

Purpose of assessments in relation to standards
- Assessments help ensure that standards are taken seriously.
- Standards and assessments guide teaching and learning.
- Assessments help individual students meet standards.
- Assessments help policymakers ensure that all students have access to a sound education.

Elements of effective assessment systems. An effective state assessment system:
- is aligned with rigorous state standards.
- addresses specific goals and purposes.
- balances validity, reliability, and efficiency.
- informs instruction and has consequences.
- has mechanisms to encourage schools and districts to align their instruction and evaluation with the state system.
- has a clearly articulated relationship with national measures of student performance.

Source: Claycomb & Kysilko, 2000

grade; he didn't know phonics. I was puzzled and relieved. After all, he excelled in reading, and his literacy skills were sophisticated for his age, a fact verified by their own standardized tests. It turned out that what he didn't know how to do (or more likely didn't want to do) were the sets of repetitive phonics exercises that he had been assigned for the past several weeks. . . . I asked how she would assess my son's ability to read and, without hesitation, she replied, "Oh he's probably the best reader in the class." (pp. 101–102)

Drawing from these observations, Kris Gutiérrez identified a number of concerns:

What is implicated in this very brief narrative is a set of complex issues that defines schooling for so many students today. . . . It is an account of the consequences of narrow views of literacy and how a teacher's understanding of literacy is complicated and constrained by mandated school curriculum that was conceptualized and implemented independent of the knowledge and practices of its students. It is an account of the ways that we understand the competence across racial, ethnic and class lines. It is an account of the consequences of the ways we measure what counts as literacy, especially, if we only see it in snapshots in discrete moments in time disconnected from the laminated, multimodal reality of literacy activity. And it is an account of how parents can mediate school policy and practices.

The challenges my son faced are all too common, but they are particularly so from non-dominant groups, especially English Learners. However, unlike so many poor and immigrant parents unfamiliar with the institutions of our country, I could mediate vigilantly and persistently, the effects of discrimination and of policies gone awry. I knew that I was the school's worse nightmare: I was more than a meddling, middle-class mother; I was a meddling, middle-class, Latina mother! This is no insignificant point; however, it is a point misunderstood (or not taken up) by policy makers. (p. 102)

The teacher's behavior in Kris Gutiérrez's description seems to fit with the lament of David Olson (2004) that teachers are being positioned less as professionals and more as persons to implement pre-set programs. In other words, pre-set programs, either explicitly or implicitly, define (or dictate) what counts for teachers and, in turn, for students. In terms of what counts for students, many scholars have noted how standardized and regulated approaches result in the marginalization and displacement of the knowledge, language, and culture of students from "nondominant groups" (Gutiérrez, 2004). For instance, as Gutiérrez (2008) observes elsewhere, in her paper "Developing a Sociocritical Literacy in the Third Space," standardized and scripted literacy frameworks—what she describes as "'marketplace reforms' . . . that bring the business principles of efficiency, accountability, quality, and choice to establish the education agenda" (p. 148)—deepen divides between home and school, exclude students from exploring more critical perspectives, and fail to provide students with opportunities to collectively and critically design new social futures. She goes on to note how "such reforms employ the 'sameness as fairness' principle, making it easier to roll back small gains in educational equity and implement the 'color blind' practices of English-only, one-size-fits-all curricula and policies and practices driven by high-stakes assessment" (Gutiérrez, 2008, p. 148; see also Crosland, 2004; Gutiérrez & Jaramillo, 2006).

Recently critical race theorists and postcolonial scholars have similarly described the inherent and entrenched forms of inequality perpetuated through literacy standards and assessments. For example, building on Au's (2009) argument that standardized tests are "mechanism[s] for the (re)production of socioeconomic and educational inequality" (Au, 2009, p. 140), Eve Tuck and Julie Gorlewski (2016) argue that "standardized examinations have a long, well-documented history of justifying and reproducing discrimination. Although cloaked in the guise of objectivity and swathed in the myth of meritocracy, high-stakes assessments are forms of racist ordering" (p. 201). By "re-instantiat[ing] fictions associated with race and achievement" (Tuck & Gorlewski, 2016, p. 207), rigid and regulated approaches to literacy disproportionately place certain students over others.

Arguably, the notion of a one-size-fits-all test or set of teaching materials may befit a model of literacy that discounts diversity and community-based, student-centered approaches that meaningfully connect with students' lives. Indeed, this regulated reader approach runs counter to findings of selected colleagues' observations of successful school programs. For example, in his book *Possible Lives*, Mike Rose (1995) suggests that meaningful teaching and instruction, as a dynamic, ongoing, and contingent process, cannot be standardized.

As one teaches, one's knowledge plays out in social space, and this is one of the things that make teaching such a complex activity. As studies of teaching cognition have

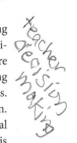

shown, and as we saw in the classrooms that we visited, teaching well means knowing one's students well and being able to read them quickly and, in turn, making decisions to slow down or speed up, to stay with a point or return to it later, to underscore certain connections, to use or forgo a particular illustration. This decision-making operates as much by feel as by reason; it involves hunch, intuition, at best, quick guess.

There is another dimension of the ability to make judgments about instruction. The teachers we observed operate with knowledge of individual students' lives, of local history and economy, and of social-cultural traditions and practices. They gain this knowledge in any number of ways: living in the communities in which they work; getting involved in local institutions and projects; drawing on personal and cultural histories that resemble the histories of the children they teach; educating themselves about the communities and cultures of the students before them; connecting with parents and involving parents in schooling; seeing students as resources and learning from them.

. . . This quality of reflective experimentation, of trying new things, of tinkering and adjusting, sometimes with uneven results, sometimes failing, was part of the history of many of the classrooms in *Possible Lives*. (pp. 419, 421)

Rather than education consisting of a cycle of testing, teaching, and inspection tied to external forces (a model of the regulated reader that pursues pre-set targets), reading and writing might be enlivened by a flow that connects to the students' worlds—their lived experiences, local ways of knowing, diverse literacies and interests.

In this age of reform, standards and testing have assumed more prominence. In turn, teaching practices have been realigned with testing, and reading and student learning have become increasingly regulated. We can illustrate how the orientation to pre-set testing often flies in the face of a diverse curriculum, teacher professionalism, and student-centered learning that is responsive to individual differences and needs. For example, tests such as Dynamic Indicators of Basic Early Literacy Skills (DIBELS) have become influential with their increased use throughout the United States. DIBELS was developed to screen, monitor, and assess outcomes of the elements extrapolated from the National Reading Panel (NRP, 2000) report. The test developers suggest that DIBELS can be used as a means of screening students to identify those who are at risk, to monitor progress in selected areas for instructional emphasis, and to measure the outcome of students' progress as readers. In so doing, DIBELS links the means with the ends—in particular, by suggesting that it can be administered to repeatedly assess student literacy development while serving as a measure of outcomes. But the use of DIBELS to screen students, monitor their progress, and measure their outcomes fails to separate outcomes from the means of achieving them; consequently, what DIBELS measures and what teachers teach become one and the same thing.

A number of problems can occur as a result. The DIBELS tests and other accountability measures define what is taught and the outcomes that are measured so that progress may *not* be much more than what was tested and taught. In other words, although students may be performing better on tests (i.e., tests that assess phonemic awareness, phonics, vocabulary, fluency, and comprehension/retelling), they may not be progressing in terms of larger goals for literacy (e.g., developing expanded uses of various literacies to serve a range of purposes) (Goodman, 2006; Pearson, 2006; Tierney & Thome, 2006).

In turn, in adopting the mode of responding to externally prescribed reform mandates, a teacher assumes more the role of a technician than a professional. Gerry Duffy (1990), in his presidential address to the National Reading Conference, suggested: "Empowering teachers means creating the conditions in which teachers can make up their own minds, do their best work, and define their own context." Quoting teacher colleague Bruce Burke, Duffy (1990) then asked: "Do we do this? Do we invest in the minds of teachers? Do we help them make up their own minds, do their own best work, define their own context? Or do we invest in our theories, programs, and procedures in the expectation that teachers will compliantly follow" (p. 15)? McNeil's report (2000) on Houston's reform efforts in part provides an answer.

> They tried to teacher-proof the curriculum with a checklist for teaching behaviors and the student minimum competency skills tests. By so doing, they have made schools exceedingly comfortable for mediocre teachers who like to teach routine lessons according to a standard sequence and format, who like working as de-skilled laborers not having to think about their work. They made being a Texas public school teacher extremely uncomfortable for those who know their subjects well, who teach in ways that engage their students, who want their teaching to reflect their own continued learning. (p. 187)

With these shifts, too often the tests become the program. This should not come as any surprise, as it has happened repeatedly in cases where high-stakes assessment is enlisted in schools. In past studies of the impact of testing on teaching, George Madaus (1988, 2001), Sharon Nichols and David Berliner (Nichols & Berliner, 2007), and others suggest that such testing contributes to a form of teaching to the test, whereby the curriculum begins to emulate the test and reading is regulated (in a fashion that may be quite restrictive) to enhance performance. Forms of monitoring, such as RTI (Response to Intervention) and a Value-Added Model, only seem to perpetuate this alignment with testing, maintaining pre-set regimens of instruction (teaching to the test) aimed at regulating student learning rather than engaging in a diverse array of learning possibilities (Fuchs & Fuchs, 2006; McCaffrey et al., 2003).

While the one-size-fits-all approach to reading may advance an impression of assured quality control, this regulated reader framework is in danger of displacing education that connects and is relevant to what students know and do in their everyday lives. It has the potential to preserve forms of literacy that are out of step with the dynamic networking and transactions that students conduct everyday as they interact with others, including family, friends, and other human resources.

Furthermore, the pursuit of a regulated reader model does not capitalize on the natural dynamics of engagements within and across individuals and communities in the digital age, where readers measure their success in terms such as relevance. The pursuit of "culturally free" curriculum and assessment seems flawed. In lieu of "culture-free" standardized testing and curricula, it would seem preferable to aspire to experiences with literacy that are diverse and involve culturally relevant meaning making rather than rigidly imposed, static sets of guidelines for thinking and communicating. Indeed, the notion of a "relevant reader"—in opposition to a regulated reader—would seem to fit better with the engagements and exchanges offered in a digital, multifaceted, and diverse world aspiring to be culturally relevant or reciprocal (Ladson-Billings, 1997; Li, 2008).

References

Allington, R., & Cunningham, P. (1996). *Schools that work: Where all children read and write* (1st ed.). Allyn and Bacon.

Au, W. (2009). *Unequal by design: High-stakes testing and the standardization of inequality.* Taylor & Francis.

Campbell, D. T. (1976). *Assessing the impact of planned social change.* Public Affairs Center, Dartmouth College.

Carr, W., & Kemmis, S. (1986). *Becoming critical: Education, knowledge, and action research.* Falmer Press.

Claycomb, C., & Kysilko, D. (2000). The purposes and elements of effective assessment systems: The policy framework. *State Education Standard, 1*(2), 6–11.

Congress of the United States, House Committee on Education and the Workforce. (1998, July 17). *Education at a crossroads: What works and what's wasted in education today* (Report of the Subcommittee on Oversight and Investigations of the Committee on Education and the Workforce. The 105th Congress of the United States).

Duffy, G. G. (1990). What counts in teacher education? Dilemmas in educating empowered teachers. In J. Zutell & S. McCormick (Eds.), *Learner factors/Teacher factors: Issues in literacy research and instruction. 40th yearbook of the National Reading Conference* (Proceedings of the Annual Meeting of the National Reading Conference, Miami, Florida, November 27–December 1) (pp. 1–18). National Reading Conference.

Duffy, G., & Hoffman, J. V. (2002). Beating the odds in literacy education: Not the "betting on" but the "bettering of" schools and teachers. In B. Taylor & P. D. Pearson (Eds.), *Teaching reading: Effective schools, accomplished teachers* (pp. 361–373). Erlbaum.

Fuchs, D., & Fuchs, L. S. (2006). Introduction to response to intervention: What, why, and how valid is it? *Reading Research Quarterly, 41*(1): 93–99.

Goodman, K. (Ed.). *The truth about DIBELS* (pp. v–xix). Heinemann.

Gutiérrez, K. (2004). Literacy as laminated activity: Rethinking literacy for English learners. In J. Worthy, B. Maloch, J. V. Hoffman, D. L. Schallert, & C. M. Fairbanks (Eds.), *53rd yearbook of the National Reading Conference.* (pp. 101–114). National Reading Conference.

Guttiérez, K. (2008). Developing a sociocritical literacy in the third space. *Reading Research Quarterly, 43*(2), 148–164. doi: 10.1598/RRQ.43.2.3

Haney, W. (1993). Testing and minorities. In L. Weis & M. Fine (Eds.), *Beyond silenced voices: Class, race, and gender in United States schools* (pp. 45–74). SUNY Press.

Hargreaves, A., & Shirley, D. (2007, December 21). The coming age of post-standardization. *Education Week, 27.* www.edweek.org/ew/articles/2007/12/21/17hargreaves_web.h27 .html

International Reading Association. (2002). *Evidence-based reading instruction: Putting the National Reading Panel report into practice* (pp. 232–236). International Reading Association.

Kincheloe, J. L. (1991). *Teachers as researchers: Qualitative inquiry as a path to empowerment.* Routledge. doi: 10.4324/9780203801550

Ladson-Billings, G. J. (1997). *The dreamkeepers: Successful teachers of African-American children.* Jossey-Bass.

Li, G. (2008). *Culturally contested literacies: America's "rainbow underclass" and urban schools.* Routledge.

Linn, R. L., Baker, E. L., & Betebenner, D. W. (2002). Accountability systems: Implications of requirements of the No Child Left Behind Act of 2001. *Educational Researcher, 31*(6), 3–16. doi: 10.3102/0013189X031006003

Lyon, G. R., & Chhabra, V. (2004). The science of reading research. *Educational Leadership, 61*(6), 12–17. www.ascd.org/publications/educational-leadership/mar04/vol61 /num06/The-Science-of-Reading-Research.aspx

Madaus, G. F. (1988). The influence of testing on the curriculum. In L.N. Tanner (Ed.), *Critical issues in curriculum: 87th Yearbook of the National Society for the Study of Education.* University of Chicago Press.

Madaus, G. F., & Clarke, M. (2001). The adverse impact of high stakes testing on minority students: Evidence from one hundred years of test data. In G. Orfield & M. L. Kornhaber (Eds.), *Raising standards or raising barriers? Inequality and high stakes testing in education* (pp. 85–106). Century Foundation Press.

McCaffrey, D. F., Lockwood, J. R., Koretz, D. M., & Hamilton, L. S. (2003). Evaluating Value-Added Models for teacher accountability. RAND Corporation. www.rand.org /content/dam/rand/pubs/monographs/2004/RAND_MG158.pdf

McNeil, L. M. (2000). *Contradictions of school reform: Educational costs of standardized testing.* Routledge. doi: 10.4324/9780203900451

Miller, J. (1990). *Creating spaces and finding voices: Teachers collaborating for empowerment.* SUNY Press.

National Academy of Education. (1999, March). *Recommendations regarding research priorities: An advisory report to the National Educational Research Policy and Priorities Board.* National Academy of Education. web.stanford.edu/~hakuta/www/archives /syllabi/Docs/NAE_NERPP.PDF

National Educational Research Policy and Priorities Board. (1999). *Investing in learning: A policy statement with recommendations on research in education by the National Educational Research Policy and Priorities Board.* U.S. Department of Education. files.eric .ed.gov/fulltext/ED431036.pdf

National Reading Panel. (2000, April). *Teaching children to read: An evidence-based assessment of the scientific research literature on reading and its implications for reading instruction* (NIH P.N. 00–4769). U.S. Department of Health and Human Services, Public Health Service, National Institutes of Health and the National Institute of Child Health and Human Development. www.nichd.nih.gov/publications/pubs/nrp/smallbook

National Research Council. (1999). *Improving student learning: A strategic plan for educational research and its utilization*. Committee on a Feasibility Study for a Strategic Education Research Program & Commission on Behavioral and Social Sciences and Education. National Academy Press. www.nap.edu/login.php?record_id=6488&page =https%3A%2F%2Fwww.nap.edu%2Fdownload%2F6488

National Research Council. (2002). *Scientific research in education*. Committee on Scientific Principles for Education Research (Shavelson, R. J., & Towne, L., Eds.) & Center for Education, Division of Behavioral and Social Sciences and Education. National Academy Press. www.nap.edu/catalog/10236/scientific-research-in-education

New London Group. (1996). A pedagogy of multiliteracies: Designing social futures. *Harvard Educational Review, 66*(1), 60–93. doi: 10.17763/haer.66.1.17370n67v22j160u

Nichols, S. L., & Berliner, D. C. (2007). *Collateral damage: How high stakes testing corrupts America's schools*. Harvard Education Press.

No Child Left Behind Act of 2001, P.L. 107–110, 20 U.S.C. §6319 (2002).

Olson, D. R. (2004). The triumph of hope over experience in the search for "what works": A response to Slavin. *Educational Researcher, 33*(1), 24–26. doi: 10.3102/0013189X033001024

Pappas, C. C., & Zecker, L. B. (Eds.). (2001). *Teacher inquiries in literacy teaching-learning: Learning to collaborate in elementary urban classrooms*. Erlbaum.

Pearson, P. D. (2006). Foreword. In K. Goodman (Ed.), *The truth about DIBELS* (pp. v–xix). Heinemann.

Pressley, Michael. (2001). What I have learned up until now about research methods in reading education. In D. L. Schallert, C. M. Fairbanks, J. Worthy, B. Maloch, & J. V. Hoffman (Eds.), *54th yearbook of the National Reading Conference* (pp. 22–43). National Reading Conference.

Québec Ministère de l'Éducation. (2001). *Teacher training: Orientations, professional competencies* (New directions for success). Gouvernement du Québec. www.education .gouv.qc.ca/fileadmin/site_web/documents/dpse/formation_ens_a.pdf

Rogers, T., Winters, K. L., Bryan, G., Price, J., McCormick, F., House, L., Mezzarobba, D., & Sinclaire, C. (2006). Developing the IRIS: Toward situated and valid assessment measures in collaborative professional development and school reform in literacy. *The Reading Teacher, 59*(6), 544–553. doi: 10.1598/RT.59.6.4

Rogoff, B., Turkanis, C., Goodman, K. S., & Bartlett, L. (Eds.). (2001). *Learning together: Children and adults in a school community*. Oxford University Press.

Rose, M. (1995). *Possible lives: The promise of public education in America*. Houghton Mifflin.

Schoenfeld, A. F. (2002). Making mathematics work for all children: Issues of standards, testing and equity. *Educational Researcher, 31*(1), 13–25. doi: 10.3102/0013189X031001013

Schofield, A., & Rogers, T. (2004). At play in fields of ideas: Teaching, curriculum, and the lives and multiple literacies of youth. *Journal of Adolescent and Adult Literacy, 48*(3), 238–248.

Schon, D. A. (1983). *The reflective practitioner: How professionals think in action*. Basic Books.

Shannon, P., Edmondson, J. E., & O'Brien, S. (2002). Expressions of power and ideology in the National Reading Panel. In D. L. Schallert, C. M. Fairbanks, J. Worthy, B. Maloch, & J. V. Hoffman (Eds.), *51st yearbook of the National Reading Conference* (pp. 383–395). National Reading Conference.

Taylor, B. M., Pressley, M. P., & Pearson, P. D. (2002). Research-supported characteristics of teachers and schools that promote reading achievement. In B. Taylor & P. D. Pearson (Eds.), *Teaching reading: Effective schools, accomplished teachers* (361–373). Routledge. doi: 10.4324/9781410612489

Taylor, D. (1998). *Beginning to read and the spin doctors of science: The political campaign to change America's mind about how children learn to read.* National Council of Teachers of English.

Tierney, R. J. (2001). An ethical chasm: Jurisdiction, jurisprudence, and the literacy profession. *Journal of Adolescent & Adult Literacy, 45*(4), 260–276.

Tierney, R. J., & Bond, E. (1998). *Standards: Problematic assumptions, faulty ideals and the disintegration of teaching, learning and testing?* educ.ubc.ca/about/tierney/NCTE_standards.pdf

Tierney, R. J., & Thome, C. (2006). Is DIBELS leading us down the wrong path? In K. S. Goodman (Ed.), *The truth about DIBELS* (pp. 50–59). Heinemann.

Trinder, L., & Reynolds, S. (Eds.). (2000). *Evidence-based practice: Critical appraisal.* Blackwell Science.

Tuck, E., & Gorlewski, J. (2016). Racist ordering, settler colonialism, and edTPA: A participatory policy analysis. *Educational Policy, 30*(1), 197–217. doi: 10.1177/0895904815616483

Warburton, W. P., & Warburton, R. N. (2001). Should the government sponsor training for the disadvantaged? In P. De Broucker & A. Sweetman (Eds.), *Towards evidence-based policy for Canadian education* (pp. 69–100). McGill-Queen's University Press.

9.2 THE ERA OF REFORM: CONTESTATION AND DEBATE

Educational reform has often placed literacy at the center both of efforts to improve education and even of political movements. Broadly, educational reform has been embedded in and across debates over ideology, nationhood, public education, standards and accountability, and civil rights (operationalized as equity along ethnic, racial, and gender lines). In terms of literacy, reform has been the center of debates on a whole range of issues (the content or canon of topics and texts that should be read, censorship, and curriculum versus child-centered teaching methods), but they all pale in comparison to the question of the optimal way to teach beginning reading, especially as that question is framed as a code-emphasis (phonics first and fast) versus meaning-emphasis (focus on sense-making) debate. Reading reform has also served as the epicenter of interventions related to supporting special needs students and students from diverse backgrounds, espousing what has been deemed as "best practice" informed by "science" for students at the bottom of the achievement distribution. In the mid-1990s in particular, it took center stage in the worldwide educational theater of developments that saw a number of debates erupting, many of which were concerned with unresolved issues from prior decades associated with the fervent interests and strong views of parents, educators, and ideological reformers.

Broad Issues of Educational Development for Society: Addressing Inequities

At one level, the issues of educational development and reform are tied to broader issues of educational achievement and the benchmarking of performance and educational investments. It has become commonplace for international comparisons to spur national ambitions for educational improvement. For example, periodic international assessments of achievement are offered in conjunction with the Program for International Student Assessment (PISA)—an international assessment under the auspices of the Organization for Economic Co-operation and Development (OECD) that measures 15-year-old students' reading, mathematics, and science literacy every 3 years. Figure 9.2 includes a subsample of the 2018 results, revealing the percentage of 15-year-olds at Level 2. Established as the baseline level of scientific literacy, Level 2 defines the level of achievement on the PISA scale at which students begin to demonstrate the scientific knowledge and skills that will enable them to participate actively in life situations related to science and technology. As you can discern, most developed countries are above the OECD average; consequently, concerns over the ranking of the United States when compared to those of other countries has motivated reform. Additional PISA data compare students in terms of a range of diversity indices as well as the

Figure 9.2. Percentage of 15-Year-Old Students at Level 2 or Above in the PISA Reading Assessment, 2018

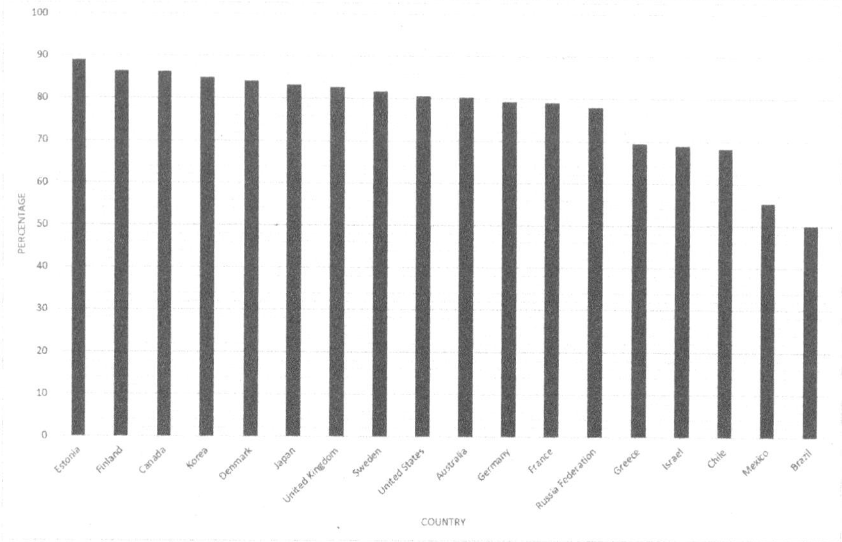

Source: Schleicher, 2019

circumstances of schooling (hours of instruction, class size, teacher qualifications, etc.) (Schleicher & OECD, 2019).

In many countries, poverty and location are intertwined with matters of educational performance. In the age of global and national audits, the circumstances and performances of various groups are also mapped by location, background, and educational investment. The data (see Figure 9.3) have revealed that, to a large extent, achievement coincides with investment.

The performance of schools on PISA correlates highly with economic investment in education in those countries. Further, they follow the same trend when these data are examined within countries by ethnicity, socioeconomic circumstances, or location. Examinations of the national assessment of reading performance, such as the National Assessment of Educational Progress in the United States (National Assessment of Educational Progress, 2019), reveals the same pattern of reading performance by different groups in different locations (see Figures 9.4 and 9.5).

Predictably, lower performing schools tend to be located in economically struggling communities. Unfortunately even as the rich get richer, these schools often receive less funding. Consider the case of the Milwaukee schools, where African American students in poorer economic circumstances tend to perform poorly and receive less funding per student than their wealthier counterparts in the suburban neighborhoods in the same school district. This trend is also apparent in data from throughout Asia, especially those dealing with massive populations spread across urban and remote areas such as China, Indonesia, and India.

Figure 9.3. Excellence and Equity: Student Achievement in PISA and Socioeconomic Parity Index

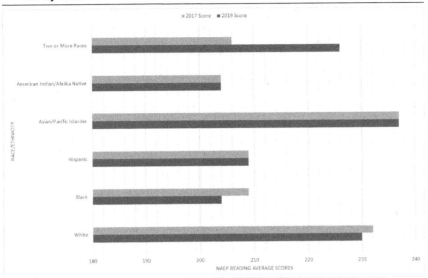

Source: Schleicher, 2019

Figure 9.4. Changes in 8th-Grade NAEP Reading by Race/Ethnicity

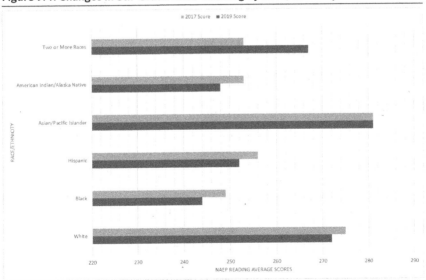

Source: National Assessment of Educational Progress, 2019

Figure 9.5. District/Jurisdictions with Scores for 2019 in NAEP Reading at Grade 8 for Overall and Selected Student Groups

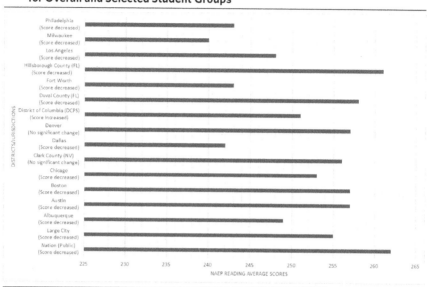

Source: National Assessment of Educational Progress, 2019

The Reform Debate: A Focus on Teachers, Curriculum, Testing, and Accountability

While there is considerable debate about funding, it does seem that policymakers tend to deflect the solution to matters regarding the quality of teaching, curriculum, and accountability. In Australia, for instance, the *Review of Funding for Schooling—Final Report* (or Gonski Review Report; see Gonski, 2011; Senate Select Committee on School Funding, 2014) recommendations tried to address the huge disparities in funding received by schools. In Australia, economically privileged students often attended schools that received more than three times the funding of students from more economically challenged circumstances attending local public schools. In other countries, such circumstances are repeated, and, unfortunately, the funding differentials remain the same as governments deflect attention to the failures of schools including issues of teacher quality or curriculum, and so on. In the area of curriculum, these included:

- The resurfacing of age-old debates around the best approach to teaching reading. Essentially, this amounted to a debate between approaches that were tied to either a whole language philosophy or a phonics orientation.
- Debates tied to empowerment over "process writing" approaches, as advocated by Donald Graves and the National Writing Project, and a "Genre approach" (with origins in Australia).

- Issues tied to the quality of teachers and their preparation, especially in areas such as phonics.

In the area of testing, these prompted discussions related to:

- Matters of accountability and student advancement and advocacy— concerns over which resulted in the propagation of national and state examinations. Such examinations included audits of student progress across the grades and put forward the possibility of student retention.
- Concerns about the merits of authentic, more informal classroom-based and learner-centered assessments, such as formative assessment and portfolios.

Researchers were not spared from these spurious attacks—indeed, research discussions were perhaps the most perplexing, eliciting entrenched views tied to positivism rather than debate and the possibility of complementary consideration. In other words, there was a politicized shift from multiple research paradigms to an arbitrary (and, in some countries, politically favored and legislated) establishment of quantitative studies enlisting randomized trial comparisons. Nowhere was this preference for quantitative approaches leading to causal inferences more evident than in the reading reforms initiated in the United States by the Clinton (the Reading Excellence Act and its focus on "reliable, replicable research") and the Bush (the Reading First arm of No Child Left Behind and its focus on Scientifically Based Reading Research) administrations. These became the gold standard of what was needed to define the merits of educational endeavors or reading approaches and to limit the research funding. The advancement of the bias toward quantitative studies enlisting randomized comparisons of different treatment/methods pushed to the margins the energetic and diverse engagement of qualitative and critical approaches or formative research, which had fueled teacher–researcher engagements. Such views also shifted pedagogy away from situated and formative models to those that were prescribed, scripted, and carefully monitored to assure treatment fidelity. At the same time, they vied to displace local and statewide curricula in the pursuit of an indirect and implicit national curriculum informed by notions of "best practice" (as identified in studies that passed muster as experimental).

Furthermore, select groups engineered and profited from these developments to their own advantage. These included special educators and psychologists who assumed prominent roles in advocating and deciding reading pedagogy and directions for research. In most countries, to secure their students' futures (see Kohn, 1998), historically privileged parents were also keen to ensure that the interests of their children would not suffer. To this end, tougher standards and tests were seen by some as necessary to stem the rising tide of ever-widening gaps in educational access (Ellwein et al., 1988; Shephard et al., 2009; Tucker & Codding, 2002). Those in the literacy research community who aligned themselves with certain uncontested developments likewise flourished and profited, while others were made to suffer and were sidelined. As some developments (e.g., digital) proceeded, those that were apt to be contested went underground. Indeed, in the United States, some of these practices later became the site of an inspector general investigation, which exposed the biases and deliberate exclusionary practices of the office of the U.S. Secretary of Education (Center for Education Evaluation and Regional Assistance, 2008; Office of the Inspector General, 2006).

As we have suggested, during this period of imposition, a great deal of focus was placed on teachers and their qualifications, including the alignment of teacher education preparation with the doctrine of best practice (Walsh et al., 2006). University teacher education programs were subjected to scrutiny and evaluation, even as government legislatures sought funding for alternatives that avoided university preparation such as Teach for America, Australia, and China. Practicing teachers also faced shifting expectations, as they were threatened with termination depending on their performance. The notion and measurement of "value added," using students' test performance as evidence, was introduced as a means of evaluating a teacher's effectiveness and as a basis for salary incentives and teacher retention (McCaffrey et al., 2003). Likewise, schools and school districts were identified as successful or failing by league tables and rankings for public consumption, and perhaps school closings or takeover.

The impacts of these shifts on schooling were predictable. Testing assumed a high-stakes profile, which perpetuated more intensive and extensive teaching for the test and a privileging of some students over others. A rhetoric around the "achievement gap" replaced learning opportunities and diversity. In turn, students, schools, and teachers were deemed as failing rather than the system itself.

In parallel with these developments was a neoliberal agenda arguing for school choice and ways by which the private sector could enhance the investment in education for children from economically advantaged circumstances. Worldwide, we began seeing a growth in private schools, parents enlisting their resources to supplement support for their children (e.g., tutoring; in Canada, Australia, and China, a very large percentage of high school students receive out-of-school tutoring support). Perhaps predictably, the end result was a shift from a focus on diverse approaches for a diverse population to single- and often simple-minded approaches to closing the achievement gap, such as fixing the teachers and schools but never the system. And all the while, we witnessed growing inequities in education in different countries for select groups, including those of low-income in rural and urban areas, Indigenous populations, and select recent migrant groups. At times the system has been subjected to questioning with regard to the widening achievement gap, but more often these select groups are the recipients of greater blame and fewer resources.

A Look at the Systems in Play

Dealing with school reform requires dealing with the frameworks that undergird the reform as well as engaging in a form of political campaigning, often using rhetorical ploys to persuade the public of the merits of an initiative. Reform efforts may be deemed legally valid and legitimate by a consultative process that informs the public as the initiatives proceed. Criticisms may at times be stemmed by selecting people of certain persuasions to support developments and by cutting off funding or other support for groups that do not comply with the proposed reform (i.e., those who might tout, pursue, or advocate for alternatives). Local resistance may be tempered into compliance with such threats to cut funding.

Universities were not exempted from this leveraging. In the 1980s, research groups such as the Center for the Study of Reading (CSR) were expected to align with the national agenda that was becoming increasingly politicized. The research group at CSR made a genuine effort to do so by developing an important report, "Becoming a Nation of Readers," under the leadership of Richard Anderson, Elfrieda Hiebert, Judith Scott, and Ian Wilkinson (Anderson et al., 1985). This report was more eclectic and not compromised. As we discuss next, later initiatives in the United States and a number of other countries (e.g., United Kingdom, Australia) were less "hands-off," especially in terms of governmental control of the focus of commissioned reports and their authorship. In some cases, some university projects seemed to pursue initiatives (e.g., test developments, reading programs) more for financial gain than aligned with scholarly ethics.

In a historical analysis of these relationships, David (Pearson, 2007) described the model undergirding this period of reform as "power-coercive":

> [The power coercive model] entails a number of practices with which we have become all too familiar in recent years. We coerce people to change when we use laws, court rulings, and legislative or executive mandates as our primary policy levers. Accountability systems may or may not belong in the power-coercive category. I think it depends on whether such systems offer any choice and adaptability in the way that educators are expected to use the key policy levers in those systems: assessments, standards, criteria for selecting materials and/or professional development providers. If there is little or no adaptability, then users end up in a closed system with few degrees of freedom in shaping a local implementation; in this case, the system has, for all practical purposes, the force of mandate. If, on the other hand, there are options in the manner in which these key policy levers can be adapted to the local context, the system can have the look and feel of the learning communities typical of the normative-reeducative approach. (pp. 15–16)

Visually, David depicted the research approach in the following manner (Figure 9.6). As David summarized:

> Scientific research is the driver of the system and the basis on which we establish standards for curriculum, assessment, and professional development activities. Then monitoring tools (to ensure fidelity in standards-based reform) and sanctions (to motivate schools and teachers to higher achievement and stricter adherence to reforms) are added to keep the system moving. (pp. 23–24)

Figure 9.6. The "Power-Coercive" Model

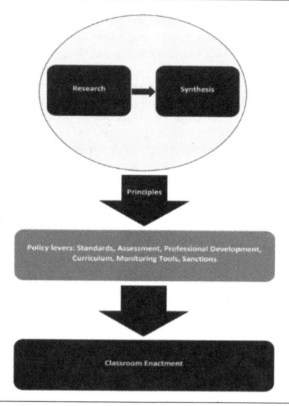

Source: Pearson, 2007

In more specific terms, he suggested that the reform undertaken in recent years in the United States was aligned with this model. For instance, Pearson described the events that coincided with the No Child Left Behind Act of 2001 (NCLB, 2002), in the following terms:

Sometime in the mid to late 1990s, a new force and a new paradigm began to take shape. It was first visible in a new discourse stimulated by research supported by the National Institute for Child Health and Human Development. We began to see and hear a "new" brand of experimental work that had been quietly but steadily gathering momentum for over a decade (Lyon & Chhaba, 1996). This was experimentalism reborn from the 1950s and 60s, with great emphasis placed upon "reliable, replicable research," large samples, random assignment of treatments to teachers and/or schools, and "tried and true" outcome measures. Its aegis was in the experimental rhetoric of science and medicine and in the laboratory research that was so prominent in those earlier periods. Although the reading education community did not broadly accept this effort, it found a very sympathetic ear in the public policy arena.

Research synthesis as a new policy tool. This new research paradigm became officially codified by the appearance, in rapid succession, of two research syntheses—the publication of the report of the National Academy of Science's Committee on Preventing Reading Difficulties (PRD) (Snow, Burns, & Griffith, 1998) and the report of the National Reading Panel (NRP) (2000). The PRD report was conducted in the tradition of "best evidence" syntheses: well established scholars meet, decide on the issues, the domain of relevant research, and some subdivision of labor, do the work, write up the results, and turn the manuscript over to a set of editors to bring some synthetic clarity to the entire effort. As such, it considered a range of studies conducted within very different research traditions using very different research methods. The result was a strong plea for a balanced view of reading instruction, but with a special nod to phonemic awareness and phonics first and fast.

Authorized by congressional mandate, the National Reading Panel report used what they considered to be the most "scientific" review approaches (i.e., meta-analysis, at least wherever they could) available to them to distill from existing research what is known about the efficacy of teaching phonemic awareness, phonics, fluency (instantiated as either guided reading instruction or independent reading), comprehension, and vocabulary; additionally, they investigated the status of the research base on teacher education and professional development and attempted to review research on technology and literacy. (pp. 21–22)

As David detailed in his paper, a key precursor to the reform effort was a narrowing of the definition of scientific research to studies enlisting randomization trials only. This narrowed definition was part of coordinated attempts to shift the focus in beginning reading toward direct instruction of phonemic awareness via commissioned reports directed by and emphasizing that orientation.

It is notable that the reform developments in literacy were dominated by a number of educators aligning with the National Reading Panel Report and the "Simple View of Reading" (Gough & Tunmer, 1986)—tied to a stage-wise developmental approach that emphasized teaching the code, especially phonemic analysis and phonics (see Ehri, 2020; Goswami & Bryant, 1990; Gough et al., 1981; Juel & Midden-Cupp, 2000; Perfetti & Hart, 2002; Eagleton, 1983a). This stressed a bottom-up rather than a meaning-centered emphasis for beginning reading, along with texts engineered to interface with the readers' development (e.g., Hiebert, 2017). The emphasis on comprehension took somewhat of a backseat to these developments, except in terms of text-centered efforts to enrich a reader's background knowledge and vocabulary. The research expanded and more clearly positioned vocabulary learning as simultaneous and interfaced with reading comprehension development and learning to read (Beck et al., 2013; Kamil, 2004; Kamil & Hiebert, 2005; Hiebert & Kamil, 2007; McKeown & Beck, 2014; Nagy, 2005; Nagy & Scott, 2000). Predictably, certain lines of research over others, as well as curriculum and pedagogy developments, favored this emphasis.

Likewise, the prescriptive nature of these efforts was enhanced by the enlistment of mandated tests authored by persons who were involved in defining the parameters of the initiative and reflective of this narrowing of what should be taught (Office of the Inspector General, 2006).

The Growth of Standards-Based Reform

Concurrent with these developments, the discourse shifted to highlighting the achievement gap and the necessity for standards. As Sarah Mosle (1996) reported in her *New York Times Magazine* article "The Answer Is National Standards,"

> What distinguishes the current standards movement from past hortatory rhetoric is that it emphasizes equal opportunity as much as achievement, through a national curriculum—goals on which both liberals and conservatives should be able to agree. (para. 12)
>
> The sensitivity to children's needs and differences, the ability to inspire intellectual curiosity and excitement exist independent of method. Schools should be allowed to use whatever approach they would like and then be held accountable for the results on substantive, content-based exams that are geared to the curriculum. (para. 47)

Around the time of Mosle's article, Rob and a colleague (Tierney & Bond, 1998) analyzed the rhetoric of the standards movement, especially that of professional groups such as the International Reading Association (IRA; now the International Literacy Association) and the National Council of Teachers of English (NCTE). Looking across 30 articles that appeared in the Council chronicle, *Reading Today*, and occasional pieces in other releases, we found at least four major rhetoric ploys:

1. Borrowing the discourse of critics in a decontextualized and distorted fashion, or not providing the evidence to warrant assertions. These assertions included:
   a. the standards will take into account and, in fact promote, diversity and equity;
   b. the creation of standards is a dynamic process;
   c. the standards will create a vision, not mandates; and
   d. the movement is being initiated and directed from the bottom up.
2. Calls to "get with the program," via the use of the following:
   a. praise and motivational rhetoric;
   b. fear tactics;
   c. bandwagoning—that is, claiming that everybody is joining the movement; and
   d. expert involvement.
3. Misrepresenting the role and value of consensus.
4. Silencing, filtering, or marginalizing critics.

Standards were precursors to tests and other controls. During the George W. Bush administration, for instance, the Academic Achievement for All Act, or Straight A's, implemented incentives—including federal regulatory exemptions and bonus funding—for participating states and districts to develop and meet their own standards. As William J. Bennett and Chester E. Finn Jr. (1999), two key political strategists and contributors to George W. Bush's education platform, stated just prior to Bush's first term:

Those states that produce the promised results would get their "performance agreement" renewed and earn a bonus. Those that fail would be thrown back into the regulatory briar patch.

. . . the Straight A's proposal is promising because under it the federal government would align itself with many of the best ideas in American education: greater accountability, more choice, more competition, higher standards.

Congress now has a choice between two very different conceptions of the federal role in K-12 schooling." (Bennett & Finn Jr., 1999, paras. 2, 6, & 8)

Reflecting on such developments, Sharon Nichols and David Berliner (2007) found a major shift toward rhetoric of standards in discussions of education by politicians and the media around 1995. Tracking media discussions across major U.S. newspapers, Nichols and Berliner noted how there was a dramatic shift in references beginning in 1995 from discussions of educational opportunity to discussions of education for achievement. They also found that government reports around this time had plentiful mentions of achievement and scant mentions of educational opportunities. Such rhetoric is consistent with the underlying logic of a marketplace as a means of controlling (in this case, incentivizing) curricular reform. But notice that this logic soon leads to the same teaching to the test practices outlined earlier; after all, if test scores are the coin of the realm, then getting to practice taking the test is the most direct path to greater rewards.

The most recent instantiation of these developments in the United States has been the heralded and hotly debated Common Core State Standards Initiative (NGA & CCSSO, 2010). According to the Common Core website:

The Common Core is a set of high-quality academic standards in mathematics and English language arts/literacy (ELA). These learning goals outline what a student should know and be able to do at the end of each grade. The standards were created to ensure that all students graduate from high school with the skills and knowledge necessary to succeed in college, career, and life, regardless of where they live. Forty-two states, the District of Columbia, four territories, and the Department of Defense Education Activity (DoDEA) have voluntarily adopted and are moving forward with the Common Core.

For years, the academic progress of our nation's students has been stagnant, and we have lost ground to our international peers. Particularly in subjects such as math, college remediation rates have been high. One root cause has been an uneven patchwork of academic standards that vary from state to state and do not agree on what students should know and be able to do at each grade level.

Recognizing the value and need for consistent learning goals across states, in 2009 the state school chiefs and governors that comprise CCSSO and the NGA Center co-ordinated a state-led effort to develop the Common Core State Standards. Proponents of the Common Core State Standards claimed that these were voluntary national (i.e., not federal) standards, with curricula to achieve the standards to be designed through collaboration among teachers, school chiefs, administrators, and other experts, the standards provide a clear and consistent framework for educators. Opponents pointed out that their voluntary status was undermined by an Obama-era program (part of the broad recovery package designed to bring the United States out of the 2008 recession) that required adoption of the CCSS in order to receive funding.

Lest the integrity of the standards were challenged, the Common Core writers asserted that they were informed by the highest, most effective standards from states across the United States and countries around the world. The standards were touted as defining the knowledge and skills students should gain throughout their K-12 educa-tion in order to graduate high school prepared to succeed in entry-level careers, intro-ductory academic college courses, and workforce training programs.

The standards claimed to be:

1. Research- and evidence-based
2. Clear, understandable, and consistent
3. Aligned with college and career expectations
4. Based on rigorous content and application of knowledge through higher-order thinking skills
5. Built upon the strengths and lessons of current state standards
6. Informed by other top performing countries in order to prepare all students for success in our global economy and society (NGA & CCSSO, 2019)

How widespread are such reform efforts? Initially, in the United States, for example, over 80% of states aligned with the Common Core initiative. Over time, however, support has dwindled, as many states have become concerned with how the standards represented the federal control of the curriculum as well as the curriculum itself. Strange bedfellows of conservative and states' rights advocates united with anti-testing coalitions to express their concerns and to leverage noncompliance with the standards. Their objections ranged from state-level opposition to federal control of teaching and mandated curriculum to con-cerns over what were included as guidelines for texts and reading skills and strategies (Hess, 2014).

Elsewhere in the world, similar concerns have been raised but do not seem to have thwarted several countries from pursuing a similar agenda of standards and testing initiatives. For example, in Australia, the Ministerial Council on Education, Employment, Training and Youth Affairs (MCEETYA) assumed an approach to educational development tied to similar sentiments—enlisting a bully pulpit to advance their agenda with a lure of funding and mobilizing fears of a stricter regime of control. As the Hon. Dr. David Kemp MP, Minister for Education, Training and Youth Affairs, suggested to the Curriculum Corporation's 6th National Conference (Kemp, 1999):

> If we are to have a school system for the next millennium, which meets the expectations and has the confidence of the Australian community, then we must have mechanisms in place that allow us to measure the key outcomes of all Australian schools and report these outcomes to the Australian community. We need to make clear our expectations for all schools—government and non-government schools alike.

A standards-based approach informed by "select" research fitted the dominant framework that politicians in a number of countries enlisted. This approach holds that standards should be research-based, and that schools and school staff should be focused on developing students using these standards—and be held accountable for doing so. In other words, teachers and teachers' professional development were seen as needing to be aligned with these standards. Further, standards should proceed nationally rather than in an uneven fashion, state by state. Again, the system for doing so was largely by legislative fiat, imposed top-down and uniformly rather than locally or diversely.

Accordingly, as standards and testing assumed prominence, teaching practices were realigned with testing. And, in turn, tests became a way to monitor and also bridge to practices of ensuring accountability as well as compliance. For example, tests often became the means and the ends befitting a principle espoused by Donald Campbell that high-stakes assessments can corrupt the relationship between teaching and testing (Campbell, 1975). As discussed earlier (see Regulated Reader), some contend it was advanced with approaches to learning tethered to tests such as Dynamic Indicators of Basic Early Literacy Skills (DIBELS), used as a means of screening students and to monitor progress in selected areas for instructional emphasis.

Essentially, these reform efforts were seen as displacing diverse and situated curricula that met local needs, and sidelining teacher professionalism, teacher research, and classroom-based assessment. Too often, the tests became the program. This is not surprising, however, as it has happened repeatedly in cases where high-stakes assessments are enlisted in schools. In his examinations of past studies of the impact of testing on teaching in the United States and the UK, George Madaus (1988) suggests such testing contributes to a form of teaching to the test in a fashion whereby the curriculum begins to emulate the test.

These developments were not apolitical. The emphases on what research counted and what themes were gleaned could have been predicted given the makeup of the reviewers and the leanings of the group overseeing the effort. Indeed, special interest groups of parents and educators, formed to address the needs of students with reading difficulties, were major advocates for such emphases. Perhaps among the more notable of these groups were those focused on what some might consider a pathologization of reading, such as occurred with those

LOOKING TO NEUROSCIENCE FOR SOLUTIONS: A BRIDGE TOO FAR

Reading scholars have a history of inquiring into the nature of the reading process by delving into the workings of the brain. They have attempted to do so through a range of methods, including studies of eye movements (Hogaboam, 1983; Rayner, 1998); observations of oral reading; and most recently, magnetic resonating technology (which attempts to signify how brain activity couples with linguistic inputs as readers process written texts). Despite the problems with the reliability of brain scan data (e.g., with extrapolations that measures of electronic response match the phenomena of brain activity measured), educators have embraced the possibilities that this technology might pin down the regions of the brain involved in the acts of reading and reading development.

Unfortunately, the bridge resulting from the passion and interests of educators may have stretched too far. Despite advances in the technology and the precision in measuring what the technology yields in measurable (i.e., visual) form, the claims offered still seem to exceed what has been shown. Further, they appear to ignore other research that would seem to supersede these findings—positioning the interpretation or inferences drawn from the data as faulty.

One can find many examples of findings going beyond what neuroscience offers and the data indicate. For instance, although the data emanating from MRIs (tracking learners' responses to coding) may have succeeded in imaging responses to decoding, it is a long way from confirming the view that reading proceeds first from the translation of visual cues of letters into sounds and then eventually builds to meaning. Support for this linear process represents group aspirations more than a firm grounding in neuroscience. Statements by groups such as the International Dyslexia Association (2020a) and others reflecting such views in relation to dyslexia are problematic.

Compounding this questionable logic is support for findings that suggest that teaching decoding results in shifts in brain activity aligned with successful readers. Again, the research in this area seems to flirt with implications that go beyond measurable data. Take, if you will, the claims reflected in the statement offered by Petscher et al. (2020). As they stated:

> Research has clearly indicated that skilled reading involves the consolidation of orthographic and phonological word forms. . . . Work in cognitive neuroscience has indicated that a small region of the left ventral visual cortex becomes specialized for this purpose. As students learn to read, they recruit neurons from a small region of the left ventral visual cortex within the left occipitotemporal cortex region (i.e., visual word form area) that are tuned to language-dependent parameters through connectivity to perisylvian language

areas.... This process provides an efficient circuit for grapheme–phoneme conversion and lexical access allowing efficient word-reading skills to develop. These studies have provided direct evidence for how teaching alters the human brain by repurposing some visual regions toward the shapes of letters, suggesting that cultural inventions, such as written language, modify evolutionarily older brain regions. Furthermore, studies have suggested that instruction focusing on the link between orthography and phonology promotes this brain reorganization (e.g., Dehaene, 2011). (p. S268)

Or consider the claims by Shaywitz (2003) that MRI frequency data suggest that written language must first be converted to oral language. Building to this point, Shaywitz begins: "The reader must somehow convert the print on a page into a linguistic code—the phonetic code, the only code recognized and accepted by the language system" (p. 50) of the brain. Having been "translated into the phonetic code, printed words are now accepted by the neural circuitry already in place for processing spoken language. Decoded into phonemes, words are processed automatically by the language system" (Shaywitz, p. 51). Linking this to MRI data, Shaywitz concludes:

We used fMRI (functional magnetic resonance imaging, SGP) to study boys and girls who were struggling to learn to read and who then received a year-long experimental reading program. The final set of images obtained one year after the intervention had ended was startling. Not only were the right-side auxiliary pathways much less prominent but, more important, there was further development of the primary neural systems on the left side of the brain.... [T]hese activation patterns were comparable to those obtained from children who had always been good readers. We had observed brain repair. (Shaywitz, 2003, pp. 85–86)

A similar claim was made by Simos et al. (2002), who found that intensive phonics instruction was responsible for improvements in functional brain imaging. However, as Rosenberger and Rottenberg (2002) suggest, "reservations may be in order" regarding the claim that "a 'deficit in functional brain organization' has been 'reversed' by remedial training" (p. 1140). The data highlighted by Simos et al. and others—illustrating how remedial instruction leads dyslexic children to do "what normal readers do naturally" (p. 1140)—does not necessarily demonstrate proficiency, then, but rather merely indicates "that the subject is doing something different (or differently)" (Rosenberger & Rottenberg, 2002).

Moreover, research from neuroscience would also suggest that the process does not follow the linear order from symbol to sound to meaning. Instead, it engages "higher-order" processes tied to the cortex and its engagement in meaning making, involving more "top-down" processing (such as predictions). In his popular book *On Intelligence*, Jeff Hawkins (2004) reviews the work in neuroscience and touts the role of predictions in governing sensory attention and processing—in a fashion more akin to an executive role than the linear progression suggested by proponents of the "Simple View of Reading." (It is noteworthy that Ulric Neisser earlier argued for the key role of predictions in his landmark 1976 book *Cognition and Reality*, setting the stage for studies of cognition.)

In a similar vein, Strauss et al. (2009) suggested that there was a failure of much of this research to reckon with other findings. As they stated:

> So, the new view is that the brain is not a prisoner of the senses—rather, on the basis of stored knowledge, it predicts experience before it happens. It uses the senses selectively as it makes sense of the experiences it is having with the world.
>
> The functional MRI studies which claimed to show that the brain uses letter-sound relationships as it reads, and that reading is essentially matching letters with sounds, were based on an inadequate understanding of human brain function. The studies indeed demonstrated that a sufficiently advanced machine can reveal brain sites where letter-sound processes occur. But they were misinterpreted to imply that nothing else of significance to reading is going on when the reader transacts with a whole, meaningful text. (p. 032)

Or, as Elliott (2020) noted,

> Confusion seems particularly evident in this discipline, where beguiling references to brain scans and the brightly colored pictures of brain activation seem to reduce the critical faculties of many. Many fail to understand that the contribution of neuroscience to the practical task of assessment and intervention of reading disability is still rudimentary (and scientific understandings continue to be undermined by methodological difficulties and the selective use of evidence. . . .
>
> Misunderstandings have been fueled by the internet, where neuroscientific research on dyslexia is frequently characterized by "distortions, simplifications, and misrepresentations" (Worthy, Godfrey, Tily, Daly-Lesch, & Salmerón, 2019, p. 314). An absence of criticality reflects a form of neuroseduction, whereby neuroscientific accounts increase the likelihood that one will be persuaded by explanations or conclusions that are not justified by the facts. . . . Principal among these for dyslexia, perhaps, is the erroneous belief that brain imaging can be employed for the purpose of differential assessment and intervention rather than this being an aspiration for the future (that may ultimately "be proven to be unfeasible" (Ozernov-Palchik, Yu, Wang, & Gaab, 2016, p. 52). (p. S66)

involved in some of the groups advocating for addressing students diagnosed as dyslexiac. They touted various studies emanating from the neurosciences as supporting their advocacy for a code emphasis, aligning their efforts to translate such research into practice. But such has not been without a significant amount of contentiousness as to whether the evidence and logic warranted the claims (see box). When all is said and done about the implications for this mind-stretching research on brain activity as a function of reading and its subprocesses, we still expect the efficacy of pedagogical approaches to be tested in the crucible of the classroom, not inferred from deep analyses of the pathway from print to meaning for expert adult readers (Shanahan, 2020).

Confirming an Alternative: Reflective Practice

In the United States and elsewhere, the number of detractors has increased as results of improvement have not been forthcoming and local authority has been displaced. Indeed, in the United States, this critique appears to be arising from growing concern over federal versus local control of education, and the lack of national improvement on international comparison. Counterexamples are evident in countries such as Finland (Sahlberg, 2015), where the educational approach undergirds its premier performances on international comparisons of educational achievement. As Hargreaves and Shirley (2007) commented:

> Imagine you are a newly appointed education official in a nation looking for policies to study and adopt in its school system. A couple of options stand out. Country A offers extensive measurements of learning gains for millions of pupils in all its public schools, generates only fair to poor academic outcomes, and ranks near the bottom of 21 industrialized countries in child well-being in a recent UNESCO study. Country B has no system of national testing at all, but its children are consistently at the top of tests used for international comparisons, and it is among the world leaders in the child-well-being rankings.
>
> Which model looks the most attractive? Country A is great for number-crunchers and advocates of "data-driven decisionmaking," but produces poor outcomes and yawning achievement gaps for students. Country B has world-class standards of living and learning for students, but is data-impoverished in comparison to country A. (paras. 5–6)

They suggest:

> In places like Finland and Canada, the world is increasingly embracing a second theory of change that we call "post-standardization." This new theory pays more attention to developing teachers' capacity to meet higher standards, rather than emphasizing the paper standards themselves. It replaces imposed standardization and privatization with networks and peer-driven improvement. Assessment for summative quality assurance is replaced by assessment for learning, where data are used to inform ongoing

decisions to produce better outcomes. In this second theory of change, the teaching profession is a high-caliber resource for and responsible partner in modernization, not an obstacle to be undermined.

It's time to accept that standardization has gone down like a lead balloon, utterly failing to inspire teachers, students, or the public at large. Post-standardization, on the other hand, inspires people's commitment to and capacity for change by connecting a visionary future to a sense of pride in the best of one's past. New economic and social needs beckon, and existing strategies are self-evidently exhausted. Other countries are beating better paths, and it's time for America to follow their lead. The future is not going to be soulless or standardized. Why should our schools be? (Hargreaves & Shirley, 2007, paras. 14–15)

By contrast, many educators remain attracted to the notion of teachers as reflective practitioners.[1] Indeed, a number of teacher groups have formed their own coalitions in an effort to engage with and support one another in their pursuits. For example, under the Whole Language Umbrella there is a consortium of networked groups (e.g., Center for Expansion of Language and Thinking, Teachers Applying Whole Language, etc.) exploring advances in literacy research, theory, and practice. Around the world, groups affiliated with the International Literacy Association and other professional groups have a history of supporting development aligned with reflective practice.

As reflective practitioners, teachers assume roles in which classroom practices are more emergent than predefined, with special emphasis given to practices arising from teachers' transactions with their students, as well as other considerations. In these roles, a teacher may be informed by various readings of past research, but these readings are apt to be critical. The teacher's instructional approach is therefore informed by an array of sources, including the teacher's past experience, the experiences of others, and notions of literacy. Furthermore, instructional adjustments may be made in an ongoing fashion, based on a form of continuous and recursive decisionmaking, as the teacher pursues a scaffolding of learning and uses indicators of the success of certain supports and activities. Figure 9.7 represents an attempt to identify these dimensions and their possible impacts.

Apart from reflective practice having a long history, recent studies of effective schools have supported this approach. Indeed, the now historic Bullock report (1975) from the UK stated:

In our view, teachers should be involved not only experimenting with the outcomes of research, but also in identifying the problems, setting up hypotheses and carrying out the collection and assessment of data. We should particularly like to see more action research . . . for we believe that this form of activity holds considerable promise for the development of new practices in school. (p. 553)

The notion of reflective practice and learner-centered assessment is also consistent with recommendations made by Hoffman (1991), Taylor et al. (1999),

Figure 9.7. Characterization of Reflective Practice

Overall Characteristics

- Nonstandardized, ongoing, and transactional (cf. meaning making).
- Teacher as researcher, informed by array of sources and engaged in a dynamic relationship with students and stakeholders as well as literacies. Teaching is ongoing and complex.
- Teacher as a professional, working in collaboration with parents, students, and colleagues.

Reform Mode

- Inside-out, school- and classroom based, student based, and community based.
- *Sources:* Various observations and sources of data may inform teaching. Local consideration of assessment needs and the development of assessment and evaluation tools in collaboration with colleagues.
- Assumes findings not generalizable, nontransferable, but can inform work in a case-like fashion.

Potential Impacts

- Responsive, dynamic curriculum.
- Greater teacher, student, parent decisionmaking and investment/ownership.
- Nonstandardized and open-ended model of literacy and literacy instruction.
- Qualitative research, action research, and other forms of inquiry—no longer stepchildren.
- Across students and settings, a range of literacy experiences and practices derived from a consideration of sociocultural possibilities, interests, and needs.
- Accountability allows for a range of measures across students and schools.
- Assessment follows from and is in partnership with learning; it is not the determiner of what is taught and learned.

Taylor et al. (2002), and Taylor et al. (1999). For example, based on a review of the literature, Hoffman described eight attributes of effective schools:

1. a clear school mission;
2. effective instructional leadership and practices;
3. high expectations;
4. a safe, orderly, and positive environment;
5. ongoing curriculum improvement;
6. maximum use of instructional time;
7. frequent monitoring of student progress; and
8. positive home-school relationships. (Hoffman, 1991, p. 911–950)

Relatedly, following their analyses of studies examining effective schools, Taylor and her colleagues (2002) found commonalities across the studies distinguishing effective literacy programs as those in which teachers work together and

Table 9.1. Some School Level Factors Responsible for High Achievement in High Poverty Schools

Factors and Focus	Hope: Successful High Poverty Urban Schools	CIERA: Study of Successful High Poverty Schools	Successful Texas Schoolwide Programs	Chicago Schools
Student improvement goals	☐	☐	☐	☐
School leadership	☐			☐
Teacher collaboration	☐	☐	☐	☐
Student data–based decisionmaking	☐	☐	☐	☐
Professionalism and innovation	☐	☐	☐	☐
Parent-school-community connections	☐	☐	☐	☐

Source: Extrapolated from Taylor et al., 2002, p. 369.

use their observations to develop instructional plans along with customized ways to assess them (Table 9.1).

In a similar vein, Rogers et al. (2006) have argued for assessments that are situated. As they describe, a situated assessment is:

> collaboratively developed and used in the context of a particular reform effort and is meant to benefit teachers who use it by informing their instruction. We contrast this to standardized measures that are used solely for accountability rather than for professional development. (p. 544)

In conjunction with their project, Rogers et al. (2006) describe a university-school collaboration to develop the comprehension strategy development of middle-graders. In pursuing the project, they report their arrival at a collaborative engagement among researchers, teachers, and school board consultants for the development of an assessment tool directed at school-specific interests and situations. As they maintain, by pursuing situated assessments, they saw themselves able to:

> respond to the growing demand for assessment approaches that are sensitive to the contexts in which they are used, build on notions of consequential and transactional validity, and allow for critical inquiry into the relationship between curriculum and instruction. This approach also supports and encourages teachers and school administrators who set their own goals for accountability and improvement in literacy. (p. 552)

In terms of the view that teaching involves partnership building, a number of educators have proposed models that entail engaging in meaningful, educationally sound, and ethical partnerships with students, other teachers, and parents—an approach that is formative and transactional (Figure 9.8). This would be consistent with the participatory approach advocated by Barbara Rogoff and colleagues (Rogoff et al., 2001) as well as Deb Butler and Leyton Schnellert (Butler & Schnellert, 2012; Butler et al., 2008), in which engaging with professional personnel and the public as research is planned, pursued, and contemplated in terms of its influence.

As Luke (2004) posited, teachers and teacher educators should strive to be somewhat akin to the cosmopolitan, suggesting that "what is needed is a teacher whose stock and trade is to deal educationally with cultural 'others,' with the kinds of transnational and local diversity that are now a matter of course" (pp. 1438–1439). It is as Purcell-Gates (2006), Rose (1995), and others have advocated: A teacher is someone who develops an understanding of the cultural worlds of students and their communities, and who also has the ability to help improvise within and across these spaces for the betterment of individuals and groups. Such a description would be consistent with the two sets of attributes of teaching detailed by Taylor et al. (2000) (Figure 9.9).

In a fashion befitting reflective teaching, John Guthrie and his colleagues have explored student engagement and proposed an "Index of Reading Engagement" that teachers might enlist to rate their students. The index guides the rating of students in terms of active engagement in reading based on behavior, internal motivation, and cognitive pursuits (see Guthrie, 2004; Guthrie, Hoa et al., 2007; Guthrie, McRae, & Klauda, 2007; Wigfield & Guthrie, 1997; and Wigfield et al., 2008).

Figure 9.8. Model for Collaboration

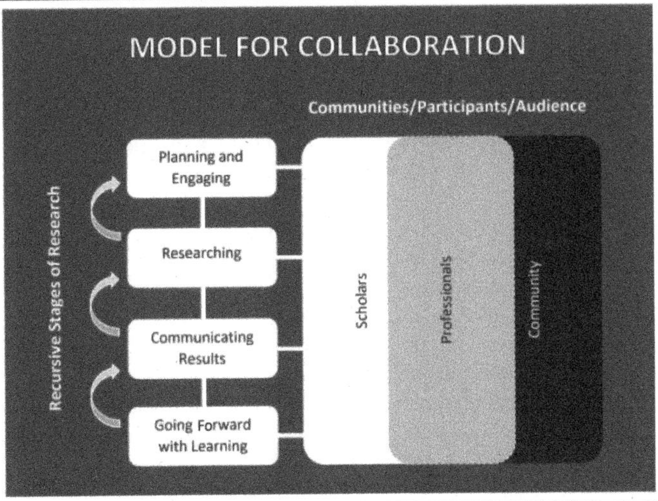

Figure 9.9. Two Sets of Criteria Used to Rate Teacher Accomplishment

Elements of Culturally Responsive Teaching

1. Views teaching as art
2. Views self as community member
3. Faith students can be successful
4. Helping build links between students' worlds, community, nation, etc.
5. Builds from students' knowledge rather than inserts knowledge
6. Engages in student interactions that are sincere and supportive
7. Connects with all students
8. Develops a learning community
9. Supports collaborative learning engagements
10. Respects the (re)creation of knowledge and sharing
11. Explores knowledge critically
12. Passionate about content
13. Develops students, skill repertoire
14. Recognizes the complexity and varied nature of expertise
15. Students are respected as competent
16. Scaffolds students learning
17. Teaching and learning the classroom focus
18. Extends students' learning and thinking
19. Draws on extensive knowledge about the students, issues, and topics explored

Elements of Effective Instruction

1. Purposeful
2. Enthusiastic
3. Task driven
4. Pursues students' engagement
5. Expeditious approach to teaching and learning
6. Ensures time is devoted to reading/language arts
7. Regular and repeated emphasis on skills and strategies
8. Pursues high success
9. Manages classroom well
10. Creates and maintains positive classroom environment
11. Expects student success
12. Makes efforts to address students incurring difficulties
13. Positive reinforcement effectively enlisted
14. Effective pacing of instruction and depth of learning
15. Supports learning with modeling and scaffolding
16. Context-based skills development
17. Additional support for readers in need
18. Student self-regulation supported
19. Balance of instruction
20. Extensive reading and writing of connected texts
22. Challenging and meaningful activities appropriate for learners and goals

Developed from Taylor et al., 2000

The Status Quo, Decentralized and Centralized Reform

Globally, educational reform has struggled with issues of centralization versus decentralization relative to policies and practices and their implementation. If you look at educational development in Asia, for example, there seems to be predominately governmental control of most educational decisions despite some variations across countries. King and Guerra (2005), drawing from World Bank data, developed the following portrayal (Table 9.2).

Table 9.2. OECD World Bank Survey (2003)

	Cambodia	China	Indonesia	Philippines	Thailand
Instructional Matters					
Design program of study	Central gvmt	Central gvmt	Central gvmt	Central gvmt	Central gvmt
Defining course content	Central gvmt	Central gvmt	Central gvmt	Central gvmt	Central gvmt
Choosing textbooks	Central gvmt	Local gvmt and schools	Schools	Schools	Schools
Teaching methods	Schools	Schools	Schools	Schools	Schools
Grouping Students	Schools	Schools	Schools	Schools	Schools
Support activities for students	Central Gvmt	Schools	Schools	Schools	Schools
Setting qualifying exam	Central gvmt	Central & Local gvmt	Central gvmt	Central gvmt	Central gvmt & School
Assessing students' work	Central gvmt	Schools	Schools	Schools	Schools
Management					
Hiring teachers and principals	Central gvmt	Local gvmt	Central & Local gvmt	Intermediate govt	Central gvmt
Salaries	Central gvmt	Central gvmt & school	Central gvmt	Central gvmt	Central gvmt
Careers	Central gvmt	School	School	Intermediate gvmt	Intermediate gvmt & school
Resource decisions	Central gvmt	Local gvmt	Central gvmt	Central gvmt	Central gvmt

Source: OECD, 2003

In Closing

Educational reform—especially literacy reform—can be looked at through various lenses. Specifically, reform developments can be looked in terms of:

- the rationale behind the reform initiative;
- the historical developments that lead up to the reform;
- the views and rhetoric informing these developments and how they position the state, schools, teachers, students, and parents;
- the politics of education, including who is privileged;
- the role of research (what and whose research counts);
- teacher professionalism;
- local versus national versus global considerations and governance;
- the interests served and not served by the reform initiative; and
- the views of reading perpetuated by the reform, including the skills, strategies, and approach to teaching and testing.

Over the last 25 years, there has been a shift in the systems in place for controlling schooling, leading to an emphasis on prescriptive practices, a return to positivism and the search for best practice, and uniform standards and accountability. Matters of diversity and teacher professionalism and decisionmaking were displaced as rhetorical ploys and political shifts coalesced, legislating and funding renewed interests for standardized, top-down control of education. These developments occurred in Western nations especially, though not exclusively. Indeed, educational reform efforts in many countries appear to be aligned with a similar approach, which entails legislated, prescribed educational practices (i.e., a top-down approach) drawing selectively from research findings en route to developing standards and accountability via testing. In particular, many countries have experienced an ongoing battle over curriculum matters such as phonics and whole language.

In terms of research, positivist research in search of best practice has sidelined more critical, situation-specific, and participatory classroom and sociocultural studies. For those of us who have been advocates of reflective and participatory practice, we found ourselves in the role of critics and sometimes adversaries—positioned either as outcasts or as non-scholarly and noncompliant. Jerome Harste (1998) captured these sentiments when he discussed his encounters with the changing political climate in the October 1998 *NCTE Council Chronicle* entitled "A Model of Difference." As Harste stated:

> I think we are in a McCarthy era in reading and it concerns me.
>
> All of a sudden we are supposed to be pleased with research reports on reading that take us back to a Bloomfield view of reading. Reports in which reading is not being seen as an instance of language. That is why they need not review this literature.

Goodman doesn't exist. Reports in which reading and writing relationship research, other than the early literacy stuff, can be ignored. Now Graves doesn't exist. These are decisions that strike at the very heart of our profession. What is particularly insidious is that all of this is being done in the name of science.

Recently, I was asked to respond to Preventing Reading Failure in Young Children at AERA where a panel of the researchers presented sections of this final report published by the National Reading Council.

Specifically, I criticized the report on its many flawed conceptions of reading. I argued that the report positioned itself as having ended the reading wars and in so doing perpetuated the myth that the problems with reading in this country are a result of whole language and phonics wars and that somehow this mess has weakened reading instruction and resulted in declining literacy scores. I suggested that the panel visit schools so they could see for themselves that there is not enough whole language going on in this country to have affected reading scores either positively or negatively. I concluded this first point by arguing that I thought they had the big picture wrong. My second criticism rested on their conception of the reading process. While their exact definition of reading is rather slippery, for the most part they advocate a linguistic model of reading where "real reading" begins with phonological awareness and graphophonemic processing. Everything else is cast as a factor that effects reading. . . . My third criticism of the document was that it posed itself as a document about pedagogy when it was really about power. I used the fact that the report's conclusions already had become legislative action as data to support this hypothesis.

When I got done with my critique, several respected colleagues expressed their disappointment with my remarks. One said he just couldn't understand what it was I disliked about this report. Another said it was a little bit like having a skunk show up at a rose garden party. Still another thought it was most unfortunate I took the position I did and that I should use my position as vice president of NCTE to get behind the report.

. . . Now I personally know that these colleagues of mine have broader views of reading than are reflected in this report. But why, I ask, is no one speaking out? (p. 220)

Optimistically, we may be witnessing some developments that might foreshadow some shifting and new alternatives. These include:

- a growing emphasis on and political lobbying for educational options and local control, together with the reestablishment of a more problem-based, topically oriented, and diverse curriculum with local origins (as opposed to a uniform, academic skill–based curriculum tied to national goals);
- an increased responsiveness by universities to alternative forms of assessment criteria from aspiring applicants;

- growing momentum for mixed methods and participatory forms of research and design-based studies;
- a resurgence in critical studies, especially tied to issues of race, gender, class, economic circumstances, and epistemologies;
- a growing regard for teachers and their professionalism as they pursue ways to connect with their students and colleagues;
- recognition of the importance of a culture of collaboration and learning in schools:
- increased interest in student-led decisionmaking;
- a reorientation of literacy via the integration of digital technologies, with more participatory, socially networked, multilayered, and multimodal learning opportunities; and
- an interest in developing globally astute learners with 21st-century dispositions, understandings, and strategies.

That said, despite these developments, expansive educational developments and change are often elusive—especially when they are pursued in systems that serve other interests and perpetuate the privilege of some over others. At times, such initiatives have faced obstacles when they have failed to address the politics of change, including attitudes, self-interests, and the gravitational forces delegating a more centralized (i.e., undemocratic) authority or a specific form of best practice. Unfortunately, audits of initiatives have sometimes appeared to be sidelined by the power dynamics of institutions, media portrayals of schools and failing students, or the changing commitments and values of authorities. Therefore, even when audits of educational endeavors have illuminated shortcomings in educational programs, substantive change has still proved challenging when faced with competition from other interests and a lack of "true" commitment.

Many of us have been involved in such encounters. Take, if you will, an evaluation of Milwaukee City Schools (Tierney et al., 2008). A team of us were asked to audit the reading services, questioning the lack of funding to inner-city schools as well as the lack of coordinated support for reading. This proved disheartening, especially given the historical privileges of certain well-funded schools and the power given to special education and school psychology (Tierney et al., 2008). Or consider the review of Indigenous education at the University of Sydney (SEG Indigenous Education Review Working Group, 2011). Despite an extensive audit revealing major shortfalls, preexisting institutional forces and historical racism including among university executives proved insurmountable. With some other deans and key Indigenous faculty, analyses were undertaken of the access and graduation rates of Aboriginal and Torres Strait Islanders within each degree program (as well as other features, such as hiring patterns and research). The audit found major shortcomings in access and graduation rates, especially for selected faculties over time, despite significant government funding. While progress seemed promising (and heralded), significant forward progress proved quite modest, especially in certain faculties. It was as if the follow-up to critical analyses was embraced by some but shelved by others.

Educational change and the disruption of systemic forces are also often countered by political maneuvering befitting preexisting biases fueled by pre-set agendas. For example, in a discussion of the Australian government's efforts to meet the needs of their diverse student body (i.e., immigrant and indigenous), a portrayal by Morgan et al. (in press) highlights the disingenuous nature of many of the government's efforts. They make visible how government positions achievement results as a means of discounting and displacing diversity goals with forms of assimilation that advance national agendas perpetuating mainstreaming, accentuating inequities and dismissing situated cultural responses. As we have noted, in the United States, during the No Child Left Behind and Reading First initiatives, the Inspector General's Office exposed similar biases, including efforts by key figures in the U.S. Office of Education to support some groups over others from endorsements for funding in conjunction with reading reform.

Today's literacy scholars are often faced with views by non-educators of what

> The politicization of reading and literacy is particularly evident in the ways in which some educators market ideas and suggestions for reform as "best practice." For example, in Australia, Jennifer Buckingham has been hugely influential positioning her own reading program (multilit.com/about/our-expertise/jennifer-buckingham/). In the United States, Emily Hanford uses blogs and tweets to selectively represent her position on dyslexia as well as what she deems essential reading pedagogy (e.g., Hanford, 2018; Loewus, 2019). The politicization of their position is most apparent in their efforts to introduce legislation in several states, mandating certain emphases to the exclusion of eclecticism and restrictions on the role of teacher decisionmaking.

should be taught and emphasized in ways that are questionable—even if represented as aligned with the "science of reading." In this regard, certain educators seem to have had the ear of politicians as they market their wares (e.g., ideas and suggestions for reform) as best, if not essential practices. At times they appear to have considerable media influence regardless of their credentials or conflict of interests. Disagreements with their position often have resulted in Twitter attacks and other forms of critique in ways that advance oppositional rather than collegial dialogue. Indeed, the recent efforts by the International Literacy Association to advance a collection of papers on the science of reading seemed to fall prey to more disagreement than ecumenicalism as some authors and their followers used the platform to continue their questionable attacks on teachers and the field of literacy (see box, "The Search for the "Science of Reading"; International Literacy Association, 2020).

The Search for the "Science of Reading"

The notion of a science of reading (SOR) dates back several hundred years. In recent history, it has become politicized, employed in lobbying efforts for certain practices over others. The International Dyslexia Association, for example, enlists the term almost as a means of marketing (International Dyslexia Association, 2020b). It is as if the science of reading has become a label—not unlike that of "organic" applied to our foods. Further it is labeling that different groups might appropriate as armament as they continue to pursue a war over what should be taught, when, and how.

When the editors of the *Reading Research Quarterly* invited scholars to submit articles to address this topic, we had envisioned more debate and adamant views. We predicted poorly. The contributors were restrained in their general characterization of the state of reading instruction, the preparation of teachers, and the state of student achievement. Our reading of the separate articles suggested that there was a general consensus that we were "not there yet" relative to science being able to offer guidance to teachers about teaching and learning for diverse classrooms and learners. For those contributors drawing from neuroscience, they were more sanguine rather than certain of the educational implications of such findings. Likewise, the reverence that some scholars had held for the "simple view of reading (SVR)," espoused by Gough and Tunmer (1986), was downplayed—especially when Gough et al. (1996) were quoted as declaring "only a fool would deny that reading is complex. Reading clearly involves many subprocesses, and those subprocesses must be skillfully coordinated" (p. 1). It seemed that all the contributors, regardless of the origins of their perspectives, questioned the state of the science of reading. Most notably, they shied away from the translation of research to practice and the implementation of suggestions of practice for all.

Indeed, it seemed that there was little disagreement about the limitations of the present state of the science of reading—especially in terms of providing guidance for teachers. In their essay on the science of reading, David Yaden, David Reinking, and Peter Smagorinsky (in press) argue the narrow focus on reading is misguiding and misdirected. They raise concerns about the conceptualization of the science of reading. Specifically they suggest that SOR:

> relies on a limited conception of science; ignores relevant environmental factors; and . . . uncritically accepts experimentation as the only valid approach to social science inquiry in literacy . . . leading to the oversimplification of understanding the nature of the reading process, of teaching reading, and of conducting research into effective reading pedagogies. The conception of science embedded in SOR research reduces reading to a technical

exercise that eliminates critical variables that follow from how the vicissitudes of living in a complex physical and social world contribute to how people read, why they read, and how they experience reading instruction.

Or, as Tim Shanahan in his contribution, "What Constitutes a Science of Reading Instruction," noted:

Making predictions about what kinds of instruction will be effective on the basis of basic research is a fraught enterprise. When the predictions are incorrect, they encourage poor pedagogy. When they are sound, their value can only be determined by their consistency with the findings of instructional studies. As such, the predictions reinforce what we learn from instructional studies, strengthening our trust in those pedagogical findings through their consonance with the predictions. Again, this does not denigrate the value of basic research for identifying potential pedagogical innovations or insightful explanations that could lead to even greater future innovation. Yet, no matter how good the ideas of basic research, they must be tried out instructionally and shown to be beneficial in improving reading ability or its dispersion in some way before they should be recommended to educators and policymakers. (Shanahan, 2020, p. 241)

Even Mark Seidenberg and his colleagues seemed more set on suggesting future directions, needs, and hypotheses than they were in providing certainties (Seidenberg et al., 2020). Indeed, Seidenberg, who had spurred considerable media attention (e.g., Hanford, 208; Seidenberg, 2017) and some of the debates around the need for a science of reading, affirmed that we lacked answers that could guide reading instruction. Seidenberg and his colleagues advocated the need to move forward with multiple, cross-disciplinary endeavors; studies of teaching practices; avoidance of a narrow focus (e.g., on phonics); more studies on what might be done in different contexts to enhance early learning; a focus on all learners; and an examination of the systems in place that might enhance or detract from improvements to practice.

Such tempered responses were echoed in the paper by those involved in the Reading for Understanding report for the National Academy of Education (Cervetti et al., 2020). Offering a cautionary note about the Simple View of Reading, Cervetti et al. stated:

the temptation to draw implications for pedagogy must be tempered by a countervailing cautionary disposition to avoid drawing unwarranted inferences about the efficacy of pedagogical alternatives that have not themselves been rigorously examined. One of the important limitations of the public "science of reading" debate has been the use of just such unwarranted inferences. Caution is particularly appropriate in this discussion of research that has highlighted the importance of the language component of the SVR. (p. 168)

In a similar vein, Pat Alexander (2020) argued:

The reality is that reading does not begin or end with phonics or whole-word instruction (Seidenberg, 2013). It is far broader and more complex. Reading, broadly conceived, is any interaction between a person—be it a child, adolescent, or adult—and written language. . . . That interaction can involve written language at many levels, from words and sentences, to paragraphs, to entire volumes. . . . Also, reading can be performed for many reasons, from purely personal to largely academic, and in many contexts, both in and out of school, as well as online or in print.

This reconceptualization of reading also requires some adjustment in what qualifies as text. Certainly, texts still encompass many well-known, traditional forms, such as works of fiction, exposition, folk tales, picture books, biography, and poetry. Yet, for today's students, fondly referred to as the iGeneration or iGens, many nontraditional, nonacademic, and ever-evolving forms of text are part of their reading experiences. Those alternative texts commonly found online and in social media include text messages, tweets, blogs, websites, memes, and podcasts. (p. 90)

It was impressive that most contributors questioned whether or not they were in a position to make strong claims from their own research about teaching practice. At times, they seemed to question the evidence supporting some of their own cases for doing so. For instance, a compelling critique of the attacks on the quality of teachers and their preparation was pursued by James Hoffman, Michiko Hikida, and Misty Sailors. Hoffman et al. (2020) questioned the bases, credentials, and posture of many critics of teacher education at the same time as they argued for more voice for teachers and teacher educators and suggested the worth of design experiments. As they stated:

The SOR is being used to silence the literacy teacher preparation community through its unfounded claims regarding what matters, what is known, and what must be done. To question these claims or inquire into their scientific base (as many have done) is met with charges of ignorance, incompetence, and/or ideological bias. . . . Those silenced are not only teacher educators preparing the future generations of teachers but also teachers and students, especially in schools serving linguistically rich and culturally diverse communities. Also, as we argued earlier, the silencing withholds the truth from the public regarding the complexity of the field's work to improve practice.

For the literacy teacher preparation profession, the SOR version of science works to corrupt our efforts to become better at what we do. The science that matters in growing more powerful literacy teacher preparation practices is the version of science that invites us to imagine, dialogue, design, and innovate. (p. 264)

Numerous contributors argued a range of similar concerns about the gaps in the research from the populations that are addressed and the adjustments to systems and the fluidity of change (e.g., Milner, 2020; Woulfin & Gabriel, 2020). Additionally, as Stephen Graham (2020) argued, there was a concern about the curriculum frameworks and their shortcomings:

If teachers are to use reading and writing instruction more regularly in mutually supportive ways, this must be championed by multiple parties, including policymakers, professional organizations, and school administrators. How much time and attention teachers devote to such instruction is dictated in part by national, state, district, and school policies. It is unlikely that current reading and writing practices will change to accommodate more connected reading and writing activities if the importance of these practices is not understood and advocated by all constituents . . . classroom change involves more than creating better teachers. It also involves creating better systems. This will not happen magically. (p. 42)

If we ask the proverbial question, "Are we there yet?" the answer is an agreed upon "No." The science of reading might be better positioned as an ecumenical pursuit for inquiry-based educational endeavors rather than a competition for converts to prescribed practices or a prescribed marketing label. Hopefully, we can continue to learn together rather than view the science of reading as a race to a set destination.

The politicization of reading and literacy research has extended throughout the modern period—especially as politicians, the media, commercial interests and certain groups have lobbied for what seems like pre-set views. Most notably, the debate about beginning reading methods has involved diehard advocates, with passions that at times seem like manipulative practices especially relative to what is and is not endorsed as best practice. In the 1960s, despite the finding from the major federally funded comprehensive study that supported eclecticism and no one best approach to teaching reading, advocates of a restricted phonics emphasis seemed intent on cherry-picking conclusions to support their position (Bond & Dykstra, 1967). In the 1990s, efforts to do the same manifested in a narrow view of what research might be funded, what research might count, and the basis for determining best practice. In the United Kingdom, Australia, and the United States, key reports were written by groups or individuals with preexisting allegiances to such an advocacy, and counters to such reports were dismissed (e.g., Adams, 1994; National Reading Panel, 2000; Rowe, 2005). It was noticeable in the studies that informed such syntheses that certain findings were excluded as evidence and national and state achievement data were interpreted in ways that were questionable and designed to advance certain arguments over others. For instance, in the 1990s, lagging achievement results were erroneously attributed to the recent literature-based approaches and other practices. Further, longitudinal studies that confirmed the limitations of a restricted emphasis on decoding were avoided. Adding to such biases, exclusionary practices—including the "blackballing" of opposing views and approaches—also occurred. Unfortunately, despite efforts to move beyond the "reading wars" (Ewing, 2006; Flippo, 2012; Snyder, 2008), research has taken more of a back seat to reform initiatives or has been enlisted only selectively in the interest of changes that seem more tied to political interests or what seems akin to passionate partisan advocacies (e.g., Lyon, 2000). As Peter Johnston and Donna Scanlon noted in their report entitled "An Examination of Dyslexia Research and Instruction, with Policy Implications" for the Literacy Research Association:

> the idea that there is a settled science that has determined the only approach to the teaching of reading, is simply wrong. There is no evidence that the highly scripted approaches . . . are more effective than other approaches. (Johnston & Scanlon, 2020, p. 12)

Perhaps these forces will be countered with a reawakening to the concerns raised in earlier periods—when a multiplicity of research approaches was embraced and the commitment to best practices was countered with considerations of the rich but varied backgrounds, circumstances, needs, and interests of students at the hands of professional educators. As Duffy and Hoffman (2002) remarked:

> Classrooms and schools . . . are multilayered and vary from context to context. One size does not fit all. So when we impose the seductively simple idea of implementing "research-based" correlates, we see only superficial improvements in teaching and only get gains in low-level literacy skills.
>
> Creating substantial forms of instructional effectiveness and substantive forms of literacy achievement requires that we examine the deeper structures guiding teachers' and school leaders' enactment of teaching. This enacting is not a simple matter of technical competence with observed correlates of effectiveness. Rather, the best teachers weave a variety of teaching activities together in an infinitely complex and dynamic response to the flow of classroom life, and the best school leaders weave school conditions together in an infinitely complex response to life in schools. It is more like orchestration than a straightforward implementation. (p. 376)

Such views align with the views espoused by the International Literacy Association when they discussed "evidence-based" practice. As IRA's position indicated:

> Time and again, research has confirmed that regardless of the quality of a program, resource, or strategy, it is the teacher and learning situation that make the difference

(Bond & Dykstra, 1967/1997). This evidence underscores the need to join practices grounded in sound and rigorous research with well-prepared and skillful teachers. . . .

In its simplest form, evidence-based reading instruction means that a particular program or collection of instructional practices has a record of success. That is, there is reliable, trustworthy, and valid evidence to suggest that when the program is used with a particular group of children, the children can be expected to make adequate gains in reading achievement. . . . In addition to evaluating the quality of the data by which programs or practices are judged, teachers also must ask if the children in their classroom closely resemble the children from whom the evidence was collected. . . . [I]f the answer to all of these questions is yes, then teachers might conclude that there is a good fit and that their children might be expected to make similar achievement gains with the same program or practice. If, however, the answer to some or all of our questions is no, then it is difficult to predict whether similar results might be achieved. The quest to find the "best programs" for teaching reading has a long and quite unsuccessful history. . . . The challenge that confronts teachers and administrators is the need to view the evidence that they read through the lens of their particular school and classroom setting. (International Reading Association, 2002, pp. 232–236)

Likewise, in a statement of the Board of the International Literacy Association prefacing the 2020 science of reading discussion, the organization offered a similar position:

The sciences of our readings are complex, dynamic and multidimensional. Reading educators in their efforts to support diverse literacy learners need to adroitly, discerningly and adeptly support reading development attuned to different circumstances. In our classrooms, it would be amiss not to draw upon multiple sciences—psychological, sociological, and others. Educators must navigate different circumstances from an embrace of offerings from all of the sciences.

Final Word

Viewed through a wide lens, reform developments fit with the overall metaphor of waves. Befitting the ocean metaphor, there is both beauty and ugliness in what might be encountered. One can relish the earnest desire of educators to improve learning. However, there is a danger in the adamancy if it is done without respecting the elements involved, including:

1. the different backgrounds and needs of learners;
2. the teacher as a professional;
3. local knowledge to guide, adjust, and customize any reform effort;
4. an understanding of the goals of the project in terms of achieving sustained and transferable abilities; and
5. how these elements all connect in time and space with people in different ways.

Ideally, literacy pursuits could integrate support for a reform agenda that also rewards teachers and educators for their innovations and critical reflexivity. Those advancing teacher professionalism should be heralded, especially those engaged in the ongoing pursuits directed at improving practices and frameworks for literacy development. Certainly, some exciting new curricular possibilities emerged, including the "New Basics and Rich Literacy Tasks" developed by Allan Luke and Peter Freebody (Education Queensland, 2000a&b; Freebody & Luke, 1990; Luke, 1999). In terms of meeting the needs of at-risk students and monitoring their efforts, initiatives such as *Reading Recovery* (Clay, 1993; Pinnell et al., 1988) and *Success for All* (Slavin et al., 1996) reflect unparalleled initiatives in terms of success.

From a disciplinary orientation, we are also seeing support for "content-rich" teaching, with approaches like "The Seeds of Science/Roots of Reading" (e.g., Pearson et al., 2010) as well as those that involve sociocultural frameworks, as seen in the approaches proposed for the 2025 National Assessment of Educational Progress (National Assessment Governing Board, 2020) and the pursuit of scenario-based assessment (Sabatini et al., 2016; Sabatini et al., 2019).

In addition, we are seeing creative studies of reform forces, as literacy educators continue to explore the development of learning communities (Rogoff et al., 2001), and various new lens are enlisted to expand our understandings of literacy education across time, place, and people. For example, in her book *Place Stories: Time, Space and Literacy in Two Classrooms*, Margaret Sheehy (2008) examined literacy practices related to school change within the framework of "place" that may enable or obstruct school reform, change, and development. Via discourse analyses, Rachel Gabriel (2019) traced the evolution of reform movements such as those advocated by proponents for dyslexia, while Stornaiuolo et al. (2017) explored dimensions such as emergence, uptake, resonance, and scale. Bringing these elements to the surface, they argue, serves as a way of capturing "different kinds of relations among people and things—whether in horizontal, vertical, rhizomatic, or other relationships—systems that (re)produce, exacerbate, and/or challenge social inequities" (p. 84).

There are also new perspectives, technologies, and practices. In terms of perspectives, critical theory and global developments are contributing to major shifts in our orientation, focus, and paths forward. For example, critical theory represents ways of challenging the systemic forces in place that reproduce privilege and perpetuate discriminatory practices. In terms of technology, the advent of online literacies has entailed a shift in the digital from a palate of tools to a portal through which we engage with our informational, social, and media worlds (social, economic, cultural, scholarly and political). In terms of practices, there are significant shifts afoot in our views of learning and research on learning. In particular, there is a growing appreciation of the situatedness of learning, including research shaped by sociocultural understandings of literacy practices and their diverse underpinnings for different peoples (e.g., Flood & Anders, 2005; Gunderson, 2007; Hare, 2013, 2016; Henry, 2017; Marshall & Toohey, 2010; Rogers & Soter, 1997; Rogers et al., 2006; Shapiro, 1996; Shapiro et al., 2002).

Befitting these developments, there has also been a shift to research that is action oriented and geared toward formative pursuits, rather than toward the pre-set and prescriptive (Anderson & Shattuck, 2012; Design-Based Research Collaborative, 2003; Bradley & Reinking, 2008; Stahl et al., 2019). Such pursuits involve forms of participatory engagements (Jenkins, 2009) and strategies for engaging with our world through a multidisciplinary lens that capitalizes and builds on the different expertises of various fields of study (e.g., Halliday & Martin, 1993; Shanahan & Shanahan, 2008). Growing out of grounded studies of literacy practices, views of comprehension have expanded to embrace disciplinary reading—tied to how experts in different fields (e.g., physics, chemistry, geography, history, medicine, computer science) might read, problem solve, and conduct their inquiries. As Shanahan and Shanahan (2008) suggested, this entails a shift to literacy in the future that is more differentiated in meeting the changing needs of learners. As they stated, it involves "a literacy curriculum that directly guides students to better meet the particular demands of reading and writing in the disciplines than has been provided by traditional conceptions of content-area reading" (p. 57).

These developments befit this whirlpool of activity around participatory learning, disciplinary comprehension, project-based learning, and design experiments. Further, they capitalize on the virtual tools afforded by digital engagements, exploring the different ways of knowing reflected across a planet of varied and diverse peoples with different interests and ways of seeing the world.

References

Adams, M. (1994). *Beginning to read: Thinking and learning about print*. MIT Press.

Allington, R. L. (2002). *Big brother and the national reading curriculum: How ideology trumped evidence*. Heinemann.

Allington, R., & Cunningham, P. (1996). *Schools that work: Where all children read and write* (1st ed.). Allyn and Bacon.

Anders, P. L., & Guzzetti, B. (2005). *Literacy instruction in the content areas*. Erlbaum.

Anderson, R. C., Hiebert, E. H., Scott, J. A., & Wilkinson, I. A. G. (1985). *Becoming a nation of readers: The report of the Commission on Reading*. The Center for the Study of Reading, National Institute of Education, National Academy of Education.

Anderson, T., & Shattuck, J. (2012). Design-based research: A decade of progress in education research? *Educational Researcher, 41*(1), 16–25.

Beck, I. L., McKeown, M. G., & Kucan, L. (2013). *Bringing words to life: Robust vocabulary instruction* (2nd ed.). Guilford.

Bennett, W. J., & Finn Jr., C. E. (1999, June 23). Idea whose time has come: 'Straight A's.' *Los Angeles Times*. www.latimes.com/archives/la-xpm-1999-jun-23-me-49295-story.html#null

Berman, B. (2004, April). *What works clearinghouse*. Speech delivered to TQE grant holders at AIR: American Institutes for Research, U.S. Department of Education.

Blair, J. (2004). Congress orders thorough study of teacher education programs. *Education Week, 23*(25), 13.

Bond, E., Tierney, R. J., Bertelsen, C. B., & Bresler, J. (1997). *A confluence of agendas and power relationships: Student-led conferences*. Paper presented at the National Reading Conference, Phoenix, AZ.

Bond, G. L., & Dykstra, R. (1967). The cooperative research program in first-grade reading instruction. *Reading Research Quarterly, 2*(4), 5–142. doi: 10.2307/746948

Boruch, R. F., & Mosteller, F. (2002). Overview and new directions. In F. Mosteller & R. F. Boruch (Eds.), *Evidence matters: Randomized trials in education research* (pp. 1–14). Brookings Institution Press.

Bradley, B. A., & Reinking, D. (2011). A formative experiment to enhance teacher-child language interaction in a pre-school classroom. *Journal of Early Childhood Literacy, 11*(3), 362–401.

Brown, J. S., Collins, A., & Duguid, P. (1989). Situated cognition and the culture of learning. *Educational Researcher, 18*(1), 32–42. doi: 10.3102/0013189X018001032

Bullock, A. (1975). *A language for life.* Report of the Committee of Inquiry appointed by the Secretary of State for Education and Science. London: Her Majesty's Stationery Office.

Burtless, G. (2002). Randomised field trials for policy evaluation: Why not in education? In F. Mosteller & R. Boruch (Eds.), *Evidence matters: Randomized trials in education research* (pp. 179–197). The Brookings Institute.

Butler, D. L., & Schnellert, L. (2012). Collaborative inquiry in teacher professional development. *Teaching and Teacher Education, 28*, 1206–1220.

Butler, D. L., Schnellert, L. & Higginson, S. (2008, April). Fostering agency and co-regulation: Teachers using formative assessment to calibrate practice in an age of accountability. Paper presented at the American Educational Research association, New York.

Campbell, D. T. (1975). Assessing the impact of planned social change. In G. Lyons (Ed.), *Social research and public policies: The Dartmouth/OECD conference* (pp. 3–45). Dartmouth College, The Public Affairs Center.

Carr, W., & Kemmis, S. (1986). *Becoming critical: Education, knowledge, and action research.* Falmer Press.

Center for Education Evaluation and Regional Assistance. (2008). *Reading first impact study: Interim report.* Institute of Education Sciences/U.S. Department of Education.

Cervetti, G. N., Pearson, P. D., Palincsar, A. S., Afflerbach, P., Kendeou, P., Biancasosa, G., Higgs, J., Fitzgerald, M. S., & Berman, A. L. (2020). How the Reading for Understanding Initiatives' research complicates the simple view of reading invoked in the science of reading. *Reading Research Quarterly, 55*(S1), 161–171.

Clay, M. M. (1993). *Reading recovery: A guidebook for teachers.* Heinemann.

Clay, M. M. (1998). *By different paths to common outcomes.* Stenhouse.

Claycomb, C., & Kysilko, D. (2000). The purposes and elements of effective assessment systems: The policy framework. *State Education Standard, 1*(2), 6–11.

Cobb, P., McClain, K., de Silva Lamberg, T., & Dean, C. (2003). Situating teachers' instructional practices in the institutional setting of the school and district. *Educational Researcher, 32*(6), 13–24. doi: 10.3102/0013189X032006013

Cochran-Smith, M., & Lytle, S. L. (1993). *Inside/outside: Teacher research and knowledge.* Teachers College Press.

Coles, G. (2002). *Great unmentionables: What national reading reports and reading legislation don't tell you.* Heinemann.

Cunningham, J. W. (2001). The National Reading Panel report. *Reading Research Quarterly, 36*(3), 326–335. doi: 10.1598/RRQ.36.3.5

de Broucker, P., & Sweetman, A. (Eds.). (2001). *Towards evidence-based policy for Canadian education.* John Deutsch Institute for the Study of Economic Policy, Queen's University.

Dehaene, S. (2011). The massive impact of literacy on the brain and its consequences for education. *Human Neuroplasticity and Education, 117*, 19–32, 237–238.

Department of Education and the Arts, Queensland Government. (2005). *Queensland curriculum, assessment and reporting framework*. Department of Education and the Arts, Strategic Policy and Education Futures, Queensland Government.

Department of Education, Australian Government. (2007). *Employment and workplace relations. National goals for Indigenous education*.

Department of Education, Government of Western Australia, School Curriculum and Standards Authority. (2006). *Curriculum Improvement Program–Phase Two*. Government of Western Australia. www.det.wa.edu.au/education/curriculum/CIP2/

Department of Education, Tasmanian Government. (2005). *The essential learnings assessing guide*. The Tasmanian Government. www.asec.purdue.edu/lct/HBCU/documents/Assessguide.pdf

Duffy, G. G. (1990). What counts in teacher education? Dilemmas in educating empowered teachers (Presidential address of the Annual Meeting of the National Reading Conference, Miami, FL). In J. Zutell & S. McCormick (Eds.), *Learner factors/teacher factors: Issues in literacy research and instruction, 40th yearbook of the National Reading Conference* (pp. 1–18). National Reading Conference.

Duffy, G. G., & Hoffman, J. V. (2002). Beating the odds in literacy education: Not the "betting on" but the "bettering of" schools and teachers? In B. Taylor & P. D. Pearson (Eds.), *Teaching reading: Effective schools, accomplished teachers* (pp. 361–373). Erlbaum.

Education Queensland. (2000a). *Literate futures: Report of the literacy review for Queensland state schools. Education Queensland*. Education Queensland.

Education Queensland. (2000b). *New Basics: Curriculum organizers*. Education Queensland.

Ehri, L.C. (2020). The science of learning to read words: A case for systematic phonics instruction. *Reading Research Quarterly, 51*(S1), 45–60.

Elliott, J. G. (2020). It's time to be scientific about dyslexia. *Reading Research Quarterly, 55*(S1), S61–S75. doi: 10.1002/rrq.333

Ellwein, M. C., Glass, G. V., & Smith, M. L. (1988). Standards of competence: Propositions on the nature of testing reforms. *Educational Researcher, 17*(8), 4–9.

Ewing, R. (2006). *Beyond the reading wars: A balanced approach to helping children learn to read*. Primary English Teachers Association Australia (PETAA).

Fisher, D., Frey, N., & Lapp, D. (2015). Learning cycles that deepen students' interactions with text. *Voices from the Middle, 22*(4), 15–19. www.ncte.org/library/NCTEFiles/Resources/Journals/VM/0224-may2015/VM0224Learning.pdf

Flippo, R. F. (2012). *Reading researchers in search of common ground* (2nd ed.). Routledge.

Flood, J., & Anders, P. L. (Eds.). (2005). *Literacy development of students in urban schools: Research and policy*. International Reading Association.

Freebody, P., & Luke, A. (1990). Literacies programs: Debates and demands in cultural context. *Prospect, 5*(3), 7–15.

Fullan, M. (2015). *The new meaning of educational change* (5th ed.). Teachers College Press.

Gabriel, R. (2019). Converting to privatization: A discourse analysis of dyslexia policy narratives. *American Educational Research Journal, 57*(1), 355–358.

Gonski, D. (2011). *Review of funding for schooling—Final report*. Department of Education, Employment, and Workplace Relations, Government of Australia. docs.education.gov.au/system/files/doc/other/review-of-funding-for-schooling-final-report-dec-2011.pdf

Goswami, U., & Bryant, P. (1990). *Phonological skills and learning to read*. Psychology.

Gough, P., Juel, C., & Roper/Schneider, D. (1983). Code and cipher: A two-stage conception of initial reading acquisition. In J. A. Niles & L. A. Harris (Eds.), *Searches for meaning in reading/language processing and instruction* (pp. 207–211). National Reading Conference.

Gough, P. B., Hoover, W. A., & Peterson, C. L. (1996). Some observations on a simple view of reading. In C. Cornoldi & J. Oakhill (Eds.), *Reading comprehension difficulties: Processes and intervention* (pp. 1–13). Erlbaum.

Gough, P. B., & Tunmer, W. E. (1986). Decoding, reading, and reading disability. *Remedial and Special Education, 7*(1), 6–10. doi: 10.1177/074193258600700104

Graham, S. (2020). The sciences of reading and writing become more fully integrated. *Reading Research Quarterly, 55*(1), 35–44.

Gunderson, L. (2007). *English-only instruction and immigrant students in secondary schools: A critical examination.* Erlbaum.

Guthrie, J. T. (2004). Reading engagement index. cori.umd.edu/measures/REI.pdf

Guthrie, J. T., Hoa, A. L. W., Wigfield, A., Tonks, S. M., Humenick, N., & Littles, E. (2007). Reading motivation and reading comprehension growth in the later elementary years. *Contemporary Educational Psychology, 32*, 282–313.

Guthrie, J. T., McRae, A., & Klauda, S. L. (2007). Contributions of concept-oriented reading instruction to knowledge about interventions for motivations in reading. *Educational Psychologist, 42*, 237–250.

Gutiérrez, K. (2004). Literacy as laminated activity: Rethinking literacy for English learners. In J. Worthy, B. Maloch, J. V. Hoffman, D. L. Schallert, & C. M. Fairbanks (Eds.), *53rd yearbook of the National Reading Conference* (pp. 101–114). National Reading Conference.

Halliday, M. A. K., & Martin, J. R. (Eds.). *Writing science: Literacy and discursive power.* Falmer Press, 1993.

Haney, W. (1993). Testing and minorities. In L. Weis & M. Fine (Eds.), *Beyond silenced Voices: Class, race, and gender in United States schools* (pp. 45–74). SUNY Press.

Hanford, E. (2018, September 10). Hard words: Why aren't kids being taught to read? APM Reports. www.apmreports.org/episode/2018/09/10/hard-words-why-american-kids -arent-being-taught-to-read

Hanford, E. (2019, August 22). At a loss for words: How a flawed idea is teaching millions of kids to be poor readers. *APM Reports.* www.apmreports.org/episode/2019/08/22 /whats-wrong-how-schools-teach-reading

Hare, J. (2013). What I can learn about Indigenous storytelling traditions that I might apply to the teaching of graphic novels written by Indigenous authors? In T. Dobson, K. James, & C. Leggo (Eds.), *Handbook of secondary English* (pp. 33–39). Pearson Canada.

Hare, J. (2016). Indigenous pedagogies in early learning: Linking community knowledge to school based settings. In A. Anderson, J. Anderson, J. Hare, & M. McTavish (Eds.), *Language, learning and culture in early childhood: Home, school and community contexts* (pp. 197–213). Routledge.

Hargreaves, A., & Shirley, D. (2007, December 21). The coming age of post-standardization. *Education Week, 27.* www.edweek.org/ew/articles/2007/12/21/17hargreaves_web.h27 .html

Harste, J. (1998). A model of difference. *NCTE Council Chronicle 8*, 220.

Hawkins, J. (with Blakeslee, S.). (2004). *On intelligence* (1st ed.). Times Books.

Henry, A. (2017). Culturally relevant pedagogies: Possibilities and challenges for African Canadian Children (Special issue: Twenty-year retrospective of culturally relevant pedagogy, G. Ladson-Billings, & A. Dixon (Eds.)). *Teachers College Record, 119*(1), 1–27.

Hess, F. (2014, Fall). How the common core went wrong. *National Affairs, 45.* www
.nationalaffairs.com/publications/detail/how-the-common-core-went-wrong#:~:text
=Third%2C%20critics%20have%20raised%20concerns%20that%20the%20
Common,the%20Gettysburg%20Address%20and%20the%20Declaration%20of%20
Independence

Hiebert, E. H. (2017). The texts of literacy instruction: Obstacles to or opportunities for
educational equity? *Literacy Research: Theory, Method, and Practice, 66(1),* 117–134.

Hiebert, E. H., & Kamil, M. (2007). Teaching and learning vocabulary.: Bringing research to
practice. New York: Taylor & Francis.

Hoffman, J. V. (1991). Teacher and school effects in learning to read. In R. Barr, M. L. Kamil,
P. Mosenthal, & P. D. Pearson (Eds.), *Handbook of reading research* (Vol. 2, pp. 911–
950). Longman.

Hoffman, J. V., Hikida, M., & Sailors, M. (2020). Contesting science that silences: Amplifying equity, agency, and design research in literacy teacher preparation. *Reading Research Quarterly, 55(S1),* S255–S266. doi: 10.1002/rrq.353

Hogaboam T. W. (1983). Reading patterns in eye movement data. In K. Rayner (Ed.), *Eye
movements in reading: Perceptual and language processes* (pp. 309–332). Academic Press.

International Dyslexia Association. (2020a). W2–Dyslexia and the brain: Understanding
the neuroscience of reading development and disability (webpage). International Dyslexia Association. dyslexiaida.org/w2/

International Dyslexia Association. (2020b, February). The science of reading: A response
to the *New York Times* (webpage). International Dyslexia Association, *9*(1). dyslexiaida
.org/the-science-of-reading-a-response-to-the-new-york-times/

International Literacy Association. (2020a). Science of reading. *Reading Research Quarterly,
55*(s1). Wiley Company.

International Literacy Association. (2020b). *ILA launches landmark literacy research resource and related digital events: A statement from the ILA Board.* ILA.

International Reading Association. (2002). *Evidence-based reading instruction: Putting
the National Reading panel report into practice* (pp. 232–236). International Reading
Association.

Jenkins, H. (2009). *Confronting the challenges of participatory culture: Media education for
the 21st century.* The MIT Press.

Johnston, P. (2003). Assessment conversations. *The Reading Teacher, 57*(1), 90–92. Reprinted in S. J. Barrentine & S. M. Stokes (Eds.). (2005). *Reading assessment: Principles and practices for elementary teachers* (2nd ed., pp. 74–76). International Reading
Association.

Johnston, P. , & Scanlon, D. (2020). An examination of dyslexia research and instruction, with policy implications. Literacy research report for Literacy Research
Association.

Juel, C., & Minden-Cupp, C. (2000). Learning to read words: Linguistic units and instructional strategies. *Reading Research Quarterly, 35*(4), 458–492.

Juel, C., & Roper/Schneider, D. (1981). The growth of letter-sound correspondence knowledge in first grade and its relation to reading achievement and programs. Paper presented at the Annual Meeting of the National Reading Conference December 2–5,
Dallas, TX.

Kamil, M. L. (2004). Vocabulary and comprehension instruction: Summary and implications of the National Reading Panel findings. In P. McCardle and V. Chhabra (Eds.),
The voice of evidence in reading research (pp. 213–234). Paul H. Brookes.

Kamil, M., & Hiebert, E. (2005). Teaching and learning vocabulary: Perspectives and persistent issues. In E. H. Hiebert and M. L. Kamil (Eds.), *Teaching and learning vocabulary: Bringing research to practice* (pp. 1–23). Erlbaum.

Kemp, D. (1999, May). *Outcomes reporting and accountable schooling.* Speech delivered to the Curriculum Corporation's Sixth National Conference, Australia.

Kincheloe, J. L. (1991). *Teachers as researchers: Qualitative inquiry as a path to empowerment.* Routledge.

King, E. M., & Guerra, S. C. (2005). Education reforms in East Asia: Policy, process, and impact. In *East Asia decentralizes: Making local government work* (pp. 179–208). The International World Bank for Reconstruction and Development/The World Bank.

Kohn, A. (1998). Only for my kid: How privileged parents undermine school reform. *Phi Delta Kappan, 79*(8), 568–577.

Ladson-Billings, G. (1994). *The dreamkeepers: Successful teachers of African American children.* Jossey-Bass.

Lather, P. (2003, April). *This IS your father's paradigm; Government intrusion and the case of qualitative research in education.* Guba Lecture, presented at the American Educational Research Association Annual meeting, Chicago, IL.

Linn, R. L., Baker, E. L., & Betebenner, D. W. (2002). Accountability systems: Implications of requirements of the No Child Left Behind Act of 2001. *Educational Researcher, 31*(6), 3–16. doi: 10.3102/0013189X031006003

Loewus, L. (2019). What teachers should know about the science of reading (Video and Transcript). *Education Week.* blogs.edweek.org/teachers/teaching_now/2019/03/what _teachers_should_know_about_the_science_of_reading_video_and_transcript.html

Loveless, T., Peterson, P., Boruch, R., Cook, T., Gueron, J., Hyatt, H., & Mosteller, F. (1999). Can we make education policy on the basis of evidence? What constitutes high quality educational research and how can it be incorporated into policymaking? A Brookings Press Forum. The Brookings Institution.

Luke, A. (1999). Education 2010 and new times: Why equity and social justice still matter, but differently. Education Queensland online conference. October 20, 1999.

Luke, A. (2004). Teaching after the market: From commodity to cosmopolitan. *Teachers College Record, 106*(7), 1422–1443.

Lyon, G. R. (2000, January/February). Why reading is not a natural process. *LDA Newsbriefs.* www.ldonline.org/article/6396/

Lyon, G. R., & Chhabra, V. (2004). The science of reading research. *Educational Leadership, 61*(6), 12–17. www.ascd.org/publications/educational-leadership/mar04/vol61 /num06/The-Science-of-Reading-Research.aspx

Madaus, G. F. (1988). The influence of testing on the curriculum. In L. N. Tanner (Ed.), *Critical issues in curriculum: 87th yearbook of the National Society for the Study of Education.* (pp. 83–121). University of Chicago Press.

Madaus, G. F., & Clarke, M. (2001). The adverse impact of high stakes testing on minority students: Evidence from one hundred years of test data. In G. Orfield & M. L. Kornhaber (Eds.), *Raising standards or raising barriers? Inequality and high stakes testing in education* (pp. 85–106). Century Foundation Press.

Marshall, E., & Toohey, K. (2010). Representing family: Community funds of knowledge, bilingualism, and multimodality. *Harvard Educational Review, 80*(2), 221–242.

Massey, D. (2005). *For space.* SAGE.

McCaffrey, D. F., Lockwood, J. R., Koretz, D. M., & Hamilton, L. S. (2003). Evaluating Value-Added Models for teacher accountability. RAND Corporation. www.rand.org /content/dam/rand/pubs/monographs/2004/RAND_MG158.pdf

McCormick, S., & Zutell, J. (2011). *Instructing students who have literacy problems* (6th ed.). Pearson.

McKeown, M. G., & Beck, I. L. (2014). Effects of vocabulary instruction on measures of language processing: Comparing two approaches. *Early Childhood Research Quarterly, 29*(4), 520–530.

McNeil, L. M. (2000). *Contradictions of school reform: Educational costs of standardized testing.* Routledge. doi: 10.4324/9780203900451

Miller, J. (1990). *Creating spaces and finding voices: Teachers collaborating for empowerment.* SUNY Press.

Milner, H. R. (2020). Disrupting racism and whiteness in researching a science of reading. *Reading Research Quarterly, 55*(S1), S249–S253. doi: 10.1002/rrq.347

Morgan, A., Reid, N., Freebody, P. (in press). Literacy and linguistic diversity in Australia. In L. Verhoeven, S. Nag, C. Perfetti, & K. Pugh (Eds.), *Global variation in literacy development.* Cambridge University Press.

Mosle, S. (1996, October 27). The answer is national standards. *New York Times Magazine,* sec. 6, pp. 45–47, 57, 68. www.nytimes.com/1996/10/27/magazine/the-answer-is -national-standards.html

Mosteller, F., & Boruch, R. F. (2002). *Evidence matters: Randomized trials in education research.* Brookings Institution Press.

Nagy, W. (2005). Why vocabulary instruction needs to be long-term and comprehensive. In E. H. Hiebert & M. L. Kamil (Eds.), *Teaching and learning vocabulary: Bringing research to practice* (pp. 27–44). Erlbaum.

Nagy, W., & Scott, J. (2000). Vocabulary processes. In M. Kamil, P. Mosenthal, P. D. Pearson, & R. Barr (Eds.), *Handbook of reading research* (Vol. 3, pp. 269–284). Erlbaum.

National Academy of Education. (1999, March). *Recommendations regarding research priorities: An advisory report to the National Educational Research Policy and Priorities Board.* National Academy of Education. web.stanford.edu/~hakuta/www/archives /syllabi/Docs/NAE_NERPP.PDF

National Assessment Governing Board. (2020). *Reading framework for the 2025 National Assessment of Educational Progress.* U.S. Department of Education. www .naepframeworkupdate.org

National Assessment of Educational Progress. (2019). National Report Card: 2019 NAEP Reading Assessment. www.nationsreportcard.gov/highlights/reading/2019/

National Early Literacy Panel. (2008). *Developing early literacy: Report of the National Early Literacy Panel: A scientific synthesis of early literacy development and implications for intervention.* National Institute for Literacy.

National Educational Research Policy and Priorities Board. (1999). *Investing in learning: A policy statement with recommendations on research in education by the National Educational Research Policy and Priorities Board.* U.S. Department of Education. files.eric .ed.gov/fulltext/ED431036.pdf

National Governors Association Center for Best Practices (NGA), & Council of Chief State School Officers (CCSSO). (2019). *The Common Core State Standards Initiative.* www.corestandards.org/about-the-standards/. Original standards released June 2010.

National Reading Panel. (2000 April). *Teaching children to read: An evidence-based assessment of the scientific research literature on reading and its implications for reading instruction* (NIH P.N. 00-4769). U.S. Department of Health and Human Services, Public Health Service, National Institutes of Health and the National Institute of Child Health and Human Development. www.nichd.nih.gov/publications/pubs/nrp/smallbook

National Research Council. (1999). *Improving student learning: A strategic plan for educational research and its utilization.* Committee on a Feasibility Study for a Strategic Education Research Program & Commission on Behavioral and Social Sciences and Education. National Academy Press. www.nap.edu/catalog/6488/improving-student -learning-a-strategic-plan-for-education-research-and

National Research Council. (2002). *Scientific research in education.* Committee on Scientific Principles for Education Research (Shavelson, R. J., & Towne, L., Eds.) & Center for Education, Division of Behavioral and Social Sciences and Education. National Academy Press. www.nap.edu/catalog/10236/scientific-research-in-education

Neisser, U. (1976). *Cognition and reality: Principles and implications of cognitive psychology.* W. H. Freeman.

Newkirk, T. (Ed.). (1992). *Workshop 4 by and for teachers: The teacher as researcher.* Heinemann.

New London Group. (1996). A pedagogy of multiliteracies: Designing social futures. *Harvard Educational Review, 66*(1), 60–93. doi: 10.17763/haer.66.1.17370n67v22j160u

New South Wales Department of Education. (2018). *Aboriginal education policy* (Policy No. PD/2008/0385/V03). Implemented 2008; original draft from 2005. education.nsw.gov .au/policy-library/policies/aboriginal-education-and-training-policy

New South Wales Government, NSW Education Standards Authority (NESA). (2007). *Using A to E grades to report student achievement.* NESA Assessment Resource Centre. arc.nesa.nsw.edu.au/go/gen-info

Nichols, S. L., & Berliner, D. C. (2007). *Collateral damage: How high-stakes testing corrupts America's schools.* Harvard Education Press.

No Child Left Behind Act of 2001, P.L. 107–110, 20 U.S.C. § 6319 (2002).

OECD. (2020). Education at a glance 2019: OECD Indicators. OECD Publishing. www .oecd-ilibrary.org/education/education-at-a-glance-2020_69096873-en

Office of the Inspector General. (2006). The Reading First program's grant application process: Final Inspection Report (ED-016/113-F0017).

Olson, D. R. (2004). The triumph of hope over experience in the search for "What works": A response to Slavin. *Educational Researcher, 33*(1), 24–26. doi: 10.3102/0013189X033001024

Pappas, C. C., & Zecker, L. B. (Eds.). (2001). *Teacher inquiries in literacy teaching-learning: Learning to collaborate in elementary urban classrooms.* Erlbaum.

Paré, A. (2004, September). *Professionalism and teacher education in Québec.* Paper presented at the European Conference on Education Research, Crete, Greece.

Parker, S. (2019). A brief history of reading instruction. www.parkerphonics.com/post/a -brief-history-of-reading-instruction

Pearson, P. D. (2007). An historical analysis of the impact of educational research on policy and practice: Reading as an illustrative case. In D. W. Rowe et al. (Eds.), *56th yearbook of the National Reading Conference* (pp. 14–40). National Reading Conference.

Pearson, P. D., Moje, E., & Greenleaf, C. (2010). Science and literacy: Each in the service of the other. *Science, 328*, 459–463.

Perfetti, C. A., & Hart, L. (2002). The lexical quality hypothesis. In L. Verhoeven, C. Elbro, & P. Reitsma (Eds.), *Precursors of functional literacy* (pp. 189–213). John Benjamins.

Petscher, Y., Cabell, S. Q., Catts, H. W., Compton, D. L., Foorman, B. R., Hart, S. A., Lonigan, C. I., Phillips, B. M., Schatschneider, C., Steacy, L. M., Terry, N. P., & Wagner, R. K. (2020). How the science of reading informs 21st-century education. *Reading Research Quarterly, 55*(S1), 267–282.

Pinnell, G. S., DeFord, D. E., & Lyons, C. S. (1988). *Reading Recovery: Early intervention for at risk first graders.* Educational Research Service.

Pressley, M. (2001). What I have learned up until now about research methods in reading education. In D. L. Schallert, C. M. Fairbanks, J. Worthy, B. Maloch, & J. V. Hoffman (Eds.), *54th yearbook of the National Reading Conference* (pp. 22–43). National Reading Conference.

Purcell-Gates, V. (2006). What does culture have to do with it? In J. Hoffman, D. L. Schallert, C. M. Fairbanks, J. Worthy, & B. Maloch (Eds.), *55th yearbook of the National Reading Conference* (pp. 43–59). National Reading Conference.

Rayner, K. (1997). Understanding eye movements in reading. *Scientific Studies of Reading, 1*(4), 317–339. doi: 10.1207/s1532799xssr0104_2

Rayner, K. (1998). Eye movements in reading and information processing: 20 years of research. *Psychological Bulletin, 124*(3), 372–422. doi: 10.1037/0033-2909.124.3.372

Reitsma, P. (1983a). Printed word learning in beginning readers. *Journal of Experimental Child Psychology, 36*(2), 321–339.

Reitsma, P. (1983b). Word-specific knowledge in beginning reading. *Journal of Research in Reading, 6*(1), 41–56.

Rogers, T., Marshall, E., & Tyson, C. (2006). Dialogic narratives of literacy, teaching and schooling: Preparing literacy teachers for diverse settings. *Reading Research Quarterly, 41*(2), 202–224.

Rogers, T., & Schofield, A. (2005). Things thicker than words: Portraits of youth multiple literacies in an alternative secondary program. In J. Anderson, M. Kendrick, T. Rogers, & S. Smythe (Eds.), *Portraits of literacy across families, communities and schools: Intersections and tensions* (pp. 205–220). Erlbaum.

Rogers, T., & Soter, A. (1997). *Reading across cultures: Teaching literature in a diverse society.* Teachers College Press.

Rogers, T., Winters, K. L., Bryan, G., Price, J., McCormick, F., House, L., Mezzarobba, D., & Sinclaire, C. (2006). Developing the IRIS: Toward situated and valid assessment measures in collaborative professional development and school reform in literacy. *The Reading Teacher, 59*(6), 544–553.

Rogoff, B., Turkanis, C. G., & Bartlett, L. (Eds.). (2001). *Learning together: Children and adults in a school community.* Oxford University Press.

Rose, M. (1995). *Possible lives: The promise of public education in America.* Houghton Mifflin.

Rosenberger, P. B., & Rottenberg, D. A. (2002). Does training change the brain? *Neurology, 58*(8), 1139–1140. doi: 10.1212/WNL.58.8.1139

Rowe, K., & National Inquiry into the Teaching of Literacy (Australia). (2005). Teaching reading: Report and recommendations. Department of Education, Science and Training. research.acer.edu.au/tll_misc/5

Ruddell, R. B., & Unrau, N. J. (1994). Reading as a meaning-construction process: The reader, the text and the teacher. In R. Ruddell, M. Ruddell, & H. Singer (Eds.), *Theoretical models and processes of reading* (4th ed, pp. 996–1056). International Reading Association.

Sabatini, J., O'Reilly, T., Weeks, J., & Steinberg, J. (2016, April). *The validity of scenario-based assessment: Empirical results.* Paper presented at the annual meeting of the National Council on Measurement in Education, Washington, DC.

Sabatini, J., O'Reilly, T., Weeks, J., & Wang, Z. (2019). Engineering a twenty-first century reading comprehension assessment system utilizing scenario-based assessment techniques. *International Journal of Testing.* doi: 10.1080/15305058.2018.1551224

Sahlberg, P. (2015). *Finnish lessons 2.0: What can the world learn from educational change in Finland?* Teachers College Press.

Schleicher, A. The Organisation for Economic Co-operation and Development (OECD). (2019). *PISA (The Programme for International Student Assessment) 2018: Insights and interpretations.* OECD Publishing. www.oecd.org/pisa/PISA%202018%20Insights%20 and%20Interpretations%20FINAL%20PDF.pdf

Schoenfeld, A. H. (2002). Making mathematics work for all children: Issues of standards, testing and equity, *Educational Researcher, 31*(1), 13–25. doi: 10.3102/0013189X031001013

Schofield, A., & Rogers, T. (2004). At play in fields of ideas: Teaching, curriculum, and the lives and multiple literacies of youth. *Journal of Adolescent and Adult Literacy, 48*(3), 238–248.

Schon, D. A. (1983). *The reflective practitioner: How professionals think in action.* Basic Books.

SEG Indigenous Education Review Working Group (Tierney, R., Peck, C., Llewellyn, G., Taylor, R., Sharma, M., Mooney, J., Blanchard, M., Payne, T., & Paynter, S.). (2011). Indigenous participation, engagement, education and research strategy, University of Sydney, November. www.academia.edu/9680700/Indigenous_Participation _Engagement_Education_and_Research_Strategy_University_of_Sydney

Seidenberg, M. (2017). *Language at the speed of sight: How we read, why so many can't, and what can be done about it.* Basic Books.

Seidenberg, M. S., Borkenhagen, M. C., & Kearns, D. M. (2020). Lost in translation? Challenges in connecting reading science and educational practice. *Reading Research Quarterly, 55*(S1), 119–130.

Senate Select Committee on School Funding, Parliament of Australia. (2014). *Executive summary: Equity and excellence in Australian schools.* Parliament of Australia. www .aph.gov.au/Parliamentary_Business/Committees/Senate/School_Funding/School _Funding/Report/a03

Shanahan, T. (2020). What constitutes a science of reading instruction? *Reading Research Quarterly, 55*(S1), 235–247.

Shanahan, T., & Shanahan, C. (2008). Teaching disciplinary literacy to adolescents: Rethinking content area literacy. *Harvard Education Review, 78*, 40–59.

Shannon, P., Edmondson, J. E, & O'Brien, S. (2001). Expressions of power and ideology in the National Reading Panel. *51st yearbook of the National Reading Conference*, (51), 383–395.

Shapiro, J. (1996). Home literacy environment and meta-literate awareness. In K. Reeder, J. Shapiro, H. Goelman, & R. Watson (Eds.), *Literate apprenticeships: The emergence of language and literacy in the preschool years* (pp. 29–52). Ablex.

Shapiro, J., Anderson, J., & Anderson, A. (2002). Storybook reading: What we know and what we should consider. In O. Saracho & B. Spodek (Eds.), *Contemporary perspectives in early literacy* (pp. 77–97). Information Age Publishing.

Shavelson, R., Phillips, D. C., Towne, L., & Feuer, M. J. (2003). On the science of education design studies. *Educational Research, 32*(1), 25–28.

Shaywitz, S., Shaywitz, B., Pugh, K., Skudlarski, P., Fulbright, R. K., Constable, R. T., Bronen, R. A., Fletcher, J. M., Liberman, A. M., Shankweiler, D. P., Katz, L., Lacadie, C., Marchione, K. E., & Gore, J. C. (1996). The neurobiology of developmental dyslexia as viewed through the lens of functional magnetic resonance imaging technology. In G. R. Lyon & J. M. Rumsey (Eds.), *Neuroimaging: A window to the neurological foundations of learning and behavior in children*. Paul H. Brookes.

Shaywitz, S. E. (2003). *Overcoming dyslexia: A new and complete science-based program for reading problems at any level* (1st ed.). A. A. Knopf.

Sheehy, M. (2009). *Place stories: Time, space and literacy in two classrooms*. Hampton Press.

Shepard, L., Hannaway, J., & Baker, E. (2009). *Standards, assessments, and accountability: Educational policy white paper*. National Academy of Education www.naeducation.org/

Simos, P. G., Fletcher, J. M., Bergman, E., Breier, J. I., Foorman, B. R., Castillo, E. M., et al. (2002). Dyslexia-specific brain activation profile becomes normal following successful remedial training. *Neurology, 58*, 1203–1213.

Slavin, R. E. (2002). Evidence-based education policies: Transforming educational practice and research. *Educational Researcher, 31*(7), 15–21. doi: 10.3102/0013189X031007015

Slavin, R. E., Madden, N. A., Dolan, L. J., & Wasik, B.A. (1996). *Every child, every school: Success for all*. Corwin.

Snow, C. E., Burns, M. S., & Griffin, P. (Eds.). (1998). *Preventing reading difficulties in young children: A report of the National Research Council*. National Academy Press. files.eric.ed.gov/fulltext/ED416465.pdf

Snyder, I. (2008). *The literacy wars: Why teaching children to read and write is a battleground in Australia*. Allen & Unwin.

Stahl, N., King, J., & Lampi, J. P. (2019, Spring). Expanding approaches for research: Design research. *Journal of Developmental Education, 42*(3), 29–31.

Stornaiuolo, A., Smith, A., & Phillips, N. C. (2017). Developing a transliteracies framework for a connected world. *Journal of Literacy Research, 49*(10), 68–91.

Strauss, S. L., Goodman, K. S., & Paulson, E. J. (2009). Brain research and reading: How emerging concepts in neuroscience support a meaning construction view of the reading process. *Educational Research and Review, 4*(2), 021–033.

Subcommittee on Oversight and Investigations of the Committee on Education and the Workforce, House Committee on Education and the Workforce. (1998, July 17). *Education at a crossroads: What works and what's wasted in education today* (Subcommittee report). U.S. House of Representatives (105th Congress, Second Session). files.eric.ed.gov/fulltext/ED431238.pdf

Taylor, B., Pearson, P., Clark, K., & Walpole, S. (1999). *Beating the odds in teaching all children to read*. CIERA Report 2-006. University of Michigan.

Taylor, B. M., Pearson, P. D., Clark, K., & Walpole, S. (2000). Effective schools and accomplished teachers: Lessons about primary-grade reading instruction in low-income schools. *Elementary School Journal, 101*(2), 121–165.

Taylor, B. M., Pressley, M. P., & Pearson, P. D. (2002). Research-supported characteristics of teachers and schools that promote reading achievement. In B. Taylor & P. D. Pearson (Eds.), *Teaching reading: Effective schools, accomplished teachers* (361–373). Routledge. doi: 10.4324/9781410612489

Taylor, D. (1998). *Beginning to read and the spin doctors of science: The political campaign to change America's mind about how children learn to read*. National Council of Teachers of English.

Tierney, R. J. (1998a). Literacy assessment reform: Shifting beliefs, principled possibilities, and emerging practices. *The Reading Teacher, 51*(5), 374–390. Also published in S. J. Barrentine & S. M. Stokes (Eds.) (2005), *Reading assessment: Principles and practices for elementary teachers* (2nd ed., pp. 23–40). International Reading Association.

Tierney, R. J. (1998b). Testing for the greater good: Social injustice and the conspiracy of the proficiency standards. *The Council Chronicle, 8*(2), 16–20.

Tierney, R. J. (2001). An ethical chasm: Jurisdiction, jurisprudence, and the literacy profession. *Journal of Adolescent & Adult Literacy, 45*(4), 260–276.

Tierney, R. J., Allington, R., Carry, D., Karbon, J. (Technical advisor), & Thome, C. (2008). *Toward a literacy action plan for Milwaukee Public Schools.* Report of the external literacy review team for Milwaukee Public Schools and Wisconsin State Department of Education. www.academia.edu/9690765/Toward_a_Literacy_Action_Plan_for_Milwaukee_Public_Schools_Report_of_the_External_Literacy_Review_Team

Tierney, R. J., Carter, M. A., & Desai, L. E. (1991). *Portfolio assessment in the reading-writing classroom.* Christopher-Gordon Publishers.

Tierney, R. J., Clark, C., Fenner, L., Herter, R. J., Simpson, C. S., & Wiser, B. (1998). Portfolios: Assumptions, tensions, and possibilities. *Reading Research Quarterly, 33*(4), 474–486. doi: 10.1598/RRQ.33.4.6

Tierney, R. J., Crumpler, T., Bond, E., & Bertelsen, C. (2003). *Interactive assessment: Teachers, students and parents as partners.* Christopher Gordon Publishers.

Tierney, R. J., & Rogers, T. (2004). Assessment: Process/Content/Design/Critique: Generative and dynamic evaluation in a digital world. *The Reading Teacher, 58*(2), 218–221. doi: 10.1598/RT.58.2.10

Tierney, R. J., Wile, J. M., Moss, A. G., Reed, E. W., Ribar, J. P., & Zilversmit, A. (1993). *Portfolio evaluation as history: A Report on the evaluation of the history academy for Ohio teachers* (Occasional Paper). National Council for History Education, Inc. files.eric.ed.gov/fulltext/ED371978.pdf

Trinder, L., & Reynolds, S. (Eds.). (2000). *Evidence-based practice: A critical appraisal.* Blackwell Science.

Tucker, M., & Codding, J. (2002). *Standards for our schools: How to set them, measure them, and reach them.* Jossey-Bass.

Walsh, K., Glaser, D., & Wilcox, D. D. (2006). *What education schools are not teaching about reading, and what elementary schools are not learning.* National Center for Teacher Quality.

Wigfield, A., & Guthrie, J. T. (1997). Relations of children's motivation for reading to the amount and breadth of their reading. *Journal of Educational Psychology, 89,* 420–432.

Wigfield, A., Guthrie, J. T., Perencevich, K. C., Taboada, A., Klauda, S. L., McRae, A., & Barbosa, P. (2008). Role of reading engagement in mediating effects of reading comprehension instruction on reading outcomes. *Psychology in the Schools, 45,* 432–445.

Woulfin, S., & Gabriel, R. E. (2020). Interconnected infrastructure for improving reading instruction. *Reading Research Quarterly, 55*(S1), S109–S117. doi: 10.1002/rrq.339

Yaden, D., Reinking, D., & Smargorinsky, P. (in press). The Trouble with Binaries: A Perspective on the Science of Reading. *Reading Research Quarterly.*

NOTE

1. See, for example, Schon's 1983 work *The Reflective Practitioner: How Professionals Think in Action.* This piece has also been discussed at length by a number of educators (e.g., Carr & Kemmis, 1986; Cochran-Smith & Lytle, 1993; Clay, 1998; Kincheloe, 1991; Miller, 1990; Newkirk, 1992; Ladson-Billings, 1994; Pappas & Zecker, 2001).

10   The Digital Wave

10.1   THE DIGITAL READER/MEANING MAKER

Being a digital reader/meaning maker involves more than reading, researching, and exchanging information online. It involves negotiating everyday life within a world where the media shapes who we are, what we know, how we access information, our expressions of ourselves, and our various negotiations with others (e.g., personal, professional, social, political, economic, cultural). Being a digital reader is not a fixed or static destination but an everchanging journey, involving relative, fluid, and multifaceted engagements. In some ways, digital readers are likely to be involved in a conglomeration of engagements that draw on their digital web-based meaning-making skills, especially their abilities to navigate the multiple dimensions of visual and text material within and across websites. In addition, they enlist various social strategies and plays as they engage socially on different platforms with different groups (e.g., friends and family, colleagues and project teams, affiliation groups or solicited others) by text and image, synchronized and asynchronized with prescribed and less prescribed parameters perhaps dealing with people from different language groups and cultures more or less accessible and familiar with the digital frames. They need to navigate search engines, multilayered images, and texts as they consider and weigh possible avenues and platforms for meaning making and their own networked exchanges through multiple lenses—that is, as constructivist, strategic, writerly, social, and global readers. Indeed, researchers studying the digital reader have drawn on these frames to delve into and recommend approaches for digital meaning making.

Information Explorer

The digital reader, in keeping with the broader notion of the reader as a constructivist and composer, is an information explorer. Befitting constructivist notions of meaning making, the exploration of digital sources of information requires engaging in text and media worlds that are multilayered, using a myriad of strategies. One key strategy is a form of forward inferencing (akin to prediction) both within and across texts, using criteria such as relevance, interconnectedness, and coherence to guide one's consideration of ideas. According to research on web users (e.g., Coiro & Dobler, 2007), one of the key distinctions of successful online comprehension is tied to the more frequent use of forward inferencing (versus backward inferencing)—as prompted by a hypertext link.[1] As Coiro and Dobler suggest, "internet reading seems to demand more attempts to infer, predict and evaluate reading choices . . . to prompt some readers to orient themselves in a new and dynamic three-dimensional space . . . to figure out how to get back to where they 'were.'" (p. 234). They suggest that the self-regulation of online comprehension seems tied to a similar set of recursive strategies of past models of composing (e.g., Tierney & Pearson, 1983). Online comprehension involves planning within and across websites, predicting and following leads, monitoring how and where to proceed and evaluating relevance and judging merits. As Coiro and Dobler explain:

> Our findings suggest that the greater complexities in online reading comprehension may result largely from a process of self-directed text construction; that is, the process online readers use to comprehend what they read as they search for the Internet text(s) most relevant to their reading needs.
>
> On one level, we observed skilled readers engaged in an ongoing "self-directed" planning process involving a series of inferences about what would best fit with their internal representation of the text's meaning. Simultaneously, on a second level, these readers constructed their own external texts. Each decision about which link was most relevant involved constructing the next element in the text they built. We observed readers actively anticipating and monitoring the relevancy of each new text unit, while quickly deciding whether to continue to add that text to their own external text by following deeper links within a page or to exclude that text and search elsewhere by clicking the back button as a fix-up strategy, for example. At the end of the reading session, it became clear that each reader had constructed not only his or her internal understanding of a certain text but had also constructed a unique external representation of the Internet texts most applicable to their needs. (p. 51)

They contrast this with:

> Readers who do not strategically plan and anticipate where they are headed within open Internet spaces may end up constructing a disjointed collection of random texts as opposed to a systematic compilation of carefully chosen texts from which to sift out a relevant point. Thus, an increased need to make forward inferences about text appeared to compound an already complex process of making bridging inferences about content in a manner that may prompt additional complexities to the process of reading online. (Coiro & Dobler, 2007, p. 53)

Essentially, it appears that there are at least three intertwined abilities and dispositions linked to successful explorations by the digital reader/meaning maker: (1) the ability to move forward adroitly with predictions and forward inferencing across digitally based information sources; (2) the ability to enlist knowledge of topics and their structures, including their possible web architecture; and

(3) a disposition and focus that serves to cluster, connect, or bring together ideas in accordance with the digital reader/meaning maker's own goals. Befitting the discussion of a writerly reader, these require drawing information together from multiple sources in a way that is focused and deft rather than a random, snatch-and-grab of ideas (Eagleton, 2001; Sutherland-Smith, 2002). It is important, then, how meaning makers position themselves (including in terms of their goals, focus, perspective, and authority), engage in forward-forecasting, rapidly discern relevance, and integrate their own knowledge. Digital reading/meaning making demands a high degree of self-regulated navigation, an ability to retain and revisit, focus on, and weave together or manage multiple inputs.

The presentation of digital information often involves complex patterns that may include stacks of texts and images that are sectioned off and posted within web templates with links, or those that are linear or temporally sequenced, or arranged in a host of other ways that may be altered during compilation and use or search and presentation. Just as form and function interplay with any architectural space, so does the form, patterning, or management of ideas influence the meaning making that occurs in digital spaces. As researchers have predicted and found, such meaning making is not always trouble free as one moves from one site to another and across layers. Indeed, with the web, depending on the sophistication of the meaning makers, they may become lost, find themselves at a dead end, or miss what they perceive to be a key data point or relationship. Indeed, meaning makers may have experiences similar to being in a labyrinth (Snyder, 1996). Again, unless the digital reader/meaning maker retains control of their navigational pursuits, their meaning making is prone to being overrun. It is essential that the digital reader/meaning maker has the strategies and agency to navigate and build toward, from, and on multilayered and multimedia communications and expressions of self and others, as well as to evaluate the sources and credibility of located information. The architecture of online material, especially that with hyperlinks, thumbnails, and annotations, seems to prompt the use of such features, albeit with varying success across meaning makers in terms of assisting with the navigation of the texts. For example, in their studies of e-books and adolescent engagement, Teresa Dobson and her colleagues (e.g., Dobson, 2007; Luce-Kapler et al., 2006) stress that hypertextual presentations within hypertext novels may prompt overly text-centered meaning making. Dobson suggests that there may be a need to prompt readers' greater consciousness of their approach to these texts to enrich meaning makers' engagements.

Social Player

Although digital reading may occur on laptop machines and may appear more individual than social, digital reading/meaning making should be more of a human social endeavor than one driven by machines. In reality, digital reading has become increasingly social. It requires vigilance so that digital readers are not coerced but have agency and positionality in their social engagements, networks, collaborations, and community engagements. (This is not always straightforward, as digital ancillaries can fashion information searches and news releases to outside sources with profiles with certain ideological biases intent on advancing their own agendas.)

Indeed, in his pursuit of studies examining the participatory nature of digital engagement, Henry Jenkins has noted how digital meaning making involves socio-political-cultural dimensions—ranging from the intimate and personal to the global and intercultural.[2] Along these lines, Jenkins and his colleagues (2009) introduced the notion of participatory culture, prompted in part to reflect the social meaning making occurring across digital environments (see box). As Jenkins et al. emphasize, "participatory culture shifts the focus of literacy from individual expression to community involvement. The new literacies almost all involve social skills developed through collaboration and networking" (p. xiii).

As studies of social media suggest, digital meaning makers may explore communities and in doing so adopt one or more personae as they position themselves with others and their worlds in a fashion growing out of their subjectivities, alliances, choices, and so on. Sometimes meaning makers' engagement in constructing selves or multiple personae in the company of others forms an embodied experience of digital environments—a secondary engagement with or participation in the worlds constructed across or within or by layers of text and other media. For example, observations of students engaged in instant messaging suggest that the digital medium supports a fluid form of identity construction. In particular, Lewis and Fabos (2005) found that when adolescents instant message with one another, they can shift identity almost simultaneously. As they stated, "they enact identities that depend upon a running analysis of the online and off-line contexts" (p. 494). The authors describe how adolescents shift their interactions to fit their relationship and stance with each other as they instant message (e.g., from confidante to advisor to cynic to empathetic supporter with the different participants), doing so in a way that is consistent with their overall sense of identity and understanding of the dynamics of the relationships.

Similarly, in the research on hypertext and gaming, Squire (2006) and Gee (2005a & b; 2013a & b) look at how readers move from print to image to virtual or real environments, suggesting that their experiences and interfacing with tools within and across those spaces and worlds may simulate opportunities to perform in situations and try on identities. As Squire (2006) and Gee (2005a & b; 2013a & b) suggest, certain virtual environments (e.g., Sim worlds and world-building games) may perpetuate certain political ideologies and ways of interacting with and constructing the world, which may contribute to identity formations. Squire, for example, contends that "games focus our attention and mold our experience of what is important in a world and what is to be ignored. The game designers' choices, particularly of what to strip away from a world, can be read as ideological when considered in relation to other systems" (pp. 21–22).

Literacy spaces almost inevitably privilege some lenses, epistemologies, and ideologies over others. As studies of affiliation groups indicate, digital spaces may not always be apolitical or utopian. Indeed, they can be alienating and dismiss members depending on their affiliation with certain persons and ideas. The digital meaning maker therefore needs to be conscious of the norms and conventions of the digital social groups with which they might engage. As Bryson et al. (2006) suggest, one might find a haven or a prison, or have a sense of belonging or dislodgement, in such spaces. Similarly, it has been argued that these new literacy spaces may be predisposed to certain ways of exploring or defining self. In other words, certain literacy spaces may be predisposed to certain ideologies over others, subordinating certain worldviews and ways of knowing (Bruce & Hogan, 1998). As Boldt et al. (2015) note:

> from a post-human perspective on affect and emergence, humans are not merely "using" materials in mediated activity; rather, humans and materials enter into affective relationships and intensities, the nature of which is often not prescribed. Foldings of the human and non-human are constant and complicated; people "use" things and things "use" people, and these movements and relations can be rife with affective movements. (p. 436)

Building on the sociopolitical functioning of digital resources has both promise and peril. As several groups of scholars—Rogers et al. (2015), Alvermann et al. (2001), Hull and Nelson (2005), and Schneider et al. (2020)—have shown and argued, access to digital resources offers students the possibility of propelling their literacy practices across spaces and in and out of schools, blurring traditional boundaries and forms of literacy practices. These spaces also allow students to "juxtapose and transform genre practices for critical purposes, engage in the playful instability of genres, selves, and messages, and re-narrate their stories and identities in the process" (Rogers et al., p. 29).

Digital social spaces can be tricky to navigate, depending on the parties involved and the purpose and manner of negotiations. Interpersonally, readers can be involved in banter that can proceed less than wittingly. For example, as we operate globally, these matters have additional potential complications as norms and conventions shift—especially when digital pursuits may be colonizing or operate disrespectfully in the interest of some but not others. A form of shuttle diplomacy tied to an ethic of respectfulness may be needed to marry the norms of the community with the interests of those outside. Otherwise, these interests can easily collide or compete within and across such spaces, revealing potentially emancipatory practices to be colonizing instead.

In Closing

The roles and expectations for readers have changed with the ongoing advances in and uses of technology. Reading has shifted as digital engagements have moved from positioning the reader as a recipient and consumer of ideas to a creator, architect, collaborator, producer, and director—enlisting digital images, videos, texts within an ever-growing expanse of multilayered modules that afford a palette for shifting social relationships. The digital reader/meaning maker's engagements can range from what might be considered constructivist processes in complex multilayered knowledge areas to forms of social play that can extend to critical and artistic consumption and expressions that are more fluid than fixed. For the digital reader/meaning making, there is a forward dynamic process, often akin to ongoing improvisation as new ways to engage with ideas and one another are adopted. Consistent with these characteristics, Spiro et al. (2007) describe digital meaning makers as "being conductors (or jazz improvisers), rapidly bouncing excerpts from rich video clips off of each other" (p. 98). They further emphasize that if the material is somewhat familiar and rich in content, meaning makers "capitalize on their affinity for this mode of 'quick-cutting' across dense images (cf. Stephens, 1998)—and their accustomedness to nonlinear processing . . . to criss-cross between many video excerpts to speed up and deepen the process of building interconnected knowledge from experience (Spiro et al., p. 98).

These engagements might be described as multivocal as readers engage with multiple personae both within and across texts or digital spaces, building sets of virtual relationships with both imagined and real worlds and people. Plus, these engagements occur in the context of navigating and journeying through worlds. Readers cultivate ideas and spur meanings using range of texts wherein ideas are explored and mixed, created and critiqued, savored and digested and used as fuel for future expressions and further considerations.

As Deuze et al. (2012) suggested in their article "A Life Lived in the Media":

> Media become a playground for a search for meaning and belonging—not just by consumption. . . . by producing, co-creating, redacting and remixing . . . we do not see people as hapless victims of this seemingly disjointed worldview. We locate the potential power of people to shape their lives and identities and produce themselves (and therefore each other) in media. (p. 6)

One should not underestimate and discount the agility, flexibility, and creativity needed to do so. Considered through a critical lens, the digital reader/meaning maker is not operating rotely (at least, in the non-school world) as they rapidly position themselves as performative inquirers with others in a fashion that is discerning of the relevance and discursive as they are involved in ongoing dialogical provocations and opportunities. At one level (or perhaps across all levels), these engagements involve conversations with oneself in the company of others. They involve constructions that are performative and discursive. At another level, they are akin to conversations that may entail reflective meaning making and negotiations (e.g., across a set of emails or text messages or texts authored by others). At yet another level, digital meaning making involves others—imagined or real. It might entail trying to understand what the author wanted you to think or act upon and coming to terms with your own goals, understandings, and actions. It might entail exploring possible worlds and imagining or re-imagining possibilities for oneself. Finally, at a more macro level, it is tied to how we are networked and positioned with others in the context of both local and global exchanges. It mirrors or perhaps makes more attainable the metaphors of reader as composer and semiotician, perhaps even inevitable. Digital meaning making involves a sociosemiotic form of transmediation across various sources, multiple layers, and interfaces involving various positioning of forms of text and images as planning, aligning, revising and monitoring occur recursively (e.g., Lemke, 1993; Reinking, 1997; Siegel, 1995; Spiro 2006a & b, 2007).

References

Alvermann, D. E., Hagood, M. C., & Williams, K. B. (2001, June). Image, language, and sound: Making meaning with popular culture texts. *Reading Online.* www.readingonline.org /newliteracies/lit_index.asp?HREF=/newliteracies/a ction/alvermann/index.html

Beach, R., & Tierney, R. J. (2016). Toward a theory of literacy meaning making within virtual worlds. In S. E. Israel & G. G. Duffy, (Eds.), *Handbook of research on reading comprehension* (2nd ed., pp. 135–165). Guilford.

Boldt, G., Lewis, C., & Leander, K. M. (2015). Forum: Moving, feeling, desiring, teaching. *Research in the Teaching of English, 49*(4), 430–441.

Bruce, B. C., & Hogan, M. (1998). The disappearance of technology: Toward an ecological model of literacy. In D. Reinking, M. C. McKenna, L. Labbo, & R. Kieffer (Eds.), *Handbook of literacy and technology: Transformations in a post-typographic world* (pp. 269–281). Erlbaum.

Bryson, M. (2006). New media, sexual subcultures, and a critical perspective on research problematics, practices, and possibilities. *Journal of Gay & Lesbian Issues in Education, 3*(4), 109–118. doi: 10.1300/J367v03n04_11

Bryson, M., MacIntosh, L., Jordan, S., & Lin, H. (2006). Virtually queer? Homing devices, mobility, and un/belongings. *Canadian Journal of Communication, 31*(4), 791–814. doi: 10.22230/cjc.2006v31n4a1795

Burbules, N. C., & Callister, T. A. (1996). Knowledge at the crossroads: Some alternative futures of hypertext learning environments. *Educational Theory, 46*(1), 23–50.

Burnett, C. (2015a). (Im)materalising literacies. In J. Rowsell & K. Pahl (Eds.), *The Routledge handbook of literacy studies* (pp. 520–531). Routledge.

Burnett, C. (2015b). Investigating children's interactions around digital texts in classrooms: How are these framed and what counts? *Education 3–13, 43*(2), 197–208. doi: 10.1080/03004279.2013.800576.

Burnett, C., & Merchant, G. (2014). Points of view: Reconceptualising literacies through an exploration of adult and child interactions in a virtual world. *Journal of Research in Reading, 37*(1), 36–50. doi: 10.1111/jrir.12006

Callow, J. (2008). Show me: Principles for assessing students' visual literacy. *The Reading Teacher, 61*(8), 616–626. doi: 10.1598/RT.61.8.3

Coiro, J., & Dobler, E. (2007). Exploring the online reading comprehension strategies used by sixth-grade skilled readers to search for and locate information on the internet. *Reading Research Quarterly, 42*(2), 214–257. doi: 10.1598/RRQ.42.2.2

Coiro, J., Knobel, M., Lankshear, C., & Leu, D. J. (2008). Central issues in new literacies and new literacies research. In J. Coiro, M. Knobel, C. Lankshear, & D. Leu (Eds.), *Handbook of research in new literacies* (pp. 1–22). Routledge.

Collins, A., Brown, J. S., & Larkin, K. (1980). Inference in text understanding. In R. J. Spiro, B. C. Bruce, & W. F. Brewer, (Eds.), *Theoretical issues in reading comprehension: Perspectives from cognitive psychology, linguistics, artificial intelligence, and education* (pp. 385–410). Erlbaum.

Deuze, M., Blank, P., & Speers, L. (2012). A life lived in media. *Digital Humanities Quarterly, 6*(1), 37. www.digitalhumanities.org/dhq/vol/6/1/000110/000110.html

Dobson, T., & Luce-Kapler, R. (2005). Stitching texts: Gender and geography in *Frankenstein* and *Patchwork Girl. Changing English, 12*(2), 265–277. doi: 10.1080/13586840500164540

Dobson, T. M. (2007). Constructing (and deconstructing) reading through hypertext: Literature and the new media. In A. Adams & S. Brindley (Eds.), *Teaching secondary English with ICT*, pp. 80–97. Open University Press.

Dyson, A. H. (1995). Writing children: Reinventing the development of childhood literacy. *Written Communication, 12*(1), 4–46. doi: 10.1177/0741088395012001002

Eagleton, M. (2001). *Factors that influence Internet inquiry strategies: Case studies of middle school students with and without learning disabilities.* Paper presented at the annual meeting of the National Reading Conference, San Antonio, TX.

Gee, J. P. (2005a). Good video games & good learning. *Phi Kappa Phi Forum, 85*(2), 33–37.

Gee, J. P. (2005b). Learning by design: Good video games as learning machines. *E-Learning and Digital Media, 2*(1), 5–16. doi: 10.2304/elea.2005.2.1.5

Gee, J. P. (2013a). *Good video games & good learning: Collected essays on video games, learning and literacy* (2nd ed.). Peter Lang.

Gee, J. P. (2013b). *The anti-education era: Creating smarter students through digital learning.* Palgrave Macmillan.

Hull, G. A., & Nelson, M. E. (2005). Locating the semiotic power of multimodality. *Written Communication, 22*(2), 224–261. doi: 10.1177/0741088304274170

Ito, M., Gutiérrez, K., Livingstone, S., Penuel, W., Rhodes, J., Salen, K., Schor, J., Sefton-Green, J., & Watkins, S. C. (2013). Connected learning: An agenda for research and design (a research synthesis report of the Connected Learning Research Network). Digital Media and Learning Research Hub. www.researchgate.net/publication /265232707_Ito_M_Gutierrez_K_Livingstone_S_Penuel_W_Rhodes_J_Salen_K _Schor_J_Sefton-Green_J_Watkins_C_2013_Connected_Learning_An_Agenda_for _Research_and_Design_Irvine_CA_The_Digital_Media_and_Learning_Research_H

James, C. (2014). *Disconnected: Youth, new media, and the ethics gap.* MIT Press.

Jenkins, H., Clinton, K., Purushotma, R., Robison, A. J., & Weigel, M. (2009). *Confronting the challenges of participatory culture: Media education for the 21st century* (A John D. and Catherine T. MacArthur Foundation Report on Digital Media and Learning). MIT Press. mitpress.mit.edu/books/confronting-challenges-participatory-culture

Jenkins, H., Ford, S., & Green, J. (2013). *Spreadable media: Creating value and meaning in a networked culture.* New York University Press.

Leander, K. M., & Boldt, G. (2013). Rereading "A pedagogy of multiliteracies": Bodies, texts, and emergence. *Journal of Literacy Research, 45*(1), 22–46.

Lemke, J. (1993). Intertextuality and educational research. *Linguistics and Education, 4*(3/4), 257–268.

Lenhart, A. (2015, April). *Teens, social media & technology overview 2015: Smartphones facilitate shifts in communication landscape for teens* (Pew Research Center Report). Pew Research Center. www.pewresearch.org/wp-content/uploads/sites/9/2015/04/PI _TeensandTech_Update2015_0409151.pdf

Leu, D. (2006). New literacies, reading research, and the challenges of change: A deictic perspective. In J. Hoffman, D. L. Schallert, C. M. Fairbanks, J. Worthy, & B. Maloch (Eds.), *55th yearbook of the National Reading Conference* (pp. 1–20). National Reading Conference.

Lewis, C., & Fabos, B. (2005). Instant messaging, literacies, and social identities. *Reading Research Quarterly, 40*(4), 470–501.

Livingstone, S. M., & Sefton-Green, J. (2016). *The class: Living and learning in the digital age.* New York University Press.

Luce-Kapler, R., Dobson, T., Sumara, D., Iftody, T., & Davis, B. (2006). E-literature and the digital engagement of consciousness. In J. Hoffman, D. L. Schallert, C. M. Fairbanks, J. Worthy, & B. Maloch (Eds.), *55th yearbook of the National Reading Conference* (pp. 171–181). National Reading Conference.

Marwick, A. E., & Boyd, D. (2014). Networked privacy: How teenagers negotiate context in social media. *New Media & Society, 16*(7), 1051–1067. doi: 10.1177/1461444814543995

Masny, D. (2012). Multiple literacies theory: Discourse, sensation, resonance and becoming. *Discourse: Studies in the Cultural Politics of Education, 33*(1), 113–128. doi: 10.1080/01596306.2012.632172

Masny, D., & Cole, D. R. (2012). *Mapping multiple literacies: An introduction to Deleuzian literacy studies.* Continuum.

Massey, D. (2005). *For space.* SAGE.

Mayer, R. E. (in press). *Multimedia learning* (3rd ed.). Cambridge University Press.

McGinley, W. (1992). The role of reading and writing while composing from sources. *Reading Research Quarterly, 27*(3), 226–248. doi: 10.2307/747793

Mitchell, C. (2011). *Doing visual research.* SAGE.

Mitchell, C. (2011). What's participation got to do with it? Visual methodologies in 'girlmethod' to address gender-based violence in the time of AIDS. *Global Studies of Childhood, 1*(1), 51–59. doi: 10.2304/gsch.2011.1.1.51

Mitchell, C., De Lange, N., & Moletsane, R. (2017). *Participatory visual methodologies: Social change, community and policy.* SAGE.

Mitchell, C., & Murray, J. (2012). Social networking practices and youth advocacy efforts in HIV awareness and prevention: What does methodology have to do with it? *Educational Research and Social Change, 1*(2), 26–40.

Moletsane, R., Mitchell, C., & Smith, A. (2012). *Was it something I wore? Dress, identity, materiality.* HSRC Press.

Napoli, M., & Sychterz, T. (2015). Graphic novels come alive in a sixth grade classroom. In V. S. Yenika-Agbaw & T. Sychterz (Eds.), *Adolescents rewrite their worlds: Using literature to illustrate writing forms.* Rowman & Littlefield.

National Academy of Education. (2013). *Adaptive educational technologies: Tools for learning, and for learning about learning,* G. Natriello (Ed.). Washington, DC.

New London Group. (1996). A pedagogy of multiliteracies: Designing social futures. *Harvard Educational Review, 66*(1), 60–92. doi: 10.17763/haer.66.1.17370n67v22j160u

Pangrazio, L. (2013). Young people and Facebook: What are the challenges to adopting a critical engagement? *Digital Culture & Education, 5*(1), 34–47.

Parks, M. R. (2010). Social network sites as virtual communities. In Z. Papacharissi (Ed.), *A networked self: Identity, community, and culture on social network sites* (pp. 104–123). Routledge. doi: 10.4324/9780203876527

Phelan, M. (2014). *Around the world.* Penguin.

Pickering, A. (1995). *The mangle of practice: Time, agency, and science*. University of Chicago Press.

Reinking, D. (1997). Me and my hypertext: A multiple digression analysis of technology and literacy (sic). *The Reading Teacher, 50*(8), 626–643.

Rogers, T., Winters, K., LaMonde, A. M., & Perry, M. (2010). From image to ideology: Analysing shifting identity positions of marginalized youth across the cultural sites of video production. *Pedagogies: An International Journal, 5*(4), 298–312.

Rogers, T., Winters, K. L., Perry, M., & LaMonde, A. M. (2015). *Youth, critical literacies, and civic engagement*. Routledge.

Schneider, J. J., King, J. R., Kozdras, D., & Welsh, J. L. (2020). Fast and slow literacies: Digital and compositional conundrums in a post-truth era. *Literacy Research: Theory, Method, and Practice, 69*(1), 320–338. doi:10.1177/2381336920937275

Sefton-Green, J. (2013). *Learning at not-school: A review of study, theory, and advocacy for education in non-formal settings*. MIT Press.

Siegel, M. (1995). More than words: The generative power of transmediation for learning. *Canadian Journal of Education, 20*(4), 4.

Snyder, I. (1996). *Hypertext: The electronic labyrinth*. New York University Press.

Spiro, R. (2006a). The "new Gutenberg revolution": Radical new learning, thinking, teaching, and training with technology . . . bringing the future near. *Educational Technology, 46*(1–4, 6), 3–5.

Spiro, R. J. (2006b). The post-Gutenberg world of the mind: The shape of new learning. *Educational Technology, 46*(2), 3–4.

Spiro, R. J., Collins, B. P., & Ramchandran, A. (2007). Reflections on a post-Gutenberg epistemology for video use in ill-structured domains: Fostering complex learning and cognitive flexibility. In R. Goldman, R. Pea, B. Barron, & S. J. Derry (Eds.), *Video research in the learning sciences* (pp. 93–100). Erlbaum.

Spiro, R. J., Collins, B. P., Thota, J. J., & Feltovich, P. J. (2003). Cognitive flexibility theory: Hypermedia for complex learning, adaptive knowledge application, and experience acceleration. *Educational Technology, 43*(5), 5–10.

Spivey, N. N. (1984). *Discourse synthesis: Constructing texts in reading and writing* (Monograph). International Reading Association.

Squire, K. (2006). From content to context: Videogames as designed experience. *Educational Researcher, 35*(8), 19–29. doi: 10.3102/0013189X035008019

Street, B. V. (2006). New literacies, new times: How do we describe and teach the forms of literacy knowledge, skills, and values people need for new times? In J. Hoffman, D. L. Schallert, C. M. Fairbanks, J. Worthy, & B. Maloch (Eds.), *55th yearbook of the National Reading Conference* (pp. 21–42). National Reading Conference.

Sutherland-Smith, W. (2002). Integrating online discussion in an Australian intensive English language course. *TESOL Journal, 11*(3), 31–35.

Thomas, A. (2007). *Youth online: Identity and literacy in the digital age. New literacies and digital epistemologies, vol. 19*. Peter Lang.

Tierney, R. J. (2009a). Agency and artistry of meaning makers within and across digital spaces. In S. E. Israel & G. G. Duffy, (Eds.), *Handbook of research on reading comprehension* (2nd ed., pp. 261–288). Routledge.

Tierney, R. J. (2009b). Literacy education 2.0: Looking through the rear view mirror as we move ahead. In J. Hoffman & Y. Goodman (Eds.), *Changing literacies for changing times: An historical perspective on the future of reading research, public policy, and classroom practices* (pp. 282–300). Routledge.

Tierney, R. J., Bond, E., & Bresler, J. (2006). Examining literate lives as students engage with multiple literacies. *Theory into Practice, 45*(4), 359–367. doi: 10.1207/s15430421tip4504_10

Tierney, R. J., & Pearson, P. D. (1983, May). Toward a composing model of reading. *Language Arts, 60*(5), 568–580.

Tierney, R. J., & Shanahan, T. (1991). Research on the reading-writing relationship: Interactions, transactions, and outcomes. In R. Barr, M. L. Kamil, P. Mosenthal, & P. D. Pearson (Eds.), *Handbook of reading research* (Vol. 2, pp. 246–280). Longman.

10.2 THE DIGITAL WAVE³

Introduction

In Stanley Kubrick's renowned 1968 science fiction film *2001: A Space Odyssey*, a computer named HAL (Heuristically Programmed Algorithmic Computer) controls operations on a group of scientists' extraordinary venture into space. Demonstrating his artificial intelligence capabilities—which include natural language processing, voice and face recognition, and an ability to reason as well as make judgments—HAL introduces himself to the crew: "I am a HAL 9000 computer. I became operational at the H-A-L plant in Urbana, Illinois on the 12th of January, 1992." The film's plot hinges on the crucial moment when the crew's judgment is perceived as conflicting with HAL's logic, at which point HAL proceeds to override them—in some cases by cutting off their life support. While the movie is set in the future, it is noteworthy that the technology as well as the human-interface tensions had already emerged at the time of its release. In conjunction with its imagined journey into deep space, the film was thus adept at envisioning developments with computers that now seem commonplace—anticipating the shifts in our digital worlds and the more pervasive and encompassing role of computers and the media in our lives.

It is interesting that the film situated HAL's origins in Urbana—the home of the University of Illinois, where Rob and David spent several years involved in interdisciplinary pursuits with scientists engaged in advancing digital developments. The University of Illinois was a hub of some major developments in the use of computers as learning tools, and many of these pursuits drew on work in reading comprehension and digital teaching approaches to explore natural language processing in particular. Indeed, 1968—the year of the film's release—represents a historic marker in terms of one of the university's more noted developments, PLATO (Programmed Logic for Automated Teaching Operations). Developed in the 1960s by a team at the Computer-based Educational Research Laboratory (CERL), PLATO offered a multiuser platform with random access capability, including precursors to what are now recognized as chat rooms, touch screens, visual and audio interfaces, and various gaming functions (i.e., role-playing avatars and precursors to Dungeons and Dragons, Warcraft, and others). Not surprisingly, PLATO spurred a large and formidable digital community of users, akin to affinity groups, throughout the period of its use until 2006.

Like the other developments in this book, the digital advances we see today have their origins in waves that began to take form over 100 years ago. The realization of their power and influence on our literacies lives, however, only took a recognizable shape in the last 40 years with technological improvements, software developments and breakthroughs in design—most notably with the introduction of hypertext and its multimodal capabilities (as can be instantiated on the Internet, games, etc.). We begin with a discussion of some of the more significant early waves of technology and software development before shifting to the superwave that changed the path of digital literacy: hypermedia, which changed our literacies forever. It changed how we make meaning, how we engage with one another, how we develop our personal and cultural identities. and how we as humans interact with machines.

Introduction to Digital Technologies

Prior to what we have designated as the digital advance, digital technology was seen as a complement to learning rather than an integrated component of it. Educational technology focused on how programmable technologies could be used as aids to learning. Broadly speaking, these included programmed learning–based analyses of the sequence of learning; technological adjuncts to learning (e.g., clicker responses, when teaching is interrupted by a polling of students); and an emphasis in schools on teaching coding (sometimes coupled with instruction on robotics and simulations). In terms of literacy, programs focused on designing aids for reading and writing development. For example, we saw a range of software developments to support writing (e.g., Quill, initially developed by Andee Rubin and Bertram Bruce) and reading development (e.g., speech recognition by Don Nix and his colleagues).

However, these appeared to operate as adjuncts to classroom learning, with the goal of increasing reading or writing fluency (Nix et al., 1998; Rubin & Bruce, 1984, 1985). At the same time, studies of the computer-based reading have perseverated on comparisons between on-screen and off-screen reading of the text equivalent of reading PDF documents. Even nowadays there is a tendency to do such comparisons while ignoring the various forms that digital texts can assume (e.g., Delgado et al., 2018; Singer & Alexander, 2017). Furthermore—and, perhaps, ironically—most of the measures enlisted to assess students' reading and writing progress alongside these aids and forms were and sometimes still are paper and pencil. It is only quite recently that tests reflected and integrated digital forms.

In the latter half of the 20th century, developments in hardware and software spurred shifts related to data analysis and word processing. Earlier breakthrough inventions of transistors, chip technology, connectivity, portability, and computer programming languages initially set the stage for the digital spaces that are nowadays pervasive in our everyday lives. A sampling of some key developments in hardware and software is shown in Figure 10.1.

Digital Literacies: Hypermedia, World Wide Web, and New Literacies

The advent of hypermedia had an impact of tidal wave proportions, especially to our literacies. Indeed, the term "digital literacies" arose in tandem with the advent of and access to hypermedia and their confluence with the aforementioned developments. These new technologies and forms of architecture for digital spaces afforded multimodal possibilities that, over the last 30 years, have intertwined with shifts in our literacies and our personal, social, economic, and political lives. They

Figure 10.1. Key Developments in Hardware and Software

Hardware Developments

1820s–1830s: Charles Babbage creates designs for the first mechanical computers with memory, operational procedures, conditional jumps, and so on. Although left undeveloped, the designs were foundational to later developments.

1936: Alan Turing introduces the notion of a universal machine, the Turing machine, for computing anything. Some suggest this was the basis for the modern computer.

1937: J. V. Atanasoff, a professor of physics and mathematics at Iowa State University, attempts to build the first computer without gears, cams, belts, or shafts.

1939: Hewlett-Packard is founded by David Packard and Bill Hewlett in a garage in Palo Alto, California.

1947: William Shockley, John Bardeen, and Walter Brattain of Bell Laboratories invent the transistor, an electronic switch with solid materials and no need for a vacuum.

1947–49: The first functional computers are developed—for example, the Harvard Mark 1 and the Manchester Mark 1 (nicknamed "The Baby").

1958: Jack Kilby and Robert Noyce unveil the integrated circuit, known as the computer chip.

Software: Computer Language Developments, Connectivity, and Advent of Personal Computers

1953: Grace Hopper develops the first computer language, COBOL (Common-Business-Oriented Language).

1954: The FORTRAN computer language (FORmula TRANslation) is introduced, beginning its wide use for statistical analyses.

1956: Informational processing language is developed by Newell, Shaw, and Simon at Carnegie Mellon Institute of Technology and the Rand Corporation.

1958: The programming language LISP is developed and used by a number of artificial intelligence scholars as a better fit for language representation, making links, and offering connective links with recursive functions.

1964: Douglas Engelbart shows a prototype of the modern computer that is more accessible to a wider public, with a mouse and a graphical user interface (GUI).

1967: LOGO is developed at the research firm Bolt, Beranek and Newman, and Seymour Papert advocates for its use in schools. In his 1980 book *Mindstorms: Children, Computers and Powerful Ideas*, Papert discusses using computers in conjunction with constructivist ideas.

1969: C Programming Language is used by a group of developers at Bell Labs to produce the Unix operating system, addressing compatibility issues across multiple platforms. Unix became the operating system of choice among mainframes at large companies and government entities.

1971: Alan Shugart from IBM invents the floppy disk, allowing data to be shared among computers.

1973: Robert Metcalfe at Xerox develops Ethernet for connecting multiple computers and other hardware.

1974–77: A number of personal computers are introduced and made available to the public (e.g., Altair, IBM 5100, Radio Shack's TRS-80).

(continued)

Figure 10.1. (continued)

1975: Following a *Popular Electronics* feature on the Altair 8080, Paul Allen and Bill Gates write software for the Altair, using the new BASIC language. On April 4, Gates and Allen form their own software company, Microsoft.

1976: Steve Jobs and Steve Wozniak roll out the Apple I, the first computer with a single-circuit board—thus starting Apple Computer.

1978: VisiCalc, the first computerized spreadsheet program, is introduced.

1979: Bob Barnaby, with MicroPro International, releases WordStar—the first word processing program.

1981: The first IBM personal computer, code-named "Acorn," is introduced.

1983: Apple's Lisa is the first personal computer with drop-down menu and icons.

1986: Compaq brings the Deskpro 386 to market. Its 32-bit architecture provides personal computer users with speeds comparable to mainframes.

1990s: Mobile devices (laptops and smartphones) become possible as transistor technologies, lithium batteries, and so on improve—following developments by Microsoft, Research in Motion, Nokia, Apple, and others.

---

have provided the foundational structures for what became known as the World Wide Web and Internet, the basis for social media platforms (from Facebook to Instagram), and the hub for online gaming communities. And, as technology itself has shifted—replacing the mainstay of static print with such multimodal, multilayered interconnections—we in turn have become increasingly tethered to new digital tools that have redesigned how ideas are represented and accessed. In particular, the development of HyperCard and hypertext had a monumental influence on the nature and shape of literacy today by providing the means for the multimodal and multilayered architecture of text. Such shifts were harbingers of what has been deemed a "post-typographic world," wherein type and visuals co-communicate ideas and information (e.g., Reinking et al., 1998). As Reinking et al. noted in the introduction to the landmark edited volume *Handbook of Literacy and Technology: Transformations in a Post-Typographic World*, there were four significant shifts:

1. "Electronic and printed texts are qualitatively different" (p. xxiv).
2. "There is an important sociocultural and historical dimension to considering the relation between technology and literacy" (p. xxv).
3. "The new technologies of electronic reading and writing are slowly but steadily transforming classrooms, schools, and instruction" (p. xxv).
4. "There is a dearth of research and scholarship available to understand and guide technological transformations of literacy" (p. xxvii).

These developments also occurred in tandem with an emerging interdisciplinary interest in how readers make meaning of extended text, how they navigate multilayered, multimodal presentations of information, and how they produce, consume, and communicate ideas. From its early days, the digital advance involved scholars engaged in literacy research to explore language and text processing and programming language (i.e., to process how text and the architecture of complex ideas are navigated by learners and experts). This overlapped with what we have outlined as the cognitive turn, bringing together scholars such as linguists, cognitive scientists, text analysts, and a number of the first and second generations of artificial intelligence researchers. By developing the construct of the oral and written language scripts and plans that humans use to organize experience and ideas, researchers in artificial intelligence (e.g., Roger Schank and Robert Abelson) were able to develop approaches to language processing—relying on research emanating from cognitive science.[4]

Hypermedia

It is notable that these developments undergirded what we have identified as the advent of digital literacies: hypermedia. The development of hypertext and its influence on literacy was profound. Hypertext provides a means to express ourselves in ways that reflect more directly the complexity of our thinking and the interrelatedness of ideas. Hypertext allows authors and groups of authors to link information together, create paths through a corpus of related material, annotate existing texts, and create notes that point readers either to bibliographic data or to the body of reference material. At the same time, hypertext blurs the distinction between author and reader by inviting readers to navigate their way via links including perhaps their own additions. As Yankelovich et al. (1985) note, "Hypertext can allow the creation of an automated encyclopedia of sorts: readers can browse through linked, cross-referenced, annotated text in an orderly but sequential manner" (p. 18). Additionally, as users create texts, they develop spaces for themselves and others—reflecting Vygotsky's (1978) notion that tools such as language or other sign symbols mediate our interactions with the world. In particular, with the advent of hypertext, users have access to an authoring tool that allows for the following:

- unfolding ideas through buttons, scrolling, and other means by which authors can stage when and where ideas are displayed;
- creating links between ideas (e,g., embeddings) that allow for various forms of relationships (i.e., definitional, illustrative, or critical), such that compositions or textual spaces are, as Bolter (2001) has argued, "pulsing networks of ideas";
- providing multimodality—the dynamic and graphic presentation of ideas by interfacing alphabetic texts with nonlogocentric media, such as graphics, animation, or video;
- supporting access to resources and their incorporation in ways that are both malleable and complex;
- furthering a relationship with readers that is collaborative and portfolio-esque, as stacks offer multiple layers and multiple explorations and engagements; and
- affording asynchronized access to ideas and communications.

In terms of literacy, as Hull and Nelson (2005) stated:

> All about us, there are unmistakable signs that what counts as a text . . . have already changed and radically so—in this our age of digitally-afforded multimodality . . . it's possible now to easily integrate words with images and sound and music and movement in order to create digital artifacts that do not necessarily privilege linguistic forms of signification, but rather that draw upon a variety of modalities—speech, writing, image, gesture, sound—to create different forms of meaning. . . . through a process of braiding (Mitchell, 2004) or orchestration (Kress & van Leeuwen, 2001), a multimodal text can create a different system of signification, one that transcends the collective contribution of its constituent parts. More simply put, multimodality can afford not just a new way to make meaning, but a different kind of meaning. (pp. 224–225)

[margin handwriting: multimodality]

As Siegel (1995) likewise suggested, these multimedia explorations have "a generative power that comes from juxtaposing different ways of knowing . . . as a way of positioning students as knowledge makers and reflective inquirers" (p. 473). Or, as Witte (1992) noted, "the influence of alternative intertexts on the constructive processes increases dramatically as the multiple voices of distinct constructive semioses mix on what might be called the battleground of the 'trace.' It is for this reason that . . . all discourse . . . is fundamentally dialogical" (pp. 287–288). The dynamic afforded by hypertext relates to what Forman (1998) has described as "the type of constructive conflict we deem to be the power of this multisymbolic approach to education" (p. 187). It corresponds to a kind of semiotic engagement that provides students access to multiple symbol systems, which allow for ongoing learning through analogies or metaphor. As Lemke (2015) contends, when students interact with multimedia text, there is "an amplifying effect."

With the multilayering and intermingling of text forms with images, hypertext prompted a shift that carried with it new requirements for meaning making. It was as if meaning makers were confronted with an expanding set of new genres to navigate. Further, as meaning makers shifted from working with a single text to those of connected multiple texts, involving new forms of syntheses or remixing, their active roles become more apparent. For example, based on her work and that of her colleagues across a number of studies examining synthesizing from multiple print sources, Spivey (1997) suggests that with HyperCard and hypertext the following applies:

> People make across-text linkages and topical jumps, and they generate relations from one text to another as they do their transformation. The kind of intertextual connections that are so visible when people work in Hypertext environments are the kinds of transformations that we have been considering. . . . (pp. 209–210)

Essentially, with the introduction of hypertext, technology expanded beyond being a tool that expedited data analysis and word processing to a platform that supported different forms of representation, communication, and meaning

Figure 10.2. Key Developments in the Digital Advance

Key developments in the digital advance included the advent of hypermedia (hypertext and HyperCard) and the widespread access to this software with the release of the Macintosh computer. A sampling of these developments include:

1963: Ted Nelson coins the terms hypertext and hypermedia to represent linked content and developed a text-editing system.

1960s and 1970s: Various incarnations of IN emerge as tools for linking documents and communities with shared interests (e.g., Abdrie van Damm at Brown University and Tom Englebart at Stanford Research Institute).

1980: Tim Berners-Lee creates ENQUIRE, an early hypertext database system, somewhat like a wiki but without hypertext punctuation. Wiki is not invented until 1987.

1980s: A number of experimental "hyperediting" functions in word processors and hypermedia programs emerge, with many features similar to what became the World Wide Web.

1982: Peter J. Brown of the University of Kent develops the first significant hypertext system for personal computers.

1980: Robert Busso, an Italian Jesuit priest, with support from the founder of IBM, develops a tool for pursuing massive searches on Thomas Aquinas work and publishes the *Index Thomisticus*.

1983: Ben Shneideman (University of Maryland) and his colleagues develop the HyperTies system, which is commercialized and used to create the first commercial electronic book, *Hypertext Hands-On!*

1986: Bill Atkinson creates HyperCard, released by Apple in August.

1987: With the understanding that it would be given for free on all Macs, Apple releases HyperCard with Macintosh computers. Apple also provides high school students in Apple Classrooms of Tomorrow with beta versions of HyperCard for the purpose of pursuing multimedia projects, enabling them to enlist random accessible laser discs as complements to the Macintosh computers.

1989: Tim Berners-Lee, a scientist at CERN (Conseil Européen pour la recherche nucléaire), proposes and later prototypes a new hypertext project in response to a request for a simple, immediate, information-sharing facility to be used among physicists working at CERN and other academic institutions. He calls the project the "WorldWideWeb."

Late 1990s: HyperCard of hypertext more broadly becomes a key influence in the design of the web.

making.[5] In many ways, hypertext was the architecture for ways of knowing and interacting with new norms and conventions befitting multimodal forms mixing image and text. Despite its initial clunkiness, it garnered momentum in the 1980s before proliferating in the early 1990s, as the advent of the World Wide Web (made possible through hypertext) gave everyday users the opportunity to engage with the technology (see Figure 10.3).

With the emergence of the web browser—and its explosion from only 500 known web servers in 1993 to over 10,000 in 1994—hypertext became the basis for what became our web-based digital engagements. These engagements, as John

Figure 10.3. Web Development, Multimedia, and Gaming

1985: The first dot-com domain name is registered on March 15, years before the World Wide Web would mark the formal beginning of Internet history. The Symbolics Computer Company, a small Massachusetts computer manufacturer, registers Symbolics.com. More than 2 years later, only 100 dot-coms had been registered.

1990: Tim Berners-Lee, a researcher at CERN, the high-energy physics laboratory in Geneva, develops Hypertext Markup Language (HTML), giving rise to the World Wide Web.

1993: The Pentium microprocessor advances the use of graphics and music on PCs.

1994: PCs become gaming machines as Command & Conquer, Alone in the Dark 2, Theme Park, Magic Carpet, Descent, and Little Big Adventure are among the games to hit the market.

1996: Sergey Brin and Larry Page develop the Google search engine at Stanford University.

1999: The term wi-fi becomes part of the computing language, and users begin connecting to the Internet without wires.

2001: Apple unveils the Mac OS X operating system, which provides protected memory architecture and preemptive multitasking, among other benefits. Not to be outdone, Microsoft rolls out Windows XP, which has a significantly redesigned GUI (GRAPHICAL USER INTERFACE).

2004: Mozilla's Firefox 1.0 challenges Microsoft's Internet Explorer, the dominant web browser. Facebook, a social networking site, launches.

2005: YouTube, a video sharing service, is founded. Google acquires Android, a Linux-based mobile phone operating system.

2006: Apple introduces the MacBook Pro, its first Intel-based, dual-core mobile computer, as well as an Intel-based iMac. Nintendo's Wii game console hits the market.

2007: The Blackberry, iPhone, and other companies bring many computer functions to the smartphone.

Callow (2010) suggested in his comparison of screen and page-based texts, entailed the following:

> The web page has multiple hyperlinks—we see them both on the top and side menu bars and in more content-specific subheadings or tabs placed about the main body of text. There has been much research done on online comprehension skills and the choices made by students when navigating the Internet for information. Locating relevant information and critically evaluating hyperlinks are key skills in an online environment. If we compare the print page to the web page, in some ways the use of the smaller call-out boxes on the bottom right of the double page does a similar job to the hyperlinked tabs on the web page. Each takes the reader to more specific information. From a reader's point of view, how are either the call-out boxes or the hyperlinks supporting a clear understanding of information about the topic? Do they elaborate on the information or extend and present more depth? They may be purely decorative, tangential or, at worst, irrelevant to the main topic. (p. 109)[6]

Figure 10.3 provides an overview of these developments.

Web-Based Explorations

The proliferation of the web and its use for meaning making in the digital realm spurred the emergence of studies of learning in hypermedia environments. For example, Coiro and Dobler (2007) examined the online comprehension strategies (via think-alouds, responses to semi-structured interview tasks and other responses) of successful 6th-grade comprehenders. Students engaged with a pre-set Internet site dealing with the topic of tigers as an assignment prompting search engine usage. The architecture of the online material, especially with hyperlinks and the use of thumbnails and annotations, seemed to prompt the use of such features to assist with the navigation of the texts. Based on their findings, Coiro and Dobler suggested that one of the key distinctions between online and offline comprehension is tied to the more frequent use of forward inferencing (versus backward inferencing)—prompted at the point of a hypertext link. They link this usage to a more multilayered inferential engagement among online meaning makers:

> The skilled readers in our study engaged in a multi-layered inferential reading process that occurred across the three-dimensional spaces of Internet text . . . combining traditionally conceived inferential reasoning strategies with a new understanding that the relevant information may be "hidden" beneath several layers of links on a website as opposed to one visible layer of information in a printed book. (p. 234)

They also suggested that "internet reading seems to demand more attempts to infer, predict and evaluate reading choices . . . to require readers to orient themselves in a new and dynamic three-dimensional space . . . to figure out how to get back to where they were" (Coiro & Dobler, 2007, p. 234). Thus, they concluded, the self-regulation of online comprehension seems tied to a similar set of recursive strategies of past models of composing (e.g., Tierney & Pearson, 1983). Online comprehension involves planning within and across websites, predicting and following leads, monitoring how and where to proceed, and evaluating relevance and judging merits. They noted that there were physical dimensions associated with these activities (e.g., scrolling, clicking) and speculated that the online environment might be more demanding and complex than offline. In some ways, these results support the characterization of online comprehension as more likely to be aligned within the author(s) frame(s) or labyrinth(s) at the same time as it entails agility with navigating, searching, selecting, and integrate across sources. As Coiro and Dobler noted:

> Our findings suggest that the greater complexities in online reading comprehension may result largely from a process of self-directed text construction; that is, the process online readers use to comprehend what they read as they search for the Internet text(s) most relevant to their reading needs.

On one level, we observed skilled readers engaged in an ongoing "self-directed" planning process involving a series of inferences about what would best fit with their internal representation of the text's meaning. Simultaneously, on a second level, these readers constructed their own external texts. Each decision about which link was most relevant involved constructing the next element in the text they built. We observed readers actively anticipating and monitoring the relevancy of each new text unit, while quickly deciding whether to continue to add that text to their own external text by following deeper links within a page or to exclude that text and search elsewhere by clicking the back button as a fix-up strategy, for example. At the end of the reading session, it became clear that each reader had constructed not only his or her internal understanding of a certain text but had also constructed a unique external representation of the Internet texts most applicable to their needs. (p. 241)

They contrasted this observation with:

Readers who do not strategically plan and anticipate where they are headed within open Internet spaces may end up constructing a disjointed collection of random texts as opposed to a systematic compilation of carefully chosen texts from which to sift out a relevant point. Thus, an increased need to make forward inferences about text appeared to compound an already complex process of making bridging inferences about content in a manner that may prompt additional complexities to the process of reading online. (p. 241)

In Coiro and Dobler's study, the online demands of meaning making appeared to prompt what they labeled forward inferencing, or a form of making predictions, as meaning makers attempted to navigate the layers of text or information that the text template and online navigational tools might suggest. Forward inferencing seems to arise in conjunction with an interest in determining where links might lead and in assessing the possible saliency of what may be uncovered, especially by a hyperlink. When using search engines, the students often relied on annotations offered with hyperlinks derived from the search as a means of assessing degree of relevance or the likelihood that an identified site would yield more or less relevant results.

Coiro and Dobler (2007) further conjectured that online comprehension could be differentiated from offline comprehension in a number of ways. First, as meaning making proceeded online, it involved knowledge of topic and knowledge of print informational text structures akin to offline comprehension; in contrast, it involved knowledge of informational website structures as well as search engines. This knowledge influenced how they navigated the text, including the physical nature of their approach (e.g., returns to the home page). Second, online comprehension involved—to a degree—similar and different inferential strategies. In response to questions that were set, the meaning makers' use of context and other text cues was akin to that of offline comprehenders when exploring texts. But, as suggested, there was more forward inferencing involved as one chose what path to follow.

Teresa Dobson's research on reading hypertext novels showed similar findings—especially with regard to the nature of the influence of hypertext architecture on the approach and strategies of the meaning maker. She and her colleagues have done extensive probing of adolescents' responses to selected hypertext novels that are literary in nature (e.g., Dobson, 2007; Dobson & Luce-Kapler, 2005; Luce-Kapler et al., 2006). Their observations of and comments by her students indicated that hypertext novels provoked more self-consciousness of the reader's role in meaning making and a great deal of emphasis on reading in a way that might be considered text dependent or author-centric. She suggested, in her subsequent work with wikis, that meaning makers engaged in their own development of these structures seem to shift in their attitude (Dobson, 2004). As she stated:

> in my current work with students reading Hypertexts and writing collaboratively and individually) in malleable "wiki" writing spaces, I often find those who are exceedingly critical of Hypertext structures as readers become wholly engaged as writers, often delighting in engaging the rhetorical ploys they previously eschewed. (pp. 17–18)

Observations of high schoolers from the Apple Classrooms of Tomorrow who were engaged in hypertext projects suggested similar tendencies (Galindo et al., 1989; Tierney et al, 1997). Students displayed a preoccupation with the architecture of ideas (especially with images) and the possibility of engaging the use of special effects (e.g., animation) drawn from their exposure to pop culture. They appeared to approach hypertext with more questions and more interest and more concern over form (e.g., the layering of material with links and interface with video) than they did the regular print-based projects. They viewed the advantage of the hypertext as allowing them to design a space that affords different forms of engagement for others (e.g., especially with a kind of edginess). Perhaps more profound was the lasting effect on the students. When interviewed several years later, it was obvious that for these early users, these projects constituted far more than an engagement with a new genre or access to enlivened integration of image and text. The technology was a springboard into a life that was shaped by new affordances with new forms of literacy. This shift went beyond performing meaning making drawn from the web—it affected how they integrate its uses personally, in their studies, and professionally (Tierney et al., 2006).

In recent years, studies of digital reading have expanded to address a range of other dimensions, including the ability of students to make critical judgments of the material that they might access—for example, judgments related to its credibility. In a study of a large pool of students from a range of schools, Turner et al. (2020) explored the approach—especially the means of evaluation—that students enlisted for judging web-based resources en route to suggesting how educators might better prepare them to do so. In a study comparing how historians, professional fact checkers, and undergraduates evaluate online information and arrive at judgments of credibility, Sam Wineburg and Sarah McGrew found that historians and students often fell victim to easily manipulated features of websites—reading vertically within a website to evaluate its reliability. In contrast, fact checkers read laterally or across sites and were able to evaluate the veracity of information more accurately and quickly (Wineburg & Mc Grew, 2019).

Living in the Media: Embodiment[7]

For many of us nowadays, digital technologies permeate our lives. As Rob and Richard Beach (2018) suggested:

> Our daily lives are inseparable from the events and affordances of our handheld devices, Web-based interactions, and participation in various virtual spaces. We are in the media age; our existence as individuals, groups, and societies occurs in various media rather than with media. (p. 136)

We enlist digital tools 24/7 as information retrieval devices, vehicles for communications and transactions, portals for entertainment and culture, platforms for building social and identity relationships, and launchpads for how we position and identify ourselves and engage with our virtual experiences on screen (especially in conjunction with virtual associations, such as role-playing in games like Second Life and other settings) (see also Thomas, 2007; Kim, 2016; Schallert et al., 2016; Serafini, 2015; Serafini & Gee, 2017). We also pay for goods and services online; and our work life often has the feel of being in a digital studio with an array of tools—akin to having a palette on our computers. We have moved from fixed usage of unidimensional software that constrain our responses to sites that involve critical and creative responses, including forms of vicarious participation, reaction, or networking—synchronized and asynchronized. As Hepp and Krotz (2014) aptly summarized, we operate in "mediatized worlds . . . structured fragments of social lifeworlds with a certain binding intersubjective knowledge inventory, with specific social practices and cultural thickenings. Mediatized worlds are the everyday concretization of media cultures and media societies" (p. 8).

Perhaps more significant, our digitally based social lives are not just extended by digital exchanges; they are integral to our identity formations and our experiences as social beings at various levels (both local and global, intimate and afar). Our digitally based social engagements—emails, text messaging, direct and indirect communications by web chats, social media, or professional networks, and collaborative projects or exchanges within local or global communities—have contributed to a heightening of collaboration and forms of shared, "spreadable" (see Jenkins et al., 2013; Serafini, 2015), and collective meaning making. Our digital engagements have become our portals to the world—transactions with fellow meaning makers, or collaborators—virtually and face-to-face, synchronized and asynchronized. For instance, Henry Jenkins and his colleagues (Jenkins et al., 2006) introduced the notion of participatory culture to describe the social meaning making emerging across digital environments As they noted, "participatory culture shifts the focus of literacy from individual expression to community involvement. The new literacies almost all involve social skills developed through collaboration and networking" (p. xiii). Adding to this, platforms for online learning have often provided avatars and other forms of scaffolding to support different forms of collaborations.

More intimately, the social spillover to identity and personae play extends to text messages and avatars, the formation of affinity groups, and the collaborative nature and possibilities of Internet projects. For example, Lewis and Fabos (2005) found that when adolescents instant message, they may shift their personae and identity to match a perceived relationship or exhibit a desire to attempt such a shift. As Lewis and Fabos stated, "they enact identities that depend upon a running analysis of the online and offline contexts" (p. 494). Wade and Fauske (2004), from their observations of online discussions, suggest individuals are "not passive reproducers in creating their identities, their use of language and other social choices . . . language choices can be thought of as strategies designed to achieve particular goals in a particular context" (p. 140).

In a related vein, as Sefton-Green (2013) found, youth compose by appropriating different elements from various sources for their own creative and sometimes critical use via "remixing" content for their own signature compositions to be shared with others. A number of researchers studying youth responses to and uses of media (e.g., Beach et al., 2017; Napoli & Sychterz, 2015; Phelan, 2014; Unsworth, 2008; Wiesner, 2006) have noted similar forms of appropriation and adaptation in conjunction with students' enlistment and adaptation of digital modes, as well as their instantiations of responses—from aesthetic and other forms of engagement—with a range of multimodal texts.

In the digital realm, meaning-making spaces for expressing ideas have proliferated (e.g., text messaging, tweets, blogs, chat rooms, listservs, and affinity groups, and in combinations of online and offline spaces that can extend one's community, collaborators, or audience). These spaces are not all the same; some can serve simply as a means of checking on schedules, locations, or facts or for exchanging information or sharing or uniting with people with similar interests (akin to fan clubs or groups of fellow gamers). As such, these engagements can be incidental or more substantial. For example, Ito et al. (2013) explored digital media and its role in shaping identity and affinity (e.g., through connections made via fan culture). But these engagements can also be supportive, subversive, or even perverse—seeking allegiance to certain causes or used to bully, shame, or exclude.

Indeed, the issue of audience or fellow meaning makers can become especially pronounced if they extend beyond an intended audience or consumer or user. Participation and postings may be less restricted than intended and less sacrosanct as presupposed. If exchanges are across cultures, they are apt to involve a myriad of negotiations, attempts, and transactions—especially when image and text and a host of semiotic meaning offerings may not fall outside of the possibly egocentric indulgences of digital correspondents. Glynda Hull and Amy Stornaiuolo (2014), in an article on cosmopolitan literacies, offered a powerful demonstration of these dimensions through the digital video and text exchanges they recorded between Indian and New York high schoolers as the students explored each other's worlds.

Alternatively, several scholars (Rogers & Winters, 2006; Alvermann, 2008, 2011, 2015; 2019, Alvermann et al., 2012; Hull & Nelson, 2005) have argued that providing access to these multimedia environments may open up new and transformative spaces and identities. Students are afforded the possibility of having their literacy practices travel across spaces, in and out of schools—to "juxtapose and transform genre practices for critical purposes, engage in the playful instability of genres, selves, and messages, and re-narrate their stories and identities in the process" (Rogers & Winters, p. 29). In some ways, these multiple engagements befit the view of meaning makers as a kind of multivocal and multiperspectival pursuer of understandings, akin to what was suggested by Barthes, or other views of the social construction of multiple meanings. That is, the meaning maker is engaged in constructing selves or multiple personas in the company of others—as a form of embodiment. Lorri Neilsen Glenn (2012) contends that these "symbolic resources not only help adolescents to make sense of their experiences, but they also offer opportunities for trying on or taking up often multiple and conflicting roles or identities. In this way, a text is both a window and a door" (p. 13).

In their study of primary students' engagements in a virtual world, Burnett and Merchant (2014) illustrated in detail how students can navigate various spaces in such a multiplicative fashion.[8] As they describe:

> The virtual world in this case was "Barnsborough," a secure virtual world built by virtuallylearning.co.uk in the Active Worlds Educational Universe (www.activeworlds .com). Developed by a group of educators, researchers and consultants, it was designed to provide opportunities for children to engage in literacy activities within a meaningful and motivating context (Merchant, 2009, 2010). "Barnsborough" itself is a three-dimensional simulation of a deserted town, which children can explore, visiting interconnected locations such as sewers, a park, the town hall, an Internet cafe, military headquarters and an old castle. As they move around the world, they encounter clues hinting at why the town is deserted in the form of dropped notes, Internet sites, graffiti, posters and so on. Children are represented as avatars on-screen and have access to an online chat function through which they can communicate with others. Chat items appear not only above avatars' heads but also on an ongoing scrolling chatlog at the bottom of the screen. They can access other functions, such as teleporting or flying between different locations. (p. 38)

They note in particular how "incidents, individuals, objects or places are not completely in either the material or virtual world, and nor do they jump between. Instead, the virtual seems to inflect the material and vice versa" (p. 38). As they demonstrate in their example of one student:

John could be seen as in a "world of his own" but not in the sense that his exploration of the virtual world sets him apart from the rest. He moves both in the classroom and in Barnsborough; his laptop is both a physical object in the classroom and the portal to the virtual world; he interacts with others both in and out of world. At the same time, the classroom frames not only what he does in physical space but also what he does online. The "world of his own" is perhaps the one he helps construct as he operates across both environments and helps sustain a space that allows both movement and stillness, both autonomy and compliance, both material and virtual actions. Importantly then, these are not parallel plural places inhabited by parallel plural identities. Instead, as Law writes, we can understand this in terms of a multiplicity that "implies that different realities overlap and interface with one another. Their relations, partially coordinated, are complex and messy" (Law, 2004, p. 61). (p. 43)

Burnett and Merchant (2014) detail how offline and online engagements can seem inseparable. As they suggest, there is a mobility to ideas, rather than a boundedness; the students' engagements seemed changing and fluid due to the interactions, relationships, and trajectories created through the meshing of online and offline spaces; and students drew from both offline and online experiences to layer their virtual experiences. As the authors explain, John's online and offline engagements support each other:

> John reads and responds to the chatlog in the light of his particular journey through Barnsborough or talks to his friends, he fuses together action and interaction both in-world and in the classroom. We see this as he switches between "doing as he is told" in class and continuing, surreptitiously, with his investigation of Barnsborough. An analysis of his online/offline activity as binary or separate events is insufficient. Instead, we suggest it is helpful to see him as enacting a kind of "layered presence" (Martin et al., 2012), in space that is both online and offline, both schooled and not-schooled.
>
> In unpacking this, we can begin to identify some of the things that are latent within the experience of John, which we could see as "folded" (Deleuze, 2001) into what he does as he interacts with the text. For example, folded into his interactions in and around Barnsborough is his prior experience of different kinds of texts, his experience of using virtual worlds or online texts, the way he has positioned himself, or has been positioned, in relation to literacy in the classroom and also of course, his understandings of classrooms, military headquarters, castles and so on, as well as his relationships with other children and adults. (p. 44)

This intersection between online and offline spaces is consistent with studies of cross-cultural understandings that have been observed in chat rooms, Twitter exchanges, and other forms of media. As Beach and Myers (2001) have argued and as various studies by Myer and his colleagues (Myers & Beach, 2001; Myers et al., 1998, 2000) have demonstrated, these literacies give meaning makers the tools for representing themselves and their communities as well as those to engage with others and their communities. This gives meaning makers the potential to enhance their understandings of self, other, and a diverse range of communities, in accordance with the portrayals and the frames undergirding the participations. As Levin (1996) and Turkle (1995) have noted, however, it also risks sustaining forums and practices that befit the norms of some but not others. Indeed, some online discussions may verge on or cross into unethical territory, colonizing or perpetuating certain views over others and resulting in the rallying, silencing, alienating, or marginalizing of individuals and groups.

Indeed, the complex nature of these spaces and how individuals and groups are located in and displaced by them are apparent in studies of how historically marginalized groups form communities. For example, studies of a sense of community achieved among lesbians via email listervs, blogs, and other spaces have demonstrated how individual members may become dislodged or marginalized within the community, depending on their performances as members of the group and the norms that are applied or develop across time (e.g., Bryson et al., 2006; Wincapaw, 2000). Bryson et al. suggest that one might find a haven or a prison, a sense of belonging or a sense of dislodgement in such spaces.

In other studies of digital communities that explore digital users' portrayals of certain personae, some users have been observed constructing a "discoursal self" to convey a certain identity related to the values, beliefs, and power relations of that space. This is distinct from an "authorial self," constructed through uses of certain writing techniques or content, or an "autobiographical self," evoked through sharing autobiographical events through writing, which result in their identities to others as "perceived writers" (Burgess & Ivanič, 2010, p. 237–241). Users construct such identities in a fashion that is ongoing or tied to events or practices mediated by the social networking platform (e.g., the use of hashtags). For instance, as the sociological papers of Damarin (1995) and Grint and Gill (1995) indicate, certain ways of interacting with technologies define particular types of gender identity. Michael Tierney (1995) (working with systems) and Hapnes and Sorenson (1995) (in studies of hacking) similarly suggest that the behavior associated with computer usage and naming may be aligned with ways of defining masculinities.

Gaming

Even more overtly, embodiment occurs in gaming and digital animations such as anime, manga, and their followings or fans. With the advent of interactive media, especially in the form of simulations and hands-on virtual engagements, especially games and so on, Squire (2006), Gee (2003, 2005), Black (2008), Steinkuehler (2008), and others describe how students' exploration of others and their worlds assume forms of embodiment with customized identities and new hybrid forms of text. They can be looked at, as suggested by the New London Group (1996), in terms of hybridity or as "articulating in new ways, established practices and conventions within and between different modes of meaning . . . (of discourses and genres), . . . cutting across boundaries of convention and creating new conventions" (p. 29). They may thereby serve as powerful means to explore new ideas and worlds. As Squire (2006) and Gee (2003, 2005) suggest, in the context of these digital spaces gamers can experience new environments and situations with tools, identities, and ideologies to explore problem solving. Squire, for example, argues that "games focus our attention and mold our experience of what is important in a world and what is to be ignored. The game designers' choices, particularly of what to strip away from a world, can be read as ideological when considered in relation to other systems" (pp. 21–22).

Games should not be underestimated in terms of the worlds, opportunities to explore, and the kinds of problem solving that they afford and invite users to experience. Games often coexist and align with forms of print media or other games, operating across these various modes simultaneously or as they develop to market themselves or related products. Games also often involve state-of-the-art visual effects and virtual engagements to simulate otherworldly encounters. These worlds are often rooted in fantasy genres—enlisting scenarios, tools, and characters that befit extraordinary environments that can be metaphorically or directly compared with real-world places. A large number of games thus present a mangling of fantasy and reality and are aligned with plots (e.g., blade runners) wherein players are transported across virtual and "real worlds" within the game. For instance, cyberpunk involves engagements in various configurations of real places such as buildings, roadways, subways, and the terrain typical of locations (often cities). In such games, players are faced with situation-specific, real-world circumstances including the people and events, including crises and catastrophes, that do or may occur, as well as the choice of solutions or resources that might be at hand.

Yet despite the illusion of "openness" and options, these world games represent ideological leanings and systemic tendencies tied to matters of violence and policing, personal and community responsibility, and constructions of race and gender. Most games have a following that extends to a network of other gamers that are in collaboration or competition with one another, or are serving as expert advisors to other players or critics of the games themselves on technical and social fronts. The world of gaming is not without major flaws. Indeed, issues have been raised with regard to the stereotyping of women and minorities and the rampant use of violence. Studies point to the violence and degradation that games perpetuate (e.g., Dill et al., 2008; Lynch et al., 2016). Moreover, the gaming industry itself has been found to have a history of gender biases (e.g., Jenson & de Castell, 2018).

Matters of Equity, Empowerment, and Ethics

As our digital literacies expand and growing numbers of communities become wired or gain wireless access to the Internet, it becomes well-nigh essential that individuals and groups neither be sidelined from participating nor constrained in ways that limit their ability to do so creatively and critically. In other words, individuals should be given: (1) access, which may carry certain technical requirements; as well as (2) opportunities, or the license to contribute creatively and critically as pursue personal and group goals. Further, if students are to be participants and not spectators, they need opportunities to collaborate, communicate, acquire, sift through, create, and critique ideas as well as to solve problems.

These notions of participation and the capital nature of these new literacies are consistent with the declaration of principles on building the information society that was the focus of the 2003 World Summit on the Information Society (WSIS, 2003).[9] However, taking your place as a participant may not be as straightforward as the WSIS invitation might suggest. Economic circumstances and/or social constructions of engagement with these technologies might preclude the possibility of access. Intranational differences within both developed and developing countries highlight that issues of access are limited for economically challenged groups and individuals (United Nations, 2006). Even within developed countries, such as the United States, participation has often been limited by personal economic circumstances. These inequities were brought to the surface on a global scale when public health restrictions resulting from the COVID pandemic forced schools to provide education online.

A great deal has been written in the media and popular press about how digital literacies can contribute to cultural continuity or disruption, expansion or erosion, and self-determination or imperialism. It has been shown that certain literacy practices may have preferential leanings and perspectives—such as Western, gendered, racist, and fantastical—that may prove alienating or perpetuate certain biases or distortions of reality. Indeed, these literacies can alternate between being sites of contestation for freedom of expression, citizenship journalism, and open exchange and those for vehicles for control, surveillance, or enculturation. Sometimes even digital projects that are viewed under the banner of empowerment are pursued without adequate consultation and community support, favoring instead the interests, pursuits, and passions of commercial or even scholarly enterprises. In this way, even those touted as critical may be actively overriding local considerations, governance, or ethics (Bruce & Hogan, 1998; Lam et al., 2012; Lewis Ellison et al., 2016; Omrod, 1995; Rowsell et al., 2017).

Digital Developments and Education

Digital advances have yielded major advances in literacy—especially when literacy is viewed as broadly encompassing multimodal engagements as well as those with the web and social media. Consider, for example, the lasting and wide-ranging literacy benefits and opportunities resulting from the provision of state-of-the-art digital access in the educational context. Longitudinal studies of those students engaged in project-based work using multimedia platforms (i.e., to explore and compose meaning) have been shown to have clear advantages related to achievement, identity, strategies, and tools for learning, problem solving, discovering, and communicating. In their 10-year study of students from Apple Classrooms of Tomorrow, Rob and his colleagues Ernest Bond and Jane Bresler (2006) argued that by providing students with the resources and tools required to engage in rich explorations of and with new literacies, the Apple learning sites afforded greater means of access and participation, as well as more opportunities for personal, cognitive, and social engagements. For these students from economically challenged backgrounds, these possibilities were akin to "genres of power"—providing students with new texts, and new ways of negotiating meaning and ways of knowing. The literacies were also transformative in terms of students' everyday lives—especially when compared with peers without such opportunities. Indeed, the students were able to develop cutting-edge uses for technology in meaningful situations. By virtue of being trusted with the tools, authority, and agency within their classroom and among peers, students were able to mobilize and develop these literacies in ways that interfaced with the social fabric of their lives within and outside school and into the future.

Repeatedly, studies of the digital affordances in classrooms have identified problems that seem to persist. For example, Cynthia Selfe and Gail Hawisher (2004) reported on a 5- to 6-year study that involved interviews with over 300 individuals. From their subset of 20 case studies, they deduced a number of themes—bringing to the fore not only the extent to which digital literacies are closely enmeshed with everyday life (perhaps for the entirety of one's lifespan), but also how certain factors (e.g., race, gender, economic circumstances) can contribute to the empowerment of some and not others. They describe how sustained engagement with the productive use of digital technologies contributes in positive (i.e., personally, socially, educationally, and economically advantageous) ways to various aspects of certain people's lives, including enhancing their imagined potential for fuller, creative, and critical participation in society. Since Selfe and Hawisher's work, we have also seen how, on a national scale, participation can foment widespread acceptance of distortions of reality for uncritical consumers of digital disinformation—including our students.

These studies especially highlight the premium placed on the economic advantage afforded by students' skill at engaging in digital, new literacy spaces. Both of the aforementioned studies support the finding that power and literacy are inextricably linked, and that the development of flexible and robust digital literacy practices may need to recognize and be built on their multiple connections to social and cultural practices. In a similar vein, Lam et al. (2012), in a review of emerging studies dealing with migration, cross-border studies, and mobility, noted how digital affordances gave voice to students with tools that afforded transliteracy possibilities. As they stated:

> Studies of youth practices with digital media indicated that some young people of migrant backgrounds are using online media to express and construct their multilayered identifications, develop linguistic and social resources through local and translocal networks, and reference and contest the language and cultural ideologies coming from their home and host societies. (p. 210)

Unfortunately, in school settings, meaningful or engaging digital learning may be more the exception than the rule. Though it seems paradoxical, many school sites may not support the transition of these new literacies in ways that might fully realize their potential, precluding any shifts in power dynamics that might occur (Sheehy, 2007). In some cases, then, what may be accessible outside of school appears to have surpassed what most students in schools have the opportunity to access and explore. As a result, any affordances of digital literacies that do cross over to school may not have the same saliency or worth. As Street (2006) argued, outside of schools there is often an interest in global issues, networking, multimodality, flexibility, and so on, whereas inside schools there is often an emphasis on stability and unity. Indeed, in some situations, these new literacies are framed as discrete skills—such as programming, responsible Internet usage, or presentation strategies—rather than as learning tools with complex palettes of possibilities for students to access in a myriad of ways. It is as if rather than being supported in learning *with* technology—using a range of multimodal literacy tools (supported by these technologies) in the pursuit of learning—students are merely being asked to "learn the technology." What Squire (2006) argued 15 years ago may well still hold true: The integration of digital resources with learning within most schools falls short of what digital-based games are already achieving—that is, situated learning, with an array of visual resources and an accessible network of others, tied to developing expertise and understanding through performance.

Nevertheless, as digital engagements with various media are increasingly considered literacies, there seems to be a potential for curricularizing these media that have been predominantly outside the purview of traditional schools (except perhaps in terms of addressing their possible negative effects—e.g., violence, wasted time). This curricularizing involves advocating for the use of media from so-called informal settings (e.g., home, arcade, etc.) to school settings. Whereas the use of the media (e.g., games, video, digital cameras, mobile technologies, Internet, smart phones, blogs, etc.) has been left to individuals and society to define and use, schools have tended to redefine their use through a somewhat interventionist orientation. Lost in this crossover to schools may be the social and cultural possibilities—for example, exploring constructions of identity, democratization, social interchanges, and so forth, as well as a more semiotic perspective on everyday use of media. These possibilities have increased, especially with the advent and widespread use of digital tools, digital video, and mobile devices (that allow for more interchanges or complex gaming or narratives). However—and also not surprising—the potential and use of digital media in one setting may not be transferable to another. The transfer of students' engagements with these literacies outside of school may not fit well with in-school demands or norms.

As Bransford et al. (2000) summarized in their review of learning with technology for the National Research Council:

> In general, technology-based tools can enhance student performance when they
> are integrated into the curriculum and used in accordance with knowledge about

learning. But the existence of these tools in the classroom provides no guarantee that student learning will improve, they have to be part of a coherent education approach (p. 216). . . . Much remains to be learned about these technologies. (p. 230)

If we are to move forward, we would hope that educators build on what we have learned to date. In this regard, the online experience arising with the COVID-19 pandemic may be quite telling. Within the first month of the World Health Organization's declaration of a pandemic, over 100,000 faculty members at Canadian universities were forced to pivot to online education in the first two weeks, with many depending on platforms such as Zoom for class meetings. As Tony Bates (2020) noted, the results were mixed. Many educators reluctantly adopted online platforms with little knowledge of (and sometimes a disregard for) online education, while students struggled with the isolation that sometimes is experienced as well as the mode of engagements demanded of them. Too often, educators proceeded with online tools either blindly or formatively, learning as they went—in the hopes of deftly and effectively deploying or enlisting digital tools and spaces. Unfortunately, teachers and students were unprepared. They were not able to support various forms of participation (i.e., for groups and individuals) for a range of learning pathways, processes, and products, and fell short of providing the scaffolding or other tools and forms of support and consultation. And, unsurprisingly, we saw evidence again for how economic strata have created digital castes, as schools and homes had access to very different levels of hardware, software, Internet, and developmental support.

There are alternative proposals for how change might proceed more deliberatively, based on the discussions and pursuits of digital learning that have occurred to date. For example, in accordance with what might be considered a relevance principle, a number of educators have advanced approaches to digital literacy grounded in users' worlds. In their article "New Literacies and Community Inquiry," Bertram Bruce and Ann Bishop (2008) apply the lens of progressive education, especially that of John Dewey, to their considerations of the relationship of new literacies to community inquiry. In particular, they examine how community inquiry shapes and is shaped by digital literacies. Adopting a range of views of what might constitute community and the types of inquiries with which the community might become involved, Bruce and Bishop detail progressive educators' views of inquiry situated within and derived from different communities' needs and goals, as negotiated in a reciprocal fashion between individuals and groups.

Within this Deweyian framework, technologies are seen as tools for problem solving and, as such, can take various forms. They might be best viewed "as representing the ongoing processes of community inquiry" (Bruce & Bishop, 2008, p. 716) or learning, and should be considered in terms of their adapted use for inquiry. Technologies might also help achieve community goals through the emerging notion of community informatics (which addresses how technologies support community needs in areas such as health and civic engagement). In a rich, complex, and illustrative manner, Bruce and Bishop provide several vignettes of how community inquiry proceeds and how new literacies have engaged and developed in different settings. Dwyer (1996), in his reflections on the Apple Classrooms of Tomorrow (ACOT) project that he directed, also stressed the importance of a community that recognizes and supports the possibility of reimagining selves across digital spaces and other literacy fields or spaces. This requires a view of schooling that emphasizes the transformation and assessment of knowledge that is performance based and affords access to and support for multiple representations of ideas.

Similarly, and perhaps most notable, has been the formulation of the notion of the "new literacies" model proposed by a group of largely critical literacy theorists identifying themselves as the New London Group. Emphasizing relevance, this model included two components: (1) the notion that global communication requires multiple channels and media; and (2) the idea that multiple literacies are constituted by, and constitutive of, the multiplicity of cultures and linguistic contexts in which literacy practices occur (New London Group, 2000). As we detailed in the Critical Wave chapter, multiliteracies represented a way to conceptualize how literacies are situated within a changing social world—one that involves a growing diversity of literacy practices, an increasingly diverse population, and an expanding variety of exchanges that require different registers, semiotic understandings, and social engagements.

The proponents of multiliteracies argued for an approach to learning that was social, situated within the embodied participation of individuals and groups, and therefore embedded "in social, cultural and material" (New London Group, 1996, p. 82) contexts. In so doing, they added momentum to the social turn at the same time as they fused it with multimodal digital developments and a design orientation—combining literacy(ies) practices with transformative, critical, and relevant engagements and overt teaching and understandings of design features. They argued for a shift from verbocentric notions of literacy to a more semiotic framing of multiple modes, wherein students are engaged in reengineering and transforming the digital resources that they access. This perspective continues to evolve and gain traction; for instance, a group of U.S. scholars has developed a proposal tied to notions of connected learning with similar tenets (Ito et al., 2013).

Discussion

With the advent of digital literacies, the embrace of the new and multiple literacies might be viewed as stating the obvious. However, it may not be as straightforward as it seems—especially as one considers the history of literacy research and theorizing. Several scholars have argued and shown that the literacy field has tended to maintain a tradition of theorizing literacy and studying texts in a fashion that is singular and separate from the growing fabric of digital literacies with which most of us engage as primary and constant sources. Despite laudatory reports that social semiotic analysis achieves some understanding of the nature and power of multimodal exchanges, oftentimes these analyses seem more focused on the instrumental and regulatory functions of digital realms rather than on the interactive and personal implications and effects. The literacy field still seems disconnected from the actual meaning-making processes and emergences (ideational and social) that are happening via and within multilayered and multimodal affiliations and texts. Further, with some exceptions (e.g., Henry Jenkins and his collaborators), the field has tended to focus on the individual versus group-as-meaning-maker. While studies of digital literacy are beginning to embrace community dynamics and the ensemble style of engagements—as well as consider multiple-text situations and their multilayeredness and linkages—the predominant theories and models of meaning making tend to stick to the individual and one or a few threads. The study of literacy has yet to fully embrace the fabric and the composing processes of the ensemble.

This focus on the thread rather than the fabric has the potential to inflate the significance of the trace or individual detail while limiting (and perhaps distorting) its relationship to meaning making—thereby misrepresenting reading as a monological experience. Yet as Lemke (1998) posits, "Literacies are legion. Each one consists of interdependent social practices that link people, media objects, and strategies for meaning making" (p. 312). Indeed, we are constantly navigating and building ever-expanding and intermeshed webs of meaning as we engage with others and ourselves across face-to-face and other forms of communication, virtual and real, synchronized or not. We are similarly faced with a flood of daily weblike encounters, involving arrays of different transactions (and co-constructions) as we engage with our colleagues, coworkers, and others in various time zones. At times, one retreats and hopes for reprieve from the deluge and a quiet day in solitude.

Moreover, webs and networks themselves are rarely separate from one another, although we do enact forms of selective engagement, sorting, and so on as we begin our day—perhaps checking and responding to emails, pursuing projects, relaxing as we peruse listservs. Such multitasking may involve a mix of direct and indirect or synchronized or non-synchronized developments—it may be that some matters are paused and resumed later as one moves on or connects with others in a form of joint advancement. Therefore, as we move across or within networks and weblike engagements, we are sifting, linking, sampling, and following leads and paths. At the same time, we are layering and affiliating as we pursue for ourselves and others various confirmations, understandings, plans, commitments, answers, directions, or acknowledgments. This is also the world of our students.

The diversity of possibilities that might arise from these hypermedia environments captured the imagination of a range of scholars, from cognitivists to semioticians to sociolinguisticians, as they envisioned the potential affordances of these digital forms. In her seminal paper "Toward a Multifaceted Heuristic of Digital Reading to Inform Assessment, Research, Practice, and Policy," Julie Coiro (2020) has posited four dimensions to help characterize the possible ways reading comprehension might proceed and present itself for the digital reader. These include characteristics of text, reader, activity, and context:

Text	Context
■ Informational text ■ Hybrid text ■ Multimedia ■ Multimodal text ■ On-screen text ■ Hypertext ■ Hypermedia ■ Internet text ■ Augmented text ■ Literacy text	■ Response format » Multiple choice » Selected responses » Short construction typed » Audio recorded response » Video recorded response » Extended construction typed » Extended construction design form ■ Contextual design considerations » Timed or untimed » Individual, partner, or group » Engagement with real people or avatars » Face-to-face, remote, or virtual » Self-selected or other-selected » Personal or task goals
Reader ■ Cognitive capabilities ■ Reading and language competencies ■ Reading dispositions and motivations ■ Sociocultural identities	■ Contextual features of community » School-based experience » After-school experience » Home-based experience » Community-based experience ■ Medium platform » Single page » Object » Bound pages
Activity ■ Simple-text activity ■ Multiple-texts activity ■ Multiple-texts activities across multiple media and/or platforms ■ Critical media literacy activity ■ Online research and inquiry activity ■ Digital creation activity	» Multiple pages or objects » Digital device » Software or app » Virtual world » Headset-based virtual reality » Augmented reality

Accordingly, Coiro suggests digital meaning-making experiences entail different affordances and possibilities as readers engage with multiple texts, for different purposes, and across different situations (e.g., both varied and dynamic).

Spiro (1987; 2006a/b; see also Spiro et al., 2007) also proposes an approach to meaning making that extends to the meaning maker's ability to navigate across multiple inputs with a great deal of speed and efficiency. As he suggests, meaning making across digital material depends on a fluidity and an ability to discern relevance and glean meanings almost at a glance. Describing digital meaning makers as "being conductors (or jazz improvisers), rapidly bouncing excerpts from rich video clips off of each other" (Spiro et al., p. 98), Spiro (2006b) emphasizes that if the material is somewhat familiar and rich in content, meaning makers will:

> capitalize on their affinity for this mode of "quick-cutting" across dense images (cf. Stephens, 1998)—and their accustomedness to nonlinear processing . . . to crisscross between many video excerpts to speed up and deepen the process of building interconnected knowledge from experience. (Spiro, 2006b, p. 11)

To some extent, the agility and flexibility needed to do what Spiro describes requires that meaning makers have some preexisting knowledge of the topics, familiarity with the genres, and skill at efficiently discerning relevance across texts. They would need to be engaged as performative inquirers, with others, and in a fashion that is discursive and discerning.

Perhaps these same meaning-making abilities are involved when viewing visual art—especially impressionist paintings. We can savor the detail at the same time considering it in relation to the composite. As we move from engagement to engagement, from one text to another, or from one website to the next, we engage with the elements and, rather carefully weighing the separate elements, we discern the whole. This is akin to a kind of Gestaltism, but in a way that involves more of a leap in meaning making. The impressionistic discernment of multiple sites and texts might also be tied to seeing other composites of the same work. But the discernment of these composites may or may not be immediately interrelated. These processes may or may not be tied to crisscrossing a domain, searching for the best fit, or finding relevance, as Spiro has described, in complex knowledge circumstances. They may instead be tied to achieving a composite specific to a moment, person, or the goals, interests, or satisfaction of one's pursuits—at least for now.

As communication theorists indicate and research confirms, literacy involves relationships with texts and media that are both personal and social rather than detached or individualistic, and these relationships proceed/function on multiple and interrelated levels. At one level (or perhaps across all levels), such engagements involve conversations with one's self in the company of others. It involves, as Butler suggests, constructions that are performative and discursive (Butler, 1993, 1997). At another level, it is akin to a conversation that may entail a form of reflective meaning making tied to negotiations (e.g., across a set of emails or text messages or texts authored by others). For example, it might entail trying to understand what the author—either imagined or real—wanted you to think or act. It might entail exploring possible worlds and imagining or re-imagining possibilities for self. At a more macro level, these engagements interrelate with how we are networked and positioned with others, in both local and global spaces. These engagements thus occur in the context of navigating and journeying worlds—cultivating ideas and spurring meanings, using a range of texts where ideas are explored and mixed, created and critiqued, savored and digested, and used as fuel for expression of further considerations.

One should not discount the affordances and effects of technological developments. As many have noted, digital spaces bring to the fore affordances that should not be understated. However, as Owston (1997) emphasizes, "no medium, in and of itself, is likely to improve learning. . . . The key to the Web appears to lie in how effectively the medium is exploited" (p. 29). Certainly, digital spaces may afford alternative ways to interact with ideas and others, including self. And, in terms of meanings, we seem to be on the frontier of a new form of public knowledge, with the advent of citizen journalism, and open access publications—perhaps a world less filtered, with shifting notions of authorship, authority, and copyright as well as new ways of making, archiving, and curating texts and news (see Willinsky, 2006).

Nor should one shy away from a theory or model of meaning making that captures how meanings are transacted within and among groups and individuals within these groups. This might entail building on discussions to date that highlight how digital learning might be authentic, interactive, collaborative, resource rich, and inquiry driven. As Reinking (1997) suggested as he contemplated the significance of hypertext and how digital learning is positioned in schools:

> the computer is much more than a new device for displaying textual information or for teaching children how to read and write. It is instead a revolutionary new vehicle for textual communication that, if fully appreciated for its own merits unencumbered by lingering biases for print, can act as catalyst to bring people closer together in a democratic and relentlessly conditional pursuit of knowledge, understanding, and enjoyment. To realize this potential, we will be best served by setting our imaginations free from seeing a computer as a machine that lacks the warmth and security of a book, seeing it instead as a technological alternative providing almost unlimited potential to operationalize the humanistic values that fuel our noblest conceptions of literacy. (p. 642)

It might involve examining ways to capitalize on students who have only known a world with digital engagements. It might also entail considering such pursuits as those of Mayer and Moreno (2002), who developed principles to undergird the enlistment and juxtaposition of animation and other modes of delivery in some fields of learning (e.g., looking at the possibilities of simulations). As James Gee (2005, 2011) has discussed, educators might learn from the power of games, including how they afford players active engagements in simulations of real and contrived worlds. Through games and simulations, players might learn to discern and discriminate between symbolic representations, interpret meanings, practice problem solving in scenarios, and enact critically reflexivity.

The embodied engagements within and across these spaces occur in a range of ways—from quite broad, even global, to quite narrow and intrapersonal. They can involve engagement across social worlds and exchanges of ideas done in a fashion akin to the exchange of goods or capital, resembling at times forms of encroachment, absorption, or adoption (involving what could be forms of colonization or hybridization). They can involve exchanges of thoughts or ideas for oneself or in the context of schooling. Literacies may involve forms of mobilities that offer individuals multiple ways to locate or dislocate themselves as they relate to or interact within and across different spaces in different ways. Jean Baudrillard (1981), an early theorist about "hyperreality," suggested that we live in a world drained of authenticity as a result of the illusions perpetuated by the media and mass-produced environments (e.g., malls, amusement parks, automobiles, etc.). The end result, he argued, was an almost complete blurring of reality and unreality.

Furthermore, if meaning making is envisioned as a form of embodiment, there may need to be a shift in how we construct the meaning maker and the strategies that they employ. Cognitive-based models of meaning making tend to suggest major phases such as planning, inferencing, connecting, and monitoring. Perhaps, rather than perpetuate a "within the head" form of individualism, our models should be reconsidered so that they are more aligned with the embodied and collective engagement of meaning makers—including how students transact meanings with one another as they engage with, access, co-plan, co-author, search and explore, position, share, guide, reflect, recycle, and sustain. Meaning makers are not alone. Students move in and out of groups or operate in all manner of fashions—unified or dispersed, in concert or in disarray. Even in solitude, meaning makers may view themselves as operating in multiples, especially as they interact with texts of others and their own selves. We should recognize what some have termed the ensemble nature of meaning making—namely, the social nature of meaning making, akin to a form of group coauthoring—and enlist terms that represent a better fit with such engagements. We might also recognize the shifts that are occurring as we more readily travel between local and languages (Martin & Rizvi, 2014). Moving forward, we might view meaning making through lenses that recognize the social nature of these processes and products of coauthorships and reflect the shifting affiliations, negotiations, and mediations they entail.

In the digital realm, educators should remain cognizant of the toxic effects of media that is neither filtered nor carefully attributed. There is a need for an orientation to media that is critical and constructive—one that prepares students to deal with societal issues and problems and equips them with the tools to judge the arguments, claims, evidence, and underlying logic and ideology of digital encounters. Further, students should be prepared and equipped to do so in respectful, anti-colonial ways—advancing civility, deliberation, and accommodation. As Renee Hobbs (2010) discussed:

> Existing paradigms in technology education must be shifted towards a focus on critical thinking and communication skills and away from "gee-whiz" gaping over new technology tools. We must consider the balance between protection and empowerment and respond seriously to the genuine risks associated with media and digital

technology. . . . We must help people of all ages to learn skills that help them discriminate between high-quality information, marketing hype, and silly or harmful junk. (p. xii)

To effectively and strategically participate in these realms, students require the tools by which they can make discerning judgments of what is posted on digital sites, social media, or news outlets, especially about the credibility of any assertions, the merit of the motives, and the representations that are made in accordance with their match with the laws and norms of a civil society.

References

Alvermann, D. E. (2008). Commentary: Why bother theorizing adolescents' online literacies for classroom practice and research? *Journal of Adolescent & Adult Literacy, 52*(1), 8–19.

Alvermann, D. E. (2011). Moving on, keeping pace: Youth's literate identities and multimodal digital texts. In S. Abrams & J. Rowsell (Eds.), *Rethinking identity and literacy education in the 21st century.* National Society for the Study of Education Yearbook (vol. 110, part I, pp. 109–128). Columbia University, Teachers College.

Alvermann, D. E. (2015). Being in the moment: Implications for teaching and young people's digital literacies. *Journal of Adolescent & Adult Literacy, 58*(8), 625–631.

Alvermann, D. E. (2019). The power of discourse: CML and "The tantrum that saved the world." *International Journal of Critical Media Literacy, 1*(1), 128–136.

Alvermann, D. E., Marshall, J. D., McLean, C. A., Huddleston, A. P., Joaquin, J., & Bishop, J. (2012). Adolescents' web-based literacies, identity construction, and skill development. *Literacy Research and Instruction, 51*(3), 179–195.

Alvermann, D. E., Moon, J. S., & Hagood, M. C. (1999). *Popular culture in the classroom: Teaching and researching critical media literacy.* International Reading Association. doi: 10.4324/9781315059327

Bates, T. (2020, December 16). A review of online learning in 2020 (Blog post). *Online Learning and Distance Education Resources* (Website). Tony Bates and Contact North/ Contact Nord. www.tonybates.ca/2020/12/16/a-review-of-online-learning-in-2020/

Baudrillard, J. (1981). *Simulations.* Semiotext(e).

Beach, R., Castek, J., & Scott, J. (2017). Acquiring processes for responding to and creating multimodal digital productions. In D. Hinchman & D. Appleman (Eds.), *Adolescent literacies: A handbook of practice-based research.* (pp. 292–309). Guilford.

Beach, R., & Myers, J. (2001). *Inquiry-based English instruction: Engaging students in life and literature.* Teachers College Press.

Beach, R., & O'Brien, D. (2015). Fostering students' science inquiry through app affordances of multimodality, collaboration, interactivity, and connectivity. *Reading & Writing Quarterly: Overcoming Learning Difficulties, 31*(2), 119–134, doi: 10.1080/10573569.2014.962200.

Beach, R., & Tierney, R. J. (2016). Toward a theory of literacy meaning making within virtual worlds. In S. Israel (Ed.), *Handbook of research on reading comprehension* (Vol. 2, pp. 135–164). Guilford.

Black, R. W. (2008). Just don't call them cartoons: The new literacy spaces of anime, manga and fanfiction. In J. Coiro, M. Knobel, C. Lankshear, & D. L. Leu. (Eds.),

Handbook of research on newl (pp. 583–610). Erlbaum/Taylor & Francis Group. doi: 10.4324/9781410618894

Bolter, J. D. (2001). *Writing spaces: The computer, hypertext, and the history of writing.* Erlbaum.

Bransford, J. Brown, A. L., & Cocking, R. R. (2000). (Eds.). *How people learn; Brain, mind, experience, and school.* National Academy Press.

Bruce, B. C., & Bishop, A. P. (2008). New literacies and community inquiry. In J. Coiro, M. Knobel, C. Lankshear, & D. L. Leu. (Eds.), *Handbook of research on new literacies* (pp. 699–742). Erlbaum/Taylor & Francis Group. doi: 10.4324/9781410618894

Bruce, B. C., & Hogan. M. (1998). The disappearance of technology: Toward an ecological model of literacy. In D. Reinking, M. C. McKenna, L. Labbo, & R. Kieffer (Eds.), *Handbook of literacy and technology: Transformations in a post-typographic world.* (pp. 269–281). Erlbaum.

Bryson, M., MacIntosh, L., Jordan, S., & Lin, H. (2006). Virtually queer? Homing devices, mobility, and un/belongings. *Canadian Journal of Communication, 31*(4), 791–814. doi: 10.22230/cjc.2006v31n4a1795

Burbules, N. C., & Callister, T. A. Jr. (1996). Knowledge at the crossroads: Some alternative futures of hypertext environments for learning. *Educational Theory, 46*(1), 23–50.

Burgess, A., & Ivanič, R. (2010). Writing and being written: Issues of identity across time-scales. *Written Communication, 27*(2), 228–255.

Burnett, C. (2014). Investigating pupils' interactions around digital texts: a spatial perspective on the "classroom-ness" of digital literacy practices in schools. *Educational Review, 66,* 2, 192–209.

Burnett, C., & Merchant, G. (2014). Points of view: Reconceptualising literacies through an exploration of adult and child interactions in a virtual world. *Journal of Research in Reading, 37*(1), 36–50.

Butler, J. (1993). *Bodies that matter: On the discursive limits of "sex."* Routledge.

Butler, J. (1997). *Excitable speech: A politics of the performative.* Routledge.

Callow, J. (2010). Spot the difference: The changing nature of page-based and screen-based texts. *Australian Screen Education (St. Kilda, Vic.),* (58), 106–110.

Char, C., & Hawkins, J. (1987). Charting the course: Involving teachers in the formative research and design of the Voyage of the Mimi. In R. Pea & K. Sheingold (Eds.), *Mirrors of minds: Patterns of experience in educational computing* (pp. 141–167). Ablex.

Cognition and Technology Group at Vanderbilt. (1990). Anchored instruction and its relationship to situated cognition. *Educational Researcher, 19*(5), 2–10.

Coiro, J. (2020). Toward a multifaceted heuristic of digital reading to inform assessment, research, practice, and policy. *Reading Research Quarterly, 56*(1), 9–31. doi: 10.1002/rrq.302

Coiro, J., & Dobler, B. (2007). Exploring the online comprehension strategies used by sixth grade skilled readers to search for and locate information on the Internet. *Reading Research Quarterly, 42,* 214–257.

Collins, A., Brown, J. S., & Larkin, K. (1980). Inference in text understanding. In R.J. Spiro, B. C. Bruce, & W. F. Brewer (Eds.), *Theoretical issues in reading comprehension: Perspectives from cognitive psychology, linguistics, artificial intelligence, and education* (pp. 385–410). Erlbaum.

Costanzo, W. (1994). Reading, writing and thinking in an age of electronic literacy. In C. L. Selfe & S. Hilligosi (Eds.), *Literacy and computer: The complications of teaching and learning with technology* (pp. 195–219). MLA.

Csordas, T. (1999). Embodiment. In G. Weiss & H. Haber (Eds.), *Perspectives on embodiment*. Routledge.

Curwood, J. S., & Cowell, L. L. H. (2011). iPoetry: Creating space for new literacies in the English curriculum. *Journal of Adolescent & Adult Literacy, 55*(2), 110–120. doi: 10.1002/jaal.00014

Damarin, S. (1995). Technologies of the individual: Women and subjectivity in the age of information. *Research in Technology and Philosophy, 13*, 185–200.

Delgado, P., Vargas, C., Ackerman, R., & Salmerón, L. (2018). Don't throw away your printed books: A meta-analysis on the effects of reading media on reading comprehension. *Educational Research Review*, 25, 23–38. doi: 10.1016/j.edurev.2018.09.003

Dill, K. E., Brown, B. P., & Collins, M. A. (2008). Effects of exposure to sex-stereotyped video game characters on tolerance of sexual harassment. *Journal of Experimental Social Psychology, 44*(5), 1402–1408. doi: 10.1016/j.jesp.2008.06.002

Dobson, T. M. (2004, May 27–30). Reading wikis: E-literature and the negotiation of reader/writer roles. Canadian Society for Studies in Education Annual Meeting, Winnipeg, MN.

Dobson, T. M. (2007). Constructing (and deconstructing) reading through hypertext: Literature and the new media. In A. Adams & S. Brindley (Eds.), *Teaching secondary English with ICT*, pp. 80–97. Open University Press.

Dobson, T. M., & Luce-Kapler, R. (2005). Stitching texts: Gender and geography in *Frankenstein* and *Patchwork Girl. Changing English, 12*(2), 265–277.

Dwyer, D. (1996). The imperative to change our schools. In C. Fisher, D. Dwyer, & K. Yocam (Eds.), *Education and technology: Reflections on computing in classrooms* (pp. 15–34). Jossey Bass.

Dyson, A. (1988). Negotiations among multiple worlds: The space/time dimensions of young children's composing. *Research in the Teaching of English, 22*(4), 355–390.

Dyson, A. (1995). Writing children: Reinventing the development of childhood literacy. *Written Communication, 12*(1), 4–46.

Ede, L. S., & Lunsford, A. A. (1990). *Singular texts/plural authors: Perspectives on collaborative writing*. Southern Illinois University Press.

Forman, G. (1998) Multiple symbolization in the Long Jump Project. In C. Edwards, L. Gandini, & G. Forman (Eds.). *The hundred languages of children: The Reggio Emilia approach—Advanced reflections* (2nd ed., pp. 171–188). Ablex.

Galindo, R., Tierney, R. J., & Stowell, L. (1989). Multi-media and multi-layers in multiple texts. In J. Zutell & S. McCormick (Eds.), *Cognitive and social perspectives for literacy research and instruction, 39th yearbook of the National Reading Conference*. National Reading Conference.

Gee, J. P. (2003, 2005). *What video games have to teach us about learning and literacy*. Palgrave MacMillan.

Gee, J. P. (2011, June 13). Good video games and good learning (Blog post). academiccolab .org/resources/documents/Good_Learning.pdf

Gee, J. P. (2013). The anti-education era: Creating smarter students through digital learning. St. Martin's Press. In J. Giaquinta, J. Bauer, & J. Levin. (1993). *Beyond technology's promise*. Cambridge University Press.

Genishi, C. (1988). Kindergartners and computers: A case study of six children. *The Elementary School Journal, 89*(2), 185–201.

Grint, K., & Gill, R. (Eds.). (1995). *The gender-technology relation: Contemporary theory and research*. Taylor and Francis.

Hapnes, T., & Sorenson, K. (1995). Competition and collaboration in male shaping of computing. In K. Grint & R. Gill (Eds.), *The gender-technology relation: Contemporary theory and research* (pp. 174–191). Taylor and Francis.

Hawisher, G., & Selfe, C. (Eds.). (2000). *Global literacies and the World Wide Web*. Routledge.

Hepp, A., & Krotz, F. (Eds.). (2014). *Mediatized worlds: Culture and society in a media age*. Palgrave Macmillan.

Hobbs, R. (2010). *Digital and media literacy: A plan of action: A white paper on the digital and media literacy recommendations of the Knight Commission on the Information Needs of Communities in a Democracy*. Aspen Institute.

Hull, G. A., & Nelson, M. E. (2005). Locating the semiotic power of multimodality. *Written Communication, 22*(2), 224–261. doi: 10.1177/0741088304274170

Hull, G. A., & Stornaiuolo, A. (2014). Cosmopolitan literacies, social networks, and "proper distance": Striving to understand in a global world. *Curriculum Inquiry, 44*(1), 15–44.

Ito, M. (2005). Technologies of the childhood imagination: Yugioh, media mixes, and everyday cultural production. In J. Karaganis & N. Jerimijenko (Eds.), *Structures of participation in digital culture* (pp. 88–110). Duke University Press.

Ito, M., Gutiérrez, K., Livingstone, S., Penuel, B., Rhodes, J., Salen, K., Schor, J., Sefton-Green, J., Watkins, S. C. (2013). *Connected learning: An agenda for research and design*. Digital Media and Learning Research Hub.

Jenkins, H. (2006). Confronting the challenges of participatory culture: Media education for the 21st century. The MacArthur Foundation. files.eric.ed.gov/fulltext/ED536086.pdf

Jenkins, H., Ford, S., & Green, J. (2013). *Spreadable media: Creating value and meaning in a networked culture*. New York University Press.

Jenson, J., & de Castell, S. (2018). "The entrepreneurial gamer": Regendering the order of play. *Games and Culture, 13*(7), 728–746. doi: 10.1177/1555412018755913

Kim, G. M. (2016). Transcultural digital literacies: Cross-border connections and self-representations in an online forum. *Reading Research Quarterly, 51*(2), 199–219. doi: 10.1002/rrq.131

Kinzer, C., & Leu, D. (1997). The challenge of change: Exploring literacy and learning in electronic environments. *Language Arts, 74*(2), 126–136.

Kinzer, C. K., with the Cognition and Technology Group at Vanderbilt. (1991a). *Integrated media: Toward a theoretical framework for using their potential*. Proceedings of the Multimedia Conference, SEP: Washington, DC.

Kinzer, C. K., with the Cognition and Technology Group at Vanderbilt. (1991b). Technology and the design of generative learning environments. *Educational Technology, 31*, 34–40.

Kinzer, C. K., with the Cognition and Technology Group at Vanderbilt. (1992). The Jasper experiment: An exploration of issues in learning and instructional design. *Educational Technology Research and Development, 40*, 65–80.

Knobel, M., & Lankshear, C. (2005). New literacies: Research and social practice. In B. Maloch, J. M Hoffman, D. L. Schallert, C. M. Fairbanks, & J. Worthy, (Eds.), *54th yearbook of the National Reading Conference* (pp. 22–50). National Reading Conference.

Kress, G. (1997). *Before writing: Rethinking paths into literacy*. Routledge.

Kress, G. (1998). Visual and verbal modes of representation in electronically mediated communication: The potentials of new forms of text. In I. Snyder (Ed.), *Page to screen: Taking literacy in the electronic era* (pp. 53–79). Allen & Unwin.

Kress, G. (2003). *Literacy in the new media age*. Routledge.

Kress, G., & van Leeuwen, T. (2001). *Multimodal discourse. The modes and media of contemporary communication*. Arnold.

Labbo, L. D. (1996). A semiotic analysis of young children's symbol making in a classroom computer center. *Reading Research Quarterly, 31*(4), 356–385. doi: 10.1598/RRQ.31.4.2

Lam, W. S. E., Warriner, D. S., Poveda, D., & Gonzalez, N. (2012). Transnationalism and literacy: Investigating the mobility of people, languages, texts, and practices in contexts of migration. *Reading Research Quarterly, 47*(2), 191–215. doi: 10.1002/RRQ.016

Lambert, J. (2002). *Digital storytelling: Capturing lives, creating community*. Digital Diner Press.

Landow, G. P. (Ed.). (1994a). *Hyper/text/theory*. Johns Hopkins University Press.

Landow, G. P. (Ed.). (1994b). *Hypertext 2.0: The convergence of contemporary critical theory and technology*. Johns Hopkins University Press.

Lanham, R. (1993). *The electronic word: Democracy, technology, and the arts*. University of Chicago Press.

Lankshear, C., & Knobel, M. (2003). *New literacies: Changing knowledge and classroom learning*. Open University Press and McGraw Hill.

Leander, K., & Sheehy, M. (2004). *Spatializing literacy research and practice*. Peter Lang.

Lemke, J. (2001). Travels in hypermodality. *Visual Communication, 1*(3), 299–325. doi: 10.1177/147035720200100303

Lemke, J. L. (1998). Metamedia literacy: Transforming meanings and media. In D. Reinking, M. McKenna, L. Labbo, & R. Kieffer (Eds.), *Handbook of literacy and technology: Transformations in a post-typographic world* (pp. 283–301). Erlbaum.

Lemke, J. L. (2015). Feeling and meaning: A unitary bio-semiotic account. In P. P. Trifonas (Ed.), *International handbook of semiotics* (pp. 589–616). Springer. doi: 10.1007/978-94-017-9404-6_27

Leu, D. (2006). New literacies, reading research, and the challenges of change: A deictic perspective. In J. M. Hoffman, D. L. Schallert, C. M. Fairbanks, J. Worthy, & B. Maloch (Eds.), *55th yearbook of the National Reading Conference* (pp. 1–20). National Reading Conference.

Levin, B. B. (1996). Learning from discussion: A comparison of computer-based versus face-to-face case discussions. Paper presented at the American Educational Research Association Annual Meeting, New York.

Lewis, C., & Fabos, B. (2005). Instant messaging, literacies, and social identities. *Reading Research Quarterly, 40*(4), 470–501. doi: 10.1598/RRQ.40.4.5

Lewis Ellison, T., Noguerón-Liu, S., & Solomon, M. (2016). Co-constructing place, space, and race: African American and Latinx participants and researchers' representations of digital literacy research in the South. *Journal of Literacy and Technology, 17*(3), 62–99.

Luce-Kapler, R., Dobson, T., Sumara, D., Iftody, T., & Davis, B. (2006). E-literature and the digital engagement of consciousness, In J. M. Hoffman, D. L. Schallert, C. M. Fairbanks, J. Worthy, & B. Maloch. (Eds.), *55th yearbook of the National Reading Conference* (pp. 171–181). National Reading Conference.

Lynch, T., Tompkins, J. E., van Driel, I. I., & Fritz, N. (2016). Sexy, strong, and secondary: A content analysis of female characters in video games across 31 years. *Journal of Communication, 66*(4), 564–584. doi: 10.1111/jcom.12237

Martin, F., & Rizvi, F. (2014). Making Melbourne: Digital connectivity and international students' experience of locality. *Media, Culture & Society, 36*(7), 1016–1031.

Mathison, M. (1996). Writing the critique, a text about a text. *Written Communication, 13*(3), 314–354.

Mayer, R., & Moreno, R. (2002). Animation as an aid to multimedia learning. *Educational Psychology Review, 14*(1), 87–99.

McEneaney, J. E. (2006). Agent-based literacy theory. *Reading Research Quarterly, 41*(3), 352–371.

McGinley, W. (1992). The role of reading and writing while composing from sources. *Reading Research Quarterly, 27*(3), 226–249.

Merryfield, M. (2003). Using electronic discussions to enhance academic learning. Teaching Online, EOS Publishing.

Miall, D. S. (1999). Trivializing or liberating? The limitations of hypertext theorizing. *Mosaic, 32*(2), 157–171. www.umanitoba.ca/publications/mosaic/backlist/1999/june/miall.pdf

Myers, J., & Beach, R. (2001). Hypermedia authoring as critical literacy. *Journal of Adolescent & Adult Literacy, 44*(6), 538–546.

Myers, J., Hammond, R., & McKillop, A. M. (1998). Opportunities for critical literacy and pedagogy in student-authored hypermedia. In D. Reinking, M. McKenna, L. Labbo, & R. Kieffer (Eds.), *Literacy and technology: Transformations in a post-typographic world* (pp. 63–78). Erlbaum.

Myers, J., Hammond, R., & McKillop, A. M. (2000). *Connecting, exploring, and exposing the, literacy: Challenging the school standard* (pp. 85–105). Teachers College Press.

Napoli, M., & Teresa Sychterz, T. (2015). Graphic novels come alive in a sixth grade classroom. In V. Yenika-Agbaw & T. Sychterz (Eds.), *Adolescents rewrite their worlds: Using literature to illustrate writing forms.* Rowman & Littlefield.

Neilsen Glenn, L. (2012). Touchstone chapter: Playing for real: Texts and performing identity. In D. Alvermann & K. Hinchman (Eds.), *Reconceptualizing the literacies in adolescents' lives: Bridging the everyday, academic divide* (3rd ed.) (pp. 3–28). Routledge.

New London Group. (1996). A pedagogy of multiliteracies: Designing social futures. *Harvard Educational Review, 66*(1), 60–92.

Nix, D., Fairweather, P., & Adams, B. (1998). Speech recognition, children, and reading. Paper presented at the CHI '98 Conference Summary on Human Factors in Computing Systems, 245–246. Association for Computing Machinery. doi: 10.1145/286498.286730

Nyce, J. (1997). Conventions in hypertext. In J. Smith & F. Halasz (Eds.), *Hypertext '87* (pp. 184–199). University of North Carolina Press.

Ormrod, S. (1995). Leaky black boxes in gender/technology relations. In K. Grint & R. Gill (Eds.), *The gender-technology relation: Contemporary theory and research* (pp. 31–47). Taylor and Francis.

Owston, R. D. (1997). The World Wide Web: A technology to enhance teaching and learning? In *Educational Researcher, 26*(2), 27–33. American Educational Research Association.

Pahl, K., & Rowsell, J. (2005). *Understanding literacy education: Using new literacy studies in the elementary classroom.* SAGE.

Phelan, M. (2014). *Around the world.* Penguin.

Postman, N. (1993). *Technopoly: The surrender of culture to technology.* Vintage Press.

Reilly, B. (1996). New technologies, new literacies, new problems. In C. Fisher, D. Dwyer, & K. Yocam (Eds.), *Education and technology: Reflections on computing in classrooms* (pp. 203–220). Jossey Bass.

Reinking, D. (1998). Introduction: Synthesizing technological transformations of literacy in a post-typographic world. In D. Reinking, M. C. McKenna, L. D. Labbo, & R. D. Kieffer (Eds.), *Handbook of literacy and technology: Transformations in a post-typographic world* (pp. x–xxxii). Erlbaum.

Reinking, D. (1997). Me and my hypertext: A multiple digression analysis of technology and literacy (sic). *The Reading Teacher, 50*(8), 626–643.

Reinking D., McKenna, M. C., Labbo, L. D., & Kieffer, R. D. (Eds.). (1998). *Handbook of literacy and technology: Transformations in a post-typographic world.* Erlbaum. doi: 10.4324/9781410603791

Richardson, W. (2006). *Blogs, wikis, podcasts, and other powerful web tools or classrooms.* Corwin Press.

Rogers, T., & Schofield, A. (2005). Things thicker than words. Portraits of youth multiple literacies in an alternative secondary program. In J. Anderson, M. Kendrick, T. Rogers, & S. Smythe (Eds.), *Portraits of literacy across families, communities and schools. Tensions and intersections* (pp. 205–220). Erlbaum.

Rogers, T., & Winters, K. (2006). Using multimedia to support the literacies and lives of struggling youth. Paper presented at Canadian Society for Studies in Education. York University, Ontario, Canada, May 2006.

Rowsell, J. (2013). *Working with multimodality: Rethinking literacy in the digital age.* Routledge. doi: 10.4324/9780203071953

Rowsell, J., Morrell, E., & Alvermann, D. E. (2017). Confronting the digital divide: Debunking brave new world discourses. *The Reading Teacher, 71*(2), 157–165. doi: 10.1002/trtr.1603

Rubin, A., & Bruce, B. C. (1984). *Quill: Reading and writing with a microcomputer* (Reading Education Report No. 48). University of Illinois at Urbana-Champaign, Center for the Study of Reading/Bolt, Beranek, and Newman.

Rubin, A., & Bruce, B. C. (1985). *Learning with QUILL: Lessons for students, teachers and software designers* (Reading Education Report No. 60). University of Illinois at Urbana-Champaign, Bolt, Beranek, and Newman, Inc., & The U.S. National Institute of Education.

Ruiz, J., Mintzer, M., & Leipzig, R. (2006). The impact of e-learning in medical education. *Academic Medicine, 81*(3), 207–212.

Schallert, D. L., Song, K., Jordan, M. E., Lee, S., Park, Y., Kim, T., Cheng, A. J., Chu, H.-N. R., Vogler, J. S., & Lee, J. E. (2016). Shifts in trajectories in thought communities and "wobbly" identities enacted in computer-mediated classroom discussions. *International Journal of Educational Research, 80*, 49–59.

Schank, R. C., & Abelson, R. P. (1977). *Scripts, plans, goals and understanding: An inquiry into human knowledge structures.* Erlbaum.

Sefton-Green, J. (2006). Youth, technology and media cultures. In J. Green & A. Luke (Eds.), Rethinking learning: What counts as learning and what learning counts. *Review of Research in Education* (pp. 279–306). American Educational Research Association.

Sefton-Green, J. (2013). *Learning at not-school: A review of study, theory, and advocacy for education in non-formal settings.* MIT Press.

Selfe, C., & Hawisher, G. E. (2004). *Literacy lives in the informational age: Narratives of literacy from the United States.* Erlbaum.

Serafini, Frank. (2015). Multimodal Literacy: From Theories to Practices. *Language Arts. 92*(6), 412-423.

Serafini, F, & Gee, E. (2017). Remixing multiliteracies: Theory and practice from new London to new times. New York: Teachers College Press. ISBN: 9780807758649

Sheehy, M. (2007). Can the literacy practices in an after-school program be practiced in school? A study of literacies from a spatial perspective. Unpublished manuscript.

Siegel, M. (1995). More than words: The generative power of transmediation for learning. *Canadian Journal of Education, 20*(4), 455–475.

Singer, L. M., & Alexander, P. A. (2017). Reading on paper and digitally: What the past decades of empirical research reveal. *Review of Educational Research, 87*(6), 1007–1041. doi: 10.3102/0034654317722961

Slatoff, W. (1970). *With respect to readers: Dimensions of literary response.* Cornell University Press.

Snyder, I. (Ed.). (1998). *Page to screen: Taking literacy into the electronic era.* Routledge. doi: 10.4324/9780203201220

Spiro, R. J. (2006a). The "new Gutenberg revolution": Radical new learning, thinking, teaching, and training with technology. *Educational Technology, 46*(1), 3–4.

Spiro, R. J. (2006b). The post-Gutenberg world of the mind: The shape of the new learning. *Educational Technology, 46*(2), 3–4.

Spiro, R. J., Collins, B. P., & Ramchandran, A. (2007). Reflections on a post-Gutenberg epistemology for video use in ill-structured domains: Fostering complex learning and cognitive flexibility. In R. Goldman, R. Pea, B. Barron, & S. J. Derry (Eds.), *Video research in the learning sciences* (pp. 93–100). Erlbaum.

Spiro, R. J., Collins, B. P., Thota, J. J., & Feltovich, P. J. (2003). Cognitive flexibility theory: Hypermedia for complex learning, adaptive knowledge application, and experience acceleration. *Educational technology 44*(5), 5–10.

Spiro, R. J., Coulson, R. L., Feltovich, P. J., & Anderson, D. K. (1988). *Cognitive flexibility theory: Advanced knowledge acquisition in ill-structured domains* (Tech. Rep. No. 441). University of Illinois, Center for the Study of Reading.

Spiro, R. J., & Jehng, J. C. (1990). Cognitive flexibility and hypertext: Theory and technology for the nonlinear and multidimensional traversal of complex subject matter. In D. Nix & R. J. Spiro (Eds.), *Cognition, education, and multimedia: Explorations in high technology* (pp. 163–205). Erlbaum.

Spiro, R. J., Vispoel, W. L., Schmitz, J., Samarapungavan, A., & Boerger, A. (1987). Knowledge acquisition for application: Cognitive flexibility and transfer in complex content domains. In B. C. Britton & S. Glynn (Eds.), *Executive control processes* (pp. 177–200). Erlbaum.

Spivey, N. N. (1997). *The constructivist metaphor: Reading, writing and the making of meaning.* Academic Press.

Squire, K. (2006). From content to context: Videogames as designed experiences. *Educational Researcher, 35*(8), 19–29.

Steinkuehler, C. A. (2008). Cognition and literacy in massively multiplayer online games. In J. Coiro, M. Knobel, C. Lankshear, & D. L. Leu (Eds.), *Handbook of research on new literacies* (pp. 611–634). Erlbaum/Taylor & Francis Group. doi: 10.4324/9781410618894

Stephens, M. (1998). *The rise of the image, the fall of the word.* Oxford University Press.

Sterne, J. (1999). Thinking the internet: Cultural studies versus the millennium. In S. Jones (Ed.), *Doing internet research: Critical issues and methods for examining the net* (pp. 257–288). SAGE.

Street, B. (1984). *Literacy in theory and practice.* Cambridge University Press.

Street, B. (2003). What's "new" in New Literacy Studies? Critical approaches to literacy in theory and practice. *Current Issues in Comparative Education, 5*(2), 1–14.

Street, B. V. (2006). New literacies, new times: How do we describe and teach forms of literacy knowledge, skills, and values people need for new times? In J. M. Hoffman, D. L. Schallert, C. M. Fairbanks, J. Worthy, & B. Maloch (Eds.), *55th yearbook of the National Reading Conference* (pp. 21–42). National Reading Conference.

Tierney, M. (1995). Negotiating a software career: Informal workplaces and the "lads" in a software installation. In K. Grint & R. Gill (Eds.), *The gender-technology relation: Contemporary theory and research* (pp. 192–209). Taylor and Francis.

Tierney, R. J. (2009). Agency and artistry of meaning makers within and across digital spaces. In S. Israel & G. Duffy (Eds.), *Handbook of research on reading comprehension*, (pp. 261–288). Routledge.

Tierney, R. J., Bond, E., & Bresler, J. (2006). Examining literate lives as students engage with multiple literacies: The thread, the needle and the fabric. *Theory into Practice* issue on literacies of and for a diverse society: Curriculum, instruction and multiple literacies, 45(4), 359–367.

Tierney, R. J., Kieffer, R. D., Whalin, K., Desai, L. E., & Moss, A. G. (1992). *Computer acquisition: A longitudinal study of the influence of high computer access on students' thinking, learning, and interactions.* ACOT Report #16, Apple Computer, Inc.

Tierney, R. J., Kieffer, R., Whalin, K., Desai, L., Moss, A. G., Harris, J. E, & Hopper, J. (1997). Assessing the impact of hypertext on learners' architecture of literacy learning spaces in different disciplines: Follow-up studies. Reading online, *Electronic Journal of the International Reading Association.*

Tierney, R. J., & Pearson, P. D. (1983). Toward a composing model of reading. *Language Arts, 60*(5), 568–580.

Tierney, R. J., & Shanahan, T. (1991). Research on the reading-writing relationship: Interactions, transactions, and outcomes. In R. Barr, M. L. Kamil, P. Mosenthal, & P. D. Pearson (Eds.), *Handbook of reading research* (Vol. 2, pp. 246–280). Longman.

Turkle, S. (1995). *Life on the screen.* Simon and Shuster.

Turner, K. H., Hicks, T., & Zucker, L. (2020). Connected reading: A framework for understanding how adolescents encounter, evaluate, and engage with texts in the digital age. *Reading Research Quarterly, 55*(2), 291–309. doi: 10.1002/rrq.271

United Nations (UN) and the United Nations Conference on Trade and Development (2006). *Information economy report 2006: The development perspective.* United Nations Conference on Trade and Development.

Unsworth, L. (2011). Comparing and composing digital re-presentations of literature: Multimedia authoring and meta-communicative knowledge. In L. Unsworth, Len (Ed.), *New literacies and the English curriculum* (pp. 186–212). Continuum.

Van Leeuwen, T. (1999). *Speech, music, sound.* Macmillan.

Vygotsky, L. S. (1978). *Mind in society.* Harvard University Press.

Wade, S. E., & Fauske, J. R. (2004). Dialogue online: Prospective teachers' discourse strategies in computer-mediated discussions. *Reading Research Quarterly, 39*(2), 134–160.

Wiesner, D. (2006). *Flotsam.* Houghton Mifflin.

Wineburg, S., & McGrew S. (2019). Lateral reading and the nature of expertise: Reading less and learning more when evaluating digital information. *Teachers College Record,* 121 (11).

Willinsky, J. (2006). *The access principle: The case for open access to research and scholarship.* MIT Press.

Wincapaw, C. (2000). The virtual spaces of lesbian and bisexual women's electronic mailing lists. *Journal of Lesbian Studies,* 4, 45–59. https://www.researchgate.net/publication/288737213_Gender_Race_Sexuality

Winograd, T. (1980). What does it mean to understand language? *Cognitive Science, 4*(3), 209–241. doi: 10.1207/s15516709cog0403_1

Winograd, T., & Flores, F. (1987). *Understanding computers and cognition: A new foundation for design.* Addison-Wesley.

Winograd, T., & Flores, F. (1987). On understanding computers and cognition: A new foundation for design. *Artificial Intelligence, 31*(2), 250–261. doi: 10.1016/0004-3702(87) 90026-9

Witte, S. P. (1992). Context, text, intertext: Toward a constructivist semiotic of writing, *Written Communication, 9*(2), 237–308.

Wittgenstein, L. (1953). *Philosophical investigations.* Macmillan.

World Summit on the Information Society (WSIS). (2003). Building the information society: A global challenge in the new millennium (Declaration of Principles Doc WSIS-03/Geneva/Doc/4-E). World Summit on the Information Society. www.itu.int/wsis /docs/geneva/official/dop.html

Yankelovich, N., Meyrowitz, N., & van Dam, A. (1985). Reading and writing the electronic book. *Computer, 18*(10), 15–30. doi: 10.1109/MC.1985.1662710

NOTES

1. The notion of forward inferencing within and across texts and digital sources is consistent with a form of progressive refinement of meaning, as postulated by Collins et al. (1980). Similarly, it reflects the findings of researchers examining reading and writing as forms of composing involving multiple sources (e.g., McGinley, 1992; Spivey, 1984).

2. Jenkins builds on the work of Ann Dyson (1995), who suggested, based on her extensive ethnographic work with young learners through a sociocultural lens, that a major developmental challenge is not simply to create a unified text world but to move among multiple worlds and coordinate across multiple space/time structures toward defining self and how one is placed in the company of others. As Dyson stated: "Children are not first and foremost learners; they are first and foremost people living the complexities of their day-to-day lives" (p. 36). As children engage with texts, they seek to "imagine" relationships and situate themselves socioculturally and ideologically.

3. This chapter befits a moment in time, given what appears to be the everchanging, deictic nature of our digital literacies (Leu, 2000).

4. Many of the major computer laboratories that focused on teaching and learning with digital resources were developed by early cognitivists—specifically those with an interest in information processing and reading and writing research. Stanford University and Xerox Research Laboratory in Palo Alto were two such think tanks for some of these developments. At Stanford, for instance, Terry Winograd's (Winograd, 1980; Winograd & Flores, 1987) study of knowledge access and use proved foundational to two of his students who later founded Google. John Seely Brown, along with scholars like David Rumelhart, helped Roy Pea establish the Stanford Human Sciences and Technologies Advanced Research Institute. Elsewhere, John Bransford advanced the Learning Technology Center and the Cognition and Technology Group at Vanderbilt University and later at the University of Washington. Other notable units were established at Bank Street College, Northwestern University, and the University of Connecticut, alongside a host of collaborative initiatives with the major computer companies (e.g., Microsoft, Apple, IBM) and selected foundations (e.g., MacArthur Foundation, George Lucas Foundation, Gates Foundation). These engagements spurred interest in educational matters, but also contributed to immensely fertile

discussions of and developments related to digital spaces that encompassed multimodal, multimedia-based, multilayered, and networking of ideas and people.

In turn, a number of scholars at the Center for the Study of Reading (e.g., Andrew Ortony, Phil Cohen, Allan Collins, Bertram Bruce) were also members of the emerging field of artificial intelligence. They brought to the center cutting-edge thinking regarding computer-based reasoning and communication. Mostly, these scholars were interested in whether we might be able to define how we make meaning. In this pursuit, they asked whether our understandings might be formulated in ways that might be replicated on computers. To develop these scripts and delve into these issues in preliminary ways, they drew on a mix of schema-based determinations of background knowledge along with knowledge of pragmatics, semantics, and syntactical structures. (Similarly, Noam Chomsky was initially hired by the Massachusetts Institute of Technology in the hopes that he might apply his theories of language development and use to computers.) To program a computer to understand natural language, researchers and institutions sought to draw on cognitive studies of reading comprehension of extended text.

5. The first hypermedia application is generally considered to be the Aspen Movie Map, implemented in 1978. The Movie Map allowed users to arbitrarily choose which way they wished to drive in a virtual cityscape (in two seasons, derived from actual photographs) and 3D polygons.

6. Burbules and Callister (1996) warn:

many readers of Hypertext end up browsing or performing the textual equivalent of "channel surfing": quickly scanning or surveying randomly accessed information, in very short snippets, with no overall sense of coherence or meaning for what they are exposed to. A novice encountering a complex Hypertext system for the first time cannot possibly know what information the system contains, without happening to come across it through searching or guesswork. (pp. 24–25)

Similarly, Ilana Snyder (1998) argued that with hypertext, meaning makers may be constrained by a kind of labyrinth and proceed gingerly from one text to the next and one link to the next—lest they become lost, at a dead end, or miss what they perceive to be a key item.

7. Embodiment here denotes Csordas's (1999) use of the term—"an existential condition" (p. 143) that grows out of subjectivities, alliances, and choices, and influences one's engagement with ideas, the strategies one employs, and how one connects with others.

8. Drawing on Massey's (2005) theory of space and the work of Leander and Sheehy (2004), Cathy Burnett and colleagues (Burnett, 2014; Burnett & Merchant, 2014) have similarly highlighted the power of online interactions across borders, including those involving virtual worlds.

9. The declaration (WSIS, 2003) began with a common vision:

Principle 1: We, the representatives of the peoples of the world, assembled in Geneva from 10–12 December 2003 for the first phase of the World Summit on the Information Society, declare our common desire and commitment to build a people-centred, inclusive and development-oriented Information Society, where everyone can create, access, utilize and share information and knowledge, enabling individuals, communities and peoples to achieve their full potential in promoting their sustainable development and improving their quality of life, premised on the purposes and principles of the Charter of the United Nations and respecting fully and upholding the Universal Declaration of Human Rights.

The principles go on to argue for participation "where human dignity is respected" and where we access these informational technologies in order to:

> reduce many traditional obstacles, especially those of time and distance, for the first time in history [making] it possible to use the potential of these technologies for the benefit of millions of people in all corners of the world . . . as tools and not as an end in themselves. . . . Under favourable conditions, these technologies can be a powerful instrument, increasing productivity, generating economic growth, job creation and employability and improving the quality of life of all. They can also promote dialogue among people, nations and civilizations. (WSIS, 2003, Principles 8 & 9)

11   The Global Wave

11.1   THE GLOBAL READER

How do you view yourself as global? You may not be aware of doing so every day, but in multiple ways we engage with the world—through the lens of both a telescope and a microscope as we examine our surroundings, look out the windows at the landscape, check the weather, or indulge in the outdoors or intermingle with others. Many of us are global news junkies, continental and intercontinental travelers as well as planetary consumers—attending to world affairs and ever conscious of our footprint. Even as we open our computers, we are apt to have emails or other forms of exchange that have global trajectories. For those of us who are deemed foreigners, we may find ourselves interacting with family, friends, and colleagues about both worldly and local issues as we contemplate planetary, national, and local circumstances, including our engagements and how we are coping with our realities. These are family, friends, and colleagues located thousands of miles apart, sometimes in transit. Yet, nowadays, it is as if we are in the same neighborhood or near to one another as we share a focus on issues that are both local and planetary in scope.

Along with our histories—including events and new technologies, the media, our countries' global ambitions and behaviours—we change as individuals as we travel across and adjust to global and local terrains and respond to the various forces that we experience. Some of these global forces are economic; others occur at the intersection of local and global as well as via personal connectivity with colleagues, family, and friends across cultures and locations. As we engage with our worlds and the world moves forward, we are learning to read ourselves and our worlds more discerningly—perhaps as an ally, advocate, activist, or reactionary as we recalibrate our views of the planet and its diversities. As a literacy educator, then, what does it mean to be a global reader?

In his "Critical Global Literacies" column for NCTE's *English Journal*, Bogum Yoon (2018) highlighted the importance of the global:

> We no longer live in an isolated world; we live in a global era. Understanding dynamic human practices around the world is a necessity, not an option. Given that there is no "official" curriculum standard on global literacy, English teachers' agency to provide

opportunities for students to expand their understanding of the world in their ELA classes becomes quite important. By linking local and global issues and adding global perspectives to traditional and multicultural texts, teachers can offer students more opportunities to envision "alternative ways of thinking and living" and to challenge global issues (Short, 2011, p. 145). When teachers invite students to become critical members of the global community with the lens of critical global literacies, possibilities open. (p. 94)

We would offer what might be a bolder proposal: Global meaning making should be integral to all of our reading. Our engagement with global matters goes beyond comparative analyses or a reading to learn about others; it involves reading ourselves and our worlds in the company of other readers and other cultures— thereby recognizing "the others of our selves" (Bhabha, 1994, p. 560). Moreover, it involves reading the systems at play that limit or liberate, nurture or destroy. Critically oriented global meaning making is not passive but action oriented, re- quiring us to act responsibly on our readings.

Defining our reading as global may seem foreign, but it is not. Our reading of worlds is lifelong and life-wide. We are constantly crossing borders; as we do so, we read events either vicariously or as a participant, consumer, or connoisseur— with an eye to understanding the systems at play and the relationships among people, places, and events. Reading is not a simple act of retrieval but a form of cultural study and engagement. Readers, students as well as adults, are akin to researchers—conscious of the perspectives, positionalities, gaps, slants, and biases that inform their ongoing meaning making. Their contemplations may involve an aversion and opposition to or, alternatively, a resonance with calls for engaged support, action, or even activism. Approaching engagements globally, from multi- ple perspectives, affords meaning makers opportunities to observe and participate aesthetically or vicariously, efferently and critically, with events, settings, charac- ters, and issues.

Further, reading globally compels meaning makers to grapple with their own positionalities and identities, and to reach out for other perspectives to scrutinize the cauldron of sociopolitical forces involved in different circumstances. While it requires a consideration of how others see the world—hearing their voices and examining their ways of thinking—it also helps us to see ourselves, uncovering what may have gone unnoticed, misunderstood, or ignored. This may occur with as little effort as inviting others to bring their different knowledge sources to the reading; alternatively, it may necessitate a more strategic invitation to outsiders with different interests and histories to inform one's reading. Such transforma- tive readings can shape one's own life or reading of others. It can occur as one participates in everyday events, engaging with different persuasions or attitudes or history. It might entail being faced with confrontations or circumstances that are racist, sexist, gendered, or in other ways discriminatory.

Being global involves the everyday, requiring forms of multicultural cosmo- politanism including nuanced knowledge of others (e.g., norms, conventions, language) to connect. It may involve forms of border crossing or cross-boundary negotiations through translanguaging (e.g., Horowitz, 2012; Nelson et al., 2016) and language fusions or playful line stepping (Gutiérrez et al., 2017) that capitalize on readers' plural identities and abilities to move across or interweave communities.

Texts and media can contribute to global considerations—from the simplest of picture books to graphic novels; from realistic to historical, fantasy, and science fiction to nonfiction, self-help guides, and naturalist writing; and from print media to films to online and social media productions—even Twitter feeds. Arguably, in these political times, global meaning making is integral to one's reading of news releases, opinion pieces, and the writings of politicians. But it is also how we support, dismiss, or position ourselves as an ally, adversary, or passive observer of forms of discrimination or advantage for one group over another.

Take, if you will, James Baldwin's (1974) novel *If Beale Street Could Talk.* Baldwin's story moves readers across multiple perspectives, cultures, and worlds. It is not just a story of love between an African American couple, as told by a wife, or that of love within a family, as told by a daughter. It is a story of families; of the broader society of humanity; of intolerance, and unconscionable racism. It is a story that engages readers in complex social dynamics within and across individuals, families, communities, and cultures. As readers encounter these various dynamics, they are transacting with and across cultures, bringing their own selves and their societal experiences to the text—especially as they contemplate the events and the cultural forces in play. In this way, as Baldwin seems to suggest, Beale Street is not just one place, within one story.

Similarly, consider some of the powerful Indigenous historical novels, such as Australian Aboriginal educator Eric Willmott's (1988) book *Pemulwuy: The Rainbow Warrior.* The novel recounts the story of Australian Aboriginal resistance to British occupation—a story kept invisible both to outsiders and across generations of Australian immigrants. Or take scholar and author Larissa Y. Behrendt's (2004) work *Home*—a modern-day account of her experiences, as an urban Aboriginal, in visiting her place of heritage in a remote rural area where her community experienced horrific treatment. These stories reveal the current circumstances and dynamics of cultural experiences across time and place; they are educative, provocative, and may be transformative. For Australian readers, these texts might serve as antecedents to a reconsiderations of the systemic forces that have shaped the population culturally, including the unacceptable racism that persists. For North American readers, Thomas King's (2012) work *The Inconvenient Indian: A Curious Account of Native People in North America,* may provide a similar platform. His account introduces readers to a world that that they might claim to know, but likely narrowly or monoculturally.

Many of us who read these stories are reading them not just as powerful narratives, but as accounts of societies that may be invisible or that may have been (and may remain) violent. Moreover, our readings reveal how the worlds of others are also part of "our worlds" and "our selves" (Bhabha, 1994). They afford forms of transformative engagements in terms of understanding and situating our social and cultural time and place, including recognizing and, I would hope, interrogating and challenging the systems that may still contribute to persisting cultural and planetary affronts.

Cultural considerations, on a global scale or those that involve border crossings, are pervasive in our lives as a result of our associations, links, and interests—to the point that they verge on planetary considerations. Our lives involve forms of trafficking as we attend to time zones, climate flows, migration, languages, health, trade, and politics. At times—such as with many of the events over the past few years—historical developments occur that reverberate throughout our lives, challenge the status quo, and make forms of global meaning making more overt. For example, consider the news in the spring of 2019 of the murder of some 50 New Zealanders of Muslim faith by an Australian white supremacist. The event brought to the surface a range of issues existing in our lives, including concerns over global terrorism and the rising white supremacist movement; the consequences of our interconnectedness with global media; and debates around the precipitousness of hate speech, from tweets to blogs (e.g., of individuals, such as PewDiePie, or those tied to political policy speeches, such as Trump). Yet in the midst of these concerns, New Zealand prime minister Jacinda Ardern reminded us of the need for a moral compass—that is, the need to embrace one another as one, with all our differences. One of the most poignant moments occurred when, immediately following the tragic event, she stated:

> Clearly what has happened here is an extraordinary and unprecedented act of violence. . . . Many of those who would have been directly affected by this shooting may be migrants to New Zealand. They may even be refugees here. They have chosen to make New Zealand their home, and it is their home. . . . They are us. . . . The people who were the subject of this attack today, New Zealand is their home, they should be safe here. The person who has perpetuated this violence against us is not. They have no place in New Zealand. ("Christchurch mosque," 2019)

As with other global affairs, this horrid event triggered discussions of xenophobic developments in various venues around the world, from classrooms to media to town meetings to informal conversations with friends. For some, it entailed interrogating the white supremacy movement, the growth of anti-Muslim sentiment, and the spread of nationalism—scrutinizing how these developments are fueled by certain political factions and policies. For others, it spurred contemplating the role of media conglomerates, including Facebook and YouTube, as vehicles for trafficking hate speech—specifically through their failure to balance profitability with social responsibility, free access with censorship, and cultural diversity with respect. Some New Zealanders in particular questioned whether or not the country was as inclusive as it had been purported to be. Issues of firearms also resurfaced, and Prime Minister Ardern introduced legislation to revamp the country's gun laws. Australia interrogated its current role in advancing racism and the conditions for white supremacy. Adolescents reckoned with the role of social media, including the norms with regard to language used on certain sites. The United States examined the president's role and use of social media in inciting the event. Globally, xenophobic attitudes, especially Islamophobic prejudices, were interrogated, and matters of responsiveness and responsibilities (especially moral and humanistic) to one another remotely or in our immediate worlds were brought to the fore.

A reader might view the event as creating a new site for engagement—a space that might include:

- Exploring the event through a range of social frames, including religious freedom and coexistence; immigration; individual expression, social responsibility, and censorship; and liberty and violence against humanity and community.
- Contemplating cultural developments and the flow of people and ideas along with global fusion, adaptation, translanguaging, border crossing, and various forms of displacement.
- Unpacking the sociopolitical conditions that undergird these developments.
- Being responsive; reading oneself and one's positioning as detached or complicit; as an ally, activist, or actionist.

[handwritten margin note: considering global events]

Engaging in global reading therefore involves contemplating ourselves in the company of others, deliberating on the sociopolitical and physical conditions that exist within and across the precincts of a community, country, and the planet itself. Such dynamics may play out in our everyday exchanges locally or may manifest themselves globally. Influences that shape readers and the objects of readings and writings may exist separately or be woven together in a tapestry of events, patterned by sociopolitical circumstances or affordances. Though our specific circumstances differ, we all live across societies—from the local to the planetary—exploring and contemplating ourselves and others, deliberating on the social, political, cultural, and physical conditions of our worlds, and, at times, crossing borders as we engage with global affairs patterned by those conditions. Our readings involve multilayered, critical self-examinations—forms of reflexivity as well as activism as we contemplate our positionality and roles as well as our responsibilities and responsive possibilities. If examined systematically, matters of complicities, responsibility, and possible responses will arise.

Arguably, global readers/meaning makers transact with themselves and others as they contemplating the road ahead—with an eye to the systems at play across the spaces and times available to them and their collaborators. They engage with both a global telescope and a microscope, attending to media coverage of worldly matters while scrutinizing their own affairs and those of their communities. Such scrutiny should be as sensitive to local circumstances as it is to the broader systems at play—whether they be the Internet architecture that undergirds the traffic of communications, or the norms that relate to the incidental exchanges or updates on events among colleagues, family members, and friends.

These layered interfaces could be viewed as the local and global existing in combination, transacting, or trafficking within or across borders. They could include a number of topics anchored in the local but with an obvious global reach—including questions of Western interference in the affairs of other countries; nationalism, populism, sovereignty, and trade within and across regions; intellectual property and extraditions; and matters of internationalizing and indigenizing. These topics, though local in origin, may also be tied to a network of global interests and matters of alignment with regard to one's position and role—befitting cultural considerations of self in the company of others and a moral reckoning of interests.

Thus, global reading involves our mobilization and search for traction as we address local concerns that also may extend to regions, nations, and the planet. It is not uncommon nowadays to witness different publics taking the initiative to be engaged in local and global activism on social, political, and environmental issues. In the past years, for example, we have witnessed a range of movements—including the advent of global student reading, networking, and activism on issues such as gun control and climate change.

For these reasons, global explorations should be pursued carefully; they should be well researched, consultative, and informed by an interrogation of one's position, interests, and potential roles. The contemplations of global readers should be reflexive and scrutinized, and any resulting actions should be pursued in ways that are supportive, not narcissistic or presumptuous. Actions should respect situatedness, befitting the indigenous nature of communities and the particular circumstances at play. Global reading should extend to activism that is grounded in and consistent with ecological considerations and cultural respectfulness of local circumstances. It should involve critical analyses that stem from thoughtful explorations of multiple resources, viewpoints, and approaches; it should aim to understand sociopolitical circumstances; and it should demonstrate a reflexivity and recognition of oneself and one's position as insider-outsider, ally, or partner—especially as one strives to leverage and support the needs and interests of others in a manner reverent of cultural practices.

Essentially, global meaning making involves leveraging an ecology anchored in the recognition of multiple voices—the pursuit of a multitopia that advances unity, but not at the cost of uniformity or suppression. It engages readers in a form of shared and transformative decisionmaking that involves a critical reflexivity of one's world as experienced through events and writings and encounters with media (Tierney, 2017). Global meaning making goes beyond being able to recant, connect, or even compare and contrast. As Rob has discussed in other papers (Tierney, 2018, 2020), global reading is not scripted; however, there are some dimensions that are commonplace. It entails methods and strategies of critical analysis, including the following:

- Contemplating one's self and one's global presence, positionality, and purview

- Exploring multiple resources, viewpoints, and approaches
- Reading across time and space, including into, beneath, and beyond
- Probing sociopolitical currents
- Moving from connoisseur to activist
- Bridging and leveraging information and knowledge

Moreover, for each of us it involves dealing with and traversing cultures—whether within or across places, with various peoples, across our planet.

Global readings and consultations also entail a form of shuttle diplomacy tied to nuanced meaning making. They require inferencing, translating, situating, discerning, questioning, discussing, linking with, reconsidering, rereading, rethinking, composing, and acting on. They involve accessing and weighing information that might be gleaned from multiple readings, multiple informants, and multiple sources, such as selected websites, tweets, and listservs; blogs, news bulletins, and papers (including developing drafts) related to ongoing projects; and various exchanges with friends and colleagues. Moreover, befitting forms of activism and advocacy, global reading involves navigating "tricky" spaces in support of others, including challenging the hegemonies and perhaps one's own complicity with systemic biases whether they be tied to racism, ethnocentrism, gender, colonialism, or economic privilege (Andreotti & de Souza, 2011; Smith, 2005; Spivak, 1990, 1999; Stein 2018; Tierney, 2018, 2020). At times when societal unrest or anxieties arise from events in their worlds, thoughtful and nonjudgmental spaces might be considered (Kay, 2018) or what Arao & Clements (2013) and Ali (2017) refer to as the necessary "brave" spaces—engagements that build understandings of ourselves (individually and collectively) in the interests of our local and planetary diversities.

References

Ali, D. (2017). Safe spaces and brave spaces: Historical context and recommendations for student affairs professionals. NASPA Policy and Practice Series. NASPA. https://www.naspa.org/images/uploads/main/Policy_and_Practice_No_2_Safe_Brave_Spaces_DOWNLOAD.pdf

Andreotti, V., & de Souza, L. M. T. M. (2011). *Postcolonial perspectives on global citizenship education*. Routledge.

Arao, B., & Clemens, K. (2013). From safe spaces to brave spaces: A new way to frame dialogue around diversity and social justice. In L. Landreman (Ed.), *The art of effective facilitation: Reflections from social justice educators* (pp. 135–150). Stylus.

Baldwin, J. (1974). *If Beale Street could talk*. Dial Press.

Behrendt, L. (2004). *Home*. University of Queensland Press.

Bhabha, H. K. (1994). *The location of culture*. Routledge.

Gutiérrez, K. D., Cortes, K., Cortez, A., DiGiacomo, D., Higgs, J., Johnson, P., Lizárraga, J., Mendoza, E., Tien, J., & Vakil, S. (2017). Replacing representation with imagination: Finding ingenuity in everyday practices. *Review of Research in Education, 41*(1), 30–60.

Horowitz, R. (2012). Border crossing: Geographic space and cognitive shifts in adolescent language and literacy practices. In H. Romo, C. Garrido de la Caleja, & O. Lopez (Eds.), *A bilateral perspective on Mexico-U.S. migration* (pp. 147–164). Universidad Veracruzana and The University of Texas at San Antonio, UTSA—Mexico Center.

Kay, M. R. (2018). *Not light, but fire: How to lead race conversations in the classroom.* Stenhouse.

King, T. (2012). *The inconvenient Indian: A curious account of native people in North America.* University of Minnesota Press.

Nelson, N. E., Barrera, E. S., Skinner, K., & Fuentes, A. M. (2016). Language, culture and border lives: Mestizaje as positionality/Lengua, cultura y vidas de frontera: El mestizaje como posicionalidad. *Cultura y Educación, 28*(1), 1–41. doi: 10.1080/11356405.2014.980121

New Zealand Herald. (2019, March 15). Christchurch mosque shootings: New Zealand prime minister Jacinda Ardern describes one of "darkest days." www.nzherald.co.nz /nz/news/article.cfm?c_id=1&objectid=12213100

Short, K. G. (2011). Building bridges of understanding through international literature. In A. W. Bedford & L. K. Albright (Eds.), *A master class in children's literature: Trends and issues in an evolving field* (pp. 130–148). National Council of Teachers of English.

Smith, L. T. (2005). On tricky ground: Researching the Native in the age of uncertainty. In N. K. Denzin & Y. S. Lincoln (Eds.), *The SAGE handbook of qualitative research,* 3rd ed. (pp. 85–108). SAGE.

Spivak, G. C. (1990). *The post-colonial critic: Interviews, strategies, dialogues.* Routledge.

Spivak, G. C. (1999). *A critique of postcolonial reason: Toward a critique of the vanishing present.* Harvard University Press.

Stein, S. (2017). The persistent challenges of addressing epistemic dominance in higher education: Considering the case of curriculum internationalization. *Comparative Education Review, 61*(Suppl. 1), S25–S50.

Tierney, R. J. (2017). Multitopia: Global citizenship across diverse spaces. *Global Commons Review, Fall 1,* Paulo Freire Institute-UCLA, 75–81. www.globalcommonsreview.org /download/b972f6ad34fcd2e33307646455838a6a189728.pdf

Tierney, R. J. (2018). Toward a model of global meaning making. *Journal of Literacy Research, 50*(4), 397–422. doi: 10.1177/1086296X18803134

Tierney, R. J. (2020). Notes on global reading: Critical cultural traversals, transactions and transformations. In L. I. Misiaszek (Ed.) *Exploring the complexities in global citizenship education: Hard spaces, methodologies, and ethics* (pp. 36–68). Routledge. www .academia.edu/40450420/Notes_on_global_reading_critical_cultural_traversals _transactions_and_transformations

Willmott, E. (1988). *Pemulwuy: The rainbow warrior.* Bantam Press.

Yoon, B. (2018, September). Critical global literacies: Critical global perspectives in the English curriculum. *English Journal, 108*(1), 92–94.

11.2   THE GLOBAL WAVE

Our global engagements are undergoing significant shifts—akin to awakenings—that include the following:

- Awakening to our place in the universe and on the planet;
- Awareness of the world as ever changing;
- Acknowledgment of and respect for ecology and diversity including people, languages, and ways of knowing;
- Recognition of how we negotiate our pursuits in the world—as we reposition ourselves and others in ways that afford possibilities of expression and engagement and afford others their voices, rights of self-determination and sovereignty rather than subjugation, oppression, colonizing or displacement;
- Recognition of ourselves as global persons with virtual and concrete connections with rights and responsibilities as global citizens defined in different ways but respectful of others and their ways.

These shifts move us toward a new form of multiculturalism, befitting a world committed to pluralism and the tenets of ecology, diversity, transliteracies, and cosmopolitanism (Stornaiuolo et al., 2017; Stornaiuolo & Nichols, 2019). The shifts represent a postcolonial orientation that interrogates the mobility of ideas, especially the bridges between local and global as well as the relationship between colonial structures and Indigenous peoples. They represent the pursuit of respect, recognition, reconciliation, and accommodation versus that of patrimony, marginalization, discrimination, and assimilation.

Our Place on the Planet

Worldly engagements are dynamic and have been across time. Migration from Africa by Homo erectus began 2.5 million years ago. Current estimates reflect that there are 250 million immigrants globally. For thousands of years, through colonization, exploration, and oppression, nations have been involved in border crossings and pilgrimages in search of trade, possessions, or better lives. The world seems as if it is always in a state of change and exchange, as trade ebbs and flows, and people experience variable degrees of freedom, opportunity, and possibilities as they move between countries or within their own communities, neighborhoods, and media hubs.

The world of literacy is no exception. For better and worse, the history of literacy has operated "hand in glove" with matters pertaining to globalization—a link that dates back several millennia. It is a history tied to trade, migration, empire building, the spread of ideas, and matters of faith. It has as well been tied to conquest and cooperation—where literacy has been critical to social, political, cultural, linguistic, and economic development.

Literacy is a combination of pursuits—for interdependencies, relationships, and mutuality, both locally and globally. It has involved developments and exchanges in ideas largely supported by trade, colonization, and corporate interests across a world once navigated by caravans and now by bandwidth, featuring a combination of alliances and the growth of international agencies and affinity groups clustered or networked in our ever-changing, virtual worlds.

Alliances and Networks

To some extent, alliances set the stage for shared planetary engagements and pursuits. At a macro-political level, our interdependencies are realized through international groups such as the United Nations (UN) and other agencies. These groups are established to formulate, realize, monitor, moderate, and facilitate global activities (e.g., labor mobility, trade, crisis management, medical support, educational development, and meeting social needs, such as poverty). The UN, for example, helps with the formulation and traction of global declarations through participating countries' ratification of principles related to basic literacy, informational technology, and human rights (e.g., World Summit, 2005). Nowadays, these and other networks are increasingly salient whenever we are dealing with a health pandemic, natural disasters, migration, food crises, literacy campaigns, or other essential and immediate needs. These networks of international and national affiliates have acted as organizing forces contributing to how developments are orchestrated within and across countries. They offer developments tied to a planetary perspective, affording coordination and collaboration and, increasingly, respect and advocacy for diversity, including ways of knowing and languages.

Less formally, networks have coalesced around shared interests and common goals—piggybacking on developments and issues that arise. For example, in the 1970s, there was a global civil rights network that connected the U.S. Black Panther movement with mobilizing social rights initiatives by the Aboriginal and Torres Strait Islander community in Australia, the Maori community in New Zealand, the anti-apartheid movement in South Africa, as well as movements in Asia. More recently, the Black Lives Matter movement has bridged to groups worldwide as a way of mobilizing against systemic racism. Protests against police brutality have resonated with the plight of Maoris, Australian Aboriginal and Torres Strait Islanders, Thais, Nigerians, and other groups in Europe, Eurasia, Asia, and Latin America. Across countless initiatives, we have seen the emergence of numerous virtual spaces for dialogue and to exchange resources and support. Indeed, oftentimes these networks are supported by and operate exclusively in virtual spaces.

In terms of literacy, among the most notable networks has been the International Reading Association, established in the 1950s. Now called the

International Literacy Association (ILA), it was created to be a professional organization of reading educators and scholars that touted itself as international and committed to literacy research and practice worldwide. In a developmental fashion, the International Literacy Association, often in collaboration with the United Nations Educational Social and Cultural Organization (UNESCO) and various other nonprofit organizations, has been responsible for major developments in literacy in different parts of the world—especially through ILA's seven international affiliates (Africa, Europe, Asia, Latin America, the Caribbean, Oceania, and Eurasia). These grassroots networks have thousands of affiliates that work across their continents and within nations to advance literacy support for educators. For example, the Africa network has affiliates in over 50 African countries that come together for a biannual Pan-African Conference and most recently in an initiative, "Context Matters," jointly sponsored by CODE (a Canadian NGO supporting global literacy) and ILA in an effort to advance literacy research for Africans by Africans (code.ngo/approach/research-initiatives/). In addition, many of the African affiliates are pursuing a range of initiatives under the umbrella of their national reading associations. In Nigeria, under the leadership of Chukwuemeka Eze Onukaogu and his colleagues (such as Gabriel Egbe, Chinwe Muodumogu), teacher leadership as well as literacy for social change have been foci. In Uganda, various book projects supported by CODE and Room to Read (a U.S. organization) and other initiatives have been launched under the leadership of Annette K. Mpuga, Loy Tumusiime, Harrison Kiggundu, and Sam Andema. In Kenya, under the leadership of Hellen Inyega and Margaret Muthiga, the Association of Reading of Kenya was a partner in a Reading Kenya project. In South Africa, the Literacy Association of South African Reading Association has been under the leadership of Janet Condy and Carol Bloch. In Botswana, the Reading Association of Botswana has been led by Penny Moanakwene and Arua E. Arua.

Trade

The exchange of goods, the spread of ideas and philosophy are one of the key foundations to achieving a global presence and connections tied to meeting local needs. Trade has been the cornerstone of global developments for thousands of years. Indeed, trade and access to goods have been one of the major catalysts for migration, alliance building, and colonization. At the same time that global diversity was being enhanced by trade, however, it was also being diminished— especially as empires (e.g., Spain, Portugal, Holland, Britain) advanced colonization, subjugation, enculturation, conversion, and education of peoples in the colonizer's image. Literacies were not exempted; indeed, they were a tool for colonization by controlling what was written and recorded as well as who read, what, why, and how.

Nowadays, although colonial forces can be difficult to dislodge as a result of their deep roots, a number of countries are divesting themselves of their colonial past. At the same time, other interests are taking hold. For example, foreign aid has become a new tool of countries such as China and the United States seeking in-fluence in different regions. Multinational corporations including groups such as Internet providers (e.g., Amazon, Alibaba, Google, Mozilla, Apple, and Samsung) or industries such as those in petroleum or automobile manufacturing (e.g., BP, Exxon, Royal Dutch, Volkswagen, and Toyota) use investments to leverage access and advantage. Global powers including the United States, Britain, Europe, and, increasingly, China have enormous clout in part achieved by trade.

In terms of literacies, the global trade in ideas has shifted from paper to vir-tual productions that are mass-produced by governments, corporations, or forms of cottage industry. Indeed, the advent of the Internet has led to a massive global production of ideas and their access. This shift has included the sources of produc-tion and the character of trade, but also has led to changes in the nature of con-sumerism, communication around events, and cultural sharings. These exchanges can lead to global encounters that support, disrupt, or alienate.

Trade in Scholarly Ideas and Educational Practices

In the scholarly domain or in terms of the global knowledge economy, trade seems to be more under the control of certain groups with a bias toward the West that is quite dated. Of relevance to historical scholarship in literacy, scholars world-wide (including U.S. and Chinese literacy scholars) traveled to work with Wilhelm Wundt in Germany as psychological studies of reading were being pursued in the 1850s. This seeding of psychology across countries accounts for much of the in-tellectual character and foci of literacy today. In the 1900s, scholarly exchanges occurred with developmentalists in Italy and France as well as among British, German, and French sociologists. These account for many of the developmental and sociological frames of reference that scholars now enlist in their inquiries re-lated to educational endeavors. Likewise, in terms of schooling, these early schol-ars developed a reverence, verging on a monopoly, for the teaching of Western thought in school. Subjects such as history, economics, and literature were almost exclusively Western (also discussed in Chapter 1: "The Enculturated Reader").

A number of sociologists and international scholars would contend that nowadays global scholarship has not internationalized; instead, it remains Western. The local is excluded if it falls outside of this realm. Certainly, looked at through the lens of a global economy, literacy has been and still is to a large extent controlled by Western interests. It is as if the global knowledge economy serves Western interests exclusively. Indeed, when Westerners turn the lens on themselves, the sidelining of and exclusion of non-Westerners is apparent. Global forces are not innocent, nor are they neutral. Scholarly Western interests seem complicit with what Santos (2013) has suggested as epistemicide or the extinc-tion of non-Western ways of knowing or an approach to engagement that involves forms of epistemological imposition or reeducation (in a way that seems quite contrary to aspirations that disavow colonizing others). Rather, non-Westerners are positioned as scholarly outsiders—guests in the global scholarly community who are granted access or voice in the global knowledge economy so long as they can represent themselves in a Western image. Despite a significant non-Western readership and a large number of non-Western submissions to Western journals, articles by non-Westerners are rarely accepted and in turn rarely published. If they are published, they are expected to align with and pursue frames involving Western scholarly pursuits and perspectives.

Thus, although the Western scholarly community may tout global values, its approach befits assimilative interests rather than an accommodation of diversity. Editorial boards of the key Western journals consist primarily of Western scholars, and articles are written with an American slant. There appears to be little attempt to respect the readership of Eastern and Southern countries, or to support their local epistemologies. In other words, there appear to be few accommodations for supporting "foreign" research pursuits in the global competition for status in the knowledge economy market. The end result is that Eastern and Southern scholars are encouraged to reshape their research enterprises for Western audiences. Indeed, the competitiveness of some countries presents a palpably different orientation, which is often narcissistic.

Postcolonial critiques abound as scholars have recognized this bias and its consequences. As Santos has noted (2007, 2008, 2013), our support of Western ways of knowing and Western science alone may contribute to the loss of global locals and non-Western ways of knowing—in effect leading to a form of knowledge genocide. As Raewyn Connell (2007) argued in her book *Southern Theory: The Global Dynamics of Knowledge in Social Science* and discussed in conjunction with an essay she cowrote entitled "Toward a Postcolonial Comparative and International Education," there is a huge imbalance that has led to a sidelining and ignorance of non-Western inquiry and ways of knowing. This void in global ways of knowing suggests the need for:

> knowledge projects that decenter the global North in knowledge production, undermine the uneven power relations that naturalize the intellectual division of labor, provincialize the universalist ontology and epistemology that underpin official knowledge, and revalue knowledges that have been subjugated by global hegemony. (Takayama et al., 2017, p. S13)

This plight of non-Western scholars reflects the lament First Nations Coastal Salish writer Lee Maracle (1993) expressed in his book *Ravensong*: "Where do you begin telling someone that their world is not the only one" (p. 72)?

Similarly, the major trading routes for the exchange of educational practices across countries are predominantly Western. Emanating from Australia were the seeds of critical literacy from Bronwyn Davies, Carmen Luke, Allan Luke, and others, as well socio-semiotics perspectives that fueled genre-based approaches stemming from Michael Halliday and James Martin. Elsewhere in the Pacific,

New Zealand educators, such as Sylvia Ashton Warner, introduced educators to organic teaching approaches; Warwick Elley engaged in "book flood" initiatives; and Marie Clay together with other New Zealanders advanced Reading Recovery worldwide. (Reading Recovery eventually became perhaps the most successful approach for students who were at risk of falling behind as readers at an early age.) Other New Zealanders, such as Donald Holdaway and David Doake, introduced the shared book experience as a major practice for beginning reading.

Additionally, South America—especially Brazil—was foundational to critical literacy and community-based literacy work in accordance with the theories and projects of Paulo Freire and Augusto Boal. Emilia Ferreiro from Mexico contributed a pioneering study on early literacy development. In Europe, Italy was a major source of child and community-centered education in conjunction with the Montessori approach and Reggio Emilia project, while French and German sociologists provided frameworks for examining sociopolitical dimensions of literacy. And emanating from the UK were major curriculum initiatives and understandings of language learning under the guidance of James Britton and Michael Halliday—from both a sociolinguistic and sociological perspective (e.g., Basil Bernstein). A number of UK educators were also pioneers in advancing drama education (e.g., Dorothy Heathcote, Cecily O'Neill, and Gavin Bolton).

Cross-National Studies

This same trend to Westernization befits the interests being served by cross-national studies, at least until recently. Indeed, the study of global developments has a history of capturing the imagination of Western educators. In part, such studies were spurred by the recognition that the world offered a "natural" global laboratory that afforded explorations of differences and possibilities beyond those reflected within one country or region alone. From 1950 to the early 1970s, a number of researchers embraced these cross-national studies, viewing literacy as having enormous potential to explore global issues.

For example, Scribner and Cole (1981) explored the vexing question of the role of reading in terms of whether differences in literacy yielded reasoning differences. To do so, they delved into cultures with distinct differences in terms of the nature and role of print in their communities. Similarly, in the context of exploring reading achievement and learning to read and write, other studies delved into areas such as the roles of print in different cultures, language differences, and cultural norms. In his book *The Teaching of Reading and Writing* published for UNESCO, William S. Gray (1956) explored the nature and role of languages in learning to read, including examining eye movements across various written languages. Others examined gender differences and achievement; still others explored variations in practice such as differences in achievement arising from differences in the starting age of schooling (e.g., Preston, 1962).

> For example, in 1962, Foshay et al. published a large-scale international study comparing the performance of 13-year-old students across 12 countries. Then, in 1973, Robert Thorndike conducted a comparison of 15 countries, relating differences in reading achievement to a range of factors that varied across the countries.
>
> During this same period, John Downing argued for the creation of comparative reading as a field of study (in conjunction with the publication of his 1973 book *Comparative Reading*, in which he had scholars from different countries portray their reading practices).

A number of scholars also pursued cross-national comparisons of reading achievement differences in which they attempted to correlate reading achievement differences to various factors in each country or post-hoc considerations of emphases. In a similar fashion, studies of written composition and literature teaching were conducted and likewise related to practices and values of various countries (e.g., Purves, 1973). Further, the interest in cross-national studies remains today. For example, capitalizing on the differences in language, contemporary scholars explore some of the cross-national differences in reading due to language differences (e.g., orthographic, phonological, and morphological) and cultural norms (e.g., Chen et al., 2014; Zhang et al., 2014).

Development Pursuits

Across the globe there are countless educators involved in on-the-ground literacy efforts. Although their work may not be fully evidenced in terms of the major scholarly outlets, its impact on others in their regions has been substantial—in terms of mobilizing and networking and moving the literacy field forward with a more planetary orientation informed by a postcolonial perspective. In particular, a number of Western literacy educators have been major advocates and allies in the advancement of literacy. They work in collaboration with international groups such as UNESCO, CODE, the Global Alliance on Books, the Soros Foundation, USAID, World Bank, and others, along with selected local communities (e.g., Indigenous groups in Southern countries).

In the West, for instance, the leadership of scholars such as Daniel Wagner and his International Literacy Institute at the University of Pennsylvania has been substantial with UNESCO and other groups (Wagner, 2011, 2017: 2018a & b). Likewise, the efforts of Irwin Kirsch have had tremendous influence. Kirsch is the director of the Center for Global Assessment at Educational Testing Service and manages the Literacy Assessment and Monitoring Program with the UNESCO Institute for Statistics, the Reading Expert Group for the Organization for Economic Co-operation and Development (OECD), and the Programme for

International Student Assessment (PISA). In terms of adult literacy in particular, Tom Stitch has been involved in efforts in this area globally. And, in his past capacity as director of International Relations for the International Reading Association (1995–2003) and now as CEO for CODE, Scott Walter has supported major literacy development in Eurasia and especially in Africa.

Other literacy scholars have been involved in a range of global development initiatives involving professional development with some help from nongovernmental organizations (NGOs). For example, Misty Sailors and James Hoffman have been engaged in major development efforts in Malawi, Liberia, and Mozambique (e.g., Sailors et al., 2019; Sailors & Hoffman, 2018). Bonnie Norton, Margaret Early, and Maureen Kendrick, together with African colleagues, have been involved in a major Storybook digital initiative in Africa with primary school teachers to promote multilingual literacy in their classrooms (i.e., using the mother tongue as a resource; see Norton & Tembe, 2020). Marlene Asselin has been engaged in Ethiopia, linking schools with libraries (Asselin, & Doiron, 2013). Victoria Purcell-Gates, Rebecca Rogers, and others have been engaged in Latin America (Purcell-Gates, 2007; Rogers, 2017; Trigos-Carillo & Rogers, 2018). And a number of scholars have been involved with the George Soros Foundation in some 50 countries in an effort to advance the critical reading skills of persons living in authoritarian societies.

Rise of Global Studies: Cosmopolitanism and Global Citizenship

Development is never one-way; it always involves negotiations between the parties involved and the interests that are being served. It is especially so when different norms apply and the goals and project activities encounter resistance to efforts of change and the manner in which such change might proceed. In *The Teaching of Reading and Writing*, Gray (1956) recounts the resistance encountered by rural communities to literacy programs—until programs shifted to address the direct needs of the community. George Soros encounters resistance to his efforts to advance the critical reading skills in different countries based on questions about his political motives. Such negotiations and the issues that are brought to the fore represent matters salient to the implementation of development initiatives and the interests served. They also offer areas of considerable importance to study.

Some of the most significant and complex global studies may be those seeking to understand the interfaces between local and global across time and space that occur as globalization is spurred. Take, if you will, the work drawing on cosmopolitanism that has surfaced as ways of characterizing the nature of our global experiences. The evolution of the notion of cosmopolitanism can be traced to views expressed by ancient Greek and Chinese philosophers as well as to Emmanuel Kant and discussions of global scholars from anthropology, sociology, philosophy, and education (see Nussbaum, 1997).[1] Most recently, it has also been implemented by postcolonial theory analyses, the growing interest in digital connectivity, and the surge of interest in matters of mobility and definitions of global citizenship. Despite some detractors, the term cosmopolitanism has come to befit the aspiration of worldliness for people pursing a morality aligned with global development projects.

So, what is cosmopolitanism? Its definition is complicated by being "in between" Western critical theoretical considerations and postcolonial theory. As Fazal Rizvi (2009a) remarked, cosmopolitanism is "a political philosophy, a moral theory and a cultural disposition" (p. 253); or, as Martha Nussbaum (1997) has suggested, cosmopolitanism is critical reflection and reflexivity, paired with an identification with the global human community and the ability to imagine across cultural differences. The chameleon nature of cosmopolitanism befits a disposition to cultures that is respectful, relative, and best when self-directed (rather than universal or imposed or portrayed by outsiders). The dilemma for literacy scholars is that aspirations to engage in the development of cosmopolitanism or propose a cosmopolitan politic find themselves on the tricky ground of cultural crossover by cultural interlopers.

The cross-national study by Glynda Hull, Amy Stornaiuolo, and Urvashi Sahni (2010) as described in their article "Cultural Citizenship and Cosmopolitan Practice: Global Youth Communicate Online" further explored these matters as part of a project directed at empowering young women via the Internet in ways that reflect a mix of global ambitions and local considerations. Undergirding the study is the notion of cosmopolitanism (borrowing from Appiah, 2006) as affording "compass in a world that is at once radically interconnected and increasingly divided . . . [that] can both uphold local commitments and take into consideration larger arenas of concern" (Hull et al., 2010, p. 331). Moreover, they argue, "social networking sites, along with the online and off line experiences that accompany them, can be a digital proving ground for understanding and respecting difference and diversity in a global world as well as fostering the literacies and communication practices through which such habits of mind develop" (p. 332). The project itself argues for a form of global citizenship as the aspiration and vehicle by which young people are invited to examine, interrogate, and share their pasts with peers in other countries, enlisting digital images and texts. Specifically, they attempted to examine the following questions: "How do young people develop cosmopolitan habits of mind and attitudes toward others? What are the social and cultural processes that characterize the development of cultural citizenship? What kinds of educative spaces, especially those online, might facilitate such processes? And what forms and designs do communicative practices take in such spaces?" (p. 337).

As Hull et al. (2010) recounted, there were tensions that arose when individual empowerment and community considerations or consultations were not aligned—especially if consulting with the community might conflict with or undermine the "critical" aims of the project. As they brought to the fore in this and other studies, when one crosses borders, issues of influence, respect, reciprocity, and diversity are difficult to navigate. The multilayered engagements of people and goods are complex and at times involve paradoxical circumstances. They may demand situation-specific, interpersonal, respectful, and responsive approaches that are iterative, collaborative, formative, inclusive, and critically reflexive. In terms of definitions of cosmopolitanism, then, Hull and her colleagues establish it as fluid and culturally relevant—with a consideration of a world as entailing frequent and ongoing border crossings.

That said, as one moves across nations or cultures, navigating one's place is tricky and needs an orientation to the other that involves a fuller consideration of ethics.[2] For example, an Indigenous ethical lens would suggest the need for trustworthiness, respect for individuals and community, and informed engagement and agreement throughout any research enterprise. As Maori scholar Linda Smith (2005) commented:

> For indigenous and other marginalized communities, research ethics is at a very basic level about establishing, maintaining, and nurturing reciprocal and respectful relations, not just among people as individuals but also with people as individuals, as collectives and as members of communities, and with humans who live in and with other entities in the environment. The abilities to enter pre-existing relationships; to build, maintain, and nurture relationships; and to strengthen connectivity are important research skills in the indigenous arena. They require critical sensitivity and reciprocity of spirit by a researcher. (p. 97)

From a postcolonial perspective, this requires for many of us who are Westerners a step back—befitting the kind of critique that Ali Abdi offered on the work in global citizenship. Abdi (2015) warns against a predisposition dominated by Western values:

> As much as anything else, the Western-constructed new global citizenship education scholarship reflects a neocolonial or perhaps more accurately, a decolonial character that should not be totally detached from the old tragedies of the mission civilsatrice (Said, 1993) that presumed, without much evidence, a European predestination to save non-cultured natives from themselves. . . . What we should not discount though, is the need to see beyond the fog of the still problematically benevolent political correctness as the creators of the new scholarship are somehow oblivious in turning the gaze upon themselves and societies. (p. 16)

Similarly, as Vickers (2018) recently argued, we need an orientation that does not advance a marginalization and colonization of other. There is need for a form of shuttle diplomacy, wherein a culture of research might develop that has local relevance while being both locally and globally situated and connected. It befits the kind of horizontal negotiations across persons suggested by Campano and his colleagues (2010). At the same time it suggests a fuller consideration of appropriate engagements with others that possibly extends to a fuller range of stakeholders with a variety of expectations of the norms for and integrity of transactions. Moreover, as Hull and Stornaiuolo (2014) have shown in an extension of their aforementioned work, exchanges across cultures involve complex responses, especially given the meanings and their semiotic possibilities. Interpretations may not align even if occurring in good faith or pursued with considerations of proper distance and hospitality (discussions of which extend beyond the considerations of proper distance and hospitality in conjunction with cosmopolitanism presented here).

Moving Forward

The nature and scope of globalization and literacy are gaining ground as a planetary orientation with a critical theoretical lens (especially postcolonial). There is a sense of a growing global shared mission—one that challenges circumstances that detract from global support for diverse ideas, ways of knowing, and languages. There appears to be a coming together across communities to stem the extinction of languages and ways of knowing, and to eradicate those systemic and pervasive structures of racism, inequity, and diminished human rights. Such is apparent in the admonishment that "context counts," the call for research and development by and for locals, the global reach of Black Lives Matter and other movements, and the considerations of Indigenous concerns and ways of knowing.

There seems to be a mobilized global advocacy that is more respectful than patronizing, more planful and committed to ensuring the self-determination of stakeholders, and potentially more long-term than incidental. Such a global mission can bridge to, between, from, and across local communities in ways that position literacy development devotees more organically; it can be less prone to perpetuating forms of colonialism, objectification, commodification, and patrimony. This is an orientation that entails a more transactional approach, befitting Giddens's (1999) notion of a global dialectic between "global/local, integration/fragmentation and structure/agency" (Singh et al., 2005, p. 4). But is it a place where diversity is supported, or is it a space where global has been redefined in a fashion that is colonizing?

Consistent with a planetary disposition and aligned with a postcolonial orientation, a shift to global meaning making has been suggested. This orientation resonates with the notion that all reading is foreign—involving a transaction of one's world with others. It redefines reading as global in nature, highlighting the need to interrogate the cultural positioning represented in texts, whether they be narratives or expositions or news releases or academic research (Perry, 2018; Tierney, 2018a, 2018b, 2020). As previously stated:

> Global meaning making involves transactions that are situated and not standardized anchored in ethics aligned with respect, reciprocity and ecological global eclecticism. . . . Global meaning making entails cultural protagonism. For those engaged

in international pursuits, it entails straddling multiple locals in different countries, including spaces where racism, classism, and ethnic and various other forms of discrimination may be deep-seated, almost intractable and perhaps perpetuated unless challenged. . . . address(ing) the tug of war between homogeneity and heterogeneity, privilege and responsibility, global and local. (Tierney, 2018a)

Global meaning making also extends to being an activist, advocate, and ally, confronting and disrupting the hegemonies that privilege some but limit others (see box). It fits with helping learners explore their voice—challenging or disrupting hegemonies (as has been occurring in accordance with the activist pursuits emanating on the critical and digital research fronts, challenging racism and other systemic forms of violence, prejudice, and bias) (see Curwood & Gibbons, 2010; Rogers et al., 2015; Stornaiuolo & Thomas, 2018). Global meaning making relates to those efforts occurring globally and within various nations, such as the reconciliation efforts with First Nations communities in Canada (Truth and Reconciliation Commission of Canada, 2015), antiracist pursuits in the United States, and the challenges to systemic institutional biases against Indigenous persons occurring within universities in various countries (e.g., Parata & Gardiner, 2020). It is aligned with Andreotti and de Souza (2011), building on Spivak (1990, 1999) and Stein (2017), who have argued for a global orientation that entails disrupting the normative—to interrogate ideas, especially in terms of the systems colonizing the world (e.g., hegemonic, ethnocentric, ahistorical, paternalistic) and our complicities with their systemic continuation.

Accordingly, one of the foundations of such global meaning-making research engagements befits Freirean notions of the empowerment or conscientization of the community participants involved. As Patti Lather (1986) stated in her arguments for what she termed catalytic validity:

> My concern is that efforts to produce social knowledge that is helpful in the struggle for a more equitable world pursue rigor as well as relevance. Otherwise, just as my concern is that efforts to produce social knowledge that is helpful in the struggle for a more equitable world pursue rigor as well as relevance "pointless precision" (Kaplan, 1964) has proven to be the bane of the conventional paradigm, the rampant subjectivity inherent in the more phenomenologically based paradigms will prove to be the nemesis of new paradigm research. (pp. 67–68)

With the advent of globalization and critical reflexology and ecology, notions of integrity, respect, and reciprocity need to be advanced in ways that move across time and space and people. As we engage with one another in the interest of providing support that has integrity, the complexities and multilayered nature of the clashes between the local and global arise, as evident when some of the paradoxes and dilemmas are confronted as scholarly pursuits rub shoulders with local interests. Researchers are not innocent but shape how people and ideas are positioned and might be codified and commodified. Research fields are at risk of becoming agents that can dispossess some and privilege others. Consideration of global ethics will bring to the fore the consideration that when we cross borders, we need to interrogate our processes and positionings. Matters of influence, respect, reciprocity, and diversity are essential if credibility is to be maintained.

The multilayered engagements of people and goods are complex and at times involve paradoxical circumstances. They may demand situation-specific, interpersonal, respectful, and responsive approaches that are iterative, collaborative, formative, inclusive, and critically reflexive. Certainly, these complexities should not be avoided, denied, or hidden. They suggest notions of responsibility and responsiveness and the democratization of research—a shift from objectification and "study of" to a personalization, embodiment, enlivenment, and "study with" approach.

Unfortunately, our maps to date do not seem to fully address the transactional nature of or a full list of the elements involved in doing this kind of cross-cultural work. We do know that we should avoid disguising ourselves as allies or third-party reporters as we appropriate and commodify and assume the role of a global trader in the knowledge economy. Such work is done without a genuine license to do so by the individual or the community involved and without a fuller appreciation and reckoning with the sociological and epistemological dynamics and influences across time, place, individuals, and communities.

Global Citizenship, Ecopedagogy, Ways of Knowing, Pluriversality, Language Revitalization, and Open Access Publishing

Global initiatives on a number of fronts are grappling with how to pursue a world anchored in respect for diversity. These initiatives include deliberations on the notion of global citizenship; the pursuit of what has been termed ecopedagogy; delving into diverse ways of knowing; the revitalization of languages; and "open access" publishing.

Global Citizenship

Concurrent with discussions of cosmopolitanism, global mobility, nationalism, and internationalism, a number of individuals and groups have contemplated forms of global citizenship (e.g., Oxley & Morris, 2013; Pashby et al., 2020; Schattle, 2008; Stein, 2015; UNESCO, 2015). These discussions have been attempting to break new ground by unpacking aspirations that acknowledge our global nature and engagements with different groups in a fashion that is ecumenical. These formulations are far-ranging, reflecting deliberations that attempt to draw together liberal humanistic perspectives and postcolonial critiques—even neoliberal considerations. They represent a fusion of historical consciousness with critical reflexivity, especially with regard to anti-colonial, anti-imperialist, and antiracism objectives, as well as efforts to resist practices and modes of objectification, commodification, universalism, individualism, and neoliberalism. They aspire to appreciate the complexities and differences in the realities, interests, histories, and epistemologies of diverse cultures, and advocate for the voices and sovereignty of others (Said, 1993; Santos, 2013). Global citizenship wrestles with and seeks to uncover false statements, bias, witnessing, and pursuits that result in objectification rather than respectfulness (Smith, 1999, 2005). It deviates from universalism and nationalism, as it vies for approaches to studying the "other" that are multiple rather than singular (and allied with while still distanced from)—rather than those that are presumptuously intimate or subordinating.

Nevertheless, approaches to this issue still struggle with the paradoxes entailed in a model of global citizenship that is fixed rather than fluid. As noted by Pashby et al. (2020) in their analyses of the typologies of approaches to global citizenship, the questions being addressed have shifted from:

> How can we teach students the values that will support democracy, fairness and progress for all humanity? How can we encourage students to take responsibility for people beyond their own nation's borders? What kinds of activities can enable students to connect with and understand global issues so that they can be helpful in solving them (e.g., climate change, migration, economic globalization)? How can learning about other cultures prepare people to work and collaborate more effectively and efficiently across cultural difference? How can global learning be more systemically incorporated into curriculum and assessed through evaluation? (p. 158)

To questions such as:

> How can we imagine a responsibility *toward* others (both human and other-than-human beings) rather than a responsibility *for* others? What kinds of analyses can enable students to understand how they are a part of global problems, and how they can work to mitigate or eradicate these problems at a structural level (e.g., the impact of consumption levels on climate change, the role of Western military interventions in prompting migration, the racialized and gendered international division of labor, etc.)? Whose definitions of citizenship tend to dominate in GCE (Global Citizenship Education) discourses, and why? How might we redefine and repurpose the concept of global citizenship to advocate for more inclusive forms of representation, and the redistribution of resources? How can our ideas of global citizenship be informed not just by the national citizenship formations of Western nation-states, but also of other countries and other kinds of political communities (e.g., Indigenous nations)? How can we learn to learn from different ways of knowing in order to imagine the world differently? (p. 158–159)

And, finally, to questions that address the paradoxes of this framework, such as:

> How has the modern/colonial ontology restricted our horizons and what we consider to be possible, desirable, intelligible and imaginable? What kinds of denials and

entitlements keep us not only intellectually but also affectively invested in this ontology? What can engender a stream of connections and a sense of care and commitment towards everything that overrides self-interest and insecurities and is not dependent on convictions, knowledge, identity or understanding? What would it look and feel like if our responsibility to all living beings on the planet was not a willed choice, but rather something "before will"? What kinds of experiences can enable students to see and sense how they can be simultaneously part of global problems, and part of global solutions? Is it even possible to imagine a definition of global citizenship not premised on conditional forms of inclusion, or shared values? If citizenship is not a universalizable concept, then how might we nonetheless use it in strategic ways, while remaining conscious of its significant limitations, potential harms, and the partiality of any particular approach? How can we open ourselves up to being taught by different ways of being in order to experience and sense the world differently, being aware of misinterpretations, idealizations and appropriations that are likely to happen in this process? (Pashby et al., 2020, p. 159–160)

Ecopedagogy

Simultaneously with these developments in global citizenship, an ecological disposition that embraces diversity is also being advanced, through advocacy for what has been termed ecopedagogy (e.g., Grigorov & Fleuri, 2012; Kahn, 2009; Misiaszek, 2015; 2018). The notion of ecopedagogy has its roots in Brazil among critical pedagogy activists, especially Paulo Freire (Freire, 2004; Gadotti, 2000), whose views explored the possibilities of a collective humanity and opposition to the neoliberal tendencies that override considerations of others and the planet. As Angela Antunes and Moacir Gadotti (2005) observe:

> Ecopedagogy is not just another pedagogy among many other pedagogies. It not only has meaning as an alternative project concerned with nature preservation (Natural Ecology) and the impact made by human societies on the natural environment (Social Ecology), but also as a new model for sustainable civilization from the ecological point of view (Integral Ecology), which implies making changes on economic, social, and cultural structures. (p. 13)

Coupled with concerns about the disintegration of the planet and our cultures, ecopedagogy brings to the fore a range of issues, from dealing with problems of inequity in society to climate change. It entails advocacy for human rights as well as the rights of nature. As Freire (2004) highlighted, ecopedagogy places "reading the world" ahead of "reading the word." Moreover, it highlights our planetary roles and responsibilities to one another and to place as we adopt multiple perspectives attuned to supporting and respecting (rather than diminishing or extinguishing) our diversity. It aligns with notions of pluriversality discussed next.

Cultural Ways of Knowing, Pluriversality

Increasingly, colonized communities are mobilizing goals of reestablishing the currency of their cultural ways of knowing—befitting postcolonial critiques and in alignment with United Nations Declarations such as those pertaining to education and, more recently, Indigenous rights (UN et al., 2013; World Conference, 1990). These pursuits are not straightforward, as prevailing forces perpetuate a privileging of colonizing forces over Indigenous rights and knowledges. As Assié-Lumumba (2017) noted in her discussions of African ways of knowing (focusing on Nigeria), the repositioning of Nigeria's Indigenous ways of knowing is immensely complex, given the ongoing reverence for colonizing forces. As she stated:

> Contemporary African education has suffered from several fundamental problems. One of them is the forced juxtaposition of the European and the African systems of education on a hierarchical basis, with the European system on the top and the only one considered legitimate. While it was denied agency, the African system was not successfully eradicated by colonial policy. Individuals and groups are forced to resolve the tension between the two without the benefit of consistent, systemic, and sustained policy that attempts to create a constructive dialogue between them. Another major problem is the lack of systematized and appropriated mechanisms to permanently invigorate the Indigenous system as the foundation and using it with confidence, thereby unfreezing Africa's empowering and positive cultural reference, which was denied free agency for the purpose of justifying transatlantic enslavement and colonial domination. (p. 11)

The reality is that non-Western ways of knowing are disappearing—becoming extinct faster than the diversity of species as the broken links among individuals, communities, cultures, and places increase. Efforts to decolonize—along with those to revitalize cultural ways of knowing—struggle to mount campaigns to challenge the domination of Western ways of knowing. At the same time, burgeoning studies of Indigenous ways of knowing have made the differences between Indigenous methodologies and Western traditions clearer (see box; see also Battiste, 1998; Battiste & Henderson, 2000; Bishop, 1994; Nakata, 2001, 2004; Ocholla, 2007; Rigney et al., 2015; Rigney & Hattam, 2018; Smith, 1999; Smith, 2000, 2015).

Even in countries that have succeeded in making progress, the promotion of cultural ways of knowing requires ongoing concerted efforts to develop understandings of how to advocate for and support them. New Zealand Maori have held the view that advocating for cultural ways of knowing is not to displace one epistemology with another, but rather a matter of positioning Indigenous knowledge as significant or primary—with the possibility of it being separate, fused, or integrated with Western ways of knowing. In discussing New Zealand's success in terms of establishing a Maori-based educational focus, Maori scholar Graham Hingangaroa Smith (2000) has argued, "We ought to be open to using any theory and practice with emancipatory relevance to our Indigenous struggle" (p. 214). As Ghiso et al. (2016) further suggest, it should involve:

As Martin Nakata (2007) has detailed, Indigenous knowledge is different in the following ways:

- the range and role of different sources of knowledge—experience, observation, history, language, stories, dreams, nature, and animals;
- the nature of the state of knowledge—its animations, permanency, or changeability; its state of flux; and its relationship to the past, present, and future;
- the position of knowing within the community collective; and
- the basis for how knowledge and knowing are validated and used.

Indigenous knowing represents a significant shift from Western reductionism and objectification. It instead embraces holistic reflections that involve spiritual connections and a high degree of interrelatedness of people and their worlds. As Indigenous scholars indicate, this positions knowledge as less fixed, befitting an orientation to the world that is ecological, involving an intimacy between people and their natural worlds (Battiste & Henderson, 2000).

the robust multilingual counterpublics of their students' home and neighbourhood communities into the curriculum. This may initially be done through developing partnerships with local organizations and viewing parents and community leaders as partners who have critical knowledge about the potential role of education in a participatory democracy. (p. 24)

Drawing from work based in Argentina, it might also involve a democratization of education via h*orizontalidad* (Campano et al., 2010)—to "reorganize the hierarchical template of politics and construct new forms of participatory democracy. This process of horizontalidad is both the 'end' and the 'means to an end'" (p. 278). In African countries, given their different histories with colonization and their own regional diversities, repositioning epistemologies would require similar but distinct and complex considerations that are respectful of regional differences, varying tribal interests, disparate religious affiliations, and the ways in which local versus colonial knowledges are positioned and viewed (Onukaogu, 2011). In Australia, promoting cultural ways of knowing seems to demand a combination of activism, education, and positioning—such as making Aboriginal ways of knowing visible, fomenting activism that seeks formal recognition of the Aboriginal and Torres Strait Islanders and their ways of knowing (Sovereign Union, 2019), or engaging in other forms of leveraging to re-secure Aboriginal peoples' roles.

Similarly, a horizontal orientation is consistent with a shift in literacies away from being exclusionary, marginalizing and perpetuating deficit models of others (e.g., Bloome et al., 2014). By drawing upon vertical and horizontal knowledges,

Gutiérrez and Barbara Rogoff argue for a syncretic orientation and in so doing being able to "rupture the gap between in school and out-of-school learning" (Gutiérrez, 2014, p. 49), crossing into the everyday to leverage repertoires of learning practices befitting the movement across borders (Gutiérrez & Rogoff, 2003).

As the word "pluriversality" implies, threats to our future emanating from colonizing forces that advance some literacies over others have been challenged as our literacies are examined, enlisting a combination of lenses from postcolonial critique to affect theory and other lenses.[3] For example, Mia Perry (Perry, 2020; Perry & Pullanikkatil, 2019; Escobar, 2018) draws on various lenses: affect theory (Leander & Ehret, 2019), humanism and critical theory (Campano, 2007; Campano, & Damico, 2007; Campano et al., 2013; Janks, 2020); ecology and ubuntu (e.g., Dillard, 2019; Le Grange, 2015); the role of arts, music, and performance (e.g., Medina & Wohlwend, 2014); a form of ethico-onto-epistemology (Song, 2020), as well as transliteracies (Stornaiuolo et al., 2017) to interrogate the nature and place of literacies in terms of issues of place and time. Perry challenges the colonizing forces that contribute to the domination of Western forms of literacy, especially the positioning of peoples and places, and questions the disruption of sociocultural linkages (between people and place and with one another) that Western literacy imposes on all people to the advantage of those persons and communities invested in these Western ways versus others with a different view and orientation to the world. Perry argues:

> The project of pluriversal literacies is not to eliminate print text but rather to find ways to incorporate a much broader understanding of relational human experience . . . this development in literacies theory requires an acceptance of contradictions and of new types of alliances and relations across peoples, traditions, and onto-ethico-epistemologies. Beyond ways of being, this call infers rethinking relations and affects across types of being. . . . After all, we share one globe, and to acknowledge multiple ways and types of being in this world compels the field of global literacy education to support multiple ways of making meaning and engaging in that shared world (Perry, 2020).

Language Revitalization

As concerns have grown about planetary disregard for diversity and the impact of global colonizing influences on cultures, we have seen the rise of developmental efforts, especially among Indigenous groups, to reestablish their languages and ways of knowing in hopes of avoiding the loss of identity and cultural links that join people across generations with place. In some places these efforts have made significant progress and have helped retain at least a foothold against the overwhelming domination of languages such as English, Spanish, Mandarin, and Arabic, as well as a counter to projects and ongoing efforts to maintain or expand on the dominance of a particular language (e.g., as can be seen with exporting Mandarin on a global scale by Hanban and the Confucius Institutes). Projects to revitalize languages and ways of knowing have emerged in various countries with at least some success. By establishing legal mandates, these attempts have reestablished ancestral languages as integral to cultural identity and educational programs—ensuring their place in society through teaching. In terms of literacy, these efforts have spurred a range of research pursuits focused on language revitalization as well as knowledge projects exploring multilingualism in a world involving migrations, border crossing, and various forms of transliteracies (Gutiérrez et al., 1999; Nelson et al., 2016; Rizvi, 2009b).

A key element in this effort to stem the tide of loss involves support for cultural practices from tales presented through dance, music, or art to language revitalization. In a conversation with Lester-Irabinna Rigney, a Nurungga man who grew up on Point Pearce Mission on the Yorke Peninsula in South Australia, Lester discussed the language revitalization efforts that occurred in his own community. When asked the question, what did the restoration of your ancestral language afford?, his response pointed to cultural affirmation and cultural ways of knowing. He suggested that he now had words that fit with his worlds (across physical, social, political, spiritual, and economic spheres). Words in English defined the world in ways that were familiar but seemed foreign or ill-fitting. Further, his experience with the notion of country entailed an animated, living country—rather than one that is separate and objectified. It is one explored in tandem with ancestral practices passed on via elders, such as through song and shared meaning making.

Open access

All of these aforementioned global developments are intertwined and will be propelled by what may be emerging as a major global force—the advent of open access publishing. The adoption of open access in different countries and by various consortia and institutions represents a major shift in the flow of ideas. Indeed, depending on where one is standing, the barriers that inhibit who reads what, when, and how seem to be crumbling. Open access represents a shift from limited access to reading material (especially scholarly material) to free access to those materials without the restrictions of a financial market that controls which countries or populations can obtain access to information.

Open access may be a breakthrough comparable to movable print in 11th-century China, Gutenberg's printing press in 15th-century Europe, or worldwide digital modes of representation at the cusp of the 21st century. Global access means that the proprietorship of ideas enforced by copyright laws in a publisher-controlled monopoly is giving way to an article economy privileging author rights. Moreover, we are seeing a shift to a form of global readership that advances literacy as anchored in a broad view of public readership, a stronger commitment to academic freedom, and diversity.

As pressure has increased to meet the needs of all, especially those parts of the world that have been locked out of the publisher-controlled global economy of knowledge, challenges to the Western domination of that global knowledge economy have arisen. In our own world of literacy research publications, research has been dominated by North America and Europe, at least in terms of acceptance rates, publications, citations, and representation on editorial boards. Even closer to home in the literacy field, within the International Literacy Association, this domination of the production of knowledge has occurred despite the fact that the majority of the subscribers to ILA's three journals—*Reading Research Quarterly*, *The Reading Teacher*, and *Journal of Adolescent and Adult Literacy*—are from outside the United States and Europe.

Open access is not just a dream for the future, but a development that is under way and gathering momentum. One example: The University of California system of 11 campuses challenged the dominant hold of Netherlands-based Elsevier Publishing on journals in the natural and medical sciences by severing subscriptions to Elsevier journals. In March 2021, the dispute was settled with the university and its faculties agreeing to pay publication costs in return for Elsevier granting free public access to all articles authored by UC faculty. The fundamental principle is that since the scholarship was made possible by public funds, the general public should have free access to the information generated by those funds. A small but significant effort on behalf of the Literacy Research Association, when it was still the National Reading Conference, was a resolution passed in 2008 (Beach et al., 2007; NRC, 2008) advocating for open access for all literacy scholarship. A world of ideas once Western and privatized seems to be giving way to a world of ideas both global and freely accessible.

And, as John Willinsky (2005) suggested in his book *The Access Principle: The Case for Open Access to Research and Scholarship*:

> The case for open access is multifaceted. It draws on the spirit of copyright law, the mandate of scholarly associations, the promise of global knowledge exchanges, the right to know, the prospect of enhanced reading and indexing, the improved economic efficiencies of publishing, and the history of the academic journal, which speaks to the courage—and risk—of new ventures at opening this world of learning. . . . How knowledge circulates has always been vital to the life of the mind, which all of us share, just as it is vital, ultimately, to the well-being of humanity. (p. 206)

Final Comments

Our lives personally interface with globalization on a daily basis—socially, culturally, economically, physically, intellectually, and historically. In some ways, the global and local are fused. Increasingly, our lives are shaped by border crossings (many of us are or are from immigrants) as well as through engagements with ourselves in the context of others. This fusing fits with descriptions of various forms of criss-crossing, hip-hop, and translanguaging by meaning makers across their communities. That is, as people brush against other cultures, their engagements reflect recent descriptions of cross-border meaning making and the boundary negotiations that exist through translanguaging (e.g., Horowitz, 2012; Nelson et al., 2016) and line stepping. As Gutiérrez et al. (2017) note, these crossings occur when:

> an individual deliberately and consciously pushes against society's ideological constraints. Rather than seeing boundaries as static, we recognize their dynamism . . . identifying and testing a line, the line-stepper learns how and where lines are permeable and the available latitude in their enforcement. (p. 53)

Global research is essentially a study of ourselves, this planet, and the societies with whom we exchange. As Appadurai (2001) has commented, this is not just a matter of ecumenicalism and generosity. It requires suspending certainty and opening oneself up to debate and differences and grassroots internationalism as a crucible for emergent new forms of global engagements.

References

Abdi, A. A. (2015). Decolonizing global citizenship education. In A. A. Abdi, L. Shultz, & T. Pillay (Eds.), *Decolonizing global citizenship education* (pp. 11–26). Sense. doi: 10.1007/978–94-6300-277-6

Andreotti, V., & de Souza, L. M. T. M. (2011). *Postcolonial perspectives on global citizenship education*. Routledge.

Antunes, A. and Gadotti, M. (2005). Eco-pedagogy as the appropriate pedagogy to the Earth Charter process. *Earth Charter in action, part IV: Democracy, nonviolence, and peace*, 135–137. earthcharter.org/wp-content/assets/virtual-library2/images/uploads/ENG-Antunes.pdf

Appadurai, A. (2001). Grassroots globalization and the research imagination. In A. Appadurai, B. T. Mandémory, P. Rekacewicz, A. Huyssen, & A. Mbembe (Eds.), *Globalization* (pp. 1–21). Duke University Press.

Appadurai, A., Mandémory, B. T., Rekacewicz, P., Huyssen, A., & Mbembe, A. (2001). *Globalization*. Duke University Press.

Appiah, K. A. (2006). *Cosmopolitanism: Ethics in a world of strangers*. W. W. Norton.

Asselin, M., & Doiron, R. (2013). *Linking literacy and libraries in global communities*. www.ashgate.com/isbn/9781409452843

Assié-Lumumba, N. T. (2017). The Ubuntu paradigm and comparative and international education: Epistemological challenges and opportunities in our field. *Comparative Education Review, 61*(1), 1–21. doi: 10.1086/689922

Association of Canadian Deans of Education (ACDE). (2014). *Accord on the internationalization of education*. Association of Canadian Deans of Education. csse-scee.ca/acde/publications-2/#internationalization

Australian House of Representatives Standing Committee on Indigenous Affairs. (2017, December). *The power of education: From surviving to thriving: Educational opportunities for Aboriginal and Torres Strait Islanders students*. www.aph.gov.au/Parliamentary_Business/Committees/House/Indigenous_Affairs/EducationalOpportunities/Final_Report

Battiste, M. (1998). Enabling the autumn seed: Toward a decolonized approach to Aboriginal knowledge, language and education. *Canadian Journal of Native Education, 22*(1), 16–27.

Battiste, M., & Henderson, J. Y. (2000). *Protecting Indigenous knowledge and heritage: A global challenge*. Pirich.

Beach, R., Carter, A., East, D., Johnston, P., Reinking, D., Smith-Burke, T., & Stahl, N. (2007). Resisting commercial influences on accessing scholarship: What literacy researchers need to know and do. In D. W. Rowe, R. T. Jimenez, D. L. Compton, D. K. Dickinson, Y. Kim, K. M. Leander, & V. J. Risko (Eds.), *56th yearbook of the National Reading Conference* (pp. 96–110). National Reading Conference.

Bhabha, H. K. (2004). *The location of culture*. Routledge.

Binkley, M. R., Rust, K., & Williams, T. (Eds.). (1996). *Reading literacy in an international perspective: Collected papers from the IEA Reading Literacy Study*. U.S. Dept. of Education, Office of Educational Research and Improvement, National Center for Education Statistics.

Bishop, A. (2009). *Becoming an ally: Breaking the cycle of oppression in people*. Fernwood.

Bishop, R. (1994). Initiating empowering research? *New Zealand Journal of Educational Studies, 29*(2), 175–188.

Bloome, D., Averill, J., Hill, H., & Ryu, S. (2014). Ideologies and their consequences in defining literacies—An essay. In P. J. Dunston, S. K. Fullerton, C. C. Bates, P. M. Stecker, M. Cole, A. Hall, D. Herro, & K. Headley (Eds.), *63rd yearbook of the Literacy Research Association*. (pp. 61–78). Literacy Research Association.

Boorstin, D. J. (1989). *Hidden history: Exploring our secret past*. Vintage Books.

Campano, G. (2007). *Immigrant students and literacy: Reading, writing, and remembering*. Teachers College Press.

Campano, G., & Damico, J. S. (2007). Doing the work of social theorists: Children enacting epistemic privilege as literacy learners and teachers. *Counterpoints, 310*, 219–233.

Campano, G., Ghiso, M. P., & Sánchez, L. (2013). "Nobody knows the . . . amount of a person": Elementary students critiquing dehumanization through organic critical literacies. *Research in the Teaching of English, 48*(1), 98–125.

Campano, G., Honeyford, M. A., Sánchez, L. & Zanden, S. V. (2010). Ends in themselves: Theorizing the practice of university–school partnering through horizontalidad. *Language Arts, 87*(4), 277–286.

Castells, M. (1996). *The information age: Economy, society and culture* (Vol. 1). Blackwell.

Castells, M. (1997). *The information age: The power of identity* (Vol. 2). Blackwell.

Castells, M. (1998). *The information age: End of millennium* (Vol. 3). Blackwell.

Certeau, M. de, & Rendall, S. (Trans.) (1984). *The practice of everyday life*. University of California Press.

Chen, X., Anderson, R. C., Li, H., & Shu, H. (2014). Visual, phonological, and orthographic strategies in learning to read Chinese. In X. Chen, Q. Wang, & Y. C. Luo (Eds.), *Reading development and difficulties in monolingual and bilingual Chinese children* (pp. 23–47). Springer.

Chomsky, N. (1989). Propaganda, American-style. In C. Watner (Ed.), *I must speak out: The best of the voluntaryist, 1982–1999* (pp. 223–225). Fox & Wilkes.

Choudry, A. (2015). *Learning activism: The intellectual life of contemporary social movements*. University of Toronto Press.

Collins, R. (1998). *The sociology of philosophies: A global theory of intellectual change*. Harvard University Press.

Connell, R. (2007). *Southern theory: The global dynamics of knowledge in social science*. Polity.

Curwood, J. S., & Gibbons, D. (2010). "Just like I have felt:" Multimodal counternarratives in youth-produced digital media. *International Journal of Learning and Media, 1*(4), 59–77.

Dillard, C. B. (2019). You are because I am: Toward new covenants of equity and diversity in teacher education. *Educational Studies, 55*(2), 121–138.

Downing, J. (Ed.). (1973). *Comparative reading*. Macmillan.

Drucker, P. F. (1969). *The age of discontinuity: Guidelines to our changing society*. Harper and Row.

Duff, P., & Talmy, S. (2011). Language socialization approaches to second language acquisition: Social, cultural, and linguistic development in additional languages. In D. Atkinson (Ed.), *Alternative approaches to Second Language Acquisition* (pp. 95–116). Routledge.

Escobar, E. (2018). *Designs for the pluriverse: Radical interdependence, autonomy, and the making of worlds*. Duke University Press.

Foshay, A. W., Thorndike, R. L., Hotyat, F., Pidgeon, D. A., & Walker, D. A. (1962). *Educational achievements of thirteen-year-olds in twelve countries: Results of an international research project, 1959–1961*. UNESCO Institute for Education.

Freire, P. (2004). *Pedagogy of indignation*. Paradigm Publishers. doi: 10.4324/9781315632902

Friedman, T. L. (2008). *Hot, flat and crowded: Why we need a green revolution—and how it can renew America*. Farrar, Straus & Giroux.

Gadotti, M. (2000). *Pedagogia da terra* (5th ed.). Peirópolis.

Galla, C. K. (2017). Materials development for Indigenous language revitalization: Pedagogy, praxis and possibilities, In E. McKinley & L. T. Smith (Eds.), *Handbook of Indigenous education* (pp. 1–19). Springer. doi: 10.1007/978-981-10-1839-8_12-1

Ghiso, M. P., Campano, G., Player, G., & Rusoja, A. (2016). Dialogic teaching and multilingual counterpublics. *International Perspectives on Dialogic Theory and Practice, 16*, 1–26. doi: 10.17239/L1ESLL-2016.16.02.05

Giddens, A. (1999). *Runaway world: How globalization is reshaping our lives*. Profile.

Goodwin, S. (2012, August 23 to 25). *Conducting action research in an "evidence-based" policy environment*. Australian Qualitative Research Conference, Embodying good research: What counts and who decides? at Charles Darwin University, Australia.

Gramsci, A. (1982). *Selections from the prison notebooks*. Lawrence & Wishart.

Gray, W. S. (1956). *The teaching of reading and writing: An international survey*. UNESCO.

Grigorov, S., & Fleuri, R. (2012). Ecopedagogy: Educating for a new eco-social intercultural perspective. *Visão Global, Joaçaba, 15*(1–2), 433–454. editora.unoesc.edu.br/index.php/visaoglobal/article/view/3435/1534

Gutiérrez, K. (2014). Syncretic approaches to literacy learning; Leveraging horizontal knowledge and expertise. In P. J. Dunston, S. K. Fullerton, C. C. Bates, P. M. Stecker, M. Cole, A. Hall, D. Herro, & K. Headley (Eds.), *63rd yearbook of the Literacy Research Association*. (pp. 48–60). Literacy Research Association.

Gutiérrez, K. D., Baquedano-López, P., & Tejeda, C. (1999). Rethinking diversity: Hybridity and hybrid language practices in the third space. *Mind, Culture and Activity, 6*(4), 286–303. doi: 10.1080/10749039909524733

Gutiérrez, K. D., Cortes, K., Cortez, A., DiGiacomo, D., Higgs, J., Johnson, P., Lizárraga, J., Mendoza, E., Tien, J., & Vakil, S. (2017). Replacing representation with imagination: Finding ingenuity in everyday practices. *Review of Research in Education, 41*(1), 30.

Gutiérrez, K. D., & Rogoff, B. (2003). Cultural ways of learning: Individual traits or repertoires of practice. *Educational Researcher, 32*(5), 19–25.

Hampton, E. (1995). Toward a redefinition of Indian education. In M. Battiste & J. Barman (Eds.), *First Nations education in Canada: The circle unfolds* (pp. 5–42). University of British Columbia Press.

Hare, J., & Davidson, S. F. (2016). Learning from Indigenous knowledge in education. In D. Long & O. P. Dickason, (Eds.), *Visions of the heart: Canadian Aboriginal issues* (4th ed., pp. 241–262). Oxford University Press.

Henry, A. (2015). "We especially welcome applications from visible minorities": Reflections on race, gender and life at three universities. *Race, Ethnicity and Education, 18*(5), 589–610.

Horowitz, R. (2012). Border crossing: Geographic space and cognitive shifts in adolescent language and literacy practices. In H. Romo, C. Garrido de la Caleja, & O. Lopez (Eds.), *A bilateral perspective on Mexico-United States migration* (pp. 147–164). Universidad Veracruzana and The University of Texas at San Antonio, UTSA—Mexico Center.

Hull, G. A., & Stornaiuolo, A. (2014). Cosmopolitan literacies, social networks, and "proper distance": Striving to understand in a global world. *Curriculum Inquiry, 44*(1), 15–44. doi: 10.1111/curi.12035

Hull, G., Stornaiuolo, A., & Sahni, U. (2010). Cultural citizenship and cosmopolitan practice: Global youth communicate online. *English Education, 42*(4), 331–367.

Janks, H. (2020). Critical literacy in action: Difference as a force for positive change. *Journal of Adolescent & Adult Literacy, 63*(5), 569–572.

Kahn, R. (2009). *Critical pedagogy, ecoliteracy, & planetary crisis: The ecopedagogy movement.* Peter Lang.

Kendrick, M. (2016). *Literacy and multimodality across global sites.* Routledge. (Literacies Series). www.routledge.com/products/9780415859790

Kim, G. M. (2016). Transcultural digital literacies: Cross-border connections and self-representations in an online forum. *Reading Research Quarterly, 51*(2), 199–219. doi: 10.1002/rrq.131

King, J. E. (2017). 2015 AERA Presidential Address: Morally engaged research/ers dismantling epistemological nihilation in the age of impunity. *Educational Researcher, 46*(5), 211–222. doi: 10.3102/0013189X17719291

Kubota, R. (2009). Internationalization of universities: Paradoxes and responsibilities. *Modern Language Journal, 93*(4), 612–616.

Kubota, R., & Lehner, A. (2004). Toward critical contrastive rhetoric. *Journal of Second Language Writing, 13*(1), 7–27. doi: 10.1016/j.jslw.2004.04.003

Lam, W. S. E. (2013). Multilingual practices in transnational digital contexts. *TESOL Quarterly, 47*(4), 820–825. doi: 10.1002/tesq.132

Lam, W. S. E. (2014). Literacy and capital in immigrant youths' online networks across countries. *Learning, Media and Technology, 39*(4), 488–506. doi: 10.1080/17439884.2014.942665

Lam, W. S. E., Warriner, D. S., Poveda, D., & Gonzalez, N. (2012). Transnationalism and literacy: Investigating the mobility of people, languages, texts, and practices in contexts of migration. *Reading Research Quarterly, 47*(2), 191–215. doi: 10.1002/RRQ.016

Lather, P. (1986). Issues of validity in openly ideological research: Between a rock and a soft place. *Interchange, 17*(4), 63–84. doi: 10.1007/BF01807017

Leander, K. M., & Ehret, C. (Eds.). (2019). *Affect in literacy learning and teaching: Pedagogies, politics and coming to know.* Routledge.

Le Grange, L. (2015). Ubuntu/botho as ecophilosophy and ecosophy. *Journal of Human Ecology, 49*(3), 301–308.

Li, G. (2006). *Culturally contested pedagogy: Battles of literacy and schooling between mainstream teachers and Asian immigrant parents.* SUNY Press.

Lo, L. N. (1991). State patronage of intellectuals in Chinese higher education. *Comparative Education Review, 35*(4), 690–720. doi: 10.1086/447070

Luke, A. (2011). Generalizing across borders: Policy and the limits of educational science. *Educational Researcher, 40*(8), 367–377. doi: 10.3102/0013189X11424314

Luke, A., Shield, P., Théroux, P., Tones, M., & Villegas, M. (2012). *Knowing and teaching the Indigenous other: Teachers' engagement with Aboriginal and Torres Strait Islander cultures* (Research report from Australian Commonwealth Government, Department of Employment, Education and Workplace Relations for the evaluation of the Stronger Smarter Learning Communities Project, 2009–2013). eprints.qut.edu.au/53510/2/53510.pdf

Mahuika, R. (2008). Kaupapa Maori theory is critical and anti-colonial. *MAI Review 3*, Article 4. www.review.mai.ac.nz

Manzon, M. (2011). *Comparative education: The construction of a field.* Hong Kong: Comparative Education Research Centre. doi: 10.1007/978-94-007-1930-9

Maracle, L. (1993). *Ravensong.* Press Gang Publishers.

Martin, F., & Rizvi, F. (2014). Making Melbourne: Digital connectivity and international students' experience of locality. *Media, Culture & Society, 36*(7), 1016–1031. doi: 10.1177/0163443714541223

Medina, C. L., & Wohlwend, K. E. (2014). *Literacy, play and globalization: Converging imaginaries in children's critical and cultural performances.* Routledge.

Misiaszek, G. W. (2015). Ecopedagogy and citizenship in the age of globalisation: Connections between environmental and global citizenship education to save the planet. *European Journal of Education, 50*(3), 280–292. doi: 10.1111/ejed.12138

Misiaszek, G. W. (2018). *Educating the global environmental citizen: Understanding ecopedagogy in local and global contexts.* Routledge.

Moll, L. C., Amanti, C., Neff, D., & Gonzalez, N. (1992). Funds of knowledge for teaching: Using a qualitative approach to connect homes and classrooms. *Theory into Practice, 31*(2), 132–141. doi: 10.1080/00405849209543534

Morgan, B. (2019). Beyond the guest paradigm: Eurocentric education and aboriginal peoples in NSW. In E. A. McKinley & L. T. Smith (Eds.), *Handbook of Indigenous education* (pp. 111–128). Springer Singapore. doi: 10.1007/978-981-10-3899-0_60

Mullis, I. V. S., Martin, M. O., Foy, P., Hooper, M., International Association for the Evaluation of Educational Achievement (IEA), & Boston College, TIMSS & PIRLS International Study Center. (2017a). *PIRLS 2016 International results in reading.* International Association for the Evaluation of Educational Achievement.

Mullis, I. V. S., Martin, M. O., Foy, P., Hooper, M., International Association for the Evaluation of Educational Achievement (IEA), & Boston College, TIMSS & PIRLS International Study Center. (2017b). *ePIRLS 2016: International results in online informational reading.* International Association for the Evaluation of Educational Achievement.

Nakata, M. (2001). Another window on reality. In B. Osborne (Ed.), *Teaching diversity and democracy* (pp. 331–353). Common Ground Publishing.

Nakata, M. (2004). Ongoing conversations about Aboriginal and Torres Strait Islander research agendas and directions. *Australian Journal of Indigenous Education, 33*(2004), 1–6. doi: 10.1017/S1326011100600807

Nakata, M. (2007). *Disciplining the savages: Savaging the disciplines.* Aboriginal Studies Press.

National Reading Conference. (2008). *NRC resolutions concerning publication of scholarship in on-line, open- access outlets.* https://www.literacyresearchassociation.org/assets /docs/Websitedocs/nrc_digital%20publication_ad%20hoc%20resolution%20dec%20 2008.pdf

Nederveen Pieterse, J. (2009). *Globalization and culture: Global mélange* (2nd ed.). Rowman & Littlefield.

Nelson, N., Barrera, E. S., Skinner, K., & Fuentes, A. M. (2016). Language, culture and border lives: Mestizaje as positionality/Lengua, cultura y vidas de frontera: El mestizaje como posicionalidad. *Cultura y Educación, 28*(1), 1–41. doi: 10.1080/11356405.2014.980121

Norton, B. (2000). *Identity and language learning: Gender, ethnicity and educational change.* Longman/Pearson Education.

Norton, B., & Early, M. (2011). Researcher identity, narrative inquiry, and language teaching research. *TESOL Quarterly*, Special Issue: Narrative Research in TESOL.

Norton, B., & Tembe, J. (2020). Teaching multilingual literacy in Ugandan classrooms: The promise of the African Storybook. *Applied Linguistics Review.* doi: 10.1515/ applirev-2020-2006

Nozaki, Y. (2009). Orientalism, the West and non-West binary, and postcolonial perspectives in cross-cultural research and education. In M. Apple, W. Au, & L. Gandin (Eds.), *The Routledge international handbook of critical education* (pp. 382–390). Routledge. doi: 10.4324/9780203882993

Nussbaum, M. C. (1994). Patriotism and cosmopolitanism. *Boston Review, XIX*(5), 3–16.

Nussbaum, M. C. (1997). *Cultivating humanity: A classical defense of reform in liberal education.* Harvard University Press.

Ocholla, D. (2007). Marginalized knowledge: An agenda for Indigenous knowledge development and integration with other forms of knowledge. *International Review of Information Ethics, 7*, 236–245. www.i-r-i-e.net/inhalt/007/26-ocholla.pdf

Onukaogu, C. (2011, August). *Literacy and transparent elections in Africa: Lessons, issues and challenges of the Nigerian experience.* Paper presented at the 9th Pan African Literacy Conference, Gaborone, Botswana.

Oxley, L., & Morris, P. (2013). Global citizenship: A typology for distinguishing its multiple conceptions. *British Journal of Educational Studies, 61*(3), 301–325. doi: 10.1080/00071005.2013.798393

Parata H., & Gardiner, H. (2020, September 19). Letter to Rt Hon Sir Anand Satyanand Chancellor Te Whare Wānanga o Waikato investigating racism. www.waikato.ac.nz /major-projects/taskforce/Parata-Gardiner-Report.pdf

Pashby, K., da Costa, M., Stein, S., & Andreotti, V. (2020). A meta-review of typologies of global citizenship education. *Comparative Education, 56*(2), 144–164. doi: 10.1080/03050068.2020.1723352

Perry, M. (2018). Unpacking the imaginary in literacies of globality. *Discourse: Studies in the Cultural Politics of Education, 41*(4), 574–586. doi: 10.1080/01596306.2018 .1515064

Perry, M. (2020). Pluriversal literacies: Affect and relationality in vulnerable times. *Reading Research Quarterly*. doi: 10.1002/rrq.312

Perry, M., & Pullanikkatil, D. (2019). Transforming international development. *Impact, 2019*(9), 30–32.

Popkewitz, T. S., & Rizvi, F. (2009). Globalization and the study of education. *Yearbook of the National Society for the Study of Education, 108*(2), 1–3. doi: 10.1111/j.1744-7984 .2009.01157.x

Postlethwaite, T. N., & Ross, K. N. (1992, November). *Effective schools in reading: Implications for educational planners: An exploratory study.* The International Association for the Evaluation of Educational Achievement.

Preston, R. G. (1962). The reading achievement of German and American students. *School and Society, 90*, 350–354.

Purcell-Gates, V. (2007). *Cultural practices of literacy: Case studies of language, literacy, social practice, and power.* Erlbaum.

Purves, A. (1973). *Literature education in ten countries: An empirical study. International Studies in Evaluation.* National Council of Teachers of English.

Reinking, D. (1996). Reclaiming a scholarly ethic: Deconstructing "intellectual property" in a post-typographic world. In D. J. Leu, C. K. Kinzer, & K. A. Hinchman (Eds.), *Literacies for the 21st Century: Research and practice. 45th yearbook of the National Reading Conference* (pp. 461–470). National Reading Conference.

Rigney, D., Bignall, S., & Hemming, S. (2015). Negotiating indigenous modernity. Kungun Ngarrindjeri Yunnan—Listen to Ngarrindjeri speak. *Alternative, 11*(4), 334–349.

Rigney, L., & Hattam, R. J. (2018, April). *Toward a decolonizing culturally responsive pedagogy?* Paper presented at the American Educational Research Association annual meeting, New York.

Rizvi, F. (2009a). Towards cosmopolitan learning. *Discourse: Studies in the Cultural Politics of Education, 30*(3), 253–268.

Rizvi, F. (2009b). Global mobility and the challenges of educational research and policy. *Yearbook of the National Society for the Study of Education, 108*(2), 268–289. doi: 10.1111/j.1744-7984.2009.01172.x

Rizvi, F., & Lingard, B. (2010). *Globalizing education policy.* Routledge. doi: 10.4324/9780 203867396

Robertson, R. (1992). *Globalization: Social theory and global culture.* SAGE.

Robertson, S. L., & Dale, R. (2009). The World Bank, the IMF, and the possibilities of critical education. In M. Apple, W. Au, & L. Gandin (Eds.), *The Routledge international handbook of critical education* (pp. 23–35). Routledge. doi: 10.4324/9780203882993

Rogers, R. (2017, November 29). *Literacy research, racial consciousness, and equitable flows of knowledge.* Presidential address at the Literacy Research Association, Tampa, FL. www.youtube.com/watch?v=1oyZ2altlqk

Rogers, T., Winters, K. L., Perry, M., & LaMonde, A. M. (2015). *Youth, critical literacies, and civic engagement.* Routledge.

Said, E. W. (1979). *Orientalism.* Vintage Books.

Said, E. W. (1993). *Culture and imperialism.* Knopf.

Sailors, M., Hoffman, J. V., Goia, E., Ngomane, J., Sitoe, A., & Modesto, H. (2019). Affordances of mentoring on preservice teacher language and literacy learning in Mozambique. *Journal of Adolescent & Adult Literacy, 63*(2), 127–133.

Sailors, M., Hoffman, J. V., & International Literacy Association. (2018). *Literacy coaching for change: Choices matter.* International Literacy Association.

Santos, B. de Sousa. (2007). Beyond abyssal thinking: From global lines to ecologies of knowledges. *Review-Fernand Braudel Center for the Study of Economies, Historical Systems, and Civilizations, 30*(1), 45–89.

Santos, B. de Sousa. (Ed.). (2008). *Another knowledge is possible: Beyond Northern epistemologies*. Verso.

Santos, B. de Sousa. (2013). *Epistemologies of the south: Justice against epistemicide*. Paradigm. doi: 10.4324/9781315634876

Schattle, H. (2008). Education for global citizenship: Illustrations of ideological pluralism and adaptation. *Journal of Political Ideologies, 13*(1), 73–94. doi: 10.1080/13569310701 822263

Schriewer, J. (2004). Multiple internationalities: The emergence of a word-level ideology and the persistence of idiosyncratic world-views. In C. Charle, J. Schriewer, & P. Wagner (Eds.), *Transnational intellectual networks: Forms of academic knowledge and the search for cultural identities* (pp. 473–533). Campus Verlag.

Schriewer, J., & Martinez, C. (2004). Constructions of internationality in education. In G. Steiner-Khamsi (Ed.), *The global politics of educational borrowing and lending* (pp. 29–53). Teachers College.

Schulte, B. (2004). East is east and West is west? Chinese academia goes global. In C. Charle, J. Schriewer, & P. Wagner (Eds.), *Transnational intellectual networks: Forms of academic knowledge and the search for cultural identities* (pp. 307–322). Campus Verlag.

Scribner, S., & Cole, M. (1981). *The psychology of literacy*. Harvard University Press.

Seda Santana, I. (2000). Literacy research in Latin America. In R. Barr, M. Kamil, P. Mosenthal, & P. D. Pearson (Eds.), *Handbook of research in reading* (pp. 41–52). Erlbaum.

Shi, L. (2012). Rewriting and paraphrasing source texts in second language writing. *Journal of Second Language Writing, 21,* 134–148.

Shi, Z., & Li, C. (2018). Bourdieu's sociological thinking and educational research in Mainland China. In Mu, G.M., Dooley, K. & Luke, A. (Eds.), *Bourdieu and Chinese education* (pp. 45–61). Routledge.

Shu, H., Anderson, R. C., & Zhang, H. (1995). Incidental learning of word meanings while reading: A Chinese and American cross-cultural study. *Reading Research Quarterly, 30*(1), 76–95.

Singh, M., Fenway, J., & Apple, M. (2005). Globalizing education: Perspectives from above and below. In M. Apple, J. Fenway, & M. Singh (Eds.), *Globalizing education: Policies, pedagogies and politics* (pp. 1–30). Peter Lang.

Smith, G. H. (1990). Research issues related to Maori education, paper presented to NZARE Special Interest Conference, Massey University, reprinted in 1992, *The Issue of Research and Maori*, Research Unit for Maori Education, the University of Auckland. www.rangahau.co.nz/research-idea/27/

Smith, G. H. (2000). Protecting and respecting Indigenous knowledge. In M. Battiste (Ed.), *Reclaiming Indigenous voice and vision* (pp. 209–224). University of British Columbia Press.

Smith, G. H. (2015, April). Transforming research: The Indigenous struggle for social, cultural, and economic justice within and through education. Paper presented at The American Educational Research Association Annual Meeting, Chicago, IL.

Smith, L. T. (1999). *Decolonising methodologies: Research and Indigenous peoples*. University of Otago Press.

Smith, L. T. (2005). On tricky ground: Researching the Native in the age of uncertainty. In N. K. Denzin & Y. S. Lincoln (Eds.), *The SAGE handbook of qualitative research* (3rd ed., pp. 85–108). SAGE.

Song, A. Y. (2020). An ethico-onto-epistemological approach to literacy research. *Journal of Literacy Research, 52*(2), 231–237.

Sovereign Union. (2019). "Uluru statement from the heart"—Wording and video reading (from the Referendum Council at Uluru, May 26, 2017), Sovereign Union: First Nations Asserting Sovereignty (website). nationalunitygovernment.org/content/uluru-statement-heart

Spivak, G. C. (1990). *The post-colonial critic: Interviews, strategies, dialogues.* Routledge.

Spivak, G. C. (1999). *A critique of postcolonial reason: Toward a critique of the vanishing present.* Harvard University Press.

Stein, S. (2015). Mapping global citizenship. *Journal of College and Character, 16*(4), 242–252. doi: 10.1080/2194587x.2015.1091361

Stein, S. (2017). The persistent challenges of addressing epistemic dominance in higher education: Considering the case of curriculum internationalization. *Comparative Education Review, 61*(Suppl. 1), S25–S50.

Stornaiuolo, A., & Nichols, T. P. (2019). Cosmopolitanism and education. *Oxford encyclopedia of education, online.* www.academia.edu/39153381/Cosmopolitanism_and_Education?email_work_card=view-paper

Stornaiuolo, A., Smith, A., & Phillips, N. C. (2017). Developing a transliteracies framework for a connected world. *Journal of Literacy Research, 49*(10) 68–91.

Stornaiuolo, A., & Thomas, E. E. (2018). Restorying as political action: Authoring resistance through youth media arts, *Learning, Media and Technology, 43*(4), 345–358. doi: 10.1080/17439884.2018.1498354

Takayama, K. (2009). Progressive education and critical education scholarship in Japan: Toward the democratization of critical educational studies. In M. Apple, W. Au, & L. Gandin (Eds.), *The Routledge international handbook of critical education* (pp. 354–367). Routledge. doi: 10.4324/9780203882993

Takayama, K., Sriprakash, A., & Connell, R. (2017). Toward a postcolonial comparative and international education. *Comparative Education Review, 61*(S1), S1–S24. doi: 10.1086/690455

Talmy, S. (2015). A language socialization perspective on identity work of ESL youth in a superdiverse high school classroom. In N. Markee (Ed.), *Handbook of classroom discourse and interaction* (pp. 353–368). Wiley Blackwell.

Thorndike, R. L. (1973) *Reading comprehension education in fifteen countries. International Studies in Evaluation,* Halstead Press.

Tierney, R. J. (2018a). Toward a model of global meaning making. *Journal of Literacy Research, 50*(4), 1–26. independent.academia.edu/RobTierney/Papers

Tierney, R. J. (2018b). Global educational research in Western times: The rise and plight of China. *Frontiers of Education in China, 13*(2),163–192. www.academia.edu/37171936/Global_Educational_Research_in_Western_Times_The_Rise_and_Plight_of_Chinese_Educational_Research

Tierney, R. J. (2020). Notes on global reading: Critical cultural traversals, transactions and transformations. In L. I. Misiaszek (Ed.) *Exploring the complexities in global citizenship education: Hard spaces, methodologies, and ethics* (pp. 36–68). Routledge. www.academia.edu/40450420/Notes_on_global_reading_critical_cultural_traversals_transactions_and_transformations

Tierney, R. J., & Kan, W. (2016). Knowledge globalization within and across the People's Republic of China and the United States: A cross-national study of internationalization of educational research in the early 21st century. *American Educational Research Journal,* *53*(6), 1759–1791. doi: 10.3102/0002831216678320

Torres, C. A. (2015). Global citizenship and global universities: The age of global interdependence and cosmopolitanism. *European Journal of Education, 50*(3), 262–279. doi: 10.1111/ejed.12129

Trigos-Carrillo, L., & Rogers, R. (2018). Latin American influences on multiliteracies: From epistemological diversity to cognitive. *Literacy Research: Theory, Method, and Practice,* *66*(1), 373–388.

Truth and Reconciliation Commission of Canada. (2015). *Honouring the truth, reconciling* *for the future: Summary of the final report of the Truth and Reconciliation Commission* *of Canada.* www.trc.ca

United Nations, Australian Human Rights Commission, & National Congress of Australia's First Peoples. (2013). *United Nations Declaration on the Rights of Indigenous Peoples:* Adopted by the United Nations General Assembly on 13 September 2007. www.un.org /esa/socdev/unpfii/documents/DRIPS_en.pdf

United Nations Conference on Trade and Development. (2006). *Information economy report: 2006.* United Nations.

United Nations Educational, Scientific and Cultural Organization (UNESCO). (2015). *Global citizenship education: Topics and learning objectives.* UNESCO. unesdoc.unesco .org/images/0023/002329/232993e.pdf

Vickers, E. (2018). Book review: The strong state and curriculum reform, edited by Leonel Lim and Michael W. Apple, with response from the book's contributors. *London Review of Education,* 16(*2*): 336–344. doi: doi.org/10.18546/LRE.16.2.12

Wagner, D. A. (2011). What happened to literacy? Historical and conceptual perspectives on literacy in UNESCO. *International Journal of Educational Development, 31*(3), 319–323.

Wagner, D. A. (2017). Children's reading in low-income countries. *The Reading Teacher,* *71*(2), 127–133.

Wagner, D. A. (2018a). Technology for education in low-income countries: Supporting the UN Sustainable Development Goals. In I. Lubin (Ed.), *ICT-supported innovations in* *small countries and developing regions: Perspectives and recommendations for international education* (pp. 51–74). Springer.

Wagner, D. A. (2018b). *Learning as development: Rethinking international education in a* *changing world.* Routledge.

Wagemaker, H., Polydorides, G., & Martin, M. (Eds.). (1994). *Gender differences in reading.* IEA, The Hague, The Netherlands.

Willinsky, J. (1998). *Learning to divide the world: Education at empire's end.* University of Minnesota Press.

Willinsky, J. (2005). *The access principle: The case for open access to research and scholarship.* MIT Press.

World Conference on Education for All: Meeting Basic Learning Needs. (1990). *World declaration on education for all and framework for action to meet basic learning needs.* Adopted by the World Conference on Education for All: Meeting Basic Learning Needs, Jomtien, Thailand, 5–9 March 1990. Inter-Agency Commission (UNDP, UNESCO, UNICEF, World Bank) for the World Conference on Education for All.

World Summit on the Information Society, Stauffacher, D., Kleinwächter, W., & United Nations ICT Task Force. (2005). *The World Summit on the Information Society: Moving from the past into the future*. UN.

Zhang, J., Lin, T.-J., Wei, J., & Anderson, R. C. (2014). Morphological awareness and learning to read Chinese and English. In X. Chen, Q. Wang, & Y. C. Luo (Eds.), *Reading development and difficulties of monolingual and bilingual Chinese children* (pp. 3–22). Springer.

Other Internet Resources

Active mobile broadband subscriptions per 100 inhabitants (Graph illustrating growth of mobile devices, smartphones). en.wikipedia.org/wiki/Mobile_phone#/media/File:Active_mobile_broadband_subscriptions_2007-2014.svg

DeCarlo, S. (Ed.). The *Fortune* global 500. *Fortune*. fortune.com/global500/

Global Internet usage (Wikipedia page entry). en.wikipedia.org/wiki/Global_Internet_usage

Knowledge economic index (Wikipedia page entry). en.wikipedia.org/wiki/Knowledge_Economic_Index

List of social networking websites (Wikipedia page entry). en.wikipedia.org/wiki/List_of_social_networking_websites

Matthews, C. (2014, October 5). Fortune 5: The most powerful economic empires of all time. *Fortune*. fortune.com/2014/10/05/most-powerful-economic-empires-of-all-time/

NOTES

1. Nussbaum's (1997) approach to cosmopolitanism is critical and tied to an orientation that is aligned with a politic of a common humanity that is committed to diversity—as she notes, "recognizing the equal humanity of the alien and the other" (p. 24). But some would suggest that her approach has the potential to be culturally bound in ways that are prescribed rather than relative to different cultural ways of knowing—that is, counter to a cosmopolitanism that embraces postcolonial theory or other viewpoints that position time, space, and materiality quite differently.

2. Interestingly, in Canada, pertinent and relevant ethical guidelines for international work are oftentimes connected with Indigenous ethics. For example, the Canadian government's research guidelines clearly identify the guidelines for international work as being tied to the principles governing research with First Nations communities in Canada (see ethics.gc.ca/eng/home.html).

3. The term *pluriversal* was traced to a meeting in Chiapas when Indigenous persons decrying their displacement rallied behind a plea for a world that embraces diverse lands and their peoples, or as they stated, "*un mundo donde quepan muchos mundos*," or a world in which many worlds fit.

Part III

EBB AND FLOW

12 **Research Currents**

WAVES OF LITERACY RESEARCH FRAMES, METHODS, AND CLAIMS

The history of reading/literacy research (in terms of theoretical frames and methodology) is tantamount to a tour of epistemological developments over the last 150 years. For whatever reason, literacy research has sparked the interest of a wide range of experts from various disciplines, including

- anthropologists, historians, and sociologists with interests from exploring the earliest uses of representation from tokens to print to studies of the dynamics of meaning making in the complexity of schools or the intricate networks supporting digital sense-making;
- linguists, psycholinguists and sociolinguists interested in language and social development;
- psychologists observing and delving into reading processes and the interrelationships among the variables identified;
- critical theorists pursuing systemic analyses and change using various lens; and
- teachers committed to meeting the needs of learners and advancing their reading abilities.

These explorations have occurred in every corner of the planet and enlisted various frames to do so (e.g., physiological, psychological, political, social, cultural, economic, linguistic). Hence, tracing these traditions also requires one to examine diverse epistemological frames, including positivism, post-positivism, post-structuralism, and various interpretive as well as critical frames. It is a journey across disciplines, across the different faculties within a university, and across the diverse areas of study associated with the rise of not only education as a discipline, but also reading, and now literacy, as a major preoccupation of teaching and learning.

Although modern incarnations of reading research have drawn from various traditions and movements, it is fair to conclude that psychology, in all of its sub-specializations, has exerted the most dominant influence on literacy studies, as indeed much of this volume documents. Since the 1950s continuing into the present day, there has been a strong emphasis on quasi-experimental work tied to psychological frames, though this work has increasingly been challenged by constructivist research and more recently socio-cultural-political analyses. Indeed, the history of literacy has experienced significant shifts that have been revolutionary in concert with shifts in the nature of literacy demands as well as the politics of knowledge. Research has shifted as our literacies have expanded, including becoming increasingly digital. At the same time, our understandings of literacy have advanced as researchers and theorists have responded to the challenges presented by positivism and behaviorism and the shifts emanating from cognitive, cultural, situative, and sociocultural variations. And the influences from other fields have been even more varied, embracing cultural, political, economic, philosophical, literary, interpretive, and critical frames.

HISTORICAL SNAPSHOTS

Snapshots of the history of literacy research over time can be found in a myriad of sources and scholarly analyses rooted in different traditions. In terms of reading and literacy, overviews of this field of research are apparent in occasional historical analyses of key works and some of their antecedents. In the last century, these include historical markers of developments in psychological and pedagogical studies of reading, such as Edmund Burke Huey's 1908 book, *The Psychology and Pedagogy of Reading*, which many deem the first attempt at an account of reading research. Yet there also exists an array of other important syntheses, such as William S. Gray's 1956 review for UNESCO, *The Teaching of Reading and Writing: An International Survey*; the annual reviews that accompanied the *Reading Research Quarterly* that first appeared in the 1960s; and various research syntheses such as edited handbooks and government-sponsored initiatives focusing on theoretic models, theories of reading, and the gleaning of best practices.

Most recently, snapshots of the field have also included a number of bibliometric analyses of the journal articles found across key research journals in the field, which are now quite extensive. For example, a study by Parsons, Gallagher, and colleagues at George Mason University pursued analyses of the articles published between 2009 and 2014 in the nine leading reading research journals (Parsons et al., 2016). The research team found that there were over 1,200 articles published during this period. Yet what does this mean in terms of overall research activity? If we factor in data on acceptance rates and other journals, the number of reading/literacy research studies is estimated to be over 1,000 studies every year. In terms of theoretical frames and methodologies, the dominant psychological orientation appears to persist, albeit mixed with social constructivism. In terms of methodology, experimentation tied to quantitative student assessments likewise dominates.[1] It is also interesting to note that the leading journals are all Western (mostly from the United States), drawing from Western theorists. In a follow-up examination of scholarship in literacy, Parsons et al. (2020) expanded the number and scope of the journals that were reviewed and the nature of the analyses itself, especially to afford comparisons between journals predominantly intended for a research audience versus practitioner audience. Their findings reinforced some of what they had discerned earlier in terms of a wide of range of topics and the enlistment of a predominantly socio-constructivist perspective where the frame could be identified. Certainly, the journals intended for the research audience remained dominated by quantitative studies, although some journals seem more eclectic. Practitioner journals and the hybrid journals were not so dominated by any one approach, nor were they focused on decoding, phonemics, and spelling as many of the research journals have been. Especially for the practitioner journals, their analyses suggested there was some movement in the field away from the traditional comparative quantitative studies derived from a "simple view of reading" with its emphasis on decoding and assessing the effects of selected instructional approaches to a more sociocultural frame and critical literacies using a mix of paradigms with an emphasis on comprehension, multiple literacies, bilingual/ELL, and writing.

WAVES OF RESEARCH AND METHODOLOGICAL DEVELOPMENTS IN THE MODERN PERIOD

With the major shifts in the lenses enlisted by researchers and theorists, our understanding of literacy changed. In particular, the status, acceptability, and accommodation of different paradigms have shifted over time in conjunction with researchers seeking new illumination. For instance, the rise of constructivism coincided with the perceived failure of positivism to address complex issues in education and the behaviorist aversion to delving into meanings that were neither fixed nor measurable (e.g., the layers of meaning making that shape and define the cultures of learning, and how learning develops). Social constructivism acknowledged subjectivities, perspectival and situated descriptions of interactions, and the importance of participatory research. This emerged alongside a growing recognition of the power of qualitative studies to address complexities and capture the interactions among language, culture, and thought, within and across time and spaces, in multilayered and a multi-perspectival fashion.

At the same time, with these developments there has been considerable debate about the merits of one paradigm over another, or the possibility of their complementarity. Some positivists reject constructivism as true science—deeming it incompatible in terms of its views of knowledge as well as the logic and nature of its research pursuits. At times, positivist researchers have characterized constructivist research as flawed due to its acknowledged subjectivity, selectivity, and approach. Indeed, some have vehemently opposed the use of findings from constructivist research to guide policy or practices. Other scholars, however, accepted the clear differences in views of knowledge and science, as well as methodologies and findings—acknowledging the possibilities of the different contributions that might arise from a dialogue across approaches. Mostly, these scholars appeared to do so within a positivist or a post-positivist constructivist frame, enlisting the tools of another while remaining consistent with their epistemological orientation. In this regard, they strived to conjoin the approaches by enlisting either a mix of methodologies or a kind of hybridization of approaches, while acknowledging the merits of findings from both paradigms and being restrained about their claims, especially beyond the situation and nature of their study. For these reasons, it should be stressed that the contrast in these approaches is rooted in epistemological differences—in positivism versus constructivism. It is not quantitative versus qualitative—nor does it entail empirical versus nonempirical or interventionist versus noninterventionist methodologies. Rather, this debate stems from how researchers position themselves and their research pursuits, in terms of reasoning and knowledge claims.

METHODOLOGICAL WAVES

Across time, certain methodologies have predominated, beginning with an emphasis on correlational studies that later merged somewhat with quasi-experimental investigations and multiple correlational approaches. While these persist, in the late 1900s, a wave of socio-cultural-political perspectives surged in tandem with qualitative, formative, and design-based research as well as studies seeking transformative change.

Correlational Studies

Dating back to the advent of psychology as a field of study in the 1850s, the 1950s and 1960s saw a preoccupation with measurement—a preoccupation that gained momentum with a proliferation of tests designed to measure reading and other abilities. In turn, these tests spurred a large number of correlational studies examining the interrelationships among variables, such as comparing measures of student variables or teacher variables with measures of achievement to emphasize their relationship and interdependency. The logic seems to be to assess stability of association among these variables. While some studies focused on predictors of early reading development, others focused on reading comprehension and predictors (e.g., intelligence and vocabulary). Still others focused on broader teacher and student variables, such as years of experience, teacher knowledge, or the relationship between classroom engagements and achievement. As an early and comprehensive case, consider some of the analyses of the report of the Coordinating Center of the Cooperative Research Program in First-Grade Reading Instruction in the 1960s. Though coordinated by Guy Bond and Robert Dykstra, these analyses involved a number of the world's leading researchers—all in search of the best method of teaching beginning reading. In their study, as shown in Table 12.1., Bond and Dykstra (1967) reported a number of correlations among a host of predictor

Table 12.1. The Cooperative 1st-Grade Studies: Summary of Correlations Between Key Pre-Measures and the Stanford Paragraph Meaning Test for Each of the Six Treatments

Measures	Basal	Initial Teaching Alphabet	Basal + Phonics	Language Experience	Linguistic	Phonic/ Linguistic
Murphy Durrell Phonemes	.46	.53	.52	.41	.50	.57
Murphy Durrell Letters	.52	.58	.55	.51	.55	.59
Metropolitan Word Meaning	.30	.38	.44	.19	.27	.32
Metropolitan Listening	.23	.29	.38	.18	.27	.33
Pitner-Cunningham Intelligence Test	.42	.52	.56	.43	.48	.52

variables (e.g., letter names, letter sounds, auditory discrimination, visual discrimination) and between those predictors and end of 1st-grade achievement outcomes (scores on reading tests) across different beginning reading approaches. Even though Bond and Dykstra were careful to warn readers to refrain from attributing causal claims to these correlation associations, many publishers and practitioners appeared to be inspired by the strength and persistence of these correlations to develop curricula that emphasized teaching letter names and sounds systematically.

In accordance with the emerging concern that the teacher variable was key, studies then began to focus on measuring teacher and student behavior. The preoccupation with correlational analyses examining interrelationships between teacher and student behaviors and performance especially increased in the 1970s. Synthesizing a host of studies examining teachers and reading achievement, Rosenshine and Stevens (1984) repeatedly found that some variables seemed positively related to test performance. This included the amount of academic content covered, which correlated between .40 and .70, and a strong relationship between student engagement in academic activities (.30 and .40).[2]

Of course, correlational analyses do not confirm causality. But the strength of the relationship prompted an attention to the possibility of one variable's influence on another. Correlational studies went hand in hand with, or were often followed by, studies wrestling with causation—setting up comparisons to show that a difference might be due to shifts or differences in the comparison group. Unfortunately, most comparison groups were not purely one group or the other, and studies enlisting random assignments of individuals to groups for purposes of comparisons were not without their problems. For example, as the next section discusses, random assignments were often an awkward imposition on classrooms, and randomness was no assurance that differences did not exist across groups.

Nonetheless, the research did offer some insights simply as a result of pursuing the endeavor or by way of explaining the results.

Quasi-Experimental Comparative Studies of Treatments

Comparisons based on systematic comparisons (via the random assignment of subjects to conditions) were perceived by some as the aspirational gold standard for educational endeavors. The dilemma with such comparisons, however, is that they may not be feasible to set up and, if established, tend to reflect rarified circumstances.

Unlike laboratory scientists, educational researchers engage in the "real world" that requires them to both factor in and contend with a myriad of situation-specific issues. In the real world of educational research, most studies demand a careful crafting to local circumstances and depend on the access researchers are able to negotiate and likely any promises of non-obtrusiveness. Imagine you wanted to compare students who received intensive decoding instruction with those who received a meaning-centered orientation. The reality is that it is difficult to have such a random assignment of students or teachers. While students are usually pre-assigned to classes by schools and teachers, teachers normally cannot teach more than one class and be expected to employ different pre-set approaches set up for systematic comparisons. At a minimum, the fidelity to what normally occurs in the classroom in different ways may need to be checked. At the same time, the progress across the range of student learning will need to be monitored—especially with regard to abilities and experiences.

Apart from negotiating arrangements with school personnel, there are other matters to address, such as plans for ongoing data collection. Initially, most researchers conducting comparative studies enlisted standardized tests—until they recognized how insensitive such tests were to measuring changes, especially if developments were subtle. So they shifted to assessments focused on what was being taught and pursued in the classroom. If not more important, there was the inclusion of other measures (e.g., delayed post-tests, transfer measures) as researchers became increasingly focused on whether students retained what was taught, sustained their use of strategies and skills, and whether or not they might transfer newfound abilities to other reading or learning situations.

Once the data are collected, further consideration needs to be given to analyses. Assuming the data are in the form of interval data, a researcher might pursue a simple t-test for comparing groups on measures—or an analysis of variance, which can extend the comparison of groups across time and other variables, such as ability. Typically, researchers look for significant differences, usually at the .05 or .01 level, so that they can say that the groups are likely to be different with a level of confidence of approximately 95 or 99%. If the researcher finds that there are *interaction effects* (e.g., significant ability by treatment effects), the story of the differences includes a discussion of how the effects vary by the treatment and the variable (e.g., ability). Researchers may find, but rarely did, that the effects are not interactional but rather consistent, regardless of ability.

Shift to More Formative Studies

While experimental and quasi-experimental studies are still pursued today (in fact, in the United States, the Institute of Education Sciences places a high priority on both efficacy studies and randomized control trials as a prerequisite to policy recommendations for particular interventions), many researchers have shifted to approaches that are more fluid and nimble. A common approach within the 30-year-old field in the learning sciences, where it goes by the name of design research, as well as literacy studies, where it is more commonly called formative experimentation, is to frame a line of inquiry as an iterative time series of probes that enable the research team to draw inferences about facets of the learning phenomena under examination. The research team monitors developments as they proceed and makes adjustments based on what they are learning in real time. These approaches also enlist an array of measures—in the hopes of observing concurrent evidence of change (including changes in student strategies as revealed through introspective techniques such as think-alouds, etc.) as well as assessing how and to what extent students have changed independently and across situations. As the data may involve both interval measures and frequency data tied to categorical analyses, there is a need for both parametric and non-parametric analyses.[3]

In studies of the effectiveness of reading strategies, for example, comparisons might involve slight variations of the strategies and comparisons to a control group. These might include: pre- and post-measures, plus ongoing measures of learning during and after the intervention; a pedagogical protocol (involving teacher or student explanations, explorations, practices, etc.); explorations of the differences that occur across students of varying abilities or backgrounds; analyses to assess the effects of treatments over time and texts, across students of different abilities; a consideration of convergences (e.g., the relationship between think-alouds and classroom performance with the results of the measures); and a positioning of findings as *situated*—that is, representing findings as demonstrations rather than prescribed generalizations dependent on similarities in circumstances. In addition, studies were aligned with theoretical and other developments associated with the different waves (e.g., cognitive, learning to learn, social, critical). In studies of reading comprehension, measures of the reader's prior knowledge became commonplace as a schema theoretic orientation became dominant. As metacognition and learning to learn undergirded the pursuit of strategy research, so studies included multiple measures of effects beyond just measures of the immediate impact of interventions. Studies examined long-term effects in an effort to determine whether learnings were sustained over time and explored measures intended to assess any transfer or generalized learning that might have been spurred.

Qualitatively Oriented Research, Design-Based Studies, Longitudinal Research, Case Studies, Postpositivism, and Mixed Methods

As positivist approaches failed to address more complex classroom dynamics, along with a myriad of other facets to which researchers were attracted, many researchers began to shift to less constrained qualitative analyses. Interest in qualitatively oriented research, or mixed methods, also occurred as researchers shifted to studies of language development (e.g., literacy acquisition) and reading–writing connections (e.g., studies of comprehension and composing) and the social dynamics of learning. This shift seemed to initiate a period of discovery involving more intense, extensive, and creative observations and data that befit the research goal of understanding the ongoing meaning making of readers and writers and to search for ways to capture emergent possibilities. Recalls, retellings, think-alouds, and a host of different observation and probing techniques were pursued. As these were mostly open-ended, they demanded that the researcher be contemplative and discerning about how to view, analyze, code, and represent the data. Certainly, one might have counted some of the variables, but the open-ended data often offered much more. Mostly, there was a shift away from predetermined measures to approaches that might afford deeper and more complex considerations of the meaning making that might occur. Among the treasure troves of approaches were case studies of young learners as parents and educators pursued longitudinal studies of reading and writing development (e.g., Chomsky, 1969; Dyson, 1988; Ferreiro & Teberosky, 1982; Harste et al., 1984; King et al., 1981; Teale & Sulzby, 1986). They brought to the foreground the socio-cognitive and linguistic abilities and aptitudes of young learners as they negotiated and appropriated various literacies to meet their needs and expand their worlds.

Case Studies

Case studies became increasingly enlisted as stand-alone studies or as complements to multifaceted pursuits. They became used as an opportunity to engage in studies of one or more individuals or a group or groups to either provide illustrations, demonstrations, or perhaps to generate hypotheses or check on existing and looming possible generalizations. They could offer the possibility of providing descriptive details and observations in an effort to portray a learner in different circumstances en route to suggesting a possible frame of reference against which the learner might be profiled. Case studies might be used simply to detail characteristics of a learner and done in a way that includes situational specifics. Alternatively, it can be used in a way that befits more emergent formulations of themes or frames that might connect elements of the case. The approach to case studies requires a reiterative style of progressive refinement while enlisting social, cultural, linguistic, historical, and political considerations across time and space foregrounding elements and providing backgrounds so that one can discern the forest and the trees as well as one's material interactions. While case studies can focus on or incorporate data or measures including survey data, most case studies tend to be qualitative, pursuing descriptive detail. At times, they are coupled with other methods as they serve to spur or confirm other studies. In literacy research, case studies of learners, classrooms, and communities are commonplace with some exemplars that enlist socio-linguistic or socio-constructivist frames to guide both observations and analyses. Some exemplars include studies by Ann Haas Dyson (e.g., 1988), Douglas Hartman (1995), and Victoria Purcell-Gates and her colleagues (2011).

Longitudinal Studies

Longitudinal studies of literacy involving extended studies of one or more individuals or groups over time have proven themselves key to understanding development, moving us from speculation about changes to tracing them across time. As researchers enlisting longitudinal approaches will attest, they glean developmental insights from longitudinal investigations that studies simply comparing learners across ability level or ages will not provide—indeed, that might prove to be misguiding. Longitudinal studies involve an extended commitment involving close observations of learners over time enlisting the appropriate lens, samplings of behavior, different artifacts, and measures to do so repeatedly for purposes of comparison. In addition, they can involve measures and data for the same student or students across time and in ways that afford legitimate comparability. Such pursuits are not straightforward and require a major investment in time. However, the returns can be immense and offer new insights into the nature of development. Certainly, the field of literacy has been enriched significantly by breakthroughs from such studies across the ages—from studies of language acquisition, early reading and writing development, to reading to learn to advanced literacy development. Longitudinal studies have contributed significantly to our understandings of young learners' reading and writing development. Likewise, longitudinal studies of reading development across the elementary grades have highlighted the advantages of a meaning-centered approach over a code emphasis as students moved beyond the 3rd grade.

Postpositivist Frames

In contrast to enlisting a positivistic approach, researchers also became more interested in subjectivities and demonstrations of learning than in objectivity and generalizability. Essentially, research approaches shifted toward participatory, introspective, and explorative, rather than aiming for objective and definitive results. Increasingly, quasi-experimental work included observational studies enlisting qualitative tools, formative approaches, and measures such as retellings, think-alouds, or debriefings. Consultation with participants was thus seen

> In a number of his studies, Rob found debriefings to prove invaluable. As he states: "Debriefings can make the invisible visible. I would tell the students what I was exploring and ask them for feedback. The feedback was rich and illuminating. For example, in one study I presented some readers (identified as not-as-able readers when compared with others) with passages in which errors had been inserted (i.e., words or phrases that did not make sense in terms of the meaning). These readers did not appear to notice the errors as they read or recalled the text; however, once we debriefed them, they pointed out where they noticed the inserted errors" (Raphael & Tierney, 1981). In a study looking at the effects of reading and writing on critical thinking, such debriefings afforded corroboration that substantiated the key findings that reading and writing together contributed to thinking critically (Tierney et al., 1989).

as clarifying—correcting results rather than confounding or corrupting them. Retellings involved extensive analyses of what appeared to be explicit recall as well as researcher inferences and were often followed by debriefings with the students.

Essentially, as scholars delved into the role and nature of literacy within a sociocultural frame, they found themselves shifting paradigmatically. Observational engagements and conversations with readers and writers as they read and wrote enabled researchers to witness and, in turn, depict the layers of social negotiations and transactions within learners' heads and on paper—demonstrating the union of social networks with meaning-making processes and products over time. The raw research material involved detailed observations, which sometimes were dependent on video or recorded data, classroom artifacts, and researcher observations. And, despite the modest numbers of students being observed, there were massive amounts of data.

It is important to recognize that the shift in methodology encompassed a change in the knowledge claims that emanated from these pursuits. A constructivist approach is not driven to confirm but to understand, to postulate, and to discover. The researcher's knowledge and critical reflections are key and prominent factors as he or she interacts with participants and shares observations, discernments, and, for select cases, notes. Certainly, validity and reliability still matter, but they take different forms. The validity of data is tied to usability rather than generalizability and relies on the extent to which the data can be explained and for which it can be accounted. The reliability of data is evidenced by the verifiable, concrete manner of data presentation. That is not to say that there is no analysis; there is, rather, an inductively oriented form of reasoning with constructivist and phenomenological approaches as opposed to the deductive reasoning involved in positivist approaches.[4] Furthermore, there is a different approach to interpretation as different frames and lenses applied to the data function hand in hand with attempts to discern themes. At times, these interpretations lend themselves to examinations of the data via forms of transmediation—such as enlisting art, narrative, or poetry as a way of uncovering previously undisclosed meanings or interpretations (e.g., Irwin, 2008; Irwin & Springgay, 2008; Leggo, 2008; Norman, 2008; Springgay, 2008; Van Maanen, 1988). Some scholars prefer to view interpretivism as integral to going beyond phenomenology (e.g., Finlay, 2009).[5]

Mixed Methods, Model Building, and Path Analysis

Nowadays, a large number of studies incorporate a blend of the aforementioned approaches—combining observations and quantitative analyses with follow-up probes—a mix of focused comparisons of quantitative and qualitative data. In hopes of determining the relationship between variables based on their shared variances, model building is increasingly common. Building on multiple correlations between variables and their interrelationships with one another and recent advances in statistical methods, researchers have subjected data from their studies or data accessible in data repositories (e.g., national and state test and survey) to a range of multivariate analyses as a means of suggesting how salient variables are related to one another in a fashion akin to creating what has been described as path models. Oftentimes these models depicting the constellation are then checked for their applicability with a closer look at the interplay of variables through case studies or other forms of scrutiny. Consider a researcher interested in how reading and writing are related to other measures such as science achievement (D), mathematic ability (C), general reading ability (B) and critical thinking (A); they might examine how the data from a national pool generate correlations looking for the best fit between these variables. In the end, they develop a path model (see Figure 12.1) indicating the interrelationships that best coincide with accounting for their shared variances or intercorrelations.

Then, consistent with a mixed methods approach, a follow-up or verification of the model is pursued, perhaps with case studies to examine how these abilities work together for different students in different situations. Essentially, the follow-up serves two purposes: (1) to check on whether the model represents a reasonable fit to different cases or circumstances; and (2) to provide a more complex description of the relationship between the variables, at times highlighting the limitations and possible applications of the mathematically derived path model.

Perhaps not dissimilarly, models that pull together the interrelationships between variables are enlisted in attempts at syntheses or meta-analyses where researchers look across studies in an effort to extract if there are some common tendencies especially related to the effects of different practices across the different populations studied to date. For example, various researchers might have explored studies examining class size and its relationship to learning or different organizational structures within school, or the overall efficacy of different approaches to teaching and learning. A researcher might gather together a substantial corpus

Figure 12.1. Example of a General Path Model

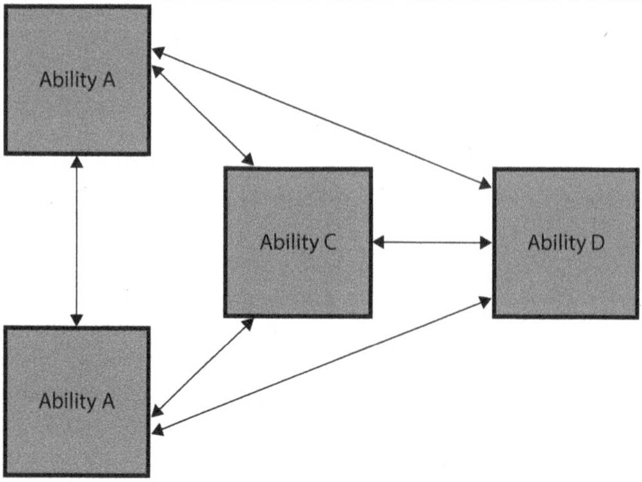

of studies exploring culturally responsive pedagogy and with it the effects on attitudes, values, and so on. They might look to see if they could determine from
these studies whether there are trends in the effect sizes across studies to declare
the overall worth of these practices. During a period of reform tied to mandating
best practices and evidence-based approaches, educators often defaulted to these
studies to guide this advocacy, and a number of researchers garnered reputations
for such pursuits (e.g., Hattie, 2008; Marsh et al., 2006).

Classroom-Based Mixed Methods

Oftentimes, classroom-based research follows other pathways—such as from close
study to larger studies. For example, both of us have been involved in a host of
studies that began with close observational work as a prelude to possible interventions. The observational work was key to unpacking some of the possible and plausible features of the interventions in an effort to get an early reading of the "active
ingredients" that might be most important to the efficacy of a multi-component
intervention. For example, following intensive close study of portfolios in a small
number of classrooms and in response to a large school district's effort to initiate
portfolio use as well as monitor its implementation and influences, Rob and his
colleagues set up a study comparing portfolio use across classrooms over time.
By implementing a staggered start approach, we were able to engage with and
compare classrooms initiating portfolio use with those classrooms that had yet
to enlist them (Tierney et al., 1991). David and his colleagues at the Lawrence
Hall of Science (Pearson & Billman, 2016) employed formative experiments to
determine which features of a 1st-grade literacy-in-science intervention showed

sufficient promise, as indexed by short-term probes, to make it into the first substantive version of the intervention. In this way, they went into the final version of the intervention with a set of features that all showed promise.

Similarly, the observational work done by Rob and his colleagues in the Apple Classrooms of Tomorrow enabled then to take note of the changing views of text, particularly as hypermedia tools for composing multimedia websites became available (Tierney et al., 1998). This blend of approaches also benefitted their collaborative observations and research on how reading and writing work together to enhance critical thinking. Following extensive and intensive observations that involved following and talking with students as they engaged in reading and writing projects, they engaged in a quasi-experimental pursuit, examining the combined effects of reading and writing on thinking critically (Tierney et al., 1989). To pursue this comparison, they selected topics that would likely provoke critical thinking and engage a reader. In terms of setup, they first asked students to write an essay on a topic. Following this exercise, they gave around 12 students the opportunity to read an editorial on the topic prior to being given a chance to revise. The remainder of the students were not provided with any reading to do—they were simply asked to write and revise. The two key elements that emerged were the writing that the students did, including the revisions (especially the various types of revisions), and the students' explanations of their thinking as they read, as they wrote, and as they revised. The analyses of the differences across the students in each case, with evidence from the revisions and debriefings, demonstrated the power of reading and writing in combination. Essentially, the reading and writing study offered what some might consider a mixed methods approach—combining a quasi-experimental approach with case studies of a range of rich, open-ended data for selected individuals from comparison groups. At that time, the hope was that this research design/approach appealed to a broader, more mixed audience of scholars, such as those with positivist leanings or constructivists interested in a more complex, organic approach that included a form of responsive evaluation. It was hoped that it met the standards of both groups. Again, however, despite the use of comparisons styled after positivism, the research approach was anchored in constructivist logic (e.g., having findings presented as situated demonstrations rather than overgeneralizations on a universe of readers and writers). While quantitative data were reported, they were represented in a fashion that was contextualized by rich examples.

Various forms of mixed methods have propagated over the last 30 years as theorists enlisting various tools and perspectives have borrowed from different theorists or searched for explanations that account for their observations. Increasingly, approaches to research design involve a mix of methods and approaches, which are participatory, critical, or verging on activism. Further, mixed research has also combined with efforts to be multi-perspective and fluid (e.g., through the transmediating function of using different modes to explore data, as with arts-based research or various digital representations, such as fluid animations of the ongoing, ever-changing states of factors including the agency of material objects).

Critical Analyses, Reflexivity, and Participatory Research

As qualitative research and the social turn advanced, increasing numbers of re-searchers identified and made visible the social processes and political dynamics in operation by the enlistment of analyses involving social, cultural, critical and postcolonial critiques. To these ends, various forms of sociological analyses, often enlisting forms of discourse analyses, were pursued in the interests of examining the forces at work—norms, conventions, representations, positioning. Oftentimes, they were examined enlisting various frames to do so—especially critical ones such as cultural constructions, gender considerations, racial and ethnic matters. In turn, they served to unpack the dynamics of such as hegemonies or power rela-tions in play (e.g., Bloome & Green, 2015; Bourdieu & Thompson, 1991; Cook-Gumperz & Gumperz, 1992; Dyson, 1988;. Gee, 1990; Gilmore & Marshall, 2019; Gutiérrez, 2008; Heath, 1983; Marshall, 2018; McDermott, 1974; Philips, 1983; Purcell-Gates, 1995; Purcell-Gates et al., 2011; Rex et al., 2010; Scribner & Cole, 1981).

At a more macro level, a number of critical theorists have engaged with stud-ies of education in conjunction with critiques of education and power as well as studies involving counter-hegemonic pursuits (i.e., recognition, redistribution, mobilization, resistance, empowerment, and other forms of activism tied to trans-formative goals). In the West, the work of Marxist theorists, such as Michael Apple, are especially notable (see Apple, 2010, 2012, 2014; Apple et al., 2009; Apple et al., 2010), along with the initiatives of African American, feminist, queer theorist, and indigenous scholars, as well as those examining youth resistance (e.g., Tuck & Yang, 2014). Also, in terms of transformative approaches, the work on teacher action research advanced by academics such as Schön (1983), Kincheloe (2003), Shor (1980), McNiff (1993, 2013) and classroom teachers (e.g., Lassonde & Israel, 2008) has been exemplary.

These sociocultural lenses were employed so researchers were not spared from turning a critical lens on themselves—interrogating their positioning and the eth-ics and integrity of research approaches. These critiques reframed and questioned the notion of a fair witness divested of cultural moorings, encouraging researchers to look beyond being empathetic or antagonistic to adopting approaches that are responsible, respectful, reciprocal, participatory, democratic, and reflexive relative to their biases, backgrounds, motives, and so on.

Emerging from these developments are new expectations for research, espe-cially studies involving teacher action or inquiry-driven studies and other forms of democratic, action-oriented research approaches. These expectations befit a critical turn that requires researchers to direct the lens on themselves and ap-proach research with an ethic and consciousness of not only self but also others. In the mid-1980s, those who were the objects of anthropological research spoke back and questioned not just how they had been positioned in studies but also how their cultures were being described in ways that sometimes reflected colo-nialist and racist tendencies. More recently, Takayama et al. (2017), in conjunction with critiques of comparative education, suggested that research findings were blinkered by Northern construction of other cultures and perpetuated colonial construction. Along with indigenous scholars and others, Takayama et al. argue for an approach to research *of* others, *with* others—that is, research conducted under the control of Indigenous persons and in a manner that is respectful, consultative, and engaging with regard to communities. Patti Lather (1986) offered a similar critique of key ethnographic work—arguing that while it may have been empathetic and rigorous, it failed to add the possibility of transformative goals with participants. She offered the term "catalytic validity" (Lather, p. 67) as a way of highlighting the importance of both researcher and participant engagement together as a form of member checking, "responsive evaluation," or shared transformational pursuits.

Despite the advent of socially transformative and activist research in the interests of others, such research sometimes crosses ethical boundaries especially when respect and consultation and a community and participants' interests are displaced by the researcher's interests and approach. Research endeavors can move beyond local interests to serve the interests of others as if the research itself is a commodity (i.e., if the ownership is transferred to the researcher and to the academic outlets or policymakers that operate outside of the community).

With teacher research, the relationship to practice is transparent. The position of teacher as decisionmaker becomes prominent and, in some ways, radical, especially when contrasted with top-down reform efforts or outside, pre-set, interventionist approaches. However, teacher research is not always straightforward. It often requires developing a teacher's trust as well as their confidence in their decisionmaking, reflections, and students.

In the 1980s, Rob and David (Tierney et al., 1988) collaborated with colleagues from the Center for the Study or Reading and an Illinois State University (in Bloomington-Normal) team comprised of Professor David Tucker in reading education and several K-6 teaching faculty at the Lab School in a teacher research community. Each teacher teamed up with a research partner to undertake a unique teacher research project. The research projects were interesting in their own right, but the most important finding from the study was the value of the teacher research community as a catalyst for professional development and teacher learning.

In Rob's collaborations attempting to advance teacher-based inquiry in student-directed learning environments in the United States and China (Tierney, 2015; Tierney et al., 1988), he found it key to have teachers reflect positively on their endeavors as they consider what they wish their students to pursue. If they focus too much on their behaviors rather than on their goals for their students, teachers tend to become more inhibited in their thinking. For example, if the goal is to advance students' access and sharing of ideas, the teacher would be encouraged to explore how to engage the students in doing so rather than focusing extensively on their own behaviors. Should they seek the researcher's counsel, advice should be provided in a way that engages the teacher in reflexivity and decisionmaking and avoids judgment or direction. The research goal is to work with what the teachers are already pursuing, not with what others might impose. Hence, such research begins in classrooms, wherein researchers talk about the possibilities and observe and reflect on students in a way that is formative rather than evaluative. The goal is transformative and the approach is established in a manner whereby change and impact are not afterthoughts, but integral to the pursuit from the outset. The orientation is participatory and responsive—befitting forms of democratic processes. Table 12.2 differentiates formative teacher inquiry from outsider research.

In a different fashion, project evaluation research and development may also be closely aligned with transformational and formative goals. At times, the collective possibility of change from such evaluation is thwarted depending on how the evaluation is positioned, especially if existing systemic forces and values subvert the pursuit. For example, Rob, other deans, and staff were asked to evaluate the state of Indigenous education at the University of Sydney as a basis for setting future directions (SEG Indigenous Education Review Working Group, 2010). The approach involved iterative consultation and frequent data mining from various

Table 12.2. Dimensions Contrasting Outsider A Priori Oriented Research vs. Formative Teacher Inquiry

	Outsider Research	Teacher-Researcher
Goal setting	Pre-set questions and goals by researcher(s)	Emergent classroom-based interests, concerns, questions by teacher(s)
Method	Uniform Standardized protocols Imposed on circumstances	Customized shaped by classroom teacher(s) and ongoing pursuits Adapted to situation
Participants	Assigned predesigned tasks	Designed and formative learning engagements fitted to students' interests, ongoing learning, and teaching pursuits
Measures	Primarily pre-set and standardized	Mixture of some pre-set and some emerging
Observations	Predetermined	Ongoing and recursive
Findings	Pronouncements of measurable and objective outcomes	Iterative consideration of processes and outcomes (likely to be qualitative and quantitative) and related to feedback afforded by students and others en route to follow-up for purposes of meeting teachers' perceived discernments of students' needs
Conclusions	Seeking generalizable or transferable findings to other situations	Tentative and tied to situation including approach to exploration

sources, including sources embedded in the academic units under our review. The goal was to develop a document that would inspire stakeholder confidence, as well as generate data that would be useful both broadly and to specific units within the university. Hence, the data was intended to be useful for students, the Indigenous community, the faculties within the university, and for administrators. To afford a comparative understanding, the data presented several years in terms of participation and completion of degree programs by Aboriginal and Torres Strait Islanders within the different faculties, as well as in terms of the hiring and retention of Aboriginal and Torres Strait Islanders within the university. Such data was then compared with data for students from different ethnicities as well as for universities across Australia. The final document was intended to spur deliberative and transformative change by the university and the various units within the university. It did and did not. Although it was seen as an invaluable resource, there were regressive institutional forces aligned with deep-seated interests in approaches that were not transformative but aligned with assimilative models that maintain existing colonial vestiges.

There are a range of other examples of advocacy and activist research and development in literacy research, especially in the digital areas. Engaging in a form of design research with high school and homeless youth in the city of Vancouver through the creation of film, drama, and other arts projects, Theresa Rogers and her colleagues (2015) describe how youth enlist new and critical literacies, especially through the multimodal possibilities afforded by various digital media, to engage with various publics and speak out about societal issues (including the public's faulty constructions of youth). Their project demonstrated a form of reflective and responsive engagement in ways that spurred a form of cultural criticism and civic engagement by youth. As Rogers et al. describe, they explored the claims of youth "as expressions of resistance to the inheritance of the broken promises of democratic citizenship and their ability to imagine new possibilities of public engagement" (Rogers et al., p. 2). The youth did so, they state, "through multimodal intertextuality—the mix of genres, forms, and modes that functioned as discursive resources for creating counter narratives. . . . [Thereby] juxtaposing and hybridizing and remixing" (p. 102). In terms of theoretical frames, Rogers et al. enlisted notions of the translocal to highlight various forms of engagements. While these engagements, along with the process of locality, may be "emergent and fragile," they represent the "struggles" of youth as well as their "resistance and subversions" (p. 112). The authors note in particular how media resources offered the youth vehicles for participating, resisting, and speaking for themselves as citizens against national and global impositions. Because this work is at the intersection of global and local, they suggest, it befits the convergent space that the media affords.

Similarly, Claudia Mitchell (Mitchell, 2011; Mitchell & Murray, 2012) have pursued similar forms of design research on the use of a range of digital resources as well as other media to support the engagement of high school youth—in Southern Africa (i.e., Rwanda, Ethiopia, South Africa, and Kenya) and Canadian First Nations communities—in some significant social issues, ranging from

HIV-AIDS to violence against women. Mitchell locates this work as "social policy 'from the ground up': Youth participation and social change through digital media,"[6] and has encouraged youth to enlist images, websites, and other multimodal digital platforms to spur dialogue around difficult issues concerning their everyday lives. Despite the complexities inherent in such research, Mitchell has pursued a range of provocative design experiments in which young people have been invited to participate in forms of activism involving public disclosures. They posit that, unless young people are given a more significant voice in participating in policy dialogues about their own health and well-being, the programs themselves are destined to fail.

In a digital communication network setting in conjunction with a global project, Glynda A. Hull et al. (2010) report a project directed at empowering young women via the Internet in ways that address a number of issues stemming from their efforts to study cosmopolitanism—in particular, whether cosmopolitanism can afford "a compass in a world that is . . . is resiliently hopeful, asserting that people can both uphold local commitments and take into consideration larger arenas of concern." They explore whether "online and offline experiences that accompany them, can be a digital proving ground for understanding and respecting difference and diversity in a global world as well as fostering the literacies and communication practices through which such habits of mind develop" (pp. 1–2). The project itself argues for a form of global citizenship as the aspiration and vehicle by which young people are invited to examine, interrogate, and share their past with young people in other countries, enlisting digital images and texts, which is new for many of them. As they state: "through an examination of the participation offline and online of a group of teen-aged girls from India in an international social networking project designed to promote cosmopolitan habits of mind" (p. 337), they attempted to examine the following questions: "How do young people develop cosmopolitan habits of mind and attitudes toward others? What are the social and cultural processes that characterize the development of cultural citizenship? What kinds of educative spaces, especially those online, might facilitate such processes? And what forms and designs do communicative practices take in such spaces?" (p. 337). Their observations of the students' projects and their interactions (virtual and face-to-face) with other students, families, and communities poignantly consider the semiotic dissonance that arises across and within communities between students and their schools, students and their families, and communities and students from across the world. Using a semiotic perspective to examine the meaning making transacted between the various parties, they bring to the fore the complexities of pursuing cross-cultural studies for insiders and outsiders especially in the differences with which ways cosmopolitanism and transliteracies may be reckoned (Hull & Stornaiuolo, 2014).

Whether it be discussions of the tweets of politicians or the coverage of the press or the video clips of police brutality, digitally based examinations now mediate societal considerations, studies in the digital domain are proliferating in conjunction with sociopolitical interrogations of media, social media, and videos capturing community developments. As Rogers et al. (2015) and Mitchell and her colleagues (Mitchell, 2011; Mitchell et al., 2017; Moletsane et al., 2012) have argued, art, media, and other resources prompt civic engagement due to their transmediating features and the fluid, shifting, and embodied possibilities that they provide. As observers of events have noted, the use of various mobile digital resources has undergirded social movements and enhanced civic engagement and political protests—through "resource mobilization, repertoires of contention, opportunity structure, and the framing function of movement messaging" (Epstein, 2015, p. 15). As these ideas move across global networks, they may proliferate in either a filtered or mutated form without regard for differences, or incongruences including how they might be considered locally.

Complementarity

David, in reflecting on the various "wars" that the reading field has experienced over issues such as instructional approaches to early reading instruction (Pearson, 2004, 2007), theories of the reading process (Kamil & Pearson, 1979), and research paradigms and methods (Pearson, 1980, 2004), offers a view of what might be called research complementary or compatibilism. Writing in 2007 (pp. 25–27) for the *National Reading Conference Yearbook*, here's what David had to say about complementarity among research methods. Alas, the concerns—and the recommendations—still hold today. The need for complementary is as strong as ever.

In the current research context, literacy scholars find themselves "between a rock and a hard place." The official views of research promulgated by the federal government in its research programs administered within the Department of Education are weighted toward quantitative and experimental work. At the same time, the work of many, perhaps even most, literacy researchers and doctoral students in research training programs is decidedly qualitative, narrative, and/or ethnographic in character. An impending crisis? A confrontation of the immovable object and the irresistible force? Or just the exclusion of a wide array of literacy scholars from federally funded research efforts? I would bet on the exclusion, but I hope and argue for a rapprochement among methods and even epistemologies.

Regarding science, my fundamental claim has always been that reading research can never be truly rigorous, indeed truly scientific, until and unless it privileges all of the empirical and theoretical methodologies that characterize the scientific disciplines. Included among those methodologies would surely be experimentation and of course randomized field trials of the sort that are being proposed for several federally sponsored programs, but the range of scientific methods would extend to careful descriptions of phenomena in their natural settings (just like Darwin did and just like today's environmental scientists do), examinations of natural correlations among variables in an environment, just to see what goes with what, natural experiments in which we take advantage of the differences that serendipity and the normal course of events have created between two or more settings that are otherwise remarkably similar—the most common form of this effort in education being outlier studies and the even more common approach in public health's epidemiological studies, data gathered in the name of theory building and evaluation—just to see if we can explain the nature of things, design experiments in which we adopt a planful, incremental approach to knowledge refinement, with each successive step building carefully on what was learned in the last.

As good as randomized experiments are for determining the overall efficacy of interventions, they are very short on details about the interventions, such as why, how, for whom, and under what conditions interventions work. For that, we need complementary methods, and this is where qualitative methods come into play. Donald Campbell, one of the foremost design methodologists of the 20th century, and the coauthor of the infamous book on quasi-experiments (Campbell & Stanley, 1963), the classic treatment of threats to internal and external validity, recognized this need for complementarity.

> To rule out plausible rival hypotheses we need situation-specific wisdom. The lack of this knowledge (whether it be called ethnography, program history, or gossip) makes us incompetent estimators of program impacts, turning out conclusions that not only are wrong, but are often wrong in socially destructive ways.
>
> There is the mistaken belief that quantitative measures replace qualitative knowledge. Instead, qualitative knowing is absolutely essential as a prerequisite for quantification in any science. Without competence at the qualitative level, one's computer printout is misleading or meaningless. (Campbell, 1984, pp. 141–142)

We hear a lot of talk about randomized field trials in medical and pharmaceutical research, and we are advised to follow their lead. I agree. But if we follow medicine and pharmacology, then we should follow them all the way down the road of science. Let's remember that before researchers in those fields get to the last leg, the final 10 percent, of the journey, which is when they invoke randomized field trials in anticipation of advocacy and policy recommendations, they have already used a much wider range of methodologies, including much observation, description, examinations of relationships, and just plain messing around (that is a technical term used by scientists to describe what they spend most of their time doing) to travel the first 90 percent of that journey. So let's talk about complementarities and convergence among methods rather than competition and displacement of one worldview with another. This is the message of the report on educational research by a committee empanelled by the National Academy of Science (Shavelson & Towne, 2002), a message I heartily endorse.

If we rush too soon to the last 10 percent of the journey and enamor ourselves of randomized field trials for their own sake, we are likely to end up conducting expensive experiments on interventions that were not worth evaluating in the first place. A drug company would never think of conducting a randomized field trial on a new drug that had not gone through a thorough basic research phase in which biochemical theories, tryouts on nonhuman organisms, correlational research on chemical components of the drug in the natural environment; and probably some serendipitous case studies of individual subjects who volunteered to use the drug out of desperation all played a key role. We should ask no less of educational interventions and programs. An intervention that is based on bad theory or no theory is not likely to yield a significant contribution to practice in the long run. To know that something worked without a clue about how and why it worked does not advance either our scientific or professional understanding of an educational issue. We cannot afford blind experimentation and horse races with interventions of unknown theoretical characteristics. As our candidates for randomized field trials, we want treatments and interventions that have gone through these various stages of scientific development.

As a profession we have fallen into a methodological trap. We have become so attached to our methodologies and to their epistemological (some would say ideological) underbellies that we, as individuals, are likely to begin our work by looking for a question that fits our methodological preferences, rather than the other way around. This does not serve our profession well, for it allows us to address questions that may or may not be of great relevance to policy and practice. We must return to the ethic of insisting that just as form follows function in language, so methods must follow questions in research. And if we do not, as individuals, possess the range of methodological expertise to address different sorts of questions, then we ought to align ourselves with scholarly communities in which such expertise is distributed among its members.

NOWADAYS: PURSUING, SHARING, AND FOLLOWING UP RESEARCH STUDIES

Research exists within systems that contribute to its position, placement, and utility. Certain topics may be more popular than others, and certain findings may be sought in support of political agendas. These matters can be quite controversial, especially as answers to questions and pursuit of certainty, particularly related to best practice or silver bullets, may override the science's power to reckon with situated complexities.

Despite the status afforded positivistic approaches, it is doubtful that researchers will retreat from enlisting a range of approaches stemming from their embrace of the research pursuit with and in the communities with which they engage. The approaches to research have shifted in notable ways. While older traditions remain, a great deal of research has become more intimate, transparent, and formative. Research now befits the values of educators operating in a collective fashion, reflecting: (1) ethics that are not only respectful, but also transformative and participatory; (2) approaches that are collaborative, formative, situation based, realistic, negotiated, trustworthy, intimate, subjective, and reflexive; (3) observations and data that are sound, thick, sometimes open-ended, and grounded; (4) findings that are presented concretely and illuminated via astute analysis schemes; and (5) conclusions and follow-up that suggest rather than inform practice, research, and theory.

References

Apple, M. W. (2010). *Global crises, social justice, and education*. Routledge. doi: 10.4324/9780203861448

Apple, M. W. (2012). *Knowledge, power, and education: The selected works of Michael W. Apple*. Routledge. doi: 10.4324/9780203118115

Apple, M. W. (2014, November). *The task of the critical scholar/activist in education*. Keynote presented at the Philosophy of Education Society of Australasia Conference 2014. www.youtube.com/watch?v=0HA7Lgv8rTI

Apple, M. W., Au, W., & Gandin, L. A. (2009). *The Routledge international handbook of critical education*. Routledge. doi: 10.4324/9780203882993

Apple, M. W., Ball, S. J., & Gandin, L. A. (2010). *The Routledge international handbook of the sociology of education*. Routledge. doi: 10.4324/9780203863701

Beach, R., & Tierney, R. J. (2016). Toward a theory of literacy meaning making within virtual worlds. In S. E. Israel & G. G. Duffy (Eds.), *Handbook of research on reading comprehension* (2nd ed., pp. 135–165). Guilford. https://www.academia.edu/39016530/Toward_a_theory_of_literacy_meaning_making_within_virtual_world

Bloome, D., & Green, J. (2015). The social and linguistic turns in studying language and literacy. In J. Rowsell & K. Pahl (Eds.), *The Routledge handbook of literacy studies* (pp. 19–34). Routledge.

Boas, F. (1911). *Handbook of American Indian languages*. United States Government Printing Office (Smithsonian Institution, Bureau of American Ethnology).

Boas, F. (1912). Changes in the bodily form of descendants of immigrants. *American Anthropologist, 14*(3), 530–562. doi: 10.1525/aa.1912.14.3.02a00080

Boas, F. (1914). Mythology and folk-tales of the North American Indians. *Journal of American Folklore, 27*(106), 374. doi: 10.2307/534740

Boas, F. (1922). Report on an anthropometric investigation of the population of the United States. *Journal of the American Statistical Association, 18* (138), 181–209.

Boas, F. (1938). *The mind of primitive man* (Rev. ed.). Macmillan.

Boas, F. (1940). *Race, language and culture*. Macmillan.

Boas, F. (1945). *Race and democratic society*. Augustin.

Boas, F. (2004). *Anthropology and modern life*. Transaction Publishers. First published in 1928.

Bond, G. L., & Dykstra, R. (1967). The cooperative research program in first-grade reading instruction. *Reading Research Quarterly, 2*(4), 5–142. doi: 10.2307/746948

Bourdieu, P., & Thompson, J. B. (Trans.) (1991). *Language and symbolic power*. Harvard University Press.

Chomsky, C. (1969). *The acquisition of syntax in children from 5 to 10*. MIT Press.

Comber, B., & Simpson, A. (2001). *Negotiating critical literacies in classrooms*. Erlbaum. doi: 10.4324/9781410600288

Cook-Gumperz, J., & Gumperz, J. J. (1992). Changing views of language in education: The implications for literacy research. In R. Beach, J. L. Green, M. L. Kamil, & T. Shanahan (Eds.), *Multidisciplinary perspectives on literacy research* (pp. 151–179). National Council of Teachers of English.

Crumpler, T. & Tierney, R. J. (1995). Literacy research and rhetorical space: Reflections and interpretive possibilities. Research monograph. www.academia.edu/9699516/Literacy_Research_and_Rhetorical_Space_Reflections_and_Interpretive_Possibilities.

Denzin, N. K., & Giardina, M. D. (Eds.). (2016). *Qualitative inquiry through a critical lens*. Routledge.

Dyson, A. H. (1988). Negotiating among multiple worlds: The space/time dimensions of young children's composing. *Research in the Teaching of English, 22*(4), 355–390.

Epstein, I. (2015). Introduction: The global dimensions of contemporary youth protest. In I. Epstein (Ed.), *The whole world is texting: Youth protest in the information age* (pp. 1–24). Sense.

Ferreiro, E., & Teberosky, A. (1982). *Literacy before schooling*. Heinemann Educational Books.

Finlay, L. (2009). Debating phenomenological research methods. *Phenomenology & Practice, 3*(1), 6–25. doi: 10.29173/pandpr19818

Gee, J. P. (1990). *Social linguistics and literacies: Ideology in discourses*. Falmer Press.

Gilmore, L. & Marshall E. (2019). *Witnessing girlhood: Toward an intersectional tradition of life writing*. Fordham University Press.

Gutiérrez, K. D. (2008). Developing a sociocritical literacy in the third space. *Reading Research Quarterly, 43*(2), 148–164. doi: 10.1598/RRQ.43.2.3

Harste, J. C., Woodward, V. A., & Burke, C. L. (1984). *Language stories & literacy lessons*. Heinemann Educational Books.

Hartman, D. (1995). Eight readers reading: The intertextual links of proficient readers reading multiple passages. *Reading Research Quarterly, 30*(3), 520–561.

Hattie, J. (2008). *Visible learning: A synthesis of over 800 meta-analyses relating to achievement*. Routledge.

Heath, S. B. (1983). *Ways with words: Language, life, and work in communities and classrooms*. Cambridge University Press.

Hull, G. A., & Stornaiuolo, A. (2014). Cosmopolitan literacies, social networks, and "proper distance": Striving to understand in a global world. *Curriculum Inquiry, 44*(1), 15–44.

Hull, G. A., Stornaiuolo, A., & Sahni, U. (2010, July). Cultural citizenship and cosmopolitan practice: Global youth communicate online. *English Education, 42*(4), 331–367. www.hullresearchgroup.info/wp-content/uploads/2011/12/Cultural-Citizenship-and-Cosmopolitan-Practice-Global-Youth-Communicate-Online.pdf

Irwin, R. L. (2008). Communities of a/r/tographic practice. In S. Springgay, R. Irwin, C. Leggo, & P. Gouzouasis (Eds.), *Being with a/r/tography* (pp.71–80). Sense.

Irwin, R. L., & Springgay, S. (2008). A/r/tography as practice-based research. In S. Springgay, R. Irwin, C. Leggo, & P. Gouzouasis (Eds.), *Being with a/r/tography* (pp. xix–xxxiii). Sense.

Kincheloe, J. L. (2003). *Teachers as researchers: Qualitative inquiry as a path to empowerment* (2nd ed.). Routledge. doi: 10.4324/9780203497319

King, M., Rentel, V., Pappas, C., Pettegrew, B., & Zutell, J. (1981). *How children learn to write: A longitudinal study*. The Ohio State University Research Foundation.

Lassonde, C. A., & Israel, S. E. (2008). *Teachers taking action: A comprehensive guide to teacher research*. International Reading Association.

Lassonde, C. A., Ritchie, G. V., & Fox, R. K. (2008). How teacher research can become your way of being. In C. A. Lassonde & S. E. Israel (Eds.), *Teachers taking action: A comprehensive guide to teacher research* (pp. 3–14). International Reading Association.

Lather, P. (1986). Issues of validity in openly ideological research: Between a rock and a soft place. *Interchange, 17*(4), 63–84. doi: 10.1007/BF01807017

Lather, P. (2006). Paradigm proliferation as a good thing to think with: Teaching research in education as a wild profusion. *International Journal of Qualitative Studies in Education, 19*(1), 35–57. doi: 10.1080/09518390500450144

Leggo, C. (2008). Autobiography: Researching our lives and living our research. In S. Springgay, R. Irwin, C. Leggo, & P. Gouzouasis (Eds.), *Being with a/r/tography* (pp. 3–24). Sense.

Lincoln, Y. S., & Guba, E. G. (1985). *Naturalistic inquiry.* SAGE.

Malinowski, B. (1913). *The family among the Australian Aborigines: A sociological study.* University of London Press. archive.org/details/familyamongaustr00mali/page/n8

Malinowski, B. (1944). *A scientific theory of culture and other essays.* University of North Carolina Press.

Malinowski, B. (2013). *Argonauts of the Western Pacific: An account of native enterprise and adventure in the archipelagoes of Melanesian New Guinea* (Enhanced ed.). Waveland Press. Original work published 1922.

Marsh, H. W., Martin, A. J., & Hau, K-T. (2006). A multimethod perspective on self-concept research in educational psychology: A construct validity approach. In M. Eid & E. Diener (Eds.), *Handbook of multimethod measurement in psychology* (pp. 441–456). American Psychological Association.

Marshall, E. (2018). *Graphic girlhoods: Visualizing education and violence.* Routledge.

McDermott, R. P. (1974). Achieving school failure: An anthropological approach to illiteracy and social stratification. In G. Spindler (Ed.), *Education and cultural process: Toward an anthropology of education* (pp. 82–118). Holt, Rinehart, & Winston.

McLaren, P., & Kincheloe, J. L. (Eds.). (2007). *Critical pedagogy: Where are we now?* Peter Lang.

McNiff, J. (1993). *Teaching as learning: An action research approach.* Routledge.

McNiff, J. (2013). *Action research: Principles and practice* (3rd ed.). Routledge. doi: 10.4324/9780203112755

Mitchell, C. (2011). What's participation got to do with it? Visual methodologies in "girl-method" to address gender-based violence in the time of AIDS. *Global Studies of Childhood, 1*(1), 51–59. doi: 10.2304/gsch.2011.1.1.51

Mitchell, C., & Murray, J. (2012). Social networking practices and youth advocacy efforts in HIV awareness and prevention: What does methodology have to do with it? *Educational Research and Social Change, 1*(2), 26–40.

Norman, R. (2008). The art of poetry and narrative with and between lived curriculum: Autobiographic a/r/tography. In S. Springgay, R. Irwin, C. Leggo, & P. Gouzouasis (Eds.), *Being with a/r/tography* (pp. 33–44). Sense.

Parsons, S. A., Gallagher, M. A., & the George Mason University Content Analysis Team. (2016). A content analysis of nine literacy journals, 2009–2014. *Journal of Literacy Research, 48*(4), 476–502. doi: 10.1177/1086296X16680053

Parsons, S. A., Gallagher, M. A., Leggett, A. B., Ives, S. T., & Lague, M. (2020). An analysis of 15 journals' literacy content, 2007–2016. *Journal of Literacy Research, 52*(3), 341–367.

Pearson, P. D. (2007). An historical analysis of the impact of educational research on policy and practice: Reading as an illustrative case. In D. W. Rowe, R. T. Jiménez, et al. (Eds.), *56th yearbook of the National Reading Conference* (pp. 14–40). National Reading Conference.

Pearson, P. D., & Billman, A. (2016). Reading to learn science: A right that extends to every reader. In Z. Babaci-Wilhite (Ed.), *Human rights in STEM education* (pp. 17–34). Sense Publishers.

Philips, S. U. (1983). *The invisible culture: Communication in classroom and community on the Warm Springs Indian reservation.* Longman.

Purcell-Gates, V. (1995). *Other people's words: The cycle of low literacy.* Harvard University Press.

Purcell-Gates, V., Perry, K. H., & Briseño, A. (2011). Analyzing literacy practice: Grounded theory to model. *Research in the Teaching of English, 45*(4), 439–458.

Raphael, T. E., & Tierney, R. J. (1981). The influence of topic familiarity and the author-reader relationship on detection of inconsistent information. In M. Kamil (Ed.), *Directions in reading: Research and instruction* (pp. 40–50). National Reading Conference.

Rex, L. A., Bunn, M., Davila, B. A., Dickinson, H. A., Ford, A. C., Gerben, C., & Carter, S. (2010). A review of discourse analysis in literacy research: Equitable access. *Reading Research Quarterly, 45*(1), 94–115. doi: 10.1598/RRQ.45.1.5

Rogers, T., Winters, K. L., Perry, M., & LaMonde, A. M. (2015). *Youth, critical literacies, and civic engagement.* Routledge.

Rosenshine, B. & Stevens, R. (1984). Classroom instruction in reading. In P. D. Pearson, R. Barr, M. L. Kamil, & P. Mosenthal (Eds.), *Handbook of reading research* (pp. 745–798). Longman.

Schön, D. A. (1983). *The reflective practitioner: How professionals think in action.* Basic Books. doi: 10.4324/9781315237473

Scribner, S., & Cole, M. (1981). *The psychology of literacy.* Harvard University Press.

SEG Indigenous Education Review Working Group (Tierney, R. J., Peck, C., Llewellyn, G., Taylor, R., Sharma, M., Mooney, J., & Blanchard, M.). (2010, November). *Indigenous strategic framework report.* University of Sydney. www.academia.edu/9680700 /Indigenous_Participation_Engagement_Education_and_Research_Strategy _University_of_Sydney

Shor, I. (1980). *Critical teaching and everyday life* (1st ed.). South End Press.

Springgay, S. (2008). An ethics of embodiment. In S. Springgay, R. Irwin, C. Leggo, & P. Gouzouasis (Eds.), *Being with a/r/tography* (pp. 153–166). Sense.

Springgay, S., Irwin, R., Leggo, C., & Gouzouasis, P. (Eds.). (2008). *Being with a/r/tography.* Sense.

Stocking, G. W. (Ed.). (1983). *Observers observed: Essays on ethnographic fieldwork.* University of Wisconsin Press.

Stocking, G. W. (Ed.). (1989). *A Franz Boas reader: The shaping of American anthropology, 1883–1911* (Midway Reprint). University of Chicago Press.

Takayama, K., Sriprakash, A., & Connell, R. (2017). Toward a postcolonial comparative and international education. *Comparative Education Review, 61*(S1), S1–S24. doi: 10.1086/690455

Teale, W. H., & Sulzby, E. (1986). *Emergent literacy: Writing and reading.* Ablex.

Tierney, R. J. (1992). The eye of the bumble bee: A multifaceted view of literacy or on matters of subjectivity, knowledge claims, the art of method and ethics in literacy research. In C. Kinzer & D. Leu (Eds.), *Literacy research, theory and practice: Views from many perspectives.* National Reading Conference Yearbook, Illinois.

Tierney, R. J. (2009). Literacy education 2.0: Looking through the rear view mirror as we move ahead. In J. Hoffman & Y. Goodman (Eds.), *A historical perspective on the future of reading research, public policy and classroom practices* (pp. 282–300). Routledge.

Tierney, R. J. (2015). Integrative research review: Mapping the challenges and changes to literacy research. *Annual proceedings of the Literacy Research Association, 63*, 20–35.

Tierney, R. J., Carter, M. A., & Desai, L. E. (1991). *Portfolio assessment in the reading-writing classroom.* Christopher-Gordon Publishers. independent.academia.edu/RobTierney /Books

Tierney, R. J., Kieffer, R., Whalin, K., Desai, L., Moss, A. G., Harris, J. E., & Hopper, J. (1998). Assessing the impact of hypertext on learners' architecture of literacy learning spaces in different disciplines: Follow-up studies. *Reading Online.* International Reading Association. eric.ed.gov/?id=ED416439

Tierney, R. J., Soter, A., O'Flahavan, J. F., & McGinley, W. (1989). The effects of reading and writing upon thinking critically. *Reading Research Quarterly, 24*(2), 134–173. doi: 10.2307/747862

Tierney, R. J., Tucker, D. L., Gallagher, M., Crismore, A., & Pearson, P. D. (1988). The Metcalf Project: A teacher-researcher collaboration in developing reading and writing instructional problem-solving. In J. Samuels & P. D. Pearson (Eds.), *Innovation and change in reading classrooms* (pp. 207–226). International Reading Association. independent.academia.edu/RobTierney/Papers

Tuck, E., & Yang, K. W. (2014). *Youth resistance research and theories of change.* Routledge. doi: 10.4324/9780203585078

Van Maanen, J. (1988). *Tales of the field: On writing ethnography.* University of Chicago Press.

NOTES

1. See the anthropologic explorations by Franz Boas (1911, 1912, 1914, 1922, 1938, 1940, 1945, 2004/1928) and his students, such as George Stocking (1983, 1989) and Margaret Mead (i.e., studies intent on elevating the visibility and understanding of societies and the dynamics of ongoing social and culture interactional foundations of difference and change). Bronislaw Malinowski (1913, 1944, 2013/1922) sustained observational work in the sociological studies in education, rooted initially in Chicago.

2. A simple correlation, if squared, gives you a measure of the shared variance. For further discussions of graphing, see: mste.illinois.edu/courses/ci330ms/youtsey/scatterinfo .html.

3. It was only in the last 40 years that sociologists and constructivists enlisting ethnographic tools began to gain any leverage. Indeed, for many years, quasi-experimentalism overshadowed and thwarted qualitative research paradigm developments as they sought "truths" or generalizable findings perhaps downplaying situatedness and not making visible complexities of schooling,

4. Data are sometimes represented categorically, with nominal or ordinal classifications. It may be suggested that these categories have a relationship to matters of degree or data that appears to assume the qualities of ratio or interval data. For example, oftentimes people will develop categorical systems as they review their data or rubrics. Usually the former will be nominal or ordinal, with the latter perhaps interval. But there is an important distinction in measurement between data—depending on whether it is categorical or comparative in terms of magnitude or degree. The nature of the classificatory scheme should be presented in a manner grounded in how it is collected and verified by participations and how they might be analyzed. One might find differences in perspective relative to weight, their discreteness and interrelationship, and validity as well as the reliability of informed rubric scorers.

5. According to Finlay (2009):

Van Maanen (1990) suggests that when description is mediated by expression, including nonverbal aspects, action, artwork, or text, a stronger element of interpretation is involved. However, drawing on Gadamer's ideas, he distinguishes between interpretation as pointing to something (interpretation suited to phenomenological description) and interpretation as pointing out the meaning of something by imposing an external framework (such as when offering a psychoanalytic interpretation). Ricoeur has made a similar distinction between the "hermeneutics of meaning-recollection" which, he says, aims for greater understanding of the thing to be analyzed in its own terms, where meanings are brought out and the "hermeneutics of suspicion," which involves deeper interpretations needed to challenge surface accounts (Ricoeur, 1970). (Finlay, 2009, p. 11)

6. See Mitchell's faculty web page at McGill University: www.mcgill.ca/dise/claudia -mitchell.

13   History Unaccounted

A Personal Retrospective on Waves of Development

We have employed the metaphor of waves to characterize our account of the major developments in literacy theory, research, practice, and (occasionally) policy, as well as to highlight how these developments overtake, recede, and merge with—fully displace—each other. To extend the metaphor, we suggest that engaging in these developments is like surfers waiting alongside others to catch a wave. You often wait until you see a wave that appears to be rideable before you surge forward, seeking to achieve momentum with and from the wave and for you and the wave to become one. And all the time, keeping an eye out for others—fellow riders.

The Cognitive Wave

When the cognitive wave surged with studies on meaning making and the role of background knowledge, we were captivated by the notion that the reader, not the text, was at the core of the meaning-making process—the construction, not extraction, of information from the text was the name of the game. Instead, the studies by Dick Anderson and his Center for the Study of Reading colleagues taught us that readers create meanings with texts, enlisting their background knowledge and the ideas suggested by the text to create a model of what the text means by extracting, inferring, predicting, and integrating ideas. The work of John Bransford, Allan Collins, and our down-the-hall colleague Rand Spiro was transformative; they aligned with and extended the notions of psycholinguists and constructivist views of learning and development, such as Ken Goodman and Frank Smith, to the act of comprehension.

Rob here: Along with conversations with Ken and Yetta Goodman as well as Jerry Harste and Bob Carey, there were two books that were classics for me: John Bransford's *Human Cognition*, which walked the reader through the experiments demonstrating the constructivism of readers, and Frederick Bartlett's pioneering work *Remembering*, which was the main precursor to cognition. Together, these authors turned my views of meaning making "inside out." I was tantalized with the proposed power of the mind during reading—especially the mental images and vicarious participatory engagement that readers experienced, or the sense of epiphany when ideas were grasped anew.

David here: Bransford's *Human Cognition* was equally as formative for me as it was for Rob, but my second truly influential book came out 5 years early—Frank Smith's *Psycholinguistics and Reading* from 1971. The most important insight for me was the complementarity of comprehension and learning—that comprehension is what happens when things are clicking along on all cylinders and learning is what happens when there is a clunk—something that seems awry and hence requires an active search of one's store of knowledge and activation of monitoring processes to set things right again.

Learning to Learn Wave

As educators, the call to engage in research on teaching comprehension was a rallying cry that we readily embraced, recruiting other reading educators along the way. Many of our fellow educators were like-minded (Patty Anders, James Cunningham, Pat Cunningham, Connie Bridge, Mary Jane Cera, Catherine Thome, Taffy Raphael, Annemarie Palincsar, Peter Johnston, James Mosenthal, Jill Lazansky-Moffatt, Margie Leys, Jane Hansen, Allan Neilsen, Linda Fielding, Linda Fenner, William McGinley, Theresa Rogers, Doug Hartman, Cynthis Bertelsen, Ron Kieffer, Tom Crumpler, David Tucker, Diane Schallert, Joseph Vaughan, Dorsey Hammond, Laurie Desai, Pat Enciso, David Hayes, Margaret Sheehy, Mark Carter, John O'Flahavan, James Wile, Michael Gee, Laurie Stowell, Trika Smith-Burke, Marie Clay, Brian Cambourne, Judith Rivalland) were not just willing, but compelled and impassioned to engage with learners and teachers in classrooms. The crucible of the classroom, not the clarity of the laboratory, would be the site of our work. Figuring out how to help students learn to learn was to witness a moment when a student makes a breakthrough that far outpaces your teaching. The learning to learn wave shifted the site of research as well as the leading actors, and most important, why we do research. The mission became akin to advancing the "intelligence" of learners— to open up the mindfulness of readers, provide them with strategies to advance their comprehension, and help readers learn to learn without relying on us as teachers.

Reading–Writing Wave

The third wave involved reading–writing relationships and prompted a shift in my positioning in the ocean of ideas. We started attending meetings with scholars who were unpacking writing processes, authorship, and personae. These included cognitivists, such as Linda Flower and John Hayes, literary theorists and rhetoricians delving into authorship and audience, and writing educators such as Donald Murray and Don Graves. A number of these scholars became close friends, including Tony Petrosky, Richard Beach, Arthur Applebee, Alan Purves, Stephen Witte, Sarah Freeman, Donald Graves, Glynda Hull, Rebecca Kaplan, and Nancy Spivey.

Rob here: In the early 1980s, I had the very good fortune of having two graduate students (Mary Ellen Giacccobe and Susan Sowers) who had worked closely with Don Graves and Don Murray. Both had worked at Atkinson Academy in

New Hampshire, where Don Graves explored his ideas for teaching writing. They invited me to visit the school, where I was stunned by the elementary students' process-oriented writing and collaborative approaches to meaning making—as well as by the ways they wrestled with their text, filtering the advice of their teachers and peers. These interactions took me far beyond myself as I shifted from being a reading educator to a literacy educator. As I traveled into the world of writing, it was as if I had crossed the border into another country—one that offered so much to learn and would illuminate my views on literacy and learning.

The Social Wave

The fourth wave involved yet another set of revelations as a result of my engagements with those literacy colleagues with backgrounds in sociolinguistics and the nature and power of student ensembles. Colleagues such as David Bloome, Vicki Purcell-Gates, Judith Green, Muriel Saville-Troike, David Fernie, and Rebecca Kantor had been immersed in examining the social dimensions of reading and learning.

Rob here: My own interest in the social had been emerging in concert with an interest in social constructivism and moreover my fascination with drama education, the vicarious nature of reading alongside an awareness of the role of collaboration—especially via the rich work of Cecily O'Neill, Pat Enciso, and Ann Haas Dyson in unpacking the multidimensional (including social) and dynamic meaning making of young children. Initially, however, I was more an observer than a participant in the social wave, as I had positioned the social as a fixed variable that influenced reading and writing. A friend, Judith Green, recognized my naivete and educated me. Her sharing of her observation of the social and political dynamics of the everyday was integral to my realization that social dynamics were crucial to meaning making rather than separate from them. This shift in thinking was major; it entailed reconceptualizing reading and writing as social practices occurring "outside of the head," rather than restricting them to mental processes occurring "inside the head." It also was foundational to the next wave, which recognized our socially constituted states and the systemic forces that shape power and perpetuate forms of social privilege, including biases regarding race, ethnicity, class, gender, and disabilities.

David: My journey into the social was gradual. It started with my exposure to doctoral students at Illinois. I'll mention two, because they were early in the journey, but there are so many others. I got to be on the dissertation committee of Kathy Au, who showed us how relying on social and cultural practices that students bring to the classroom can boost their opportunities to learn culturally relevant and culturally neutral content and processes. Also, Annemarie Palincsar, who showed us that when teachers share authority with students for shaping the conversations in classrooms, it can help everyone grow in competence and confidence. Also, John O'Flahavan, who took a great risk by promoting teacherless discussion groups (talk about sharing power and authority!). Michigan State colleagues Taffy Raphael and James Gavalek introduced me to the Vygotsky space. Another Michigan State colleague, Susan Florio-Ruane, cotaught a course with me that marinated me in a new discourse that included Clifford Geertz and local knowledge, Jim Gee's notions of the Social Mind, and Bruner's ideas about scaffolding to give me the theory to go along with the practices I was acquiring by hanging around really smart graduate students.

The Critical Wave

The fifth wave involved lenses informed by the social frames and emerged from the work of critical theorists and sociologists especially colleagues such as Michael Apple, Patty Lather, Allan Luke, Suzanne Damarin and Roger Slee. It afforded critical examinations of the systemic forces operating in our worlds, including how we are constructed and positioned. These lenses unpacked the constructions of identity and position in schools and across our various institutions, in conjunction with deconstructing the power dynamics controlling affordances, opportunities, possibilities, and license. Critical frames exposed the hegemonies and the forces that subjugate, isolate, quarantine, and limit. The critical wave represents a challenge to ourselves and society of the systems (especially related to literacy practices) that perpetuate the social reproduction of the discriminatory privileges of class, race, ethnicity, and gender—a call for advocacy and agency.

The Assessment Wave

The assessment wave involved a dramatic shift in both the role and the technology of testing. Assessment had been a uniform, standardized tool, developed by outsiders to measure, judge, sort, and compare. It involved instruction focused on test preparation. For us, the assessment wave was spurred by discontent with the negative impacts of these types of assessment on literacy practices. A key moment occurred when we asked the questions, If we were to assess assessment, how would we judge it? If we could change assessments, how would we?

Rob here: When I realized that assessment should support student learning and teaching, I found myself moving away from state-imposed, standardized, or teacher-developed tests. Instead, I found myself drawn to approaches wherein learners were engaged in assessing themselves with criteria they pursued with increasing discernment. The assessment wave represented a shift in what we assessed and especially in how learners were positioned toward assessment in a fashion befitting learning.

David here: I have spent a lot of time trying to build assessments, even those used for accountability, that reflect what we know about the nature of reading. I tried to do this in Illinois with the IGAP reading assessment, with New Standards, and for the National Assessment of Educatonal Progress. Alas! It is still a work in progress.

The Era of Reform

Arguably, educational philosophy and ideologies achieve traction by adopting and implementing policies that dictate the nature and shape of literacy teaching and learning. My discussion of the era of reform focuses on developments that have gained traction since the 1990s, reflecting efforts to leverage changes in reading instruction and the focus of reading research in terms of what was taught and how. These have included efforts to control the research agenda and the nature of research, as well as efforts to mandate reading methods (and, in turn, control teaching practices) using tests as a high-stake means of accountability. Arguably, such controls were problematic, undermining the professionalism of educators, challenging the integrity of researchers, and realigning teaching and learning with tests.

The Digital Wave

The digital wave has been quite seismic—a virtual tidal wave with its far-reaching impact. For both of us, it began with our graduate days where we worked in programming, using large mainframes to run statistical analyses. The advent of desktop publishing followed by the introduction to technology platforms offered us portals to a world with an ever-enlarging depository of ideas via the Internet. It has emerged as a multimodal palette for production, communication, engagement, and communication systems, operating locally and globally for both professional and personal purposes. Nowadays, our lives are in the media and increasingly dependent on digital exchanges for economic, social, cultural, political, or educational purposes. It has changed the face of literacy for those of us in the field and continues to do so as we live within the media world, contemplate its changing nature, and perhaps contribute to its future.

The Global Wave

The global wave represents a confluence of developments, or a coming together of perspectives and ways of existence across spaces, times, and values. It combines the past with the present and future. It relates to the lives of all of us within and across communities, states, provinces, territories, and regions. It reckons that even if we are quarantined or distanced from others, our lives involve global engagements—whether we are attending to news; adapting to different norms and conventions as we interact with our neighbors and visitors; traveling or crossing geographic borders; engaging with different groups to provide security, nourish, or comfort; or participating in the trade of ideas or goods or values. The global builds on the critical wave of examining the systems at work that position and control the trade and value of goods as well as people and identities, both culturally and economically. Befitting a planetary orientation, the global is aligned with ecological tenets that emphasize how our diversity is crucial to existence, yet increasingly under threat—as species are diminished, languages disappear, and certain epistemologies devalued. It builds on a world that recognizes transliteracies and the criss-crossing that occurs as we navigate across the terrains and borders of our worlds. Personally, it involves seeing the world with the help of friends such as Australian Aboriginals Lester-Irabinna Rigney, Bob Morgan, and John Evans, as well as Maori such as

Graham Hingangaroa Smith, as well as global scholars such as Fazal Rizvi, Ruth Hayhoe, Leslie Lo, Greg Misiaszek, Lauren Misiaszek, Carlos Torres, as well as Chukwuemeka Eze Onukaogu, Caroline Hamilton, Changyun Kang, Chen Liqen, Sude, and Kan Wei. From a literacy perspective, it involves "reading the world(s)," as Freire advocated, and moving forward in a fashion tied to valuing diversity in ways that upend the penchant for standardization, assimilation, and colonization.

HISTORY UNACCOUNTED

Waves Missed

Our collective and independent journeys took place across many years and many spaces around the globe. For David it began in 1964 in a 5th-grade classroom in Porterville, California. For Rob, it began in the late 1960s in Australia as a teacher and then in the United States when our paths crossed. Rob's journey has been more global than David's, but David was truly engaged in the Interstate Commerce of Ideas across his many years in the educational field. We do believe that the developments we have witnessed have earned the attribute label of revolutionary and the category label waves; they challenged the conventional wisdom and they flowed and merged with one another. Our experiences with these waves are somewhat idiosyncratic, both for us in tandem and for each of us individually. We readily admit our account, as a history is closer to the personal and tentative end of the continuum rather than the public and definitive pole. Certainly, it is not comprehensive; we have omitted major developments, perspectives, and players. Our confessional and provisional list of omissions includes affective dimensions, adult literacy, culturally relevant and culturally sustaining pedagogy, second language reading, bilingual reading development and pedagogy, literary theory, tutoring, adolescent and children's literature, the language arts—speaking, listening, spelling and word study, diagnosis and correction, reading disability, work-related literacies, language teaching, professional development of teachers, and the supervision and administration of reading programs. We know there are more. More significantly, we have omitted the work of countless colleagues. We offer our apologies—both to those we have omitted and to those we haven't (fearing that we may not have gotten you right!). Ah, were there but world enough and time!

A Major Missing Wave

We cannot leave our analysis of shortcomings without reminding our readers that we have yet to directly address one of the most important developments in reading scholarship over the past half century—the dramatic increase in production and popularity of handbooks that systematically review the literature. The handbook movement in reading began in the early 1980s with the publication of the first volume of the *Handbook of Reading Research*, edited by David and three co-editors, Rebecca Barr, Michael Kamil, and Peter Mosenthal. At the time it appeared, there were only two substantial handbooks in the education and development fields: *The Handbook of Research on Teaching* and the *Mussen Handbook of Child Development*. David and his colleagues felt that reading research had reached the point at which a systematic cataloguing of the field was warranted on key topics like the basic processes of reading (word identification, comprehension, metacognitive development) and instructional practices, along with ample treatment of theory and history. Since that initial entry into the handbook phenomenon, the reading field has seen the publication of many more handbooks on much more specific topics within reading, including

- *Handbook of Reading Research*, P. David Pearson, Rebecca Barr, Micahel Kamil, Peter Mosenthal, Peter Afflerbach, Elizabeth Moje, and Nonie Lesaux, 1984, 5 volumes
- *Handbook of Reading Comprehension Research*, 2006, Susan Israel and Gerald Duffy, 2 volumes
- *Handbook of Reading Disability Research*, Anne McGill-Franzen and Richard Allington, 2011
- *Handbook of Reading Interventions*, 2011, Rollanda O'Connor & Patricia Vadsayu
- *Handbook of Individual Differences in Reading*, Peter Afflerbach, 2016

And when the umbrella is cast wider to include literacy and the language arts, the expolosion is even more spectacular. We can't list all the titles, but some of the more prominent include,

- *Handbook of Early Literacy Research*, Susan Neuman and David Dickinson, 2001, 3 volumes
- *Handbook of Research on New Literacies*, Julie Coiro, Michele Knobel, Colin Lankshear, Donald Leu, 2014
- *Handbook of Research on the Teaching of the English Language Arts*, Diane Lapp, Douglas Fisher, Fames Flood, Julie Jensen, & James Squire, 4 editions
- *Handbook of Research on Teaching Literacy through the Communicative and Visual Arts*, Diane Lapp, James Flood, Shirley Brice Heath, 2004, 2 editions
- *Handbook of Literacy and Diversity*, Lesley Morrow, Robert Rueda, Diane Lapp, 2009
- *Handbook of Adolescent Literacy Research*, Leila Christenbury, Randy Bomer, & Peter Smagorinsky, 2009
- *Handbook on Research in Writing*, Charles Bazerman, 2008
- *Handbook of Writing Research*, Charles MacArthur, Steve Graham, & Jill Fitzgerald, 2008, 2 editions

The handbook phenomenon creates a resource for the field of reading as a part of the broader scope of the English language arts or literacy. Handbooks are both repositories of and artifacts for historical analysis. When David and his colleagues recruited chapter authors for the first handbook, they charged them with the responsibility to look both backward to the history of a topic, like metacognitive development, and forward to the kind of scholarship that remains to be done on that topic. Thus, handbooks are the first place to look if a reader wants an historical perspective on a topic related to the nature or pedagogy of reading. But now that there are multiple handbooks available, as well as multiple editions of a single handbook, these resources become a primary source for future historians to examine when they want to analyze trends for a specific facet of reading research, theory, practice, or policy. Indeed, the various handbooks of reading proved invaluable to us in pulling together this volume.

New Waves for Future Histories

We have been products, agents, and provocateurs as these waves have swelled, crested, and surged. An extension of the ride are the varying accounts that you share—but, undeniably, our histories are the same but varied, and even our account feels incomplete and apt to change as our perspectives shift. Certainly, as we read other histories by our colleagues past and present, we find resonance, complementarities, and differences. We would be remiss not to recommend some of these historical accounts to you—including rementioning some that we have cited. Most notable, we began with discussions of three landmark books—Edmund Burke's *Psychology and Pedagogy of the History of Reading* (Huey, 1908), Nila Banton Smith's *American Reading Instruction* (Smith, 1934), and William S. Gray's *The Teaching of Reading and Writing* (Gray, 1956). Wonderful complements to these books are Douglas Hartman's address on Huey given at the Literacy Research Association meeting in which he adopts Huey's persona to trace his life (Hartman & Davis, 2002); the recent examination by James Hoffman and Donna Alvermann of the nature and influence of Nila Banton Smith over time enlisting Foucault's approach to genealogy combined with various developments (Hoffman & Alvermann, 2020); and Ralph Staiger's follow-up to William S. Gray's book *The Teaching of Reading and Writing* published as a postscript with the original (Gray, 1956). There are numerous other historical discussions that should not be overlooked, such as those examining reading instruction for specific populations in certain eras such as pursued by Joy Monaghan's discussion of reading instruction in colonial times, Arlette Willis's discussion of literacy education in Calhoun Colored School between 1892 and 1945 (Willis, 2002), Pearson and Goodin's history of silent reading in the twentieth century (Pearson & Goodin, 2010), and Bob Jerrold's history of the International Reading Association, now the International Literacy Association (Jerrolds, 1977). Broader in scope are histories of English education by Arthur Applebee (Applebee, 1974), George Hillocks's review of written composition research (Hillocks, 21986), the regular and recurring editions of *Theoretical Models and Processes* shepherded by Robert Ruddell and his many colleagues since 1970, beginning with his co-founder Harry Singer, his regular and recurring co-editor Norm Unrau, and many others (Donna Alvermann, Misty Sailors, and Martha Rapp Ruddell). books on the history of reading and its pedagogy (e.g., Manguel, 1996; Mathews, 1966; Smith, 2002). There are countless other articles that could be mentioned, but one that has some convergences with our own is the article by James King and Norm Stahl that examines our modern history through the lenses of their graduate students engaging with Thomas Kuhn's discussion of paradigm shifts as well as guided interrogation of developments and practices (King & James, 2012). We could go on, but perhaps this list sufficiently acknowledges that we are not supposing that our account and form of genealogical analyses are exclusive.

Please access the related website (literacyresearchcommons.org: username *TCPWavesofLiteracy*, password *Tierney&Pearson*), which includes video lectures, taped conversations between the coauthors, and an invitation to extend our literacy research commons.

References

Applebee, A. (1974). *Tradition and reform in the teaching of English*. National Council of Teachers of English.

Gray, W. S. (1956). *The teaching of reading and writing: An international survey*. UNESCO.

Hartman, D. K., & Davis, D. H. (2008). Edmund Burke Huey: The formative years of a scholar and field. *57th yearbook of the Literacy Research Association* (pp. 41–55). Literacy Research Association.

Hillocks, G. (1986). *Research on written composition: New directions for teaching*. National Conference on Research in English and Educational Resources Information Center.

Hoffman, J., & Alvermann, D. (2000). What a genealogical analysis of Nila Banton Smith's *American reading instruction* reveals about the present through the past. *Reading Research Quarterly, 55*(2), 251–289.

Huey, E. B. (1908). *Psychology and pedagogy of reading*. Macmillan.

Jerrolds, B. W. (1977). *Reading reflections: The history of the International Reading Association*. International Reading Association.

King, J. R., & Stahl, N. A. (2012). Toward systematic study of the history and foundations of literacy. *Reading Psychology, 33*(3), 241–268. doi: 10.1080/02702711.2010.507647

Manguel, A. (1996). *A history of reading*. Alfred Knopf.

Mathews, M. M. (1966). *Teaching to read, historically considered*. University of Chicago.

Monaghan, E. J. (2007). *Learning to read and write in colonial America*. University of Massachusetts Press.

Pearson, P. D., & Goodin, S. (2010). Silent reading pedagogy: An historical perspective. In E. H. Hiebert & D. R. Reutzel (Eds.), *Revisiting silent reading: New directions for teachers and researchers* (pp. 3–23). IRA.

Singer, H., & Ruddell, R. B. (1970). *Theoretical models and processes of reading*. Newark, DE: International Reading Association.

Smith, N. B. (1934, 1965, 1986, 2002). *American reading instruction: Its development and its significance in gaining a perspective on current practices in reading* (Rev. ed.). International Reading Association.

Venezky, R. L. (1984). The history of reading research. In P. D. Pearson, R. Barr, M. L. Kamil, & P. Mosenthal (Eds.), *Handbook of reading research* (pp. 3–38). Longman.

Willis, A. I. (2002). Literacy at Calhoun Colored School: 1892–1945. *Reading Research Quarterly, 37*(1), 8–44.

Index

About the Authors

Robert J. Tierney is emeritus dean and emeritus professor of the Faculty of Education at the University of British Columbia, past dean of the Faculty of Education and Social Work at the University of Sydney, and a visiting distinguished scholar at Beijing Normal University.

P. David Pearson is the Evelyn Lois Corey Emeritus Professor of Instructional Science in the Graduate School of Education at the University of California, Berkeley.